CALIFORNIA ALMANAC
4th Edition

James S. Fay, Senior Editor

Stephanie W. Fay, Text Editor

Ronald J. Boehm, Publisher

Published by

Pacific Data Resou

Cover photograph: Tom Till

ISBN 0-944158-01-3

OFFICE OF THE GOVERNOR
State of California

July 6, 1989

The complexity and continuing growth of
California greatly enhances the need for a comprehensive and authoritative reference of the
facts and statistics concerning the Golden
State.

The California Almanac addresses this need
by providing an extensive compilation of the
many facets of California's social, political,
business and educational dimensions. This
almanac serves as a vital reference tool for
all segments of society -- from the student to
the professional to the curious fact-seeker.

This almanac serves to enhance our under-
standing and knowledge of the Golden State, and
I encourage all Californians to take advantage
of its wealth of information.

Most cordially,

George Deukmejian

George Deukmejian

ABOUT THE EDITORS

James Fay is a Professor of Political Science at California State University. He grew up in New York and lived in the South and the Midwest prior to moving to California in 1970. His interests focus on California Politics, political parties, election law, and political films. After graduating from Georgetown University, Mr. Fay spent two years as a lieutenant in the army. He has an M.A. from the New School for Social Research, a Ph.D. from the University of Michigan and a J.D. from Hastings College of the Law. He has been an Adjunct Professor at Hastings College of the Law and at the University of San Francisco School of Law. In 1981, with Kay Lawson, he established the California Committee for Party Renewal, a multipartisan group whose purpose is to strengthen the state's political parties. Mr. Fay lives in Berkeley with his wife, Stephanie, the text editor, and their son Alexander. Their older son, Eric, works in New York.

Stephanie Fay grew up in Milwaukee, Wisconsin. She came to California via New York City and Ann Arbor, Michigan, among other places, earning an A.B. from Hunter College and an A.M. from the University of Michigan. After receiving a Ph.D. in American literature from the University of California at Berkeley, she taught composition classes at the University of California at Berkeley and at Davis and worked as a free-lance editor. She is now on the staff of the University of California Press, where she edits illustrated books on a variety of scholarly subjects. In her free time she jogs in the Berkeley hills, putters in the garden, and keeps her pencils sharp for the next edition of the *Almanac*.

Ron Boehm is the President of ABC-Clio, and Co-Founder and President of Intellimation, two Santa Barbara based companies involved in multimedia educational publishing. He was a co-founder of Pacific Data Resources, while working on a joint JD-MBA at U.C. Hastings and U.C. Berkeley.

TABLE OF CONTENTS

ACKNOWLEDGEMENTS

The Editors would like to thank those who helped with the computerized preparation of the *California Almanac*. Neal Schaefer redesigned our database on a new system as well as supervised the entire computer entry/formatting and page setting process from start to finish. (Thanks also to his wife Barbi for patiently doing without a husband for those last few weeks.) Loren Saunders did a large part of the data entry and helped troubleshoot various Macintosh related problems. Amy Eberhard worked countless hours and contributed a large portion of the data entry and proofreading. Andy Vort was another significant contributor in the data entry department. Marlys Boehm and Barbi Schaefer also helped with the proofreading. Richard Bass and John Graham worked on the cover and provided technical assistance for the manual layout and paste up. Much thanks to all of these people who's diligent labors made this edition possible.

The Editors take the usual responsibility for omissions and errors.

* *

Pacific Data Resources has worked to provide California Almanac readers with the latest available data in each section of the book. In some cases, the basic sources, government agencies and private groups, are two to three years late in producing their reports, a delay reflected in the data. While Pacific Data Resources has also worked to ensure accuracy in the California Alamanac, it is impossible to guarantee every number or fact among the thousands here.

Readers who wish to suggest changes in the data can fill in one of the forms in the back of the California Almanac and send it to the Editors.

CALIFORNIA
ALMANAC

COUNTIES

N

0 20 40 60 80 100
miles

Del Norte

Siskiyou

Modoc

Humboldt

Trinity

Shasta

Lassen

Tehama

Plumas

Mendocino

Glenn

Butte

Sierra

Colusa

Sutter

Yuba

Nevada

Lake

Placer

Napa

Yolo

El Dorado

Sonoma

Sacramento

Solano

Amador

Alpine

Marin

Contra Costa

San Joaquin

Calaveras

San Francisco

Alameda

Tuolumne

San Mateo

Santa Clara

Stanislaus

Mariposa

Mono

Santa Cruz

Merced

Madera

San Benito

Fresno

Monterey

Inyo

Kings

Tulare

San Luis Obispo

Kern

Santa Barbara

San Bernardino

Ventura

Los Angeles

Orange

Riverside

San Diego

Imperial

Historical Atlas of California, 1974. University of Oklahoma Press. Reprinted by permission.

Population

The population boom of the 1980s continues unabated in California, primarily because of migration. The natural increase of births over deaths accounts for 41 percent of the state's population growth since 1980, but 59 percent has resulted from migration into the state. Although some immigrants (about one-sixth) come from elsewhere in the United States, the overwhelming majority (the remaining five-sixths) are newcomers to this country who have settled in the Golden State. These new Californians are a mix of poorly educated economic refugees, many from south of the border, and well-educated individuals from a host of nations, particularly those of Asia. The healthy economy in California, which provides low-skilled as well as high-technology jobs, has been the magnet drawing many of these migrants.

As has been the case for several decades, Los Angeles and San Diego counties are experiencing the greatest population growth, with San Bernardino, Riverside, and Orange counties picking up smaller but still significant numbers of new residents. In Northern California, Sacramento County is still showing rapid growth, along with the Central Valley counties of Fresno, San Joaquin, and Stanislaus. In the San Francisco Bay Area, Alameda, Contra Costa, and Santa Clara counties are growing, but not nearly as fast as Southern California counties. A few counties, bucking the trend, have declining or relatively stable populations. These are San Francisco (losing) and Alpine and Marin (stable). People seem to be moving more to those areas of the state where housing is still relatively affordable, and in time the unavailability of affordable housing may limit some of the population upsurge. For now, however, even sky-high housing costs do not appear to be checking the population boom.

As migration swells the state's population, the number of Hispanics and Asians in California is increasing more rapidly than many demographers had predicted. As of 1988, Hispanics represented 24 percent of the state's population and Asians, Pacific Islanders, and Indians 9 percent.

Where can we expect the biggest and smallest population increases in the next three decades? The greatest increase in population will take place in the Los Angeles-Orange-Ventura area, though the rate of growth there will be relatively slow. Similarly, the San Francisco Bay Area, which will add 1.5 million new residents, will add them at a slow rate--only two-thirds the state's average growth rate. The future boom areas, in both absolute numbers and rate of growth, will be the Inland Empire, the San Joaquin Valley, the eleven-county greater Sacramento area, and San Diego. If you want to move to an area that will not grow much in the next three decades, try the northern coastal area, northeastern California, or the central coast. Elsewhere, expect to see crowds. By 2020 the state's population will probably be 40 million.

RESIDENT POPULATION OF CALIFORNIA AND THE UNITED STATES

	United States			California			California as a Percent of U.S.
		Decennial or Annual Change			Decennial or Annual Change		
Year*	Population	Number	Percent	Population	Number	Percent	
1850	23,192,000	6,100,000	36%	93,000†	-	-	0.4%
1860	31,443,000	8,300,000	36%	380,000	287,000	245%	1.2%
1870	39,818,000	8,400,000	27%	560,000	180,000	47%	1.4%
1880	50,156,000	10,300,000	26%	865,000	305,000	54%	1.7%
1890	62,948,000	12,800,000	26%	1,213,000	348,000	40%	1.9%
1900	75,995,000	13,000,000	21%	1,485,000	272,000	22%	2.0%
1910	91,972,000	16,000,000	21%	2,378,000	893,000	60%	2.6%
1920	105,711,000	13,700,000	15%	3,427,000	1,049,000	44%	3.2%
1930	122,775,000	17,100,000	16%	5,677,000	2,250,000	66%	4.6%
1940	132,457,000	9,682,000	8%	6,950,000	1,273,000	22%	5.2%
1950	151,868,000	19,411,000	15%	10,643,000	3,693,000	53%	7.0%
1960	179,979,000	28,111,000	19%	15,863,000	5,220,000	49%	8.8%
1970	203,984,000	24,005,000	13%	20,039,000	4,176,000	26%	9.8%
1980	227,255,000	23,271,000	11%	23,780,000	3,741,000	19%	10.5%
1981	229,637,000	2,382,000	1.0%	24,265,000	485,000	2.0%	10.6%
1982	231,996,000	2,359,000	1.0%	24,783,000	518,000	2.1%	10.7%
1983	234,284,000	2,288,000	1.0%	25,308,000	525,000	2.1%	10.8%
1984	236,477,000	2,193,000	0.9%	25,780,000	472,000	1.9%	10.9%
1985	238,736,000	2,259,000	1.0%	26,358,000	578,000	2.2%	11.0%
1986	241,107,000	2,371,000	1.0%	27,001,000	643,000	2.4%	11.2%
1987	243,419,000	2,312,000	1.0%	27,662,900	662,000	2.5%	11.4%
1988	245,807,000	2,388,000	1.0%	28,314,500	651,600	2.4%	11.5%
1989††	247,117,000	NA	NA	28,662,000	NA	NA	11.6%

* July. † The 1848 non-Indian population estimated to be 14,000. †† January.
1.1,90 Sources: *California Statistical Abstract*; California Department of Finance, Population Research Unit; & U.S. Bureau of the Census, *Historical Statistics of the United States and Current Population Reports*.

CALIFORNIA POPULATION BY RACE
1988

Race	Number	Percent of Population
White	16,955,100	60.9%
Hispanic	6,588,800	23.7%
Asian & other	2,506,700	9.0%
Black	1,806,700	6.5%
Total	27,857,300	100%

1.2,90 Source: California Dept. of Finance, State Census Data Center, Current Population Survey, March 1989.

COMPONENTS OF CHANGE IN CALIFORNIA'S CIVILIAN POPULATION 1970-1989
(in thousands)

Year	Civilian Population	Births	Deaths	Natural Increase	Net Migration	Net Change From Preceding Year
1970	20,039	358	165	193	101	294
1975	21,249	316	171	145	228	375
1976	21,653	323	170	153	248	404
1977	22,075	342	168	174	248	422
1978	22,566	350	173	177	314	491
1979	22,991	368	177	191	234	425
1980	23,509	390	180	210	303	519
1981	23,758	403	186	216	303	516
1982	24,244	420	185	236	264	485
1983	24,765	430	188	241	279	521
1984	25,257	436	188	248	255	492
1985	25,769	447	195	252	265	512
1986	26,388	470	202	270	352	618
1987	27,021	482	203	279	358	633
1988	27,694	503	209	294	371	673
1989	28,360	505	216	289	377	666

1.3,90 Source: California Department of Finance, Population Research Unit, *Report E-6*, and *California Statistical Abstract*, 1988.

CALIFORNIA'S PROJECTED POPULATION BY RACE/ETHNICITY 1970-2020

Year	Caucasian	Hispanic	Asian/ Other	Black
1970	78%	12%	3%	7%
1980	67%	19%	7%	8%
1990	58%	25%	10%	7%
2000	52%	29%	12%	7%
2010	46%	34%	13%	7%
2020	41%	38%	14%	7%

1.4,90 Source: California Dept. of Finance, Population Research Unit, *Report 88P-4*.

SECTION 1 NOTE

The average household in California in 1989 has 2.68 persons; nationwide the average size of households is 2.64 persons.

1.5,90

1910-2020 AGE DISTRIBUTION BY PERCENT
(Both Sexes)

Age	Percent Distribution										
	1910	1920	1930	1940	1950	1960	1970	1980	1990	2000	2020
Under 5 years	8.1	8.0	7.1	6.6	10.4	11.1	8.2	7.2	7.9	6.7	6.6
5 to 9 years	7.4	8.2	8.2	6.3	8.0	10.2	9.6	7.0	8.3	7.2	6.8
10 to 14 years	7.3	7.6	7.5	6.9	6.2	9.0	9.8	7.6	6.9	7.8	6.8
15 to 19 years	8.2	7.1	7.6	7.9	5.9	7.0	9.1	9.0	6.5	7.9	6.5
20 to 24 years	9.8	8.0	8.4	8.3	7.3	6.3	8.7	10.0	7.5	7.0	6.8
25 to 29 years	10.4	9.0	8.7	8.9	8.7	6.5	7.3	9.4	8.1	6.1	6.7
30 to 34 years	9.5	8.9	8.5	8.4	8.4	7.1	6.1	8.5	8.7	6.7	7.3
35 to 39 years	8.4	9.0	8.6	8.1	8.2	7.7	5.8	6.6	8.6	7.7	7.2
40 to 44 years	7.3	7.7	7.8	7.5	7.2	6.8	6.1	5.3	7.5	8.0	5.9
45 to 49 years	6.2	6.8	6.9	7.0	6.4	6.2	6.2	4.9	5.7	7.7	5.4
50 to 54 years	5.0	5.7	5.8	6.4	5.7	5.2	5.4	5.1	4.6	6.7	5.8
55 to 59 years	3.5	4.4	4.5	5.3	4.9	4.5	4.7	5.1	4.2	5.0	6.3
60 to 64 years	3.1	3.5	3.7	4.3	4.3	3.7	3.9	4.2	4.1	3.9	6.3
65 to 69 years	2.2	2.4	2.7	3.3	3.5	3.3	3.1	3.5	3.8	3.2	5.5
70 to 74 years	1.5	1.7	1.9	2.3	2.4	2.5	2.4	2.7	2.9	3.0	4.3
75 to 79 years	0.9	1.0	1.0	2.4	2.2	1.6	1.7	1.9	2.2	2.5	2.6
80 to 84 years	0.4	0.5	0.5	*	*	0.8	1.1	1.2	1.4	1.6	1.6
85+	0.2	0.2	0.3	*	0.4	0.5	0.7	0.9	1.0	1.4	1.6
Not reported	0.4	0.3	0.2	-	-	-	-	-	-	-	-
Median	29.3	31.1	31.4	33.0	32.1	30.0	28.1	29.9	32.8	35.4	36.7

* Included in the preceding age category.
1.6,90 Source: 1980 U.S. Census, & California Department of Finance, Population Research Unit, *Report 86-3*.

CALIFORNIA POPULATION BY MARITAL STATUS
(Population Aged 15 Years and Older)
1988

	Males		Females		Total	
	Number	Percent	Number	Percent	Number	Percent
Single	3,441,900	32%	2,574,800	24%	6,016,700	28%
Married	5,954,600	56%	5,870,800	54%	11,825,400	55%
Separated	256,800	2.4%	374,500	3.4%	631,200	2.9%
Divorced	738,000	7.0%	1,120,700	10.3%	1,858,700	8.7%
Widowed	206,500	1.9%	928,400	8.5%	1,134,900	5.3%
Total	10,597,800	100%	10,869,200	100%	21,466,800	100%

1.7,90 Source: California Dept. of Finance, State Census Data Center, March 1989, unpublished Current Population Survey data.

SECTION 1 NOTE

If California were a separate nation, it would have the 30th largest population in the world, smaller than Colombia's but larger than Canada's.

1.8,90

COUNTY POPULATIONS BY AGE AND SEX, 1985					
County	Percent Under 5 Years	Percent Under 18 Years	Percent 18-64	Percent 65 and Over	Percent Male	Percent Female
Alameda	7.7	25.0	64.0	11.0	48.7	51.3
Alpine	5.4	21.3	71.6	7.2	53.2	46.8
Amador	5.9	22.4	60.0	17.5	50.9	49.1
Butte	7.3	23.1	60.7	16.2	48.5	51.5
Calaveras	6.0	22.4	61.4	16.2	49.2	50.7
Colusa	10.2	29.1	54.9	16.0	49.9	50.1
Contra Costa	7.4	25.3	64.5	10.3	48.7	51.3
Del Norte	8.9	27.5	58.5	14.0	50.1	49.9
El Dorado	7.5	24.8	64.3	11.0	50.0	50.0
Fresno	10.3	30.5	59.2	10.2	49.2	50.8
Glenn	8.7	28.5	57.8	13.7	50.1	49.9
Humboldt	7.9	24.9	63.3	11.8	49.7	50.3
Imperial	11.0	33.9	56.6	9.6	49.5	50.5
Inyo	7.2	24.1	58.0	17.9	49.3	50.7
Kern	10.0	30.5	60.2	9.3	51.0	49.0
Kings	11.8	32.8	58.4	8.8	50.7	49.3
Lake	6.6	21.1	57.8	21.0	48.8	51.2
Lassen	7.4	24.7	65.4	9.9	55.3	44.7
Los Angeles	9.2	27.6	61.7	10.7	48.9	51.1
Madera	9.4	31.3	58.2	10.5	50.2	49.8
Marin	5.4	19.0	70.5	10.6	48.8	51.2
Mariposa	6.0	23.4	61.1	15.4	51.2	48.8
Mendocino	8.5	27.5	60.0	12.5	49.5	50.5
Merced	12.3	34.5	56.8	8.6	50.0	50.0
Modoc	7.8	26.6	59.3	14.1	49.8	50.2
Mono	7.6	24.4	69.4	6.1	55.8	44.2
Monterey	8.9	27.2	63.9	9.0	51.7	48.3
Napa	6.5	22.9	62.6	14.5	48.9	51.1
Nevada	7.0	23.0	62.6	14.4	49.2	50.8
Orange	8.0	25.6	65.5	9.0	49.3	50.7
Placer	7.3	25.4	62.7	11.9	48.9	51.1
Plumas	7.4	25.6	61.0	13.4	50.1	49.9
Riverside	8.7	27.1	58.7	14.2	48.8	51.2
Sacramento	8.2	26.0	63.7	10.3	48.8	51.2
San Benito	9.3	31.3	59.3	9.4	49.1	50.9
San Bernardino	9.3	29.8	60.9	9.4	49.5	50.5
San Diego	7.9	25.0	64.3	10.7	50.8	49.2
San Francisco	6.1	17.3	66.5	16.3	49.2	50.8
San Joaquin	9.6	29.7	59.8	10.5	48.8	51.2
San Luis Obispo	6.7	21.8	65.3	12.8	51.9	48.1
San Mateo	7.0	22.1	65.5	12.4	48.6	51.4
Santa Barbara	7.4	23.6	64.9	11.5	49.0	51.0
Santa Clara	8.0	25.7	66.4	7.9	49.6	50.4
Santa Cruz	8.2	24.5	63.9	11.6	49.1	50.9
Shasta	7.8	26.8	60.9	12.3	48.7	51.3
Sierra	7.2	23.1	59.8	17.1	50.5	49.5
Siskiyou	8.0	26.4	58.9	14.7	49.7	50.3
Solano	8.8	28.5	63.9	7.6	51.2	48.8
Sonoma	7.3	24.7	62.0	13.3	48.1	51.9
Stanislaus	9.1	29.2	59.5	11.3	48.6	51.4
Sutter	9.1	28.0	60.1	11.1	49.2	50.8
Tehama	7.8	26.1	59.0	14.9	49.2	50.8
Trinity	7.1	25.3	61.8	12.9	50.4	49.6
Tulare	10.5	32.5	57.4	10.1	49.0	51.0
Tuolumne	6.4	22.5	62.4	15.1	51.9	48.1
Ventura	8.4	28.6	62.5	8.9	49.6	50.4
Yolo	7.6	23.8	66.7	9.5	49.9	50.1
Yuba	9.6	29.5	60.3	10.3	50.3	49.7
State Totals	**8.5**	**26.5**	**62.8**	**10.7**	**49.3**	**50.7**

1.9,90 Source: Cal. Dept of Finance, Population Research Unit, *Report 86-P-3*.

County	Total Persons	White	Black	Percent Black	Spanish origin	Percent Spanish origin	American Indian	Eskimo	Aleut
Alameda	1,105,379	740,612	203,612	18.4	129,962	11.8	7,252	124	70
Alpine	1,097	932	3	0.3	42	3.8	145	1	-
Amador	19,314	18,411	152	0.8	917	4.7	336	-	-
Butte	143,851	134,030	1,702	1.2	7,542	5.2	2,034	20	8
Calaveras	20,710	19,912	74	0.4	911	4.4	318	1	-
Colusa	12,791	10,284	74	0.6	2,493	19.5	194	-	-
Contra Costa	656,380	534,628	60,172	9.2	55,820	8.5	3,811	50	29
Del Norte	18,217	16,004	52	0.3	1,018	5.6	1,295	5	1
El Dorado	85,812	82,400	296	0.3	3,971	4.6	723	6	10
Fresno	514,621	379,279	25,339	4.9	150,790	29.3	4,716	20	11
Glenn	21,350	18,901	54	0.3	2,532	11.9	350	3	-
Humboldt	108,514	99,489	543	0.5	3,736	3.4	5,694	12	8
Imperial	92,110	51,467	2,310	2.5	51,384	55.8	1,367	5	3
Inyo	17,895	15,910	26	0.1	1,084	6.1	1,605	3	1
Kern	403,089	309,372	21,152	5.2	87,026	21.6	5,981	9	18
Kings	73,738	54,103	3,583	4.9	19,827	26.9	722	3	-
Lake	36,366	34,027	350	1.0	1,882	5.2	799	5	2
Lassen	21,661	19,354	757	3.5	1,417	6.5	628	2	4
Los Angeles	7,477,503	5,073,617	943,968	12.6	2,066,103	27.6	47,234	389	497
Madera	63,116	47,715	2,174	3.4	16,916	26.8	1,043	-	2
Marin	222,568	206,118	5,477	2.5	9,204	4.1	742	20	9
Mariposa	11,108	10,431	72	0.6	504	4.5	356	-	1
Mendocino	66,738	61,646	345	0.5	3,688	5.5	2,364	9	2
Merced	134,560	104,377	6,806	5.1	34,054	25.3	1,068	11	12
Modoc	8,610	8,042	14	0.2	356	4.1	346	-	-
Mono	8,577	7,994	16	0.2	405	4.7	334	-	-
Monterey	290,444	200,035	18,825	6.5	75,129	25.9	2,889	21	17
Napa	99,199	90,856	887	0.9	8,636	8.7	715	8	2
Nevada	51,645	50,450	73	0.1	1,532	3.0	504	2	1
Orange	1,932,709	1,669,314	25,287	1.3	286,339	14.8	12,782	105	64
Placer	117,247	110,243	402	0.3	8,211	7.0	1,121	6	4
Plumas	17,340	16,443	163	0.9	636	3.7	498	-	-
Riverside	663,166	544,771	30,857	4.7	124,417	18.8	7,140	31	33
Sacramento	783,381	632,777	58,951	7.5	74,141	9.5	8,669	108	50
San Benito	25,005	17,179	60	0.2	11,430	45.7	176	3	-
San Bernardino	895,016	737,545	47,813	5.3	165,863	18.5	9,967	79	38
San Diego	1,861,846	1,514,006	104,452	5.6	275,177	14.8	14,355	115	146
San Francisco	678,974	395,081	86,414	12.7	83,373	12.3	3,358	120	70
San Joaquin	347,342	264,038	19,176	5.5	66,565	19.2	3,419	21	17
San Luis Obispo	155,435	140,386	2,726	1.8	14,792	9.5	1,726	29	31
San Mateo	587,329	458,489	35,487	6.0	73,339	12.5	2,383	60	38
Santa Barbara	298,694	247,695	7,767	2.6	55,356	18.5	2,654	31	17
Santa Clara	1,295,071	1,017,854	43,716	3.4	226,611	17.5	8,312	104	90
Santa Cruz	188,141	164,709	1,461	0.8	27,648	14.7	1,465	26	24
Shasta	115,715	110,697	723	0.6	3,455	3.0	2,610	10	10
Sierra	3,073	2,999	3	0.1	196	6.4	46	-	-
Siskiyou	39,735	36,574	602	1.5	1,891	4.8	1,479	5	1
Solano	235,203	174,181	27,785	11.8	24,773	10.5	1,947	23	11
Sonoma	299,681	277,991	3,466	1.2	20,824	6.9	3,435	31	28
Stanislaus	265,900	233,557	3,124	1.2	39,889	15.0	3,167	16	12
Sutter	52,246	42,893	562	1.1	6,098	11.7	585	2	-
Tehama	38,888	37,128	63	0.2	2,127	5.5	598	4	1
Trinity	11,858	11,204	13	0.1	319	2.7	453	-	-
Tulare	245,738	180,080	3,548	1.4	73,298	29.8	2,535	10	13
Tuolumne	33,928	32,023	377	1.1	1,781	5.2	592	5	2
Ventura	529,174	425,688	11,199	2.1	113,192	21.4	4,825	39	35
Yolo	113,374	92,990	1,945	1.7	19,342	17.1	1,154	18	34
Yuba	49,733	41,962	2,231	4.5	4,367	8.8	1,139	4	3
State Totals	23,667,902	18,030,893	1,819,281	7.7	4,544,331	19.2	198,155	1,734	1,480

1.10.90 Source: U.S. Bureau of the Census, *1980 U.S. Census.*

CALIFORNIA POPULATION AND POPULATION DENSITY BY COUNTY 1989				
	Population		Population Density	
County	Number as of January 1, 1989	Rank in State	Residents per Square Mile	Rank in State
Alameda	1,252,400	6	1,709	4
Alpine	1,190	58	1.6	58
Amador	29,150	47	49	35
Butte	176,700	25	106	22
Calaveras	32,400	45	32	40
Colusa	15,500	52	13	48
Contra Costa	775,500	9	1,057	7
Del Norte	20,400	49	20	45
El Dorado	124,100	30	72	29
Fresno	621,200	13	104	24
Glenn	23,600	48	18	46
Humboldt	116,800	31	33	39
Imperial	115,700	32	27	41
Inyo	18,200	51	1.8	57
Kern	526,600	14	65	33
Kings	96,000	34	69	30
Lake	52,100	40	41	36
Lassen	28,800	46	6.3	52
Los Angeles	8,650,300	1	2,131	3
Madera	83,800	35	39	37
Marin	231,900	22	446	11
Mariposa	14,800	53	10	49
Mendocino	76,900	37	22	43
Merced	173,900	26	88	27
Modoc	9,375	55	2.3	56
Mono	9,800	56	3.2	55
Monterey	349,300	17	105	23
Napa	107,600	33	142	17
Nevada	78,800	36	81	28
Orange	2,280,400	3	2,916	2
Placer	160,400	27	113	21
Plumas	20,050	50	7.8	50
Riverside	1,014,800	7	141	18
Sacramento	988,300	8	1,005	8
San Benito	35,250	44	25	42
San Bernardino	1,324,600	5	66	31
San Diego	2,418,200	2	568	9
San Francisco	731,700	10	16,260	1
San Joaquin	460,300	15	327	14
San Luis Obispo	211,900	24	64	34
San Mateo	632,800	12	1,394	5
Santa Barbara	348,400	18	127	20
Santa Clara	1,440,900	4	1,107	6
Santa Cruz	229,900	23	524	10
Shasta	143,100	28	38	38
Sierra	3,600	57	3.8	54
Siskiyou	43,750	43	6.9	51
Solano	321,100	20	388	12
Sonoma	371,600	16	236	15
Stanislaus	347,500	19	232	16
Sutter	62,500	38	103	25
Tehama	47,250	42	16	47
Trinity	14,000	54	4.4	53
Tulare	300,200	21	62	32
Tuolumne	49,000	41	22	43
Ventura	653,600	11	353	13
Yolo	137,000	29	132	19
Yuba	57,300	39	90	26
State Totals	28,662,000	---	183	---

1.11,90 Source: California Dept. of Finance, Population Research Unit, *Report 89-E-1*, and Pacific Data Resources.

County	1970	1980	1970-1980 Change	1989	1980-1989 Change
CALIFORNIA POPULATION AND PERCENT CHANGE IN POPULATION, BY COUNTY 1970-1989					
Alameda	1,071,446	1,097,580	2.4%	1,252,400	14.1%
Alpine	484	1,093	125.0%	1,190	8.9%
Amador	11,821	19,261	62.9%	29,150	51.3%
Butte	101,969	143,150	40.3%	176,700	23.4%
Calaveras	13,585	20,442	50.4%	32,400	58.5%
Colusa	12,430	12,738	2.4%	15,500	21.7%
Contra Costa	556,116	650,155	16.9%	775,500	19.3%
Del Norte	11,580	18,210	28.8%	20,400	12.0%
El Dorado	45,833	85,202	94.0%	124,100	45.7%
Fresno	413,329	506,977	22.6%	621,200	22.5%
Glenn	17,521	21,333	21.0%	23,600	10.6%
Humboldt	99,692	108,486	8.8%	116,800	7.7%
Imperial	74,492	91,708	23.1%	115,700	26.2%
Inyo	15,571	17,871	14.7%	18,200	1.8%
Kern	330,234	400,506	21.2%	526,600	31.5%
Kings	66,717	73,819	10.0%	96,000	30.0%
Lake	19,548	36,507	86.0%	52,100	42.7%
Lassen	16,796	21,674	29.0%	28,800	32.9%
Los Angeles	7,041,980	7,441,302	5.6%	8,650,300	16.2%
Madera	41,519	63,078	51.8%	83,800	32.9%
Marin	208,652	217,114	4.0%	231,900	6.8%
Mariposa	6,015	11,055	83.7%	14,800	33.9%
Mendocino	51,101	66,751	30.6%	76,900	15.2%
Merced	104,629	134,252	28.3%	173,900	29.5%
Modoc	7,469	8,618	15.3%	9,375	8.8%
Mono	4,016	8,589	113.8%	9,800	14.1%
Monterey	247,450	289,252	16.9%	349,300	20.8%
Napa	79,140	96,783	22.2%	107,600	11.2%
Nevada	26,346	51,510	96.4%	78,800	53.0%
Orange	1,421,233	1,919,264	35.0%	2,280,400	18.8%
Placer	77,632	117,293	51.0%	160,400	36.8%
Plumas	11,707	17,365	48.0%	20,050	15.5%
Riverside	456,916	660,012	44.0%	1,014,800	53.8%
Sacramento	634,373	780,391	23.0%	988,300	26.6%
San Benito	18,226	24,910	36.6%	35,250	41.5%
San Bernardino	682,233	877,481	28.6%	1,324,600	51.0%
San Diego	1,357,854	1,858,217	36.8%	2,418,200	30.1%
San Francisco	715,674	674,073	5.8%	731,700	8.5%
San Joaquin	291,073	346,821	19.1%	460,300	32.7%
San Luis Obispo	105,690	154,732	46.4%	211,900	36.9%
San Mateo	557,361	581,698	4.3%	632,800	8.8%
Santa Barbara	264,324	296,996	12.3%	348,400	17.3%
Santa Clara	1,065,313	1,283,043	20.4%	1,440,900	12.3%
Santa Cruz	123,790	186,873	50.9%	229,900	23.0%
Shasta	77,640	114,779	47.8%	143,100	24.7%
Sierra	2,365	3,069	29.7%	3,600	17.3%
Siskiyou	33,225	39,715	19.5%	43,750	10.2%
Solano	171,989	230,228	33.8%	321,100	39.5%
Sonoma	204,885	292,190	42.6%	371,600	27.2%
Stanislaus	194,506	265,571	36.5%	347,500	30.8%
Sutter	41,935	52,247	24.5%	62,500	19.6%
Tehama	29,517	38,876	31.7%	47,250	21.5%
Trinity	7,615	11,849	55.6%	14,000	18.2%
Tulare	188,322	243,060	29.0%	300,200	23.5%
Tuolumne	22,169	33,921	53.0%	49,000	44.4%
Ventura	378,497	527,942	39.4%	653,600	23.8%
Yolo	91,788	113,305	23.4%	137,000	20.9%
Yuba	44,736	49,671	11.0%	57,300	15.4%
State Totals	**20,039,000**	**23,769,000**	**18.6%**	**28,662,000**	**20.6%**

1.12,90 Source: California Department of Finance, Population Research Unit, *Report 89-E-1.*

PROJECTED POPULATION OF CALIFORNIA COUNTIES, 1990-2020				
County	1990	1995	2000	2020
Alameda	1,270,858	1,323,694	1,361,190	1,498,828
Alpine	1,264	1,401	1,645	2,475
Amador	29,616	33,303	36,813	51,154
Butte	183,233	202,574	221,868	296,135
Calaveras	32,271	37,853	42,804	62,440
Colusa	16,392	17,973	19,355	23,049
Contra Costa	768,829	824,296	870,558	1,026,353
Del Norte	19,711	20,372	20,774	21,199
El Dorado	123,072	141,064	158,532	228,961
Fresno	628,998	683,213	733,982	954,037
Glenn	24,881	26,491	27,953	32,005
Humboldt	116,916	118,972	119,982	118,060
Imperial	119,063	131,551	143,011	184,060
Inyo	18,612	18,751	18,784	19,174
Kern	539,598	602,081	662,641	859,746
Kings	101,339	109,767	116,198	140,687
Lake	59,529	70,691	80,884	121,267
Lassen	26,394	27,774	29,527	35,584
Los Angeles	8,543,687	8,885,846	9,132,563	10,119,311
Madera	89,275	102,608	115,522	164,732
Marin	230,137	234,383	236,518	232,660
Mariposa	15,742	18,043	20,340	29,381
Mendocino	80,246	86,437	92,202	113,945
Merced	186,271	211,916	238,209	339,585
Modoc	10,009	10,890	11,727	14,934
Mono	9,609	10,026	10,598	12,654
Monterey	363,956	396,182	424,312	514,299
Napa	109,961	116,700	123,180	147,481
Nevada	83,181	98,853	113,809	167,429
Orange	2,302,123	2,463,752	2,559,246	3,043,973
Placer	159,424	181,985	203,741	287,973
Plumas	20,706	22,289	23,775	27,877
Riverside	1,022,046	1,177,125	1,349,961	1,941,125
Sacramento	993,938	1,091,299	1,183,990	1,511,721
San Benito	36,859	43,023	48,677	65,259
San Bernardino	1,281,983	1,476,210	1,660,980	2,287,881
San Diego	2,387,842	2,630,296	2,852,513	3,664,719
San Francisco	773,558	781,454	763,794	684,185
San Joaquin	482,854	550,573	611,979	837,674
San Luis Obispo	228,957	267,066	302,208	421,020
San Mateo	636,265	650,617	656,870	662,890
Santa Barbara	364,764	390,129	407,392	461,013
Santa Clara	1,487,727	1,569,902	1,639,959	1,877,131
Santa Cruz	239,740	263,816	286,114	374,912
Shasta	148,167	164,351	179,628	227,345
Sierra	3,732	3,951	4,143	4,844
Siskiyou	44,459	45,897	47,079	51,105
Solano	313,778	353,708	391,399	520,938
Sonoma	369,905	401,580	429,053	530,443
Stanislaus	341,605	380,409	418,198	563,153
Sutter	63,552	68,278	71,997	85,841
Tehama	49,735	54,830	59,631	77,389
Trinity	14,765	15,881	16,921	21,019
Tulare	315,992	354,645	393,436	549,678
Tuolumne	49,477	57,736	64,643	85,927
Ventura	663,734	726,279	784,465	987,638
Yolo	134,074	143,657	152,170	182,103
Yuba	57,658	60,671	63,173	69,316
State Totals	28,771,169	30,995,714	32,852,616	39,618,536

1.13,90 Source: California Dept. of Finance, Population Research Unit, *Report 86-P-3*.

PROJECTED POPULATION OF CALIFORNIA COUNTIES
1985 to 2000
Ranked By Projected Numerical & Percent Change

Rank	County	Numerical Change	Rank	County	Percent Change
1	Los Angeles	1,047,267	1	Lake	67%
2	San Diego	720,910	1	Nevada	67%
3	San Bernardino	574,584	3	Riverside	65%
4	Riverside	529,359	4	Calaveras	60%
5	Orange	471,345	4	San Benito	60%
6	Sacramento	290,192	6	San Luis Obispo	59%
7	Santa Clara	239,852	7	Tuolumne	58%
8	San Joaquin	195,275	8	Amador	57%
9	Ventura	184,262	9	San Bernardino	53%
10	Kern	182,047	10	Mariposa	52%
11	Alameda	164,203	11	El Dorado	51%
12	Fresno	157,789	11	Madera	51%
13	Contra Costa	152,960	13	Merced	48%
14	Solano	116,200	14	Placer	47%
15	Stanislaus	113,295	14	San Joaquin	47%
16	Tulare	112,937	16	Solano	42%
17	San Luis Obispo	112,107	17	Tulare	40%
18	Monterey	94,616	18	Alpine	39%
19	Sonoma	93,652	19	Kern	38%
20	Merced	77,709	20	Kings	37%
21	Santa Barbara	72,788	20	Stanislaus	37%
22	Santa Cruz	71,816	22	Shasta	36%
23	Placer	65,336	23	Butte	35%
24	Butte	57,863	23	Imperial	35%
25	El Dorado	53,825	23	Tehama	35%
26	Shasta	47,935	26	San Diego	34%
27	Nevada	45,518	26	Santa Cruz	34%
28	San Mateo	40,278	28	Colusa	32%
29	Madera	39,223	28	Sacramento	32%
30	Imperial	37,010	30	Ventura	31%
31	Lake	32,580	31	Monterey	29%
32	Kings	31,299	32	Sonoma	28%
33	San Francisco	28,796	33	Fresno	27%
34	Yolo	28,165	34	Mendocino	25%
35	Yuolumne	23,838	35	Plumas	24%
36	Napa	19,179	35	Trinity	24%
37	Mendocino	18,403	37	Modoc	23%
38	San Benito	18,182	37	Sutter	23%
39	Calaveras	16,002	37	Yolo	23%
40	Tehama	15,324	40	Orange	22%
41	Sutter	13,497	40	Santa Barbara	22%
42	Amador	13,410	42	Contra Costa	21%
43	Marin	10,413	42	Glenn	21%
44	Yuba	8,874	44	Lassen	20%
45	Humboldt	6,981	45	Sierra	19%
46	Mariposa	6,942	46	Napa	18%
47	Lassen	4,925	47	Santa Clara	17%
48	Glenn	4,757	48	Yuba	16%
49	Colusa	4,657	49	Alameda	14%
50	Plumas	4,576	49	Mono	14%
51	Siskiyou	4,275	51	Los Angeles	13%
52	Trinity	3,319	52	Del Norte	11%
53	Modoc	2,228	53	Siskiyou	10%
54	Del Norte	1,974	54	Humboldt	7%
55	Mono	1,296	54	San Mateo	7%
56	Sierra	648	56	Marin	5%
57	Alpine	460	57	San Francisco	4%
58	Inyo	386	58	Inyo	2%
	The State	6,487,539		The State	24.6%

1.14,90 Source: Cal. Dept. of Finance, Population Research Unit, *Report 86-P-3.*

POPULATION OF CALIFORNIA COUNTIES AND CITIES*, 1987 & 1989					
County/Cities	1987	1989	County/Cities	1987	1989
Alameda	1,214,100	1,252,400	**Contra Costa (cont.)**		
Alameda	70,300	77,200	Lafayette	22,500	22,850
Albany	15,100	16,500	Martinez	28,800	30,700
Berkeley	106,900	106,400	Moraga	15,500	16,150
Dublin	21,500	23,550	Orinda	17,250	17,550
Emeryville	4,630	5,025	Pinole	15,000	15,900
Fremont	157,400	169,000	Pittsburg	41,600	43,750
Hayward	101,100	104,500	Pleasant Hill	29,950	31,750
Livermore	54,400	56,800	Richmond	78,700	82,000
Newark	38,000	39,250	San Pablo	21,350	21,700
Oakland	356,200	356,300	San Ramon	27,450	33,800
Piedmont	10,350	10,450	Walnut Creek	62,100	62,600
Pleasanton	46,350	52,000	Unincorporated	140,400	147,400
San Leandro	66,300	67,500	**Del Norte**	19,450	20,400
Union City	49,900	49,900	Crescent City	3,460	3,420
Unincorporated	115,700	118,000	Unincorporated	16,000	16,950
Alpine	1,200	1,190	**El Dorado**	110,000	124,100
Unincorporated	1,200	1,190	Placerville	7,375	8,100
Amador	24,150	29,150	South Lake Tahoe	21,850	22,050
Amador	150	180	Unincorporated	80,800	93,900
Ione	2,750	5,600	**Fresno**	588,300	621,200
Jackson	3,280	3,700	Clovis	42,000	46,750
Plymouth	790	910	Coalinga	7,825	8,225
Sutter creek	2,000	2,120	Firebaugh	3,910	4,050
Unincorporated	15,200	16,650	Fowler	3,020	3,080
Butte	167,400	176,700	Fresno	294,400	317,800
Biggs	1,460	1,480	Huron	3,660	3,780
Chico	33,750	36,450	Kerman	4,240	4,850
Gridley	4,220	4,260	Kingsburg	6,025	6,800
Oroville	10,100	10,550	Mendota	6,800	6,925
Paradise	25,100	26,250	Orange Cove	4,580	4,720
Unincorporated	92,800	97,700	Parlier	6,600	8,050
Calaveras	28,800	32,400	Reedley	13,750	14,850
Angels Camp	2,410	2,580	Sanger	14,700	15,550
Unincorporated	26,400	29,800	San Joaquin	2,050	2,100
Colusa	14,950	15,500	Selma	13,500	14,300
Colusa	4,860	5,050	Unincorporated	161,700	159,400
Williams	1,780	1,870	**Glenn**	22,850	23,600
Unincoroporated	8,325	8,550	Orland	4,480	4,720
Contra Costa	734,500	775,500	Willows	5,250	5,300
Antioch	51,800	57,600	Unincorporated	13,150	13,550
Brentwood	6,100	6,825	**Humboldt**	113,600	116,800
Clayton	4,830	6,825	Arcata	14,350	15,050
Concord	108,000	110,100	Blue Lake	1,300	1,300
Danville	28,150	30,000	Eureka	24,650	25,150
El Cerrito	23,400	23,450	Ferndale	1,450	1,450
Hercules	11,600	14,550	Fortuna	8,450	8,900

1.15.1,90

SECTION 1 NOTE
In California, 82 percent of the population lives in 15 counties, 89 percent in 20 counties.

1.16,90

POPULATION OF CALIFORNIA COUNTIES AND CITIES*, 1987 & 1989

County/Cities	1987	1989	County/Cities	1987	1989
Humboldt (cont.)			**Los Angeles (cont.)**		
Rio Dell	2,840	2,900	Baldwin Park	62,200	63,300
Trinidad	410	420	Bell	28,150	28,250
Unincorporated	60,200	61,700	Bellflower	59,500	60,900
Imperial	107,700	115,700	Bell Gardens	37,700	38,300
Brawley	18,250	19,650	Beverly Hills	34,300	34,300
Calexico	18,500	19,550	Bradbury	910	930
Calipatria	2,670	3,030	Burbank	91,000	93,800
El Centro	28,400	31,650	Carson	88,400	88,800
Holtville	4,900	5,100	Cerritos	57,900	58,400
Imperial	4,120	4,720	Claremont	36,000	36,550
Westmorland	1,830	1,990	Commerce	12,500	11,700
Unincorporated	29,150	30,000	Compton	92,800	93,000
Inyo	17,950	18,200	Covina	42,450	43,250
Bishop	3,550	3,680	Cudahy	20,050	20,700
Unincorporated	14,400	14,500	Culver City	40,750	40,950
Kern	496,200	526,600	Downey	86,700	86,800
Arvin	8,325	8,750	Duarte	21,100	21,350
Bakersfield	153,400	161,800	El Monte	93,900	95,400
California City	3,450	4,150	El Segundo	15,400	15,750
Delano	19,850	21,150	Gardena	50,200	50,900
Maricopa	1,250	1,240	Glendale	156,900	166,100
McFarland	6,250	6,550	Glendora	43,200	47,400
Ridgecrest	24,850	28,650	Hawaiian Gardens	12,050	12,350
Shafter	7,525	7,650	Hawthorne	62,900	67,400
Taft	6,075	6,225	Hermosa Beach	19,400	19,750
Tehachapi	4,650	5,325	Hidden Hills	1,960	1,950
Wasco	11,050	11,400	Huntington Park	51,200	51,200
Unincorporated	249,600	263,800	Industry	390	370
Kings	85,700	96,000	Inglewood	102,900	102,300
Avenal	4,700	9,075	Irwindale	1,060	1,230
Corcoran	7,250	11,050	La Canada Flintridge	20,750	20,800
Hanford	25,400	29,400	La Habra Heights	5,350	5,450
Lemoore	13,000	13,350	Lakewood	76,600	76,500
Unincorporated	35,400	33,150	La Mirada	42,550	42,600
Lake	50,000	52,100	Lancaster	68,000	82,200
Clearlake	10,650	10,800	La Puente	33,400	33,550
Lakeport	4,240	4,480	La Verne	29,150	30,500
Unincorporated	35,100	36,850	Lawndale	27,050	27,300
Lassen	25,400	28,800	Lomita	20,150	20,300
Susanville	6,725	7,075	Long Beach	406,200	419,800
Unicorporated	18,700	21,750	Los Angeles	3,311,500	3,400,500
Los Angeles	8,403,500	8,650,300	Lynwood	53,400	53,700
Agoura Hills	18,500	19,400	Manhattan Beach	35,100	35,150
Alhambra	73,100	74,900	Maywood	24,600	24,650
Arcadia	49,250	49,100	Monrovia	33,550	34,000
Artesia	14,950	14,950	Montebello	59,100	58,200
Avalon	2,420	2,490	Monterey Park	62,900	64,600
Azuza	36,800	38,250	Norwalk	89,600	90,800

1.15.2,90

SECTION 1 NOTE

In 1988, California had an estimated 10,182,700 households.

1.17,90

POPULATION OF CALIFORNIA COUNTIES AND CITIES*, 1987 & 1989					
County/Cities	1987	1989	County/Cities	1987	1989
Los Angeles (cont.)			**Mendocino**	74,700	76,900
Palmdale	33,100	45,850	Fort Bragg	5,850	5,975
Palos Verdes Estates	15,050	15,000	Point Arena	450	440
Paramount	41,850	44,450	Ukiah	13,400	14,000
Pasadena	130,800	132,200	Willits	4,400	4,520
Pico Rivera	59,300	57,300	Unincorporated	50,600	52,000
Pomona	117,800	119,900	**Merced**	166,400	173,900
Rancho Palos Verdes	46,000	46,000	Atwater	21,300	21,950
Redondo Beach	64,400	64,700	Dos Palos	4,260	4,370
Rolling Hills	2,130	2,090	Gustine	3,660	4,040
Rolling Hills Estate	7,900	7,875	Livingston	6,650	7,150
Rosemead	46,900	47,700	Los Banos	12,800	13,100
San Dimas	29,600	32,500	Merced	48,850	53,600
San Fernando	20,250	20,700	Unincorporated	68,900	69,700
San Gabriel	33,700	34,900	**Modoc**	9,325	9,375
San Marino	13,900	13,800	Alturas	3,150	3,020
Santa Clarita	109,300†	115,700	Unincorporated	6,175	6,350
Santa Fe Springs	15,450	16,400	**Mono**	9,275	9,800
Santa Monica	96,100	96,500	Mammoth Lakes	4,465	4,740
Sierra Madre	11,150	11,250	Unincorporated	4,810	5,050
Signal Hill	8,175	8,150	**Monterey**	341,200	349,300
South El Monte	19,000	18,700	Carmel-by-the-Sea	4,990	4,990
South Gate	78,700	79,200	Del Rey Oaks	1,570	1,780
South Pasadena	24,400	24,500	Gonzales	4,130	4,040
Temple City	32,050	31,900	Greenfield	5,975	6,625
Torrance	140,200	142,200	King City	7,175	7,575
Vernon	90	80	Marina	28,100	30,100
Walnut	23,750	26,400	Monterey	31,100	31,550
West Covina	93,400	94,200	Pacific Grove	16,500	16,600
West Hollywood	38,450	38,400	Salinas	97,500	101,900
Westlake Village	7,325	8,025	Sand City	200	220
Whittier	72,800	74,100	Seaside	37,550	36,700
Unincorporated	1,061,100	1,006,400	Soledad	6,575	6,650
Madera	79,300	83,800	Unincorporated	99,900	100,600
Chowchilla	6,000	5,950	**Napa**	105,200	107,600
Madera	26,900	27,300	Calistoga	4,340	4,390
Unincorporated	46,350	50,500	Napa	56,300	57,900
Marin	227,600	231,900	St. Helena	5,025	5,100
Belvedere	2,320	2,320	Yountville	3,180	3,060
Corte Madera	8,450	8,625	Unincorporated	36,350	37,150
Fairfax	7,325	7,500	**Nevada**	72,400	78,800
Larkspur	11,350	11,350	Grass Valley	8,750	8,825
Mill Valley	13,200	13,400	Nevada City	2,840	2,930
Novato	45,950	47,500	Unincorporated	60,800	67,000
Ross	2,750	2,740	**Orange**	2,193,600	2,280,400
San Anselmo	12,000	12,000	Anaheim	242,200	244,300
San Rafael	45,600	46,450	Brea	32,950	33,550
Sausalito	7,550	7,575	Buena Park	65,800	66,200
Tiburon	8,225	8,350	Costa Mesa	89,900	92,900
Unincorporated	62,900	64,000	Cypress	42,850	45,350
Mariposa	13,850	14,800	Fountain Valley	55,600	56,100
Unincorporated	13,850	14,800	Fullerton	110,100	111,700

1.15.3,90

POPULATION OF CALIFORNIA COUNTIES AND CITIES*, 1987 & 1989

County/Cities	1987	1989	County/Cities	1987	1989
Orange (cont.)			**Riverside (cont.)**		
Garden Grove	134,100	134,800	Rancho Mirage	8,150	8,900
Huntington Beach	186,800	188,700	Riverside	199,000	209,700
Irvine	94,100	100,500	San Jacinto	11,750	13,750
Laguna Beach	18,800	24,550	Unincorporated	294,700	342,200
La Habra	48,500	49,000	**Sacramento**	928,700	988,300
La Palma	16,150	16,100	Folsom	19,250	25,650
Los Alamitos	12,100	12,150	Galt	7,250	7,875
Newport Beach	67,800	69,900	Isleton	900	910
Orange	103,300	106,400	Sacramento	327,200	339,900
Placentia	39,150	41,650	Unincorporated	574,200	613,900
San Clemente	34,800	39,100	**San Benito**	32,400	35,250
San Juan Capistrano	23,750	24,500	Hollister	16,800	18,100
Santa Ana	227,400	237,300	San Juan Bautista	1,450	1,640
Seal Beach	27,400	27,350	Unincorporated	14,150	15,550
Stanton	28,100	28,350	**San Bernardino**	1,167,200	1,324,600
Tustin	43,100	46,800	Adelanto	4,700	5,850
Villa Park	6,950	6,950	Barstow	20,550	21,100
Westminister	73,300	73,300	Big Bear Lake	5,825	6,375
Yorba Linda	42,600	47,900	Chino	52,000	56,800
Unincorporated	326,000	354,800	Colton	31,650	37,700
Placer	144,900	160,400	Fontana	60,000	78,000
Auburn	8,525	9,400	Grand Terrace	9,875	10,850
Colfax	990	1,050	Highlands	25,900	26,850
Lincoln	5,975	6,400	Loma Linda	12,600	13,950
Loomis	5,725	6,075	Montclair	23,300	25,800
Rocklin	12,250	15,400	Needles	5,200	5,475
Roseville	31,600	37,900	Ontario	113,600	124,300
Unincorporated	79,900	84,100	Rancho Cucamonga	80,400	104,700
Plumas	19,550	20,050	Redlands	54,200	59,800
Portola	2,070	2,160	Rialto	56,400	64,300
Unincorporated	17,450	17,900	San Bernardino	140,900	153,700
Riverside	886,200	1,014,800	Twentynine Palms	10,800†	11,150
Banning	17,200	19,150	Upland	58,900	63,900
Beaumont	8,000	9,150	Victorville	24,750	31,700
Blythe	7,775	8,150	Unincorporated	410,300	422,400
Cathedral City	23,550	29,050	**San Diego**	2,240,700	2,418,200
Coachella	13,650	14,550	Carlsbad	55,300	62,000
Corona	47,050	61,000	Chula Vista	120,300	128,000
Desert Hot Springs	9,125	10,650	Coronado	24,700	24,600
Hemet	30,350	33,350	Del Mar	5,050	5,125
Indian Wells	2,290	2,590	El Cajon	82,900	86,400
Indio	30,950	34,300	Encinitas	85,452	53,100
Lake Elsinore	12,250	14,950	Escondido	86,900	99,000
La Quinta	8,200	10,200	Imperial Beach	25,150	25,950
Moreno Valley	79,300	101,300	La Mesa	51,500	53,000
Norco	23,200	25,200	Lemon Grove	22,450	22,750
Palm Desert	17,100	19,450	National City	54,700	56,500
Palm Springs	31,500	31,950	Oceanside	101,000	117,600
Perris	11,250	15,150	Poway	39,150	43,100

POPULATION OF CALIFORNIA COUNTIES AND CITIES*, 1987 & 1989					
County/Cities	1987	1989	County/Cities	1987	1989
San Diego (cont.)			Santa Barbara	341,800	348,400
San Diego	1,022,400	1,086,600	Carpinteria	11,700	12,500
San Marcos	23,250	33,850	Guadalupe	5,375	5,625
Santee	50,200	52,400	Lompoc	31,750	32,800
Solana Beach	24,132	14,700	Santa Barbara	79,100	79,500
Vista	50,900	61,700	Santa Maria	52,000	53,700
Unincorporated	315,216	391,700	Solvang	3,970	4,180
San Francisco	742,700	731,700	Unincorporated	157,900	160,100
San Francisco	742,700	731,700	Santa Clara	1,407,900	1,440,900
San Joaquin	435,700	460,300	Cambell	33,900	34,500
Escalon	3,730	4,130	Cupertino	38,650	39,650
Lodi	45,800	49,200	Gilroy	27,450	29,550
Manteca	37,150	39,650	Los Altos	27,200	27,350
Ripon	6,100	7,100	Los Altos Hills	7,850	8,025
Stockton	185,000	192,300	Los Gatos	27,950	28,200
Tracy	27,300	29,400	Milpitas	43,900	46,450
Unincorporated	130,700	138,400	Monte Sereno	3,400	3,440
San Luis Obispo	198,200	211,900	Morgan Hill	21,450	23,800
Arroyo grande	13,300	14,050	Mountain View	62,200	63,500
Atascadero	20,850	22,700	Palo Alto	56,600	57,000
El Paso De Robles	14,700	16,400	San Jose	719,500	738,400
Grover City	10,600	11,450	Santa Clara	89,300	90,900
Morro Bay	9,825	10,150	Saratoga	29,900	30,250
Pismo Beach	6,950	7,575	Sunnyvale	115,200	116,700
San Luis Obispo	38,300	41,050	Unincorporated	103,600	103,200
Unincorporated	83,600	88,600	Santa Cruz	220,400	229,900
San Mateo	617,100	632,800	Capitola	9,950	10,250
Atherton	7,875	7,950	Santa Cruz	46,900	49,800
Belmont	24,950	25,000	Scotts Valley	7,850	9,075
Brisbane	3,030	3,050	Watsonville	28,550	30,250
Burlingame	27,000	27,250	Unincorporated	127,100	130,500
Colma	710	710	Shasta	133,800	143,100
Daly City	82,500	85,400	Anderson	7,850	8,175
East Palo Alto	18,850	18,850	Redding	52,700	59,800
Foster City	27,550	29,750	Unincorporated	73,200	75,100
Half Moon Bay	8,100	8,825	Sierra	3,470	3,600
Hillsborough	11,000	11,200	Loyalton	1,180	1,180
Menlo Park	27,550	28,200	Unincorporated	2,290	2,420
Millbrae	20,600	20,850	Siskiyou	42,300	43,750
Pacifica	37,100	37,850	Dorris	890	910
Portola Valley	4,370	4,530	Dunsmuir	2,140	2,170
Redwood City	59,400	61,600	Etna	810	800
San Bruno	34,900	35,550	Fort Jones	590	620
San Carlos	26,300	26,950	Montague	1,560	1,560
San Mateo	83,500	85,100	Mount Shasta	3,330	3,550
South San Francisco	51,700	52,400	Tulelake	880	890
Woodside	5,575	5,700	Weed	2,900	3,000
Unincorporated	54,300	56,100	Yreka	6,600	6,825

1.15.5,90

SECTION 1 NOTE
Los Angeles is the most heavily populated county in the U.S.; San Diego is the fifth most heavily populated and Orange County the sixth.

1.18,90

POPULATION OF CALIFORNIA COUNTIES AND CITIES*, 1987 & 1989

County/Cities	-1987-	-1989-	County/Cities	-1987-	-1989-
Siskiyou (cont.)			**Tehama (cont.)**		
Unincorporated	22,650	23,450	Unincorporated	27,600	29,100
Solano	291,300	321,100	**Trinity**	13,550	14,000
Benicia	21,850	24,350	Unincorporated	13,550	14,000
Dixon	10,400	10,750	**Tulare**	287,900	300,200
Fairfield	70,200	76,100	Dinuba	11,300	12,000
Rio Vista	3,320	3,400	Exeter	6,800	7,475
Suisun City	16,450	19,450	Farmersville	6,075	6,050
Vacaville	58,700	64,500	Lindsay	8,100	8,275
Vallejo	92,400	103,300	Porterville	24,650	27,000
Unincorporated	17,950	19,300	Tulare	27,350	29,650
Sonoma	349,100	371,600	Visalia	62,700	68,800
Cloverdale	4,440	4,620	Woodlake	5,225	5,400
Cotati	4,500	5,175	Unincorporated	135,700	135,700
Healdsburg	8,500	9,250	**Tuolumne**	42,950	49,000
Petaluma	39,150	41,850	Sonora	4,170	4,560
Rohnert Park	31,400	33,350	Unincorporated	38,750	44,450
Santa Rosa	103,000	111,600	**Ventura**	619,300	653,600
Sebastopol	6,325	6,500	Camarillo	45,700	48,300
Sonoma	7,250	7,950	Fillmore	10,950	11,200
Unincorporated	144,600	151,300	Moorpark	17,550	24,900
Stanislaus	320,600	347,500	Ojai	7,725	7,900
Ceres	18,000	22,300	Oxnard	124,000	128,000
Hughson	3,090	3,130	Port Hueneme	20,300	20,700
Modesto	138,500	152,100	San Buenaventura	87,500	90,800
Newman	3,420	3,470	Santa Paula	23,450	24,000
Oakdale	10,150	10,950	Simi Valley	94,300	99,800
Patterson	5,700	7,575	Thousand Oaks	98,900	104,400
Riverbank	6,950	7,700	Unincorporated	89,000	93,600
Turlock	34,750	39,700	**Yolo**	126,500	137,000
Waterford	3,280	3,450	Davis	41,300	44,250
Unincorporated	96,800	97,100	West Sacramento	27,350†	27,550
Sutter	59,500	62,500	Winters	3,610	4,190
Live Oak	3,680	4,100	Woodland	34,700	39,000
Yuba City	22,300	24,600	Unincorporated	46,850	22,050
Unincorporated	33,500	33,750	**Yuba**	54,900	57,300
Tehama	45,050	47,250	Marysville	11,250	11,850
Corning	5,525	5,700	Wheatland	1,780	1,890
Red Bluff	11,550	12,050	Unincorporated	41,850	43,600
Tehama	380	390			
State Totals				**27,292,300**	**28,662,000**

* January 1.   † 1988 data.

1.15.6,90 Source: California Dept. of Finance, Population Research Unit, *Report 89-E-1*.

SECTION 1 NOTE

In California, 41 percent of the population lives in cities with populations over 100,000, 57 percent in cities with populations over 50,000, 70 percent in cities with populations over 25,000, 75 percent in cities with populations over 10,000, and 77 percent in cities with populations over 5,000.

1.19,90

SECTION 1 NOTE

The average age of California men is 30.2, of women 31.6.

1.20,90

POPULATION OF THE TEN LARGEST CITIES IN CALIFORNIA 1987 AND 1989

Cities	1987		1989	
	Population*	Percent Change from 1986	Population*	Percent Change from 1988
Los Angeles	3,311,500	1.8%	3,400,500	1.0%
San Diego	1,022,400	2.0%	1,086,600	2.7%
San Jose	719,000	1.2%	738,400	1.4%
San Francisco	742,000	0.9%	731,700	-0.7%
Long Beach	406,000	2.4%	419,800	1.3%
Oakland	356,200	0.9%	356,300	0.1%
Sacramento	327,200	2.9%	339,900	1.6%
Fresno	294,000	3.7%	317,800	3.4%
Anaheim	242,200	1.7%	244,300	0.5%
Santa Ana	227,400	0.4%	237,300	2.5%

* January 1.
1.21,90 Source: California Dept. of Finance, Population Research Unit, press release.

TEN LARGEST AND SMALLEST COUNTIES IN CALIFORNIA, 1989

Largest	Population	Smallest	Population
Los Angeles	8,650,300	Alpine	1,190
San Diego	2,418,200	Sierra	3,600
Orange	2,280,400	Modoc	9,375
Santa Clara	1,440,900	Mono	9,800
San Bernardino	1,324,600	Trinity	14,000
Alameda	1,252,400	Mariposa	14,800
Riverside	1,014,800	Colusa	15,500
Sacramento	988,300	Inyo	18,200
Contra Costa	755,500	Plumas	20,050
San Francisco	731,700	Del Norte	20,400

1.22,90 Source: Cal. Dept. of Finance, Popu. Research Unit, *Report 89-E-1.*

SECTION 1 NOTE

The greater Los Angeles area is the second largest metropolitan area in the U.S. The greater San Francisco Bay Area is the fourth largest.
1.23,90

SECTION 1 NOTE

As of 1987 California had 4 of the top 15 cities in the U.S.: Los Angeles (2), San Diego (7), San Francisco (12), and San Jose (14).
1.24,90

TEN FASTEST-GROWING CALIFORNIA CITIES WITH 50,000 TO 200,000 POPULATION 1989

Rank	City	Population*	Percent Change from Previous Year†
1	Corona	61,000	16.8%
2	Fontana	78,000	11.6%
3	Moreno Valley	101,300	11.5%
4	Lancaster	82,200	10.3%
5	Vista	61,700	9.6%
6	Rancho Cucamonga	104,700	9.5%
7	Oceanside	117,600	9.1%
8	Pleasanton	52,000	7.7%
9	Redding	59,800	7.4%
10	Escondido	99,000	6.2%

* January 1. † Percent change calculated using unrounded data.
1.25,90 Source: California Dept. of Finance, Population Research Unit, *Report 89-E-1*.

TEN FASTEST-GROWING CALIFORNIA CITIES WITH POPULATIONS LESS THAN 50,000 1989

Rank	City	Population*	Percent Change from Previous Year†
1	Corcoran	11,000	43.0%
2	San Marcos	33,800	28.7%
3	Ione	5,600	23.3%
4	Perris	15,200	22.4%
5	Ceres	22,300	18.6%
6	Victorville	31,700	17.7%
7	Adelanto	5,800	17.4%
8	Palmdale	45,900	17.3%
9	Lake Elsinore	15,000	16.9%
10	Hercules	14,500	15.0%

* January 1. † Percent change calculated using unrounded data.
1.26,90 Source: California Dept. of Finance, Population Research Unit, *Report 89-E-1*.

SECTION 1 NOTE

California has 41 cities with populations over 100,000. There are 182 such cities in the U.S.

1.27,90

METROPOLITAN AREAS IN CALIFORNIA GROWTH PROJECTIONS 1986-2000		
Rank in U.S. in Population Growth	Metropolitan Area	Expected Population Growth 1986-2000
1	Los Angeles - Long Beach	1,017,000
3	Riverside - San Bernardino	724,000
7	Anaheim - Santa Ana	567,000
8	San Diego	558,000
12	Oakland	341,000
15	San Jose	322,000
17	Sacramento	310,000
28	San Francisco	187,000
29	Oxnard - Ventura	186,000
39	Vallejo - Fairfield - Napa	133,000
40	Santa Rosa - Petaluma	127,000

Note: The top 40 growth areas in the U.S. are ranked. 10 of the top 40 growth areas are in California.
1.28,90 Source: National Planning Association, Press Release June 29, 1988.

RANKING OF CONSOLIDATED METROPOLITAN AREAS IN THE UNITED STATES		
Rank	Area	Population
1	New York	18,053,800
2	Los Angeles	13,470,900
3	Chicago	8,146,900
4	San Francisco	5,953,100
5	Philadelphia	5,890,600
19	San Diego	2,285,000
28	Sacramento	1,336,500
64	Fresno	597,400
72	Bakersfield	504,500
79	Stockton	443,500
104	Salinas	343,100
106	Santa Barbara	340,900
109	Modesto	327,400
117	Visalia	291,600
176	Merced	165,800
203	Redding	135,600
240	Yuba City	115,800

Note: The Census Bureau Ranks 282 Metropolitan areas in the U.S.
1.29,90 Source: U.S. Bureau of the Census Press Release CB 88-157, 1988.

URBANIZATION OF THE CALIFORNIA POPULATION 1850-1980			
Year	Percent of Population Urbanized	Year	Percent of Population Urbanized
1850	7.4	1920	67.9
1860	20.7	1930	73.3
1870	37.2	1940	71.0
1880	42.9	1950	80.7
1890	48.6	1960	86.4
1900	52.3	1970	90.9
1910	61.8	1980	91.3

1.30,90 Source: California Dept. of Finance, *Report 86-P-3, 1986.*

POPULATION BREAKDOWN BY AGE   1988

California   United States

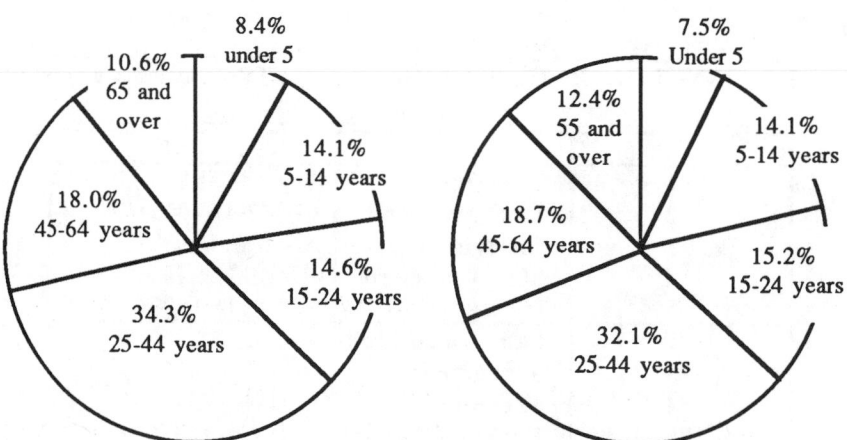

1.31,90 Source: U.S. Census Bureau, *Report P-25, 1044.*

SECTION 1 NOTE
Foreign born Californians make up 15.1 percent of the state's population.

1.32,90

SECTION 1 NOTE
The 1980 population center of California is 35 degrees 28 minutes 48 seconds North and 119 degrees 26 minutes 28 seconds West. The location is near Buttonwillow (Kern County).

1.33,90

Vital Statistics

Vital statistics are the basic numerical records of human biology (births, deaths, fertility) and human decision (marriages, divorces, abortions). California's vital statistics mirror many, but not all, of the broad trends observable in the nation as a whole.

AIDS, which has become a significant health problem for the state of California, will probably be listed among the ten leading causes of death when the 1989 statistics are released. The California Department of Health Services estimates that by 1990 the medical system will be treating 20,000 AIDS patients. AIDS is an expensive disease to treat. For those relying on nongovernmental sources to finance their care, the cost is over $42,000 per year per patient. This means that by 1990 AIDS will cost the health insurance industry almost $.5 billion annually if the $56 million in state Medi-Cal charges are included. The typical Medi-Cal AIDS patient lives for 10.2 months after the initial diagnosis. Increasingly the financial burden of paying for the care of AIDS patients has fallen to the state of California, with Medi-Cal now paying for 33 percent of AIDS patients' care, up from 19 percent in 1983. Caring for children with AIDS is more expensive than caring for adults with the disease. The children's hospital stays, at nearly $26,000 each, are almost twice as costly as those of the average adult AIDS patient.

Although health statistics indicate that AIDS in California is still primarily a disease of homosexual males (in the nation as a whole it is becoming a disease primarily of intravenous drug users), a large number of people have been infected. At the end of 1988 it was estimated that the state's cumulative caseload of AIDS patients was 17,000; this number will probably double by 1990.

All the massive health warnings about AIDS may have had some peripheral but mixed benefits in slowing the spread of related venereal diseases. Gonorrhea cases have dropped sharply (31 percent) in the past two years, although syphilis cases have doubled during the same period.

DEATHS, LIVE BIRTHS, MARRIAGES, DIVORCES AND ANNULMENTS IN CALIFORNIA, 1940-1987									
		Deaths		Live Births		Marriages		Divorces†	
Year	Population	Number	Rate*f*	Number	Rate*f*	Number	Rate*f*	Number	Rate*f*
1940	6,907,387	80,293	11.6	111,840	16.2	45,070	6.5	22,979	3.3
1950	10,586,223	98,583	9.3	244,457	23.1	79,360	7.5	38,833	3.7
1960	15,717,204	135,334	8.6	371,799	23.7	105,352	6.7	49,511	3.2
1970	20,039,000	166,382	8.3	362,652	18.2	172,388	8.6	112,942	5.6
1980	23,771,000	186,440	7.8	402,743	17.0	210,900	8.9	133,500	5.6
1981	24,216,000	184,732	7.6	420,418	17.4	217,348	9.0	133,600	5.5
1982	24,698,000	188,263	7.6	429,641	17.4	230,694	9.4	133,400	5.4
1983	25,186,000	188,018	7.5	435,722	17.3	226,800	8.8	127,500	5.1
1984	25,622,000	195,470	7.6	447,394	17.4	226,600	8.8	142,972	5.6*
1985	26,365,000	201,815	7.7	470,815	17.9	226,113	8.6	127,406	4.8
1986	26,981,000	197,538	7.3	478,822	17.7	219,000	8.1	127,600	4.7
1987	27,663,000	214,486	7.8	494,053	17.9	244,440	8.8	124,090	4.5

* Includes separations. † Includes annulments. *f* Per 100,00 population.
2.1,90 Sources: *U.S. Statistical Abstract* and National Center for Health Statistics, unpublished data, and California Department of Finance, Population Research Unit, *Report E-6A.*

LIVE BIRTHS AND INFANT, NEONATAL, FETAL, AND MATERNAL DEATHS IN CALIFORNIA, 1940-1987									
		Infant Deaths		Neonatal Deaths		Fetal Deaths		Maternal Deaths	
Year	Live Births	Number	Rate*	Number	Rate*	Number	Rate*	Number	Rate**
1940	111,840	4,428	39.5	2,846	25.4	2,280	20.4	318	28.4
1950	244,457	6,095	24.9	4,501	18.4	3,703	15.1	135	5.5
1960	37,199	8,663	23.3	6,405	17.2	4,778	12.9	107	2.9
1970	362,652	6,243	17.2	4,592	12.7	4,082	11.3	77	2.1
1980	402,720	4,451	11.1	2,886	7.2	3,594	8.9	45	1.1
1981	420,418	5,276	10.2	2,711	NA	3,481	8.3	38	0.9
1982	429,631	4,218	9.8	2,686	NA	3,333	7.8	43	1.0
1983	425,722	4,226	9.7	2,711	6.2	3,049	7.0	37	0.8
1984	447,394	4,212	9.4	2,654	NA	3,110	7.0	27	36.0
1985	470,815	4,475	9.5	2,813	6.0	3,278	7.0	36	3.8
1986	481,905	4,298	8.9	2,703	5.6	3,259	6.8	32	0.7
1987	503,655	4,530	9.0	2,767	5.5	3,504	7.0	28	0.6

* Per 1,000 live births. ** Per 10,000 live births.
Note: Birth and mortality statistics were recorded by place of occurrence from 1940 to 1944. They have since been kept by place of residence. Infant deaths occur within one year after birth. Neonatal deaths occur within 28 days after birth. Maternal deaths are those due to complications of pregnancy, childbirth and the puerperium. Fetal deaths registration is believed to be incomplete.
2.2,90 Source: State of Cal., Dept. of Health Services, *Birth, Death, and Fetal Death Records.*

BIRTHS AND DEATHS BY COUNTY, 1987				
County	Births	Birth Rate (per 1,000)	Deaths	Death Rate (per 1,000)
Alameda	20,957	17.1	9,717	7.9
Alpine	16	13.1	4	3.3
Amador	263	10.4	299	11.8
Butte	2,370	14.0	1,770	10.5
Calaveras	348	11.8	297	10.0
Colusa	261	17.6	140	9.5
Contra Costa	11,419	15.4	5,545	7.5
Del Norte	288	14.8	200	10.3
El Dorado	1,696	15.0	856	7.6
Fresno	12,391	20.8	4,602	7.7
Glenn	396	17.2	270	11.7
Humboldt	1,777	15.6	1,045	9.2
Imperial	2,279	20.9	686	6.3
Inyo	228	12.7	240	13.3
Kern	10,453	20.7	3,754	7.4
Kings	1,983	22.6	545	6.2
Lake	650	12.8	655	12.9
Lassen	371	14.0	186	7.0
Los Angeles	166,958	19.7	64,106	7.6
Madera	1,448	18.1	620	7.7
Marin	2,786	12.2	1,726	7.6
Mariposa	163	11.6	154	11.0
Mendocino	1,155	15.4	699	9.3
Merced	3,690	22.2	1,170	7.0
Modoc	126	13.5	87	9.4
Mono	145	15.8	36	3.9
Monterey	6,914	20.2	2,202	6.4
Napa	1,370	13.0	1,063	10.1
Nevada	890	12.1	620	8.4
Orange	39,060	17.6	14,153	6.4
Placer	2,114	14.2	1,179	7.9
Plumas	258	13.0	161	8.1
Riverside	17,583	19.2	8,436	9.2
Sacramento	16,727	17.7	7,331	7.7
San Benito	594	17.9	205	6.2
San Bernardino	25,516	21.2	8,938	7.4
San Diego	41,461	18.1	16,113	7.0
San Francisco	9,705	13.1	8,259	11.1
San Joaquin	8,783	19.8	3,704	8.3
San Luis Obispo	2,668	13.2	1,636	8.1
San Mateo	9,576	15.4	4,842	7.8
Santa Barbara	5,410	15.8	2,506	7.3
Santa Clara	24,518	17.2	8,327	5.9
Santa Cruz	3,803	17.1	1,748	7.8
Shasta	1,990	14.7	1,371	10.1
Sierra	54	15.9	15	4.4
Siskiyou	597	13.9	450	10.5
Solano	5,405	18.1	1,912	6.4
Sonoma	5,329	15.0	3,099	8.7
Stanislaus	6,044	18.5	2,777	8.5
Sutter	1,056	17.5	497	8.2
Tehama	657	14.3	470	10.2
Trinity	166	12.2	117	8.6
Tulare	5,898	20.2	2,299	7.9
Tuolumne	516	11.5	425	9.5
Ventura	10,872	17.3	3,769	6.0
Yolo	1,987	15.4	919	7.1
Yuba	1,238	22.2	443	8.0
State Totals	503,376	18.2	209,395	7.6

2.3,90 Source: State of California, Department of Health Services, *Birth and Death Records.*

| LIVE BIRTHS BY MONTH OF BIRTH 1987 ||
Month	Number of Births
January	40,126
February	36,925
March	41,745
April	40,996
May	42,154
June	42,568
July	44,557
August	43,672
September	44,187
October	42,982
November	40,643
December	42,821
Total Live Births	**503,376**

2.4,90   Source: California Department of Health Services, *Vital Statistics of California,* 1987.

| LIVE BIRTHS BY AGE OF MOTHER, CALIFORNIA, 1981-1987 |||||||
| | 1981 || 1985 || 1987 ||
Age of Mother	Number	Rate per 1,000	Number	Rate per 1,000	Number	Rate per 1,000
Under 15	876	1.0	890	1.0	983	1.1
15-19	55,004	53.1	50,365	52.5	53,586	55.2
20-24	137,056	118.5	136,985	121.2	135,924	123.7
25-29	129,334	115.8	149,523	126.0	158,120	134.3
30-34	73,234	68.9	94,067	79.7	107,459	85.0
35-39	20,977	26.0	33,578	32.1	40,294	35.4
40-44	3,587	5.5	4,953	6.1	6,527	7.1
44 and over	191	0.3	240	0.4	323	0.5
Not stated	159	-	215	-	160	-
Total	**420,418**	**72.0**	**470,816**	**74.6**	**503,376**	**76.6**

2.5,90 Source: California Department of Health Services, *Birth Records.*

SECTION 2 NOTE
In California 15 percent of mothers under the age of 15 receive no prenatal care until the third trimester.

2.6,90

BIRTH, DEATHS, MARRIAGE, DIVORCE, & SUICIDE RATES CALIFORNIA AND THE UNITED STATES									
Birth Rate*		Death Rate*		Marriage Rate*		Divorce Rate*		Suicide Rate†	
Year	Cal.	U.S.	Cal.	U.S.	Cal.	U.S.	Cal.	U.S.	Cal.	U.S.
1940	16.2	19.4	11.6	10.8	6.5	12.1	3.3	2.0	27.2	14.4
1950	23.1	24.1	9.3	9.6	7.5	11.1	3.7	2.6	18.1	11.4
1960	23.7	23.7	8.6	9.5	6.7	8.5	3.2	2.2	15.9	10.6
1970	18.1	18.4	8.3	9.5	8.6	10.6	5.6	3.5	18.7	11.6
1980	16.9	15.9	7.8	8.8	8.9	10.6	5.6	5.2	14.4	11.4
1987	18.1	15.7	7.4	8.7	8.8	9.9	4.5	4.8	14.0	12.7

* per 1,000 † per 100,000

2.7,90 Source: *U.S. Statistical Abstract* & U.S. Center for Health Statistics, *Vital Statistics* of the U.S., & unpublished data.

BABY BOOMS IN CALIFORNIA (in 19 year increments)			
Era	Cal. Number of Births	U.S. Number of Births	Cal. as a % of U.S.
1908-26	1,066,462	55,000,000	1.9%
1927-45	2,033,644	49,000,000	4.2%
1946-64	5,926,084	76,000,000	7.8%
1965-83	6,750,986	66,000,000	10.2%
1984-2002*	8,937,925	68,000,000	13.1%

* Estimates after 1988.

2.8,90 Source: California Dept. of Finance-Population Research Unit, unpublished report Feb. 10, 1988 & *U.S. Statistical Abstract*. U.S. Census Bureau-Population Estimates Section-unpublished data; *Vital Statistics of California*, and *California Statistical Abstract*.

CALIFORNIA LIVE BIRTHS BY RACE, 1987	
Race/Ethnicity	Percent of Births
White	45%
Hispanic	33%
Black	10%
Filipino	3%
Chinese	2%
Japanese	1%
Korean	1%
Vietnamese	1%
Pacific Islander	1%
Cambodian	0.5%
Other Asian	2%
American Indian	1%
Total	100%

2.9,90 Source: State of California, Dept. of Health Services, *Birth Records*.

	Total Number of Live Births, All Races	Nonmarital Live Births (percent)			
County		White (Non-Hispanic)	White (Hispanic)	Black	All Races
LIVE BIRTHS BY MARITAL STATUS, 1987					
Alameda	20,957	17.1	25.5	61.6	27.2
Alpine	16	*	*	*	*
Amador	263	18.4	*	*	19.4
Butte	2,370	24.7	26.1	*	25.6
Calaveras	348	18.1	*	*	18.4
Colusa	261	21.9	*	*	21.8
Contra Costa	11,419	15.3	26.6	62.9	22.2
Del Norte	288	25.9	*	*	27.4
El Dorado	1,696	20.3	31.7	*	21.2
Fresno	12,391	20.5	42.8	70.4	32.2
Glenn	396	23.9	17.1	*	23.0
Humboldt	1,777	25.6	*	*	27.3
Imperial	2,279	18.9	29.6	*	27.3
Inyo	228	19.3	*	*	24.6
Kern	10,453	23.5	38.7	68.3	31.7
Kings	1,983	15.6	37.1	49.6	25.2
Lake	650	27.5	*	*	29.2
Lassen	371	19.9	*	*	20.8
Los Angeles	166,958	18.8	39.2	66.1	33.7
Madera	1,448	19.8	40.7	*	30.9
Marin	2,786	15.3	27.4	*	17.3
Mariposa	163	21.2	*	*	20.9
Mendocino	1,155	28.2	27.7	*	30.2
Merced	3,690	20.6	32.7	49.1	24.2
Modoc	126	16.8	*	*	20.6
Mono	145	10.5	*	*	13.8
Monterey	6,914	11.3	29.2	28.0	20.0
Napa	1,370	18.5	19.4	*	18.6
Nevada	890	18.1	*	*	18.7
Orange	39,060	14.0	31.9	33.7	19.2
Placer	2,114	16.5	24.9	*	17.4
Plumas	258	19.7	*	*	20.9
Riverside	17,583	21.3	31.8	49.4	26.0
Sacramento	16,727	23.1	40.6	63.2	28.8
San Benito	594	16.3	30.8	*	24.1
San Bernardino	25,516	20.4	33.0	52.1	26.3
San Diego	41,461	16.9	32.9	47.6	23.3
San Francisco	9,705	23.3	34.3	67.2	27.5
San Joaquin	8,783	22.8	34.0	67.9	27.3
San Luis Obispo	2,668	15.1	28.1	*	17.2
San Mateo	9,576	12.4	24.9	55.5	17.7
Santa Barbara	5,410	13.1	26.7	44.8	18.8
Santa Clara	24,518	14.8	38.4	47.1	21.5
Santa Cruz	3,803	17.0	29.7	*	21.5
Shasta	1,990	26.2	*	*	26.8
Sierra	54	*	*	*	*
Siskiyou	597	20.0	*	*	21.6
Solano	5,405	17.7	21.8	48.2	22.0
Sonoma	5,329	17.1	30.2	*	19.5
Stanislaus	6,044	23.1	29.0	52.3	24.6
Sutter	1,056	22.6	29.4	*	21.6
Tehama	657	21.8	*	*	23.7
Trinity	166	21.8	*	*	22.3
Tulare	5,898	23.3	40.0	68.3	32.5
Tuolumne	516	20.0	*	*	20.0
Ventura	10,872	11.8	20.0	33.6	14.8
Yolo	1,987	23.3	31.6	*	25.5
Yuba	1,238	25.0	32.1	*	23.6
State Totals	503,376	18.2	35.8	60.7	27.1

* Sample too small to calculate percentages.

2.10,90 Source: California State Department of Health Services, *Birth Records.*

ESTIMATED LIVE BIRTHS TO UNMARRIED WOMEN AS A PERCENT OF TOTAL LIVE BIRTHS BY RACE AND AGE OF MOTHER						
	1966	1970	1976	1980	1985	1987
All Races						
All Ages	9.4	12.6	17.7	20.7	24.5	27.1
Under 15	82.5	81.5	84.8	86.5	84.2	86.0
15-17	33.6	43.8	57.6	63.7	71.6	73.7
18-19	16.7	24.4	36.1	42.0	52.2	56.2
20-24	8.4	11.4	17.6	22.6	29.6	33.9
25-29	5.2	6.0	9.4	12.5	16.9	19.6
30-34	5.3	6.5	8.0	10.7	13.9	15.7
35 and over	5.8	7.8	10.4	12.4	15.8	17.4
White						
All Ages	7.4	9.8	14.4	17.9	22.6	25.4
Under 15	73.3	70.6	48.4	83.6	83.6	85.4
15-17	25.2	34.6	50.4	57.9	68.5	70.9
18-19	13.6	19.3	29.5	36.5	47.6	52.3
20-24	6.9	9.0	13.9	18.8	26.6	31.1
25-29	4.1	4.9	7.6	10.6	15.4	18.0
30-34	4.1	5.1	7.0	9.7	13.3	15.0
35 and over	4.7	6.7	9.6	11.7	16.0	17.7
Black						
All Ages	31.6	42.3	54.8	56.5	58.2	60.7
Under 15	93.5	96.1	96.5	96.4	90.6	94.2
15-17	68.6	81.1	89.2	91.8	90.8	90.7
18-19	42.1	59.0	76.1	79.6	83.4	84.6
20-24	26.2	37.2	53.4	58.7	62.4	65.4
25-29	19.7	24.7	36.6	41.3	46.4	50.3
30-34	20.4	25.9	30.6	36.2	40.4	44.8
35 and over	19.8	23.6	29.5	36.2	38.2	41.1

2.11,90 Source: State of California, Dept. of Health Sevices, *Birth Records.*

CALIFORNIA ABORTION OVERVIEW, 1987
Approximately 304,000 abortions per year. Number of abortions increased by two percent from 1984 to 1985. 47% of abortions performed in clinics or doctors' offices, 53% in hospitals, 96% on an outpatient basis. At least 186 California hospitals perform abortions; 1, 691 facilities perform abortions. 26% of abortions performed on teenagers, down from 31% in 1980. At least 81% of Medi-Cal abortions take place in the first trimester. Medi-Cal Funded abortions cost $30,710,000 in 1987. The number of abortions paid for by Medi-Cal has declined 18% since 1977. 5,413 women had 2 or more Medi-Cal funded abortions. Teenage abortions have declined since 1986.

2.12,90 Source: California Health and Welfare Agency, Center for Health Statistics, *Medi-Cal Reports 89-01011,* 1989.

ABORTIONS* IN CALIFORNIA

Year	California	United States	California as a % of United States
1973	143,900	744,600	19%
1975	165,600	1,034,200	16%
1979	248,080	1,497,700	17%
1980	250,380	1,553,890	16%
1981	262,710	1,577,340	17%
1982	265,740	1,573,920	17%
1983	NA	1,575,000	NA
1984	297,730	1,577,180	19%
1985	304,130	1,588,550	19%

* Abortion data are based on voluntary reports and are incomplete. The Guttmacher data are based on a more complete survey of abortions than is conducted by the state but still are believed to underestimate the actual number of abortions.
2.13,90 Source: Alan Guttmacher Institute, 1989.

MEDI-CAL FUNDED ABORTIONS NUMBER, COST AND RATE

Year	Number of Abortions*	Cost per Abortion	Monthly Rate †
1977	105,550	$320	13.99
1978	98,409	$333	13.45
1979	99,412	$328	14.55
1980	103,097	$339	12.85
1981	98,513	$345	12.00
1982	91,265	$335	11.32
1983	84,144	$315	11.38
1984	79,705	$331	10.99
1985	76,929	$343	10.48
1986	79,988	$344	10.72
1987	86,116	$357	11.22

* Actual number of abortions is probably higher since many Medi-Cal claims do not report specific services rendered.
† Per 1,000 eligible women.
2.14,90 Source: State of Cal., Dept. of Health Services, *Medi-Cal Reports, #89-01011*, 1989.

SECTION 2 NOTE

In 1987 Medi-Cal funded 118,745 deliveries, 19 percent of them by cesarean section. The average cost was $1,957 per delivery.
2.15,90

NUMBER OF MEDI-CAL FUNDED ABORTIONS, BY COUNTY 1987

County	Total	County	Total
Alameda	4,852	Placer	402
Alpine	1	Plumas	37
Amador	34	Riverside	3,001
Butte	693	Sacramento	4,490
Calaveras	61	San Benito	127
Colusa	17	San Bernardino	4,580
Contra Costa	2,072	San Diego	6,214
Del Norte	73	San Francisco	2,810
El Dorado	275	San Joaquin	1,872
Fresno	3,628	San Luis Obispo	358
Glenn	84	San Mateo	1,052
Humboldt	498	Santa Barbara	3
Imperial	224	Santa Clara	3,837
Inyo	55	Santa Cruz	860
Kern	1,843	Shasta	690
Kings	214	Sierra	9
Lake	161	Siskiyou	107
Lassen	62	Solano	968
Los Angeles	27,063	Sonoma	1,103
Madera	194	Stanislaus	1,356
Marin	330	Sutter	188
Mariposa	27	Tehama	119
Mendocino	256	Trinity	28
Merced	646	Tulare	966
Modoc	15	Toulumne	108
Mono	10	Ventura	1,441
Monterey	982	Yolo	385
Napa	278	Yuba	200
Nevada	159		
Orange	3,998	**State Total**	**86,116**

2.16,90 Source: State of Cal., Dept. of Health Services, *HR 70 Summary, Maternal Care File, 1987.*

MEDI-CAL ABORTIONS BY AGE

Age	Percentage
Under 15	0.6%
15-19	25.6%
20-29	57.8%
30-34	10.5%
35-44	5.2%

Data apply only to Medi-Cal funded abortions.
2.17,90 Source: California Health and Welfare Agency, Center for Health Statistics, Medical Reports #89-01011, 1989.

ABORTIONS - CALIFORNIA AND THE NATION RATE AND RATIO				
	Rate*		Ratio†	
Year	California	U.S.	California	U.S.
1973	30.5	16.3	485	239
1980	43.7	29.3	598	428
1984	47.8	28.1	654	422
1985	47.9	28.0	640	425

* Rate per 1,000 women.   † Ratio per 1,000 live births.
2.18,90 Source: *U.S. Statistical Abstract.*

SECTION 2 NOTE
Of women who have babies in California, 75 percent receive prenatal care beginning in the first trimester, 18 percent in the second trimester, and 4 percent in the third trimester; 2 percent get no prenatal care, and 1 percent are unclassified.

2.19,90

NUMBER OF CHILDREN PLACED FOR ADOPTION IN CALIFORNIA BY TYPE OF PLACEMENT 1970-1988				
	Adoption Agencies			
Year*	Public	Private	Independent	Intercounty
1970-1971	4121	1438	2603	92
1971-1972	3012	922	2456	105
1972-1973	2488	681	2080	101
1973-1974	2020	529	2396	132
1974-1975	1971	548	2292	364
1975-1976	1998	582	2117	376
1976-1977	1794	478	2056	245
1977-1978	1571	533	1591	258
1978-1979	1679	526	1552	182
1979-1980	1685	608	2074	194
1980-1981	1704	464	2318	233
1981-1982	1442	422	2101	299
1982-1983	1708	449	2101	351
1983-1984	1776	397	2308	141
1984-1985	1848	494	2033	417
1985-1986	2042	447	2220	425
1986-1987	2285	394	2396	505
1987-1988	2174	468	2537	515

* July 1-June 30.
2.20,89   Source: California Dept. of Social Services, Statistical Services Branch, *Adoptions in California,* Annual.

TEN LEADING CAUSES OF DEATH IN CALIFORNIA IN 1987 (number, rate, & percent distribution)	
Causes of Death	**Number**
Diseases of the Heart	69,327
Malignant neoplasms	47,358
Cerebrovascular disease	15,714
Accidents and adverse effects	10,583
Chronic obstructive pulmonary disease and allied conditions	8,979
Pnemonia and influenza	8,263
Chornic liver disease and cirrhosis	3,920
Suicide	3,870
Diabetes mellitus	3,283
Homicide	2,949
All other causes	35,149
Total-All Causes	**209,395**
	Rate*
Diseases of the Heart	250.6
Malignant neoplasms	171.2
Cerebrovascular disease	56.8
Accidents and adverse effects	38.3
Chronic obstructive pulmonary disease and allied conditions	32.5
Pnemonia and influenza	29.9
Chornic liver disease and cirrhosis	14.2
Suicide	14
Diabetes mellitus	11.9
Homicide	10.7
All other causes	127.1
Total-All Causes	**757**
	Percent
Diseases of the Heart	33.1
Malignant neoplasms	22.6
Cerebrovascular disease	7.5
Accidents and adverse effects	5.1
Chronic obstructive pulmonary disease and allied conditions	4.3
Pnemonia and influenza	3.9
Chornic liver disease and cirrhosis	1.9
Suicide	1.8
Diabetes mellitus	1.6
Homicide	
All other causes	16.8
Total-All Causes	**100**

* Rates are per 100,000 estimated population.
2.21,90 Source: State of California, Dept. of Health Services, *Death Records.*

CASES OF SELECTED NOTIFIABLE DISEASES, CALIFORNIA, 1970-1988							
	1970	1980	1982	1984	1985	1986	1987	1988
Disease	Cases	Cases	Cases	Cases	Cases	Cases	Cases	Cases
Amebiasis	395	1,847	3,105	2,332	2,145	1,788	1,411	1,277
Anthrax	-	-	-	-	-	-	-	-
Botulism	2	36	29	47	42	38	27	10
Brucellosis	28	27	30	17	26	19	18	20
Cholera	NA	NA	NA	NA	NA	NA	NA	3
Coccidioidomycosis	456	631	414	417	432	435	476	434
Congenital Rubella Syndrom	NA	NA	NA	NA	NA	NA	3	1
Conjunctifvitis, Acute Newborn	21	15	24	6	23	9	6	40
Dengue	NA	NA	NA	NA	NA	NA	5	4
Diarrhea of the Newborn	72	21	23	1	14	1	18	1
Diptheria	6	-	NA	1	-	-	1	-
Encephalitis, Viral	380	128	183	172	173	146	154	134
Food & Waterborne Illness	673	1,124	NA	NA	NA	2,185	NA	NA
Food Poisoning Cases	NA	NA	521	556	636	1,130	2,149	119
German Measles (Rubella)	5,498	946	1,431	196	138	242	140	85
Hepatitis, Viral	11,484	13,004	10,727	15,012	16,554	15,452	13,195	10,506
Type A (Infectious)	9,798	6,259	4,400	7,187	7,421	7,917	7,230	6,043
Type B (Serum)	1,686	3,972	3,733	5,411	5,898	5,076	4,372	3,351
Non A - Non B	NA	NA	877	1,176	1,111	956	687	543
Unspecified	NA	2,773	1,581	1,238	2,124	1,503	897	555
Lapses of Consciousness	NA	NA	NA	NA	NA	NA	14,292	15,083
Legionellosis	NA	NA	NA	NA	NA	NA	47	62
Leprosy	55	91	77	93	155	117	110	73
Leptospirosis	7	5	1	1	1	1	1	2
Listeriosis	NA	NA	NA	NA	NA	NA	201	158
Malaria	425	741	360	362	343	420	325	331
Measles	1,979	1,051	831	327	265	486	813	818
Meningitis, Viral	1,582	1,140	1,383	1,152	1,067	1,302	1,492	1,114
Meningococcal Infections	420	258	293	234	300	356	633	585
Mumps	6,420	485	484	421	422	337	397	494
Pertussis	536	147	115	159	276	303	217	290
Plague	3	3	NA	6	0	3	NA	2
Poliomyelitis	2	2	2	1	2	1	1	-
Psittacosis	9	25	27	20	14	17	9	15
Q-Fever	15	13	22	5	7	5	6	21
Rabies, Animal	NA	NA	NA	544	552	539	402	417
Relapsing Fever	4	11	14	11	6	4	11	11
Reye Syndrom	NA	NA	NA	NA	NA	NA	4	2
Rheumatic Fever	40	15	12	6	10	14	NA	NA
Rocky Mountain Spotted Fever	2	4	5	2	3	1	3	2
Salmonellosis	2,214	2,951	3,562	3,926	4,632	5,491	5,915	5,621
Shigellosis	1,899	4,856	3,545	5,066	4,243	4,727	4,308	7,892
Streptococcal Infections	33,481	25,500	24,290	24,642	41,608	36,337	36,434	34,152
Tetanus	9	14	12	7	5	3	6	3
Toxic Shock Syndrom	NA	NA	NA	NA	NA	NA	46	53
Trichinosis	19	6	4	0	8	0	7	5
Tuberculosis	3,456	4,276	3,545	3,276	3,505	3,507	3,607	3,285
Tularemia	7	11	6	8	4	3	2	4
Typhoid Fever	62	1,241	102	112	137	142	111	142
Typhus Fever	1	2	5	8	7	6	8	10
Venereal Diseases								
AIDS	-	11	209	1,025	2,061	3,114	3,743	4,359
Chancroid	77	26	323	135	23	40	214	66
Gonorrhea, Total	104,568	135,885	112,032	106,381	112,922	111,102	93,876	64,674
Granuloma Inguinale	5	9	4	6	3	1	1	-
Lymphogranuloma Venereum	45	17	27	53	19	18	9	14
Syphilis, Total	10,982	12,270	9,950	9,462	10,928	12,034	19,161	19,654
Primary and Secondary	2,348	4,696	4,151	3,895	4,286	5,240	7,383	5,717

2.22,90 Source: California Dept. of Health Services, Infectious Disease Section, *Cal. Morbidity*.

DEATHS FROM SELECTED EXTERNAL CAUSES 1987	
Accidental Deaths	
Transport Accidents	
Motor Vehicle	5,772
Other	363
Total	**6,135**
Nontransport Accidents	
Poisoning by Solids and Liquids	1,207
Poisoning by Gases and Vapors	54
Falls	1,055
Fire and Flames	291
Drowning	523
Other	992
Total	**4,122**
Late Effects of Accidental Injury	111
Total Accidental Deaths	**10,297**
Medical Misadventures	
Surgical and Medical	70
Adverse Patient Reaction	
Surgical and Medical	153
Drugs, Medications and	
Biological Substances	12
Total	**235**
Suicide	3,861
Homicide	2,991
Legal Intervention	67
Injury, Undetermined Whether	
Accidentally or Purposely Inflicted	237
Injury Resulting From	
Operations of War	1

2.23,90 Source: California Department of Health Services, *Death Records*.

SECTION 2 NOTE
California's suicide rate of 14.0 per 100,000 people is 16 percent higher than the national rate of 12.7.

2.24,90

DEATH RATES* FOR CANCER, HEART DISEASE, AND STROKE						
	Cancer		Heart Disease		Stroke	
Year	Cal.	U.S.	Cal.	U.S.	Cal.	U.S.
1951	140	140	354	356	102	107
1961	139	150	318	363	91	106
1970	152	163	304	362	91	106
1980	169	184	280	336	70	75
1981	169	184	270	329	65	71
1982	173	187	273	326	63	68
1983	171	189	265	329	59	67
1984	173	192	263	324	59	65
1985	173	193	262	323	58	64
1986	172	195	253	318	56	62

* Deaths per 100,000 population.
  2.25,90 Source: U.S. Statistical Abstract and National Center for Health Statistics, unpublished data.

DEATHS BY MONTH OF DEATH 1987	
Month	Number of Deaths
January	19,392
February	16,728
March	18,604
April	17,383
May	17,086
June	16,668
July	16,565
August	16,637
September	16,198
October	17,628
November	17,388
December	19,418
Total Deaths	209,395

2.26,89 Source: California Department of Health Services, *Death Records.*

DEATHS BY AGE OF DECEDENT CALIFORNIA, 1981-1987						
Age of Decedent	1981		1985		1987	
	Number	Rate*	Number	Rate*	Number	Rate*
Under 1 year	4,276	1,032.4	4,475	966.3	4,520	991.9
1-4	874	62.3	885	49.8	924	49.1
5-14	941	27.3	888	24.6	904	23.2
15-24	4,956	109.9	4,511	104.4	4,623	107.8
25-44	12,170	166.4	14,377	169.7	12,134	183.1
45-64	39,234	847.9	38,725	791.0	38,654	761.9
65-74	41,391	2,725.8	44,395	2,602.9	45,374	2,473.0
75-84	46,104	6,130.9	52,433	6,055.2	97,688†	8,035.8†
85 and over	34,646	15,282.8	40,968	16,143.9	NA	NA
Age not stated	140	—	158	—	161	NA
Total	184,732	762.9	201,815	765.5	209,395	757.0

* Rates are per 100,000 population.
† All deaths aged 75 and over.
    2.27,90 Source: State of California, Department of Health Services, *Death Records*.

SUICIDES			
Year	Number	Rate*	Percent of All Deaths
1978	3,645	16.3	2.1%
1979	3,534	15.2	2.0%
1980	3,445	14.4	1.8%
1981	3,579	14.7	1.9%
1983	3,635	14.4	1.9%
1984	3,690	14.4	1.9%
1985	3,782	14.3	1.9%
1986	3,960	14.7	2.0%
1987	3,870	14.0	1.8%

* Rates are per 100,000 population.
    2.28,90 Source: California Dept. of Health Services, Center for Health Statistics, *Death Records*.

VENEREAL DISEASE, 1988				
	Syphilis		Gonorrhea	
County	Cases	Rate*	Cases	Rate*
Alameda	775	38.1	7,303	644
Alpine	0	0.0	0	0
Amador	7	0.0	8	29
Berkeley†	66	45.9	424	397
Butte	11	0.0	103	60
Calaveras	1	0.0	2	7
Colusa	3	0.0	11	74
Contra Costa	361	26.9	2,837	377
El Dorado	4	0.9	30	26
Fresno	563	24.4	2,363	390
Glenn	15	4.3	14	60
Humboldt/Del Norte	5	0.0	78	58
Imperial	68	5.4	91	82
Inyo	2	0.0	6	33
Kern	790	35.4	1,454	284
Kings	67	18.5	133	145
Lake	12	0.0	10	19
Lassen	11	0.0	5	19
Long Beach†	790	52.4	2,763	665
Los Angeles (excl L.B./Pas.)	11,229	42.3	30,036	375
Madera	197	35.5	222	272
Marin	20	3.1	161	70
Mariposa	0	0.0	0	0
Mendocino	7	0.0	42	56
Merced	63	11.9	299	177
Modoc	1	10.8	0	0
Mono	0	0.0	7	75
Monterey	246	6.6	837	242
Napa	9	3.8	39	37
Nevada	1	0.0	17	23
Orange	1,183	8.8	2,887	129
Pasadena†	120	22.7	542	411
Placer	10	2.0	42	28
Plumas	2	5.0	7	35
Riverside	373	9.2	1,287	136
Sacramento	154	5.5	2,680	279
San Benito	12	2.9	11	32
San Bernardino	378	13.2	2,408	194
San Diego	1,233	18.4	6,538	281
San Francisco	634	30.4	6,573	887
San Joaquin	664	63.9	1,379	306
San Luis Obispo	37	2.0	114	56
San Mateo	179	4.6	1,527	243
Santa Barbara	139	4.3	357	103
Santa Clara	364	7.1	2,044	143
Santa Cruz	199	17.7	309	137
Shasta	4	0.0	119	87
Sierra	0	0.0	0	0
Siskiyou	4	4.6	18	42
Solano	41	5.9	1,266	417
Sonoma	33	0.3	305	85
Stanislaus	103	12.0	668	200
Sutter	21	18.1	87	143
Tehama	14	0.0	9	19
Trinity	3	0.0	1	7
Tulare	243	23.4	691	234
Tuolumne	39	2.2	7	16
Ventura	208	12.2	405	64
Yolo	14	1.5	135	101
Yuba	31	15.9	78	138
State Totals	**21,763**	**23.6**	**81,789**	**292**

* Per 100,000 population.

† Seperate data for the cities of Berkeley, Long Beach, and Pasadena. Counties without cases are omitted.

2.29,90 Source: California Dpt. of Health Services, Sexually Transmitted Disease Section, Venereal Disease Facts, 1988.

AIDS IN CALIFORNIA FACTORS ASSOCIATED WITH THE DISEASE (ADULTS AND ADOLESCENTS)						
Patient Group	Male	(%)	Female	(%)	Total	(%)
Homosexual or Bisexual Male	13,620	82	0	0	13,620	80
Homosexual or Bisexual Male and IV drug user	1,717	10	0	0	1,717	10
IV drug user	492	3	130	28	622	4
Recipient of blood transfusion	265	2	136	29	401	2
Hemophiliac	105	1	8	2	113	1
None of above/ other causes	302	2	47	10	349	2
Heterosexual contact	92	1	142	31	234	1
Total	16,593	100	463	100	17,056	100

Note: 76% of AIDS patients are non-Hispanic Caucasion, 12% are Hispanic, 11% are non Hispanic Blacks and 1% are Asian and other groups.

2.30,90 Source: Cal. Dept. of Health Statistics, *Surveillance Report,* 1989.

AIDS IN CALIFORNIA			
Year	Cases	Deaths	% of U.S. Cases
before 1980	1	0	1
1980	12	9	NA
1981	57	51	19
1982	207	184	20
1983	685	618	24
1984	1,325	1,143	23
1985	2,385	2,026	22
1986	3,712	2,685	22
1987	4,778	2,507	20
1988	4,320	1,206	21
Total	17,482	10,429	21

2.31,90 Source: Cal. Dept. of Health Statistics, *Surveillance Report,* 1989, and U.S. Center for Disease Control in Atlanta, phone report.

AIDS IN CALIFORNIA TOP METRO AREAS		
Area	Cases	% of State Cases
San Francisco	6,684	39%
Los Angeles	6,053	35%
San Diego	1,141	7%

Note: Cases and deaths Jan. 1981 to Dec. 31, 1988.

2.32,90 Source: California Dept. of Health Statistics, *Surveillance Report,* 1989.

The California Aqueduct. Photo Courtesy of the California Department of Water
Resources.

Immigration and Visitors

After a decade of relatively slow population growth - the 1970s - California's population increased dramatically during the 1980s. From 1980 to 1987 the state added 518,000 people per year. Much of this growth, about 60 percent, has resulted from migration into the state. Fifty percent of the migrants are legal immigrants, two-thirds of them Asian and about one-third Hispanic. Another 33 percent of the migrants are illegal or undocumented immigrants, 85 percent of them Hispanic, virtually none Asian. Altogether illegals make up 6 percent of the state's total population. Finally, 17 percent of the migrants are U.S. citizens moving to California from another state.

Many people wondered what effect the 1987 federal immigration law would have on illegal immigration into the United States. Immigration and Naturalization Service statistics on illegal border crossings suggest that the law is having little impact. Economic hardship in Central America seems to be so potent a factor in immigration that a change in federal law has little dissuasive power. The preponderance of Hispanic and Asian immigrants suggests that over the next few decades the state's population will have a more distinctively Latin and Asian cast.

Most of the people who come to California are not immigrants but visitors. In 1987 visitors to the state included 30 million Americans and 6 million foreigners. In addition, over 70 million Californians traveled about in their home state during the same year. Mexico, Japan, and Canada sent the largest numbers of foreign visitors to our state. These travelers tend to be prosperous: in 1987 they spent almost $34 billion in California and generated 533,000 travel-oriented jobs and $1.5 billion in state and local taxes. Air transportation accounts for about one-quarter of their travel expenditures, restaurants and bars for another quarter. Retail stores and hotels/motels consume another 35 percent of the tourist dollar, with food stores, gas stations, and recreation businesses taking up the rest.

As long as earthquakes, fires, volcanoes, and traffic jams do not scare away the tourist, California will remain the number one destination state for both U.S. residents and international visitors.

NUMBER OF IMMIGRANTS TO THE U.S. SETTLING IN CALIFORNIA BY COUNTRY OF BIRTH
Fiscal Year 1988

County of Origin	Number	County of Origin	Number
Afghanistan	1,195	Korea	9,748
Burma	467	Laos	3,649
Canada	2,243	Mexico	53,622
China	11,273	Nicaragua	1,308
Colombia	771	Pakistan	1,009
Cuba	645	Peru	1,206
Czechoslovakia	354	Philippines	25,012
El Salvador	6,829	Poland	865
France	644	Portugal	253
Greece	236	Romania	980
Guatemala	2,726	Taiwan	4,300
Hong Kong	3,750	Thailand	2,754
India	4,576	U.S.S.R.	805
Iran	8,160	United Kingdom	2,684
Iraq	291	Vietnam	11,096
Israel	775	West Germany	1,049
Italy	371	Other	18,072
Japan	1,689		
Kampuchea	3,289	**Total**	**188,696**

3.1,90 Source: U.S. Immigration and Naturalization Service, Statistical Analysis Branch, unpublished data, 1988.

FOREIGN IMMIGRATION, 1974-1988

Year	California	New York	California as a Percent of U.S.
1974	86,821	88,068	22
1976	113,822	105,744	23
1978	146,061	100,542	24
1979	118,880	94,401	26
1982	162,982	85,048	27
1983	134,791	93,159	24
1984	140,289	NA	26
1985	155,403	104,734	27
1986	168,790	110,206	27
1987	161,164	114,194	27
1988	188,696	109,259	29

3.2,90 Source: U.S. Immigration & Naturalization Service, Statistical Analysis Branch, unpublished data.

NUMBER OF ILLEGAL IMMIGRANTS SEIZED IN CALIFORNIA 1982-1988			
	Place of Seizure		
Year	On or Near the U.S.-Mexican Border	Northern California	Total
1982*	NA	NA	450,558
1984	476,391	54,111	530,502
1985	510,165	52,213	562,378
1986	724,842	46,454	771,296
1987	555,618	15,112	570,730
1988	472,771	11,371	484,142

* Fiscal Year.
3.3,90 Source: U.S. Immigration and Naturalization Service, unpublished data.

NONIMMIGRANTS TO CALIFORNIA, 1988		
Type of Nonimmigrant	Number	California as a % of U.S.
Foreign Government	8,278	9%
Business Visitors	326,462	14%
Pleasure Visitors	1,681,196	16%
Aliens in Transit	11,681	44%
Traders and Investors	26,071	21%
Students	54,581	18%
Students' Dependents	3,169	12%
Temporary Agricultural Workers	62,172	52%
International Representatives	639	11%
Temporary Workers & Trainees	73,912	38%
Temporary Workers' Dependents	3,269	17%
Foreign Press	2,860	14%
Exchange Visitors	17,596	11%
Exchange Visitors' Dependents	5,103	14%
Fiancés of U.S. Citizens	1,283	22%
Fiancés' Dependents	144	21%
Company Transferees	8,771	14%
Company Transferees' Dependents	6,024	16%
NATO Officials	832	10%
Parolees	22,284	26%
Refugees	35,529	45%
Other	2,248	15%
Total	2,291,932	16%

3.4,90 Source: U.S. Bureau of Immigration & Naturalization, Statistical Analysis Branch, unpublished data.

PERSONS NATURALIZED AS U.S. CITIZENS IN CALIFORNIA AND NEW YORK 1974-1988

Year	California	New York	California as a % of U.S.
1974	23,460	26,359	18%
1976	31,861	40,419	17%
1978	36,544	31,840	21%
1980	39,424	29,557	25%
1982	33,658	37,122	19%
1983	33,411	32,410	19%
1984	40,490	35,049	21%
1985	70,519	37,250	29%
1986	105,284	39,571	38%
1987	82,607	32,320	36%
1988	65,397	38,457	27%

3.5,90 Source: U.S. Immigration and Naturalization Service, Statistical Analysis Branch, unpublished data.

REFUGEE RESETTLEMENT IN CALIFORNIA*

Type of Refugee	1987	% of U.S.†	1988	% of U.S.†
Southeast Asian	16,195	40%	15,632	45%
E. Europe and Soviet Union	3,109	27%	13,394	48%
Cuba, Ethiopia, and Near East	6,053	50%	5,762	43%

* Refugees who initially settle in California.
† Percent of all such refugees to the U.S. who settle in California.
3.6,90 Source: U.S. Dept. of Health and Human Services, Office of Refugee Resettlement, unpublished data.

CALIFORNIA COUNTIES WITH THE TEN LARGEST REFUGEE POPULATIONS, 1987

Rank	County	Number of Refugees
1	Los Angeles	116,000
2	Orange	58,000
3	Santa Clara	41,000
4	San Diego	32,000
5	San Francisco	30,000
6	San Joaquin	30,000
7	Fresno	26,000
8	Sacramento	25,000
9	Alameda	25,000
10	Merced	9,000

Note: 93% of the refugees in California are Southeast Asian Refugees.
3.7,90 Source: California Department of Finance, *Estimates of Refugees in California Counties and the State*, 1987.

MIGRATION BETWEEN CALIFORNIA AND OTHER STATES 1986-1987					
	To Cali-fornia	From Cali-fornia		To Cali-fornia	From Cali-fornia
New England			**South Atlantic**		
Maine	672	826	(continued)		
New Hampshire	1,101	1,006	West Virginia	636	304
Vermont	479	284	North Carolina	3,202	2,437
Massachusetts	6,909	3,484	South Carolina	1,534	1,565
Rhode Island	879	582	Georgia	3,981	4,588
Conneticut	4,014	2,910	Florida	11,809	13,059
Middle Atlantic			**East South Central**		
New York	16,570	11,097	Kentucky	1,606	1,379
New Jersey	7,565	4,419	Tennessee	2,481	771
Pennsylvania	7,519	6,677	Alabama	1,819	1,641
			Mississippi	1,469	597
East North Central			**West South Central**		
Ohio	10,053	5,538	Arkansas	1,948	3,186
Indiana	4,800	3,241	Lousiana	5,125	2,720
Illinois	17,233	5,949	Oklahoma	6,205	3,191
Michigan	11,613	6,528	Texas	30,386	17,569
Wisconsin	5,012	2,783			
West North Central			**Mountain**		
Minnesota	6,267	3,113	Montana	2,435	1,610
Iowa	3,747	1,755	Idaho	4,251	3,618
Missouri	5,146	3,747	Wyoming	2,054	921
North Dakota	1,149	378	Colorado	14,565	11,520
South Dakota	1,140	529	New Mexico	3,900	2,719
Nebraska	1,513	1,112	Arizona	15,158	15,727
Kansas	3,363	2,017	Utah	6,539	4,378
			Nevada	7,665	14,724
South Atlantic			**Pacific**		
Delaware	415	414	Washington	15,535	13,368
Maryland	3,998	2,762	Oregon	13,538	15,330
District of			Alaska	3,378	2,053
Columbia	601	790	Hawaii	5,572	2,180
Virgina	6,429	6,579	Other/Unknown	-	4,574
			Total	**339,739**	**224,249**

* Data based on driver license address changes July 1, 1986 to June 30, 1987. Outmigration data adjusted.

3.8,90 Source: California Department of Finance, Population Research Unit, unpublished report.

NET COUNTY MIGRATION 1988			
County	Net Migration	County	Net Migration
Alameda	5,712	Placer	6,711
Alpine	-10	Plumas	218
Amador	2,043	Riverside	58,606
Butte	4,297	Sacramento	18,035
Calaveras	1,911	San Benito	1,150
Colusa	293	San Bernardino	61,983
Contra Costa	14,816	San Diego	63,898
Del Norte	689	San Francisco	-5,821
El Dorado	5,929	San Joaquin	5,399
Fresno	9,650	San Luis Obispo	6,613
Glenn	298	San Mateo	3,227
Humboldt	1,373	Santa Barbara	3,276
Imperial	2,919	Santa Clara	2,998
Inyo	262	Santa Cruz	3,530
Kern	8,537	Shasta	4,843
Kings	3,247	Sierra	79
Lake	1,283	Siskiyou	731
Lassen	2,429	Solano	10,488
Los Angeles	-2,541	Sonoma	9,498
Madera	1,665	Stanislaus	10,335
Marin	2,250	Sutter	850
Mariposa	505	Tehama	1,008
Mendocino	988	Trinity	363
Merced	2,710	Tulare	3,423
Modoc	170	Tuolumne	3,850
Mono	294	Ventura	8,880
Monterey	-768	Yolo	3,317
Napa	1,555	Yuba	325
Nevada	3,036		
Orange	15,597	**Total**	**378,952**

3.9,90 Source: Cal. Department of Finance, Population Research Unit, *Report E-6.*

SECTION 3 NOTE
According to the California Department of Finance, 1,725,000 illegal immigrants in the state qualify for amnesty under federal legislation: 64 percent of them live in Los Angeles County, 8 percent in Orange County, and 9 percent in the San Francisco Bay Area.

3.10,90

TRAVELERS IN CALIFORNIA 1987 BASIC TRAVEL FACTS
105 million people traveled to or through California. 6 million of these were foreigners
71% of travelelers were California residents. 29% of travelers were from out of state. 72% of travelers in California were just on vacation or pleasure trips. $33.8 billion was spent by travelers in California (up 7.6% from 1986) California was the number one state in travel expenditures.
66% of visitors to California come by airplane. 38% of visitors to California come from the Western U.S. 45% of visitors to California are college graduates. 533,000 California jobs are generated by tourism. 4.6% of California's non-agricultural emplyment is in tourism.
$909 million in state tax revenue is generated by tourism. $582 million in local tax revenue is generated by tourism. $7.6 billion in payroll is generated by travel. 1.5 million Mexicans, 1 million Japanese, 800,000 Canadians, and 1.2 million Europeans visited California.

3.11,90 Source: *Number & Characteristics of Travelers to California in 1987-*
A report prepared for the Cal. Office of Economic Research, June 1988.

IMPACT OF TRAVEL ON CALIFORNIA COUNTIES, 1986			
County	Total Travel Expenditures (thousands)	Travel Generated Payroll (thousands)	Travel Generated Employment (jobs)	Local Tax Receipts (thousands)
Alameda	1,025,155	214,428	18,088	21,731
Alpine	13,943	2,419	281	265
Amador	27,208	4,585	628	375
Butte	73,695	13,299	1,850	1,055
Calaveras	32,233	5,338	703	347
Colusa	11,836	2,174	268	172
Contra Costa	491,586	94,760	9,901	8,620
Del Norte	52,051	9,484	1,264	707
El Dorado	273,824	47,091	5,246	6,964
Fresno	322,666	58,222	6,900	6,396
Glenn	15,422	2,840	369	222
Humboldt	112,504	19,412	2,373	2,209
Imperial	63,377	11,324	1,431	1,072
Inyo	57,362	10,573	1,479	1,361
Kern	303,929	53,135	6,443	5,929
Kings	30,842	5,601	785	438
Lake	42,314	7,966	1,030	636
Lassen	17,985	3,097	415	232
Los Angeles	5,243,703	1,063,717	85,095	148,939
Madera	47,217	8,380	1,059	625
Marin	139,042	27,293	2,363	2,851
Mariposa	123,329	20,166	2,393	2,571
Mendocino	120,523	20,573	2,712	2,650
Merced	77,881	15,050	1,970	1,181
Modoc	13,587	2,223	358	161
Mono	124,487	22,581	2,225	2,837
Monterey	684,484	126,735	12,070	21,375
Napa	166,348	33,020	3,356	4,840
Nevada	55,988	10,629	1,293	918
Orange	1,991,721	410,348	37,459	51,892
Placer	142,641	25,344	2,839	3,155
Plumas	34,818	5,977	749	451
Riverside	1,017,046	202,102	19,599	21,935
Sacramento	497,955	92,501	10,087	11,438
San Benito	20,929	4,059	476	233
San Bernardino	600,361	110,055	12,914	10,840
San Diego	2,235,715	454,471	44,574	49,383
San Francisco	2,179,095	469,900	32,552	77,598
San Joaquin	179,262	31,846	3,760	2,916
San Luis Obispo	323,750	68,069	8,316	6,535
San Mateo	680,351	136,990	9,980	17,944
Santa Barbara	461,577	90,228	9,502	12,354
Santa Clara	1,426,908	275,192	26,971	35,823
Santa Cruz	230,030	45,513	5,062	5,414
Shasta	111,120	19,505	2,356	2,089
Sierra	17,858	2,956	367	174
Siskiyou	49,021	7,897	1,046	751
Solano	122,005	21,367	2,492	2,106
Sonoma	437,546	82,374	8,651	6,248
Stanislaus	128,568	23,586	2,887	1,972
Sutter	25,698	4,767	608	352
Tehama	25,407	4,455	639	401
Trinity	17,913	2,970	393	182
Tulare	149,587	25,658	3,219	2,503
Tuolumne	55,682	9,346	1,141	927
Ventura	345,772	67,664	7,284	6,946
Yolo	78,661	14,431	1,675	1,587
Yuba	27,845	5,011	567	262
State Totals	23,379,363	4,630,697	432,544	582,118

3.12,90 Source: California Department of Commerce, *Regional and Economic Impacts of California Travel 1985 & 1986, March 1988.*

Health

For the past two decades the cost of health care has been skyrocketing, propelled by tens of billions of dollars in new government money, eye-opening advances in medical techniques and technology, and the American legal system, which has brought us seven-figure malpractice suits. Nowadays many doctors practice defensive medicine, ordering multiple tests for their patients not so much for diagnostic information as for protection from lawsuits.

The efforts of government and business to control the cost of health care and hospital stays have led to a major expansion of prepaid health plans and health maintenance organizations (HMOs) in California. Many expect these new medical organizations, which have moved away from the traditional fee-for-service model, to be the wave of the future. But several major HMOs have been unable to keep their costs under control. The giant Los Angeles-based Maxicare (the second-largest HMO in the United States) filed for bankruptcy in 1989. Shortly thereafter HEALS,the HMO based in Oakland, also ran into a cash crisis and was desperately seeking a financial angel in hopes of working out a merger. Even venerable Blue Cross has been under severe profit pressure as the contours of the health-care field shift in response to the financial strictures of both government and business.

This financial squeeze on the prepaid providers of health care may intensify as governments, which have been slow to adopt the cost-containment measures prevalent in the private sector, begin to implement them. The big winner in the California HMO competition has been Kaiser Permanente, with a membership in California of 4.4 million and healthy profits.

One problem area in the state's health-care picture is the large number of Californians without health insurance--including 12 percent of workers who are employed full-time. Of adults living in poverty, 46 percent lack health insurance. These individuals can get health care at county hospitals, but they often wait until they are seriously ill before seeking medical assistance. The governor and the state legislature are examining the problem and hope to achieve a workable solution within budgetary limits.

CALIFORNIA HEALTH SERVICES EMPLOYMENT	
1982	594,100
1983	604,200
1984	615,900
1985	619,500
1986	662,100
1987	689,600
1988	734,500
1989	736,000

4.1,90 Source: California Employment Development Dept., *Report to the Governor on Labor Market Conditions.*

NUMBER AND BED CAPACITY OF STATE LICENSED FACILITIES 1988		
Facility Type	Number	Bed Capacity
General Acute Care Hospital	522	107,584
Acute Psychiatric Hospital	63	8,084
Chemical Dependency Hospital	12	579
Skilled Nursing Facility	1,165	108,776
Intermediate Care Facility	34	2,077
Intermediate Care Facility/ Developmentally disabled	22	1,720
Intermediate Care Facility/ Developmentally disabled habilitative	204	1,413
Home Health Agency	477	0
Adult Day Health Care	50	0
Rehabilitation Clinic	7	0
Community Clinic	465	0
Psychology Clinic	14	0
Surgical Clinic	33	0
Chronic Dialysis Clinic	148	0
Free Clinic	21	0
Referral Agency	9	0
Total	3,246	230,233

4.2,90 Source: Department of Health Services, Facilities Information System, *Licensing Statistical Report, July 1988.*

SECTION 4 NOTE
In 1987, according to the National Institutes for Health, California received $658 million for biomedical research, New York $589 million, and Massachusetts $487 million.

4.3,90

INPATIENT TURNOVER IN CALIFORNIA STATE HOSPITALS FOR THE MENTALLY DISABLED, FISCAL YEAR 1987-1988				
Hospital	Inpatient Population on June 30, 1988	Admissions	Deaths*	Discharges
Atascadero	1,018	891	5	650
Camarillo	643	690	11	626
Metropolitan	801	2,834	4	2,768
Napa	1,260	1,111	23	1,106
Patton	1,122	501	7	487
Total	4,844	6,027	50*	5,637

* Inpatient deaths. Does not include two deaths on AWOL.
4.4,90 Source: California Dept. of Mental Health, Statistics and Data Analysis Section, unpublished data.

CALIFORNIA HEALTH CARE PROFESSIONALS					
	1970	1980	1983	1987	1989
Medical Doctors					
Practicing Residents*	NA	55,131	59,213	65,994	68,243
Non-residents	NA	22,661	24,312	24,179	24,689
Total	38,451	77,792	83,525	90,173	92,932
Osteopaths	NA	NA	NA	707	864
Dentists	11,410	14,346	20,347	19,500	23,383
Pharmacists	13,963	16,890	17,034	15,372	19,300
Registered Nurses					
Active††	NA	164,198	180,960	184,999	211,599
Inactive	NA	26,604	29,732	NA	28,820
Total	NA	190,802	210,692	NA	240,495
Vocational Nurses					
Active	NA	63,716	63,748	58,145	54,285
Inactive	NA	2,930	5,901	NA	NA
Delinquent**	NA	17,883	30,949	NA	NA
Total	NA	84,529	100,598	NA	NA

* Living in California   † Licensed in California, but living in another state.
†† Includes nurses living outside of California.   ** Nursing license fee unpaid.
4.5,90 Source: U.S. Statisticl Abstract, Calif. Board of Dental Examiners, Osteopathic Examiners, Registered Nurses, Vocational Nurses, Medical Quality Assurance, and Pharmacy.

SECTION 4 NOTE
According to the Statistical Bulletin of the Metropolitan Life Insurance Company, in 1986 a typical appendectomy in California cost $7,480; in the U.S. it cost $5,090.

4.6,90

COMPLAINTS AND DISCIPLINARY ACTION AGAINST CALIFORNIA HEALTH CARE PROFESSIONALS, 1988	
Medical Doctors	
Complaints Against Doctors	5,960
Licenses Revoked, Suspended, or	
Voluntarily Surrendered	77
Osteopaths	
Complaints Against Osteopaths	75
Licenses Revoked or Suspended	3
Dentists	
Complaints Against Dentists	1,852
Licenses Revoked or Suspended	7
Pharmacists	
Complaints Against Pharmacists	728
Licenses Revoked or Suspended	47

4.7,90 Source: California Boards of Dental Examiners, Osteopathic Examiners, Registered Nurses, Vocational Nurses, Medical Quality Assurance, & Pharmacy.

PHYSICIANS AND DENTISTS, NUMBER AND RATE* CALIFORNIA AND THE UNITED STATES							
	Active Physicians				Active Dentists		
	California		U.S.		California		U.S.	
Year	Number	Rate	Number	Rate	Number	Rate	Number	Rate
1980	54,082	231	413,692	184	14,346	65	121,240	55
1986	64,066	240	491,503	205	16,440	61	137,900	57

* Per 100,000 civilian population.
4.8,90 Source: U.S. Statistical Abstract.

COST OF HOSPITALIZATION IN CALIFORNIA, SELECTED STATES AND THE UNITED STATES (in dollars)						
	Average Daily Room Change		Average Cost per day		Average Cost per stay	
State	1980	1988	1980	1987	1980	1987
California	$161	$364	$362	$741	$2,395	$4,755
District of Columbia	$170	$443	$358	$722	$3,189	$5,636
Alaska	$189	$337	$408	$892	$2,276	$5,056
New York	$157	$263	$257	$493	$2,469	$4,519
Mississippi	$67	$141	$174	$354	$1,178	$2,422
United States	$127	$253	$245	$538	$1,851	$3,850

4.9,90 Source: Health Insurance Asso. of America, Survey of Hospital Semi-Private Room Charges and American Hospital Asso., Hospital Statistics (copyright).

PRINCIPAL PAYOR OF HOSPITAL COSTS				
Payor	Age 65-74	Age 74-84	Age 85+	Total
Medicare	93%	98%	97%	94%
Medi-Cal	3%	2%	1%	2%
Blue Cross/Shield	1%	*	*	*
Insurance	2%	*	*	1%
HMO/PHP	1%	*	*	*
SELF	1%	*	*	1%
Other	1%	*	*	*
Total %	**100%**	**100%**	**100%**	**100%**
Total # of Patients	**433,014**	**331,838**	**130,350**	**895,224**

4.10,90 Source: California Health Policy and Data Advisory Commission - *Health Care Costs and Older Californians*, 1986.

CALIFORNIANS NOT COVERED BY HEALTH INSURANCE PERCENT UNINSURED			
	1979	1983	1986
Children under 18	18.6%	19.9%	21.6%
Adults 18-64	16.9%	19.1%	20.9%
Children in poverty	32.0%	30.1%	32.9%
Adults in poverty	40.6%	44.8%	46.1%
Unemployed Adults	41.2%	40.6%	43.4%
Self-Employed	30.4%	33.9%	37.3%
Full-Time Year Round Worker	8.6%	8.9%	12.3%
Part-Time Worker	18.5%	24.9%	24.3%
Children			
Non-Latino White	16.4%	13.7%	15.0%
Latino	23.2%	31.8%	33.3%
Asian/ Other	20.2%	18.4%	13.3%
Black	18.8%	18.2%	29.1%
Adults			
Non-Latino White	14.7%	16.1%	15.1%
Latino	24.4%	30.7%	37.1%
Asian/ Other	18.9%	19.0%	19.9%
Black	19.2%	18.4%	25.2%

4.11,90 Source: Changes in Health Insurance Coverage of Californians 1979-1986, University of California - California Policy Seminar, 1988.

CALIFORNIA PERSONAL HEALTH CARE EXPENDITURES (In Billions of Dollars)									
Year	Hospital Care	Doctor Fees	Dentist Fees	Drugs and Sundries	Glasses	Nursing Homes	Other Prof. Services	Other Health Services	Total
1978	8.4 (41%)	5.4 (26%)	1.8 (9%)	1.8 (9%)	NA	1.4 (7%)	NA	1.7 (8%)	$20.7
1986*	23.3 (44%)	11.9 (23%)	3.8 (7%)	4.0 (8%)	1.1 (2%)	5.0 (9%)	1.8 (3%)	1.5 (3%)	$52.5

* Estimates based on national expenditures patterns.

4.12,90 Source: U.S. Health Care Financing Administration, Health Care Financing Review.

CALIFORNIA HOSPICES	
City	**Hospice**
Anaheim	Martin Lurther Hospital Hospice
Aptos	Hospice Caring Project
Auburn	Auburn Faith Hospice
Bakersfield	Kern Hospice
Barstow	Hospice of Mohave Valley
Berkeley	Community Hospice of the East Bay
Bishop	Hospice of the Owens Valley
Brownsville	Yuba Feather Home Hospice
Burbank	St. Joe Medical Center Home Hospice
Burlingame	Mission Hospice of San Mateo
Burlingame	South Bay Hospice
Camarillo	Camarillo Hospice
Canoga Park	NuMed Medical Center
Carmichael	Mercy San Juan Hospice
Cerritos	Assoiciated Health Care HHA
Cerritos	Interhealth Home Health Care
Chatsworth	Clinishare Home Health Care
Chester	Sierra Hospice
Chico	Enloe Hospice
Chico	Home Health Agency
Concord	Mt. Diablo Medical Center Hospice
Corona	Home Care Plus Hospice
Corona	Hospice of Corona-Norco-Lake Elsinore
Crescent City	Hospice of Del Norte
Daly City	Comp. Comm. Home Health and Hospice
Daly City	West Bay Home Care Service Hospice
Davis	Yolo Hospice
Deer Park	Hospice of Napa Valley
Delano	Hospice of Delano Area
Downey	Lifeline Homecare
Dublin	Hope Hospice
El Cajon	Kaiser Foundation Hospital Hospice
Encinitas	Hospice of the North Coast
Escondido	Elizabeth Hospice
Escondido	Palomar Pomerado Home Health Agency
Eureka	Hospice of Humboldt
Fairfield	Northbay Hospice
Fallbrook	Fallbrook Hospice
Fontana	Kaiser Foundation Hospice
Fort Bragg	Mendocino Coast Dist. Hospital-Hospice
Fresno	Hinds Hospital Hospice
Fresno	Hospice of Fresno at St. Agnes
Fresno	Valley Central Hospice

CALIFORNIA HOSPICES	
City	**Hospice**
Fullerton	Hospice Prog. of Hospital HHC of CA.
Fullerton	St. Jude Hospice Program
Garberville	Hospice of Southern Humboldt
Garden Grove	Town and Country Hospice
Gilroy	Center for Living with Dying
Glendale	Verdugo Hills VNA Hospice in the Home
Grass Valley	Hospice of the Foothills
Hayward	Kaiser-Hayward Hospice Program
Hemet	Ramona Visiting Nurse Asso. and Hospice
Hollister	San Benito Hospice
La Habra	Home Health Resource Center
Laguna Hills	Saddleback Coordinated Homecare
Lake Isabella	Kern Valley Hosp. Home Health
Lakeport	Hospice Service of Lake County
Lakewood	Greater Lakewood Community Hospice
Loma Linda	Loma Linda Hospice
Lompoc	Hospice of Lompoc
Long Beach	Beyond Rejection Ministries
Long Beach	Clinishare Home Health/ Hospice
Long Beach	Memorial Home Health Care Hospice
Long Beach	St. Mary Home Hospice Care
Long Beach	VNS of Long Beach Hospice in the Home
Los Alamitos	Hospice of Los Alamitos Med. Ctr.
Los Angeles	AIDS Hospice Foundation
Los Angeles	Ceders-Sinai Women's Guild Palliative Care Pgm.
Los Angeles	City of Angels Hospice Foundation
Los Angeles	Good Shepherd Hospice
Los Angeles	Greater L.A. AIDS Hospice Foundation
Los Angeles	Home Health Services Hospice
Los Angeles	Kaiser-Foundation Hospice
Los Angeles	VNA of L.A. Hospice in the Home
Los Angeles	West L.A. Med. Ctr.- Palliative Treatment
Madera	Hospice of Madera County
Merced	Hospice of Merced & Mariposa County
Modesto	Community Hospice
Montclair	VNA of Pomona
Monterey	Hospice of the Monterey Peninsula
Mt. View	Mid Peninsula Homecare and Hospice
Norwalk	Kaiser-Permanente Hospice
Oakland	Alta-Bates Herrick Hospice

4.13.2,90

CALIFORNIA'S HOSPICES	
City	**Hospice**
Oakland	American Baptist Homes - West
Oakland	Kaiser-Permanente Hospice
Orange	St. Joseph Hospital Hospice
Orange	VNA of Orange County Hospice
Oroville	Hospice of Oroville
Oxnard	Mercy Hospice of St. Johns Med. Ctr.
Palm Springs	Desert Hospital Hospice of the Desert Comm.
Palo Alto	Stanford U. Hospital - Home Health - Hospice
Panorama City	Kaiser-Permanente Hospice
Paradise	Hospice of the Ridge
Pasadena	Hospice of Pasadena
Petaluma	Hospice of Petaluma
Placerville	Snowline Hospice
Pleasant Hill	Hospice of Contra Costa
Pomona	Inland Hospice Association
Port Hueneme	Cal. Home Health Services
Poway	Horizon Hospice
Red Bluff	St. Elizabeth Community Hosp. Hospice
Redding	Mercy Hospice
Redlands	Hospice of Redlands Community Hospital
Redondo Beach	South Bay Hospital
Riverside	Riverside Hospice
Roseville	Hospice of Roseville
Sacramento	Hospice Care of Sacramento
Sacramento	Kaiser Hospice
Sacramento	Mercy Hospital Hospice
Sacramento	Sutter/ VNA Hospice Care
Sacramento	Univ. CA./ Davis Medical Center Sacramento
Salinas	Salinas Valley Hospice
San Diego	San Diego Hospice Corp.
San Francisco	Comm. Hospice/ Hospice by the Bay
San Francisco	Visiting Nurses/ Hospice San Francisco
San Jose	Hospice of the Valley
San Jose	VNA Home Health Care
San Leandro	Vesper Hospice
San Luis Obispo	Hospice of San Luis Obispo County
San Pedro	San Pedro Peninsula Home Care Hospice
San Rafael	Hospice of Marin
Santa Barbara	Hospice of Santa Barbara
Santa Barbara	Santa Barbara VNA Hospice Program

4.13.3,90

CALIFORNIA'S HOSPICES	
City	**Hospice**
Santa Clara	VNA Home Health Care Center for Living with Dying
Santa Paula	Hospice of Santa Clara Valley
Santa Rosa	Home Hospice of Sonoma County
Simi Valley	Hospice of Simi Valley
Sonoma	Valley of the Moon Hospice
Sonora	Hospice of the Sierra
Stockton	Hospice of San Joaquin
Sun City	Hospice of Sun City
Susanville	Lassen Hospice Care
Thousand Oaks	Hospice of the Conejo
Torrance	HHHC of CA. Hospice
Truckee	Tahoe Forest Hospital Hospice
Turlock	Hospice of Emmanuel
Ukiah	Hospice in Home Health Care of N. CA.
Van Nuys	National In-Home Health Services
Ventura	Bethesda Hospice/ Bible Fellowship Church
Ventura	Hospice of San Buena Ventura
Ventura	Livingston Memorial VNA
Victorville	Desert Hospice
Visalia	Hospice of Tulare County
Walnut Creek	Golden Rain Home Health Agency
Walnut Creek	Hospice for Young People
Walnut Creek	Kaiser-Permanente Hospice
West Covina	Hospice of East San Gabriel Valley
West Covina	Interhealth Home Health Care
West Covina	Queen of the Valley Hospital Hospice
Whittier	Interhealth Home Health Care
Yuba City	Valley Hospice
Yucca Valley	Hospice of Morongo Basin

* VNA is the Visiting Nurses Asso.
4.13.4,90 Source: National Hospice Organization, 1988 Guide to the Nation's Hospices.

NURSING HOME RESIDENTS	
Year	**Residents**
1980	125,000
1990	180,000
2000	238,000

4.14,90 Source: California Health Policy and Data Advisory Commission - *Health Care Costs and Older Californians*, 1986.

CALIFORNIA'S 10 LARGEST HEALTH MAINTENANCE ORGANIZATIONS (HMO), 1987

Rank	HMO	City	Members
1	Kaiser, No. Cal.	Pasadena	2,086,516
2	Kaiser, So, Cal.	Oakland	1,855,862
3	Health Net	Woodland Hills	503,148
4	Cigna	Glendale	428,531
5	MaxiCare	Los Angeles	348,655
6	PacifiCare	Cypress	208,948
7	Foundation Health	Sacramento	189,369
8	FHP, Inc.	Fountain Valley	177,002
9	TakeCare	Oakland	165,231
10	Western Health	San Diego	143,000

Note: Data as of Dec., 31, 1987.
4.15,90 Source: Group Health Association of America, unpublished data.

CALIFORNIA MEDICAL, DENTAL, PHARMACY AND VETERINARY SCHOOLS

Medical	Dental	Pharmacy	Veterinary
UC, Davis			UC, Davis
UC, Irvine			
UC, Los Angeles	UC, Los Angeles		
UC, San Diego			
UC, San Francisco	UC, San Francisco	UC, San Francisco	
Loma Linda University	Loma Linda University		
USC	USC	USC	
Stanford University			
	Univ. of the Pacific	Univ. of the Pacific	

4.16,90 Source: Pacific Data Resources.

SECTION 4 NOTE

According to the American Journal of Nursing, experienced registered nurses can make up to $49,920 per year in Los Angeles and up to $41,489 per year in San Francisco. Los Angeles nurses receive the second-highest pay in the nation, San Francisco nurses the sixth-highest.
4.17,90

SECTION 4 NOTE

California has the tenth-lowest infant mortality rate in the U.S.: 8.8 deaths per 1,000 live births. The national rate is 10.4 deaths per 1,000.
4.18,90

CALIFORNIA HEALTH FACTS AND FIGURES

6% of California children are born with a low birth weight (under 2500 grams).

11% of California mothers are teenagers.

24% of California mothers are not married.

23% of California deliveries are Cesarean.

0.9% of California children are born outside of a hospital.

5.7% of California mothers had no prenatal care or had care only in the third trimester.

Infant, fetal, and neonatal death rates for Whites, Hispanics, and Asians are about the same. Black rates are twice as high as the other groups.

8.2% of kindergarten students arrive in school needing one or more immunizations.

10% of California's population is eligible for Medi-Cal health services but only half the eligibles use the service.

The occupancy rate at California's 512 General Acute Care (G.A.C.) hospitals is 54%.

The typical patient stays 5.7 days at a G.A.C. hospital in California.

It costs $745 per day for the average patient in a California hospital and $5,041 for the typical hospital stay.

It Costs a typical patient $55 per day in a California skilled or intermediate care nursing home.

California ranks 8th among the states in physicians per capita.

22% of the nation's AIDS deaths occur in California, 21% of the cases occur in California.

California's infant, neonatal, & fetal mortality rate for whites and blacks are below the U.S. average.

California has 1,569 nursing homes with 25 or more beds for a total of 143,000 beds. There are 50 such beds for every 1,000 Californians aged 65 and older.

California has 563 full-time equivalent hospital employees for each 100 hospital patients.

The occupancy rate of California hospitals has declined from 74% in 1960 to 62% in 1986.

4.19,90 Source: California Dept. of Health Services, Health Data Summaries for California counties, 1988.

SECTION 4 NOTE

53% of the uninsured population is in the workforce, 20% are unemployed, and 27% are children under 16. Those without health insurance receive almost $2 billion in free state, county, and private health services. Hence, many of their health needs are met without insurance.

4.20,90

ALCOHOL USE BY CALIFORNIANS			
	Percent Who Drink	Percent Heavy Drinkers*	Percent Who Drink 3 or more Times a Week
Age			
18-24	87%	18%	25%
25-44	84%	12%	30%
45-64	81%	7%	40%
65+	68%	1%	30%
Sex			
Male	85%	16%	40%
Female	78%	4%	24%
Race/Ethnicity			
White	85%	9%	37%
Hispanic	76%	18%	20%
Black	74%	9%	23%
Asian and other	63%	7%	16%
Education			
Under 12 years	69%	16%	23%
12 years	83%	13%	29%
Over 12 years	86%	6%	37%
Income			
Under $15,000	75%	11%	24%
$15,000-$24,999	84%	12%	32%
$25,000-$39,999	84%	10%	32%
$40,000 +	89%	6%	46%
Total	**81%**	**10%**	**32%**

* 5 or more drinks per sitting.
4.21,90 Source: Cal. Department of Health Services, 1983 Poll Data.

SALES OF PACKAGED CIGARETTES		
Year	Sales	Packs Consumed Per Capita
1960-61	2.37 billion	147
1970-71	2.63 billion	130
1980-81	2.91 billion	121
1981-82	2.92 billion	119
1982-83	2.86 billion	115
1983-84	2.80 billion	110
1984-85	2.76 billion	106
1985-86	2.70 billion	101
1986-87	2.64 billion	97
1987-88	NA	94

4.22,90 Source: Cal. State Board of Equalization, *Annual Report 1987-1988*.

CONSUMPTION OF BEER, WINE, AND SPIRITS BY CALIFORNIANS 1950-1988								
	Beer		Wine				Spirits	
Year	Total*	Gallons Per Capita	14% Alcohol or less*	Over 14%	Cham- pagne & Sparkling Wines*	Gallons Per Capita	Distilled Spirits*	Gallons Per Capita
1950-51	167	15.4	7.3	13.7	0.4	2.0	20.0	1.8
1960-61	233	14.5	15.9	17.6	0.9	2.1	28.1	1.7
1970-71	357	17.7	44.4	13.1	4.2	3.1	45.4	2.3
1980-81	611	25.5	89.9	8.3	7.6	4.4	57.5	2.4
1981-82	611	25.0	92.8	8.4	8.2	4.5	56.1	2.3
1982-83	599	24.0	95.7	8.4	9.1	4.5	54.4	2.1
1983-84	623	24.5	98.1	8.1	10.7	4.6	53.6	2.1
1984-85	626	24.0	101.7	7.8	10.8	4.6	52.7	2.0
1985-86	635	23.8	111.4	8.2	11.5	4.9	51.0	1.9
1986-87	664	24.3	108.4	9.0	10.6	4.7	50.1	1.8
1987-88	650	23.2	107.3	8.9	9.9	4.5	48.9	1.7

* Millions of gallons.
4.23,90 Source: California Board of Equalization, *Annual Report, 1987-88*.

MARIJUANA USE IN CALIFORNIA

57% of California adults have never used it
43% of California adults have used it
73% of those who have used it have stopped using it

4.24,90 Source: Estimates based on a 1983 California Poll.

SECTION 4 NOTE

California, with 18 gallons per person, leads the nation in per capita annual consumption of bottled water. This is 3 times the national average.

4.25,90

SECTION 4 NOTE

For information on radon gas, call the Federal Environmental Protection Agency at (916) 445-1967.

4.26,90

SMOKING HABITS OF CALIFORNIANS

	Percent Current Smokers	Percent Who Formerly Smoked	Moderate Smokers*	Heavy Smokers†
Age				
18-24	34%	15%	40%	15%
25-44	32%	23%	38%	28%
45-64	32%	35%	34%	33%
65+	18%	37%	32%	24%
Sex				
Male	32%	31%	38%	31%
Female	29%	22%	36%	22%
Race/Ethnicity				
White	29%	28%	38%	35%
Hispanic	30%	25%	27%	7%
Black	44%	20%	40%	10%
Asian and other	32%	19%	40%	11%
Education				
Under 12 years	41%	25%	36%	25%
12 years	36%	24%	38%	28%
Over 12 years	23%	29%	37%	27%
Income				
Under $15,000	37%	24%	37%	20%
$15,000-$24,999	35%	23%	40%	30%
$25,000-$39,999	29%	26%	34%	33%
$40,000 +	18%	37%	38%	31%
Total	**31%**	**24%**	**27%**	**37%**

* 15-24 cigarettes per day.
† 25 or more cigarettes per day.
4.27,90 Source: California Department of Health Services, 1983 Poll Data.

PERCENT OF CALIFORNIANS WHO ENGAGE IN VARIOUS FORMS OF EXERCISE

Type of Activity	Percentage	Type of Activity	Percentage
Walking	77%	Basketball	12%
Jogging	13	Football	9
Hiking and		Soccer	7
Mt. Climbing	38	Golf	16
Downhill Skiing	18	Tennis	18
Cross Country Skiing	10	Pool Swimming	31
Water Skiing	15	Ocean, Lake, and	
Horseback Riding	13	River Swimming	59
Hunting	12	Surfing	4
Target Shooting	14	Rowing	16
Softball and Baseball	26	Sailing	10

4.28,90 Source: California Department of Health Services, unpublished study by CIC Research, 1987.

Education

California's public schools are beset by so many problems that one wonders if some of them can continue to cope. The schools must try to educate children from broken families, children distracted by drug use, and a large number of children for whom English is at best a second language. In addition, the schools must deal with shocking levels of violence and vandalism. Evidence indicates that the schools are not doing well.

Despite a high and increasing number of violent school crimes and students caught with guns and other weapons in school, the Department of Public Instruction congratulates the schools because the rate of school crime has not increased. Despite a dropout rate well above the national average, the department is "gratified" that the state's dropout rate is stable. Despite a large population of college students so poorly prepared by their high schools that they must take remedial English classes before they can progress to their regular college classes, the K-12 education establishment seems unwilling to rethink, regroup, and modify the status quo.

Comparative studies indicate that students in most other industrialized countries not only have longer school days and longer school years but also do considerably more homework than their California counterparts. Although some efforts are being made to overcome these comparative deficiencies, whether they will succeed is in doubt.

While the K-12 system is in a period of crisis and introspection, the public college and university system seems to be doing somewhat better. Private colleges have increasingly priced themselves out of the reach of all but the upper middle class, and many students who might have gone to private schools are now attending the University of California or the State University system. So popular has the University of California become that most of its campuses are at their full capacity. The U.C. regents, who had not expected the campuses to fill up so rapidly, are now exploring sites for several additional campuses. At least one will probably be in the San Joaquin Valley and perhaps one each in Northern California and the greater Los Angeles area. But where the university and the state treasury will get the billions of dollars to build, staff, and operate these new campuses has not been resolved.

Even as the University of California and the California State University system are considering expanding, they are also beginning to face another kind of difficulty: the prospect of a diminishing faculty. Many of those hired to teach in the booming 1960s are expected to retire during the next decade. The retirements should provide excellent employment opportunities for graduate students, who for the past two decades have had a hard time finding faculty openings.

SELECTED DATA ON CALIFORNIA PUBLIC AND PRIVATE SCHOOLS GRADES K-12
1975-1988

	1975-1976	1984-1985	1985-1986	1987-1988
Public School				
Districts	1,046	1,029	1,028	1,024
Schools				
Public	7,045	7,416	7,362	7,125
Private	2,668	4,969	5,457	6,270
Fall Enrollment				
Public	4,284,471	4,151,110	4,255,544	4,488,398
Private	421,647	540,127	536,920†	528,561
Teachers				
Full-time Public	187,669	173,756	179,660	197,466
Full-time Private	20,946	29,171	29,832	31,035
Part-time Private	NA	8,823	8,681	8,669
Graduates (High School)				
Public*	285,868	225,448	242,164†	237,414
Private	21,029	25,695	23,124	25,507†

* Includes day school and evening or adult high school graduates.
† 1986-1987
5.1,90 Source: California Department of Education, Educational Data Management Office, *Enrollment and Staff in California's Private Elementary and High Schools*, Enrollment Data: *California Elementary and Secondary Public Schools*.

NUMBER AND ENROLLMENT OF CHURCH-AFFILIATED KINDERGARTEN-TWELFTH GRADE SCHOOLS

School Year	Number	Enrollment
1974-1975	NA	334,200
1975-1976	NA	331,011
1976-1977	NA	337,314
1977-1978	NA	353,183
1978-1979	NA	376,210
1979-1980	NA	388,127
1980-1981	1,754	389,964
1981-1982	1,871	404,960
1982-1983	1,906	407,361
1984-1985	2,004	410,114
1985-1986	1,964	406,960
1986-1987	1,968	398,832
1987-1988	1,977	394,909

5.2,90 Source: California Department of Education, Educational Data Management, *Enrollment and Staff in California's Private Elementary Schools and High Schools*.

PRIVATE SCHOOL ASSOCIATIONS

Association of Christian Schools International 731 North Beach Blvd. La Habra, CA 90631 (213) 694-4791	**EPISCOPAL** **Episcopal Diocese of California** 1275 Sacramento St. San Francisco, CA 94108 (415) 771-6600
California Association of Independent Schools 1351 Santa Monica Mall, Suite 103 Santa Monica, CA 90401 (213) 393-5161	**LUTHERAN** **The Evangelical Lutheran Church in America** 1340 S. Bonnie Brae Los Angeles, CA 90006 (213) 387-8183
California Association of Private Special Education Schools 1121 L St., Suite 500 Sacraemento, CA 95814 (916) 722-7555	**The Evangelical Lutheran Church in America** 401 Roland Way, Suite 420 Oakland, CA 94621 (415) 430-0500
Christian Schools International 10818 Artesia Blvd. Cerritos, CA 90701 (818) 860-0556	**SEVENTH-DAY ADVENTIST** **Pacific Union Conference of Seventh-Day Adventists** 2686 Townsgate Road P.O. Box 5005 Westlake Village, CA 91359 (805) 497-9457
BAPTIST **Christian Day School Association** 9825 Woodley Ave. Sepulveda, CA 91343 (213) 894-5745	**HEBREW** **Bureau of Jewish Education** 6505 Wilshire Blvd., Suite 710 Los Angeles, CA 90048 (213) 852-1234
CATHOLIC **California Catholic Conference Division of Education** 1010 Eleventh St. Suite 200 Sacramento, CA 95814 (916) 443-4851	**Orthodox Islamic** 1635 S. Saint Andrews Place P.O. Box 18183 Los Angeles, CA 90019 (213) 296-5961

5.3,90 Source: California State Board of Education, *California/Private School Directory.*

SECTION 5 NOTE

According to a 1987 report prepared for the California Dept. of Education, 17% of the state's adults are functionally illiterate. These individuals cannot read well enough to decipher medical labels, read help-wanted ads, or fill out job applications.

5.4,90

STUDENT-TEACHER RATIO* FOR PUBLIC PRIMARY AND SECONDARY SCHOOLS IN SELECTED STATES 1987-1988	
California	22.84
Arizona	16.90
Oregon	16.87
Texas	15.97
New York	12.98
U.S. Average	16.27

* The total number of public school students divided by the total number of teachers. The California elementary school (K-8) ratio in the 1988 school year was 24.22 and the secondary school (9-12) ratio was 23.43. California ranked last nationally in pupil/teacher ratios.

5.5,90 Source: National Education Association, unpublished data.

AVERAGE CLASS SIZE*				
	1980-81	1985-86	1986-87	1987-88
Elementary Schools (K-8)	27.83	27.10	26.79	26.88
Secondary Schools (9-12)†	28.29	28.19	27.87	27.59
Selected Secondary School Courses				
English	26.74	27.28	26.89	26.59
Math	27.87	29.02	28.81	28.43
Science	27.69	28.88	28.69	28.11
Social Science	29.87	29.95	29.35	29.06

* Total Number of Students Divided by the Total Number of Classes.

† Data exclude junior high schools.

5.6,90 Source: California Department of Education, Educational Demographics Unit, Program Evaluation and Research Division, *Class Size and Pupil Teacher Ratios, 1988.*

YEARS OF SCHOOL COMPLETED BY THE ADULT* POPULATION 1987				
	California		United States	
	High School Graduate	College Graduate	High School Graduate	College Graduate
Male	79%	27%	76%	24%
Female	79%	20%	75%	17%
White	78%	23%	77%	21%
Hispanic	49%	13%	51%	9%
Black	80%	6%	64%	11%
Total	79%	23%	76%	20%

* Persons 25 years and older.

5.7,90 Source: U.S. Bureau of the Census, Current Population Reports Series P-20, No. 428.

EDUCATION LEVEL OF CALIFORNIANS 25 YEARS AND OLDER PERCENTAGE BY RACE/ETHNICITY					
	White	Asian and Other	Black	Hispanic	Total
Elementary	4.6%	14.5%	6.7%	38.1%	11.9%
High School 1-3 years	7.2%	5.1%	12.6%	15.0%	8.8%
High School 4 years	34.2%	26.7%	35.1%	25.0%	31.9%
College 1-3 years	24.3%	20.1%	32.0%	13.5%	22.4%
College 4 years	29.7%	33.6%	13.6%	8.4%	25.0%
Average Years Completed	13.4	12.5	12.6	9.5	12.6

5.8,90 Source: California Department of Finance, unpublished data.

CALIFORNIA HIGH SCHOOL ATTRITION RATE*	
Year	Rate
1970-71	19.4%
1975-76	23.9%
1980-81	30.4%
1983-84	30.5%
1984-85	31.9%
1985-86	31.7%
1986-87	32.7%
1987-88	32.2%

* Percentage of enrolled tenth graders who do not graduate three years later.
5.9,90 Source: California Department of Education, California Basic Educational Data System, Press Releases.

CALIFORNIA HIGH SCHOOL DROP OUT RATE*	
Year	Rate
1986	25.9%
1987	22.0%
1988	22.7%

* Percentage of 10th, 11th, or 12th grade students absent for 45 consecutive days, not enrolling in another school, or receiving a high school equivalency diploma.
5.10,90 Source: California Department of Education, California Basic Educational Data System, Press Releases.

SECTION 5 NOTE
In the fall of 1988, for the first time in California history, Anglo students constituted a minority in the state's public schools, with 49.2 percent of the total enrollment.

5.11,90

PUBLIC HIGH SCHOOL GRADUATES			
1971	282,866	1982	241,343
1977	278,596	1984	232,199
1978	278,553	1985	225,448
1979	262,967	1986	229,026
1980	249,217	1987	237,414
1981	242,172	1988	249,518

Note: There has been a 12% decline in the number of graduates from 1971 to 1988.
5.12,90 Source: California Department of Education, California Basic Educational Data System, unpublished data.

HIGH SCHOOL DROP-OUTS, BY ETHNIC GROUP*		
Ethnic Group	Percent	Number
White	5.9%	31,726
Hispanic	12.0%	28,746
Black	12.7%	10,850
Asian	4.8%	3,771
Filipino	5.1%	1,124
Pacific Islander	14.1%	604
American Indian	8.8%	762
Total	8.0%	77,583

* Percentage of students absent for 45 consecutive days or more and not re-enrolling or receiving a high school diploma or equivalent.
5.13,90 Source: California Department of Education, California Basic Educational Data System, press release.

AVERAGE S.A.T. SCORES OF COLLEGE-BOUND SENIORS CALIFORNIA AND THE NATION, 1972-1988							
	1972	1975	1980	1985	1986	1987	1988
Verbal							
California	464	435	424	424	423	424	424
Nation	452	434	424	431	431	430	428
Mathematics							
California	493	473	472	480	481	482	484
Nation	484	472	466	475	475	476	476
Percent of California High School Graduates Taking the S.A.T.							
	30%	36%	36%	42%	38%	46%	44%

5.14,90 Source: California Dept. of Education, California Assessment Program, 1989.

ACT MEAN SCORE
OF ACT TESTED COLLEGE BOUND STUDENTS
1972-1988

Year	English Natl.	English Cal.	Math Natl.	Math Cal.	Soc. Std. Natl.	Soc. Std. Cal.	Nat. Sci. Natl.	Nat. Sci. Cal.	Composite Natl.	Composite Cal.
1972-73	18.1	17.6	19.1	18.0	18.3	17.5	20.8	20.0	19.2	18.4
1974-75	17.7	17.3	17.6	16.9	17.4	16.9	21.1	21.0	18.6	18.2
1976-77	17.7	17.5	17.4	17.1	17.3	17.4	20.9	20.8	18.4	18.3
1978-79	17.9	18.2	17.5	17.6	17.2	17.5	21.1	21.1	18.6	18.7
1980-81	17.8	18.4	17.3	17.9	17.2	18.1	21.0	21.4	18.5	19.1
1982-83	17.8	18.4	16.9	18.0	17.1	18.1	20.9	21.3	18.3	19.1
1984-85	18.1	18.8	17.2	18.5	17.4	18.0	21.2	21.5	18.6	19.3
1985-86	18.5	18.9	17.3	18.7	17.6	18.3	21.4	21.4	18.8	19.5
1986-87	18.4	18.5	17.2	18.6	17.5	17.7	21.4	21.3	18.7	19.1
1987-88	18.5	18.5	17.2	18.6	17.4	17.6	21.4	21.3	18.8	19.1

5.15,90 Source: California Dept. of Education, Educational Planning and Information Center, unpublished data.

SCHOOL DISTRICT ENROLLMENT, 1967-1986
CHANGE IN ENROLLMENT BY RACE

District	White Enrollment (Percent) 1967	1986	% Change	Black Enrollment (Percent) 1967	1986	% Change
Los Angeles	48%	22%	-26%	22%	18%	-4%
San Diego	76%	44%	-32%	11%	18%	7%
San Francisco	42%	15%	-27%	26%	21%	-5%
Long Beach	86%	38%	-48%	7%	18%	11%
Fresno	70%	42%	-28%	9%	11%	2%
Oakland	33%	10%	-23%	52%	62%	10%

District	Hispanic Enrollment (Percent) 1968	1986	% Change	Asian Enrollment (Percent) 1968	1986	% Change
Los Angeles	20%	56%	36%	4%	8%	4%
San Diego	10%	19%	9%	2%	17%	15%
San Francisco	13%†	18%*	5%	18%	45%	27%
Long Beach	5%†	25%*	20%	2%	18%	16%
Fresno	22%††	33%*	11%	2%	14%	12%
Oakland	8%†	12%*	4%	5%	16%	11%

†   The Respective school districts.
*   Cal. Dept. of Education, Cal. Basic Educational Data System, unpublished data.
†† 1973/74
5.16,90 Source: California Dept. of Education, California Basic Educational Data Systems and National School Board Asso., *Racial Change & Desegregation in Large School Districts 1967-1986, 1988.*

SECTION 5 NOTE

In California 88 percent of the private schools are coeducational.
5.17,90

Grade Level and Content	79-80	81-82	83-84	85-86	86-87	87-88
AVERAGE TEST SCORES OF STUDENTS IN THE CALIFORNIA ASSESSMENT PROGRAM, 1979-1988						
Grade 3						
Reading	250	258	268	280	282	282
Written Language	250	260	272	285	287	254
Mathematics	250	261	274	283	285	251
Grade 6						
Reading	250	254	249	260	260	265
Written language	250	257	260	271	271	273
Mathematics	250	258	261	268	268	270
Grade 8						
Reading	NA	NA	250	243	247	252
Written Language	NA	NA	250	248	254	263
Mathematics	NA	NA	250	253	259	264
History-Social Science	NA	NA	NA	243	247	253
Science	NA	NA	NA	290	256	263
Grade 12						
Reading	63.1	63.2	62.2	62.7	63.6	250
Written Language	62.4	63.2	62.6	63.4	64.1	-
Spelling	68.8	69.5	69.4	70.1	70.6	-
Mathematics	66.8	67.7	67.4	68.7	68.7	250

- California third graders are at or slightly above the national average in reading and written language and significantly above the average in math.
- California sixth graders are slightly above the national average in reading and written language and substantially above the national average in math.
- California eight graders show a substantial decline in reading and mathematics scores from grades 6 to 8 and slight decline in written language. The decline in reading scores puts the eighth graders well below the national average in reading and slightly above the national average in math.
- By most measures, California twelfth graders are well below the national norms in written language and reading and slightly below the average in math.

5.18,90 Source: Cal. Dept. of Education, Cal. Assessment Program, Student Achievement in Cal. Schools, Annual Report.

SECTION 5 NOTE

The U.C. Berkeley School of Business, established with a gift from the Flood Family, which made a fortune in the Comstock Lode, is the nation's second oldest business school.

5.19,90

SECTION 5 NOTE

The National Scholarship Research Service in San Rafael has a list of over 200,000 scholarships, grants, and loans available to college students.

5.20,90

CHARACTERISTICS OF CALIFORNIA TEACHERS AND NON-TEACHING STAFF,1987-1988			
	Support Staff	Admin- istrators	Teachers
Racial or Ethnic Group			
American Indian or Alaskan Native	0.8%	0.9%	0.8%
Asian or Pacific Islander	3.3%	2.7%	3.5%
Filipino	0.6%	0.3%	0.7%
Hispanic	7.5%	9.5%	6.9%
Black, not of Hispanic origin	8.4%	8.8%	6.1%
White, not of Hispanic origin	79.4%	77.8%	82.2%
Sex			
Male	30.8%	59.2%	31.7%
Female	69.2%	40.8%	68.3%
Highest Educational Level			
Doctorate	3.8%	12.1%	0.8%
Master's plus 30 or more semester hours	45.4%	56.6%	21.5%
Master's degree	23.0%	20.9%	13.7%
Bachelor's plus 30 or more semester hours	20.4%	8.7%	50.6%
Bachelor's degree	4.9%	1.3%	12.0%
Less than Bachelor's degree	2.5%	0.4%	1.4%
Type of Appointment			
Tenured	76.9%	63.1%	77.3%
Probationary	11.7%	6.7%	15.5%
Long-term substitute or temporary	2.7%	0.4%	4.2%
Other	8.7%	29.8%	3.2%
Full-time	89.6%	97.3%	95.0%
Part-time	10.4%	2.7%	5.0%
Age			
Average (in years)	45.7%	47.2%	42.6%
Under 25 years	0.1%	0.0%	1.7%
25-34 years	11.4%	3.8%	20.0%
35-44 years	35.8%	36.2%	37.3%
45-54 years	32.4%	38.5%	27.3%
55 years and older	20.3%	21.4%	13.7%
Years in District			
Average (in years)	13.4%	15.6%	11.9%
1-3 years	17.4%	14.7%	24.5%
4-5 years	6.7%	5.2%	8.8%
6-10 years	18.4%	12.8%	15.8%
11-15 years	16.5%	15.6%	14.0%
16-20 years	18.1%	20.3%	17.9%
Over 20 years	22.9%	31.6%	19.0%
Total Years of Educational Service			
Average (in years)	16.9%	21.7%	14.7%
1-5 years	11.4%	1.9%	20.3%
6-10 years	15.0%	4.6%	16.3%
11-15 years	20.1%	15.7%	17.7%
16-20 years	19.0%	24.4%	17.8%
Over 20 years	34.5%	53.6%	27.9%
Total number of positions	15,582	16,544	199,872
Total number of districts	1,009	1,009	1,009
Average salary	$38,550	$50,723	$33,159

5.21,90 Source: California State Dept. of Education. *Characteristics of Professional Staff Members in California Public Schools, 1987-88.*

RACIAL COMPOSITION OF CALIFORNIA PUBLIC SCHOOL STUDENTS, TEACHERS, AND ADMINISTRATORS, 1987-88
(by percent)

	All Students	First Grade	High School Graduates	Teachers	Admin- istrators
White (non-Hispanic)	50.1	47.8	61.1	82.0	78.5
Hispanic	30.1	33.1	19.3	6.9	8.6
Asian	7.3	7.0	8.2	3.4	2.9
Black	9.1	9.0	7.9	6.1	8.6
Indian	0.8	0.6	0.7	0.8	0.5
Filipino	2.1	1.9	2.2	0.7	0.5
Pacific Islander	0.5	0.5	0.5	0.1	0.1
Male	NA	NA	NA	31.8	45.6
Female	NA	NA	NA	68.2	54.4

5.22,90 Source: California Dept. of Education, *Racial or Ethnic Distribution of Staff and Students in California Public Schools*, 1987-88.

CALIFORNIA PUBLIC SCHOOL EMPLOYEES

Type of Staff	Number	% of Total Staff
Superintendents	1,148	0.3%
Principals &		2.0%
Vice Principals	10,108	2.0%
Program Administrators	5,155	1.0%
Support Services	14,306	3.0%
Other Certificated Staff	722	0.1%
Paraprofessional	80,303	18.0%
Office Staff	45,142	10.0%
Other Classified Staff	90,967	20.0%
Teachers	197,466	44.0%
Total	445,317	100.0%

In California private schools there are 39,654 teachers and 6,436 staff. Teachers are 86% of school employees and staff are 14%.

5.23,90 Source: California Dept. of Education, Racial or Ethnic Distribution of Staff and Students in California Public Schools, 1987-88 and Enrollment and Staff in California's Private Elementry Schools and High Schools, 1986-87.

SECTION 5 NOTE

According to a nationwide study by Prof. Mark Dewalt of Susquehanna University, California has 41 one-room schools. All 41 are public schools.

5.24,90

LOS ANGELES SCHOOL SYSTEM
ENROLLMENT (1970 and 1988)

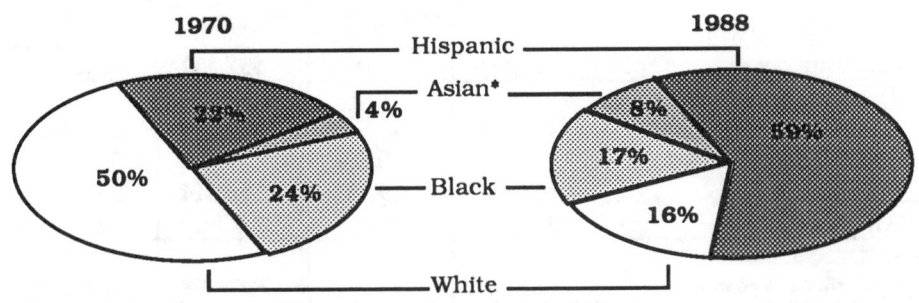

1970

1988

Hispanic

Asian*

4%

50%

24% — Black —

17%

8%

59%

16%

White

Student enrollment: 638,277

Student enrollment: 594,908

* Includes Filipino and Pacific Islander students.
  5.25,90 Source: *Los Angeles Unified School District*.

State	Average Teacher's* Salary	Rank	Average Beginning BA Teacher Salary†	Rank	Per Pupil Spending	Rank
AVERAGE TEACHERS' SALARIES, BEGINNING BA TEACHER SALARIES AND PER PUPIL SPENDING SELECTED STATES, 1988-1989						
California	$35,285	5	$21,900	2	$4,075	30
Arizona	$28,684	23	$19,300	11	$3,904	34
Oregon	$29,500	18	$18,022	23	$4,818	15
New York	$36,500	4	$20,650	4	$7,338	2
Illinois	$31,195	13	$17,804	25	$4,513	21
Texas	$26,513	31	$18,800	15	$3,842	38
Michigan	$34,419	6	$20,100	6	$4,576	19
U.S. Average	**$29,567**		**$18,557**		**$4,509**	

* Classroom teachers.   †   1987-88.
  5.26,90 Source: American Federation of Teachers, Research Dept. 1988 and National Education Association, *Estimates of School Statistics, 1988-89*.

SECTION 5 NOTE

The dim state of California high school science training was apparent in 1988, as California placed only 1 finalist out of 40 in the National Westinghouse Talent Search. New York had 19 finalists.

5.27,90

AVERAGE SALARIES FOR FULL-TIME PROFESSIONAL TEACHING STAFF IN CALFORNIA 1984-1988

Classification	Number*		Average Salary	
	1983-84	1987-88	1983-84	1987-88
Administrators	14,886	16,031	$37,557	$50,723
Teachers				
Kindergarten-Grade 8	106,940	40,927	$24,696	$32,045
Unified School Dist.	—	130,808	—	$33,238
Grades 9-12	68,084	19,474	$26,314	$34,899
All Teachers	**175,024**	**195,475**	**$24,843**	**$33,159**
Student Support				
Services Personnel	12,457	15,277	$27,798	$38,550
All Professional Staff	**202,367**	**226,783**	**$25,960**	**$34,720**

* Full-time equivalent (FTE).
5.28,90 Source: California State Department of Education, *Characteristics of Professional Staff in California Public Schools.*

PUBLIC SCHOOL CRIME IN CALIFORNIA

Year	Violent Crimes	% Change from prior year	Murder	Property crimes	% Change from prior year	Substance abuse*	% Change from prior year
1985-86	60,270	NA	15	74,669	NA	20,196	NA
1986-87	62,819	4.2%	14	71,351	-4.4%	15,999	-21.0%
1987-88	64,783	3.4%	7	74,894	5.0%	13,645	-14.7%

Year	Gun possession	% Change from prior year	Other weapons possession	% Change from prior year	Total criminal incidents	% Change from prior year
1985-86	503	NA	7,065	NA	**162,733**	NA
1986-87	642	28.0%	6,786	3.9%	**157,597**	-3.2%
1987-88	789	23.0%	7,750	14.2%	**162,061**	2.8%

Note: The crime rate in California schools dropped slightly from 1985-86 to 1987-88. The typical school has 21 crimes per year.
* Possession, sale or use of alcohol or drugs.
5.29,90 Source: California Dept. of Education School Climate Section, *Annual Reports of the School Crime Reporting System.* The reporting system began in 1985.

SECTION 5 NOTE

Residential boarding schools constitute 7 percent of California's private schools.
5.30,90

	FALL ENROLLMENTS IN CALIFORNIA COLLEGES AND UNIVERSITIES 1970-1988					
	California Community Colleges		California State Universities and Colleges		University of California	
Year	Full-time	Total	Full-time	Total	Full-time	Total
1970	282,857	826,596	166,876	241,559	103,193	109,033
1975	371,504	1,284,824	186,560	310,891	121,193	128,486
1978	285,130	1,159,819	182,817	306,175	119,315	127,881
1979	282,765	1,248,459	184,986	306,801	121,081	131,472
1980	296,188	1,384,068	191,286	313,850	126,300	135,821
1981	307,752	1,430,634	193,237	319,565	128,613	138,762
1982	308,818	1,334,119	195,571	315,814	129,667	139,138
1983	208,107	1,199,269	199,800	313,900	130,913	141,289
1984	257,056	1,102,834	200,089	316,005	133,762	144,589
1985	254,647	1,142,469	203,175	324,626	136,479	147,957
1986	265,496	1,225,375	205,262	333,424	128,492	152,065
1987	275,347	1,264,409	209,322	342,776	144,337	157,331
1988	272,665	1,277,903	217,061	355,106	149,109	161,522

5.31.1,90

	FALL ENROLLMENTS IN CALIFORNIA COLLEGES AND UNIVERSITIES 1970-1987							
	Independent Colleges & Universities		Private Two-year Colleges		Other Public Institutions		Total	
Year	Full-time	Total	Full-time	Total	Full-time	Total	Full-time	Total
1970	88,140	117,891	NA	NA	2,114	2,114	643,180	1,297,193
1975	91,196	130,773	NA	NA	NA	NA	796,506	1,900,852
1978	123,749	177,851	5,334	6,058	484	484	716,829	1,778,268
1979	129,666	189,832	6,107	6,878	1,967	1,972	726,572	1,885,414
1980	108,462	156,564	6,291	6,837	2,005	2,021	730,387	1,999,161
1981	134,329	190,947	6,837	8,012	3,315	3,315	761,965	2,015,791
1982	125,340	183,453	10,128	11,578	3,488	3,488	765,924	1,949,767
1983	113,103	166,031	NA	NA	3,604	3,622	741,962	1,877,566
1984	129,301	193,380	12,883	14,177	3,613	3,634	745,454	1,823,788
1985	131,035	193,877	11,194	12,618	NA	3,678	745,621	1,854,562
1986	136,045	193,261	9,917	12,091	NA	1,676	757,834	1,914,276
1987	113,994	172,109	9,983	12,686	NA	1,676	712,138	1,882,105

* The data for independent colleges and universities do not include all private institutions. Reporting enrollment is voluntary so totals reflect only those responding.

5.31.2,90 Source: *California Statistical Abstract* and *Governor's Budget*.

ENROLLMENT* AT PUBLIC CALIFORNIA UNIVERSITIES 1987-1988

University of California

Berkeley		San Diego	
Undergraduate	20,625	Undergraduate	12,595
Postbaccalaureate	75	Postbaccalaureate	79
Graduate	7,944	Graduate	1,699
Health Sciences	768	Health Sciences	1,098
Subtotal	29,412	Subtotal	15,471
Davis		San Francisco	
Undergraduate	14,729	Health Sciences	3,580
Postbaccalaureate	88	Santa Barbara	
Graduate	3,162	Undergraduate	15,013
Health Sciences	1,863	Postbaccalaureate	116
Subtotal	19,842	Graduate	1,889
Hastings		Subtotal	17,018
Graduate	1,300	Santa Cruz	
Irvine		Undergraduate	7,983
Undergraduate	11,442	Postbaccalaureate	120
Postbaccalaureate	249	Graduate	515
Graduate	1,583	Subtotal	8,618
Health Sciences	1,119		
Subtotal	14,393	**Total University**	
Los Angeles		Undergraduate	107,110
Undergraduate	20,024	Postbaccalaureate	1,031
Postbaccalaureate	58	Graduate	25,676
Graduate	7,722	Health Sciences	12,166
Health Sciences	3,695	Total	145,983
Subtotal	31,499		
Riverside			
Undergraduate	4,699		
Postbaccalaureate	246		
Graduate	1,162		
Health Sciences	43		
Subtotal	6,150		

California State University

Bakersfield	3,312	San Diego	26,819
Chico	13,331	San Francisco	19,141
Dominguez Hills	5,093	San Jose	19,470
Fresno	14,916	San Luis Obispo	15,468
Fullerton	16,811	Sonoma	4,592
Hayward	9,749	Stanislaus	3,541
Humboldt	5,637		
Long Beach	24,187	System Totals	
Los Angeles	15,549	In-State	257,839
Northridge	20,843	International	
Pomona	15,340	Programs	404
Sacramento	17,945	Grand Total	258,243
San Bernardino	6,095		

California Community Colleges

	Credit Courses	Noncredit Courses	Total
Headcount	1,095,361	169,048	1,264,409
ADA†	609,741	71,508	681,249

* Full-time equivalent students. Actual student enrollment is one-fourth to one-third higher.

† ADA is average daily attendance.

5.32,90 Source: 1989-1990 Report of the Legislative Analyst: *Analysis of the 1989-1990 Budget Bill.*

CALIFORNIA COMMUNITY COLLEGE ENROLLMENTS

District	County	Enrollment	District	County	Enrollment
Allan Hancock	Santa Barbara	10,912	North Orange	Orange	59,229
Antelope Valley	Los Angeles	7,724	Palo Verde	Riverside	745
Barstow	San Bernardino	1,928	Palomar	San Diego	17,775
Butte	Butte	9,557	Pasadena Area	Los Angeles	24,534
Cabrillo	Santa Cruz	11,862	Peralta	Alameda	25,624
Cerritos	Los Angeles	19,144	Rancho Santiago	Orange	31,932
Chaffey	San Bernardino	12,000	Redwoods	Humboldt	7,292
Citrus	Los Angeles	9,766	Rio Hondo	Los Angeles	12,959
Coachella Valley	Riverside	8,604	Riverside	Riverside	15,066
Coast	Orange	52,153	Saddleback	Orange	23,796
Compton	Los Angeles	4,753	San Bernardino	San Bernardino	14,916
Contra Costa	Contra Costa	33,228	San Diego	San Diego	65,566
El Camino	Los Angeles	26,041	San Francisco	San Francisco	57,283
Feather River	Plumas	1,172	San Joaquin	San Joaquin	15,417
Foothill	Santa Clara	42,241	San Jose	Santa Clara	17,483
Fremont-Newark	Alameda	8,063	San Luis Obispo	San Luis Obispo	7,029
Gavilan	Santa Clara	3,837	San Mateo	San Mateo	29,758
Glendale	Los Angeles	17,279	Santa Barbara	Santa Barbara	23,567
Grossmont-			Santa Clarita	Los Angeles	4,548
Cuyamaca	San Diego	18,607	Santa Monica	Los Angeles	21,252
Hartnell	Monterey	7,197	Sequoias	Tulare	8,383
Imperial	Imperial	4,111	Shasta	Shasta	9,103
Kern	Kern	17,001	Sierra	Placer	11,159
Lake Tahoe	El Dorado	1,467	Siskiyou	Siskiyou	2,244
Lassen	Lassen	2,008	Solano	Solano	9,498
Long Beach	Los Angeles	22,701	Sonoma	Sonoma	24,660
Los Angeles	Los Angeles	102,752	South County	Alameda	19,417
Los Rios	Sacramento	41,781	Southwestern	San Diego	12,417
Marin	Marin	16,055	State Center	Fresno	18,906
Mendocino-	Mendocino-		Ventura	Ventura	29,327
Lake	Lake	3,984	Victor Valley	San Bernardino	6,169
Merced	Merced	7,017	West Hills	Fresno	2,556
Mira Costa*	San Diego	8,570	West Kern	Kern	789
Monterey	Monterey	8,358	West Valley-		
Mt. San Antonio	Los Angeles	27,836	Mission	Santa Clara	26,499
Mt. San Jacinto	Riverside	3,745	Yosemite	Stanislaus	14,675
Napa	Napa	7,681	Yuba	Yuba	8,651
Total					1,261,359

* Revised Projection.
5.33,90   Source: Department of Finance, Demographic Research Unit, California Community College Districts, *Projection of Fall Total Enrollment, 1989.*

SECTION 5 NOTE
In addition to base salary, the average K-12 teacher in California receives additional benefits totaling 22 percent of that salary. California ranks 12th among the states in its benefit package for teachers.

5.34,90

FALL 1987 ENROLLMENT AND 1986-87 DEGREES CONFERRED IN THE FIVE SEGMENTS OF HIGHER EDUCATION††					
	Com- munity Colleges*	California State Colleges	University of California†	Total Independent Colleges and Universities	Other†† Public Insti- tutions°
Total Enrollment	1,264,409	342,776	157,331	151,844	1,847
Lower division	1,264,409	95,002	59,586	38,440	185
Upper division	-	178,985	57,493	39,146	187
Graduate	-	68,789	29,091	53,641	-
First Professional	-	-	6,810	16,115	1,475
Other	-	-	4,351	4,502	-
Degrees Conferred by Type					
Associates	34,112	-	-	2,523	-
Baccalaureate	-	44,374	22,755	19,653	137
Masters	-	8,510	5,751	14,914	-
Doctorate	-	27	2,023	2,204	-
First Professional	-	-	1,847	5,107	443
Other/Not Known	12,297	-	752	2,288	-

*   Credit enrollments only.
†   "Total University" includes Health Science, Interns and Residents, and First Professional enrollments.
°   California Maritime Academy, UC Hastings College of the Law.
†† Enrollment of Other Public Institutions for Fall 1986.
    Degrees of Other Public Institutions for 1985-86.
    5.35,90 Source: California Postsecondary Education Commission, Information Systems Library.

AVERAGE DEFAULT RATES FOR GUARANTEED STUDENT LOANS 1988-89		
Institution	Number of Schools	Average Default Rate*
Universtiy of California	10	7.5%
California State Universities and Colleges	20	13.2%
California Community Colleges	106	32.6%
Private Two-year Colleges	21	18.3%
Private Four-year Colleges	438	10.4%
Private Vocational Schools	311	32.6%
Statewide Average	-	**17.5%**

*   Percentage of students defaulting on loans.
    5.36,90 Source: *Report of the Legislative Analyst: Analysis of the Budget Bill, 1989-90.* Defaulted loans cost the State of California alone approximately $200 million in 1987.

	California Community Colleges*	California State Universities and Colleges		University of California	
Ethnicity	Under-graduate	Under-graduate	Graduate	Under-graduate	Graduate

DISTRIBUTION OF STUDENTS IN CALIFORNIA PUBLIC HIGHER EDUCATION BY ETHNICITY 1982-1988

Ethnicity	California Community Colleges* Under-graduate	California State Universities and Colleges Under-graduate	Graduate	University of California Under-graduate	Graduate
Fall 1982					
White	68.2%	70.5%	76.4%	73.0%	79.4%
Black	9.5%	6.8%	5.2%	4.0%	3.8%
Hispanic	12.5%	9.5%	7.8%	6.1%	6.1%
Asian	8.2%	11.3%	8.8%	14.8%	10.2%
American Indian	1.6%	1.9%	1.3%	2.0%	0.6%
Fall 1986					
White	66.4%	67.9%	78.2%	64.3%	77.2%
Black	7.7%	5.8%	4.2%	4.5%	3.7%
Hispanic	13.4%	9.4%	5.4%	8.4%	6.3%
Asian	11.1%	11.8%	9.1%	19.4%	10.5%
American Indian	1.4%	1.1%	1.0%	0.6%	0.6%
Fall 1988					
Male	43.3%	47.4%	39.3%	49.3%	58.8%
Female	56.7%	52.6%	60.7%	50.7%	41.2%
White	62.4%	59.3%	66.4%	58.1%	63.3%
Black	7.1%	5.3%	3.8%	4.6%	3.3%
Hispanic	15.0%	10.5%	6.8%	9.8%	5.9%
Asian	12.2%	14.6%	7.9%	23.5%	15.6%
American Indian	1.2%	0.9%	0.9%	0.8%	0.5%
Not Stated	5.0%	9.4%	14.3%	3.2%	11.4%

* Fall 1987
5.37,90 Source: U.C. Chancellor's office unpublished data, The California State University Office of the President unpublished data, The California Community Colleges Chancellor's office, Report on Enrollment, Fall 1987.

ANNUAL UNDERGRADUATE TUITION AND FEES AT SELECTED CALIFORNIA UNIVERSITIES AND COLLEGES, 1990

California Community Colleges	$100
California State Universities and Colleges	$708
University of California	$1,477
University of San Francisco	$9,102
University of Southern California	$13,350
California Intstitute of Technology	$12,489
Stanford University	$13,569

5.38,90 Source: Pacific Data Resouces, unpublished data, 1989.

		COLLEGE ENROLLMENT RATE OF CALIFORNIA HIGH SCHOOL GRADUATES 1974-1987					
		Percent Enrolling as Freshmen					
Year	Number of High School Graduates	U.C.	C.S.U.C.	Community Colleges	Total Public Colleges	Private Colleges	Total
1974	289,714	5.1%	7.6%	41.3%	54.0%	NA	NA
1975	293,941	5.3%	7.5%	43.1%	55.9%	NA	NA
1976	289,454	5.1%	7.8%	41.7%	54.6%	NA	NA
1977	285,360	5.2%	8.0%	43.3%	56.5%	3.6%	60.1%
1978	283,841	5.5%	8.4%	41.4%	55.3%	3.4%	58.7%
1979	278,548	5.8%	8.7%	42.1%	56.6%	3.4%	60.0%
1980	270,971	6.0%	9.0%	43.0%	58.0%	3.5%	61.5%
1981	260,229	6.4%	9.0%	42.1%	57.6%	3.3%	60.8%
1982	265,924	6.4%	9.0%	42.8%	58.2%	3.2%	61.4%
1983	262,160	7.0%	8.9%	37.9%	53.4%	3.4%	57.2%
1984	257,633	7.5%	8.9%	36.3%	52.7%	3.3%	56.0%
1985	251,143	7.7%	10.0%	33.0%	50.7%	3.0%	53.7%
1986	248,894	7.9%	10.2%	36.3%	54.4%	3.4%	57.8%
1987	262,921	7.7%	10.7%	34.4%	52.8%	3.4%	56.2%

* U.C. is the University of California. C.S.U.C. is the California State Universities and Colleges.

5.39,90 Source: Cal. Postsecondary Education Commission, *Cal. College-Going Rates, 1987.*

PERCENT OF PUBLIC AND PRIVATE HIGH SCHOOL GRADUATES WHO ENROLL IN THE UNIVERSITY OF CALIFORNIA AS FRESHMEN BY RACE/ETHNICITY		
	Type of High School	
Race/Ethnicity	Public	Private
White	6.4%	16.5%
Hispanic	3.8%	26.0%
Asian	17.3%	7.0%
Black	4.8%	20.7%
Filipino	12.5%	26.8%
Amer. Indian	9.4%	17.3%
Total	7.1%	13.2%

5.40,90 Source: University of California, unpublished data.

SECTION 5 NOTE
The University of California has 26 nature reserves around the state for teaching, research, and limited public visits.

5.41,90

	University of California		California State University		California Community Colleges
ENROLLMENT PROJECTIONS OF CALIFORNIA'S PUBLIC UNIVERSITIES AND COLLEGES					
Year	Graduate	Under-graduate	Graduate	Under-graduate	All Students
1987-88	28,112	116,821	68,789	273,987	1,261,359
1992-93	28,900	120,000	74,500	281,400	1,349,540
1997-98	29,100	127,600	76,300	285,000	1,465,750

5.42,90 Source: California Dept. of Finance, unpublished projections.

AVERAGE FACULTY SALARIES IN CALIFORNIA PUBLIC HIGHER EDUCATION
Academic year 1988-89

Rank	University of California	California Universities and Colleges	Community Colleges
Professor	$68,932	$55,132	-
Associate Professor	$45,240	$43,137	-
Assistant Professor	$39,559	$34,947	-
Instructor	-	$29,145	-
Average Faculty Salary	**$59,469**	**$49,220**	**$40,046**

* The California Community Colleges do not have standard faculty ranks like those at the University of California and the California State Universities and Colleges.
5.43,90 Source: Cal. Community Colleges Chancellor's office, unpublished data. *Report of the Legislative Analyst, Analysis the 1989-90 Budget Bill.*

AVERAGE FACULTY SALARIES AT THE UNIVERSITY OF CALIFORNIA, THE CALIFORNIA STATE UNIVERSTIES AND COLLEGES AND THE CALIFORNIA COMMUNITY COLLEGES

	Academic Year						
	1979-80	1980-81	1982-83	1983-84	1984-85	1985-86	1988-89
University of California	$29,559	$32,664	$35,768	$37,082	$45,799	$54,164	$59,469
California State Universities	$26,111	$29,012	$31,331	$32,652	$36,945	$43,984	$49,220
Community Colleges	$25,785	$28,273	$32,022	$32,704	NA	$38,005	$40,046

5.44,90 Source: California Postsecondary Education Commission. *Faculty Salaries in California's Public Universities 1987-1988* and Cal. Community Colleges- Chancellor's office, *Annual Staffing and Salaries Report, 1987.*

FACULTY IN CALIFORNIA PUBLIC HIGHER EDUCATION BY SEX AND ETHNICITY 1987										
	Professor		Associate Professor		Assistant Professor		Lecturer/ Instructor		All Faculty		
	U.C.	C.S.-U.C.	U.C.	C.S.-U.C.	U.C.	C.S.-U.C.	U.C.	C.S.-U.C.	U.C.*	C.S.-U.C.	Community Colleges
Sex											
Male	92%	83%	77%	67%	71%	53%	NA	44%	86%	75%	62%
Female	8%	17%	23%	33%	29%	47%	NA	56%	14%	25%	38%
Ethnicity											
White	91%	87%	87%	81%	80%	79%	NA	83%	88%	86%	85%
All Minorities	9%	13%	13%	19%	20%	21%	NA	NA	12%	14%	15%
Hispanic	2.4%	3.1%	4.1%	5.0%	5.3%	6.4%	NA	4.3%	3.2%	3.6%	5.8%
Black	1.2%	2.3%	3.1%	3.5%	2.2%	4.7%	NA	4.3%	1.7%	2.8%	5.2%
Asian	5.5%	7.0%	6.1%	9.4%	12.4%	9.2%	NA	6.5%	6.6%	7.3%	3.9%
American Indian	0.3%	0.3%	0.1%	0.7%	0.1%	0.4%	NA	2.2%	0.2%	0.5%	0.6%

* Excluding lecturers.
U.C. = University of California. C.S.U.C. = California State Universities and Colleges.
U.C. data is for Full-time Faculty. Community College data is for Contract and Regular Faculty.
5.45,90 Source: The respective University and College systems - unpublished data.

CONTRIBUTIONS TO CALIFORNIA UNIVERSITIES 1987-1988	
School	Contribution in millions
Stanford	$182
Cal Tech	$97
U.S.C.	$82
U.C.L.A.	$75
U.C. Berkeley	$67
U.C.S.F.	$38
Pomona	$34
U.C. San Diego	$32
Loyola Marymount	$27
U.C. Davis	$20
Loma Linda	$18
U.C. Irvine	$17
Pepperdine	$14
Univ. of San Francisco	$11
U.C. Total	$262
Cal State Univ. System Total	$40
State Total	**$900**

Note: Stanford led all U.S. universities in fund raising.
5.46,90 Source: Council for Aid to Education, unpublished data.

CALIFORNIA UNIVERSITY AND COLLEGE ENDOWMENTS 1988		
School	**Market Value (Millions)**	**National Rank**
Stanford	1,800	5
University of California	1,062	10
Cal Tech	425	26
Univ. of Southern California	404	27
Pomona	242	53
Occidental College	130	91
Loyola Marymount	90	112
Claremont McKenna College	80	122
Santa Clara University	77	126
Pepperdine University	67	141
Mills College	60	152
Claremont U. (Center & Grad. School)	53	166
Harvey Mudd	51	168
Scripps College	49	171
Loma Linda	45	183

5.47,90 Source: Council for Aid to Education, unpublished data.

FOREIGN LANGUAGE STUDY IN CALIFORNIA'S COLLEGES* AND UNIVERSITIES		
Language	**Number of Students Studying**	**% of All Such Language Students in the U.S.**
Arabic	434	13%
Chinese	4,324	26%
French	31,314	11%
German	13,598	11%
Ancient Greek	1,668	9%
Hebrew	1,187	8%
Italian	6,327	15%
Japanese	6,596	28%
Latin	1,613	6%
Portuguese	756	15%
Russian	3,242	10%
Spanish	59,737	15%
103 Other Languages	1,862	14%
5 European Languages	114,218	13%
Total	**132,658**	13%

* Includes 2 year colleges.
    5.48,90 Source: Modern Language Association, unpublished data.

CALIFORNIA'S LIBRARIES† (Excluding K-12 School Libraries)				
	1980	1984	1986	1988
Public Libraries	**168**	**169**	**169**	**169**
Main Libraries	162	163	163	163
Branch Libraries	559	579	587	601
(at least 1,400 square feet, at least 1 librarian and 1 clerk)				
Library Stations	393	366	340	338
(fixed outlets smaller than branches)				
Mobile Library Stops	2,112	1,799	1,855	1,785
(served by bookmobiles, etc.) (75 vehicles operated by 53 libraries in 1988)				
Total Service Outlets	**3,226**	**2,907**	**2,945**	**2,887**
Academic Libraries, **University and College***				
State	29	29	29	29
Community College	90	100	102	102
Private	43	49	53	66
Branch Libraries	NA	NA	NA	30
Total	**162**	**178**	**184**	**197**
State Agencies*				
State Institutional & School	29	38	39	49
Legal	8	19	20	NA
Medical	10	11	11	NA
Government Offices	NA	NA	NA	41
Nonprofit Special	21	42	42	NA
Total	**68**	**110**	**112**	**81**
Special Libraries*				
U.S. Armed Forces	18	16	18	20
U.S. Installations	NA	NA	NA	16
Legal	29	24	28	32
Medical	115	97	93	78
Religious	13	8	10	NA
For Profit, Special	162	169	178	131
Nonprofit Special	150	142	140	74
Total	**487**	**456**	**467**	**471**
County Law Libraries (One maintained by each county)	**58**	**58**	**58**	**58**
Total California Libraries* (excluding school libraries)	**943**	**971**	**990**	**895**

* Not all operating libraries in these categories report annually to the State Library.

† The State Library estimates that there are 1,200 libraries in California exclusive of K-12 school libraries.

5.49,90 Source: California State Library, Library Development Services Bureau, *California Library Directory, 1989.*

CALIFORNIA LIBRARY HOLDINGS, CIRCULATION AND EXPENDITURES (in thousands)						
Type of Library	Total Volumes	Circula- tion	Inter-Library Loan		Refer- ence Trans- actions	Total Expend- ditures
			Borrowed	Lent		
1985-1986*						
Public	51,543	129,275	261	239	37,271	356,086
Academic	51,374	20,016	175	296	4,538	273,985
Special	9,716	3,096	136	118	797	43,116
State Agencies	1,290	788	9	43	190	11,404
County Law	2,280	NA	NA	NA	NA	11,507
State Total	**116,203**	**153,175**	**581**	**696**	**42,796**	**696,098**
1986-1987*						
Public	52,516	131,955	270	225	34,890	381,756
Academic	53,875	21,001	189	308	4,974	302,582
Special	10,415	2,322	157	118	637	43,723
State Agencies	1,135	879	12	50	244	15,176
County Law	2,360	NA	NA	NA	NA	13,636
State Total	**120,301**	**156,157**	**628**	**701**	**40,745**	**756,873**
1987-1988*						
Public	52,594	136,082	293	259	36,627	402,425
Academic	54,230	22,046	281	409	4,487	307,699
Special	6,379	2,365	143	96	552	27,489
State Agencies	922	787	7	49	138	15,012
County Law	2,418	NA	NA	NA	NA	14,612
State Total	**116,543**	**161,280**	**724**	**813**	**41,804**	**767,237**

* Fiscal Year.

5.50,90 Source: Cal. State Library, *California Library Statistics*.

EDUCATION PROMINENT CALIFORNIANS	
Henry Cogswell	Rufus B. Kleinsmidt
Henry Durant	Robert Gordon Sproul
Robert Hutchins	Leland Stanford
David Starr Jordan	Benjamin Ide Wheeler
Clark Kerr	Joseph & Robert Widney

5.51,90 Source: Pacific Data Resources

SECTION 5 NOTE
In 1976 in California 9 percent of the schoolchildren were in private schools; in 1984 the figure was 11.7 percent; by 1988 it was 10.5 percent.

5.52,90

MAJOR UNIVERSITY LIBRARIES

Rank	University	Volumes in Library
1	Harvard	11,496,906
2	Yale	8,538,156
3	Illinois	7,377,051
4	**University of California, Berkeley**	**7,190,821**
5	Michigan	6,133,171
6	Texas	5,888,776
7	**University of California, Los Angeles**	**5,812,863**
8	Columbia	5,740,832
9	**Stanford**	**5,740,162**
38	**University of Southern California**	**2,533,850**
50	**University of California, Davis**	**2,227,255**
64	**University of California, Santa Barbara**	**1,862,167**
65	**University of California, San Diego**	**1,846,761**
99	**University of California, Riverside**	**1,369,083**
101	**University of California, Irvine**	**1,361,756**

5.53,90 Source: Association of Research Libraries, ARL Statistics 1987-88.

SECTION 5 NOTE

California high school students taking the S.A.T. exam overall receive the fourth highest scores in the U.S. Only students in New Hampshire, Oregon, and Vermont do better.

5.54,90

SECTION 5 NOTE

California high schools are among the worst in the U.S. in rate of graduation. The U.S. Dept. of education ranks California 42nd among the 50 states: only 66 percent of the state's high school students graduate.

5.55,90

SECTION 5 NOTE

Crime in the public schools--arson, vandalism, and theft--cost the state of California $24,500,000 in 1987-88.

5.56,90

SECTION 5 NOTE

California has more foreign students (50,000, or 14 percent of the U.S. total) than any other state in the nation.

5.57,90 Source: Institute of International Education, 1988.

Law and Justice

Violent crime has increased by more than 30 percent in California since 1984 after decreasing during the early 1980s. Although recently burglaries and incidents of arson have declined, the statistics for most other serious crimes, including murder, robbery, aggravated assault, and car theft, show an increase. As a consequence, arrests are up and the state's prisons are facing the pressure of a growing population of inmates. From 1978 to 1988 arrests in California rose 38 percent, and during the same period the state's prison population increased dramatically: from 21,000 to 76,000.

The costs of incarcerating those sentenced to terms in prison has necessitated a huge increase in the budget for the California Department of Corrections, from $4 to $9 billion annually. As expensive as incarceration is, analysts at the Rand Corporation have determined that it is less expensive for society to lock up criminals than to leave them on the streets, where they continue to break the law--at great cost to both individuals and communities.

Some crimes--for example, murder, rape, and aggravated assault-- are more likely to be solved than others and their perpetrators arrested. In California 52 percent of rapists, 61 percent of assailants, and 66 percent of murderers are arrested but only 28 percent of robbers, 15 percent of car thieves, and 14 percent of burglars.

Among California's cities with populations over 50,000, the three most crime ridden are Richmond, Oakland, and Berkeley, all on the eastern rim of San Francisco Bay. The three safest cities in the state are Thousand Oaks and Simi Valley, both in Ventura County, and Sunnyvale, near San Jose.

Like most states in the West, California has a relatively high overall crime rate compared with the rest of the nation. The rate of violent crime in most of the state's neighbors, including Washington, Oregon, and Arizona, is higher than in California itself, but California nonetheless is the eighth most violent state in the nation.

One area of criminal activity that has been in the headlines also shows up prominently in the arrest statistics: illicit drugs. From 1984 to 1988 felony narcotics arrests jumped from 42,000 to 115,000. These figures suggest that we are far from the goal of being the kinder, gentler nation President Bush envisions.

NUMBER OF VIOLENT CRIMES AND PERCENT CHANGE FROM PREVIOUS YEAR 1977-1988									
	Willful Homicide		Forcible Rape		Robbery		Aggravated Assualt		Total	
Year	Number	%	Number	%	Number	%	Number	%	Number	%
1977	2,481	-	10,715	-	62,207	-	77,424	-	152,827	-
1980	3,405	15.8%	13,661	12.0%	90,282	19.3%	102,555	10.4%	209,903	14.3%
1981	3,140	-7.8%	13,545	-0.8%	93,638	3.7%	97,842	-4.6%	208,165	-0.8%
1982	2,788	-11.5%	12,529	-7.5%	91,988	-1.8%	94,138	-3.8%	201,433	-3.2%
1983	2,640	-5.0%	12,092	-3.5%	85,824	-6.7%	93,933	-0.2%	194,489	-3.4%
1984	2,724	3.2%	11,702	-3.2%	84,015	-2.1%	97,209	3.5%	195,650	0.6%
1985	2,781	2.1%	11,442	-2.2%	86,464	2.9%	101,379	4.3%	202,066	3.3%
1986	3,030	9.0%	12,118	5.9%	92,513	7.0%	140,691	38.8%	248,352	22.9%
1987	2,929	-3.3%	12,114	0.0%	83,373	-9.9%	155,721	10.7%	254,137	2.3%
1988	2,947	0.6%	11,771	-2.8%	86,180	3.4%	161,082	3.4%	261,990	3.1%
1977-1988	-	18.7%	-	9.9%	-	38.6%	-	108.1%	-	71.4%

6.1,90 Source: California Department of Justice, Bureau of Criminal Statistics, *Crime and Delinquency in California.*

NUMBER OF PROPERTY CRIMES AND PERCENT CHANGE FROM PRIOR YEAR 1977-1988									
	Burglary		Motor Vehicle Theft		Total		Theft		Arson	
Year	Number	%	Number	%	Number	%	Number	%	Number	%
1977	462,736	-	144,014	-	606,750	-	NA	-	NA	-
1980	543,846	9.9%	174,548	4.4%	718,394	8.5%	910,210	7.9%	28,446	-
1981	539,809	-0.7%	162,267	-7.0%	702,076	-2.3%	920,047	1.1%	24,534	-13.8%
1982	499,468	-7.5%	164,530	1.4%	663,998	-5.4%	935,831	1.7%	20,274	-17.4%
1983	460,401	-7.8%	158,899	-3.4%	619,300	-6.7%	866,992	-7.4%	17,705	-12.7%
1984	443,634	-3.6%	161,341	1.5%	604,965	-2.3%	857,717	-1.1%	19,407	9.6%
1985	449,065	1.2%	177,330	9.9%	626,399	3.5%	892,646	4.1%	20,455	5.4%
1986	457,743	1.9%	205,602	15.9%	663,345	5.9%	913,057	2.3%	19,722	-3.6%
1987	420,182	-8.2%	229,695	11.7%	649,877	-2.0%	896,770	-1.8%	18,490	-6.2%
1988	407,555	-3.0%	265,975	15.8%	673,530	3.6%	932,715	4.0%	18,846	1.9%
1977-1988	-	-11.9%	-	84.7%	-	11.0%	-	2.5%	-	-33.7%

6.2,90 Source: California Department of Justice, Bureau of Criminal Statistics, *Crime and Delinquency in California.*

SECTION 6 NOTE
The lower court conviction is affirmed in 94 percent of criminal appeals by defendants.

6.3,90

SECTION 6 NOTE
The Los Angeles area is the bounced-check capital of the U.S.

6.4,90

NUMBER OF ARRESTS AND PERCENT CHANGE FROM PRIOR YEAR 1978-1988						
	Adult		Juvenile		Total	
Year	Number	%	Number	%	Number	%
1978	1,098,602	—	284,203	—	1,382,805	—
1979	1,147,485	4.4%	294,552	3.6%	1,442,037	—
1980	1,260,324	9.8%	282,526	-4.1%	1,542,850	—
1981	1,366,481	8.4%	265,870	-5.9%	1,632,351	5.8%
1982	1,378,695	0.9%	243,249	-8.5%	1,621,944	-0.6%
1983	1,435,788	4.1%	218,126	-10.3%	1,653,914	2.0%
1984	1,458,674	1.6%	222,047	1.8%	1,680,721	1.6%
1985	1,485,079	1.8%	230,961	4.0%	1,716,040	2.1%
1986	1,558,601	5.0%	235,880	2.1%	1,794,481	4.6%
1987	1,635,731	4.9%	223,611	-5.2%	1,859,342	3.6%
1988	1,673,864	2.3%	229,203	2.5%	1,903,067	2.4%
1978-1988	—	52.4%	—	-19.4%	—	37.6%

6.5,90 Source: California Department of Justice, Bureau of Criminal
Statistics, *Crime and Delinquency in California,* 1988.

NUMBER OF ARRESTS AND PERCENT CHANGE FROM PRIOR YEAR BY CATEGORY OF OFFENSE, 1982-1988						
	Felonies		Misdemeanors		Status Offenses*	
Offender	Number	% Change	Number	% Change	Number	% Change
Adults						
1982	302,559	3.2%	1,076,136	0.3%	—	—
1983	302,421	0%	1,133,367	5.3%	—	—
1984	315,872	4.4%	1,142,802	0.8%	—	—
1985	340,152	7.7%	1,144,927	0.2%	—	—
1986	393,790	15.8%	1,164,811	1.7%	—	—
1987	442,663	7.3%	1,213,068	4.1%	—	—
1988	469,688	11.1%	1,204,176	-0.7%	—	—
Juveniles						
1982	84,436	-9.2%	134,772	-7.3%	24,041	-12.4%
1983	71,188	-15.7%	124,421	-7.7%	22,517	-6.3%
1984	68,989	-3.1%	126,334	1.5%	26,724	18.7%
1985	73,521	6.6%	131,667	4.2%	25,773	-3.6%
1986	76,192	3.6%	134,411	2.1%	25,277	-1.9%
1987	73,583	-3.4%	124,698	-7.2%	25,332	0.2%
1988	80,758	9.8%	124,561	-0.1%	23,884	-5.7%

* Truancy, incorrigible, curfew, runaway.
6.6,90 Source: Cal. Dept. of Justice, Bureau of Criminal Statistics,
Crime and Delinquency in California, 1988.

NUMBER OF FELONY ARRESTS, 1984-1988						
	1984		1987		1988	
Crime	Number	Percent	Number	Percent	Number	Percent
Violent Crimes						
Homicide	3,896	5%	3,056	3%	3,159	3%
Rape	4,369	6	4,543	4	4,534	4
Robbery	23,109	30	23,343	22	24,284	21
Assault	43,145	56	74,705	69	84,388	71
Kidnapping	2,224	3	2,387	2	2,236	2
Total Violent Crimes	**76,743**	**100%**	**108,034**	**100%**	**118,601**	**100%**
Property Crimes						
Burglary	76,295	46%	73,756	40%	76,270	38%
Theft	51,144	31	61,960	33	68,151	34
Motor Vehicle						
Theft	23,108	14	36,275	20	43,771	22
Forgery	12,138	7	12,393	7	11,878	6
Arson	2,066	1	1,901	1	1,983	1
Total Property Crimes	**164,751**	**100%**	**186,285**	**100%**	**202,053**	**100%**
Drug Law Violations						
Narcotics	42,479	46%	91,931	63%	115,107	68%
Marijuana	21,350	23	18,722	13	16,853	10
Dangerous Drugs	27,820	30	34,252	23	36,045	21
Other	1,475	2	1,683	1	2,151	1
Total Drug Law Violations	**93,124**	**100%**	**146,588**	**100%**	**170,156**	**100%**
All Other Felony Arrests	50,243	—	55,339	—	59,636	—
Total Felony Arrests	**384,861**	**...**	**496,246**	**...**	**550,446**	**...**

6.7,90 Source: California Dept. of Justice, Bureau of Criminal Statistics, *Crime and Delinquency in California.*

CALIFORNIA'S WORST MASS MURDERERS			
Rank	**Murderer**	**Murders**	**Area**
1	Zebra Killers	73	San Francisco Bay Area
2	David Burke	43	PSA Flight 1771
3	Juan Corona	25	Yuba City
4	James Huberty	21	San Ysidro
5	Patrick Kearney	21	Southern California
6	Richard Ramirez	13	Los Angeles
7	William Bonin	13	Southern California
8	Leonard Lake and Charles Ng	12	Calaveras County
9	Herbert Mullin	11	Santa Cruz

6.8,90 Source: Pacific Data Resources.

SECTION 6 NOTE
The workload (cases filed) of the California Supreme Court has doubled since 1964.

6.9,90

NUMBER OF ADULT MISDEMEANOR ARRESTS BY OFFENSE 1983-1988						
	1983		**1987**		**1988**	
Crime	Number	%	Number	%	Number	%
Assault and Battery	46,110	4	61,285	5	63,507	5
Petty Theft	80,942	7	90,973	8	93,932	8
Checks and Credit Cards	2,089	.2	1,407	.1	1,315	.1
Drug Law Violations	92,579	8	112,573	9	122,283	10
Indecent Exposure	3,013	.3	2,612	.2	2,661	.2
Annoying Children	599	0	436	0	521	0
Obscene Matter	56	0	24	0	55	0
Lewd Conduct	7,171	.6	8,901	.7	8,084	.7
Prostitution	16,562	1	21,062	2	21,190	2
Drunk	219,818	19	191,347	16	170,888	14
Liquor Laws	29,738	3	32,465	3	29,790	3
Disorderly Conduct	10,322	.9	12,136	1	9,456	.8
Disturbing the Peace	10,956	1	9,958	.8	9,872	.8
Driving under the Influence	342,203	30	337,294	28	315,585	26
Hit-and-Run	6,053	.5	6,575	.5	6,649	.6
Traffic Violations	102,985	9	87,298	7	81,991	7
Gambling	2,174	.2	1,721	.1	1,457	.1
Nonsupport†	790	.1	816	.1	638	.1
All Other	159,207	14	234,185	22	264,302	18
Total Misdemeanor Arrests	**1,133,367**	**100**	**1,213,068**	**100**	**1,204,176**	**100**

Note: Juvenile arrests for misdemeanors would, if added to the adult total, increase it by approximately 10 percent.
6.10,90 Source: California Dept. of Justice, Bureau of Criminal Statistics, *Crime and Delinquency in California.*

DISPOSITION OF JUVENILE CASES REFERRED TO PROBATION DEPARTMENTS, 1974-1988				
Year	Closed or Sent to Other Agency	Informal Probation	Sent to Juvenile Court	Total
1974	98,657	25,951	53,724	178,332
1982	67,607	15,411	43,163	126,181
1983	59,728	15,313	41,852	116,893
1984	57,444	15,769	40,309	113,522
1985	61,022	17,654	41,752	120,468
1986	65,632	17,363	41,843	124,838
1987	66,064	17,238	41,083	124,385
1988†	59,731	14,087	30,856	104,674

† Excludes Los Angeles County.
6.11,90 Source: California Dept. of Justice, Bureau of Criminal Statistics, *Crime and Delinquency in California.*

SECTION 6 NOTE
The annual operating costs of the California Court System are $1.1 billion.

6.12,90

		Dismissed or Transferred	Remanded to Adult Court	Sent to California Youth Authority	Total
DISPOSITION OF CASES REFERRED TO JUVENILE COURTS BY PROBATION DEPARTMENTS, 1979-1988					
Year	Probation	Dismissed or Transferred	Remanded to Adult Court	Sent to California Youth Authority	Total
1979	33,464	13,838	361	470	48,133
1982	32,227	10,063	313	560	43,163
1983	32,219	8,921	212	500	41,852
1984	30,832	8,861	150	466	40,309
1985	32,409	8,807	163	413	41,792
1986	31,710	9,440	153	540	41,843
1987	28,540	9,857	119	587	41,083
1988†	22,248	8,197	152	259	30,856

† Excludes Los Angeles County.
6.13,90 Source: California Dept. of Justice, Bureau of Criminal Statistics, *Crime and Delinquency in California.*

NUMBER OF JUVENILES IN DETENTION BY SEX AND TYPE OF FACILITY 1988

	County Detention		California Youth Authority	
	Number	Percent	Number	Percent
Sex				
Male	8,287	91	8,409	96
Female	839	9	346	4
Total	**9,126**	**100**	**8,755**	**100**
Type of Facility				
Secure	6,345	70	NA	NA
Non-secure	2,781	30	NA	NA
Total	**9,126**	**100**	**NA**	**NA**

6.14,90 Source: California Dept. of Justice, Bureau of Criminal Statistics, *Crime and Delinquency in California* and California Youth Authority, *Population Movement Summary.*

SECTION 6 NOTE

The verdicts in 17 percent of all civil cases tried in Superior Court are appealed to the state courts of appeal. The verdicts in 99 percent of criminal cases are appealed.

6.15,90

SECTION 6 NOTE

In 1987 the number of Californians with permits to carry concealed firearms was 32,405. In 1988 it was 31,576.

6.16,90

NUMBER OF JUVENILES IN DETENTION 1978-1988		
Year	County Detention	California Youth Authority
1978	6,028	4,700
1982	7,508	5,811
1983	7,542	5,824
1984	8,252	6,324
1985	8,474	7,148
1986	8,598	8,249
1987	8,601	8,824
1988	9,126	8,755
Percent Change, 1978-1988	43%	86%

6.17,90 Source: California Dept. of Justice, Bureau of Criminal Statistics, *Crime and Delinquency in California*, and California Youth Authority, unpublished data.

CALIFORNIA PRISON POPULATION BY MOST SERIOUS OFFENSE, 1987				
Offense	Number of Felons	Percent of All Felons	Male	Female
Homicide	8,755	13%	8,277	478
Robbery	10,474	16%	10,094	380
Assault	4,666	7%	4,473	193
Burglary	12,276	19%	11,772	504
Theft, except auto	5,248	8%	4,476	772
Auto Theft	1,812	3%	1,767	45
Forgery	1,110	2%	794	316
Rape	2,542	4%	2,538	4
Other Sex Crimes	4,186	6%	4,125	61
Drug Offenses	11,636	18%	10,550	1,086
Escape	454	0.7%	436	18
Kidnap	919	1%	897	22
Drunk Driving	380	0.6%	458	22
Arson	293	0.4%	266	27
Possession of Weapon	911	1%	896	15
Other Offenses	436	6%	365	71
Total	**66,975**	**100%**	**62,823**	**4,152**

6.18,90 Source: California Department of Corrections, Administrative Services Division, *California Prisoners and Parolees, 1987*.

SECTION 6 NOTE
In 1987 thirty-nine Californians had permits to own machine guns. In 1988 thirty-three had such permits.

6.19,90

CALIFORNIA PRISON POPULATION Actual Population and New Commitments			
Year	New Commitments	Percent Increase From Prior Year	Actual Inmate Population
1976	6,909	20%	20,345
1978	9,325	24%	20,629
1980	11,347	15%	23,511
1981	13,932	23%	26,768
1982	15,932	14%	32,127
1983	18,401	15%	36,082
1984	18,247	-1%	40,649
1985	21,611	18%	50,511
1986	24,708	14%	59,484
1987	27,945	13%	66,975
1988	33,665	20%	76,171

6.20,90 Source: California Department of Corrections. *Movement of Prison Population by Institution.*

ESCAPES FROM STATE PRISONS AND CAMPS AND COMMUNITY BASED FACILITIES		
	Number of Escapes	
Year	Prisons and Camps	Community Based Facilities
1960	160	NA
1970	298	103
1975	114	45
1980	105	21
1981	133	133
1982	136	419
1983	114	648
1984	79	828
1985	81	915
1986	84	872
1987	89	735
1988	70	1,006

6.21,90 Source: California Dept. of Corrections, Administrative Division, Offender Information Services Branch, *Escapes from Dept. of Corrections, 1989.*

SECTION 6 NOTE
According to the National Rifle Association, nationwide 19 percent of households have handguns (1.7 per household) and 37 percent have firearms (3.2 per household). Based on these percentages, the statistics for California are as follows: 1.9 million households own handguns and 3.7 households own firearms.

6.22,90

NEW FELONS IN STATE PRISON AND CAMPS BY RACE-ETHNICITY				
Year	White	Mexican-American	Black	Other
1960	58%	17%	23%	2%
1965	55%	16%	27%	2%
1970	52%	16%	30%	2%
1975	46%	18%	34%	2%
1980	39%	24%	36%	2%
1981	36%	25%	36%	3%
1982	36%	25%	36%	3%
1983	35%	26%	36%	3%
1985	35%	27%	33%	4%
1986	32%	31%	32%	5%
1987	31%	31%	33%	6%
1988	31%	28%	37%	5%

6.23, 90 Source: California Dept. of Corrections, Administrative Services Division, Offender Information Services Branch, unpublished data.

PRISONERS ON DEATH ROW		
State	Number of Prisoners 1987	Number of Prisoners 1989
California	195	241
Texas	242	284
New York	0	0
Arizona	64	84
Total U.S.	1,874	2,183

6.24,90 Source: N.A.A.C.P. Legal Defense Fund, 1989.

FIRES IN CALIFORNIA								
Year	Number of Fires	Percent Change from Prior Year	Property Loss (millions)	Percent Change From Prior Year	Firemen		Civilians	
					Killed	Injured	Killed	Injured
1975	215,898	NA	$139	NA	14	2,115	407	2,801
1980	211,934	-1.8%	$393	182.7%	4	2,325	321	2,536
1981	192,460	-9.2%	$411	4.6%	3	1,558	349	2,144
1982	165,471	-14.0%	$406	-1.2%	7	1,329	370	2,306
1983	155,892	-5.8%	$366	-9.9%	2	935	354	1,856
1984	174,612	12.0%	$416	13.7%	3	1,225	276	2,071
1985	170,584	-2.3%	$483	16.1%	0	1,144	312	2,034
1986	159,700	-6.4%	$441	-8.7%	0	1,093	313	2,054
1987	162,036	1.5%	$668	51.5%	2	1,053	307	2,254

6.25,90 Source: California State Fire Marshall, *Annual Reports.*

PERCENT OF FIRES BY TIME OF DAY AND DAY OF WEEK, 1987			
12:01-2AM	6.0%	Sunday	14.3%
2:01-4AM	4.4%		
4:01-6AM	3.2%	Monday	13.8%
6:01-8AM	4.2%		
8:01-10AM	6.2%	Tuesday	13.8%
10:01-12PM	8.6%	Wednesday	13.9%
12:01-2PM	11.2%		
2:01-4PM	12.9%	Thursday	14.7%
4:01-6PM	13.4%		
6:01-8PM	11.7%	Friday	14.7%
8:01-10PM	10.2%	Saturday	14.8%
10:01-Midnight	8.0%		

6.26,90 Source: California State Fire Marshall, *Annual Reports*.

TYPES OF FIRES IN CALIFORNIA, NUMBER/PERCENT, 1975-1987						
Year	Building	Grass	Vehicle	Refuse	Other	Total
1975	61,853/29%	55,639/26%	34,132/16%	30,208/14%	33,887/16%	**215,719/100%**
1980	53,419/25%	53,815/25%	45,454/21%	38,147/18%	20,829/10%	**211,934/100%**
1981	48,991/25%	48,234/25%	47,862/25%	36,818/19%	10,555/ 5%	**192,460/100%**
1982	45,789/28%	34,587/21%	45,126/27%	30,072/19%	9,897/ 6%	**165,471/100%**
1983	41,620/27%	32,311/21%	44,476/29%	28,976/19%	8,509/ 5%	**155,892/100%**
1984	44,216/25%	41,042/24%	45,154/26%	33,893/19%	10,307/ 6%	**174,612/100%**
1985	44,673/26%	37,694/22%	44,510/26%	33,623/20%	10,264/ 6%	**170,584/100%**
1986	41,474/26%	32,343/20%	45,585/29%	30,386/19%	9,912/ 6%	**159,700/100%**
1987	42,413/27%	32,500/20%	46,054/28%	30,631/19%	10,439/ 6%	**162,036/100%**

6.27,90 Source: California State Fire Marshall, Annual Reports.

CRIMINAL AND NON-CRIMINAL CAUSES OF FIRES			
	Arson	Arson Suspected	Other Cause	Total Fires
Year	Number/%	Number/%	Number/%	Number/%
1975	25,071/12%	27,331/13%	163,245/76%	215,647/100%
1980	30,061/14%	30,280/14%	151,593/72%	211,934/100%
1981	27,426/14%	27,156/14%	137,878/72%	192,460/100%
1982	21,807/13%	20,618/12%	123,046/74%	165,471/100%
1983	20,823/13%	18,321/12%	116,748/75%	155,892/100%
1984	22,112/13%	22,668/13%	129,832/74%	174,612/100%
1985	22,338/13%	22,368/13%	125,878/74%	170,584/100%
1986	21,807/14%	20,754/13%	117,139/73%	159,700/100%
1987	21,431/13%	19,521/12%	121,084/75%	162,036/100%

6.28,90 Source: California State Fire Marshall, Annual Reports.

SECTION 6 NOTE
Only California skyscrapers built after 1974 are required to have complete sprinkler systems.

6.29,90

		BUILDING FIRES BY LOCATION, NUMBER/PERCENT OF TOTAL FIRES						
Year	1-2 Family Dwelling	Apart-ment House	Room-ing House	Dorm-atory	Hotel/ Motel	Mobile Home	School
1975	39,146/18%	15,796/7%	211/*	192/*	1,534/.7%	1,188/.6%	4,279/2%
1980	34,945/16%	14,432/7%	85/*	174/*	1,335/.6%	1,044/.5%	3,448/2%
1981	32,518/17%	13,943/7%	75/*	144/*	1,233/.6%	1,025/.5%	2,796/1%
1982	30,137/18%	12,378/7%	91/*	137/*	967/.6%	974/.6%	2,964/2%
1983	27,306/14%	10,973/7%	69/*	153/*	955/.6%	1,016/.6%	1,932/1%
1984	28,846/17%	12,381/7%	68/*	148/*	1,063/.6%	1,071/.6%	2,286/1%
1985	29,205/17%	12,233/7%	71/*	124/*	1,013/.6%	1,066/.6%	2,221/1%
1986	26,403/17%	12,126/8%	85/*	110/*	901/.6%	971/.6%	1,869/1%
1987	27,911/17%	12,618/8%	87/*	136/*	919/.6%	765/.5%	1,699/1%

* Negligible %.

6.30,90 Source: Califorrnia State Fire Marshall, *Annual Reports.*

	LAW ENFORCEMENT OFFICERS FELONIOUSLY KILLED, 1974-1988			
Year	California	New York	Texas	Nation
1974	9	9	9	132
1975	11	8	11	129
1976	5	4	12	111
1977	10	9	4	93
1978	12	5	9	93
1979	10	7	8	106
1980	7	11	9	104
1981	8	6	5	91
1982	7	7	9	92
1983	9	1	11	80
1984	6	5	4	72
1985	6	1	7	78
1986	3	2	5	66
1987	4	9	7	73
1988	9	4	12	78
Total	116	88	122	1,404

6.31,90 Source: F.B.I., Uniform Crime Reports, *Law Enforcement Officers Killed and Assaulted.*

SECTION 6 NOTE
The counties with the highest auto theft rates are (1) San Diego, (2) Los Angeles, (3) San Francisco, (4) Sacramento and (5) San Bernardino. Sierra and Alpine counties had the lowest rates.

6.32,90

EXPLOSIVES INCIDENTS IN CALIFORNIA 1980-1987											
	Bombings		Incendiaries		Other			Total			
Year	Number	% of All U.S.	Number	% of All U.S.	Number	% of All U.S.		Number	% of All U.S.		
1980	162	15%	105	24%	68	5%		335	12%		
1981	124	13%	149	35%	49	5%		322	14%		
1982	106	15%	58	21%	32	4%		196	11%		
1983	61	9%	23	11%	45	6%		129	8%		
1984	99	13%	31	16%	52	6%		182	10%		
1985	124	14%	33	15%	84	7%		241	11%		
1986	154	15%	38	15%	126	11%		318	13%		
1987	183	19%	31	14%	165	16%		389	17%		

6.33,90 Source: U.S. Treasury, Bureau of Alcohol, Tobacco and Firearms, *Explosives Incidents Report.*

BOMBING INCIDENTS 1987 TOP FIVE STATES	
State	Number
California	**183**
Florida	77
Illinois	69
Texas	53
New York	48
Total U.S.	**973**

6.34,90 Source: U.S. Department of the Treasury, Bureau of Alcohol, Tobacco and Firearms, *Explosives Incidents Report.*

EXPLOSIVES STOLEN IN CALIFORNIA 1980-1987					
	Number of Thefts		Pounds of Explosives		Number of Blasting Caps
Year	California	% of All U.S.	California	% of All U.S.	California	% of All U.S.
1980	18	6%	5,082	3.0%	1,708	3.0%
1981	14	6%	1,067	2.0%	901	3.0%
1982	6	3%	224	0.3%	200	0.5%
1983	10	5%	1,370	4.0%	365	1.0%
1984	11	5%	250	0.3%	979	3.0%
1985	11	5%	501	2.0%	1,060	2.0%
1986	14	8%	1,647	5.0%	1,894	6.0%
1987	4	3%	50	0.3%	330	1.0%

6.35,90 Source: U.S. Department of the Treasury, Bureau of Alcohol, Tobacco and Firearms, *Explosives Incidents Report.*

		Crime Rate			1987 Murder Rank	Murder Rate		1987 Robbery Rank	Robbery Rate		1987 Motor Vehicle Theft Rank	Motor Vehicle Theft Rate	
Rank	Metropolitan Area	1986	1987	% Change	Murder Rank	1986	1987	Robbery Rank	1986	1987	Theft Rank	1986	1987
15	Anaheim - Santa Ana	6,031	5,735	-4.9%	20	5.0	4.1	11	186	163	5	638	681
4	Bakersfield	7,593	7,443	-2.0%	2	11.1	12.0	5	273	244	10	501	475
17	Chico	6,071	5,461	-10.0%	11	4.2	9.4	23	53	56	16	328	365
1	Fresno	8,563	8,006	-6.5%	6	14.6	11.1	8	275	231	7	562	660
10	Los Angeles - Long Beach	7,406	6,784	-8.4%	1	16.9	16.6	1	594	521	2	1,226	1,246
22	Merced	5,111	4,849	-5.1%	18	6.7	4.8	18	102	88	23	229	288
9	Modesto	7,570	6,960	-8.1%	15	7.1	6.5	13	143	138	12	411	448
5	Oakland	7,551	7,439	-1.5%	8	11.6	10.0	3	393	332	8	570	641
23	Oxnard - Ventura	4,297	3,997	-7.0%	23	6.7	2.9	16	135	118	20	308	310
16	Redding	5,790	5,690	-1.7%	9	9.0	9.5	22	67	70	18	313	321
3	Riverside - San Bernardino	7,435	7,455	0.2%	3	11.4	11.7	9	242	222	3	668	809
7	Sacramento	7,437	7,234	-2.7%	7	10.4	10.6	4	303	249	4	585	699
18	Salinas - Seaside - Monterey	5,797	5,403	-6.8%	19	7.4	4.3	12	143	155	21	246	295
8	San Diego	6,463	6,990	8.2%	13	9.1	7.8	6	272	240	1	1,001	1,315
14	San Francisco	6,053	6,116	1.0%	12	9.9	8.5	2	380	344	6	606	666
21	San Jose	5,114	4,853	5.1%	22	4.1	3.4	17	121	106	14	341	386
20	Santa Barbara - Santa Maria - Lompoc	5,089	4,891	3.9%	21	3.2	3.7	20	92	78	19	283	313
12	Santa Cruz	6,922	6,347	-8.3%	16	8.3	6.2	15	133	121	15	401	371
19	Santa Rosa - Petaluma	4,940	4,926	-0.2%	17	7.3	5.4	19	90	81	22	265	290
2	Stockton	8,633	7,747	-10.3%	4	14.8	11.5	7	265	237	9	472	519
11	Vallejo - Fairfield - Napa	6,352	6,760	6.4%	14	6.2	7.7	10	186	173	11	394	470
13	Visalia - Tulare - Porterville	6,108	6,132	0.3%	5	9.1	11.5	14	140	137	17	295	329
6	Yuba City	6,635	7,384	11.3%	10	6.9	9.4	21	84	74	13	368	418
	California††	6,763	6,506	-3.8%	7	11.3	10.6	5	343	301	3	762	830
	United States	5,480	5,550	1.4%	---	8.6	8.3	---	225	213	---	508	529

CRIME RATES* AND CRIME RANKS† OF CALIFORNIA METROPOLITAN AREAS AND THE NATION

* Rate per 100,000 inhabitants. † Ranking among California's 23 Metropolitan Areas. †† Ranking among the 50 states.

6.36,90 Source: Federal Bureau of Investigation, *Crime in the U.S., Annual.*

SECTION 6 NOTE

According to research done by California Attorney Peter G. Carroll, Calfiornia lawyers pay the highest annual dues ($417) of any of the 15 largest states with mandatory bar laws. 78% of the State Bar dues go to attorney discipline matters. This is 36% more than the next highest state. It costs the California State Bar $3,811 to investigate the average complaint. This is almost three times the cost of the next most expensive state.

6.37,90

SECTION 6 NOTE

California has the eighth highest crime rate after (1) Florida, (2) District of Columbia, (3) Texas, (4) Arizona, (5) Washington, (6) Oregon, and (7) New Mexico.

6.38,90

BIG CITY CRIME IN CALIFORNIA, 1988

California Rank	National Rank	City	Number	California Rank	National Rank	City	Number
		All Serious Crime				**Murders**	
1	19	Oakland	46,978	1	15	Oakland	110
2	20	Berkeley	13,684	2	18	Inglewood	30
3	27	San Bernardino	17,673	3	20	San Bernardino	40
4	28	Fresno	34,270	4	28	Pomona	28
5	35	Stockton	20,868	5	33	Los Angeles	739
6	50	Sacramento	34,573	6	34	Stockton	41
7	51	Bakersfield	15,850	7	37	Sacramento	69
8	75	San Diego	97,036	8	44	Pasadena	22
9	78	Los Angeles	300,734	9	48	Santa Ana	38
10	79	San Francisco	66,431	10	54	Bakersfield	22
11	82	Riverside	18,416	11	57	Long Beach	57
12	85	Santa Ana	21,154	12	60	San Diego	144
13	86	Chula Vista	10,747	13	65	Fresno	39
14	89	Long Beach	34,836	14	68	Berkeley	14
15	96	Pomona	9,849	15	90	Oceanside	12
16	108	Oceanside	8,152	16	112	Sunnyvale	10
17	115	Ontario	9,244	17	117	Oxnard	11
18	116	Modesto	10,474	18	120	El Monte	8
19	118	Inglewood	7,952	19	121	Hayward	8
20	123	Anaheim	18,320	20	123	Anaheim	19
21	125	Garden Grove	10,066	21	124	Ontario	9
22	129	Hayward	7,332	22	132	Chula Vista	8
23	130	Pasadena	9,330	23	137	Riverside	13
24	137	El Monte	6,680	24	144	Garden Grove	8
25	138	Santa Rosa	6,778	25	147	Fullerton	6
26	141	Fullerton	7,314	26	151	San Jose	37
27	142	Orange	6,774	27	152	Modesto	7
28	143	Concord	7,009	28	154	Santa Rosa	5
29	151	Oxnard	8,127	29	161	Concord	5
30	152	West Covina	6,175	30	165	Glendale	6
31	167	Glendale	8,685	31	175	West Covina	3
32	169	San Jose	38,739	32	176	Orange	3
33	170	Torrance	7,265	33	177	Huntington Beach	5
34	171	Huntington Beach	9,672	34	178	Torrance	3
35	176	Fremont	6,610	35	183	Fremont	2
36	177	Sunnyvale	4,176				

Cities ranked by crime rate per 100,000 population. Data is for cities with a population of 100,000 or more.

6.39.1,90 Source: *The Detroit Free Press*, unpublished computer analysis, 1989.

SECTION 6 NOTE

On June 3, 1959, Barbara Graham was the last woman executed at San Quentin.

6.40,90

BIG CITY CRIME IN CALIFORNIA, 1988							
Rape				Robberies			
California Rank	National Rank	City	Number	California Rank	National Rank	City	Number
1	8	Oakland	498	1	15	Inglewood	965
2	41	Inglewood	92	2	19	Oakland	3,141
3	47	Fresno	231	3	24	Los Angeles	26,182
4	67	Oceanside	70	4	25	San Bernardino	1,130
5	75	El Monte	64	5	37	San Francisco	4,867
6	80	Oxnard	82	6	38	Long Beach	2,646
7	83	San Francisco	453	7	39	Pomona	745
8	84	Stockton	115	8	41	Berkeley	613
9	85	San Jose	438	9	42	Stockton	1,076
10	86	Los Angeles	2,006	10	48	El Monte	513
11	99	San Bernardino	81	11	50	Fresno	1,393
12	101	Riverside	114	12	52	Sacramento	1,574
13	102	Sacramento	182	13	59	Pasadena	600
14	104	Long Beach	218	14	62	Santa Ana	1,041
15	115	Pasadena	65	15	63	Bakersfield	656
16	123	Bakersfield	70	16	76	Riverside	750
17	124	Pomona	54	17	80	Ontario	414
18	128	Santa Rosa	45	18	94	Oceanside	317
19	130	Modesto	61	19	96	San Diego	3,204
20	131	Ontario	53	20	105	Garden Grove	377
21	132	Anaheim	107	21	110	West Covina	261
22	135	Hayward	43	22	111	Torrance	362
23	136	Berkeley	44	23	112	Anaheim	620
24	137	Fullerton	46	24	120	Oxnard	297
25	143	Garden Grove	51	25	123	Chula Vista	273
26	144	San Diego	389	26	132	Hayward	214
27	147	Santa Ana	89	27	141	Orange	194
28	148	Chula Vista	45	28	144	Fullerton	205
29	164	Orange	30	29	148	Modesto	234
30	165	Concord	31	30	158	Glendale	222
31	170	West Covina	26	31	160	Santa Rosa	135
32	171	Sunnyvale	26	32	162	San Jose	948
33	172	Huntington Beach	43	33	170	Concord	113
34	175	Torrance	30	34	178	Sunnyvale	104
35	177	Glendale	32	35	179	Huntington Beach	154
36	180	Fremont	24	36	184	Fremont	112

Cities ranked by crime rate per 100,000 population. Data is for cities with a population of 100,000 or more
6.39.2,90 Source: *The Detroit Free Press,* unpublished computer analyis, 1989.

SECTION 6 NOTE
From 1852 to 1880 San Quentin was California's only state prison.

6.41,90

BIG CITY CRIME IN CALIFORNIA, 1988

California Rank	National Rank	Serious Assaults City	Number	California Rank	National Rank	Burglary City	Number
1	16	Los Angeles	37,812	1	21	Oakland	10,962
2	18	Pomona	1,303	2	35	San Bernardino	4,226
3	24	Oceanside	1,014	3	40	Bakersfield	4,330
4	29	San Bernardino	1,375	4	42	Berkeley	2,840
5	39	Riverside	1,758	5	45	Fresno	7,632
6	44	Fresno	2,334	6	49	Stockton	4,866
7	48	El Monte	732	7	71	Riverside	4,746
8	49	Inglewood	746	8	74	Sacramento	7,515
9	55	Bakersfield	1,012	9	98	Anaheim	4,805
10	58	Ontario	782	10	104	Ontario	2,279
11	61	Oakland	2,299	11	111	Long Beach	7,426
12	64	Chula Vista	746	12	112	Pomona	2,137
13	73	San Francisco	4,255	13	123	Chula Vista	2,069
14	76	Pasadena	738	14	124	San Diego	17,536
15	78	Long Beach	2,231	15	125	Inglewood	1,722
16	80	Oxnard	708	16	130	Oceanside	1,668
17	87	San Diego	5,434	17	135	Pasadena	2,074
18	91	Berkeley	524	18	137	El Monte	1,538
19	92	Sacramento	1,658	19	139	Hayward	1,586
20	101	Hayward	479	20	140	Los Angeles	50,988
21	103	San Jose	3,266	21	144	Garden Grove	2,086
22	106	Fremont	694	22	145	Modesto	2,067
23	109	Stockton	818	23	147	Santa Rosa	1,498
24	111	Modesto	580	24	150	Santa Ana	3,589
25	131	Santa Ana	853	25	153	Oxnard	1,846
26	134	Garden Grove	473	26	157	Orange	1,401
27	140	Concord	329	27	162	Fullerton	1,426
28	144	Anaheim	696	28	163	Huntington Beach	2,377
29	150	Torrance	380	29	169	Concord	1,331
30	154	West Covina	255	30	177	West Covina	1,134
31	156	Fullerton	281	31	181	Glendale	1,610
32	159	Orange	253	32	182	Torrance	1,405
33	167	Santa Rosa	214	33	184	San Jose	6,560
34	170	Huntington Beach	370	34	186	Fremont	1,390
35	181	Glendale	222	35	190	Sunnyvale	554
36	185	Sunnyvale	134	36			

Cities Ranked by crime rate per 100,000 population. Data is for cities with a population of 100,000 or more.

6.39.3,90 Source: *The Detroit Free Press,* unpublished computer analysis, 1989.

SECTION 6 NOTE

The last log cabin courthouse in California closed at the end of 1988. The 900-square-foot courthouse in McCloud (Shasta County) was closed in a court-consolidation plan.

6.42,90

CALIFORNIA'S TEN CITIES WITH POPULATION OVER 50,000 WITH THE HIGHEST CRIME RATES, 1987		
Rank	**City**	**Crime Rate***
1	Richmond	12,852
2	Oakland	12,294
3	Berkeley	11,770
4	San Bernardino	11,295
5	Fresno	11,053
6	Vallejo	10,973
7	Sacramento	10,437
8	Bakersfield	10,309
9	Stockton	10,067
10	National City	9,444

* Per 100,000 residents.

6.43,90 Source: Federal Bureau of Investigation, *Crime in the U.S., Annual.*

CALIFORNIA'S TEN CITIES WITH POPULATION OVER 50,000 WITH THE LOWEST CRIME RATES, 1987		
Rank	**City**	**Crime Rate***
1	Thousand Oaks	3,240
2	Simi Valley	3,429
3	Sunnyvale	3,492
4	Whittier	3,857
5	Pico Rivera	4,080
6	Vacaville	4,153
7	Irvine	4,163
8	South San Francisco	4,191
9	Daly City	4,269
10	Norwalk	4,306

* Per 100,00 residents.

6.44,90 Source: Federal Bureau of Investigation, *Crime in the U.S., Annual.*

SECTION 6 NOTE
According to the FBI's Uniform Crime Reports, in 1986 and 1987 there was more reported crime associated with the U.C. Berkeley campus than with any other campus in the nation.

6.45,90

CRIMES CLEARED* IN CALIFORNIA, 1988

Crime	Clearance Rate
Willful Homicide	65.7%
Forcible Rape	51.6%
Robbery	27.6%
Aggravated Assault	60.7%
Burglary	13.7%
Motor Vehicle Theft	14.6%

* Crimes are cleared or solved when at least one person is arrested, charged with a crime, and turned over to the courts or juvenile authorities.

6.46,90 Source: California Department of Justice, Bureau of Criminal Statistics, *Crime and Delinquency in California,* 1988.

FIREARMS IN CALIFORNIA 1989

834 Gun Clubs affiliated with National Rifle Association. 6% of all N.R.A. Clubs in the United States.

2.5 to 2.7 million households own 4.3 to 4.6 million handguns.*
3.2 to 3.8 million households own 4.4 to 7.1 million rifles and 3.5 to 5.0 million shotguns.*

21,442 Licensed Firearms Dealers.
8,800 Licensed Handgun Dealers.

Handguns Sold by Licensed Dealers

1981	311,777	1985	271,953
1982	291,535	1986	254,479
1983	258,119	1987	263,203
1984	260,659	1988	274,539

* Estimates based on 1982 survey results adjusted upward to allow for population increases and actual firearms sale.

6.47,90 Source: National Rifle Association estimates and estimates based on a California Poll Survey in 1982: California Dept. of Justice, Automated Firearms and Property Systems Unit, and U.S. Department of the Treasury Bureau of Alcohol, Tobacco and Firearms, unpublished data.

SECTION 6 NOTE

Appeals court judges in New York are the highest paid in the U.S., and those in California are the second-highest paid. Superior Court Judges in California are the third-highest paid in the U.S. after those in New York and New Jersey.

6.48,90

ATTORNEYS		
Year	Number of Active Licensed Attorneys	Increase From Prior Decade
1930	10,580	-
1940	12,579	19%
1950	14,745	17%
1960	19,365	31%
1970	31,467	63%
1980	67,377	114%
1983	79,085	17% *
1985	85,281	27% †
1987	92,058	37% ††
1989	99,396	48% **

* Increase from 1980-1983 † Increase from 1980-1985
†† Increase from 1980-1987 ** Increase from 1980-1989.
 Note: California also has 13,588 licensed but inactive attorneys.
 6.49, 90 Source: California State Bar.

FEMALE AND MINORITY ATTORNEYS	
Group	% of California Attorneys
Female	24.7%
Hispanic	3.7%
Black	2.7%
Asian	2.6%
Other	0.7%
All Minorities	9.7%

6.50,90 Source: California State Bar estimates based on 1980 and 1987 surveys.

LARGEST CALIFORNIA LAW FIRMS, 1988				
California Rank	U.S. Rank	Name	Number of Lawyers/ Partners	Headquarters
1	7	Gibson, Dunn & Crutcher	680/186	Los Angeles
2	10	Pillsbury, Madison & Sutro	512/188	San Francisco
3	12	Morrison & Foerster	434/141	San Francisco
4	15	O'Melveny & Meyers	415/134	Los Angeles
5	17	Latham & Watkins	413/154	Los Angeles
6	31	Brobeck, Phleger & Harrison	348/107	San Francisco
7	54	Thelan, Marrin, Johnson & Bridges	298/86	San Francisco
8	59	Graham & James	294/129	San Francisco
9	65	Paul, Hastings, Janofsky & Walker	280/96	Los Angeles
10	78	Lillick, McHose & Charles	254/91	Los Angeles & San Francisco

6.51,90 Source: *The National Law Journal, Sept. 29, 1988.*

STATE BAR CERTIFIED SPECIALISTS 1989	
Specialty	**Number of Certified Attorneys**
Criminal Law	305
Family Law	518
Immigration Law	9
Probate, Estate Planning, and Trust Law	0
Tax Law	416
Workers' Compensation Law	669

6.52,90 Source: California State Bar, unpublished data.

PASS RATE ON STATE BAR EXAM				
Exam		**Percent Passing**	**Out of State Attorney's Exam**		**Percent Passing**
Spring	1952	61			NA
Fall	1952	53			NA
Spring	1960	40			NA
Fall	1960	54			NA
Spring	1970	51			NA
Fall	1970	56			NA
Spring	1975	43			NA
Fall	1975	61	(1 exam)	1975	70
Spring	1980	35	*Spring*	1980	42
Fall	1980	50	Fall	1980	36
Spring	1982	31	*Spring*	1982	34
Fall	1982	48	Fall	1982	26
Spring	1983	28	*Spring*	1983	26
Fall	1983	49	Fall	1983	47
Spring	1984	30	*Spring*	1984	46
Fall	1984	42	Fall	1984	32
Spring	1985	33	*Spring*	1985	44
Fall	1985	45	Fall	1985	43
Spring	1986	28	*Spring*	1986	37
Fall	1986	44	Fall	1986	41
Spring	1987	43	*Spring*	1987	53
Fall	1987	50	Fall	1987	51
Spring	1988	46	*Spring*	1988	60
Fall	1988	53	Fall	1988	47

6.53,90 Source: California State Bar.

STATE BAR DISCIPLINARY ACTIONS AGAINST LAWYERS					
Action	**1980**	**1984**	**1986**	**1987**	**1988**
Complaints against Attorneys	6,357	8,329	8,574	7,452	4,376
Attorney Investigated by Bar	929	8,867	9,302	9,043	4,724
Attorney Admonished (warned)*	12	21	13	7	3
Attorney Privately Reproved*	42	48	19	23	20
Attorney Publicly Reproved*	11	23	25	29	31
Suspension of Attorney Recommended*	53	95	86	123	133
Disbarment of Attorney Recommended*	13	18	38	56	69
Attorney Disbarred	NA	11	22	38	53
Attorney Resigned from Bar with Charges Pending	12	12	69	38	65
Starting in 1987 a stricter standard of complaints was instituted. Only contacts related to actual disciplinable offenses are listed. Starting in 1988 the backlog of complaints was eased.					

* By State Bar Court.
6.54,90 Source: California State Bar Association, 1989.

CALIFORNIA SUPREME COURT			
Justice	Date of Appointment	Appointed By	Date of Birth
Chief Justice Malcolm Lucas	1/6/87	G. Deukmejian	4/19/27
Justice Stanley Mosk	8/18/64	Pat Brown	9/4/12
Justice Allen Broussard	6/25/81	Jerry Brown	4/13/29
Justice Edward Panelli	11/2/85	G. Deukmejian	11/23/31
Justice Marcus Kaufman	2/18/87	G. Deukmejian	6/19/29
Justice David Eagleson	2/18/87	G. Deukmejian	10/4/24
Justice Joyce Kinard	3/10/89	G. Deukmejian	5/6/41

6.55,90 Source: California Supreme Court.

JUDGES	
Court	**Number**
Federal 9th Circuit*	20
Federal District Court	72
California Supreme Court	7
California Courts of Appeal	84
California Superior Courts	721
California Municipal Courts	549
California Justice Courts	66
Total	**1,519**

* In California
6.56,90 Source: California Judicial
Council and Pacific Data Resources, 1989.

JUDICIAL APPOINTMENTS BY RECENT GOVERNORS 1959-89				
Governor		Percent Women	Percent Minorities	Number of Appointments
Edmund Brown, Sr.	1959-67	2%	7%	621
Ronald Reagan	1967-75	3%	7%	645
Edmund Brown, Jr.	1975-83	16%	24%	800
George Deukmejian	1983-89	15%	13%	737

6.57,90 Source: Office of the California Governor, Appointments Section and the *Los Angeles Times*, December 5, 1982.

FEDERAL DISTRICT COURTS IN CALIFORNIA CIVIL CASES FILED BY TYPE OF CASE 1987 and 1988								
	1987				1988			
Type	U.S. Cases	% of Total Cases*	Private Cases	% of Total Cases*	U.S. Cases	% of Total Cases*	Private Cases	% of Total Cases*
Social Security	975	7%	—	---	1,034	7%	—	---
Prisoner Petitions	442	10%	1,778	5%	592	12%	2,015	6%
Forfeitures, Penalties	558	16%	—	---	665	17%	—	---
Tax Suits	423	15%	—	---	364	14%	—	---
Real Property	104	2%	163	3%	89	1%	135	3%
Labor Suits	144	11%	1,808	16%	152	13%	1,774	15%
Contracts	8,571	29%	3,602	9%	5,639	24%	3,320	8%
Torts	559	17%	1,777	5%	538	17%	1,398	4%
FELA	—	---	124	5%	—	---	139	6%
Copyrights, Patents and Trademarks	—	---	1,040	19%	—	---	1,038	17%
Civil Rights	330	14%	1,305	8%	313	13%	1,249	7%
Anti-Trust	7	26%	98	13%	3	11%	103	16%
Commerce	—	---	169	17%	—	---	238	15%
All Other Civil Cases	442	10%	1,275	9%	744	16%	1,160	8%
Total	**12,555**	**17%**	**13,139**	**8%**	**10,133**	**15%**	**12,569**	**7%**

* Percent of all cases in the nation.

6.58,90 Source: Administrative Office of the U.S. Courts, *Annual Report*.

SECTION 6 NOTE
In 1988, the average law firm in Los Angeles had 256 lawyers, in San Francisco, 267 lawyers. The average salary was $60,923 for lawyers in Los Angeles and $53,909 in San Francisco.

6.59,90

FEDERAL DISTRICT COURTS IN CALIFORNIA FELONY CRIMINAL CASES FILED BY TYPE OF CRIME 1987 and 1988				
	1987		1988	
Type	Number	% of Total Cases Filed in All Federal District Courts	Number	% of Total Cases Filed in All Federal District Courts
Embezzlement	331	15%	267	13%
Auto Theft	3	1%	13	4%
Firearms	132	7%	111	5%
Escape	113	14%	83	9%
Burlary and Larceny	331	9%	280	8%
Marijuana and Controlled Substances	482	13%	767	18%
Narcotics	329	6%	392	6%
Forgery and Counterfeiting	194	9%	141	8%
Fraud	615	9%	704	10%
Homicide	9	6%	12	8%
Robbery	333	26%	314	24%
Assault	60	9%	43	7%
Immigration	525	32%	576	30%
Traffic	104	1%	102	1%
Agricultural Acts	11	5%	6	2%
Postal Laws	16	7%	29	13%
All Other Crimes (excluding traffic offenses)	139	9%	98	6%
Total	3,727	9%	3,938	9%

6.60,90 Source: Administrative Office of the U.S. Courts, *Annual Report*.

CALIFORNIA SUPREME COURT NUMBER OF PETITIONS FILED FOR HEARING CASES PREVIOUSLY DECIDED BY THE COURTS OF APPEAL					
	Appeals*		Original Proceedings		Total Petitions for Review Filed
Year	Civil	Criminal	Civil	Criminal	
1979-1980	944	1,100	700	439	3,183
1980-1981	925	1,130	657	465	3,179
1981-1982	921	1,148	678	591	3,338
1983-1984	1,100	1,071	623	450	3,244
1984-1985	1,020	1,203	717	524	3,464
1985-1986	1,044	1,444	786	560	3,834
1986-1987	1,092	1,212	677	517	3,498
1987-1988	1,099	1,132	531	479	3,241

6.61,90 Source: California Administrative Office of the Courts, *Annual Report*.

	Death Penalty Direct	Original Proceedings		Total	Written
Year	Appeals	Civil	Criminal	Filings	Opinions
1979-1980	22	215	438	3,858	140
1980-1981	27	195	463	3,864	114
1981-1982	43	204	471	4,056	123
1983-1984	34	209	538	4,025	126
1984-1985	24	167	715	4,370	125
1985-1986	19	169	805	4,827	144
1986-1987	23	188	872	4,581	85
1987-1988	39	216	894	4,390	122

CALIFORNIA SUPREME COURT NUMBER OF FILINGS AND OPINONS 1979-1988

6.62,90 Source: California Administrative Office of the Courts, *Annual Report*.

	Appeals		Original Proceedings		Motions to	Total	Written
Year	Civil	Criminal	Civil	Criminal	Dismiss	Filings	Opinions
1979-1980	4,249	4,586	4,260	1,279	383	14,757	6,659
1980-1981	4,466	4,730	4,520	1,256	474	15,446	7,166
1981-1982	4,152	4,808	4,492	1,247	351	15,050	7,786
1982-1983	5,003	5,137	4,300	1,295	618	16,353	7,705
1983-1984	4,720	5,398	4,050	1,788	505	16,461	8,509
1984-1985	4,997	5,255	3,732	2,206	537	16,727	8,599
1985-1986	5,066	4,969	3,794	2,440	523	16,792	9,428
1986-1987	4,892	5,093	3,929	2,803	660	17,377	8,974
1987-1988	5,298	5,656	4,063	2,942	645	18,604	8,741

CALIFORNIA COURTS OF APPEAL NUMBER OF FILINGS AND OPINIONS 1979-1988

6.63,90 Source: California Adminstrative Office of the Courts, *Annual Report*.

SECTION 6 NOTE

California has five major legal newspapers and one legal magazine.

Los Angeles Daily Journal   California Lawyer
Los Angeles Lawyer
San Francisco Recorder*
San Francisco Banner Daily Journal†
Sacramento Docket

* Owned by American Lawyer Newspaper.
† Owned by Los Angeles Daily Journal.
 6.64,90 Source: Pacific Data Resources.

CALIFORNIA COURTS OF APPEAL MEDIAN TIME TO DECISION (in months)							
	Notice of Appeal to Filing of Opinion				Ready for Calendar to Filing of Opinion			
	Civil		Criminal		Civil		Criminal	
Court	1986	1988	1986	1988	1986	1988	1986	1988
District I								
Division 1	25	30	20	18	13	8	7	5
Division 2	36	29	20	18	22	10	6	6
Division 3	21	30	20	17	7	8	7	4
Division 4	22	27	19	14	11	4	7	2
Division 5	22	30	17	14	7	6	6	3
District II								
Division 1	12	14	16	13	2	2	1	2
Division 2	17	17	11	14	3	2	1	2
Division 3	15	17	15	16	4	4	2	4
Division 4	9	15	14	15	2	2	1	2
Division 5	8	18	11	15	3	3	2	3
Division 6	13	13	16	12	3	4	3	3
Division 7	14	15	11	14	4	3	3	4
District III	15	23	13	13	9	16	6	5
District IV								
Division 1	15	14	12	13	6	5	5	5
Division 2	15	16	16	16	3	5	4	4
Division 3	20	21	16	19	11	11	9	10
District V	17	17	14	11	11	7	5	4
District VI	9	31	10	21	4	4	3	9

6.65,90 Source: California Administrative Office of the Courts, *Annual Report*.

SECTION 6 NOTE
Of the 15 most populated states in the U.S., California has the third highest rate of crime after Florida and Texas.

6.66,90

CALIFORNIA SUPERIOR COURTS
NUMBER OF FILINGS
1971-1988

Year	Civil	Juvenile	Mental Health	Criminal	Appeals From Lower Courts	Habeus Corpus	Total Other Proceedings	Total
1971-72	373,000	NA	NA	65,000	NA	NA	83,000	522,000
1973-74	407,823	NA	6,412	54,635	10,215	9,625	80,887	NA
1978-79	551,393	86,295	3,573	53,955	14,414	13,008	84,950	740,933
1980-81	532,556	81,241	3,786	64,993	15,035	14,929	98,740	735,219
1981-82	532,190	79,591	4,085	67,411	16,759	15,282	103,537	738,363
1982-83	540,510	77,764	4,106	72,390	21,733	14,062	112,291	753,822
1983-84	561,916	76,033	4,749	74,567	21,313	13,221	113,850	780,863
1984-85	593,120	79,688	6,843	82,621	19,765	12,818	122,047	828,663
1985-86	619,630	84,479	7,046	95,467	19,515	13,247	135,275	876,259
1986-87	636,762	86,717	7,180	104,929	20,242	14,197	146,548	909,984
1987-88	641,447	84,442	6,842	115,595	19,632	12,256	154,325	920,681

Note: Columns for Appeals From Lower Courts, Habeus Corpus, and Total Other Proceedings are grouped under "Other Proceedings".

6.67,90 Source: California Administrative Office of the Courts, *Annual Report*.

CALIFORNIA SUPERIOR COURTS
NUMBER OF CIVIL CASES FILED BY TYPE OF CASE
1981-1988

Year	Probate and Guardian-ship	Family Law	Personal Injury, Death, and Property Damage	Eminent Domain	Other	Total
1981-82	64,965	167,902	80,495	4,313	217,330	532,190
1983-84	65,712	164,565	96,731	1,138	233,770	561,916
1984-85	66,786	165,613	112,335	1,379	247,067	593,120
1985-86	66,287	163,962	130,347	2,080	256,940	619,630
1986-87	66,207	173,146	137,458	1,516	258,420	636,762
1987-88	68,478	173,252	132,378	2,028	265,371	641,447

6.68,90 Source: California Administrative Office of the Courts, *Annual Report*.

SECTION 6 NOTE

According to the LOS ANGELES TIMES, government drug agents have siezed more cash ($100 million) from drug dealers in Los Angeles than in any other place in the U.S.

6.69,90

CALIFORNIA MUNICIPAL AND JUSTICE COURTS CRIMINAL CASES, 1976-1988				
		Non-Traffic		
Year	Felonies	Misdemeanors (in thousands)	Infractions (in thousands)	Total Criminal
1976-77	102,849	598	49	15,022,423
1980-81	128,850	632	73	16,394,374
1981-82	134,277	633	96	16,374,824
1982-83	137,302	638	110	16,106,162
1983-84	143,480	663	114	16,567,069
1984-85	155,875	680	137	16,949,983
1985-86	175,305	704	130	16,146,629
1986-87	198,182	736	148	15,676,922
1987-88	209,252	764	170	16,057,210

6.70,90 Source: California Administrative Offices of the Courts, *Annual Report*.

CALIFORNIA MUNICIPAL AND JUSTICE COURTS NUMBER OF CRIMINAL AND CIVIL FILINGS BY TYPE OF CASE 1976-1988						
	Criminal Traffic			Civil Cases		
Year	Misdemeanors (thousands)	Infractions (millions)	Parking (millions)	Small Claims	Others	Total
1976-77	511	4.8	9.0	427,224	344,161	771,388
1980-81	650	5.3	9.6	561,908	521,374	1,083,282
1981-82	759	5.6	9.1	598,165	507,820	1,105,985
1982-83	819	5.7	8.7	565,738	494,196	1,059,934
1983-84	894	6.0	8.7	512,904	503,421	1,016,225
1984-85	1,010	6.0	9.0	521,766	518,523	1,040,289
1985-86	991	6.0	8.1	538,403	553,132	1,091,535
1986-87	1,069	6.3	7.2	537,600	577,020	1,114,620
1987-88	1,120	6.5	7.3	527,426	592,103	1,119,529

6.71,90 Source: California Administrative Office of the Courts, *Annual Report*.

SECTION 6 NOTE
Many drug enforcement officials now believe that Los Angeles is the center of the U.S. cocaine business.

6.72,90

CALIFORNIA SUPERIOR, MUNICIPAL, AND JUSTICE COURTS ESTIMATED ANNUAL COST OF TRIAL COURTS							
	Cost per Judicial Position						
Court and year	Judicial Position	Non-judicial Personnel	Services and Supplies	Indirect Costs	Total Including Court Reporter and Balliff	Total Number of Judicial Positions	Trial Court Cost (millions)
Superior							
1982-83	$70,226	$114,558	$100,546	$52,444	$402,917	NA	NA
1984-85	$83,091	$172,634	$154,959	$48,209	$534,302	753	$402
1986-87	$100,088	$167,885	$192,460	$45,122	$590,758	825	$487
1988-89	$108,160	$199,313	$128,659	$33,582	$566,703	905	$513
Municipal							
1982-83	$64,131	$140,303	$74,242	$61,259	$389,157	NA	NA
1984-85	$76,064	$195,250	$128,816	$75,106	$526,581	623	$328
1986-87	$91,179	$220,787	$160,471	$59,999	$591,802	677	$401
1988-89	$99,084	$239,678	$158,540	$68,628	$633,366	734	$465
Justice							
1984-85	-	-	-	-	-	85*	$23
1986-87	-	-	-	-	-	82*	$29
1988-89	-	-	-	-	-	76*	$29

* Part-time.
6.73,90 Source: California Administrative Office of the Courts, *Annual Report*.

CRIMINAL JUSTICE SYSTEM EXPENDITURES, 1977-1988 (in millions)												
	Law Enforcement		Prosecution		Public Defense		Courts		Corrections		Total	
Year	Cost	%	Cost	%	Cost	%	Cost	%	Cost	%	Cost	%
1977	$1,580	55	$149	5	$55	2	$280	10	$826	28	$2,888	100
1981	$2,401	55	$232	5	$84	2	$406	9	$1,241	28	$4,363	100
1982	$2,742	55	$261	5	$97	2	$469	9	$1,387	28	$4,954	100
1983	$2,982	55	$281	5	$112	2	$516	10	$1,465	27	$5,355	100
1984	$3,257	55	$308	5	$120	2	$551	9	$1,644	28	$5,878	100
1985	$3,596	54	$344	5	$138	2	$656	10	$1,944	29	$6,678	100
1986	$3,889	52	$383	5	$157	2	$753	10	$2,305	31	$7,487	100
1987	$4,243	51	$415	5	$186	2	$826	10	$2,700	32	$8,370	100
1988	$4,510	50	$453	5	$213	2	$898	10	$3,012	33	$9,087	100
% Change 1977-1988	—	185	—	204	—	287	—	221	—	265	—	215

6.74,90 Source: California Department of Justice, Bureau of Criminal Statistics, *Crime & Delinquency*.

JUDGES/LAWYERS - PROMINENT CALIFORNIANS

Rose Bird - Calif. Supreme Court	Ed Meese - Attorney General
Stephen J. Field - U.S. Supreme Court	Roger Traynor - Calif. Supreme Court
Clara Foltz - 1st Female Attorney	Earl Warren - U. S. Supreme Court
Serranus Hastings - Founded 1st Law School	

6.75,90 Source: Pacific Data Resources

FULL-TIME PUBLIC LAW ENFORCEMENT PERSONNEL IN CALIFORNIA

	Highway Patrol		City Police		County Police		College Police		Total	
Year	Offi-cers	Total	Offi-cers	Total	Offi-cers	Total	Offi-cers	Total	Offi-cers	Total
1986	5,531	7,687	29,737	41,511	16,493	24,695	682	1,326	52,443	75,219
1987	5,490	7,558	28,842	40,484	16,540	24,291	676	1,395	51,548	73,728

6.76,90 Source: Federal Bureau of Investigation, *Crime in the U.S., Annual.*

PRIVATE POLICE IN CALIFORNIA, 1985

	Detectives, Investigators	Watch Guards	Protective Service Workers	Total
Number	4,430	81,800	24,360	**110,590**

6.77,90 Source: California Department of Employment Development, *Projections of Employment 1985-1995*, 1988.

CRIMINAL JUSTICE SYSTEM PERSONNEL, 1977-1988

	Law Enforcement		Prosecution		Public Defense		Courts		Corrections		Total	
Year	No.	%	No.	%	No.	%	No.	%	No.	%	No.	%
1977	65,971	67	6,809	7	1,784	2	1,269	1	23,035	23	98,867	100
1981	69,158	68	7,184	7	1,929	2	1,393	1	22,424	22	102,088	100
1982	71,071	68	7,407	7	1,972	2	1,410	1	22,790	22	104,929	100
1983	72,317	68	7,460	7	1,992	2	1,451	1	23,536	22	107,524	100
1984	74,536	67	7,686	7	2,013	2	1,473	1	24,850	22	110,558	100
1985	74,629	64	8,072	7	2,179	2	1,501	1	28,958	25	115,340	100
1986	76,576	64	8,470	7	2,286	2	1,540	1	30,805	26	119,677	100
1987	77,015	63	8,332	7	2,406	2	1,579	1	32,729	27	122,071	100
1988	72,586	59	8,251	7	2,839	2	1,613	1	37,810	31	123,099	100
% Change 1977-1988	10%		21%		59%		27%		64%		25%	

6.78,90 Source: California Department of Justice, Bureau of Criminal Justice, *Crime and Delinquency.*

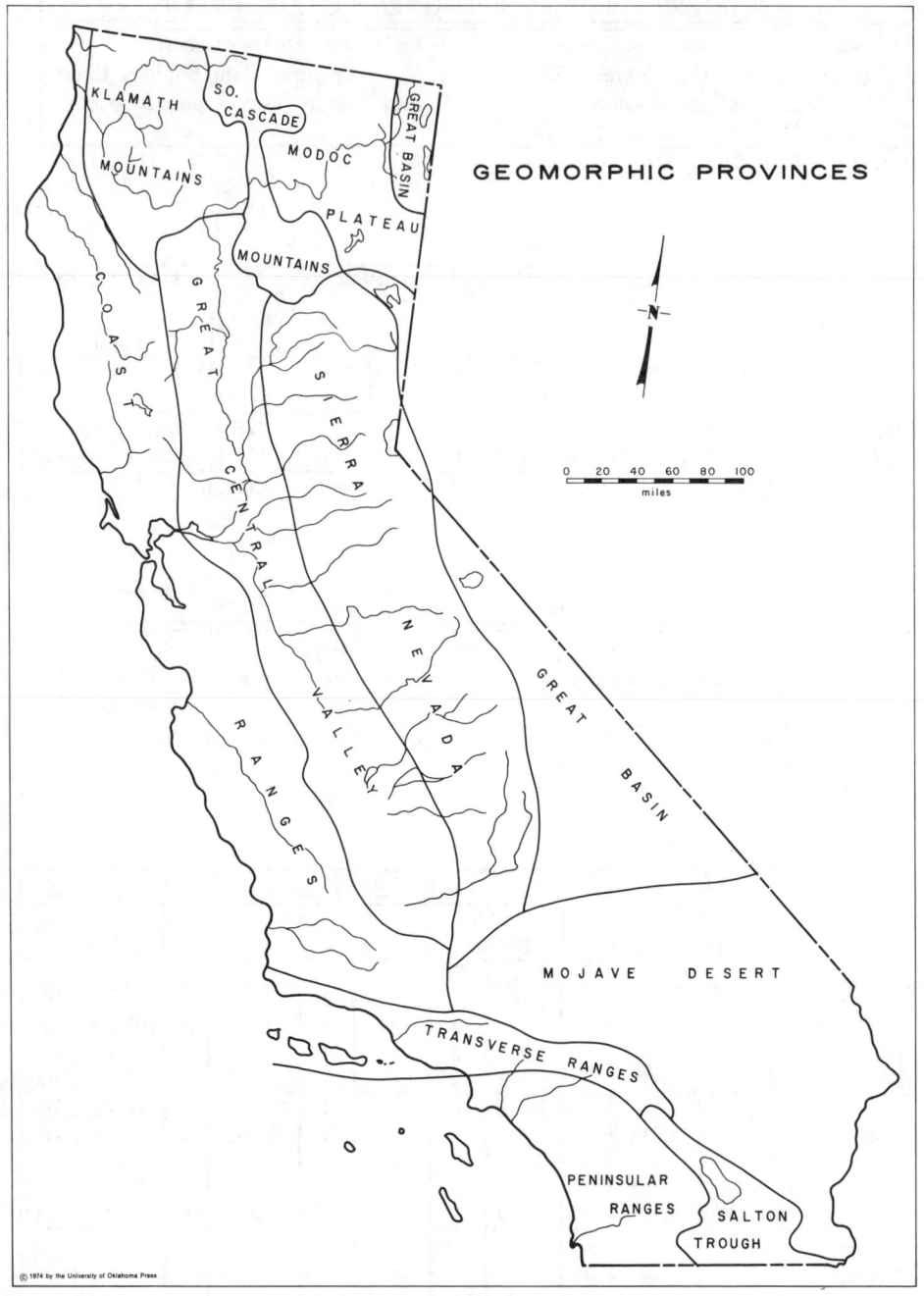

GEOMORPHIC PROVINCES

KLAMATH
MOUNTAINS

SO.
CASCADE

MODOC

PLATEAU

MOUNTAINS

GREAT BASIN

COAST

GREAT

SIERRA

CENTRAL

NEVADA

VALLEY

RANGES

GREAT

BASIN

MOJAVE   DESERT

TRANSVERSE RANGES

PENINSULAR
RANGES

SALTON
TROUGH

-N-

0 20 40 60 80 100
miles

Historical Atlas of California, 1974. University of Oklahoma Press. Reprinted by permission.

Geography and Environment

In 1989 state climatologists almost had their worst fears confirmed. They had predicted that 1989 would be the third consecutive year of severe drought. Scientists knew from the analysis of tree rings that three such years had last occurred in 1593-1595 in California, 174 years before the first mission was established in the state. Nature surprised us, however. The jet stream moved south, and March 1989 proved to be an unusually rainy month, relieving, if not totally breaking, the drought.

Without this relief Californians would have faced draconian water rationing rules. Residential cutbacks of 25 to 45 percent were to have been imposed in urban areas while farmers in several water districts faced 50 percent reductions in their water allocations. The city of Los Angeles approved a series of water conservation measures banning decorative fountains that do not use recycled water and mandating the installation of water-saving shower heads and toilets.

Los Angeles has another major environmental problem to worry about: its air. The plan passed by the Los Angeles Air Quality Management District in 1989 sent shock waves through the area. This plan, aimed at alleviating the huge smog problem in the Los Angeles basin, would ban non-radial tires, aerosol cans, starter fluid for backyard barbecues, and gasoline engines for such small appliances as lawnmowers. Refineries, bakeries, dry cleaners, breweries, furniture painters, and other businesses would have to reduce their emissions into the atmosphere significantly. After a time new automobiles would have to run on electricity or on fuels other than gasoline. Carpooling and the use of mass transit would be encouraged and the use of automobiles, the major source of smog, would in general be discouraged. People in business and government are just beginning to understand the costs and consequences of these drastic measures--as well as the costs and consequences of doing nothing.

As Los Angeles dealt with its regional air problems, the states of California and Arizona together have dealt with a mutual interstate problem, nuclear waste. A site in the Mojave Desert near Needles has been selected for the storage of low-level nuclear waste from both states. As is the pattern around the country, the state that produces more of the waste has the privilege of serving as the host site.

California has environmental experts in almost every area, and sometimes their analyses conflict. As the nation's press and political salons were aflutter with talk about the greenhouse effect, the former state climatologist Jim Goodrich dismissed the whole issue, noting that 90 percent of the temperature measurements that support the greenhouse theory are taken in cities, which are heat sinks.

LAND AND WATER AREAS OF CALIFORNIA COUNTIES					
	Water Area		Land Area		Total Area	
County	Acres	Square Miles	Acres	Square Miles	Acres	Square Miles
Alameda	59,150	92.4	469,120	733.0	528,270	825.4
Alpine	2,310	3.6	462,720	723.0	465,030	726.6
Amador	5,290	8.3	379,520	593.0	384,810	601.3
Butte	1,170	1.8	1,064,320	1,663.0	1,065,490	1,664.8
Calaveras	6,010	9.4	657,280	1,027.0	663,290	1,036.4
Colusa	1,820	2.8	737,920	1,153.0	739,740	1,155.8
Contra Costa	40,920	63.9	469,760	734.0	510,680	797.9
Del Norte	---	---	641,920	1,003.0	641,920	1,003.0
El Dorado	58,080	90.8	1,096,960	1,714.0	1,155,040	1,804.8
Fresno	21,860	34.2	3,816,960	5,964.0	3,838,820	5,998.2
Glenn	1,280	2.0	842,880	1,317.0	884,160	1,319.0
Humboldt	16,970	26.5	2,286,720	3,573.0	2,303,690	3,599.5
Imperial	200,580	313.4	2,741,760	4,284.0	2,942,340	4,597.4
Inyo	4,400	6.9	6,458,240	10,091.0	6,462,640	10,097.9
Kern	11,720	18.3	5,217,280	8,152.0	5,229,000	8,170.3
Kings	25,990	40.6	892,800	1,395.0	918,790	1,435.6
Lake	45,120	70.5	803,840	1,256.0	848,960	1,326.5
Lassen	91,700	143.3	2,910,080	4,547.0	3,001,780	4,690.3
Los Angeles	12,330	19.3	2,598,400	4,060.0	2,610,730	4,079.3
Madera	2,000	3.1	1,372,160	2,144.0	1,374,160	2,147.1
Marin	43,500	68.0	332,800	520.0	376,300	588.0
Mariposa	3,490	5.5	931,200	1,455.0	934,690	1,460.5
Mendocino	2,360	3.7	2,244,480	3,507.0	2,246,840	3,510.4
Merced	16,450	25.7	1,268,480	1,982.0	1,284,930	2,007.7
Modoc	158,990	248.4	2,618,880	4,092.0	2,777,870	4,340.4
Mono	48,030	75.0	1,937,920	3,028.0	1,985,950	3,103.0
Monterey	70	0.1	2,127,360	3,324.0	2,127,430	3,324.1
Napa	24,890	38.9	485,120	758.0	510,010	796.9
Nevada	9,090	14.2	625,920	978.0	635,010	992.2
Orange	1,960	3.1	500,480	782.0	502,440	785.1
Placer	52,780	82.5	911,360	1,424.0	964,140	1,506.5
Plumas	30,980	48.4	1,644,800	2,570.0	1,675,780	2,618.4
Riverside	42,260	66.0	4,593,280	7,177.0	4,635,540	7,243.0
Sacramento	20,660	32.3	629,120	983.0	649,780	1,015.3
San Benito	710	1.1	893,440	1,396.0	894,150	1,397.1
San Bernardino	21,120	33.0	12,883,840	20,131.0	12,904,960	20,164.0
San Diego	16,360	25.6	2,723,200	4,255.0	2,739,560	4,280.6
San Francisco	29,500	46.1	28,800	45.0	58,300	91.1
San Joaquin	17,420	27.2	901,760	1,409.0	919,180	1,436.2
San Luis Obispo	6,560	10.2	2,122,240	3,316.0	2,128,800	3,326.2
San Mateo	49,130	76.8	290,560	454.0	339,690	530.8
Santa Barbara	4,260	6.7	1,752,320	2,738.0	1,756,580	2,744.7
Santa Clara	8,880	13.9	833,280	1,302.0	842,160	1,315.9
Santa Cruz	400	0.6	280,960	439.0	281,360	439.6
Shasta	33,420	52.2	2,430,720	3,798.0	2,464,140	3,850.2
Sierra	380	1.0	613,120	958.0	613,500	959.0
Siskiyou	4,030	6.3	4,039,680	6,312.0	4,043,710	6,318.3
Solano	28,930	45.2	529,280	827.0	558,210	872.2
Sonoma	11,900	18.6	1,010,560	1,579.0	1,022,360	1,597.6
Stanislaus	13,580	21.2	960,000	1,500.0	973,580	1,521.2
Sutter	---	---	388,480	607.0	388,480	607.0
Tehama	---	---	1,904,640	2,976.0	1,904,640	2,976.0
Trinity	20,260	31.6	2,042,240	3,191.0	2,062,500	3,222.6
Tulare	4,390	6.9	3,096,320	4,838.0	3,100,710	4,844.9
Tuolumne	11,960	18.7	1,455,360	2,274.0	1,467,320	2,292.7
Ventura	8,040	12.6	1,184,640	1,851.0	1,192,680	1,863.6
Yolo	---	---	661,760	1,034.0	661,760	1,034.0
Yuba	1,340	2.1	407,680	637.0	409,020	639.1
State Totals	1,356,780	2,120.5	100,206,720	156,573.0	101,563,500	158,693.2

7.1,90 Source: California Regional Framework Study Committee for Pacific Southwest Interagency Committee Water Resources Council, *California Regional Framework Study, Base Year 1985*.

AIR POLLUTION							
Number of Days per Year with Unhealthful Air*							
Basin	**1979**	**1981**	**1983**	**1984**	**1985**	**1986**	**1987**	**1988**
South Coast†	193	187	153	175	158	164	162	178
San Joaquin Valley	59	69	38	61	53	59	64	73
Southeast Desert	109	121	104	92	111	115	101	124
San Diego	66	78	61	51	50	42	40	45
Sacramento Valley	20	19	12	23	18	24	24	36
South Central Coast	73	85	58	46	44	59	31	55
San Francisco Bay Area	15	8	21	22	9	5	14	5
Lake Tahoe	0	0	0	0	0	0	0	0
Mountain Counties	8	12	6	5	8	0	0	7
Great Basin	0	0	0	0	0	0	0	0
North Central Coast	0	2	0	0	0	0	0	0
North Coast	0	0	0	NA	NA	NA	NA	NA
Northeast Plateau	0	0	0	0	0	0	1	0
County								
Alameda County	NA	NA	NA	NA	NA	5	7	4
Fresno County	NA	36	27	42	34	39	43	43
Kern County	NA	50	20	26	27	33	46	56
Kings County	NA	0	1	0	2	0	2	3
Lake County	NA	0	0	0	0	0	0	0
Los Angeles County	NA	NA	NA	NA	NA	159	148	165
Orange County	NA	NA	NA	NA	NA	53	42	45
Placer County	NA	NA	NA	NA	NA	4	7	13
Riverside County	NA	NA	NA	NA	NA	117	122	131
Sacramento County	NA	18	12	23	18	22	17	31
San Bernardino County	NA	NA	NA	NA	NA	145	141	153
San Joaquin County	NA	4	9	4	5	3	1	4
Santa Barbara County	NA	3	7	4	3	1	2	0
Santa Clara County	NA	NA	NA	NA	NA	1	12	2
Stanislaus County	NA	11	5	13	10	2	18	5
Sutter County	NA	NA	NA	NA	NA	2	1	2
Tulare County	NA	2	4	3	6	13	8	4
Ventura County	NA	85	58	45	44	59	31	55
Yolo County	NA	NA	NA	NA	NA	2	3	0

* Ozone concentration of .12 parts per million (ppm) or more for at least 1 hour per day.

† Los Angeles and Orange Counties and the most heavily populated areas of Riverside and San Bernardino Counties.

7.2,90 Source: California Air Resources Board, Technical Support Division, 1989.

SECTION 7 NOTE
California's largest land fill is Puente Hills in Los Angeles County, which accepts 13,000 tons of garbage every day.

7.3,90

	OZONE (SMOG) AIR POLLUTION TRENDS AS INDICATED BY AVERAGE MAXIMUM CONCENTRATIONS†					
Year	San Francisco Bay Area	South* Coast	San Diego	San Joaquin Valley	Sacramento Valley	Southeast Desert
1976	4.2	13.6	6.3	6.1	NA	NA
1978	4.3	14.6	6.6	6.9	NA	NA
1980	4.3	14.1	6.8	7.3	6.5	9.3
1981	4.2	13.1	6.8	7.1	6.3	9.0
1982	4.4	12.9	6.9	6.9	6.3	8.7
1983	4.5	12.5	6.9	6.9	6.2	8.6
1984	4.4	12.7	6.9	7.0	6.3	8.9
1985	4.2	12.3	6.8	7.1	6.5	8.5
1986	4.1	12.0	6.8	7.4	6.6	8.3
1987	4.3	11.9	6.7	7.6	6.8	8.4

† Three-year moving averages of May-October mean daily maximum-hour concentrations in parts per hundred million (pphm). Three-year moving averages are assigned to the middle year of the three-year period.

* Orange County and the most heavily populated areas of Los Angeles, Riverside, and San Bernardino Counties.

7.4,90 Source: California Air Resources Board, Technical Support Division, July 1989.

	CARBON MONOXIDE AIR POLLUTION TRENDS AS INDICATED BY AVERAGE MAXIMUM CONCENTRATIONS†				
Year	San Francisco Bay Area	South* Coast	San Diego	San Joaquin Valley	Sacramento Valley
1976	NA	9.1	NA	6.9	4.2
1978	5.5	7.8	8.0	6.0	3.8
1980	4.6	7.3	6.3	5.4	3.6
1981	4.1	7.0	5.9	4.9	3.3
1982	3.8	6.9	5.9	4.5	3.1
1983	3.9	6.3	5.7	4.1	2.9
1984	4.0	6.1	5.7	4.0	3.0
1985	4.0	6.0	5.5	4.2	3.4
1986	4.2	5.7	5.7	4.4	3.4
1987	4.0	5.5	5.5	4.4	3.2

† Three-year moving averages of October-February mean daily maximum-hour concentrations in parts per million (ppm). Three-year moving averages are assigned to the middle year of the three-year period. For example, the moving average of the three periods from October 1982 through February 1985 is assigned to 1984.

* Orange County and the most heavily populated areas of Los Angeles, Riverside, and San Bernardino Counties.

7.5,90 Source: California Air Resources Board, Technical Support Division, July 1989.

CALIFORNIA'S MAJOR RIVERS - LENGTHS AND RUNOFF

River	Length† (miles)	Runoff (1000 acre ft.)††	River	Length† (miles)	Runoff (1000 acre ft.)††
Alamo	42	642*	Pit	49	2,721
Amargosa	140	NA	Rubicon	50	193
American	60	2,709	Russian	100	1,623
Bear (Nev. & Placer)	60	328	Sacramento	373	16,982
Bear (Amador)	17	37	Salinas	179	714
Big	36	280	Salmon	46	1,290
Calaveras	72	154	San Antonio	59	75
Carmel	25	142	San Benito	100	22
Carson	160	309	San Diego	50	55
Chowchilla	78	71	San Dieguito	50	45
Colorado	1,450	11,911	San Gabriel	65	148*
Cosumnes	102	379	San Gorgonio	NA	1
Cuyama (Santa Maria)	NA	16	San Jacinto	NA	13
Eel	197	6,273	San Joaquin	370	3,152
Elk	12	54	San Lorenzo	22	125
Fall (Shasta & Siskiyou)	12	NA	San Luis Rey	54	62
Fall (Butte & Plumas)	20	NA	Santa Ana	100	322
Feather	80	5,719	Santa Clara	75	216
Fresno	87	78	Santa Margarita	60	37
Garcia	32	195	Santa Maria	NA	91
Guadalupe	NA	100	Santa Ynez	NA	159
Gualala	37	530	Scott	68	471
Kaweah	45	463	Shasta	40	133
Kern	164	662	Sisquoc	45	32
Kings	176	1,633	Smith	45	2,927
Klamath	180	12,500	Stanislaus	148	1,085
Los Angeles	NA	76	Sur (Big & Little)	15	88
Lost	NA	NA	Susan	50	67
Mad	90	925	Sweetwater	45	18
Mattole	65	1,095	Ten Mile	16	520
Merced	150	963	Tia Juana	NA	39
McCloud	60	1,230	Trinity	128	3,785
Mojave	100	57	Truckee	110	568
Mokelumne	140	804	Tule	91	133
Nacimiento	65	211	Tuolumne	162	1,789
Napa	53	186	Van Duzen	75	632
Navarro	56	375	Ventura	30	68
Noyo	25	155	Walker	186	275
Otay	NA	9	White	53	NA
Owens	125	141	Whitewater	NA	19
Pajaro	100	223	Yuba	70	2,274

† Length to headwaters. †† Average annual runoff measured at point of maximum runoff.
* No average runoff data available. 1980 annual runoff data used. NA = not available.
Note: Runoff data vary depending on place of measurement.
7.6,90 Source: U.S. Geological Survey, *Gazette of Surface Waters of California*, GPO 1913; California Department of Water Resources; Pacific Southwest Interagency Committee, *River Mile Index--Water Resources of California*; U.S. Geological Survey, Water Resources Data, *California Water Year 1981*, Volumes 1-4.

CALIFORNIA RIVERS-WATER QUALITY, 1987

Good To Excellent		Medium		Poor
American	Pit	Cache	San Benito	Los Angeles
Colorado	Putah	Cuyama	San Deiguito	New Alamo
Feather	Russian	Eel	San Joaquin	Rio Honda
Kern	Sacramento	Guadalupe	San Lorenzo	San Diego
Kings	Trinity	Husana	Santa Clara	San Gabriel
Klamath	Truckee	Mad	San Luis Rey	Santa Ana
Mokelumne	Yuba	Merced	Tuolumne	Santa Margarita
Napa		Pajaro	Whitewater	Tijuana
		Petaluma		
		Salinas		
		San Antonio		

Note: The overall quality of monitored California rivers and streams has shown a 9% improvement in quality over the past few years. The average river is above minimum safety standards for swimability and fishability.

7.7,90 Source: California State Water Resources Control Board, *Water Quality Inventory for Water Years 1984 and 1985* and update.

LAKES IN CALIFORNIA

	Number			Acres		
Fishery Type	Lakes	Reservoirs	Total	Lakes	Reservoirs	Total
Coldwater	3,269	303	3,572	190,778.6	102,601.8	293,380.4
Mixed	95	325	420	3,435.1	258,564.8	261,999.9
Warmwater	137	601	738	197,501.2	213,596.4	411,097.6
Salton Sea	1	-	1	220,000.0	-	220,000.0
No Fishing	146	45	191	201,113.1	9,942.6	211,055.7
Statewide Totals	**3,648**	**1,274**	**4,922**	**812,828.0**	**584,705.6**	**1,397,533.6**

7.8,90 Source: California Department of Fish and Game, unpublished data. February 1978.

MAJOR LAKES IN CALIFORNIA*

Almanor	Don Pedro Reservoir	Nacimiento Reservoir
Anderson Reservoir	Eagle	Oroville Reservoir
Arrowhead	Elsinore	Salton Sea
Berryessa	Folsom	San Luis Reservoir
Big Bear	Goose	Shasta
Cachuma	Henshaw	Silverwood
Casaic	Honey	Tahoe
Clair Engle	Isabella Reservoir	Upper
Clear (largest natural lake)	Millerton	

* California has 3,885 lakes of ten acres or larger.

7.9,90 Source: California State Water Resources Control Board, *Water Quality Inventory for Water Years 1980 and 1981.*

CALIFORNIA'S PRINCIPLE SALINE* LAKES		
Lake	**County**	**Square Miles of Area**
Salton Sea	Riverside and Imperial	360
Goose	Modoc and State of Oregon	100
Mono	Mono	76
Owens	Inyo	35

* Saline means dissolved solids over 1,000 parts per million.
7.10,90 Source: U.S. Geological Survey, *Principle Lakes of the U.S. Circular 476*, 1963.

AGGREGATE GROSS CAPACITIES OF MAJOR RESERVOIRS IN CALIFORNIA, 1986		
Hydrographic Area	**Number of Reservoirs**	**Total Capacity (in thousands of acre-feet)**
Intrastate		
North Coastal	6	3,828
San Francisco Bay	17	808
Central Coastal	6	1,257
South Coastal	28	3,088
Sacramento Valley	47	17,179
San Joaquin Valley	31	15,128
Lahontan	8	1,775
Colorado Desert	4	702
Total	**147**	**43,764**

7.11,90 Source: California Department of Water Resources, Statewide Planning Branch, unpublished data.

MAJOR CALIFORNIA WATERFALLS			
Waterfall	**Location**	**Height**	
		feet	**(meters)**
Ribon	Yosemite National Park	1,612	(491)
Upper Yosemite	Yosemite National Park	1,430	(436)
Silver Strand	Yosemite National Park	1,170	(357)
Middle Cascade	Yosemite National Park	909	(277)
Feather	Plumas National Park	640	(195)
Bridalveil	Yosemite National Park	620	(189)
Nevada	Yosemite National Park	594	(181)
Illilouette	Yosemite National Park	370	(113)
Lower Yosemite	Yosemite National Park	320	(98)
Vernal	Yosemite National Park	317	(97)

7.12,90 Source: National Geographic Society.

PER CAPITA WATER USE
BY SELECTED COMMUNITIES

Community	Gallons per Day
Eureka	140
Redding	240
East Bay Cities	200
San Francisco	125
San Jose	170
Sacramento	300
Fresno	290
Bakersfield	345
Santa Barbara	190
Beverly Hills	325
Riverside	245
Los Angeles	190
San Diego	190

Note: Data represent the 1983-85 daily average.
7.13,90 Source: California Department of Water Resources *Bulletin 160-87*.

MUNICIPAL WATER SUPPLIES*
REPRESENTATIVE CITIES AND AGENCIES
FISCAL YEAR1986-1987

City or District	Water Production (millions of gallons)
Eureka	1,635
Santa Rosa	6,840
San Francisco	104,089
East Bay Municipal Utility District	80,115†
Santa Barbara	5,377
Santa Cruz	4,285
Metropolitan Water District of Southern California	594,978††
Long Beach	24,812
Los Angeles	229,491
Redding	4,975
San Diego	81,192
Sacramento	37,432
Fresno	29,853
Yreka	839
Tehachapi	353
El Centro	2,272

*   Gross water produced. †Gross water deliveries.
†† Total deliveries of water. Includes part of water supply for Long Beach, Los Angeles, and San Diego, listed above.
7.14,90 Source: Dept. of Water Resources, Statewide Planning Branch.

MAJOR DAMS AND RESERVOIRS OF CALIFORNIA

Name of Dam	Stream	County	Reservoir Capacity (acre-feet)
Antelope	Indian Creek	Plumas	22,600
Auburn†	M. Fork American River*	Placer	2,330,000
Beardsley	M. Fork Stanislaus River*	Tuolumne	97,500
Bethany	Tributary Feather River	Butte	4,800
Big Creek No. 7	San Joaquin River	Fresno	345,000
Big Santa Anita	Tributary Rio Hondo Creek	Los Angeles	805
Big Tujunga No. 1	Big Tujunga Creek	Los Angeles	6,000
Black Butte	Stony Creek	Tehama	370,000
Bouquet Canyon	Bouquet Creek	Los Angeles	36,505
Box Canyon	Sacramento River	Siskiyou	26,000
Bradbury	Santa Ynez River	Santa Barbara	205,000
Briones	Bear Creek	Contra Costa	67,500
Brush Creek	Brush Creek	El Dorado	1,750
Buchanan	Chowchilla River	Madera	150,000
Bucks Storage	Bucks Creek	Plumas	103,000
Buena Vista	Kern River	Kern	205,000
Calaveras	Calaveras Creek	Alameda	100,000
Camanche	Mokelumne River	San Joaquin	431,500
Camp Far West	Bear River	Placer	103,000
Casitas	Coyote Creek	Ventura	324,000
Castaic Lagoon	Castaic Creek	Los Angeles	5,700
Castaic	Castaic Creek	Los Angeles	324,000
Cedar Springs	W. Fork Mojave*	San Bernardino	75,000
Cherry Valley	Cherry Creek	Tuolumne	268,000
Clear Lake Impounding	Cache Creek	Lake	420,000
Clear Lake	Lost River	Modoc	388,500
Clifton Court Forebay	Tributary Old River	Contra Costa	28,700
Cogswell	W. Fork San Gabriel River*	Los Angeles	10,450
Courtright	Helms Creek	Fresno	123,300
Del Valle	Arroyo Del Valle	Alameda	77,100
Don Pedro	Tuolumne River	Tuolumne	2,030,000
Donnells	M. Fork Stanislaus River*	Tuolumne	64,500
El Capitan	San Diego River	San Diego	112,800
Elderberry Forebay	Castaic Creek	Ventura	28,200
Englebright	Yuba River	Nevada	70,000
Fish Barrier Pool	Feather River	Butte	600
Folsum	American River	Sacramento	1,010,000

* M. = Middle, W. = West, † Construction halted.
7.15.1,90

MAJOR DAMS AND RESERVOIRS OF CALIFORNIA

Name of Dam	Stream	County	Reservoir Capacity (acre-feet)
Frenchman Lake	M. Fork Feather River*	Plumas	55,500
Friant	San Joaquin River	Fresno	520,500
Grizzly Valley	Big Grizzly Creek	Plumas	84,371
Henshaw	San Luis Rey River	San Diego	50,000
Indian Valley	Tributary Cache Creek	Lake	300,000
Iron Canyon	Cedar Salt Log Creek	Shasta	24,300
Isabella	Kern River	Kern	842,000
Jackson Creek	Jackson Creek	Amador	22,000
Jackson Meadows	M. Fork Yuba River*	Nevada	52,500
James H. Turner	San Antonio Creek	Alameda	50,500
L.L. Anderson	M. Fork American River*	Placer	133,700
Lake Almanor	N. Fork Feather River*	Plumas	1,308,000
Lake Loveland	Sweetwater River	San Diego	25,400
Lake Spaulding	S. Fork Yuba River*	Nevada	74,800
Lake Tahoe	Truckee River	Placer	732,000
Leroy Anderson	Coyote River	Santa Clara	91,300
Lexington	Los Gatos Creek	Santa Clara	21,400
Little Grass Valley	S. Fork Feather River*	Plumas	93,000
Little Panoche Detention	Little Panoche Creek	Fresno	13,310
Long Valley	Ownes River	Mono	183,500
Los Banos Detention	Los Banos Creek	Merced	34,600
Lower Bear River	Bear River	Amador	52,000
Lower Hell Hole	Rubicon River	Placer	208,400
Mammoth Pool	San Joaquin River	Fresno	123,000
Mathews	Tributary Cajalco Creek	Riverside	182,000
McCloud	McCloud River	Shasta	35,300
Monticello	Putah Creek	Napa	1,602,000
Morris	San Gabriel River	Los Angeles	27,500
Mulholland	Weid Canyon	Los Angeles	4,000
Nacimiento	Nacimiento River	San Luis Obispo	350,000
New Bullards Bar	North Yuba River	Yuba	969,600
New Exchequer	Merced River	Mariposa	1,032,000
New Hogan	Calaveras River	Calaveras	325,000
New Lake Arrowhead	Little Bear Creek	San Bernardino	48,000
New Melones	Stanislaus River	Calaveras	2,400,000
New Upper San Leandro	San Leandro Creek	Alameda	42,000
O'Neill Forebay	San Luis Creek	Merced	57,000

* M. = Middle, N. = North, S. = South.

7.15.2,90

MAJOR DAMS AND RESERVOIRS OF CALIFORNIA

Name of Dame	Stream	County	Reservoir Capacity (acre-feet)
O'Shaughnessy	Tuolumne River	Tuolumne	340,000
Oroville	Feather River	Butte	3,540,000
Pacoima	Pacoima Creek	Los Angeles	3,900
Pardee	Mokelumne River	Amador	210,000
Parker	Colorado River	San Bernardino	648,000
Perris	Offstream	Riverside	131,000
Pine Flat	Kings River	Placer	1,113,000
Pit No. 7	Pit River	Shasta	34,000
Prado	Santa Ana River	Riverside	314,000
Pyramid	Piru Creek	Los Angeles	171,000
Rollins	Bear River	Amador	66,000
Salt Springs	N. Fork Mokelumne River*	Amador	139,400
San Antonio	San Antonio River	Monterey	350,000
San Gabriel No. 1	San Gabriel River	Los Angeles	44,600
San Joaquin Reservoir	Tributary Bonita Creek	Orange	3,000
San Luis	San Luis Creek	Merced	2,041,000
San Vicente	San Vicente Creek	San Diego	90,200
Santa Felicia	Piru Creek	Ventura	100,000
Shasta	Sacramento River	Shasta	4,552,000
Shaver Lake	Stevenson Creek	Fresno	135,300
Slab Creek	S. Fork American River*	El Dorado	16,600
Sly Creek	Lost Creek	Butte	65,050
Spring Creek Debris	Spring Creek	Shasta	5,900
Stampede	Little Truckee River	Sierra	226,500
Terminus	Kaweah River	Tulare	266,000
Thermalito Afterbay	Tributary Feather River	Butte	57,000
Thermalito Diversion	Feather River	Butte	13,300
Thermalito Forebay	Tributary Feather River	Butte	11,700
Trinity	Trinity	Trinity	2,448,000
Tulloch	Stanislaus River	Calaveras	68,400
Twitchell	Cuyama River	Santa Barbara	151,000
Union Valley	Silver Creek	El Dorado	271,000
Vermillion Valley	Mono Creek	Fresno	125,000
Warm Springs	Dry Creek	Sonoma	381,000
Whale Rock	Old Creek	San Luis Obispo	40,700
Whiskeytown	Clear Creek	Shasta	241,000
Wishon	N. Fork Kings River*	Fresno	128,000

* N. = North, S. = South.
7.15.3,90 Source: California Dept. of Water Resources, *Bulletin No. 17097, Dams within Jurisdiction of the State of California*, Dec. 1979 & *Bulletin 32-56*, 1986, updated through March 1986, and phone update.

75 MILLION ACRE-FEET OF WATER AVERAGE YEARLY RUNOFF FOR CALIFORNIA

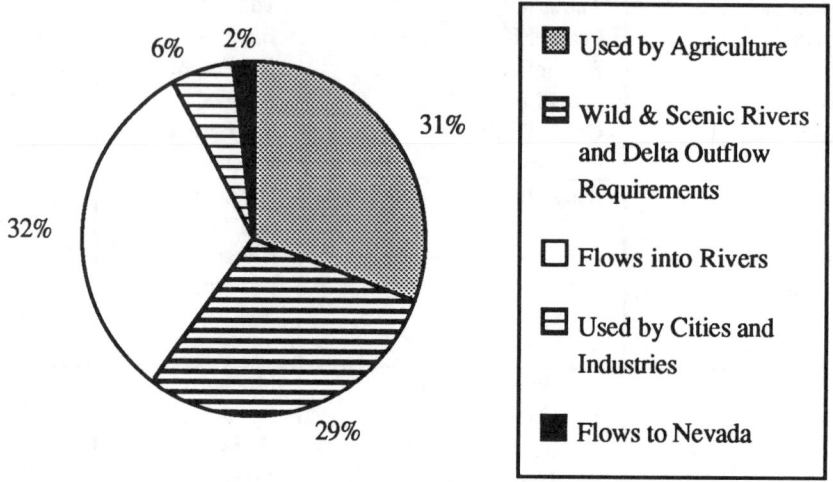

6%   2%

31%

32%

29%

▩ Used by Agriculture

⊟ Wild & Scenic Rivers and Delta Outflow Requirements

☐ Flows into Rivers

⊟ Used by Cities and Industries

■ Flows to Nevada

7.16,90 Source: California Department of Water Resources.

CALIFORNIA WATER USE			
Consumptive Use (millions of gallons per day)			
User	California	U.S.	California as a % of U.S.
Domestic	879	5,680	15%
Commercial	331	1,190	28%
Irrigation	19,300	73,800	26%
Livestock	155	2,370	7%
Industrial	312	5,157	6%
Mining	123	975	13%
Thermoelectric			
Fossil Fuel	25	3,440	1%
Geothermal	42	42	100%
Nuclear	5.6	2,720	<1%
Hydroelectric	0	0	NA
Total	72	6,200	1%

7.17,90 Source: California Dept. of Water Resources, unpublished data.

CALIFORNIA WATER USE* (millions of gallons per day)								
	Surface Water				Ground Water			
	California		United States		California		United States	
User	Fresh	Saline	Fresh	Saline	Fresh	Saline	Fresh	Saline
Domestic								
Public Supply	3,240††	-	21,000††	-	-	-	-	-
Self Supply	15	-	62	-	125	-	3,250	-
Commercial								
Public Supply	1,220††	-	5,710††	-	-	-	-	-
Self Supply	5.7	-	481	-	47	-	746	-
Irrigation								
Reclaimed Sewerage	235	-	434	-	-	-	-	-
Public & Self Supply	20,300	-	91,300	-	10,400	-	45,700	-
Livestock								
Public & Self Supply	159	-	1,450	-	41	-	3,020	-
Industrial								
Public Supply	494††	-	5,730††	-	-	-	-	-
Self Supply	105	254	18,400	3,480	326	7.9	3,930	26
Reclaimed Sewerage	2.9†	-	144†	-	-	-	-	-
Mining								
Public & Self Supply	58	25	1,270	138	108	276	1,410	626
Thermoelectric								
Public Supply	31††	-	96	-	-	-	-	-
Self Supply	412	11,700	130,000	56,000	68	-	608	-
Fossil Fuel	412	8,400	105,000	40,300	8.7	-	505	-
Geothermal	-	-		-	60	-	61	-
Nuclear	0.2	3,340	25,200	15,700	0	-	42	-
Hydroelectric**	83,800	-	3,050,000	-	-	-	-	-

*   Withdrawals, Actual use is less.   † Not necessarily fresh or saline or surface or ground water.
†† Not necessarily surface or ground water.   ** All water returned after use.
   7.18,90 Source: U.S. Geological Survey, *Estimated Use of Water in the U.S., 1989.*

SECTION 7 NOTE
CALIFORNIA'S SEVEN NATURAL WONDERS
Big Sur
Death Valley
Lake Tahoe
Mount Whitney
Pygmy Forest
Sutter Buttes
Yosemite

7.19,90

SECTION 7 NOTE
California is 140 miles wide on its southern border and 212 miles wide on its northern border.

7.20,90

CALIFORNIA LAND AREA BY USE OR MAJOR VEGETATION

Land Use or Vegetation Type	Thousand Acres	Percent
Forest		
Productive Forest	17,944	17.9
Unproductive Forest	22,216	22.2
Total Forest	**40,160**	**40.1%**
Non-Forest		
Coastal sagebrush	2,300	2.3
Inland sagebrush	3,800	3.8
Desert	23,900	23.9
Grassland	12,000	12.0
Riparian, marsh, tidelands	700	0.7
Barren	1,800	1.8
Agriculture	11,000	11.0
Urban, industrial, roads, and other	4,390	4.4
Total Non-Forest	**59,890**	**59.9%**
All Types	**100,050**	**100.0%**

7.21,90   Source: U.S. Forest Service, *California Forests: Trends, Problems & Opportunities (Resource Bulletin PnW-89), 1981.*

CALIFORNIA AND UNITED STATES MAXIMUM SNOWFALL

	Duration	Depth (inches)	Date	Place	County/State
California	1 day	67	1/5/82	Echo Summit	El Dorado
United States	1 day	75.8	4/14-15/21	Silver Lake	Colorado
California	1 month	390	Jan. 1911	Tamarack	Alpine
United States	1 month	390	Jan. 1911	Tamarack	Alpine
California	1 season	884	1906-07	Tamarack	Alpine
United States	1 season	1,122	1971-72	Rainier	Washington

GREATEST SNOW DEPTH

	Depth (inches)	Date	Place	County/State
California	451	March 11, 1911	Tamarack	Alpine
United States	451	March 11, 1911	Tamarack	Alpine

7.22,90   Source: National Oceanic and Atmospheric Administration, *Climate of Sacramento, California,* Jan. 1988.

ALL TIME BAROMETRIC PRESSURE RECORDS

	Reading	Date	Place
Highest	30.74	Feb. 17, 1883	Sacramento
Lowest	28.81	Jan. 27, 1916	Pt. Reyes

7.23,90   Source: National Weather Service, *Western Region Technical Memorandum WR-28, 1988.*

CALIFORNIA'S HIGHEST AND LOWEST TEMPERATURES

	Temperature	Date	Place	County
Highest	134°F	July 10, 1913	Death Valley	Inyo
Lowest	-45°F	Jan. 20, 1937	Boca	Nevada

7.24,90 Source: National Oceanic and Atmospheric Administration, *Environmental Information Summaries C-5, Temperature Extremes in the U.S.*

CALIFORNIA MAXIMUM RAINFALL

Duration	Depth (inches)	Date	Place	County
1 minute	0.65	April 5, 1926	Opids Camp	Los Angeles
1 hour	5.75	Jan. 27, 1981	Mining Ridge	Monterey
1 day	26.12	Jan. 23, 1943	Hoegees	Los Angeles
30 days	81.90	Dec. 1981	Camp Six	Del Norte
1 year	254.90	Oct. 1981-Sept. 1982	Camp Six	Del Norte

7.25,90 Source: Jim Goodridge, former State Climatologist, unpublished data & National Weather Service Bureau Western Region, Technical Memorandum WR-28 1983.

LEAST PRECIPITATION IN ONE YEAR CALIFORNIA AND UNITED STATES

	Precipitation (inches)	Date	Place	County
California	0.00	1913	Bagdad	San Bernardino
California	0.00	1929	Greenland Ranch	Inyo
United States	0.00	1913&1929	Same as California	

7.26,90 Source: National Oceanic & Atmospheric Administration, *Climate of Sacramento, Jan. 1985.*

SUNSHINE

City	Average % of Possible Sunshine
Eureka	50
Fresno	82
Los Angeles-City	73
Red Bluff	79
Sacramento	79
San Diego	68
San Francisco-City	67

7.27,90 Source: National Oceanic & Atmospheric Administration- *Comparative Climatic Data for the U.S. through 1981.*

	Feet Above Mean Sea Level	Normal Annual Precipitation (in inches)	Freeze Data		
Station			Date of Last Spring Freeze	Date of First Spring Freeze	Frost-Free Period (days)
CLIMATOLOGICAL DATA					
FOR REPRESENTATIVE STATIONS IN CALIFORNIA					
Alturas Ranger Station	4,400	12.45	May 29	Sep 15	108
Bakersfield	475	5.72	Jan 4	Dec 15	344
Bishop	4,108	5.61	Mar 30	Oct 10	193
Blue Canyon	5,280	67.87	Mar 29	Nov 9	224
Eureka	43	38.51	-	-	365
Fresno	328	10.52	-	-	365
Imperial	-64	2.40	-	-	365
Los Angeles Civic Center	257	14.85	-	-	365
Mt. Shasta	3,539	37.49	Apr 24	Nov 7	196
Red Bluff	342	31.72	Jan 13	-	351
Redding	502	40.95	Jan 13	Nov 12	302
Sacramento	18	17.10	Feb 5	-	276
San Diego	13	9.32	-	-	365
San Francisco	75	19.33	-	-	365
San Luis Obispo	315	23.00	-	-	365
Susanville Airport	4,146	14.29	May 15	Oct 1	138

7.28,90 Source: National Oceanic and Atmospheric Administration, *Climatological Data, California, Vol. 89, 1987* and *Climatography of the U.S. No. 81, California 1982.*

SECTION 7 NOTE

The California Aquaduct is the largest aquaduct system in the world.

7.29,90

SECTION 7 NOTE

California extends from 32° to 40° north latitude and from 114° to 124° west longitude.

7.30,90

SECTION 7 NOTE

California is 825 miles (1,325 km) long at its longest point and 345 miles (555 km) wide at its widest point, near Point Arguello.

7.31,90

SECTION 7 NOTE

California's geographic center is 35 miles (56 km) northeast of Madera.

7.32,90

		Record High and month/yr.	Record Low and month/yr.	Mean Maximum Number Days 90°F or Higher	Mean Minimum Number Days 32°F or Lower	Base 65°F	
City	Aver. Mean Temp.					Heating Degree Days	Cooling Degree Days
Alturas	46.6	107 7/60	-34 12/72	36	210	6,896	202
Auburn	60.0	113 7/72	16 12/72	74	25	3,090	1,299
Berkeley	57.2	103 9/71	25 12/72	2	0	2,951	91
Bishop	55.9	109 7/72	-7 1/74	95	144	4,313	1,037
Chico	60.9	117 7/72	13 12/72	88	36	2,878	1,414
Cloverdale	59.6	115 7/72	18 12/72	64	18	2,763	814
Colusa	61.1	113 8/78	15 12/72	94	31	2,793	1,373
Davis	60.1	113 7/72	19 1/68	76	23	2,843	1,059
Eureka	52.2	85 9/58	21 12/72	0	5	4,679	0
Fairfield	59.8	112 9/53	18 1/79	49	23	2,686	821
Fort Bragg	52.7	93 10/65	23 12/73	0	11	4,469	0
Fresno	62.3	111 7/72	19 1/63	107	29	2,650	1,671
Half Moon Bay	54.5	94 8/68	27 12/72	0	1	3,846	6
King City	58.9	113 9/55	15 1/76	32	51	2,639	406
Lakeport	57.0	112 8/71	9 12/72	80	76	3,729	831
Livermore	58.7	113 9/55	18 12/72	61	41	3,011	734
Lodi	59.9	111 6/61	19 12/72	70	31	2,861	1,001
Lompoc	57.3	106 9/78	21 12/78	2	14	2,890	87
Los Banos	61.7	112 7/61	19 1/63	97	33	2,616	1,448
Los Gatos	59.1	114 6/61	19 12/72	36	18	2,740	591
Madera	62.1	116 7/61	17 1/76	111	31	2,673	1,654
Marysville	62.2	113 6/61	20 12/72	93	17	2,551	1,639
Merced	61.7	111 7/60	18 12/67	102	32	2,653	1,465
Modesto	61.2	112 6/61	22 12/72	81	21	2,671	1,287
Monterey	56.5	103 10/80	23 12/72	2	1	3,170	48
Napa	58.6	113 7/61	20 12/72	26	21	2,749	416
Nevada City	52.7	106 7/72	-1 12/72	39	117	4,909	432
Oakland	57.4	107 6/60	23 12/30	2	1	2,909	128
Palo Alto	57.8	107 6/61	21 1/63	10	17	2,891	275
Petaluma	57.7	110 7/72	19 12/72	25	27	2,960	316
Pismo Beach	57.7	108 8/62	23 3/63	3	4	2,755	90
Red Bluff	62.8	119 7/72	20 1/75	99	22	2,486	1,904
Redding	63.8	118 8/71	20 12/72	109	20	2,544	2,139
Richmond	58.1	107 9/71	24 12/72	4	2	2,687	162
Sacramento	62.2	114 7/25	17 12/32	56	9	2,587	NA
St. Helena	58.8	115 7/72	17 12/72	55	40	2,879	644
San Francisco (Airport)	56.9	106 6/61	20 12/32	4	3	3,042	108
(Federal Building)	56.7	101 9/71	30 12/72	1	0	3,080	39
San Jose	59.7	108 7/72	21 11/76	16	6	2,439	498
San Luis Obispo	58.9	112 9/71	15 1/63	12	3	2,498	285
San Rafael	59.6	110 6/61	23 12/72	22	3	2,439	483
Santa Cruz	56.6	107 9/71	22 1/63	8	16	3,136	95
Santa Rosa	57.9	110 9/71	16 12/72	34	37	2,980	382
Sonora	58.4	113 7/72	8 12/72	83	64	3,539	1,161
Stockton	60.7	114 7/72	19 1/63	86	25	2,806	1,259
Susanville	48.8	105 8/77	-23 2/56	41	167	6,233	362
Ukiah	59.3	115 9/55	13 12/72	78	42	2,958	913
Vacaville	60.5	115 6/61	18 12/78	88	32	2,788	1,174
Visalia	63.1	111 6/61	21 1/63	104	20	2,460	1,804
Wasco	63.6	114 7/72	16 12/72	114	30	2,466	1,999
Watsonville	55.9	106 10/80	23 1/60	4	15	3,353	43
Willows	61.1	117 7/72	14 12/78	85	31	2,836	1,429
Woodland	51.8	114 7/72	20 12/72	95	23	2,709	1,321
Yosemite Park	53.5	104 8/72	-1 12/72	53	136	NA	NA
Yreka	51.8	108 8/72	-11 12/72	51	134	5,395	597

CLIMATE IN NORTHERN CALIFORNIA CITIES (TEMPERATURE) 1951-1980

7.33.1,90 Source: National Oceanic & Atmospheric Admin., *Climatography of the U.S., No. 20, 1951-1980, California.*

CLIMATE IN SOUTHERN CALIFORNIA CITIES (TEMPERATURE) 1951-1980

City	Aver. Mean Temp.	Record High and month/yr.		Record Low and month/yr.		Mean Maximum Number Days 90°F or Higher	Mean Minimum Number Days 32°F or Lower	Base 65°F Heating Degree Days	Cooling Degree Days
Bakersfield	64.9	115	7/50	20	1/63	110	0	2,128	2,347
Barstow	64.0	116	7/72	3	1/63	130	58	2,580	2,239
Beaumont	61.4	111	7/79	18	1/57	93	26	2,629	1,320
Burbank	63.7	113	9/71	22	12/78	57	6	1,679	1,292
Chula Vista	60.4	108	9/63	24	1/63	0	0	2,074	385
Corona	63.4	114	9/55	22	12/68	75	13	1,795	1,225
Escondido	62.2	108	9/71	23	12/53	41	16	2,006	980
Imperial	73.1	119	6/70	23	1/71	170	4	976	3,961
Indio	73.2	123	6/70	20	12/53	182	16	1,059	4,096
Laguna Beach	59.9	108	9/63	24	12/56	2	3	2,221	375
La Mesa	63.4	108	9/55	27	1/63	23	0	1,567	986
Long Beach	63.3	111	10/61	25	1/63	22	1	1,485	1,091
L.A. Int. Airport	61.7	110	9/63	23	1/37	5	0	1,595	728
L.A. Civic Ctr.	64.8	110	9/55	28	1/49	20	0	1,204	1,339
Needles	72.8	122	7/67	13	12/80	164	6	1,390	4,270
Newport Beach	60.7	107	9/63	28	2/66	1	0	1,954	371
Ojai	61.7	112	9/55	22	1/63	72	24	2,147	978
Oxnard	60.3	103	10/61	28	2/62	3	0	2,068	357
Palmdale	61.8	113	7/72	6	1/63	103	62	2,908	1,760
Palm Springs	72.3	123	7/79	22	1/63	180	7	1,109	3,820
Pasadena	64.3	109	9/71	23	3/78	54	1	1,550	1,299
Pomona	62.8	112	9/55	21	1/63	70	16	1,972	1,191
Redlands	63.8	115	9/71	23	12/78	99	11	1,992	1,571
Riverside	64.0	115	9/55	23	1/54	92	14	1,818	1,471
San Bernardino	64.8	117	9/71	22	12/68	110	13	1,777	1,718
San Diego	62.9	111	9/63	29	1/49	3	0	1,284	842
San Gabriel	64.3	111	9/71	26	12/78	57	4	1,532	1,281
Santa Ana	64.0	110	9/63	25	1/52	21	3	1,430	1,089
Santa Barbara	60.6	105	9/78	29	12/68	2	1	1,933	393
Santa Maria	56.9	104	7/53	20	1/76	6	24	3,054	76
Santa Monica	61.1	104	9/63	33	3/52	0	0	1,873	438
Santa Paula	61.0	109	9/63	25	12/68	16	9	2,030	596
Tehachapi	54.3	103	7/80	-4	12/67	31	97	4,494	622
Torrance	62.1	111	9/55	28	12/78	8	1	1,719	677
Tustin-Irvine	62.1	111	9/63	24	12/68	24	8	1,854	813
Upland	62.3	111	9/71	23	12/68	73	8	2,175	1,223
Victorville	60.3	112	7/72	7	1/57	104	79	3,192	1,499
Yorba Linda	63.5	114	9/55	22	12/68	53	5	1,644	1,118

7.33.2,90 Source: National Oceanic & Atmospheric Admin., *Climatography of the U.S., Nos. 20, 60 & 81,* 1951-1980, California.

SECTION 7 NOTE

The maximum wind speed ever recorded in California at a regular weather station, was 115 mph, reported at the Monterey Naval Air Station in 1951.

7.34,90

CLIMATE IN NORTHERN CALIFORNIA CITIES (PRECIPITATION) 1951-1980

City	Mean Annual Precipitation (inches)	Greatest Monthly Precipitation (inches) month/yr.		Greatest Daily Precipitation (inches) month/yr.		Mean Annual Snowfall (inches)	Greatest Monthly Snowfall (inches) month/yr.	
Alturas	12.45	6.17	10/62	1.18	1/67	39.0	43.3	1/52
Auburn	34.46	19.16	12/55	5.41	10/62	1.6	6.5	1/72
Berkeley	23.24	15.04	12/55	3.96	1/67	.0	1.0	1/76
Bishop	5.72	8.93	1/69	3.64	2/69	NA	31.9	2/69
Chico	25.93	14.44	11/73	4.46	10/62	.2	2.3	12/72
Cloverdale	43.82	25.72	1/70	8.37	10/62	.3	1.8	3/76
Colusa	15.41	8.03	1/73	3.35	10/62	.3	6.0	1/73
Davis	17.14	11.87	12/55	3.50	10/62	.1	1.1	1/73
Eureka	39.76	16.58	11/73	5.83	12/50	NA	3.0	12/35
Fairfield	20.94	13.66	12/55	4.50	10/62	.0	0.0	
Fort Bragg	39.30	19.53	2/58	3.78	1/79	.0	0.0	
Fresno	10.24	8.56	1/69	2.59	1/69	NA	2.2	1/62
Half Moon Bay	25.22	13.81	12/55	4.94	1/56	.0	0.0	
King City	11.25	7.69	12/55	3.32	1/63	.2	5.3	1/57
Lakeport	30.04	17.46	1/70	4.24	10/62	.0	4.0	1/62
Livermore	14.11	10.15	12/55	3.45	1/52	.0	0.0	
Lodi	16.27	9.45	12/55	2.44	1/67	.0	0.0	
Lompoc	13.88	10.26	2/62	4.27	10/55	.0	0.0	
Los Banos	9.00	5.47	12/55	1.88	2/58	.1	1.5	1/62
Los Gatos	25.59	26.56	12/55	8.48	12/55	.1	2.0	2/76
Madera	10.72	5.82	12/55	1.98	11/78	.1	4.0	1/62
Marysville	20.55	11.30	12/55	4.24	10/62	.0	0.5	12/72
Merced	12.05	7.71	12/55	2.10	12/55	.0	0.7	1/62
Modesto	11.70	6.34	12/55	2.72	3/78	.1	1.5	1/62
Monterey	18.34	10.04	1/52	3.85	12/55	.1	1.5	1/62
Napa	24.34	16.13	12/55	5.85	11/77	.0	0.0	
Nevada City	54.59	35.34	12/55	7.07	10/62	18.2	40.5	1/52
Oakland	18.69	11.29	12/55	5.45	10/62	NA	1.0	2/76
Palo Alto	14.77	10.56	12/55	2.77	12/55	.1	1.5	1/62
Pismo Beach	16.57	13.18	11/69	5.16	1/69	.0	0.0	
Red Bluff	22.04	11.38	2/58	4.00	11/54	NA	13.6	1/50
Redding	40.95	28.84	1/70	7.30	12/64	3.5	23.0	12/68
Richmond	21.83	14.25	12/55	3.90	12/69	.0	0.0	
Sacramento	17.87	15.04	1/62*	5.28	4/80*	.1	3.5	1/88*
St. Helena	35.24	24.32	12/55	6.83	1/67	.3	4.0	1/74
S.F.† Fed. Bldg.	20.66	11.47	12/55	3.65	3/40	NA	0.0	
S.F.† Airport	19.53	12.30	12/55	4.58	1/67	NA	1.5	1/62
San Jose	13.86	9.62	12/55	3.60	1/68	.0	0.5	2/76
San Luis Obispo	23.00	24.63	1/69	5.90	1/69	.0	0.0	
San Rafael	37.48	22.65	12/55	7.47	1/67	.0	0.0	
Santa Cruz	28.98	21.07	12/55	4.65	1/63	.1	3.0	1/57
Santa Rosa	29.88	17.89	12/55	5.04	1/66	.2	6.5	4/63
Sonora	31.02	21.69	12/55	7.10	12/55	1.2	9.0	4/55
Susanville	14.29	12.26	10/62	4.70	10/62	27.0	30.0	12/64
Ukiah	38.12	23.52	1/70	6.18	12/64	.5	5.0	1/52
Vacaville	24.29	18.38	12/55	5.85	12/55	.1	2.0	1/73
Visalia	9.86	7.72	1/69	3.70	10/74	.0	0.0	
Wasco	6.48	5.71	2/62	2.53	2/78	.1	3.0	1/62
Watsonville	21.70	14.61	12/55	5.90	9/59	.0	0.0	
Willows	17.28	10.98	2/58	3.20	11/64	.5	6.0	1/73
Woodland	17.89	11.71	12/55	3.26	12/55	.1	1.0	1/73
Yosemite Park	NA	29.73	12/55	6.92	12/55	72.7	89.0	2/69
Yreka	19.20	13.71	12/64	4.57	12/64	21.6	33.0	11/55

* Denotes 1862, 1880 and 1888 respectively.   † S.F. = San Francisco.

7.33.3,90 Source: National Oceanic & Atmospheric Admin., Climatography of the U.S., No. 20, 1951-1980, California.

CLIMATE IN SOUTHERN CALIFORNIA CITIES (PRECIPITATION) 1951-1980

City	Mean Annual Precipitation inches	Greatest Monthly Precipitation inches	mo/yr	Greatest Record Precipitation inches	mo/yr	Mean Annual Snowfall inches	Greatest Monthly Snowfall inches	mo/yr
Barstow	4.14	2.82	2/80	1.76	7/58	0.7	12.0	12/67
Beaumont	17.00	13.20	2/80	4.69	1/69	1.5	15.8	1/79
Burbank	15.78	15.19	2/80	5.30	12/65	0.0	0.1	1/66
Chula Vista	8.67	6.00	11/65	2.89	3/68	0.0	0.0	
Corona	11.60	10.90	1/69	3.66	1/69	0.0	1.0	12/68
Escondido	14.53	11.58	1/80	3.58	12/66	0.0	0.0	
Imperial	2.10	3.87	8/77	2.35	9/76	0.0	0.0	
Indio	3.14	4.23	9/76	3.16	8/77	0.0	0.0	
Laguna Beach	12.34	9.64	2/80	3.59	1/56	0.0	0.0	
La Mesa	12.56	9.70	1/80	4.25	1/79	0.0	0.0	
Long Beach	10.25	11.24	1/69	6.86	1/56	0.0	0.0	
L.A.* Int. Airport	11.59	11.07	2/62	6.19	1/56	0.0	0.0	
L.A.* Civic Ctr.	14.05	14.94	1/69	6.11	1/56	0.0	0.3	1/49f
Needles	4.39	4.72	9/76	2.55	8/51	0.0	0.0	
Newport Beach	11.09	8.34	2/69	3.82	2/69	0.0	0.0	
Ojai	21.67	25.76	1/69	7.00	1/69	0.0	0.0	
Oxnard	14.53	15.58	2/62	5.96	1/56	0.2	5.0	1/62
Palmdale	7.38	6.42	2/80	2.44	1/52	1.7	19.0	1/74
Palm Springs	5.20	6.35	11/65	2.76	9/76	0.1	1.5	1/79
Pasadena	19.29	19.70	2/80	6.51	1/56	0.0	0.0	
Pomona	17.02	16.14	2/80	6.38	1/56	0.0	0.0	
Redlands	12.89	9.91	2/69	3.41	1/69	0.1	2.0	11/64
Riverside	9.64	8.00	2/69	2.70	1/56	0.0	0.0	
San Bernardino	15.68	13.64	1/69	5.05	1/56	0.1	1.5	3/53
San Diego	9.45	7.60	12/43†	3.07	12/45°	0.0	0.0	
San Gabriel	17.76	18.16	1/69	6.93	1/56	0.0	0.0	
Santa Ana	12.60	9.86	1/52	4.22	1/56	0.0	0.0	
Santa Barbara	17.70	17.33	1/62	5.32	1/77	0.0	0.0	
Santa Maria	12.25	9.69	2/62	3.15	12/74	0.0	0.0	
Santa Monica	13.69	14.11	2/62	5.11	1/69	0.0	0.0	
Santa Paula	17.81	18.63	1/69	6.48	1/80	0.0	0.0	
Tehachapi	10.40	6.22	11/70	3.29	11/70	21.5	33.0	4/67
Torrance	13.13	13.26	1/69	6.53	1/56	0.0	0.0	
Tustin-Irvine	11.97	8.64	1/52	4.52	1/56	0.0	0.0	
Upland	19.89	19.64	1/69	6.38	1/69	0.0	0.0	
Victorville	5.00	4.45	2/80	2.33	9/76	1.6	17.0	1/74
Yorba Linda	14.46	12.58	1/69	5.20	1/56	0.0	0.0	

* L.A. = Los Angeles   † 1943   ° 1945   f 1949
7.33.4,90 Source: National Oceanic & Atmoshpheric Admin., *Climatography of the U.S., Nos. 20, 60 & 81, 1951-1980, California.*

SECTION 7 NOTE

Meteorologists estimate that in a December 1977 storm in Los Angeles County, Santa Ana winds gusted at up to 150 mph. These winds knocked down four Southern California Edison transmission towers.

7.35,90

| TORNADOES IN CALIFORNIA ||
Year	Number
1894-1899	2
1900-1909	1
1910-1919	0
1920-1929	6
1930-1939	6
1940-1949	3
1950-1959	22
1960-1969	26
1970-1979	42
1980	8
1981	3
1982	14
1983	9
1984	2
1985	3
1986	7
1987	4
1988	6

Note: Tornado reporting has become more thorough in recent years resulting in an increase in the reported number of tornadoes.

7.36, 90 Source: National Severe Storms Forecast Center, Kansas City, unpublished data.

CALIFORNIA'S MAJOR EARTHQUAKE FAULTS		
Banning	Holser (L.A. & Ventura)	Potrero (L.A.)
Big Pine (Ventura)	Honey Lake	Raymond Hill (L.A.)
Blackwater	Imperial	San Andrea
Buck Creek (Ventura)	Inglewood (L.A.)	San Antonio (L.A. & San Bern)
Calaveras	Inyo	San Cayetano (Ventura)
Calico-Mesquite	Ivanpah	San Gabriel
Canton (L.A.)	Kern Canyon	San Jacinto
Ceder Canyon	Lenwood	Santa Monica (L.A.)
Cuyama	Mission Creek	Santa Susana (L.A. & Ventura)
Death Valley	Nacimiento	Santa Ynez (Ventura)
Dry Creek (Ventura)	Newport-Inglewood	Sierra Madre (L.A. & San Bern)
Elsinore	Oakridge	Sierra Nevada
Elysian Park (L.A.)	Palos Verdes (L.A.)	South Fork Mountain
Furnace Creek	Panamint Valley	Suey
Garlock (Kern & L.A.)	Pine Mountain (Ventura)	Surprise Valley
Hayward-San Pablo	Pinto Mountain	Torrance-Wilmington (L.A.)
Healdsburg	Piru (Ventura)	Whittier-Narrows (L.A.)
Helendale		

7.37,90 Source: U.S. Geological Survey maps.

MAJOR CALIFORNIA EARTHQUAKES

Date	Locality	Magnitude (Richter scale)	Intensity (Mercalli scale*)
October 1800	Santa Cruz	NA	VII
December 8, 1812	Los Angeles	6.9	VII
December 21, 1812	Santa Barbara Channel	7.1	X
June 10, 1836	San Francisco Bay Area	6.8	X
June 1838	San Francisco	7.0	X
February 9, 1857	Los Angeles	7.9	IX
October 8, 1865	Santa Cruz	6.3	IX
October 21, 1868	Hayward	6.8	IX
March 26, 1872	Owens Valley	7.8	X-XI
November 23, 1873	Del Norte County	6.7	VIII
January 24, 1875	Lassen and Plumas Counties	5.8	VII
February 2, 1881	Monterey	5.6	VIII
April 10, 1881	Stanislaus County	5.9	VI
May 19, 1889	Contra Costa County	6.0	VIII
April 24, 1890	Hollister	NA	NA
February 24, 1892	San Diego County	6.7	VIII-IX
April 19, 1892	Solano County	6.4	IX
June 20, 1897	Santa Clara County	6.2	VIII-IX
March 31, 1898	San Pablo Bay	6.2	IX
April 15, 1898	Mendocino County	6.4	IX
April 19, 1898	Solano and Yolo Counties	6.4	IX
December 25, 1899	Riverside County	6.6	IX
April 18, 1906	San Francisco	8.3	XI
July 29, 1925	Santa Barbara	6.3	IX
March 10, 1933	Long Beach	6.3	IX
May 18, 1940	Imperial Valley	7.1	X
June 30, 1941	Santa Barbara	5.9	VIII
July 21, 1952	Kern County	7.7	XI
December 21, 1954	Eureka	6.6	NA
February 9, 1971	San Fernando	6.4	XI
October 15, 1979	Imperial Valley	6.6	IX
May 2, 1983	Coalinga (Fresno County)	6.7	VIII
April 24, 1984	Morgan Hill	6.2	VIII
November 23, 1984	25 km. N.W. of Bishop	6.1	V
July 21, 1986	Chalfant Valley (near Bishop)	6.5	VI
October 1, 1987	Whittier-Narrows	5.9	NA
November 24, 1987	Superstition Hills (Imperial City)	6.0	VII

* The Mercalli intensity scale measures the severity of an earthquake in terms of its effects on the structures in an area and on its inhabitants.

7.38,90 Source: U.S. Department of the Interior, Geological Survey, *Earthquake History of the United States, 1982*; University of California, Berkeley, Seismology Department; and California Division of Mines and Geology, *Open File Report 81-11 SAC* and *82-17 SAC* and Cal. Tech. Seismology Lab.

SECTION 7 NOTE

Four of the most significant earthquakes in U.S. history occurred in California: the San Francisco (1906), Long Beach (1933), San Fernando (1971), and Coalinga (1983) earthquakes.

7.39,90

LIKELIHOOD OF EARTHQUAKES IN CALIFORNIA

Fault Segment	Probable Richter Scale Magnitude of the Earthquake	Likelehiood of Quake Occuring in 30 Years
Olema (North of San Francisco)	8	10%
North Hayward (North of Hayward)	7	20%
South Hayward (South of Hayward)	7	20%
San Francisco Peninsula	7	20%
South Santa Cruz Mountains	6.5	30%
Central Creeping	7	10%
Parkfield	6	90%*
Cholame	7	30%
Carrizo (North of Los Angeles)	7	10%
Mojave	7.5	30%
San Bernardino Mountains	7.5	20%
Coachella Valley (Indio)	7.5	40%
Imperial	6.5	50%
San Bernardino Valley	7	50%
San Jacinto Valley	7	50%
Anza (El Centro)	7	50%

* By 1993.
The probability of a magnitude of 7.0 or larger earthquake in the San Francisco Bay area is 10% by 1988, 30% by 2000, and 50% by 2018.
The probability of a magnitude 7.5 to 8.0 earthquake on the Southern San Andreas fault in the greater southern California area is 10% by 1993, 40% by 2008, and 60% by 2018.
7.40,90 Source: U.S. Geological Survey, *Open- File Report 88-389, (1988).*

CALIFORNIA'S 11 GEOLOGICAL REGIONS

Coast Range	Klamath Mts.	Southern Cascade Mts.
Modoc Plateau	Sierra Nevada	Central Valley
Great Basin	Transverse Ranges	Mojave Desert
Salton Trough	Peninsula Ranges	

7.41,90 Source: U.S. Geological Survey Maps

SECTION 7 NOTE

In an average year 190 million acre feet of water fall on California: 71 million acre feet (37 percent) go into rivers and streams as runoff; the other 119 million acre feet evaporate or go into ground water. An estimated 600 million acre feet of water is sitting in underground ground water reservoirs in the Central Valley.

7.42,90

SECTION 7 NOTE

California's "Lost Coast" is a rugged coastal area north of Cape Mendocino.

7.43,90

CALIFORNIA'S TALLEST MOUNTAINS

Mountain	Elevation	Mountain Range
Mt. Whitney	14,495	Sierra Nevada
Mt. Williamson	14,384	Sierra Nevada
White Mountain	14,246	White Mountain
North Palisade	14,242	Sierra Nevada
Mt. Shasta	14,162	Cascades
Mt. Sill	14,162	Sierra Nevada
Mt. Russell	14,086	Sierra Nevada
Polemonium Peak**	14,080	Sierra Nevada
Split Mountain	14,058	Sierra Nevada
Mt. Langley	14,042	Sierra Nevada
Middle Palisade*	14,040	Sierra Nevada
Mt. Tyndall	14,018	Sierra Nevada
Mt. Muir	14,015	Sierra Nevada
Thunderbolt Peak	14,003	Sierra Nevada

* Also known as Disappointment Peak.
** South of North Palisade.
7.44,90 Source: *California Geology Magazine.*

NONHAZARDOUS WASTE LANDFILLED STATEWIDE*

Year	Waste Landfilled** (millions of tons)
1981	33.5
1982	34.1
1983	34.7
1984	35.3
1985	36.0
1986	36.7
1987	37.4
1988	38.1
1989†	38.8
1990†	39.5
1995†	42.5
2000†	46.9

† Estimated.
* Municipal Solid Waste sent to land fills.
** Data does not include 10% statewide recycling rate.
7.45,90 Source: California Waste Management Board, and unpublished data, 1989.

SECTION 7 NOTE

The first diamond discovered in California was found in the summer of 1848 in a creek near Placerville. It was only the tenth diamond found in North America.
7.46,90

ACTIVE CLASS I* HAZARDOUS WASTE DISPOSAL SITES

Name	Location	Materials Accepted
Chemical Waste	Kettleman Hills	Most organic & non-organic wastes
Casmalia Resources	Casmalia	Most organic & non-organic wastes
International Technology	Westmorland	Most organic & non-organic wastes
Petroleum Waste	Buttonwillow	Most organic waste

* Class I sites are expected to provide complete permanent protection to the ground and to surface water from all site wastes.

7.47,90 Source: California Dept. of Health Services, Toxic Substances Control Division, *Hazardous Waste Facilities for Recycling, Treatment, Disposal,* Dec. 1988.

NONHAZARDOUS WASTE GENERATED BY REGION

Region	Percent of Waste Generated
Northern California	1.8%
Sierra	0.5%
Bay Area	19.3%
Central Valley & Coast	10.8%
L.A., Santa Barbara, Ventura, Orange, Riverside, San Bernardino	60.3%
San Diego, Imperial	7.3%

7.48,90 Source: California Waste Management Board, *A Comprehensive Plan for Management of Nonhazardous Waste in California,* 1985.

HAZARDOUS WASTE GENERATED IN CALIFORNIA

Year	Tons of Waste
1984	1,417,762
1985	1,185,567
1986	968,133
1987	938,332
1988	916,099

7.49,90 Source: California Department of Health Services, *Hazardous Waste Information System:* unpublished data.

SECTION 7 NOTE

Three waste-to-energy incinerators now operate in California-in the City of Commerce, in Long Beach, and in Stanislaus County.

7.50,90

County	Non-Hazardous Waste Land Filled (thousands of tons/yr)	Hazardous Waste Generated (tons)	Waste Recycled (percent)	Years of Landfill Disposal Remaining by 1989	Proposed Resource Recovery (thousands of tons/yr)	Proposed new Landfill Capacity (thousands of tons/yr)	Waste Incinerated (thousands of tons/yr)
Alameda***	2,500	44,935	12	21	none	none	none
Alpine	NA	†	UNK	NA	none	none	none
Amador	21	76	UNK	22	none	none	none
Butte	132	1,947	UNK	23	none	none	none
Calaveras	18	225	UNK	<1	none	1,800	none
Colusa	20	21	UNK	9	none	none	none
Contra Costa	930	47,154	18	2	none	160,000	none
Del Norte	10	4	12	2	none	none	none
El Dorado	43	67	UNK	12	none	none	none
Fresno	580	15,385	14	12	none	4,000	none
Glenn	20	751	UNK	<1	none	none	none
Humboldt	75	426	26	12	none	none	none
Imperial	104	1,289	20	17	none	none	none
Inyo	21	55	25	45	none	none	none
Kern	728	22,010	18	87	none	35,000	none
Kings	95	2,888	UNK	6	none	4,000	none
Lake	99	15,537	UNK	21	none	none	none
Lassen	20	24	UNK	5	none	none	none
Los Angeles	14,800	373,633	10	5	none	560,000	300
Madera	79	534	10	<1	none	3,000	none
Marin	228	1,235	12	9	none	none	none
Mariposa	13	34	UNK	34	none	NA	none
Mendocino	34	538	UNK	21	none	none	none
Merced	151	3,456	UNK	12	none	none	none
Modoc	7	102	UNK	28	none	none	none
Mono	9	20	UNK	44	none	none	none
Monterey	571	4,067	UNK	27	none	none	none
Napa	190	626	33	10	none	51,000	none
Nevada	46	611	UNK	6	none	none	none
Orange	3,700	42,648	20	7	none	60,000	none
Placer	81	2,469	UNK	106	none	285	none
Plumas	11	87	UNK	8	none	none	none
Riverside	1,300	11,894	11	36	none	none	none
Sacramento	868	21,126	17	30	none	NA	none
San Benito	20	16	UNK	4	none	none	none
San Bernardino	1,582	37,960	11	4	none	520,000	none
San Diego	3,280	70,884	3	10	470	25,000	none
San Francisco	0	22,808	24	0	none	none	none
San Joaquin	519	3,890	UNK	47	none	10,000	none
San Luis Obispo	221	6,866	4	13	none	NA	none
San Mateo	675	39,222	22	1	none	62,000	none
Santa Barbara	437	7,651	11	12	none	none	none
Santa Clara	1,500	50,169	14	30	none	6,500	none
Santa Cruz	185	1,039	5	16	none	7,000	none
Shasta	128	610	UNK	57	none	none	none
Sierra	3	NA	UNK	7	††	none	none
Siskiyou	26	1,507	10	15	none	none	none
Solano	288	9,136	13	53	none	2,912	none
Sonoma	401	5,456	12	4	none	12,000	none
Stanislaus	181	9,691	15	33	none	none	200
Sutter	**	357	12	NA	**	none	none
Tehama	26	129	UNK	34	none	none	none
Trinity	6	117	UNK	16	none	none	none
Tulare	286	1,312	UNK	36	none	none	none
Tuolumne	43	208	UNK	3	none	2,000	none
Ventura	743	16,921	UNK	4	none	40,000	none
Yolo	302	4,718	UNK	13	NA	none	none
Yuba	106	490	12	12	none	none	none

* Waste amount includes deduction for recycling. † 631 tons. †† Some wastes sent to Lassen County.
** All wastes sent to Yuba County. *** Includes 750,000 tons/yr of San Francisco County's waste.
7.51,90 Source: California Waste Management Board, *County Solid Waste Management Plans.*

SECTION 7 NOTE

According to CALIFORNIA GEOLOGY magazine, California is one of the five highest-risk areas in the world for earthquakes.

7.52,90

SECTION 7 NOTE

The Federal Emergency Management Agency has estimated that a major earthquake in Southern California would kill 3,000-14,000 people, seriously injure 12,000-52,000, and cause $17 billion in property damage. A major quake in Northern California would kill 3,000-11,000 people, seriously injure 12,000-44,000, and cause $38 billion in property damage. The damage estimates for Northern California are higher because fault lines in the San Francisco Bay Area run close to a number of city centers.

7.53,90

SECTION 7 NOTE

According to the U.S. Geological Survey, Californians use 218 gallons of fresh water per person per day. The national average is 183 gallons. Eight states and the District of Columbia use more water per capita than California. The per capita domestic or household use in California is 133 gallons of fresh water per person per day. The national average is 105 gallons.

7.54,90

SECTION 7 NOTE

According to the U.S. Geological Survey, public agencies in California supply 5,310 million gallons per day of fresh water, 70 percent of it ground water, used mostly for irrigation (26 percent of all the ground water pumped in the nation is pumped in California).

7.55,90

SECTION 7 NOTE

California was hit by 124 tornadoes from 1960 through 1988. No one was killed by any of them.

7.56,90

SECTION 7 NOTE

In both 1978 and 1982, fourteen tornadoes hit California-the highest number in any one year since 1950. Tornadoes are most likely to occur during March and April and are most frequent along the Los Angeles coast and the eastern edge of the Great Valley.

7.57,90

SECTION 7 NOTE

According to the Center for Plant Conservation in Boston, 680 plants in the U.S. - 129 of them in California - are in danger of becoming extinct.

7.58,90

SECTION 7 NOTE

The highest average annual wind speed in California is 14.6 miles per hour, at Sandberg (Los Angeles County).

The lowest average annual wind speed in California is 3.27 miles per hour, at Dry Canyon Reservoir (Los Angeles County).

7.59,90

SECTION 7 NOTE

According to the Federal Environmental Protection Agency, 295 waterways in California are polluted, only 1.7 percent of those in the nation. Seventeen of the 295 are badly contaminated by toxic wastes from sewage treatment plants and industrial facilities.

7.60,90

SECTION 7 NOTE

According to the California Department of Health Services, 100,000 Californian individuals and firms are registered with the U.S. Environmental Protection Administration for the purpose of producing hazardous waste. Approximately 26,000 firms ship hazardous waste off site for treatment or disposal. In 1987, 110,000 tons of hazardous waste was exported from the state.

7.61,90

SECTION 7 NOTE

All property in California is defined with respect to one of 3 points:
Properties south of San Luis Obispo: San Bernardino Meridian
Properties at the northern tip of the state: Humboldt (City) Meridian
Properties in between: Mt. Diablo Meridian
(Each property is referenced with a longitude and latitude with those points as a base.)

7.62,90

SECTION 7 NOTE

To stop poaching or to turn in a poacher,
call (800) 952-5400
Mon.-Fri. 8AM - 5PM
You may receive a $500 reward
if your tip leads to an arrest.
You need not give your name.

7.63,90

SECTION 7 NOTE

Two of the best bird watching places in the U.S. are the Klamath and the Tule Lake national wildlife refuges in Siskiyou County.

7.64,90

Public Lands

After decades of accumulating land for national and state parks and forests, federal and state agencies seem to be settling into a period of digesting and maintaining the huge holdings for which they are responsible. National forests cover 20 percent of the state, national parks 5 percent, and state parks slightly over 1 percent. Many of these vast governmental holdings receive inadequate funds for oversight and maintenance. Given the high federal budget deficit, it is unlikely that significant increases in appropriations for forests and parks are likely. Because of this financial squeeze a number of park and forest supporters now favor raising user fees so that those who enjoy our natural treasures will bear a larger share of the burden of maintaining them.

As California's population increases, particularly in the major metropolitan areas, more attention is being given to creating local and urban parks and recreation areas. About .5 percent of the state's land (568,000 acres) is now given over to such areas, the most intensively used in the state, with 440 million visits each year. City parks, in particular, have many users: an average of over 2,000 annually per acre of park. Such heavy use has prompted both federal and state governments to allocate funds for purchasing additional urban park and recreation sites. As urban development accelerates in the state, however, such sites are increasingly expensive and land for them more difficult to find.

California, even as it struggles to locate new sites for urban parks, must also contend with a significant threat to its existing forests and parks. Forestry officials in the state and elsewhere in the industrial world have detected damage to trees that is generally attributed to air pollution. Since the Los Angeles basin has some of the worst smog in the nation, the state may be facing a long-term problem of tree damage in forest land downwind from the basin.

With the rapid increase in the state's population continuing, pressures on wildlife and plant habitats grow more intense. Since 1987 three varieties of kangaroo rat have been added to the federal list of endangered wildlife species, along with several forms of marine life, including the Shasta crayfish and the California freshwater shrimp. The California Department of Fish and Game now produces its own list of endangered, threatened, and rare plants and wildlife.

County	Total County Land Area	% Land Area Gov't Owned	Federal Owner-ship	State Owner-ship	County Owner-ship	Local Agency Owner-ship	Total Gov't Owner-ship
OWNERSHIP OF PUBLIC LANDS IN CALIFORNIA BY COUNTY (in acres)							
Alameda	469,120	23.69	6,178.08	8,064.21	30,804.26	65,765.39	111,111.94
Alpine	462,720	92.58	425,926.10	1,882.50	543.05	3.80	428,355.45
Amador	379,520	25.61	76,987.16	4,374.53	2,039.21	13,820.87	97,221.77
Butte	1,064,320	17.95	151,198.61	23,662.37	7,432.65	8,643.05	190,936.71
Calaveras	657,280	23.46	128,552.53	6,725.79	3,207.08	15,731.06	154,216.46
Colusa	737,920	17.09	111,396.08	4,182.59	3,775.92	3,741.59	126,096.18
Contra Costa	469,760	13.61	9,722.24	10,230.21	10,379.00	33,629.88	63,959.33
Del Norte	641,920	73.51	451,743.13	18,315.72	1,494.07	351.86	471,904.58
El Dorado	1,096,960	48.44	513,830.40	8,601.14	5,632.12	3,386.09	531,449.75
Fresno	3,816,960	40.33	1,476,894.75	18,739.82	18,589.82	25,172.29	1,539,396.08
Glenn	842,880	27.35	217,726.90	2,316.51	5,612.14	5,161.56	230,517.11
Humboldt	2,286,720	22.10	436,132.81	59,037.01	7,618.73	2,546.86	505,332.41
Imperial	2,741,760	60.80	1,499,402.44	106,034.16	15,579.65	46,058.34	1,667,074.59
Inyo	6,458,240	85.68	5,172,135.31	117,304.01	5,747.45	238,168.18	5,533,354.95
Kern	5,217,280	25.03	1,246,328.82	21,803.23	24,864.02	12,637.63	1,305,633.70
Kings	892,800	4.21	20,912.69	1,684.99	5,556.25	9,460.34	37,614.27
Lake	803,840	45.68	351,170.45	10,125.83	5,390.78	471.51	367,158.57
Lassen	2,910,080	63.46	1,771,503.08	68,956.62	4,608.42	1,772.01	1,846,840.13
Los Angeles	2,598,400	39.15	763,237.20	29,759.64	53,780.22	170,601.49	1,017,378.55
Madera	1,372,160	40.98	545,661.41	6,986.33	7,453.24	2,264.06	562,365.34
Marin	332,860	14.03	11,572.39	8,887.91	3,321.21	22,909.60	46,691.11
Mariposa	931,200	48.11	443,867.21	1,608.37	2,455.14	67.60	447,998.32
Mendocino	2,244,480	17.49	310,488.87	73,843.44	5,586.98	2,714.71	392,634.00
Merced	1,268,480	6.59	24,803.10	33,947.91	9,934.74	14,947.50	83,633.25
Modoc	2,618,880	66.76	1,729,305.31	13,220.08	4,682.31	1,286.44	1,748,494.14
Mono	1,937,920	79.11	1,452,195.20	14,767.19	3,139.12	63,040.50	1,533,142.01
Monterey	2,127,360	29.83	588,387.70	13,674.48	25,087.25	7,387.27	634,536.70
Napa	485,120	17.54	72,754.00	7,856.47	3,266.32	1,230.66	85,107.45
Nevada	625,920	28.33	159,486.40	5,742.86	2,605.11	9,499.33	177,333.70
Orange	500,480	22.96	64,807.56	7,317.21	8,628.10	34,145.12	114,897.99
Placer	911,360	34.50	298,532.17	5,039.93	5,016.02	5,847.17	314,435.29
Plumas	1,644,880	71.20	1,150,228.84	15,736.59	2,909.04	2,278.86	1,171,153.33
Riverside	4,593,280	59.10	2,489,120.43	100,155.08	26,326.52	112,626.59	2,714,455.23
Sacramento	629,120	8.83	15,278.55	10,545.43	13,175.42	16,528.22	55,527.62
San Benito	893,440	14.02	115,039.27	3,314.28	2,320.37	4,602.62	125,276.54
San Bernardino	12,883,840	78.17	9,619,763.18	348,063.69	44,580.40	58,269.16	10,070,951.43
San Diego	2,723,300	50.45	750,693.36	487,679.60	14,001.07	121,434.85	1,373,808.88
San Francisco	28,800	48.64	4,224.42	1,209.19	8,197.71	377.84	14,009.16
San Joaquin	901,760	5.18	9,854.50	7,732.35	11,284.41	17,826.25	46,697.51
San L. Obispo	2,122,240	16.61	308,359.70	20,340.02	20,872.51	2,982.30	352,554.53
San Mateo	290,560	18.43	274.60	7,596.78	36,370.98	9,294.88	53,537.24
Santa Barbara	1,752,320	49.66	838,546.23	6,815.20	8,340.36	16,600.38	870,802.17
Santa Clara	833,280	10.85	10,717.50	22,134.35	21,603.89	25,944.10	90,399.84
Santa Cruz	280,960	12.65	152.31	25,503.54	3,004.09	6,868.32	32,528.26
Shasta	2,430,720	41.73	978,474.02	25,070.39	6,594.77	4,308.15	1,014,447.33
Sierra	613,120	62.26	374,539.00	4,320.67	1,975.95	886.38	381,772.00
Siskiyou	4,039,680	62.91	2,516,443.61	7,977.24	9,312.01	7,861.45	2,541,594.64
Solano	529,280	8.93	15,553.37	16,358.67	3,742.51	11,611.57	47,266.12
Sonoma	1,010,560	4.03	12,355.36	14,061.12	10,102.76	4,179.68	40,698.92
Stanislaus	960,000	5.56	16,367.50	3,205.83	15,223.74	18,532.37	53,329.44
Sutter	388,480	3.88	2,591.70	5,505.31	4,549.22	2,147.89	15,064.12
Tehama	1,904,640	27.12	460,159.30	50,043.35	2,549.32	1,684.28	516,436.25
Trinity	2,042,240	72.35	1,465,593.16	4,741.00	4,080.15	3,179.74	1,477,594.05
Tulare	3,096,320	51.79	1,558,008.18	13,813.15	17,898.42	13,938.62	1,603,658.37
Tuolumne	1,455,360	77.01	1,089,237.70	6,036.54	17,442.66	8,116.77	1,120,833.67
Ventura	1,184,640	54.50	621,395.81	8,854.54	6,073.66	9,261.73	645,585.74
Yolo	661,760	8.97	31,510.00	7,117.36	4,865.66	15,874.30	59,367.32
Yuba	407,680	27.00	86,352.30	14,831.59	3,725.07	5,152.02	110,060.98
State Totals	100,206,720	50.25	46,465,167	1,953,456	617,132	1,321,719	50,357,471

* County statistics do not fully account for recent increases in Federal land totals.
8.1,90 Source: U.S. Bureau of Land Management, *Public Land Statistics*.

REAL PROPERTY OF THE U.S. GOVERNMENT IN CALIFORNIA, BY AGENCY, 1987	
Department or Agency	**Area (acres)**
U.S. Government Total	**46,465,163**
Department of Agriculture	**21,162,484**
Forest Service	21,162,055
Other	429
Department of Defense	**2,881,123**
Air Force	463,164
Army	905,277
Corps of Engineers	77,283
Navy	1,512,682
Department of Energy	**66,723**
USN Petroleum Oil Shale Reserve	58,611
Other	8,112
Department of the Interior	**22,266,555**
Bureau of Land Management	17,149,299
National Park Service	4,498,787
Bureau of Reclamation	440,703
Fish and Wildlife Service	177,651
Bureau of Indian Affairs	103
Other	12.3
Department of Transportation	**2,807**
Coast Guard	876
Federal Aviation Administration	1,931
Other Departmental Agencies	
National Aeronautics and Space Administration	1,163
International Communications Agency	1,761
Veterans Administration	2,266

8.2,90 Source: U.S. General Services Administration, unpublished data, 1989.

CALIFORNIA COASTLINE		
	Statute Miles	**Kilometers**
General Coastline	840	1,352
Tidal Shoreline*	3,427	5,514

*   Includes shoreline of outer coast, offshore islands, sounds, bays, rivers, & creeks to the head of tidewater or where tidewaters narrow to 100 feet.
8.3,90 Source: U.S. National Oceanic & Atmospheric Administration, *The Coastline of the U.S.*, 1975.

SECTION 8 NOTE
The Medicine Lake Volcano (east of Mt. Shasta) is the largest volcano cone in the West. It spreads over 900 square miles.

8.4,90

NATIONAL FOREST AREAS IN CALIFORNIA
(part 1)

Name	Headquarters	Total Area (acres)
National Forests		
Angeles	Pasadena	693,667
Calaveras Big Tree	Sonora	380
Cleveland	San Diego	566,850
El Dorado	Placerville	884,635
Inyo	Bishop	1,940,122
Klamath	Yreka	1,886,725
Lassen	Susanville	1,374,945
Los Padres	Goleta	1,962,743
Mendocino	Willows	1,079,971
Modoc	Alturas	1,979,327
Plumas	Quincy	1,400,895
Rogue River*	Medford, OR	61,031
San Bernardino	San Bernardino	818,999
Sequoia	Porterville	1,178,367
Shasta	Redding	1,634,896
Sierra	Fresno	1,412,801
Siskiyou*	Grants Pass, OR	39,689
Six Rivers	Eureka	1,118,247
Stanislaus	Sonora	1,090,039
Tahoe	Nevada City	1,211,425
Toiyabe*	Reno, NV	694,988
Trinity	Redding	1,179,098
Total National Forests		**24,209,840**
Purchase Units**		
El Dorado	Placerville	180
Northern Redwood	Eureka	145,290
Total Purchase Units		**145,470**
Utilization Projects†		
Butte Valley	Yreka	18,425
San Joaquin Pasture	Porterville	797
Total Utilization Projects		**19,222**
Research-Experiment Areas		
Fire Research Laboratory	Riverside	9
Institute of Forest Genetics	Placerville	194
San Joaquin	O'Neals	4,580
Total Research-Experiment Areas		**4,783**

* Unit is in two or more states.
** Designated for purchase.
† Areas for farm tenants.
8.5.1,90 Source: U.S. Dept of Agriculture, Forest Service, *Land Areas of the National Forest System, 1988.*

NATIONAL FOREST AREAS IN CALIFORNIA
(part 2)

Name	Headquarters	Total Area (acres)
Other Forest Areas*		
Angeles	Pasadena	468
Cleveland	San Diego	16
El Dorado	Placerville	1,683
Felton Forest Station	San Francisco	43
Humboldt Nursery Site	Eureka	223
Inyo	Bishop	649
Klamath	Yreka	716
Lassen	Susanville	267
Los Padres	Santa Barbara	355
Mendocino	Willows	12
Modoc	Alturas	95
Plant Introduction Station	Willows	209
Plumas	Quincy	521
San Bernardino	San Bernardino	707
Sequoia	Porterville	29
Shasta	Redding	84
Sierra	Fresno	134
Stanislaus	Sonora	279
Tahoe	Nevada City	123
Trinity	Redding	33
Total Other Areas		**6,646**
State Total - All Forest Area		**24,385,961**

* Areas not in a National Forest but administered by the Forest Service.
8.5.2,90 Source: U.S. Dept. of Agriculture, Forest Service, *Land Areas of the National Forest System,* 1988.

HIGHEST, LOWEST, AND MEAN ELEVATIONS

		Elevation	
		Feet	**Meters**
Highest Point	Mount Whitney	14,494	4,421
Lowest Point	Death Valley	-282	-86
Mean	State	2,900	885

8.6,90 Source: U.S. Geological Survey, *Elevations & Distances in the U.S., 1980.*

SECTION 8 NOTE

California has 9,100,000 acres (9% of the state) which have not been surveyed.

8.7,90

NATIONAL WILDERNESS AREAS IN CALIFORNIA

Name	National Forest	Total Area (acres)
Agua Tibia	Cleveland	15,933
Ansel Adams	Inyo	78,777
Ansel Adams	Sierra	151,483
Bucks Lake	Plumas	21,000*
Caribou	Lassen	20,546
Carson-Iceberg	Stanislaus and Toiyabe	158,948*
Castle Crags	Shasta	11,048
Chanchelulla	Trinity	8,200*
Cucamonga	San Bernardino	8,581
Cucamonga	Angeles	4,200
Desolation	El Dorado	63,475
Dick Smith	Los Padres	67,800
Dinky Lakes	Sierra	30,000*
Dome Land	Sequoia	93,861
Emigrant	Stanislaus	112,338
Golden Trout	Inyo	194,318
Golden Trout	Sequoia	111,146
Granite Chief	Tahoe	25,748
Hauser	Cleveland	8,091
Hoover	Inyo	9,528
Hoover	Toiyabe	39,094
Ishi	Lassen	42,866
Jennie Lakes	Sequoia	10,289
John Muir	Inyo and Sierra	581,143
Kaiser	Sierra	22,700
Manchesna Mountain	Los Padres	20,000
Marble Mountain	Klamath	242,464
Mokelumne	El Dorado	61,831
Mokelumne	Stanislaus	22,277
Mokelumne	Toiyabe	16,500*
Monarch	Sierra and Sequoia	44,896
Mt. Shasta	Shasta and Trinity	37,710
North Fork	Six Rivers	8,100*
Pine Creek	Cleveland	13,686
Red Butte	Rogue River	16,150*
Russian Peak	Klamath	12,000*
San Gabriel	Angeles	36,118
San Gorgonio	San Bernardino	58,669
San Jacinto	San Bernardino	33,408
San Mateo Canyon	Cleveland	39,540*
San Rafael	Los Padres	151,170
Santa Lucia	Los Padres	21,704
Santa Rosa	San Bernardino	19,803
Sheep Mountain	Angeles and San Bernardino	42,367
Siskiyou	Klamath, Siskiyou and Six Rivers	153,000*
Snow Mountain	Mendocino	37,000*
South Sierra	Inyo and Sierra	82,324
South Warner	Modoc	70,729
Thousand Lakes	Lassen	16,335
Trinity Alps	Klamath, Shasta, Six Rivers and Trinity	513,100*
Ventana	Los Padres	167,489
Yolla Bolly-Middle Eel	Mendocino	101,553
Yolla Bolly-Middle Eel	Trinity	38,640
Yolla Bolly	Six Rivers	11,433
State Total		**3,981,109**

* Estimates pending final map completions.

8.8,90 Source: U.S. Dept. of Agriculture, Forest Service, *Land Areas of the National Forest System,* 1988.

ESTIMATED FRESHWATER WETLAND ACRES			
County	Public	Private	Total
Alameda	400	0	400
Butte	8,375	36,992	45,367
Colusa	15,338	17,684	33,022
Contra Costa	0	5,263	5,263
Del Norte	2,560	4,975	7,535
El Dorado	0	3,069	3,069
Fresno	5,198	0	5,198
Glenn	5,112	5,896	11,008
Humboldt	2,951	8,700	11,651
Imperial	8,703	3,400	12,103
Kern	14,395	20,692	35,087
Lassen	1,000	16,000	17,000
Los Angeles	300	300	600
Madera	0	6,574	6,574
Marin	5,330	0	5,330
Merced	21,561	96,762	118,323
Modoc	14,450	0	14,450
Monterey	2,700	0	2,700
Napa	0	1,000	1,000
Nevada	1,000	3,000	4,000
Orange	300	0	300
Placer	0	1,535	1,535
Plumas	3,000	2,000	5,000
Riverside	0	2,300	2,300
Sacramento	3,160	17,950	21,110
San Bernardino	520	480	1,000
San Diego	480	0	480
San Joaquin	0	15,787	15,787
San Luis Obispo	1,090	0	1,090
San Mateo	600	0	600
Santa Barbara	230	0	230
Sierra	2,000	3,000	5,000
Siskiyou	33,750	0	33,750
Solano	11,587	46,000	57,587
Stanislaus	0	6,574	6,574
Sutter	2,590	18,159	20,749
Tulare	4,795	6,900	11,695
Ventura	500	300	800
Yolo	0	34,473	34,473
Yuba	0	6,139	6,139
Total	172,915	391,903	564,818

8.9.90 Source: California Dept. of Forestry; *FRRAP Information and Analysis System.*

SECTION 8 NOTE
In 1988, 30 million people made recreational visits to Federal Bureau of Land Management lands in California.

8.10,90

NATIONAL PARKS AND OTHER NATIONAL PARK SERVICE AREAS CALIFORNIA, 1987

Name	Area in Acres		
	Total	Federal	Non-Federal
National Parks			
Channel Islands	249,353.77	64,254.62	185,099.15
Kings Canyon	461,901.20	461,845.02	56.18
Lassen Volcanic	106,372.36	106,366.47	5.89
Redwood	110,178.03	75,324.96	34,853.07
Sequoia	402,482.38	401,877.16	605.22
Yosemite	761,170.20	759,465.25	1,704.95
National Monuments			
Cabrillo	143.94	143.94	-
Death Valley	2,067,627.68†	2,048,928.88	18,698.80
Devils Postpile	798.46	798.46	-
Joshua Tree	559,954.50	549,634.12	10,320.38
Lava Beds	46,559.87	46,559.87	-
Muir Woods	553.55	522.98	30.57
Pinnacles	16,245.44	1,654.62	10.82
National Seashore			
Point Reyes	71,045.77	64,426.97	6,618.80
National Trail System			
Pacific Crest Trail 2,600 miles	NA	NA	NA
National Wild and Scenic Rivers††			
American River, North Fork (38.3)	13,430.00	8,790.00	4,640.00
Eel River (394)	NA	NA	NA
Feather River, Middle Fork (77.6)	19,873.00	16,277.00	3,646.00
Klamath River (286	NA	NA	NA
Lower American River (23)	NA	NA	NA
Smith River (329)	NA	NA	NA
Trinity River (203)	NA	NA	NA
Toulumne River (83)	NA	NA	NA
National Recreation Areas			
Golden Gate	73,116.84	27,203.31	45,913.53
Santa Monica Mountains	150,000.00	11,921.68	138,078.32
Whiskeytown-Shasta-Trinity	42,503.46	42,448.23	55.23
National Historic Sites			
Eugene O'Neill	13.19	-	13.19
Fort Point	29.00	29.00	-
John Muir	8.90	8.90	-

†   1,938,135.37 acres in California; 110,812.73 acres in Nevada.
††   River mileage in parentheses.
    8.11,90 Source: U.S. National Park Service, *The National Park Index, 1987.*

VISITORS TO NATIONAL PARKS IN CALIFORNIA		
Year	Number of Visitors (in millions)	Percent of Total Visits to National Parks
1978	22.6	10%
1979	23.7	12%
1980	31.0	14%
1981	33.5	14%
1982	34.0	14%
1983	30.9	13%
1984	31.8	13%
1985	33.6	13%
1986	38.2	14%
1987	39.9	14%
1988	39.2	14%

Note: Yosemite is the most popular National Park in California with over 3.2 million visitors a year. The Golden Gate National Recreation Area draws 21.8 million visitors a year.
8.12,90 Source: U.S. National Park Service, *Statistical Abstract, 1988*.

FEDERAL BUREAU OF LAND MANAGEMENT WILDERNESS AREAS AND NATIONAL GAME PRESERVES	
Name	Area (acres)
Santa Lucia	1,733
Ishi	240
Manchesna Mountain	120
Trinity Alps	4,623
Yolla Bolly-Middle Eel	8,500
National Game Preserve	
Tahquitz	27,573

8.13,90 Source: U.S. Dept. of Agriculture, Forest Service, *Land Areas of the National Forest System, 1988*, and U.S. Bureau of Land Management, *Public Land Statistics, 1988*.

SECTION 8 NOTE
There are 1,884 wild free-roaming horses and 1,438 burros on Federal public lands in California.

8.14,90

SECTION 8 NOTE
California has an estimated 6,210 antelope, 385 bears, 3,205 bighorn sheep, 101,000 deer, 920 elk, 3,400 javeline wild boar, and 1,650 turkeys on Federal public lands.

8.15,90

NATIONAL WILDLIFE REFUGES††		
Name	**Acres**	**Headquarters Address**
Cibola	NA	Box AP, Blythe, CA, 92225*
Havasu	NA	Box A, Needles, CA 92363*
Imperial	NA	Box 72217, Martinez Lake, AZ 85364*
Kern		Box 670, Delano, CA 93216
Blue Ridge	NA	
Hopper Mountain	1,871	
Kern	10,618	
Pixley	5,187	
Seal Beach	911	
Klamath Basin Refuges		Rt. 1, Box 74, Tulelake, CA 96134
Bear Valley†	4,120	
Clear Lake	33,440	
Klamath Forest††	16,377	
Lower Klamath†	51,713	
Tule Lake	38,908	
Upper Klamath†	12,457	
Modoc	6,283	Box 1610, Alturas, CA 96101
Sacramento Valley Refuges		Rt. 1, Box 311, Willows, CA 95988
Butte Sink	2,800	
Colusa	4,040	
Delevan	5,633	
Sacramento	10,793	
Sutter	2,591	
Salton Sea		P.O. Box 120, Calipatria, CA 92223
Salton Sea	35,484	
Tijuana Slough	1,056	
San Francisco Bay		Box 524, Newark, CA 94560
Antioch Dunes	55	
Castle Rock	7	
Ellicott Slough	130	
Farallones	211	
Humboldt Bay	500	
Salinas River	518	
San Francisco Bay	20,000	
San Pablo Bay	12,000	
San Luis		Box 2176, Los Banos, CA 93635
Grasslands	22,000	
Kesterson	5,900	
Merced	2,562	
San Luis	7,340	

* Partly in Arizona.   † Partly in Oregon.
†† Open to Visitors, except Butte Sink, Grasslands, and Kesterson.
8.16,90 Source: U.S. Fish and Wildlife Service, *National Wildlife Refuges*, 1988.

SECTION 8 NOTE

For an exhaustive list of place names in the Golden State, see Edwin G. Gudde, CALIFORNIA PLACE NAMES (University of California Press).
8.17,90

CALIFORNIA STATE PARKS, RESERVES, HISTORIC PARKS AND RECREATION AREAS, 1988.		
Name	**County**	**Area (in acres)**
Admiral William Standley SRA	Mendocino	45.22
Ahjunawi Lava Springs SP	Shasta	6,370.58
Alamitos Beach Project	Orange	0.90
American River Bikeway Project	Sacramento	59.17
Anderson Marsh Project	Lake	872.01
Andrew Molera State Park	Monterey	4,748.98
Angel Island State Park	Marin-San Francisco	755.71
Annadel State Park	Sonoma	4,915.91
Ano Nuevo State Reserve	San Mateo	4,088.87
Antelope Valley California Poppy Reserve	Kern	1,706.22
Antelope Valley Indian Museum Project	Los Angeles	387.34
Anza-Borrego Desert State Park	Imperial-San Diego	559,451.14
Armstrong Redwoods SR	Sonoma	752.00
Asilomar State Beach	Monterey	105.44
Atascadero State Beach	San Luis Obispo	125.18
Auburn SRA	Placer-El Dorado	42,000.00
Austin Creek SRA	Sonoma	4,233.99
Azalea SR	Humboldt	30.00
Backbone Trail Project	Los Angeles	1,296.02
Baldwin Hills SRA (K. Hahn)	Los Angeles	309.72
Bale Grist Mill SHP	Napa	0.75
Big Rock Beach (Malibu)	Los Angeles	0.43
Bean Hollow State Beach	San Mateo	44.00
Benbow Lake SRA	Humboldt	975.37
Benicia Capitol SHP	Solano	0.86
Benicia SRA	Solano	455.18
Bethany Reservoir SRA	Alameda	609.23
Bidwell Mansion SHP	Butte	5.20
Bidwell River Park Project	Butte	180.00
Big Basin Redwoods State Park	Santa Cruz-San Mateo	17,035.43
Bodie SHP	Mono	486.70
Bolsa Chica State BEach	Orange	169.75
Border Field State Park	San Diego	396.88

8.18.1,90
See part 8 for source, notes, and abbreviations.

CALIFORNIA STATE PARKS, RESERVES, HISTORIC PARKS AND RECREATION AREAS, 1988		
Name	**County**	**Area (in acres)**
Bothe-Napa Valley State Park	Napa	1,923.22
Brannan Island SRA	Sacramento	225.00
Bufano Peace Statue Project	Sonoma	0.25
Burleigh Murray Ranch Project	San Mateo	1,325.45
Burton Creek State Park	Placer	1,882.83
Butano State Park	San Mateo	2,186.49
Calaveras Big Trees State Park	Calaveras-Tuolumne	5,995.49
California Citrus SHP	Riverside	173.04
Candlestick Point SRA	San Francisco	153.28
Cardiff State Beach	San Diego	22.61
Carlsbad State Beach	San Diego	24.88
Carmel River State Beach	Monterey	296.69
Carnegie SVRA	San Joaquin-Alameda	1,539.82
Carpinteria State Beach	Santa Barbara	53.06
Caspar Headlands State Beach	Mendocino	2.95
Caspar Headlands State Reserve	Mendocino	2.70
Castaic Lake SRA	Los Angeles	3,101.95
Castle Crags State Park	Shasta-Siskiyou	4,381.61
Castle Rock State Park	Santa Cruz	3,515.00
Caswell Memorial State Park	San Joaquin	258.13
Cayucos State Beach	San Luis Obispo	15.63
China Camp State Park	Marin	1,514.30
Chino Hills State Park	Orange-Riverside-San Bernardino	10,194.44
Chumash Painted Caves SRA	Santa Barbara	7.50
Clay Pit SVRA	Butte	220.14
Clear Lake State Park	Lake	565.57
Colonel Allensworth SHP	Tulare	234.84
Columbia SHP	Tuolumne	278.34
Colusa-Sacramento River SRA	Colusa	66.50
Corona del Mar State Beach	Orange	29.57
Crystal Cove State Park	Orange	4,035.13
Cuyamaca Rancho State Park	San Diego	24,698.75
D.L. Bliss State Park	El Dorado	1,236.93
Dan Blocker Beach Project	Los Angeles	13.12
Del Norte Coast Redwoods State Park	Del Norte	6,375.02
Delta Meadows	Sacramento	133.90

8.18.2,90
See part 8 for source, notes, and abbreviations.

CALIFORNIA STATE PARKS, RESERVES, HISTORIC PARKS AND RECREATION AREAS, 1988

Name	County	Area (in acres)
Dockweiler State Beach	Los Angeles	90.88
Doheny State Beach	Orange	254.59
Donner Memorial State Park	Nevada-Placer	351.48
Drum Barracks Project	Los Angeles	0.44
Durham Ferry SRA	San Joaquin	183.39
East Bay Shoreline Project	Alameda	33.00
El Capitan State Beach	Santa Barbara	132.84
El Presidio De Santa Barbara SHP	Santa Barbara	4.33
El Pueblo De Los Angeles SHP	Los Angeles	5.42
Emerald Bay State Park	El Dorado	593.19
Emma Wood State Beach	Ventura	113.15
Empire Mine SHP	Nevada	800.61
Folsom Lake SRA	El Dorado-Placer-Sacramento	17,808.98
Forest of Nisene Marks State Park	Santa Cruz	10,120.90
Fort Humboldt SHP	Humboldt	17.83
Fort Ross SHP	Sonoma	1,198.27
Fort Tejon SHP	Kern	205.50
Franks Tract SRA	Contra Costa	3,531.83
Fremont Ford SRA	Merced	114.00
Fremont Peak State Park	Monterey-San Benito	244.23
Garcia Property Project	Santa Cruz	143.52
Garrapata Beach Project	Monterey	2,810.18
Gaviota State Park	Santa Barbara	2,757.17
Gazos Creek Angling Access	San Mateo	5.94
George J. Hatfield SRA	Merced	46.50
Governor's Mansion	Sacramento	0.77
Gray Whale Cove State Beach	San Mateo	3.10
Greenwood Creek Project	Mendocino	47.22
Grizzly Creek Angling Access	San Mateo	393.45
Grover Hot Springs State Park	Alpine	538.54
Half Moon Bay State Beach	San Mateo	380.65
Harry A. Merlo SRA	Humboldt	830.00
Hearst San Simeon SHM	San Luis Obispo	161.16
Hendy Woods State Park	Mendocino	816.26
Henry Cowell Redwoods State Park	Santa Cruz	4,120.45
Henry W. Coe State Park	Santa Clara-Stanislaus	692.02

8.18.3,90
See part 8 for source, notes, and abbreviations.

CALIFORNIA STATE PARKS, RESERVES, HISTORIC PARKS AND RECREATION AREAS, 1988

Name	County	Area (in acres)
Hollister Hills SVRA	San Benito	3,323.99
Humboldt Lagoons Project	Humboldt	1,503.58
Humboldt Redwoods State Park	Humboldt	50,604.59
Hungry Valley SVRA	Los Angeles-Ventura	17,451.73
Huntington State Beach	Orange	128.95
Indian Grinding Rock SHP	Amador	135.79
Indio Hills Palms	Riverside	2,206.01
Irving Finch River Access	Glenn	4.92
Jack London SHP	Sonoma	990.69
Jedediah Smith Redwoods State Park	Del Norte	9,793.03
John Little State Reserve	Monterey	21.00
John Marsh Home Project	Contra Costa	16.45
Jug Handle State Reserve	Mendocino	772.16
Julia Pfeiffer Burns State Park	Monterey	3,562.16
Kenneth Hahn SRA	Los Angeles	309.72
Kings Beach SRA	Placer	7.74
Kruse Rhododendron State Reserve	Sonoma	317.00
L.A. County Riding & Hiking Trails Project	Los Angeles	1.76
Lake County Estates Project	El Dorado	777.73
Lake del Valle SRA	Alameda	3,731.86
Lake Earl/Lake Talawa Project	Del Norte	5,018.03
Lake Elsinore SRA	Riverside	2,975.78
Lake Oroville SRA	Butte	28,753.27
Lake Perris SRA	Riverside	5,239.98
Lake Valley SRA	El Dorado	150.00
La Purisma Mission SHP	Santa Barbara	966.98
Las Tunas State Beach	Los Angeles	3.24
Leo Carrillo State Beach	Los Angeles	2,261.74
Leucadia State Beach	San Diego	10.60
Lighthouse Field State Beach	Santa Cruz	37.60
Little River State Beach	Humboldt	111.63
Los Angeles State and County Arboretum State Reserve	Los Angeles	111.00
Los Banos Creek Project	Merced	2,475.00
Los Encinos SHP	Los Angeles	4.73
Los Osos Oaks State Reserve	San luis Obispo	85.10
MacKerricher State Park	Mendocino	2,175.42
Mailliard Redwoods State Reserve	Mendocino	242.00
Malakoff Diggins SHP	Nevada	2,884.73
Malibu Bluff Project	Los Angeles	169.66

8.18.4,90
See part 8 for source, notes, and abbreviations.

CALIFORNIA STATE PARKS, RESERVES, HISTORIC PARKS AND RECREATION AREAS, 1988

Name	County	Area (in acres)
Malibu Creek State Park	Los Angeles	5,395.07
Malibu Lagoon State Beach	Los Angeles	169.66
Manchester State Beach	Mendocino	5,268.97
Mandalay State Beach	Ventura	92.12
Manhattan State Beach	Los Angeles	50.66
Manresa State Beach	Santa Cruz	138.24
Marina Beach Project	Monterey	170.71
Marshall Gold Discovery SHP	El Dorado	274.76
McArthur-Burney Falls Memorial SP	Shasta	761.11
McConnell SRA	Merced	74.26
McGrath State Beach	Ventura	312.39
Mendocino Headlands State Park	Mendocino	379.16
Mendocino Woodlands Project	Mendocino	720.00
Millerton Lake SRA	Fresno-Madera	6,553.75
Mono Lake Tufa State Reserve	Mono	17,000.00
Montana de Oro State Park	San Luis Obispo	8,066.64
Montara State Beach	San Mateo	787.14
Monterey State Beach	Monterey	35.03
Monterey SHP	Monterey	7.58
Montgomery Woods State Reserve	Mendocino	1,323.80
Moonlight State Beach	San Diego	12.70
Morro Bay State Park	San Luis Obispo	1,964.69
Morro Strand State Beach	San Luis Obispo	33.81
Moss Landing State Beach	Monterey	60.35
Mount Diablo State Park	Contra Costa	17,336.84
Mount San Jacinto State Park	Riverside	714.17
Mount Tamalpais State Park	Marin	6,220.20
Natural Bridges State Beach	Santa Cruz	58.88
New Brighton State Beach	Santa Cruz	90.49
Ocotillo Wells SVRA	San Diego	21,107.76
Old Sacramento SHP	Sacramento	291.08
Old Town San Diego SHP	San Diego	26.85
Olompali SHP	Marin	700.00

8.18.5,90
See part 8 for source, notes, and abbreviations

CALIFORNIA STATE PARKS, RESERVES, HISTORIC PARKS AND RECREATION AREAS, 1988

Name	County	Area (in acres)
Oxnard State Beach	Ventura	25.60
Pacifica Beach Project	San Mateo	20.73
Palomar Mountain State Park	San Diego	1,897.38
Pan Pacific Park Project	Los Angeles	28.29
Patrick's Point State Park	Humboldt	634.75
Paul M. Dimmick WC	Mendocino	11.81
Pelican State Beach	Del Norte	5.15
Pescadero State Beach	San Mateo	637.89
Petaluma Adaobe SHP	Sonoma	41.43
Pfeiffer Big Sur State Park	Monterey	842.95
Picacho SRA	Imperial	6,758.69
Pigeon Point Project	San Mateo	10.70
Pio Pico SHP	Los Angeles	3.42
Pismo Dunes SVRA	San Luis Obispo	3,029.13
Pismo State Beach	San Luis Obispo	1,057.14
Placerita Canyon State Park	Los Angeles	341.72
Plumas-Eureka State Park	Plumas	4,423.30
Point Dume State Beach	Los Angeles	62.98
Point Lobos State Reserve	Monterey	1,355.12
Point Montara Project	San Mateo	6.00
Point Mugu State Park	Ventura	13,846.10
Point Sal State Beach	Santa Barbara	84.03
Point Sur SHP	Monterey	33.58
Pomponio State Beach	San Mateo	420.68
Portola State Park	San Mateo	2,294.32
Prairie Creek Redwoods State Park	Del Norte-Humboldt	13,971.90
Providence Mountains SRA	San Bernardino	5,250.46
Railtown 1897 SHP	Tuolumne	23.90
Redondo State Beach	Los Angeles	26.05
Red Rock Canyon State Park	Kern	6,103.77
Refugio State Beach	Santa Barbara	151.52
Reynolds Wayside Campground	Mendocino	65.80
Richardson Grove State Park	Humboldt	1,454.16
Rincon Point Project	Santa Barbara-Ventura	3.35
Robert H. Meyer Memorial SB	Los Angeles	37.01

8.18.6,90
See part 8 for source, notes, and abbreviations.

CALIFORNIA STATE PARKS, RESERVES, HISTORIC PARKS AND RECREATION AREAS, 1988		
Name	County	Area (in acres)
Robert Louis Stevenson Staate Park	Napa-Lake-Sonoma	3,710.92
Robert W. Crown Memorial State Beach	Alameda	132.22
Royal Palms State Beach	Los Angeles	18.07
Russian Gulch State Park	Mendocino	1,306.23
Saddleback Butte State Park	Los Angeles	3,341.13
Salinas River State Beach	Monterey	245.94
Salton Sea SRA	Riverside-Imperial	16,439.67
Salt Point State Park	Sonoma	5,676.18
Samuel P. Taylor State Park	Marin	2,708.59
San Bruno Mountains Project	San Mateo	297.60
San Buenaventura State Beach	Ventura	113.51
San Clemente State Beach	Orange	117.60
San Elijo State Beach	San Diego	42.21
San Gregorio State Beach	San Mateo	171.60
San Joaquin Valley Agricultural Museum	San Joaquin	Structure only
San Juan Bautista SHP	San Benito	6.12
San Luis Island Project	Merced	2,712.00
San Luis Reservoir SRA	Merced	23,551.00
San Mateo County Trails Project	San Mateo	2.38
San Mateo Riding and Hiking Trails Project	San Mateo	0.06
San Onofre State Beach	San Diego	2,106.79
San Pasqual Battlefield SHP	San Diego	56.49
San Simeon State Beach	San Luis Obispo	542.13
Santa Cruz County Trails Project	Santa Cruz-Santa Clara	220.35
Santa Cruz Mission SHP	Santa Cruz	1.94
Santa Monica/Pacific Ocean Park Project	Los Angeles	3.54
Santa Monica State Beach	Los Angeles	49.15
Santa Susana Mountains Project	Los Angeles	428.19
Schooner Gulch Project	Mendocino	53.62
Seacliff State Beach	Santa Cruz	85.14
Seccombe Lake SURA	San Bernardino	42.98
Shasta SHP	Shasta	20.61
Silver Strand State Beach	San Diego	339.39
Silverwood Lake SRA	San Diego	2,201.01
Sinkyone Wilderness State Park	Mendocino	6,965.02
Smithe Redwoods State Reserve	Mendocino	628.03
Sonoma Coast State Beach	Sonoma	5,052.87

8.18.7,90
See part 8 for source, notes, and abbreviations.

CALIFORNIA STATE PARKS, RESERVES, HISTORIC, PARKS AND RECREATION AREAS, 1988		
Name	County	Area (in acres)
Sonoma SHP	Sonoma	63.57
South Carlsbad State Beach	San Diego	123.71
South Yuba River Project	Nevada	1,772.15
Standish-Hickey SRA	Mendocino	1,023.88
Stanford House SHP	Sacramento	0.88
State Indian Museum	Sacramento	Incl. in Sutter's Fort
Stillwater Cove Project	Sonoma	36.27
Stone Lake Project	Sacramento	1,089.52
Sugarloaf Ridge State Park	Napa-Sonoma	2,692.34
Sugar Pine Point State Park	El Dorado	2,011.37
Sunset State Beach	Santa Cruz	301.86
Sutter's Fort SHP	Sacramento	5.80
Tahoe SRA	Placer	54.84
Thornton State Beach	San Mateo	58.01
Tomales Bay State Park	Marin	2,044.28
Topanga State Beach	Los Angeles	31.21
Topanga State Park	Los Angeles	8,964.02
Torrey Pines State Beach	San Diego	41.23
Torrey Pines State Reserve	San Diego	1,525.24
Trinidad State Beach	Humboldt	158.70
Tule Elk State Reserve	Kern	945.66
Turlock Lake SRA	Stanislaus	408.88
Twin Lakes State Beach	Santa Cruz	94.58
Van Damme State Park	Mendocino	2,169.20
Verdugo Mountain Project	Los Angeles	251.41
Ward Creek Project	Placer	173.00
Washoe Meadows State Park	El Dorado	627.73
Wassama Round House SHP	Madera	26.61
Watts Tower Project	Los Angeles	0.11
Weaverville Joss House SHP	Trinity	3.23
Westport Union Landing SB	Mendocino	40.95
Wilder Ranch State Park	Santa Cruz	4,511.34
Will Rogers State Beach	Los Angeles	86.20
Will Rogers SHP	Los Angeles	189.12
William B. Ide Adobe SHP	Tehama	3.95
William Randolph Hearst Memorial SB	San Luis Obispo	8.14
Windemere Point Project	Somoma	20.56
Woodland Opera House SHP	Yolo	0.26
Woodson Bridge SRA	Tehama	323.47
Zmudowski State Beach	Monterey	194.41
Total		1,280,782.80

* Classified units not yet under the Dept. of Parks and Recreation Management.
Abbreviations: SB: State Beach; SP: State Park; SR: State Reserve; SHM: State Historical Monument; SHP: State Historic Park; SRA: State Recreational Area; SURA: State Urban Recreation Area; SVRA: State Vehicular Recreation Area; WC: Wayside Campgrounds.
8.18.8,90 Source: California Dept. of Parks and Recreation, Acquisition Division.

CALIFORNIA PARKS AND RECREATION AREAS*

California has 12% of the State Park and Recreation land in the lower 48 states.
California has 9% of the State Park and Recreation land in the U.S.
10% of all visits to all State Park and Recreation areas occurs in California.
California collects 10% of all the revenue paid by visitors to State Park and
Recreation areas in the U.S.

* Data as of 1987.
8.19,90 Source: *U.S. Statistical Abstract, 1989.*

ATTENDANCE AT STATE PARKS IN CALIFORNIA

Year*	Number of Visitors†	Percent Change from Prior Year
1959-1960	22,194,166	-
1969-1970	43,984,960	-
1979-1980	58,024,000	-
1980-1981	63,976,030	10.3%
1981-1982	63,079,294	-1.4%
1982-1983	61,282,517	-2.8%
1983-1984	65,810,720	7.4%
1984-1985	66,476,104	1.0%
1985-1986	69,050,988	3.9%
1986-1987	72,856,593	5.5%
1987-1988	72,540,158	-0.4%

* Fiscal year, July1-June 30.
† Includes paid and estimated free use.
8.20,90 Source: California Department of Parks and Recreation, *Statistical Report* and unpublished data.

SECTION 8 NOTE

In 1986-87 the visitors to local parks numbered 22,963,170.
8.21,90

MOST POPULAR STATE PARKS, 1988	
Name	**Attendance**
Old Town San Diego State Historic Park	3,961,050
Huntington State Beach	2,768,333
Sonoma Coast State Beach	2,275,258
Carlsbad State Beach	2,174,147
Folsom Lake State Recreational Area	2,081,332
San Buenaventura State Beach	2,044,304
Bolsa Chica State Beach	1,917,761
Seacliff State Beach	1,789,459
Cardiff State Beach	1,769,591
Half Moon Bay State Beach	1,686,883
Morro Bay State Beach	1,642,605
Lake Perris State Recreational Area	1,522,593
Leo Carrillo State Beach	1,249,243
Big Basin Redwoods State Park	1,212,605
Pismo State Beach	1,178,192
Mount Tamalpais State Park	1,135,524
Torrey Pines State Reserve	1,091,710
Twin Lakes State Beach	1,062,725
San Simeon State Historic Monument	1,053,894

8.22,90 Source: California Department of Parks and Recreation, unpublished data, 1989.

LOCAL PARKS AND RECREATION AREAS				
	Cities	**Counties**	**Special Districts**	**Total**
Number of Jurisdictions with parks & rec. areas	417	53	166	636
Number of Parks & Rec areas	5,489	1,170	1,079	7,738
Number of Acres (thousands)	129	257	83	568
Annual Attendance (millions)	265	54	120	440
Average Park Size (acres)	24	219	169	73
Number of Parks (acres) per 10,000 Residents	2.8(65)	0.5(105)	0.5(NA)	2.9(213)
Park Visits per Resident	13.4	2.2	5.3	16.5
Annual Visits per acre	2,056	213	656	NA
Park & Rec Budgets as a % of Gov't Budgets	5.0%	1.3%	1.6%	NA

8.23,90 Source: California Dept. of Parks and Recreation, *Local Parks and Recreation Agencies in California, A 1987 Survey.*

HISTORIC LANDMARKS AND POINTS OF HISTORICAL INTEREST			
County	California Historic Landmarks	Items on National Register of Historic Places	Points of Historic Interest
Alameda	32	102	36
Alpine	6	0	1
Amador	23	14	5
Butte	9	18	17
Calaveras	42	11	4
Colusa	3	4	3
Contra Costa	12	16	7
Del Norte	7	8	2
El Dorado	32	14	6
Fresno	7	30	11
Glenn	2	2	16
Humboldt	13	38	4
Imperial	12	8	3
Inyo	22	14	9
Kern	46	14	9
Kings	3	4	0
Lake	8	4	6
Lassen	6	3	3
Los Angeles	91	263	42
Madera	0	1	3
Marin	13	27	4
Mariposa	8	27	3
Mendocino	7	9	5
Merced	5	12	0
Modoc	12	13	4
Mono	2	2	22
Monterey	24	37	3
Napa	17	46	10
Nevada	19	15	29
Orange	23	70	19
Placer	20	10	15
Plumas	17	3	3
Riverside	16	30	52
Sacramento	58	54	9
San Benito	5	7	2
San Bernardino	33	30	109
San Diego	66	73	10
San Francisco	43	110	12
San Joaquin	23	26	5
San Luis Obispo	12	13	1
San Mateo	36	32	31
Santa Barbara	13	26	7
Santa Clara	41	70	58
Santa Cruz	6	31	5
Shasta	19	21	13
Sierra	4	6	3
Siskiyou	7	12	11
Solano	14	17	7
Sonoma	25	40	1
Stanislaus	5	5	7
Sutter	2	0	21
Tehama	4	7	1
Trinity	2	5	2
Tulare	8	7	0
Tuolumne	20	18	4
Ventura	12	20	2
Yolo	2	16	5
Yuba	6	9	10
State Totals*	984	1,521	406

* Multiple locations for some landmarks.

8.24,90 Source: Cal. Dept. of Parks and Rec., *Cal. Historical Landmarks*; U.S. Natl. Park Service, *Nat. Register of Hist. Places, Federal Register May 24, 1988.*

INDIAN RESERVATIONS

Reservation	County	Indian* Population	Acreage
Agua Caliente	Riverside	160	24,074
Alturas	Modoc	11	20
Augustine	Riverside	0	502
Barona Rancheria	San Diego	440	5,181
Benton Paiute	Mono	82	163
Berry Creek	Butte	15	33
Big Bend Rancheria	Shasta	6	40
Big Lagoon Rancheria	Humboldt	24	9
Big Pine Rancheria	Inyo	371	279
Big Sandy	Fresno	61	77
Big Valley	Lake	175	65
Bishop Reservation	Inyo	927	875
Blue Lake Rancheria	Humboldt	28	11
Bridgeport Colony	Mono	53	40
Buena Vista	Amador	1	68
Cabazon	Riverside	25	1,462
Colusa Rancheria	Colusa	27	273
Cahuilla	Riverside	50	18,272
Campo	San Diego	110	15,010
Capitan Grande	San Diego	0	15,753
Cedarville Rancheria	Modoc	10	17
Chicken Ranch	Tuolumne	3	3
Cloverdale Rancheria	Sonoma	1	19
Cold Springs Rancheria	Fresno	158	165
Cortina Rancheria	Colusa	9	640
Coyote Valley Rancheria	Mendocino	39	58
Cuyapaipe	San Diego	0	4,100
Dry Creek Rancheria	Sonoma	35	75
Elk Valley Rancheria	Del Norte	17	48
Enterprise Rancheria	Butte	18	40
Fort Independence	Inyo	65	352
Greenville Rancheria	Plumas	279	21
Grindstone Creek Rancheria	Glenn	122	80
Hoopa Valley	Humboldt	2,449	86,728
Hoopa Valley Extension	Del Norte	NA	7,028
Hoopa Valley Extension	Humboldt	NA	NA
Hopland Rancheria	Mendocino	97	38
Inaja-Cosmit	San Diego	0	852
Jackson Rancheria	Amador	20	331
Jamul Indian Village	San Diego	33	6
Karok	Humboldt and Siskiyou	1,696	11
La Jolla	San Diego	317	8,228
La Posta	San Diego	5	3,672
Laytonville Rancheria	Mendocino	296	200
Likely Rancheria	Modoc	0	1
Lone Pine Rancheria	Inyo	189	237

* Living on the Reservation.
8.25.1,90

INDIAN RESERVATIONS			
Reservation	County	Indian* Population	Acreage
Lookout Rancheria	Modoc	16	40
Los Coyotes	San Diego	82	25,050
Manchester-Pt. Arena Rancheria	Mendocino	104	363
Manzanita	San Diego	34	3,579
Mesa Grande	San Diego	58	120
Middletown Rancheria	Lake	34	109
Mooretown Rancheria	Butte	3	109
Montgomery Creek Rancheria	Shasta	30	72
Morongo	Riverside	486	32,248
North Fork Rancheria	Madera	3	80
Pacayune Rancheria	Madera	12	29
Pala	San Diego	502	11,488
Pauma and Yuima	San Diego	108	5,877
Pechanga	Riverside	401	4,094
Pinoleville Rancheria	Mendocino	142	9
Pit River	Modoc	0	14
Potter Valley Rancheria	Mendocino	1	3
Quartz Valley	Siskiyou	7	51
Ramona	Riverside	0	560
Redding Rancheria	Shasta	36	17
Redwood Valley Rancheria	Mendocino	44	10
Resighini Rancheria	Del Norte	14	228
Rincon	San Diego	281	3,960
Roaring Creek Rancheria	Shasta	8	80
Robinson Rancheria	Lake	23	43
Rohnerville Rancheria	Humboldt	8	10
Round Valley	Mendocino	867	19,023
Rumsey Rancheria	Yolo	30	185
San Manuel	San Bernardino	21	653
San Pasqual	San Diego	55	1,380
Santa Rosa	Riverside	13	11,093
Santa Rosa Rancheria	Kings	362	170
Santa Ynez	Santa Barbara	187	99
Santa Ysabel	San Diego	258	15,527
Sheep Ranch Rancheria	Calaveras	0	1
Sherwood Valley Rancheria	Mendocino	44	292
Shingle Springs Rancheria	El Dorado	32	92
Smith River Rancheria	Del Norte	32	92
Soboba	Riverside	341	5,036
Stewart's Point Rancheria	Sonoma	29	40
Sulphur Bank Rancheria	Lake	93	50
Susanville	Lassen	145	150
Sycuan	San Diego	52	640
Table Bluff Rancheria	Humboldt	51	20
Table Mountain	Fresno	82	19
Timi-Sha	Inyo	43	NA
Torres-Martinez	Riverside and Imperial	83	24,823
Trinidad Rancheria	Humboldt	70	44
Tule River	Tulare	576	54,116
Tuolumne Rancheria	Tuolumne	132	336
Twenty-Nine Palms	San Bernardino	0	402
Upper Lake	Lake	52	19
Viejas Rancheria	San Diego	187	1,609
79 Acres	Shasta	0	79

* Living on the Reservation.
   8.25.2,90 Source: U.S. Bureau of Indian Affairs, *Tribal Information and Directory, 1988.*

ENDANGERED AND THREATENED WILDLIFE*-FEDERAL LIST

Common Name	Status	Common Name	Status
Mammals		**Reptiles (cont.)**	
Brown Bear	Threatened	Barefoot Banded Gecko	Threatened
Black-footed Ferret	Endangered	Southern Rubber Boa	Threatened
San Joaquin Kit Fox	Endangered	Alameda Whipsnake	Threatened
Salt Marsh Harvest Mouse	Endangered	Giant Garter Snake	Threatened
Southern Sea Otter	Threatened	Green Sea Turtle	Threatened
Morrow Bay Kanaroo Rat	Endangered	Leatherback Sea Turtle	Endangered
Fresno Kangaroo Rat	Endangered	Loggerhead Sea Turtle	Threatened
Gray Wolf	Endangered	Olive (Pacific) Ridley	
Guadalupe Fur Seal	Threatened	Sea Turtle	Threatened
Amargosa Vole	Endangered	**Amphibians**	
Mojave Ground Squirrel	Threatened	Siskiyou Mountain Salamander	Threatened
San Joaquin Atnelope Squirrel	Threatened	Kern Canyon Slender Salamander	Threatened
Sei Whale	Endangered	Tehachapi Slender Salamander	Threatened
Finback Whale	Endangered	Limestone Salamander	Threatened
Blue Whale	Endangered	Shasta Salamander	Threatened
Humpback Whale	Endangered	Black Toad	Threatened
Right Whale	Endangered	Desert slender Salamander	Endangered
Sperm Whale	Endangered	Santa Cruz	
Sierra Nevada Red Fox	Threatened	long-toed Salamander	Endangered
Island Fox	Threatened	**Fishes**	
Wolverine	Threatened	Lost River Sucker	Endangered
California Big Horn Sheep	Threatened	Bonytail Chub	Endangered
Peninsula Bighorn Sheep	Threatened	Mohave tui Chub	Endangered
Grey Whale	Endangered	Owens Pupfish	Endangered
Birds		Unarmored	
Short-tailed Albatross	Endangered	threespine Stickleback	Endangered
California Condor	Endangered	Lahontan cutthroat Trout	Threatened
Eskimo Curlew	Endangered	Little Kern golden Trout	Threatened
Bald Eagle	Endangered	Paiute cutthroat Trout	Threatened
American Peregrine Falcon	Endangered	Ownes tui Chub	Endangered
Aleutian Canada Goose	Endangered	Desert Pupfish	Endangered
Brown Pelican	Endangered	Colorada Squawfish	Endangered
California Clapper Rail	Endangered	Bull Trout	Endangered
Light-footed Clapper Rail	Endangered	Shortmore Sucker	Endangered
Yurna Clapper Rail	Endangered	Razorback Sucker	Endangered
San Clemente		Cottonback Marsh Pupfish	Threatened
Loggerhead Shrike	Endangered	Rough Sculpin	Threatened
San Clemente Sage Sparrow	Threatened	Modoc Sucker	Endangered
Wood Stork	Endangered	**Insects**	
California Least Tern	Endangered	Bay checkerspot Butterfly	Threatened
Inyo Brown Towhee	Threatened	Delta green ground Beetle	Threatened
Swainson's Hawk	Threatened	Valley elderberry	
California Black Rail	Threatened	longhorn Beetle	Threatened
Western Yellow-Billed Cuckoo	Endangered	El Segundo blue Butterfly	Endangered
Elf Owl	Endangered	Lange's metalmark Butterfly	Endangered
Great Grey Owl	Endangered	Lotis blue Butterfly	Endangered
Gila Woodpecker	Endangered	Mission blue Butterfly	Endangered
Guilded Northern Flicker	Endangered	Palos Verdes blue Butterfly	Endangered
Belding's Savannah Sparrow	Endangered	San Bruno elfin Butterfly	Endangered
Greater Sandhill Crane	Endangered	Smith's blue Butterlfy	Endangered
Least Bell's Vireo	Endangered	Kern primrose sphinx Moth	Threatened
Reptiles		**Gastropods**	
Blunt-nosed Leopard Lizard	Endangered	Trinity Bristle Snail	Threatened
Coachella Valley		**Crustaceans**	
Fringe-toed Lizard	Threatened	Shasta Crayfish	Endangered
Island Night Lizard	Threatened	California Freshwater Shrimp	Endangered
San Francisco Garter Snake	Endangered		

* Threatened-Any species likely to become endangered in the foreseeable future within all or a significant portion of its range.
Endangered-Any species in danger of extinction within all or a significant portion of its range. Note: There are no endangered clams in California.
Note: Ten of the 13 threatened or endangered insects in the U.S. are in California.
8.26,90 Source: *Code of Fed. Regulations, vol. 50, Sec. 17.11-12, Jan. 1989.*

ENDANGERED AND THREATENED WILDLIFE - STATE LIST			
Common Name	Status	Common Name	Status
Mammals		**Reptiles**	
Mojave Ground Squirrel	Threatened	Barefoot Banded Gecko	Threatened
San Joaquin Antelope Squirrel	Threatened	Southern Rubber Boa	Threatened
Sei Whale	Endangered	Alameda Whip Snake	Threatened
Finback Whale	Endangered	Giant Garter Snake	Threatened
Blue Whale	Endangered	**Amphibians**	
Humpback Whale	Endangered	Siskiyou Mountain Salamander	Threatened
Right Whale	Endangered	Kern Canyon Slender Salamander	Threatened
Sperm Whale	Endangered	Tehachapi Slender Salamander	Threatened
Sierra Nevada Red Fox	Threatened	Limestone Salamander	Threatened
Island Fox	Threatened	Shasta Salamander	Threatened
Wolverine	Threatened	Black Toad	Threatened
California Big Horn Sheep	Threatened	**Fishes**	
Peninsula Big Horn Sheep	Threatened	Bull Trout	Endangered
Birds		Shortnose Sucker	Endangered
Swainson's Hawk	Threatened	Razorback Sucker	Endangered
California Black Rail	Threatened	Cottonball Marsh Pupfish	Threatened
Western Yellow-billed Cuckoo	Endangered	Rough Sculpin	Threatened
Elf Owl	Endangered	**Gastropods**	
Great Gray Owl	Endangered	Trinity Bristle Snail	Threatened
Greater Sand Hill Crane	Endangered		
Gila Woodpecker	Endangered		
Guilded Northern Flicker	Endangered		
Belding's Savannah Sparrow	Endangered		

8.27,90 Source: California Administrative Code, Title 14, Section 670.5.,1988.

CEMETERIES
There are 262 special cemetery districts in California. There are over 2,000 cemeteries in the state but the total acreage is undetermined. 180 large cemeteries handle approximately 82% of all burials.

8.28,90 Source: State Controller, Annual Report 1987-88, Financial Transactions concerning Special Districts of California; California Cemetery Board; Internment Association of California.

ENDANGERED AND THREATENED PLANTS*
FEDERAL LIST

Common Name	Status
Trukee Barberry	Endangered
McDonald's rock-cress	Endangered
Contra Costa Wallflower	Endangered
Slender-Petaled Mustard	Endangered
Santa Barbara Island Liveforever	Endangered
Presido (Raven's) Manzinita	Endangered
San Clemente Island Broom	Endangered
San Diego Mesa Mint	Endangered
San Clemente Island bush-mallow	Endangered
Pedate checker-mallow	Endangered
Eureka Valley evening-primrose	Endangered
Antioch Dunes evening-primrose	Endangered
San Benito evening-primrose	Threatened
Solano (Crampton's Orcutt) Grass	Endangered
Eureka Dune Grass	Endangered
San Clemente Island Larkspur	Endangered
San Clemente Island Indian Paintbrush	Endangered
Salt Marsh's bird's beak	Endangered
Ash Meadows gumplant	Threatened
Large Flowered Fiddleneck	Endangered
Amargosa Niterwort	Endangered
Spring-loving Centaury	Threatened
San Mateo Thornmint	Endangered
Palmate-bracted birds-beak	Endangered
Loch Lomond coyote-thistle	Endangered
Slender-horned Spineflower	Endangered
Santa Cruz Cypress	Endangered
Santa Ana River woolly-star	Endangered

* Threatened - Any species which is likely to become endangered in the foreseeable future within all or a significant portion of its range.
Endangered - Any species in danger of extinction within all or a significant portion of its range.
8.29,90 Source: *Code of Federal Regulations, Vol. 50, Sec. 17.11-12,* Jan., 1989.

SECTION 8 NOTE

According to the U.S. Bureau of Land Management, 1 percent of California's federal range land is in excellent condition, 46 percent in good condition, 38 percent in fair condition, 10 percent in poor condition, and 5 percent unclassified.

8.30,90

ENDANGERED AND THREATENED PLANTS-STATE LIST*

Common Name	Status	Common Name	Status
Grasses & Allies		**Herbs Continuted**	
White sedge	Endangered	Ferris' birds-beak	Endangered
Geyser's panicum	Endangered	Seaside bird's-beak	Endangered
Colusa grass	Endangered	Cuyamaca Lake downingia	Endangered
California Orcutt grass	Endangered	Short-leaved dudleya	Endangered
San Joaquin Valley Orcutt grass	Endangered	Santa Barbara Island dudleya	Endangered
Hairy Orcutt grass	Endangered	Trinity buckwheat	Endangered
Slender Orcutt grass	Endangered	Ione buckwheat	Endangered
Sacramento Orcutt grass	Endangered	Irish Hill buckwheat	Endangered
Napa blue grass	Endangered	San Diego button-celery	Endangered
Shrubs		Loch Lomond button-celery	Endangered
Vine Hill manzanita	Endangered	Delta button-celery	Endangered
Hearst's manzanita	Endangered	Menzies' wallflower	Endangered
San Bruno Mountain manzanita	Endangered	Santa Cruz wallflower	Endangered
Pacific manzanita	Endangered	Roderick's fritillary	Endangered
Alameda manzanita	Endangered	San Clemente Island bedstraw	Endangered
Encinitas baccharis	Endangered	Boggs Lake hedge-hyssop	Endangered
Santa Catalina Island	Endangered	Algodones Dunes sunflower	Endangered
mountain-mahogany	Endangered	Otay tarplant	Endangered
Indian Knob mountainbalm	Endangered	Lake County dwarf flax	Endangered
Thorne's buckwheat	Endangered	Santa Cruz tarplant	Endangered
San Nicolas Island buckwheat	Endangered	Burke's goldfields	Endangered
Kellogg's buckwheat	Endangered	Western lily	Endangered
Nevin's barberry	Endangered	Pitkin Marsh lily	Endangered
Island barberry	Endangered	Point Reyes meadowfoam	Endangered
Santa Cruz Island bush mallow	Endangered	Shippee meadowfoam	Endangered
Herbs		Parish's slender meadowfoam	Endangered
Nipomo Mesa Lupine	Endangered	Sebastopol meadowfoam	Endangered
Tidestrom's lupine	Endangered	San Clemente Island	
Willowy monardella	Endangered	woodland star	Endangered
Many-flowered navarretia	Endangered	San Clemente island	
Amargosa nitrophilia	Endangered	bird's-foot trefoil	Endangered
Dehesa nolina	Endangered	Santa Cruz Island	
Succulent owl's-clover	Endangered	bird's-foot trefoil	Endangered
Yreka phlox	Endangered	San Francisco Popcornflower	Endangered
San Diego thorn mint	Endangered	Santa Lucia mint	Endangered
Humboldt milk-vetch	Endangered	Otay Mesa mint	Endangered
Sodaville milk-vetch	Endangered	Hickman's cinquefoil	Endangered
Peirson's milk-vetch	Endangered	Hartweg's psuedobahia	Endangered
Coastal dunes milk-vetch	Endangered	Tulare pseudobahia	Endangered
Bakersfield saltbush	Endangered	Tahoe yellow cress	Endangered
Indian Valley brodiaea	Endangered	Owens Valley checkerbloom	Endangered
Thread-leaved brodiaea	Endangered	Kenwood Marsh checkerbloom	Endangered
Kawaeah brodiaea	Endangered	Bird-footed checkerbloom	Endangered
Chinese Camp brodiaea	Endangered	Scadden Flat checkerbloom	Endangered
Stebbins' morning-glory	Endangered	Red Mountain catchfly	Endangered
Pitkin Marsh Indian paintbrush	Endangered	Slender-petaled thelypodium	Endangered
California jewelflower	Endangered	Monterey clover	Endangered
Orcutt's spineflower	Endangered	Tiburon mariposa lily	Threatened
Ashland thistle	Endangered	Howell's spineflower	Threatened
Fountain thistle	Endangered	Laguna Beach dudleya	Threatened
Presidio clarkia	Endangered	Striped adobe lily	Threatened
Vine Hill clarkia	Endangered	Sand gilia	Threatened
Merced clarkia	Endangered	Milo Baker's lupine	Threatened
Springville clarkia	Endangered		

* Endangered and Threatened plants not on the Federal list but considered at risk by the California Dept. of Fish and Game Endangered Plant Project.
8.31,90 Source: California Department of Fish and Game, Endangered Plant Project, *Endangered Plants of California, 1988.*

DISPOSAL OF PUBLIC LAND IN CALIFORNIA
1850-1956

	Acres (millions)	Percent of State Land
Grants to the State	8.8	16%
Grants to Railroads	11.6	20
Confirmation of Private Land Claims	8.9	16
Cash and Auction Sales	8.6	15
Homestead Entries	11.4	20
Desertland Entries	1.1	2
Timberland & Stone Quarry Entries	3.0	5
Mineral Entries	.6	1
Indian Tribal Lands	.1	*
Other	2.4	4
Total	**56.6**	**100%**

* Less than 1%.
8.32,90 Source: U.S. Bureau of Land Management, *Public Land Statistics*.

HUNTING AND FISHING LICENSES
1970-1988

Year	Fishing Liccenses*	Hunting Licenses	Deer and Bear Tags	Special Hunt Permits	Licensed Hunt Permits	Hunting Permits in Waterfowl Areas
1970-71	5,831,723	696,651	402,477	48,974	208	99,962
1980-81	6,314,951	555,232	326,245	490	144	82,921
1981-82	6,447,402	542,015	335,974	522	142	71,620
1982-83	6,909,936	531,944	334,412	701	144	79,859
1983-84	6,657,687	505,165	293,670	499	145	79,950
1984-85	3,656,738	487,688	264,651	4,612	140	75,854
1985-86	3,506,441	456,977	266,220	5,007	175	67,325
1986-87	3,314,766	435,522	248,447	4,149	133	46,735
1987-88	3,690,892	421,289	246,376	5,465	173	48,230

* Licenses and angling stamps.
8.33,90 Source: California Dept. of Fish and Game, License and Revenue Branch, unpublished data, and *California Statistical Abstract*.

SECTION 8 NOTE

No new counties have been formed in California since 1907. In that year Imperial County was carved out of San Diego County.

8.34,90

Federal Government Finances

Eight years with the most conservative president in decades in the White House appear to have had no dramatic effect on the federal government's expenditures except to slow slightly the rate at which governmental spending has grown. From Reagan's first budget in 1981 until his last in 1988 federal spending in California rose 48 percent, or an average of 6 percent a year. California's share of the federal largess has hovered around 12 percent of the total expended in the states, giving California a slightly larger share than its percentage of the nation's population warrants. Because California is a relatively wealthy state, this federal spending amounts to a modest income transfer from relatively poorer states to relatively prosperous California. California's businesses must be doing well, however, because their share of the total taxes paid by U.S. corporations has grown in the past few years.

Federal revenue-sharing funds have disappeared, but Washington still funnels $11.7 billion to our state and local governments. The agencies that spend the most in California are the Departments of Health and Human Services, Housing and Urban Development, and Labor. Altogether their expenditures constitute 68 percent of federal spending in the state.

All of these figures exclude hefty spending by the Defense Department, NASA, and classified military procurement programs such as the B-2 Stealth bomber and intelligence satellites. Despite the huge federal expenditures in the state, California's share of federal employees has been declining slightly and is now lower than it has been in almost thirty years.

After the 1990 census, California will probably gain six new members of the House of Representatives. Will a fifty-one member California delegation be able to work harmoniously to deliver federal dollars and programs to the state, or will the delegation continue to be divided along partisan and regional lines and find itself immobilized periodically by these divisions?

FEDERAL EXPENDITURES TO CALIFORNIA AND OTHER STATES			
Year	Expenditures to California (in billions)	Expenditures to All 50 States (in billions)	Expenditures to California as a % of Expenditures to All States
1979	$52.5	$463	11%
1980	$61.5	NA	NA
1981	$69.4	$584	12%
1982	$77.5	$627	12%
1983	$86.4	$695	12%
1984	$91.7	$725	13%
1985	$97.8	$788	12%
1986	$100.9	$830	12%
1987	$100.8	$848	12%
1988	$102.4	$884	12%

9.1,90 Source: Bureau of the Census, *Federal Expenditures by State for Fiscal Year 1988, and U.S. Statistical Abstract.*

FEDERAL EXPENDITURES TO CALIFORNIA STATE AND LOCAL GOVERNMENTS, 1984-88				
	Expenditures in California (millions)			Percent of Total U.S. Expenditures in 1988
Agency	1984	1986	1988	
Department of Agriculture	$830.3	$924.5	$1,075.0	9.5%
Department of Commerce	$24.8	$30.1	$17.7	4.8%
Department of Defense*	$1.2	$7.4	$2.5	2.2%
Department of Education	$491.7	$718.4	$807.0	8.5%
Department of Energy	$23.4	$17.4	$7.5	3.6%
Environmental Protection Agency	$259.6	$251.2	$189.0	6.4%
Equal Employment Opportunity Commission	$1.9	$1.5	$1.8	9.3%
Federal Emergency Management Agency	$74.8	$50.0	$30.0	7.2%
Department of Health and Human Services	$4,836.0	$5,639.9	$6,354.0	12.4%
Department of Housing and Urban Development	$787.8	$950.8	$987.0	8.6%
Department of the Interior	$97.2	$58.8	$52.6	3.9%
Department of Justice	$2.2	$6.5	$38.8	12.9%
Depaartment of Labor	$582.0	$652.5	$647.0	11.7%
National Endowment for the Arts	$0.9	$0.9	$1.5	4.6%
Department of Transportation	$1,251.3	$1,374.1	$1,438.0	7.9%
Department of the Treasury	$516.8	$580.6	8.5†	2.2%
Veterans Administration	$5.4	$12.8	$12.7	11.9%
Total	$9,799.0	$11,277.4	$11,676.0	10.2%

* Does not include defense contracts, procurement, or wages.   †   1987 data.

9.2,90 Source: U.S. Bureau of the Census, *Fed. Expenditures by State for Fiscal year 1988.*

FEDERAL EXPENDITURES IN CALIFORNIA
SELECTED PROGRAMS

Year	Per Capita Spending	Public* Assistance (millions)	Medicaid (millions)	General Revenue Sharing (millions)	K-12 Education (millions)	Highway Trust Fund (millions)
1979	NA	$2,811	$1,415	$774	$198	$439
1981	NA	2,037	2,094	570	324	548
1982	NA	1,823	2,108	516	348	491
1983	$3,429	1,908	2,166	529	291	526
1984	3,579	2,017	2,064	517	321	688
1985	3,710	2,007	2,408	508	378	926
1986	3,738	2,168	2,553	581	442	855
1987	3,642	2,365	2,773	0	469	794
1988	3,634	2,467	2,985	0	535	904

* Includes Aid for Families with Dependent Children (AFDC), refugee assistance and home energy assistance.

9.3,90 Source: *U.S. Statistical Abstract*; Department of the Treasury, *Federal Aid to States*, 1982; U.S. Bureau of the Census, *Federal Expenditures by State*.

TOTAL FEDERAL EXPENDITURES IN CALIFORNIA
(in billions)

Year	Grants to State and Local Governments	Salaries and Wages	Direct Payments to Individuals	Procurement	Other Programs	Total
1981	$10.0	$11.1	$25.7	$21.6	$.9	$69.4
1982	$9.0	$12.0	$28.2	$27.5	$.7	$77.5
1983	$9.2	$12.8	$31.3	$30.9	$2.3	$86.4
1984	$9.8	$13.5	$32.7	$34.2	$1.6	$91.7
1985	$10.6	$14.4	$35.4	$35.2	$2.2	$97.8
1986	$11.3	$15.1	$37.0	$35.2	$2.3	$100.9
1987	$11.0	$15.5	$39.3	$32.2	$2.8	$100.8
1988	$11.7	$16.4	$41.9	$29.5	$2.9	$102.4

9.4,90 Source: U.S. Bureau of the Census, *Federal Expenditures by State for Fiscal Year 1988*.

SECTION 9 NOTE

In 1988 Los Angeles County led the nation's 3,000 counties with $12.5 billion in federal procurement contracts. Santa Clara County was second with $4.5 billion and Orange County was sixth with $3.3 billion. With $29.5 billion in contracts, California led all states and had 15.6% of all such contracts in the U.S.

9.5,90

FEDERAL TAX RECEIPTS AND TAX RETURNS FROM CALIFORNIA

	1983	1985	1988
Individual Returns	10,744,350	11,726,433	12,393,552
Individual & Employment Tax Receipts (in billions)	$64.0	$77.2	$92.1
Individual & Employment Tax Receipts as a % of Total U.S. Individual Tax Receipts	11.4%	11.6%	11.6%
Corporate Returns	318,181	382,623	399,900
Corporate Receipts (in billions)	$7.5	$7.8	$12.2
Corporate Receipts as a % of Total U.S. Corporate Tax Receipts	10.1%	9.7%	11.1%
Total Federal Tax Receipts from California (in billions)	$76.6	$89.6	$108.3
Total U.S. Tax Receipts (in billions)	$680.5	$782.3	$935.1
California Receipts as a % of Total U.S. Tax Receipts	11.3%	11.5%	11.6%

9.6,90 Source: U.S. Internal Revenue Service, *Annual Report of the Commissioner.*

FEDERAL CIVILIAN EMPLOYMENT IN CALIFORNIA

Year	Number	% of Federal Employees in U.S.	Department of Defense	Post Office	Veterans Admini- stration	All Other
1960	240,000	10.8%	-	-	-	-
1970	304,000	11.4%	-	-	-	-
1980	298,000	10.8%	-	-	-	-
1981	302,000	11.3%	133,000	76,000	23,000	70,000
1982	300,785	11.0%	134,580	77,168	23,834	65,203
1984	307,257	10.6%	134,954	82,595	23,905	65,793
1986*	314,020	10.4%	134,351	95,373	23,164	61,224

* As of December 31, 1986.
9.7,90 Source: U.S. Office of Personnel Management; *Federal Civilian Employment in the U.S. by Geographic Area, Annual* & unpublished data.

REAL PROPERTY & BUILDINGS OWNED & LEASED TO THE FEDERAL GOVERNMENT IN CALIFORNIA

	Number of Install- ations	Owned Acres * (millions)	Build- ings	Number of Land Leases	Leased Acres (thou- sands)	Number of Install- ations	Floor Space (millions of sq. ft.)	Annual Rents PAID (millions)
Item	2,033	46.3	61,495	4,386	100	3,120	18.7	$151.2
% of U.S. Total	6.8%†	11.3%	14.3%	6.7%	11.8%	6.1%	9.0%	11.2%

† Approximately   * Excluding Alaska
9.8,90 Sources: U.S. General Services Administration, *Summary Report of Real Property Owned by the U.S. Throughout the World, Annual* and *Summary Report of Real Property Leased by the U.S. Throughout the World, Annual.*

SECTION 9 NOTE

California ranks 16th among the 50 states in per capita federal spending. The federal government spends $3,634 per person in the Golden State.

9.9,90

SECTION 10
State and Local Finances

Any close observer of California politics could sympathize with Governor George Deukmejian's decision to retire after two relatively successful terms in office. The governor's job as the state's chief budget official is becoming difficult, if not impossible, because of voter-mandated restrictions on state taxes and spending. First, the Jarvis-Gann initiative (Proposition 13) in 1978 cut local property taxes and shifted to the state government a greater part of the burden of financing local programs and schools. Then the Gann initiative (Proposition 4), passed in 1979, imposed a ceiling on the expenditures of state and local governments, with annual increases tied to inflation and the increase in population. Finally, in the fall of 1988 the voters passed Proposition 98, which required a minimum level of funding for K-12 public schools and community colleges. Sponsored by the state's teachers' unions, Proposition 98 puts K-12 schools and community colleges in a preferred position in the state budget, guaranteeing them at least 41 percent of the state budget each year. Furthermore, this school budget must increase with enrollment expansion and inflation even if state revenues are stagnant or decline because of a recession. All other state programs, such as social welfare, higher education, and law enforcement, have a lower priority in state spending. The effect of these initiatives has been to make the budgetary process very tight.

The 1988-89 budget was barely held in balance after unexpected increases in a variety of programs occurred just when a similarly unexpected decrease appeared in tax revenues from capital gains. The governor's desire to build a $900-million reserve for such emergencies as these will inevitably clash with the legislature's tendency to spend all it can.

Despite the tight controls on the state's budget approved by voters, politicians have nonetheless discovered a way to put billions of dollars into new and old programs without any short-term tax increases. This sleight of hand is accomplished by offering bonds for public approval. The voters hate taxes but love to spend money for the environment, prisons, roads, and schools--as long as they can pay for all these projects with massive bond sales. Some legislators worry that this profligate use of bonds to pay for such programs as highway construction, which used to be financed out of general revenues, will endanger the state's credit worthiness. These legislators are considering a constitutional initiative to limit the dollar amount of the bonds offered in any one year.

Only the state's economy, which continues to be buoyant, and its increasing tax revenues are holding together an increasingly fractured state budgetary process.

Tax Source	1960	1970	1980	1987	1988	1989*	1990*
STATE TAXES (in millions of dollars)							
Personal Income Tax	247	$1,152	$6,506	$13,925	$12,947	$14,728	$16,363
Sales & Use Tax	710	1,754	6,623	10,904	11,650	12,593	13,448
Bank & Corporation Tax	241	587	2,510	4,801	4,776	5,225	5,585
Motor Vehicle Fuel Tax	337	669	853	1,246	1,280	1,304	1,330
Motor Vehicle Fees	256	499	1,097	2,693	2,974	3,160	3,362
Insurance Tax	62	137	446	1,009	1,158	1,411	1,279
Cigarette Tax	65	237	290	255	251	545	863
Horse Racing Tax	36	58	128	132	146	148	160
Distilled Spirits Tax	40	90	113	101	98	96	94
Beer & Wine Tax	10	16	26	31	31	31	32
Total Taxes (billions)	**$2.2**	**$5.6**	**$20.6**	**$35.1**	**$35.3**	**$39.2**	**$42.5**

* Estimates.

Note: Prior to 1967 data calculated on cash basis, after 1967 on an accrual basis.
10.1,90 Source: Governor's Budget Summary, 1989 - 90.

	STATE EXPENDITURES		
Year	Total Expenditures* (in billions)	Expenditures per Capita	Expenditures per $100 of Personal Income
1950-51	$1.0	$95	$5.10
1960-61	$2.5	$159	$5.83
1970-71	$6.6	$327	$6.89
1980-81	$24.5	$1,031	$8.89
1981-82	$25.0	$1,031	$8.12
1982-83	$25.3	$1,022	$7.72
1983-84	$26.8	$1,059	$7.60
1984-85	$31.0	$1,201	$7.96
1985-86	$35.0	$1,327	$8.29
1986-87	$38.1	$1,410	$8.40
1987-88	$40.5	$1,462	$8.21

* Includes general fund, special fund, and select bond fund expenditures beginning in 1963-64.

10.2,90 Source: *Governor's Budget 1989-90*. Schedule S.

TOTAL STATE EXPENDITURES (1989-90 Fiscal Year)
(Excluding Selected Bond Funds)

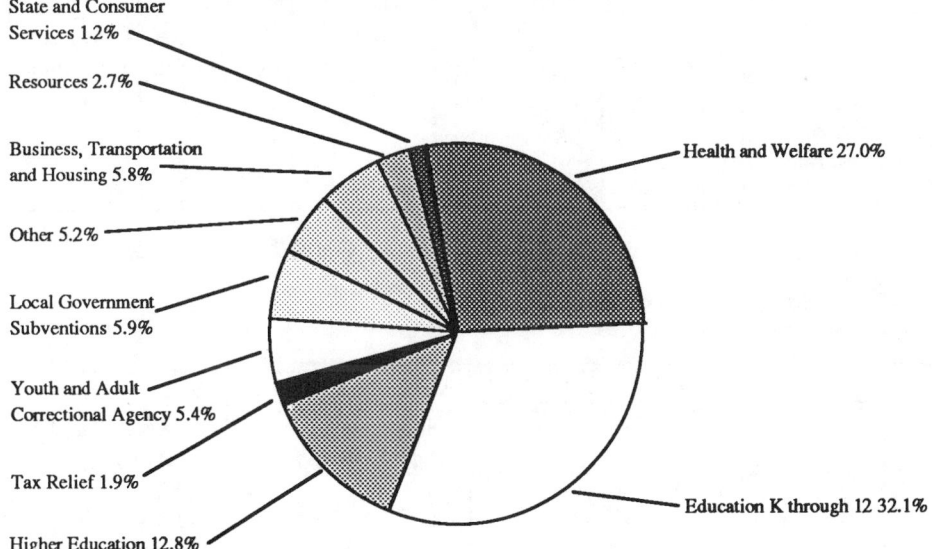

State and Consumer Services 1.2%

Resources 2.7%

Business, Transportation and Housing 5.8%

Other 5.2%

Local Government Subventions 5.9%

Youth and Adult Correctional Agency 5.4%

Tax Relief 1.9%

Higher Education 12.8%

Health and Welfare 27.0%

Education K through 12 32.1%

10.3,90 Source: Governor's Budget.

INDIVIDUAL STATE TAX RETURNS

Year	Number of Returns (in millions)	Adjusted Gross Income (in billions)	Tax Assessed (in billions)
1960	4.2	$31	$.25
1970	5.6	$63	$1.2
1980	10.3	$189	$6.5
1982	10.7	$225	$7.5
1984	11.6	$290	$9.3
1985	11.9	$306	$10.8
1986	12.2	$340	$11.4
1987	NA	NA	$13.9
1988	NA	NA	$12.9

10.4,90 Source: *Economic Report of the Governor.*

SECTION 10 NOTE

As of the end of fiscal 1987, California ranked a healthy 33 out of the 50 states in per capita debt. Each citizen owed $2,601, of which $37 was short-term and $2,565 long-term debt. Alaska led the nation with $21,285 in per capita debt.

10.5,90

CALIFORNIA TAX RATES

	Income		Sales		
	Personal	**Corporation**	**General Sales & Use**	**Gasoline per gallon**	**Cigarette per pack**
California Lowest & Highest rate in other states	1%-9.3% 0%-12%†	9.3% 0% -12%	4.75%* 0% -7.5%	9¢ 4-20.8¢	35¢ 2 - 40¢

* Plus local tax additions.
† 3 states tax income from dividends, interest, and net capital gains, not from earned or pension income.
10.6,90 Source: The Tax Foundation, April 1, 1989.

BANK AND CORPORATE TAX RETURNS

Year	Number of Returns	Net Income* (in billions)	Tax Assessed (in billions)
1961	NA	NA	$0.27
1970	NA	NA	$0.59
1980	165,183	$20.7	$2.5
1982	175,053	$10.7	$2.2
1984	208,566	$19.3	$3.1
1985	207,388	$21.1	$3.7
1986	216,677	$25.5	$3.8
1987	NA	NA	$4.8
1988	NA	NA	$4.8

* Minus net losses.
10.7,90 Source: *Economic Report of the Governor.*

COMPARATIVE PER CAPITA STATE TAXES 1987 (RANK AMONG THE 50 STATES)

State	Total Tax	Personal Income Tax	General Sales Tax	Property Tax*
California	$1,926 (9)	$673 (6)	$495 (10)	$495 (23)
New York	2,773 (3)	1,043 (2)	532 (8)	799 (7)
Texas	1,329 (36)	0	341 (31)	549 (21)
Florida	1,365 (33)	50 (46)	459 (12)	453 (28)
Pennsylvania	1,554 (24)	448 (17)	299 (38)	412 (32)
Arizona	1,595 (23)	284 (33)	554 (6)	468 (26)
Oregon	1,612 (21)	587 (8)	0	715 (8)
Nevada	1,622 (19)	0	555 (5)	360 (35)
U.S. Average	$1,665	$437	$398	$498

* 1985 data.
10.8,90 Source: U.S. Bureau of the Census, *Governments Finances in 1986 - 87.*

COMPARATIVE STATE PROPERTY TAXES 1972-1987				
State	**1972**	**1982**	**1985**	**1987**
California	**$329**	**$352**	**$420**	**$495**
New York	$288	$574	$688	$799
Texas	$153	$366	$466	$549
Arizona	$202	$330	$347	$468
Oregon	$239	$483	$617	$715
U.S. Average	**$206**	**$362**	**$435**	**$498**

10.9,90 Source: U.S. Bureau of the Census, *Government Finances in 1986-1987.*

	SENIOR CITIZENS AND DISABLED PROPERTY TAX ASSISTANCE FOR HOMEOWNERS AND RENTERS			
	Homeowners		Renters	
Year	**Number of Claimants**	**Amount of Assistance (in millions)**	**Number of Claimants**	**Amount of Assistance (in millions)**
1981	148,736	$14.2	290,799	$45.3
1984	83,001	7.7	241,874	32.4
1985	68,985	6.2	224,883	28.3
1986	57,254	5.1	206,841	24.0
1987	51,137	4.6	193,972	20.6
1988	44,414	3.7	178,417	17.3
1989*	NA	4.4	NA	17.6

* Estimated.

10.10,90 Source: *Governor's Budget, 1988-1989.*

SECTION 10 NOTE
The best-paid government employee in California is Bruce Malkenhorst, the city administrator of Vernon (Los Angeles County), which has a population of 80. He makes $162,804 per year.

10.11,90

| | | Bonds Authorized but | |
Purpose	Outstanding* (millions)	Unissued (millions)	Interest (millions)
General Fund Bonds			
Beach, Park, Recreational and			
Historical Facilities	$140	$0	$9
Park and Recreational Facilities	84	275	6
Clean Water	222	330	15
Clean Water and Water Conservation	232	45	20
Community Parklands	0	100	0
Community College			
Construction Program	55	0	3
County Correctional Facility	0	495	0
County Jail Capital Expenditure	345	150	20
Earthquake Safety & Housing	0	150	0
State Construction Program	119	0	5
First-Time Home Buyer	7.8	185	1
Fish and Wildlife Habitat			
Enhancement	26	55	2
Hazardous Substance Cleanup	45	50	3
Health Science Facilities			
Construction Program	66	0	4
Higher Education Facilities	0	400	0
State Higher Education			
Construction Program	44	0	2
Junior College Construction			
Program	10	0	1
Lake Tahoe Acquisitions Bond Act	27	55	2
New Prison Construction	726	445	55
Recreation and Fish and			
Wildlife Enhancement	18	0	1
State School Building Lease-Purchase	545	350	35
Safe Drinking Water	147	170	12
State Parklands	166	45	15
State, Urban, and Coastal Parks	146	25	11
Senior Center	45	0	4
Water Conservation and			
Water Quality	1	149	0
Total General Fund Bonded Debt	**$3,290**	**$5,700**	**$245**
Self-Liquidating Bonds			
San Francisco Harbor Improvement	$11	$0	$0.4
State School Building Aid	346	40	18
Veterans Farm and Home Building	3,021	1,020	213
State Water Facilities	1,339	180	60
Total Self-Liquidating Bonds	**$4,717**	**$1,240**	**$292**
Total Bonded Debt	**$8,007**	**$6,940**	**$537**

STATE BONDED DEBT

* As of June 30, 1988, General Obligation Bonds only. Note: Totals may not add due to rounding.

10.12,90 Source: Cal. State Controller, *State of Cal. Preliminary Annual Report, 1987-1988 FY, Cash Basis.*

County	Assessed Value 1984-1985	Assessed Value 1986-1987	Assessed Value 1988-1989
Alameda	$35,801	$45,598	$55,404
Alpine	$127	$145	$157
Amador	$970	$1,161	$1,390
Butte	$4,723	$5,346	$6,011
Calaveras	$1,182	$1,385	$1,650
Colusa	$1,177	$1,112	$1,121
Contra Costa	$29,782	$36,475	$44,649
Del Norte	$478	$500	$552
Dorado	$4,352	$5,071	$5,943
Fresno	$17,989	$20,170	$22,506
Glenn	$1,040	$1,086	$1,106
Humboldt	$3,078	$3,521	$3,960
Imperial	$2,477	$3,093	$3,685
Inyo	$999	$1,085	$1,328
Kern	$28,824	$30,794	$31,923
Kings	$2,405	$2,415	$2,723
Lake	$2,571	$2,597	$2,736
Lassen	$692	$781	$892
Los Angeles	$249,697	$294,630	$360,654
Madera	$2,729	$3,016	$3,388
Marin	$10,474	$12,563	$14,855
Mariposa	$524	$609	$680
Mendocino	$2,446	$2,738	$3,053
Merced	$4,291	$4,761	$5,206
Modoc	$471	$498	$514
Mono	$1,178	$1,199	$1,292
Monterey	$10,519	$12,422	$14,149
Napa	$3,865	$4,657	$5,620
Nevada	$2,739	$3,223	$3,806
Orange	$86,803	$105,436	$127,409
Placer	$5,889	$7,092	$9,129
Plumas	$1,200	$1,358	$1,521
Riverside	$26,815	$34,450	$44,661
Sacramento	$23,456	$29,127	$35,813
San Benito	$943	$1,183	$1,421
San Bernardino	$29,083	$36,908	$46,997
San Diego	$67,780	$85,384	$105,372
San Francisco	$30,582	$37,568	$44,446
San Joaquin	$11,476	$13,436	$15,708
San Luis Obispo	$8,081	$10,719	$13,159
San Mateo	$27,685	$33,441	$39,837
Barbara	$12,778	$15,279	$18,115
Santa Clara	$56,055	$72,212	$84,889
Santa Cruz	$7,033	$8,467	$10,015
Shasta	$4,215	$4,837	$5,488
Sierra	$193	$224	$275
Siskiyou	$1,432	$1,573	$1,691
Solano	$7,556	$8,795	$11,003
Sonoma	$13,451	$15,169	$17,947
Stanislaus	$8,497	$9,562	$11,430
Sutter	$2,222	$2,267	$2,435
Tehama	$1,373	$1,509	$1,644
Trinity	$418	$479	$526
Tulare	$6,638	$7,495	$8,778
Tuolumne	$1,446	$1,793	$2,225
Ventura	$21,548	$25,815	$31,810
Yolo	$3,850	$4,355	$5,060
Yuba	$1,251	$1,501	$1,701
State Totals	$897,322	$1,080,082	$1,301,461

ASSESSED VALUE* OF PROPERTY BY COUNTY (millions of dollars)

* Assessed value is 100% of full value.
10.13,90 Source: Cal. State Board of Equalization, *Annual Report.*

PROPERTY TAX DELINQUENCY BY COUNTY
FISCAL YEAR 1988-89

County	Current Year Property Tax Delinquency As a Percentage of Total Due*	County	Current Year Property Tax Delinquency As a Percentage of Total Due*
Alameda	4.1%	Orange	2.5%
Alpine	4.3	Placer	4.5
Amador	3.7	Plumas	2.3
Butte	3.9	Riverside	5.1
Calaveras	5.6	Sacramento	3.9
Colusa	2.0	San Benito	6.4
Contra Costa	2.9	San Bernardino	4.0
Del Norte	5.4	San Diego	3.3
El Dorado	7.2	San Francisco	-
Fresno	3.7	San Joaquin	5.0
Glenn	3.5	San Luis Obispo	3.8
Humboldt	4.7	San Mateo	2.3
Imperial	8.5	Santa Barbara	2.6
Inyo	16.1	Santa Clara	2.5
Kern	3.4	Santa Cruz	5.5
Kings	3.4	Shasta	4.7
Lake	1.1	Sierra	5.5
Lassen	6.4	Siskiyou	6.0
Los Angeles	3.8	Solano	3.1
Madera	4.7	Sonoma	3.2
Marin	3.0	Stanislaus	4.1
Mariposa	8.0	Sutter	4.1
Mendocino	6.1	Tehama	4.9
Merced	4.5	Trinity	4.0
Modoc	6.7	Tulare	4.7
Mono	7.4	Toulumne	8.2
Monterey	3.5	Ventura	2.5
Napa	3.9	Yolo	3.1
Nevada	6.3	Yuba	6.8

* Percentage is computed on the basis of all taxes extended on the county's assessment roll.

10.14,90 Source: California State Controller, *Counties of California Financial Transactions 1987-88.*

GENERAL COUNTY REVENUES*				
	1986-1987		1987-1988	
Revenue Source	Amount (millions)	% of Total Revenues	Amount (millions)	% of Total Revenues
State Aid	$5,624	36.0%	$6,101	37.0%
Federal Aid	$2,928	19.0%	$3,087	19.0%
Property Taxes	$3,656	24.0%	$4,011	25.0%
Charges For Services	$1,321	9.0%	$1,345	8.0%
Use of Money & Property	$406	3.0%	$408	3.0%
Sales Taxes	$269	2.0%	$288	2.0%
Miscellaneous Revenue	$219	1.0%	$237	1.0%
Fines & Penalties	$241	2.0%	$273	2.0%
Other Taxes	$190	1.0%	$198	1.0%
Licenses, Permits & Franchises	$167	1.0%	$185	1.0%
Other Revenue-Inter Gov't Aid	$44	0.3%	$36	0.2%
Other Financing Sources	$437	3.0%	$110	1.0%
Total Revenue	$15,503	100.0%	$16,280	100.0%

* Data for San Francisco City and County listed in city totals
10.15,90 Source: State Controller's Office, Annual Report of *Financial Transactions Concerning Counties of California.*

GENERAL COUNTY EXPENDITURES*				
	1986-1987		1987-1988	
Expenditure	Amount (millions)	Percent of Total Expenditures	Amount (millions)	Percent of Total Expenditures
Public Assistance	$5,966	40.0%	$6,381	39.0%
Public Protection	$4,005	27.0%	$4,393	27.0%
General Government	$2,092	14.0%	$2,792	17.0%
Health	$1,583	11.0%	$1,703	10.0%
Sanitation	$12	.1%	$10	.1%
Public Roads & Facilities	$726	5.0%	$686	4.0%
Recreation & Culture	$160	1.0%	$171	1.0%
Education	$171	1.0%	$188	1.0%
Debt Service	$66	.4%	$65	.4%
Total Expenditures	$14,782	100.0%	$16,389	100.0%

* Data for San Francisco City and County listed in city totals.
10.16,90 Source: State Controller's Office, Annual Report of *Financial Transactions Concerning Counties of California.*

COUNTY BONDED INDEBTEDNESS (in millions)			
County	Outstanding Debt*	County	Outstanding Debt*
Alameda	$17.1	Orange	$29.7
Alpine	$1.7	Placer	$14.4
Butte	$5.3	Riverside	$48.7
Calaveras	$.3	Sacramento	$34.9
Contra Costa	$114.7	San Bernardino	$181.0
Humboldt	$2.3	San Diego	$215.4
Kern	$38.2	San Mateo	$29.0
Kings	$3.6	Santa Barbara	$14.7
Lake	$1.2	Santa Clara	$237.6
Los Angeles	$452.0	Santa Cruz	$42.2
Madera	$6.6	Shasta	$24.6
Marin	$3.7	Solano	$43.4
Mendocino	$20.7	Sonoma	$16.1
Merced	$4.7	Sutter	$0.8
Mono	$.9	Tulare	$1.1
Monterey	$.7	Ventura	$236.9
Napa	$1.3	Yolo	$0.1
		State Total (up 15% from 1985-1986)	$1,596

* Includes future lease obligation payments, general obligation bonds, revenue bonds, and assessment bonds. County debt is about 1/10 of 1% of net county assessed property valuation.
10.17,90 Source: State Controller's Office, *Annual Report 1987-88, Financial Transactions Concerning Counties of California.*

COUNTY BONDED INDEBTEDNESS			
Year	General Obligation Bonds (millions)	Revenue Bonds (millions)	Total Bonded Debt (millions)
1940	NA	NA	$28
1950	NA	NA	$7
1960	NA	NA	$116
1970	NA	NA	$204
1980	$71	$3.6	$75
1982	$50	$14.4	$64
1984	$33	$13.9	$47
1986	$19	$6.7	$26
1988	$115*	$21.1	$136

* Increase due to Los Angeles county issuing a $96 million bond.
10.18,90 Source: State Controller's Office, *Annual Report*, Financial Transactions Concerning Counties of California.

COUNTY LEASE-PURCHASE OBLIGATIONS		
Year	Amount	Percent Change From Prior Year
1972-1973	$880,000,000	1.62%
1973-1974	$896,000,000	1.82%
1974-1975	$943,000,000	5.25%
1975-1975	$1,068,340,871	13.29%
1976-1977	$1,143,746,979	7.06%
1977-1978	$1,088,205,577	-4.86%
1978-1979	$1,018,189,228	-6.43%
1979-1980	$934,894,394	-3.27%
1980-1981	$1,010,210,100	2.57%
1981-1982	$1,256,990,574	24.43%
1982-1983	$1,315,314,325	4.64%
1983-1984	$1,383,346,799	5.17%
1984-1985	$821,541,176	-40.62%
1985-1986	$1,260,976,873	53.49%
1986-1987	$1,580,313,570	25.33%
1987-1988	$1,596,469,679	1.02%

Note: During the last decade, the traditional methods of financing capital expenditures, i.e. through "pay as you go" plans and general obligation bonds, have undergone some subtle changes. Voters' apathy to proposals for additional bonds secured by property taxes had made many officials wary of depending upon that source of financing. One of the changes that has come into increasing use is the so-called "lease-purchase" plan. In its simplest form it may consist of a non-profit corporation organized for the sole purpose of building a structure on land owned by a governmental agency. The corporation may arrange for conventional financing which in turn is secured by a long-term lease with the agency which will use the facility. The terms of the lease are sufficient to retire the debt and at its expiration title to the facility passes to the governmental agency. The magnitude of this approach to capital improvements is indicated in a continuing survey in which 21 county governments reported that the money value of leases now in effect, if continued to their termination, amounts to $1,596,469,679. Lease purchasing obligations now constitute over 91% of long term financial obligations of counties.

10.19,90 Source: State Controller's Office, Annual Report, *Financial Transactions Concerning Counties of California.*

County	1987-1988 GENERAL PROPERTY TAX DOLLAR DISTRIBUTION BY COUNTY			
	Property Tax Dollars			
County	City	County	School Purpose	Other Districts
Alameda	$0.23	$0.30	$0.24	$0.23
Alpine	-	$0.68	$0.22	$0.10
Amador	$0.04	$0.45	$0.49	$0.02
Butte	$0.08	$0.23	$0.56	$0.13
Calaveras	$0.01	$0.28	$0.56	$0.15
Colusa	$0.05	$0.36	$0.51	$0.08
Contra Costa	$0.11	$0.25	$0.33	$0.31
Del Norte	$0.02	$0.31	$0.53	$0.14
El Dorado	$0.07	$0.33	$0.39	$0.21
Fresno	$0.15	$0.30	$0.42	$0.13
Glenn	$0.07	$0.33	$0.55	$0.05
Humboldt	$0.05	$0.35	$0.45	$0.15
Imperial	$0.11	$0.33	$0.48	$0.08
Inyo	$0.02	$0.37	$0.53	$0.08
Kern	$0.06	$0.39	$0.43	$0.12
Kings	$0.08	$0.46	$0.36	$0.10
Lake	$0.03	$0.36	$0.44	$0.17
Lassen	$0.04	$0.29	$0.59	$0.08
Los Angeles	$0.19	$0.42	$0.21	$0.18
Madera	$0.04	$0.30	$0.59	$0.07
Marin	$0.13	$0.29	$0.42	$0.16
Mariposa	-	$0.33	$0.61	$0.06
Mendocino	$0.03	$0.42	$0.47	$0.08
Merced	$0.09	$0.39	$0.42	$0.10
Modoc	$0.04	$0.36	$0.54	$0.06
Mono	$0.03	$0.38	$0.33	$0.26
Monterey	$0.10	$0.27	$0.49	$0.14
Napa	$0.11	$0.32	$0.51	$0.06
Nevada	$0.03	$0.29	$0.49	$0.19
Orange	$0.12	$0.18	$0.49	$0.21
Placer	$0.07	$0.29	$0.49	$0.15
Plumas	$0.01	$0.28	$0.58	$0.13
Riverside	$0.07	$0.26	$0.37	$0.30
Sacramento	$0.12	$0.37	$0.29	$0.22
San Benito	$0.04	$0.21	$0.53	$0.22
San Bernardino	$0.09	$0.27	$0.31	$0.33
San Diego	$0.15	$0.25	$0.50	$0.10
San Francisco	-	$0.84	$0.09	$0.07
San Joaquin	$0.14	$0.39	$0.33	$0.14
San Luis Obispo	$0.07	$0.33	$0.54	$0.06
San Mateo	$0.14	$0.25	$0.50	$0.11
Santa Barbara	$0.06	$0.30	$0.47	$0.17
Santa Clara	$0.12	$0.26	$0.46	$0.16
Santa Cruz	$0.08	$0.27	$0.51	$0.14
Shasta	$0.08	$0.25	$0.57	$0.10
Sierra	$0.01	$0.63	$0.25	$0.11
Siskiyou	$0.08	$0.35	$0.52	$0.05
Solano	$0.18	$0.32	$0.29	$0.21
Sonoma	$0.09	$0.33	$0.48	$0.10
Stanislaus	$0.09	$0.26	$0.60	$0.05
Sutter	$0.09	$0.33	$0.48	$0.10
Tehama	$0.07	$0.37	$0.52	$0.04
Trinity	-	$0.37	$0.57	$0.06
Tulare	$0.08	$0.42	$0.42	$0.08
Tuolumne	$0.01	$0.40	$0.52	$0.07
Ventura	$0.08	$0.28	$0.38	$0.26
Yolo	$0.22	$0.29	$0.42	$0.07
Yuba	$0.05	$0.39	$0.45	$0.11
State Average	$0.13	$0.33	$0.36	$0.18

Note: There are no cities in Alpine, Mariposa, and Trinity Counties. San Francisco is a City-County. 10.20,90 Source: California State Board of Equalization *Annual Report*.

	State Aid		Federal Aid		Total County Revenue (in millions)
County	Amount (in millions)	% of County Revenue	Amount (in millions)	% of County Revenue	

CONTRIBUTION OF FEDERAL AND STATE AID TO COUNTY GENERAL REVENUES, 1987-1988

County	State Aid Amount (in millions)	State Aid % of County Revenue	Federal Aid Amount (in millions)	Federal Aid % of County Revenue	Total County Revenue (in millions)
Alameda	297.6	41	136.5	19	722.1
Alpine	1.5	36	0.7	16	4.2
Amador	5.7	33	1.9	11	17.1
Butte	44.7	48	22.8	24	93.8
Calaveras	6.7	33	3.1	15	20.7
Colusa	5.7	41	1.7	12	13.9
Contra Costa	141.4	34	65.5	16	418.3
Del Norte	8.5	41	4.8	23	20.9
El Dorado	25.1	33	14.5	19	76.3
Fresno	201.6	45	111.6	25	442.0
Glenn	7.7	44	3.4	19	17.5
Humboldt	34.7	44	19.3	25	78.6
Imperial	29.3	43	16.4	24	68.8
Inyo	6.7	35	2.5	13	19.1
Kern	114.5	29	66.7	17	389.9
Kings	25.0	38	13.8	21	65.6
Lake	16.1	39	7.5	18	41.4
Lassen	7.3	40	5.0	27	18.3
Los Angeles	1,997.1	36	1,086.4	20	5,531.0
Madera	27.9	44	9.7	15	63.5
Marin	37.2	32	10.8	9	116.2
Mariposa	4.4	33	2.0	15	13.4
Mendocino	27.1	42	9.5	15	64.6
Merced	50.9	41	35.1	28	124.9
Modoc	4.1	37	3.0	27	10.8
Mono	2.8	23	1.1	9	12.2
Monterey	63.9	36	24.2	14	175.2
Napa	21.8	38	6.7	12	56.9
Nevada	13.6	32	5.5	13	42.9
Orange	337.2	35	108.2	11	972.0
Placer	30.7	31	14.6	15	98.0
Plumas	6.0	30	5.9	29	20.1
Riverside	204.9	36	109.7	19	565.9
Sacramento	264.8	38	152.2	22	689.6
San Benito	7.4	41	4.1	23	18.0
San Bernardino	270.8	39	171.9	25	696.0
San Diego	479.1	43	194.2	17	1,117.5
San Francisco	257.4	12	117.8	5	-
San Joaquin	133.6	40	99.3	30	333.1
San Luis Obispo	37.4	31	9.8	8	121.7
San Mateo	101.6	34	29.3	10	298.2
Santa Barbara	63.9	31	20.5	10	205.2
Santa Clara	302.4	38	150.4	19	795.8
Santa Cruz	46.6	35	17.5	13	131.6
Shasta	37.0	39	27.6	29	95.2
Sierra	3.2	42	1.7	22	7.6
Siskiyou	14.7	36	13.2	33	40.3
Solano	67.6	44	29.5	19	154.6
Sonoma	65.1	31	25.8	12	209.5
Stanislaus	98.9	45	58.4	27	218.0
Sutter	19.2	46	8.4	20	41.9
Tehama	13.0	41	7.3	23	31.8
Trinity	5.5	37	4.8	33	14.5
Tulare	96.3	44	57.2	26	216.9
Tuolumne	11.2	35	5.6	17	32.0
Ventura	91.4	30	36.4	12	299.7
Yolo	42.8	48	18.6	21	88.4
Yuba	17.9	43	12.6	30	41.3
State Totals	**$6,101.0**	**37**	**$3,086.5**	**19**	**$16,294.5**

10.21,90 Source: State Controller's Office, *Annual Report 1987-88, Financial Transactions Concerning Counties of California.*

California Almanac

CITY REVENUES BY SOURCE (Excluding the City and County of San Francisco)				
	1986		**1988**	
Source	**Amount**	**Percent**	**Amount**	**Percent**
Taxes				
Property Taxes	$1,209,350,416	7.95%	$1,487,392,710	8.57%
Voter-approved				
Indebtedness	$98,834,770	0.65%	$107,595,185	0.62%
Sales and Use Taxes	$1,802,398,106	11.85%	$2,048,506,688	11.80%
Transportation Tax	$153,857,723	1.01%	$177,134,436	1.02%
Business License Taxes	$384,356,249	2.53%	$436,408,080	2.51%
Utility Users Tax	$580,732,943	3.82%	$687,424,434	3.96%
Other Taxes	$821,455,821	5.40%	$993,149,316	5.72%
Special Benefit Assessments	$75,640,964	0.50%	$98,404,883	0.57%
Licenses and Permits	$215,627,016	1.42%	$268,908,953	1.55%
Fines and Forfeitures	$193,711,074	1.27%	$261,194,290	1.50%
Revenues from Use				
of Money and Property	$915,676,681	6.02%	$914,526,539	5.27%
Intergovernmental Agencies	$2,172,544,019	14.28%	$1,996,741,877	11.50%
Current Service Charges				
Sewer Service Charges				
and Connection Fees	$626,061,450	4.12%	$804,654,132	4.64%
Solid Waste Revenues	$287,739,986	1.89%	$336,298,695	1.94%
Water Service Charges				
and Connection Fees	$951,365,014	6.25%	$1,104,732,950	6.37%
Electric Revenues	$2,217,850,548	14.58%	$2,531,482,363	14.59%
Gas Revenues	$130,656,784	0.86%	$133,958,503	0.77%
Airport Revenues	$247,249,019	1.62%	$277,645,980	1.60%
Ports and Harbors				
Revenues	$214,441,420	1.41%	$294,386,123	1.70%
Quasi-external				
Transactions	$165,919,263	1.09%	$167,439,338	0.96%
Other Current Service				
Charges	$705,352,824	4.64%	$960,976,310	5.54%
Other Revenues	$474,625,204	3.12%	$449,457,148	2.59%
Other Financing Sources	$454,762,960	3.72%	$817,638,909	4.71%
Total	**$15,211,210,254**	**100.00%**	**$17,356,057,842**	**100.00%**

Note: Operating transfers, pension trusts and agency, and internal service fund transactions are not included in this table. It does include general government and city-owned enterprise activities.

10.22,90   Source: State Controller's Office, *Annual Report of Financial Transactions Concerning Cities.*

CITY EXPENDITURES BY SOURCE				
(Excluding the City and County of San Francisco)				
	1986		1988	
Category	Amount	Percent	Amount	Percent
General Government				
Legislative	$204,865,768	1.47%	$233,659,694	1.42%
Management and Support	$758,864,449	5.45%	$927,958,261	5.63%
Public Safety				
Police	$2,401,405,606	17.25%	$2,815,127,574	17.08%
Fire	$1,122,555,956	8.06%	$1,263,400,883	7.67%
Emergency				
Medical Services	$80,299,567	0.58%	$98,356,410	0.60%
Street Lighting	$162,927,703	1.17%	$166,808,781	1.01%
Other	$64,474,493	0.46%	$78,236,562	0.47%
Transportation				
Streets, Highways,				
and Storm Drains	$1,082,924,910	7.78%	$1,325,786,935	8.04%
Public Transit	$139,925,427	1.00%	$167,828,945	1.02%
Airports	$270,435,516	1.94%	$365,653,315	2.22%
Ports and Harbors	$255,611,442	1.83%	$277,820,820	1.69%
Other	$218,326,612	1.57%	$273,308,508	1.66%
Community Devel.				
Planning	$151,366,422	1.09%	$195,179,905	1.18%
Construction and				
Engineering Regulation	$407,972,709	2.93%	$523,481,607	3.18%
Other	$450,869,864	3.24%	$612,337,876	3.71%
Health				
Solid Waste	$393,712,046	2.83%	$437,190,181	2.65%
Sewers	$712,879,350	5.12%	$963,276,961	5.85%
Other	$78,687,680	0.56%	$90,279,642	0.55%
Culture and Leisure				
Parks and Recreation	$744,178,879	5.34%	$909,069,231	5.52%
Libraries	$236,147,985	1.70%	$283,070,714	1.72%
Other	$207,420,565	1.49%	$319,608,667	1.94%
Public Utilities				
Water	$1,049,495,818	7.54%	$1,254,476,443	7.61%
Gas	$130,900,738	0.94%	$121,428,055	0.74%
Electric	$2,479,485,042	17.81%	$2,660,415,451	16.15%
Other	$4,122,545	0.03%	$1,999,657	0.01%
Other	$114,050,509	0.82%	$112,372,037	0.68%
Total	**$13,923,877,601**	**100%**	**$16,478,133,115**	**100%**

10.23,90 Source: State Controller's Office, *Annual Report of Financial Transactions Concerning Cities.*

CITY PROPERTY TAXES AND VOTER APPROVED INDEBTEDNESS, 1972-1988 (Excluding the City and County of San Francisco)					
Year	Property Taxes(1)	Voter-Approved Indebtedness(3)	Total	Percent Change from Prior Year	Percent of Total Revenues
1972-73	$670,239,298	-	$670,239,298	9.34	20.45
1973-74	$681,342,489	-	$681,342,489	1.66	19.27
1974-75	$748,966,540	-	$748,966,540(2)	9.93	19.26
1975-76	$844,789,660	-	$844,789,600(2)	12.79	18.81
1976-77	$928,537,507	-	$928,537,507(2)	9.91	18.46
1977-78	$1,019,400,513	-	$1,019,400,513(2)	9.79	17.12
1978-79	$483,258,294	-	$483,258,594(4)	-52.59(4)	8.00
1979-80	$708,885,090	-	$708,885,090(5)	46.69(5)	10.90
1980-81	$799,745,374	-	$799,745,374	12.82	11.13
1981-82	$812,536,735	$92,915,806	$895,452,541	11.97	8.70(6)
1982-83	$910,058,510	$96,363,897	$1,006,422,407	12.39	9.47
1983-84	$976,665,645	$101,129,532	$1,077,795,177	7.09	8.85
1984-85	$1,075,713,846	$105,360,143	$1,181,073,989	9.58	8.6
1985-86	$1,209,350,416	$98,834,770	$1,308,185,186	10.76	8.6
1986-87	$1,347,036,132	$99,825,198	$1,466,861,330	10.60	9.3
1987-88	$1,487,392,710	$107,595,185	$1,594,987,895	10.24	9.2

(1) Includes current year secured and unsecured property taxes.
(2) Included in property taxes are Los Angeles County Library and Fire Protection Services.
(3) Voter-approved indebtedness in prior years was included in property taxes.
(4) Major reduction in 1978-1979 due to passage of Prop. 13.
(5) Increase due to shift of property tax revenues from school districts to cities, (AB-8), 1979-1980.
(6) Percent is not comparable to prior year due to reporting changes.
   10.24,90   Source: State Controller's Office, *Annual Rept. of Financial Transactions Concerning Cities*, 1987-88.

		Trans-		% Change	Percent
	Sales and	portation		from	of Total
Year	Use Taxes	Tax*	Total	Prior Year	Revenues

CITY SALES USE AND TRANSPORTATION TAXES, 1972-1988
(Excluding the City and County of San Francisco)

Year	Sales and Use Taxes	Transportation Tax*	Total	% Change from Prior Year	Percent of Total Revenues
1972-73	$452,015,601	-	$452,015,601	16.48	12.19
1973-74	$519,908,375	-	$519,908,375	15.02	12.71
1974-75	$576,454,030	-	$576,454,030	10.88	12.52
1976-77	$743,030,375	-	$743,030,375	15.58	12.29
1977-78	$876,209,137	-	$876,209,137	17.92	12.20
1978-79	$996,563,283	$17,069,082	$1,013,632,365	15.68	13.30
1979-80	$1,142,815,500	$27,505,011	$1,170,320,511	15.46	14.16
1980-81	$1,214,868,791	$59,129,871	$1,273,998,662	8.86	13.42
1981-82	$1,295,490,054	$72,157,796	$1,367,647,850	7.35	13.28†
1982-83	$1,278,850,816	$102,748,139	$1,381,598,955	1.02	13.00
1983-84	$1,489,412,071	$118,066,948	$1,607,479,019	16.35	13.21
1984-85	$1,674,194,879	$130,375,777	$1,813,570,656	12.82	13.21
1985-86	$1,802,398,106	$153,857,723	$1,956,255,829	7.87	12.86
1986-87	$1,877,776,820	$157,222,381	$2,034,999,201	4.03	13.07
1987-88	$2,048,506,688	$177,134,436	$2,225,641,124	9.37	12.82

* Effective 1978-1979, sales and use tax and transportation tax were reported separately.
† Percent is not comparable to prior years due to reporting changes.
10.25,90 Source: State Controller's Office, *Annual Report of Financial Transactions Concerning Cities, 1987-1988.*

CITY BUSINESS LICENSE AND UTILITY USERS TAXES, 1972-1988
(Excluding the City and County of San Francisco)

Year	Business License Tax	Percent of Total Revenues	Utility Users Tax	% Change from Prior Year
1972-73	$95,849,942	8.02	$94,857,156	12.54
1973-74	$102,968,893	7.43	$107,465,207	13.29
1974-75	$109,774,447	6.61	$131,042,054	21.94
1976-77	$135,177,287	10.70	$163,281,455	10.68
1977-78	$148,823,849	10.10	$184,189,321	12.80
1978-79	$179,174,091	20.39	$205,477,226	11.56
1979-80	$203,104,931	13.36	$233,855,820	13.81
1980-81	$209,855,141	3.32	$280,295,756	19.86
1981-82	$235,575,769	12.26	$326,149,621	16.36
1982-83	$255,730,647	8.56	$342,743,953	5.09
1983-84	$305,869,329	19.61	$464,612,012	35.56
1984-85	$344,717,819	12.70	$557,600,193	20.01
1985-86	$384,356,249	11.50	$580,732,943	4.15
1986-87	$397,105,237	3.52	$605,745,022	4.31
1987-88	$436,408,080	9.90	$687,424,434	13.48

10.26,90 Source: State Controller's Office, *Annual Report of Financial Transactions Concerning Cities,* 1985-1986.

STATE AND FEDERAL AID TO CITIES
(Excluding the City and County of San Francisco)

	1986-1987		1987-1988	
Source	Amount (millions)	Percent of Total City Revenues	Amount (millions)	Percent of Total City Revenues
State Grants				
Motor Vehicle In-Lieu Tax	$605,727,006	3.89%	$669,818,589	3.86%
Trailer Coach In-Lieu Tax	$5,336,171	0.03%	$5,071,632	0.03%
Cigarette Tax	$63,897,915	0.41%	$62,122,258	0.36%
Homeowners Property Tax Relief	$46,665,333	0.30%	$48,922,420	0.28%
Gasoline Tax	$277,452,385	1.78%	$280,311,384	1.62%
Other State Grants	$215,824,709	1.39%	$206,884,676	1.19%
County Grants	$46,809,097	0.30%	$123,146,960	0.71%
Federal Grants				
Federal Revenue Sharing	$75,560,007	0.49%	$362,369	0.00%
Other Federal Grants	$555,571,962	3.57%	$557,889,526	3.21%
Other Taxes In-Lieu	$44,372,644	0.28%	$42,212,063	0.24%
Total Intergovernment Aid	$1,937,217,229	12.44%	$1,996,741,877	11.50%

Note: Totals may not add due to rounding.
10.27.90   Source: State Controller's Office, *Annual Report of Financial Transactions Concerning Cities.*

LONG TERM INDEBTEDNESS-OTHER THAN BONDS
(Excluding the City and County of San Francisco)

	1985-1986		1987-1988		
Type of Debt	Amount	Percent	Amount	Percent	Percent Change from Prior Year
Lease Obligation*	$3,057,883,253	87.91%	$5,008,519,319	94.87%	26.67%
Construction Financed by State and/or Federal Government	$86,428,713	2.48%	$105,501,599	2.00%	7.37%
Notes	$63,437,424	1.83%	$26,803,229	0.51%	-43.72%
Warrants	-	-	-	-	-
Loans	$52,811,544	1.52%	$37,913,162	0.72%	-3.35%
Other	$217,828,544	6.26%	$100,252,104	1.90%	27.59%
Total	$3,478,389,631	100.00%	$5,278,999,413	100.00%	25.17%

*   Lease obligations include principal and interest.
10.28.90   Source: State Controller's Office, *Annual Report of Financial Transactions Concerning Cities.*

				Percent Increase or Decrease
			Percent of the	Over Prior
Type of Bond	1986-1987	1987-1988	Total	Year

LONG TERM INDEBTEDNESS-BONDS
(Excluding the City and County of San Francisco)

Type of Bond	1986-1987	1987-1988	Percent of the Total	Percent Increase or Decrease Over Prior Year
General Obligation	$357,955,113	$407,784,874	8.19%	13.92%
Revenue	$4,104,901,452	$4,521,477,763	90.78%	10.15%
Improvement District	$50,430,875	$48,291,370	0.97%	-4.24%
Limited Obligation	$235,000	$3,230,000	0.06%	100.00%
Total	**$4,513,522,440**	**$4,980,784,007**	**100.00%**	**10.35%**

10.29,90   Source: State Controller's Office, *Annual Report of Financial Transactions Concerning Cities.*

CITY ASSESSED VALUATION, TAXES ALLOCATED, TAXES LEVIED, AND AVERAGE PROPERTY TAX EFFORT, 1973-1988
(Excluding the City and County of San Francisco)

Year	Net Assessed Valuation(1)	Taxes Allocated(2)	Taxes Levied(3)	Total	Average Property Tax Effort per $100
1973-74	$40,376,678,740	-	$702,547,293	$702,547,293	$1.74
1974-75	$44,315,255,972	-	$772,465,640	$772,465,640	$1.74
1975-76	$49,511,057,306	-	$871,594,685	$871,594,685	$1.76
1976-77	$56,993,695,389	-	$993,109,077	$993,109,077	$1.74
1977-78	$65,596,593,781	-	$1,030,191,786	$1,030,191,786	$1.57
1978-79	$69,616,676,625	$452,124,604	$66,972,361	$519,096,965	$0.75
1979-80	$82,272,565,051	$658,128,319(6)	$67,918,258	$726,046,577	$0.88
1980-81	$92,822,471,330	$754,225,176(6)	$68,270,688	$822,495,864	$0.89
1981-82	$428,124,031,052(4)	$850,639,661(6)	$77,354,093	$927,993,754	$0.22(5)
1982-83	$486,065,716,509	$953,280,268(6)	$91,078,378	$1,044,358,646	$0.21(5)
1983-84	$529,028,275,776	$1,115,077,281(6)	$101,603,568	$1,216,680,849	$0.23(5)
1984-85	$587,963,129,460	$1,171,029,879(6)	$99,883,152	$1,270,913,031	$0.22(5)
1985-86	$657,331,860,813	$1,283,684,160(6)	$98,087,635	$1,381,771,795	$0.21(5)
1986-87	$730,076,213,906	$1,401,361,701(6)	$96,145,280	$1,497,506,981	$0.21(5)
1987-88	$816,355,661,949	$1,550,753,392	$105,252,196	$1,656,005,588	0.20
1987-88	$872,368,038,644	$1,691,648,630	$124,847,717	$1,816,496,347	0.21

(1) Net of Homeowners', Business Inventory Property Tax Relief and other exemptions.
(2) Cities' share of county-wide one percent levy.
(3) As of the 1978-79 fiscal year includes only voter approved debt.
(4) In accordance with Section 135(a) of the Revenue and Taxation Code, "Assessed Value" means 25 percent of the full value to and including the 1980-81 fiscal year, and means 100 percent of full value for the 1981-82 fiscal year and years thereafter.
(5) 1981-82 average property tax effort per $100 valuation is equal to $0.88 (4x$o.22) based on the 1980-81 definition of assessed valuation which was 25 percent of full value.
(6) Effective as of 1988-89 fiscal year, Taxes Allocated and Taxes Levied include the Unitary and Operating Non-Unitary Tax Allocation.
10.30,90 Source: State Controller's Office, *Annual Report of Financial Transactions Concerning Cities,* 1987-88.

CITY EMPLOYMENT AND PAY (CALIFORNIA'S 59 LARGEST CITIES)

City	City Employ-ment*	Employ-ment Ratio†	Average Monthly Pay	City	City Employ-ment*	Employ-ment Ratio†	Average Monthly Pay
Anaheim	2,237	108	$3,168	Ontario	803	70	$2,801
Bakersfield	1,036	69	$2,679	Orange	707	70	$2,881
Berkeley	1,623	156	$2,456	Oxnard	1,074	82	$2,783
Burbank	1,147	129	$3,189	Pasadena	1,684	130	$2,771
Carson	424	48	$2,470	Pomona	771	67	$3,356
Chula Vista	693	58	$2,562	Rancho Cucamonga	213	28	$2,267
Compton	668	69	$2,312	Richmond	909	117	$2,918
Concord	641	49	$2,858	Riverside	1,860	95	$2,596
Costa Mesa	644	73	$3,222	Sacramento	3,168	98	$3,017
Daly City	481	58	$2,929	Salinas	535	55	$2,588
Downey	484	57	$2,925	San Bernardino	1,474	106	$2,546
El Cajon	559	66	$2,303	San Buenaventura	680	80	$2,541
El Monte	414	43	$3,153	San Diego	8,604	85	$2,616
Escondido	620	74	$2,813	San Francisco	23,273	311	$3,052
Fremont	865	56	$2,805	San Jose	5,051	71	$3,494
Fresno	2,462	86	$2,527	San Mateo	675	83	$2,724
Fullerton	784	72	$2,517	Santa Ana	1,803	76	$2,873
Garden Grove	695	52	$3,095	Santa Barbara	1,053	133	$2,359
Glendale	1,502	98	$3,086	Santa Clara	993	112	$3,763
Hayward	736	73	$2,822	Santa Monica	1,476	158	$3,055
Huntington Beach	1,093	60	$2,932	Santa Rosa	869	89	$2,765
Inglewood	865	84	$3,229	Simi Valley	418	47	$2,525
Irvine	658	74	$3,266	South Gate	374	46	$2,661
Lakewood	246	32	$2,473	Stockton	1,465	80	$3,057
Long Beach	5,112	129	$2,893	Sunnyvale	822	73	$3,495
Los Angeles	45,289	139	$3,120	Thousand Oaks	449	47	$2,513
Modesto	894	67	$2,569	Torrance	1,397	103	$3,337
Norwalk	273	30	$2,379	Vallejo	481	51	$3,295
Oakland	3,793	106	$2,999	West Covina	408	42	$2,619
Oceanside	761	77	$2,581				

* Full time equivalent employment.   † City employees per 10,000 population.
10.31,90 Source: U.S. Bureau of the Census, *City Employment in 1987*. Ratios calculated by the editor.

CALIFORNIA CITIES BY POPULATION CLASS, 1988

Population	Number	Percent
Under 10,000	152	34.0%
10,000-25,000	90	20.1%
25,001-50,000	94	21.0%
50,001-100,000	75	16.8%
100.001-250,000	29	6.5%
Over 250,000	7	1.6%
Total	447*	100.0%

* Excluding the City and County of San Francisco.
10.32,90 Source: California State Contoller, *Annual Report of Fiscal Transactions Concerning Cities, 1987-1988*.

Rank	City	Employees per 10,000 Population
\multicolumn{3}{c}{**THE 10 CALIFORNIA CITIES WITH THE LARGEST CITY PAYROLLS**}		
1	Santa Monica	158
2	Berkeley	156
3	Los Angeles	139
4	Santa Barbara	133
5	Pasadena	130
6	Burbank	129
7	Long Beach	129
8	Richmond	117
9	Santa Clara	112
10	Anaheim	108

10.33,90 Source: U.S. Bureau of the Census, *City Employment in 1987*. Rankings calculated by the editor.

THE 10 CALIFORNIA CITIES WITH THE SMALLEST CITY PAYROLLS

Rank	City	Employees per 10,000 Population
1	Rancho Cucamonga	28
2	Norwalk	30
3	Lakewood	32
4	West Covina	42
5	El Monte	43
6	South Gate	46
7	Simi Valley	47
8	Thousand Oaks	47
9	Carson	48
10	Concord	49

10.34,90 Source: U.S. Bureau of the Census, *City Employment in 1987*. Rankings calculated by the editor.

THE TEN CALIFORNIA CITIES WITH THE HIGHEST PAID CITY EMPLOYEES		
Rank	City	Average Monthly pay
1	Santa Clara	$3,763
2	Sunnyvale	$3,495
3	San Jose	$3,494
4	Pomona	$3,356
5	Torrance	$3,337
6	Vallejo	$3,295
7	Irvine	$3,266
8	Inglewood	$3,229
9	Costa Mesa	$3,222
10	Burbank	$3,189

10.35,90 Source: U.S. Bureau of the Census, *Public Employment in 1987*.

THE TEN CALIFORNIA CITIES WITH THE LOWEST PAID CITY EMPLOYEES		
Rank	City	Average Monthly pay
1	Rancho Cucamonga	$2,267
2	El Cajon	$2,303
3	Compton	$2,312
4	Santa Barbara	$2,359
5	Norwalk	$2,379
6	Berkeley	$2,456
7	Carson	$2,470
8	Lakewood	$2,473
9	Thousand Oaks	$2,513
10	Fullerton	$2,517

10.36,90 Source: U.S. Bureau of the Census, *Public Employment in 1987*.

THE CALIFORNIA LOTTERY

Instant Game - Scratchers
Statring Date: Oct. 3, 1985

Game Sales---Start to March 20, 1989	$4.19 billion
Payments to winners	$2.2 billion
Winners of $1 million or more	160
Number of retailers	21,082

Top Five Scratchers Winners

Paul Spencer	$15.2 million
Joan Jones	$11.8 million
Irineo Carranza	$10.1 million
Francisco Campos	$6.4 million
Eric Daily	$6.3 million

Lotto
Starting date: Oct. 14, 1986

Game Sales--Start to March 20, 1989	$2.93 billion
Payments to winners	$2.07 billion
Number of terminals	7,200

Top Five Winners

Shelby Carroll	$25.7 million
Randy Pennington	$25.7 million
Carlos Olvera	$25.1 million
Ronald Bouvia	$23.8 million
Frank Kopita	$20.6 million

Amount Paid to Education

Kindergarten to Grade 12	$2. billion
Community Colleges	$300 million
California State University System	$110 million
University of California System	$63 million
Total Paid to Education	**$2.5 billion**

10.37,90 Source: The California Lottery Commission, unpublished data.

LOTTERY TICKET SALES PER PERSON CALIFORNIA AND SELECTED STATES	
State	**Annual per Person Ticket Sales**
California	**$80**
Arizona	$54
Massachusetts	$235
Connecticut	$162
Pennsylvania	$121

10.38,90 Source: *Gaming and Wagering Business.*

COUNTY SEATS

Crescent City
Yreka
Alturas
Eureka
Weaverville
Redding
Red Bluff
Susanville
Quincy
Willows
Oroville
Downieville
Ukiah
Lakeport
Colusa
Nevada City
Yuba City
Marysville
Woodland
Auburn
Santa Rosa
Placerville
Markleeville
Napa
Sacramento
Fairfield
Jackson
San Andreas
Martinez
Bridgeport
San Rafael
Stockton
San Francisco
Oakland
Sonora
Redwood City
Modesto
San Jose
Mariposa
Santa Cruz
Merced
Hollister
Madera
Salinas
Fresno
Independence
Hanford
Visalia
San Luis Obispo
Bakersfield
Santa Barbara
Ventura
Los Angeles
San Bernardino
Riverside
Santa Ana
San Diego
El Centro

0   20   40   60   80   100
miles

Historical Atlas of California, 1974. University of Oklahoma Press. Reprinted by permission.

Social Welfare

Although a wealthy state by national standards, California has its share of the poor and those dependent on governmental aid to meet their basic needs. Some 3.5 million Californians receive Social Security benefits; the average monthly benefit for those who are retired is $523.

Another important resource for poor Californians is the Food Stamp Program, which reaches 560,000 households, about 5.6 percent of all households in the state. The national School Lunch Program serves 2 million California schoolchildren at a cost of $312 million. And 5.8 percent of the state's households, 8.8 percent of its entire population, receive AFDC (Aid to Families with Dependent Children). California's welfare payments, relatively high in general, are surpassed only by Alaska's.

A significant social welfare issue that has received a great deal of publicity in the past few years is homelessness. With no accurate county, state, and national statistics available, estimates of the number of homeless by both the government and advocacy groups vary widely. Studies indicate that from 30 to 60 percent of the homeless are individuals--most of them men--with a history of alcoholism, drug use, and mental instability. Many of these people lived for years in quiet obscurity, housed in the single-room residential hotels of large cities. When big-city mayors and local governments all across the country approved the demolition or conversion of these hotels, their residents, often with no alternative low-cost accommodations, were forced into the streets.

The California Poll survey in 1988 found that providing for the homeless was a high priority for two-thirds of Californians. Of those interviewed, 79 percent indicated a willingness to pay at least ten dollars a year in extra taxes to provide food and shelter for the homeless. Those interviewed were not asked if they would like to have an apartment for the homeless in their neighborhood, a question that would most likely have elicited a smaller percentage of support. Sometime in the next decade private and public creativity and goodwill may combine to alleviate homelessness, but more leadership will be needed for us to achieve that goal.

SOCIAL SECURITY (OASDI) BENEFICIARIES*

Category	Number	Benefits (billions)	Percent of Total U.S. Benefits
Retired	2,574,000	$13.7	9.7%
Survivors	587,000	$3.6	8.4%
Disabled	350,000	$1.9	9.2%
Total	3,511,000	$19.2	9.4%

* As of Dec., 1987.

11.1,90 Source: Social Security Administration, *Social Security Bulletin* and *U.S. Statistical Abstract*.

SUPPLEMENTAL SECURITY INCOME (SSI) RECIPIENTS AND PAYMENTS, 1989*

	California	United States	California as a Percent of U.S. Totals
Recipients			
Aged	293,543	1,431,280	21%
Blind	20,904	83,095	25%
Disabled	463,452	2,966,988	16%
Total	777,899	4,481,363	17%
Monthly Total Payments (in millions)			
Federal SSI	$137	$973	14%
State Supplements	$173	$245	71%
Total	$309	$1,218	25%

* January.

11.2,90 Source: Social Security Administration, *Social Security Bulletin*.

SUPPLEMENTAL SECURITY INCOME (SSI) RECIPIENTS BY PROGRAM, 1980-1989

Program	1980	1982	1984	1986	1989
Aged Individuals and Couples	281,068	294,570	266,300	266,794	293,543
Blind and Disabled Individuals, Couples, and Children*	368,062	392,211	385,567	413,313	484,356
Total Recipients	649,130	686,781	665,384	680,107	777,899

* Individuals under 18 years of age.

11.3,90 Source: Social Security Administration, *Social Security Bulletin; SSI State and County Data, 1982*, and California Dept. of Social Services, 1989, unpublished data.

AID TO FAMILIES WITH DEPENDENT CHILDREN (AFDC) MONTHLY PAYMENTS IN THE TEN MOST POPULOUS STATES 1988					
	Recipients		Expenditures		Average
State	Number	Percent of All U.S.	Amount (in millions)	Percent of All U.S.	Payment per Family
California	1,718,552	15.7%	$4,090	24.5%	$581
New York	1,010,780	9.2%	$2,140	12.8%	$523
Texas	507,703	4.6%	$344	2.1%	$169
Pennsylvania	538,040	4.9%	$747	4.5%	$347
Illinois	671,237	6.1%	$815	4.9%	$309
Ohio	647,730	5.9%	$805	4.8%	$298
Florida	307,053	2.8%	$318	1.9%	$240
Michigan	646,087	5.9%	$1,231	7.4%	$481
New Jersey	313,172	2.9%	$459	2.8%	$357
North Carolina	182,842	1.7%	$206	1.2%	$243

11.4,90 Source: U.S. Social Security Administration, *Monthly Benefit Statistics.*

MEDICARE AND MEDI-CAL ENROLLMENTS AND DISBURSEMENTS IN CALIFORNIA						
	Number of Enrollees/Recipients (in thousands)			Disbursements (in millions)		
	Medicare			Medicare		
Year	Hospital Insurance	Medical Insurance	Medi-Cal*	Hospital Insurance	Medical Insurance	Medi-Cal
1975	2,221	2,199	2,288	$1,230	$606	$1,723
1980	2,581	2,567	2,804	$2,774	$1,445	$3,491
1981	2,637	2,622	2,906	$3,112	$1,736	$4,140
1982	2,679	2,669	2,862	$3,634	$2,012	$4,258
1983	2,733	2,728	2,648	$4,066	$2,443	$3,784
1984	2,783	2,786	2,619	$4,636	$2,681	$3,508
1985	NA	NA	2,651	$5,099	$3,129	$3,975
1986	2,847	2,858	2,965	NA	NA	$4,412
1987	2,991	3,006	3,045	$5,510	$3,898	$4,699
1988	3,046	3,057	3,178	$5,718	$4,386	NA

* Certified eligibles.
11.5,90 Source: *U.S. Statistical Abstract; California Statistical Abstract*; U.S. Health Care Financing Administration, *Estimated Benefit Payments*; Cal. Dept. of Health Services, Center for Health Statistics, unpublished data.

NUMBER OF RECIPIENTS ON GENERAL RELIEF* AND AND AMOUNT OF EXPENDITURES IN CALIFORNIA 1977 -1988

Year	Average Monthly Number of Recipients			Average Monthly Grant		Total Annual Expenditures† (in millions)
	Family Cases	One-person cases	Total Persons	Family Cases	One-person Cases	
1977	1,956	45,112	49,846	$154	$117	$72
1980	1,014	25,722	28,041	$224	$151	$70
1981	1,034	26,979	29,282	$270	$169	$86
1982	1,039	31,973	34,281	$283	$175	$105
1983	2,483	63,059	68,766	$309	$181	$146
1984	2,150	56,764	61,674	$321	$186	$135
1985	1,980	58,967	63,510	$323	$212	$158
1986	2,150	64,703	69,638	$345	$224	$183
1987	2,197	73,146	78,318	$416	$244	$226
1988	2,228	75,332	80,455	$375	$261	$246

* County nonmedical assistance to recipients in their homes.

† Includes General Relief and other programs administered by county Welfare Departments which are financed from county indigent funds. Generally excludes the costs of county hospitals.

11.6,90 Source: Department of Social Services, Statistical Services Branch, unpublished data.

NUMBER OF CALIFORNIA PUBLIC ASSISTANCE RECIPIENTS BY PROGRAM (Average per month) 1980-1988

Year	Aid to Families with Dependent Children†			Food Stamps	General Relief*	Refugee Cash Assist- ance††
	Adults	Children	Total			
1980	443,709	930,969	1,381,298	1,432,582	28,041	NA
1981	501,290	1,006,558	1,516,846	1,593,701	29,282	11,039
1982	527,666	1,030,378	1,561,658	1,637,834	34,281	16,721
1983	546,589	1,039,778	1,589,830	1,766,869	68,766	8,021
1984	584,212	1,074,750	1,633,998	1,716,631	61,674	4,785
1985	549,274	1,092,041	1,641,315	1,618,520	63,510	4,792
1986	585,519	1,129,031	1,675,299	1,612,327	69,638	5,059
1987	555,993	1,173,564	1,729,559	1,639,400	78,318	4,483
1988	563,322	1,191,988	1,755,310	1,641,729	80,455	4,681

† Includes children in foster homes and institutions.

* Data reported prior to 1982 not comparable to current statistics due to changes in reporting procedures.

†† Data excludes persons receiving assistance from Aid to Families with Dependent Children.

11.7,90 Source: California Department of Social Services, *Public Welfare in California* & unpublished data.

FOOD STAMP PROGRAM PARTICIPANTS AND EXPENDITURES IN CALIFORNIA 1971-1988					
	Total Households Average per month		Total Participants Average per month		Total Value of
Fiscal Year	Public Assistance	Non-Assistance	Public Assistance	Non-Assistance	Food Coupons
1970-1971	279,714	77,316	907,288	239,002	$345,893,931
1971-1972	357,819	96,325	1,101,409	303,790	$431,940,858
1972-1973	350,728	88,537	1,040,031	277,111	$426,162,514
1973-1974	300,072	108,912	945,885	322,937	$469,204,693
1974-1975	302,366	157,742	978,736	471,042	$616,136,937
1975-1976	318,154	170,296	981,030	494,986	$696,321,104
1976-1977	311,445	154,012	940,248	432,912	$659,312,518
1977-1978	287,726	152,538	882,666	389,276	$631,014,666
1978-1979	409,025	165,891	1,031,569	388,182	$557,988,792
1979-1980	311,028	206,090	966,266	467,066	$511,137,275
1980-1981	348,196	240,415	1,070,601	523,100	$587,439,912
1981-1982	357,418	238,564	1,105,900	531,934	$588,910,019
1982-1983	373,768	247,716	1,185,594	581,276	$710,380,292
1983-1984	376,912	214,957	1,207,710	508,921	$683,949,557
1984-1985	363,553	187,723	1,179,057	439,463	$640,224,885
1985-1986	363,409	190,430	1,176,971	435,357	$626,172,877
1986-1987	370,657	195,062	1,194,005	445,395	$614,490,465
1987-1988	376,083	187,548	1,214,087	427,642	$658,688,992

11.8,90 Source: Department of Social Services, Statistical Services Branch unpublished data.

FOOD STAMP PROGRAM PARTICIPANTS AND EXPENDITURES IN CALIFORNIA AND THE UNITED STATES				
	Number of Recipients (in millions)		Federal Cost (in millions)	
Year	California	U.S.	California	U.S.
1975	1.52	19.2	$361	$4,386
1980	1.57	22.0	$527	$8,686
1981	1.62	22.2	$600	$10,663
1982	1.69	22.2*	$583	$11,059
1983	1.74	21.1	$739	$11,155
1984	1.59	19.8	$656	$10,703
1985	1.57	19.1	$639	$10,704
1986	1.61	19.0	$627	$10,561
1987	1.63	19.1	$610	$11,536
1988	1.66	18.7	$690	$12,270

* Includes 1.8 million people in Puerto Rico where the food stamp program was cashed out.

11.9,90 Source: *U.S. Statistical Abstract*, U.S. Department of Agriculture, Food and Nutrition Service, *Food Stamp Program*.

FEDERAL SCHOOL LUNCH PROGRAM PARTICIPANTS AND EXPENDITURES IN CALIFORNIA AND THE UNITED STATES				
	Number of Participating Pupils (in millions)		Federal Cost (in millions)	
Year	California	United States	California	United States
1975	1.49	25.3	$97	$1,289
1980	2.01	27.0	$210	$2,282
1981	2.11	27.1	$230	$2,397
1982	1.76	22.9	$251	$2,950
1983	1.77	23.4	$240	$2,399
1984	1.85	23.8	$261	$2,398
1985	1.90	23.4	$279	$2,579
1986	1.94	23.6	$296	$2,599
1987	2.00	23.9	$312	$2,799
1988	2.10	23.4	$330	$2,917

11.10,90 Source: U.S. Statistical Abstract: U.S. Dept. of Agriculture, Food and Nutrition Service, *F and S 10 Report.*

NUMBER OF CALIFORNIA WELFARE RECIPIENTS* 1970-1988		
Year	Monthly Average Number of Recipients (in millions)	Subsistence Expenditures (in billions)
1970	1.7	$1.5
1972	2.1	$2.0
1974	1.9	$2.1
1976	2.1	$2.9
1978	2.2	$3.5
1980	2.1	$4.0
1982	2.3	$5.2
1984	2.3	$5.7
1985	2.3	$6.0
1986	2.4	$6.6
1987	2.5	$6.9
1988	2.5	$7.4

* Includes General Relief, Aid to Families with Dependent Children, Supplemental Security Income, and the State Supplementary Program.
11.11,90 Source: Cal. Dept. of Social Services, Statistical Services Branch, unpublished data.

NUMBER AND CAPACITY OF LICENSED CHILD CARE FACILITIES IN CALIFORNIA 1978-1988									
	Family Day Care Homes				Day and Infant Care Centers*				
	State-Licensed		County-Licensed		Day-Care		Infant-Care†		Total
Year	Number	Capacity	Number	Capacity	Number	Capacity	Number	Capacity	Capacity
1978	2,061	8,762	15,284	61,147	3,459	154,818	29	-	224,727
1980	2,279	11,790	17,125	78,984	4,016	184,091	-	-	274,865
1982	6,895	37,971	18,938	110,207	4,705	222,164	-	-	370,342
1983	9,893	57,699	19,970	122,620	5,045	241,410	74	1,749	421,729
1984	12,265	74,147	18,817	118,321	6,459	321,422	200	4,386	513,890
1985	14,613	91,853	19,170	119,940	6,672	336,947	234	5,091	548,740
1987	15,967	108,674	19,100	127,217	7,753	401,219	NA	NA	637,110
1988	17,873	124,749	21,401	142,486	8,916	431,855	550	11,696	710,786

* State-licensed centers outside the home.

† Data for infant-care centers which are included in the day-care center totals.

Note: State Licensing figures for Family Day Care Homes are skewed by the transfer of licensing responsibilities from several counties, including Los Angeles, to the state. State licensing figures for Day-and-Infant-Care centers are skewed by the transfer of licensing responsibilities from the state Department of Education to the Community Care Licensing Section.

Approximately one-half of the non-Family Day Care Centers are located at schools.

11.12,90 Source: California Department of Social Services, Community Care Licensing Section, unpublished data.

FOSTER CARE			
Year	Number of licensed facilities	Capacity of licensed facilities*	Average Monthly Cost Per Recipient
1980	12,441	27,367	$508
1981	12,333	27,221	$562
1982	12,767	28,531	$622
1984	12,378	33,851	$685
1987	14,261	32,997	$864
1989	15,572	36,533	NA

* Most facilities operate at or near full capacity.

11.13,90 Source: California Department of Social Services, Community Care Licensing Section, unpublished data.

WELFARE BENEFITS* CALIFORNIA & SELECTED STATES		
State	Monthly Welfare Benefit	Rank
California	$633	2
New York	$539	6
Alaska	$740	1
Oregon	$420	15
Arizona	$293	34
Nevada	$330	30

* For a mother with no other income who has 2 children. 11.14,90 Source: U.S. Dept. of Health & Human Services, Family Support Division, unpublished data, 1989.

MAJOR CALIFORNIA PUBLIC PENSION FUNDS							
Plan	Assets (millions)	Unfunded Obligations (millons)	Rate of Return (Percent) 1985	1986	1987	1988	5 Year Average
Defined Benefit Plans							
State Plans							
Judges' Retirement System	$3.6	589	*	*	*	*	*
Legislators' Retirement System	$53.4	$19.6	10.7	11.5	13.0	11.0	11.3
Public Employees' Retirement System	$35,851	9,838	11.2	12.2	12.2	12.2	11.9
State Teachers' Retirement System	$20,851	14,042	11.6	16.1	10.7	10.6	12.0
University of California Retirement System	$5,260	987	7.7	13.3	9.4	12.2	9.9
Median Value for State	-	-	NA	NA	11.4	11.6	11.6
Counties							
Alameda	$614	118	8.9	10.4	15.1	13.7	11.5
Contra Costa	$539	251	9.4	11.9	14.8	9.6	11.7
Fresno	$377	62	10.0	13.1	15.1	12.6	12.2
Imperial	$52	10.3	9.6	10.5	9.4	2.0	8.5
Kern	$342	105	10.6	15.0	10.7	8.3	10.4
Los Angeles	$6,893	1,741	11.6	17.8	15.2	9.7	12.8
Marin	$192	38	10.7	11.8	13.6	10.3	11.4
Mendocino	$42	17	10.3	11.2	13.2	9.2	10.9
Merced	$102	10.1	11.5	11.3	12.7	9.1	10.6
Orange	$988	284	10.4	13.5	15.0	6.8	11.1
Sacramento	$573	95	11.2	14.5	13.9	8.6	12.0
San Bernardino	$626	147	8.9	20.4	8.0	13.4	12.1
San Diego	$711	323	7.9	11.7	18.8	12.6	11.8
San Joaquin	$317	NONE	11.0	12.1	12.0	12.4	11.7
San Luis Obispo	$83	NONE	12.3	12.8	12.4	11.4	12.2
San Mateo	$343	170	11.0	13.2	11.1	9.7	11.1
Santa Barbara	$251	NONE	13.7	24.5	17.0	4.3	14.0
Sonoma	$135	39	10.6	10.0	12.6	8.3	10.2
Stanislaus	$149	43	10.4	12.2	12.8	13.0	11.7
Tulare	$159	3	11.0	26.0	12.9	9.7	15.0
Ventura	$425	47	11.0	20.4	16.8	9.3	14.0
Median Value for Counties	-	-	NA	NA	13.2	9.7	11.7
Cities							
Alameda, Police and Fire Pension Plan 1079 & 1082	$32.3	53.8	12.0	18.5	16.5	9.0	11.1

* Pay as you go systems.
11.15.1,90

MAJOR CALIFORNIA PUBLIC PENSION FUNDS							
	Assets	Unfunded Obligations	Rate of Return (Percent)				5 Year
Plan	(millions)	(millons)	1985	1986	1987	1988	Average
Defined Benefit Plans							
City Plans (cont.)							
Albany, Fire and Police	$3.8	$10.4	9.6	16.0	9.7	9.6	10.6
Bakersfield, Firemen's Disability and Retirement	$3.2	NONE	9.7	10.4	8.4	8.5	9.5
Berkeley, Safety Employees	$0.4	$28.6	0.1	0.2	NA	NA	NA
Concord	$35.2	$4.8	NA	NA	11.5	8.2	NA
Costa Mesa, Safety Employees	$32.8	$8.0	11.1	15.8	11.8	9.9	12.0
El Cerrito	$0.8	$2.5	8.8	9.5	7.9	7.9	8.3
Emeryville	$0.2	NA	7.3	8.7	6.3	7.0	6.9
Eureka, Fire and Police	$1.1	$6.9	12.8	10.5	6.1	8.3	9.5
Fresno, Fire and Police	$115	$109	6.2	17.6	17.6	5.4	10.8
Fresno, General Service Employees	$137	$79	13.8	17.1	17.2	5.1	12.1
Irvine, Safety	$6.2	NONE	NA	11.7	9.4	9.8	6.2
Los Angeles, Fire and Police	$2,386	$3,166	10.6	18.7	16.0	8.5	13.1
Los Angeles, General Municipal Employees	$948	$600	10.6	15.6	15.2	8.9	12.2
Los Angeles, Water and Power Employees	$434	$772	10.3	12.4	11.4	8.6	10.6
Oakland, Fire and Police	$199	$642	11.7	12.0	12.0	10.6	11.4
Oakland General	$37.3	NONE	16.0	13.2	14.8	10.6	13.6
Pasadena, Fire and Police	$32.4	$140	17.0	25.2	19.6	8.2	13.3
Piedmont, Fire and Police	$4.3	$0.72	9.7	12.0	10.5	12.9	10.7
Pittsburg	$0.2	NA	10.6	9.8	6.9	6.7	9.5
Richmond, General Pension Plan	$5.1	$3.0	11.9	9.7	9.5	12.5	10.7
Richmond, Police and Fireman's Pension Plan	$26.4	$36.6	2.2	5.2	4.7	1.3	4.2

* Pay as you go systems.
   11.15.2,90

MAJOR CALIFORNIA PUBLIC PENSION FUNDS							
Plan	Assets (millions)	Unfunded Obligations (millons)	Rate of Return (Percent)				5 Year Average
			1985	1986	1987	1988	
Defined Benefit Plans (cont.)							
City Plans (cont.)							
Sacramento	$90	$86	8.2	15.9	12.7	10.5	11.4
San Diego	$606	$21	12.5	14.9	18.4	11.0	13.1
San Francisco	$2,984	$1,494	8.1	14.5	14.0	7.9	10.7
San Jose, Federated City Employees	$277	$62	11.6	11.5	13.4	10.0	11.4
San Jose, Fire and Police	$356	$22.5	10.6	10.9	14.0	10.0	11.2
Santa Barbara Police and Fire	$1.7	NONE	16.4	13.2	18.5	7.7	11.6
Median Value for Cities	-	-	NA	12.8	12.0	8.6	11.1
Special Districts							
Alameda-Contra Costa Transit District, Union Employees	$75.9	$14.9	10.9	9.5	6.9	8.2	9.3
Alameda-Contra Costa Transit District, Salaried Employees	$11.8	$6.7	10.9	9.5	7.0	8.2	9.2
Antelope Valley Hospital District	$8.9	$2.5	NA	NA	19.0	16.7	NA
Brookside Hospital Employees Retirement Plan	$14.0	NONE	NA	15.6	25.2	-3.3	7.5
Contra Costa County Water District	$8.6	NONE	11.2	13.3	9.6	11.7	11.1
East Bay Municipal Utilities District	$130.6	$18.6	16.8	20.2	13.5	5.6	11.9
Golden Gate Transit Amalgamated Retirement Board	$24.5	$5.6	8.4	7.9	12.7	19.4	12.8
Long Beach Public Transportation Co., Contract Employees	$6.0	$1.9	6.9	16.4	14.1	10.1	11.8
Long Beach Public Transportation Co., Salaried Employees	$1.5	NONE	6.7	16.8	14.6	12.0	12.6
Mesa Consolidated Water District	$0.8	$0.14	7.3	9.2	7.1	7.9	9.8
Otay Municipal Water District	$4.3	NONE	11.6	9.4	8.6	8.2	9.7
Sacramento Regional Transit, Contract Employees	$20.0	$5.7	11.1	15.1	13.9	10.4	12.5
Sacramento, Regional Transit, Non-contract Employees	$3.5	$1.3	7.1	10.3	12.3	9.6	9.0

* Pay as you go systems.
11.15.3,90

MAJOR CALIFORNIA PUBLIC PENSION FUNDS							
Plan	Assets (millions)	Unfunded Obligations (millons)	Rate of Return (Percent)				5 Year Average
			1985	1986	1987	1988	
Defined Benefit Plans (cont.)							
Special Districts (cont.)							
San Benito Hospital District	$1.5	$0.33	13.3	11.7	5.7	27.9	12.6
San Diego Transit Corporation	$29.6	$3.9	12.0	16.9	24.2	12.3	14.6
Santa Clara County Transit District	$35.3	$1.2	13.2	11.2	9.6	12.0	11.4
Southern California Rapid Transit District, Brotherhood of Railway and Airline Clerks	$19.3	NONE	16.0	20.2	10.0	7.8	12.9
Southern California Rapid Transit District, Maintenance Employees	$65.3	$0.07	16.2	19.8	10.1	8.2	13.0
Southern California Rapid Transit District, Non-contract Employees	$71.2	NONE	16.2	19.7	9.9	7.6	12.9
Southern California Rapid Transit District, United Transportation Union	$181.8	$13.5	16.0	19.9	10.0	8.2	12.9
Stockton Metropolitan Transit District	$3.1	$0.29	14.8	9.3	7.6	9.3	10.6
Truckee Sanitary District	$0.28	$0.087	NA	NA	-2.9	28.0	NA
Tulare County Housing Authority	NA	NA	NA	NA	NA	11.5	NA
Median Value for Special Districts	-	-	NA	13.3	10.0	9.6	11.9
Defined Contribution Plans							
Counties and Cities							
Adelanto	$0.1	NA	10.0	9.2	5.9	6.1	7.8
Grand Terrace	NA	NA	NA	NA	NA	5.8	NA
Irvine, General Employees Retirement Plan	$8.3	NA	NA	10.3	8.4	8.0	NA
Los Gatos	$0.8	NA	10.4	7.2	6.2	6.1	7.7
Kerman	$0.4	NA	NA	NA	10.5	-2.7	NA
Ripon	$0.6	NA	2.1	35.7	4.1	NA	NA
San Luis Obispo County	$0.33	NA	NA	7.4	7.7	7.3	NA
Median Value for Cities and Counties				9.2	6.9	6.1	7.8
Special Districts							
Arvin Edison Water Storage	$1.6	NA	NA	NA	8.2	8.3	NA
Berrenda Mesa Water District	$0.59	NA	11.7	10.2	8.9	0.8	9.1
Broadmoor Police Protection	$0.29	NA	NA	NA	5.8	4.8	NA

* Pay as you go systems.
  11.15.4,90

		Unfunded	Rate of Return (Percent)				5 Year
	Assets	Obligations	1985	1986	1987	1988	Average
Plan	(millions)	(millons)					

MAJOR CALIFORNIA PUBLIC PENSION FUNDS

Defined Contribution Plans (cont.)

Plan	Assets (millions)	Unfunded Obligations (millons)	1985	1986	1987	1988	5 Year Average
Special Districts (cont.)							
Clear Creek Community Services District	$0.17	NA	16.1	8.2	9.1	14.9	10.8
Corcoran Irrigation	NA	NA	NA	NA	NA	5.2	NA
Eastern Sierra CSD	$0.036	NA	NA	NA	7.4	7.7	NA
El Nido Irrigation District	$0.040	NA	10.1	9.7	7.0	5.5	8.2
Exeter Irrigation District	$0.21	NA	12.7	10.9	8.4	7.6	10.1
Fresno Irrigation District	$1.0	NA	11.6	11.6	10.4	9.6	10.7
Garden Grove Sanitary District	NA	NA	NA	NA	NA	6.8	NA
Glenn Colusa Irrigation District	NA	NA	NA	NA	NA	10.6	NA
Home Gardens Sanitary District	$0.15	NA	12.6	11.2	5.5	5.5	9.5
La Canada Irrigation District	$0.20	NA	15.4	6.8	0.3	6.5	7.0
La Habra Heights County Water District	$0.29	NA	9.9	8.2	7.2	7.5	8.5
Lakeside Irrigation District	$0.1	NA	10.5	9.1	7.8	6.8	9.0
Liberty Fire Protection District	$0.028	NA	12.2	10.1	11.0	3.5	9.5
Lindmore Irrigation District	$0.70	NA	12.4	11.3	9.3	7.8	10.9
North Bakersfield Recreation and Park District	$1.0	NA	14.2	19.3	17.3	6.9	13.7
North Tahoe PUC	$0.61	NA	NA	NA	-3.6	4.4	0.2
Orange County Water District	$5.6	NA	12.5	9.1	7.6	3.8	8.4
Port San Luis Harbor	NA	NA	NA	NA	NA	7.7	NA
Rainbow Municipal Water District	$0.55	NA	10.5	9.9	8.1	7.3	9.3
Red Bluff Cemetery	$0.14	NA	NA	NA	10.2	9.8	NA
Saucelito Irrigation District	$0.13	NA	10.8	10.5	8.5	7.6	9.4

* Pay as you go systems.
11.15.5,90

PHILANTROPISTS - PROMINENT CALIFORNIANS	
Avery Brundage	Harrison Gray Otis
Lillie Coit	David Packard
Louise Davies	James D. Phelan
M.H. de Young	E.W. Scripps
Carrie Doheny	Ellen Scripps
J. Paul Getty	Norton Simon
Phoebe A. Hearst	Adolph Spreckels
William Hewlett	Jane Stanford
Henry Huntington	Leland Stanford
William Kent	Aldolph Sutro
James Lick	Dr. H.H. Toland

11.16,90 Source: Pacific Data Resources

MAJOR CALIFORNIA PUBLIC PENSION FUNDS							
Plan	Assets (millions)	Unfunded Obligations (millons)	Rate of Return (Percent)				5 Year Average
			1985	1986	1987	1988	
Defined Contribution Plans (cont.)							
Special Districts (cont.)							
South Bay Hospital	$0.012	NA	NA	NA	3.3	6.8	NA
Southgate Recreation and Park District	$0.41	NA	11.2	9.2	9.9	8.2	9.7
Tranquillity Irrigation District	$0.42	NA	9.1	10.4	8.3	8.0	8.5
Truckee-Donner Recreation	$0.034	NA	NA	NA	4.7	5.3	NA
Tulare Lake Basin Water	NA	NA	NA	NA	NA	11.7	NA
Valley Center Municipal Water District	$1.6	NA	8.9	14.9	11.5	9.5	9.2
Valley Sanitary District	$0.51	NA	9.6	8.8	7.9	7.8	8.5
Wasco Recreation and Park District	$0.1	NA	11.2	4.4	27.5	7.0	11.3
West Valley Vector Control	$0.045	NA	NA	NA	1.3	12.0	NA
Yuima Municipal Water District	$0.14	NA	26.1	0.2	51.6	8.4	17.3
Median Value, Special Districts	NA	NA	NA	9.9	8.2	7.6	9.4
Median Value, All Systems	NA	NA	11.0	NA	10.5	8.3	11.1

* Pay as you go systems.
11.15.6,90

MAJOR CALIFORNIA PENSION FUNDS MEMBERS, ASSETS AND OBLIGATIONS					
		Assets	Obligations		
Type	Members	Total (billions)	Unfunded Obligations (billions)	Average per Member	Funded Ratios 1988
State	1,330,084	$62.30	$24.80	$18,678	71%
Counties	261,308	$14.60	$3.00	$11,474	83%
Cities	137,817	$11.30	$7.40	$53,666	61%
Special Districts	24,080	$0.74	$0.04	$1,737	95%
Total	1,753,289	$88.90	$35.20	$20,119	72%

11.17,90 Source: Office of the State Controller, *Annual Report of Financial Transactions - Public Retirement Systems, Fiscal Year 1987-1988.*

DISTRIBUTION OF INVESTMENTS OF THE 119 CALIFORNIA PUBLIC RETIREMENT SYSTEMS		
Category	Amount* (in billions)	Percent of Total Invested
Bonds	$45	47%
Stocks	$40	41%
Short Term Investments	$7	7%
Real Estate	$5	5%

* Amount based on total amount of system assets.

11.18,90 Source: Office of the State Controller, *Annual Report of Financial Transactions - Public Retirement Systems, Fiscal year 1987-1988.*

CALIFORNIA FOUNDATIONS AND CHARITABLE ORGANIZATIONS					
Year	Revenues (billions)	Assets (billions)	Number of Foundations and Charitable Organizations Making Annual Grants		Total Active Foundations and Public Charitable Organizations*
			Totaling More than $10,000	Totaling Less than $10,000	
1983	$13.6	$17.3	2,700	2,500	37,983
1985	$14.1	$28.8	3,965	2,771	42,568
1987	$16.4	$38.7	2,586	3,146	45,600
1989	$26.2	$42.0	3,241	3,235	50,882

* Excludes religious, educational, health care and governmental charities and foundations, which number between 20,000 and 30,000.

11.19,90 Source: California Department of Justice, Department of Charitable Trusts, unpublished 1989 data.

MAJOR FOUNDATIONS CALIFORNIA AND THE UNITED STATES			
National Rank	Foundation	State	Assets (billions)
1	Ford	New York	$4.8
2	**Getty**	**California**	**3.7**
3	Kellogg	Michigan	3.1
4	MacArthur	Illinois	2.3
5	**Packard**	**California**	**2.0**
6	Lilly	Indiana	1.9
7	Johnson	New Jersey	1.8
8	Rockefeller	New York	1.6
9	Pew	Pennsylvania	1.6
10	Mellon	New York	1.5

11.20,90 Source: The Foundation Center.

Defense and Veterans Affairs

After stalling for more than a decade, Congress finally appointed a commission to recommend the closing and consolidation of military bases. California will be severely affected when the commission's recommendations are carried out, but the overall savings to the nation should be substantial. Among the bases to be closed in California are George, Mather, and Norton air force bases, the San Francisco Presidio, and the Salton Sea Test Base. The Hunter's Point Naval Shipyard in San Francisco will also lose most of its work along with 4,225 jobs. In all 18,167 jobs will be eliminated by the base closings, and the government will save an estimated $300 million per year.

The city of San Francisco will suffer the greatest loss of jobs from the nationwide closings--one-half of all the job losses in California. More than a few individuals suspect that the generally antimilitary voting behavior of the San Francisco Bay Area congressional delegation may have led to a not-so-subtle retaliation by the U.S. Commission on Base Realignment and Closure.

Even as the state faced a loss of jobs because of base closings, it was also losing military manufacturing jobs as production runs were completed for an assortment of weapons systems. There was some question whether Congress would fund the continuing production of the B-2 Stealth bomber, at $500 million per copy. The bomber is currently being produced by Northrop Corporation in Palmdale.

The impact of U.S. arms control negotiations on the state's armaments industry is unclear at this point, but only 8.5 percent of California's gross state product is now dependent on Pentagon funding, down from 17 percent in the 1960s.

Even if big-ticket items like air force bombers, fighters, and missiles are canceled, spending by the Pentagon on high-tech military electronics in California is likely to increase--as is funding for the space program now that President Bush has committed the nation to landing astronauts on Mars in the twenty-first century.

DEFENSE CONTRACTS IN CALIFORNIA* FISCAL YEAR 1988	
Type of Contract	Dollar Amount (in billions)
Supply	$10.9
Research and Development	7.5
Service	4.2
Construction	0.8
Civil Function	0.6
Total	**$23.5**

* All prime contracts, those of $25,000 or more.
12.1,90 Source: Department of Defense, Washington Headquarters Services Directorate for Information, Operations and Reports, *Atlas/State Data Abstract for the U.S., Annual.*

				DEFENSE CONTRACTS IN CALIFORNIA, 1970-1988					
Year	Contract Awards (billions)	% of U.S.	Military & Civilian Payroll (billions)	% of U.S.	Civilian Employees (thousands)	% of U.S.	Military Personnel (thousands)	% of U.S.
1970	5.8	17	3.1	13	NA	NA	NA	NA
1980	13.9	18	5.9	16	123	14	195	14
1981	16.6	17	6.9	16	128	14	196	14
1982	22.2	22	7.7	16	128	14	198	14
1983	26.4	22	8.3	16	133	14	205	15
1984	28.5	23	8.7	16	134	14	204	15
1985	29.1	21	8.9	16	138	14	205	15
1986	27.7	20	12.5	15	135	14	209	15
1987	24.5	18	12.7	15	138	14	206	15
1988	23.5	18	13.0	15	131	14	205	15

12.2,90 Source: Department of Defense, Washington Headquarters Services, Directorate for Information, Operations and Reports, *Atlas/State Data Abstract for the U.S.*, Annual.

ROTC ENROLLMENT IN CALIFORNIA EDUCATIONAL INSTITUTIONS FALL 1988		
Year	Number of Programs	Number of Enrollees
Army	13	1,339
Air Force	9	972
Navy/Marine Corps	4	681

12.3,90 Source: Army, Air Force, & Navy ROTC Offices, 1989.

Company	Location	Value of Contract (billions)	Type of Work
McDonnell Douglas	Long Beach	2.9	Aircraft engines
Lockheed	Sunnyvale	2.4	Guided missiles
General Motors (Hughes)	El Segundo	1.8	Torpedos
Rockwell	Los Angeles	1.7	Fixed-wing aircraft
General Dynamics	Pomona	1.5	Guided missles

TOP FIVE CALIFORNIA DEFENSE CONTRACTORS FISCAL YEAR 1988

Note: 44% of prime contracts went to these five contractors.
12.4,90 Source: Department of Defense, Washington Headquarters Services, Directorate for Information, Operations and Reports, *Atlas/State Data Abstract for the U.S., Annual.*

LOCATION OF MAJOR DEFENSE EXPENDITURES FISCAL YEAR 1988

Area	Payroll (in millions)	Total Value of Prime Contracts* (in billions)	Total (in billions)
San Diego	$2,425	$1.8	$4.2
Long Beach	$534	$2.5	$3.0
Sunnyvale	$61	$2.6	$2.7
Los Angeles	$198	$2.0	$2.2
El Segundo	$62	$1.4	$1.5
Anaheim	$21	$0.9	$1.0
San Jose	$61	$0.7	$0.8
Camp Pendleton	$732	$0.9	$0.8
Fullerton	$12	$0.8	$0.8
Redondo Beach	$10	$0.7	$0.7

* Prime contracts have a value of more than $25,000.
12.5,90 Source: Department of Defense, Washington Headquarters Services, Directorate for Information, Operations and Reports, *Atlas/State Data Abstract for the U.S.*, Annual.

FALLOUT SHELTERS IN CALIFORNIA

Fallout Shelters	15,691
Spaces in Fallout Shelter	21,351,632

12.6,90 Source: Federal Emergency Management Agency, San Francisco Office, 1989, unpublished data.

ACTIVE DUTY MILITARY PERSONNEL BY COUNTY, 1989

County	Number	County	Number
Alameda	10,420	Placer	196
Alpine	0	Plumas	0
Amador	0	Riverside	5,738
Butte	73	Sacramento	9,108
Calaveras	20	San Benito	0
Colusa	0	San Bernardino	22,434
Contra Costa	2,626	San Diego	130,614
Del Norte	34	San Francisco	6,589
El Dorado	85	San Joaquin	476
Fresno	454	San Luis Obispo	222
Glenn	0	San Mateo	812
Humboldt	269	Santa Barbara	3,704
Imperial	229	Santa Clara	6,330
Inyo	0	Santa Cruz	27
Kern	5,304	Shasta	20
Kings	5,389	Sierra	0
Lake	23	Siskiyou	0
Lassen	330	Solano	14,122
Los Angeles	23,789	Sonoma	1,194
Madera	0	Stanislaus	119
Marin	1,995	Sutter	496
Mariposa	0	Tehama	21
Mendocino	45	Trinity	0
Merced	4,845	Tulare	161
Modoc	0	Tuolumne	0
Mono	553	Ventura	7,372
Monterey	21,302	Yolo	133
Napa	237	Yuba	3,168
Nevada	35		
Orange	10,887	**State Total**	**302,000**

12.7,90 Source: California Department of Finance, *Report E6-A*, 1989.

MILITARY RETIREES IN CALIFORNIA

Service	Number of Retirees	% of Retirees in the U.S.
Army	41,863	8%
Navy	85,580	22%
Marine Corps	18,849	22%
Air Force	67,447	12%
Total	**213,739**	**14%**

12.8,90 Source: U.S. Veteran's Administration *Annual Report*.

MILITARY - PROMINENT CALIFORNIANS

General John DeWitt	General George S. Patton Jr.

12.9,90 Source: Pacific Data Resources.

NUMBER OF ACTIVE DUTY MILITARY PERSONNEL AND DEPARTMENT OF DEFENSE CIVILIAN EMPLOYEES IN CALIFORNIA, FISCAL YEAR 1988

Branch of Service	Active Duty Military Personnel	Civilian Employees	Payroll* (billions)	% of All Active Duty U.S. Military
Army	27,048	16,990	$1.7	5.5%
Air Force	51,979	28,781	$3.0	12.0%
Navy and Marine Corps	125,764	77,261	$8.0	30.2%
Other Defense Activities	0	8,156	$0.2	NA
Total	**204,791**	**131,788**	**$13.0**	**15.3%**

* Including pay for reserves, National Guard and retired personnel.
12.10,90 Source: Department of Defense, Washington Headquarters Services, Directorate for Information, Operations and Reports, *Atlas/State Data Abstract for the U.S., Annual.*

MAIN LOCATIONS OF DEPARTMENT OF DEFENSE PERSONNEL IN CALIFORNIA, 1988

Location	Active Duty Military	Civilians	Total
San Diego	38,547	13,358	51,905
Camp Pendleton	31,474	2,258	33,732
Fort Ord	13,209	2,004	15,253
McClellan AFB	3,288	12,652	15,940
North Island NAS	5,674	6,631	12,305
Mare Island	2,018	10,580	12,598
Travis AFB	8,096	2,199	10,295
Long Beach	2,230	6,550	8,780
Oakland	2,250	6,504	8,754
Norton AFB	5,461	3,019	8,480

12.11,90 Source: Department of Defense, Washington Headquarters Services, Directorate for Information, Operations and Reports, *Atlas/State Data Abstract for the U.S.,* Annual.

SECTION 12 NOTE

From 1980-1989 there were no military base closings in California.

12.12,90

MAIN MILITARY INSTALLATIONS IN CALIFORNIA

Branch	Number
Navy	49
Marine Corps	8
Air Force	34
Army	13
Defense Agencies	1
Total	**105**
	(12% of Military Installations in the United States.)

12.13,90 Source: U.S. Department of Defense, *Defense Almanac*, September, 1988.

MAJOR AIR FORCE BASES IN CALIFORNIA

Name	Principal Mission	Command /Host Unit
Beale AFB	Strategic Reconnaissance	Strategic Air Command
Castle AFB	Strategic Bombing	Strategic Air Command
Edwards AFB	Research and Development	NASA, Air Force Flight Test Center
Fresno AFB	Air Defense/Interception	Air Defense, Air National Guard
George AFB	Tactical Fighters	Tactical Air Command
Los Angeles AFB	Research and Development	Space Systems Division
March AFB	Strategic Refueling	Strategic Air Command
Mather AFB	Strategic Refueling Navigation Training	Air Training Command
McClellan AFB	Research and Development	Air Force Logistics Command
Moffett NAS	Rescue and Recovery	Air National Guard
Norton AFB	Airlift	Military Airlift Command
Travis AFB	Airlift	Military Airlift Command
Van Nuys ANGB	Airlift Assistance	Air National Guard
Vandenburg AFG	Missile Launching	Strategic Air Command

12.14,90 Source: U.S. Air Force, *Guide to the Western Bases*, 1989.

MAJOR ARMY BASES IN CALIFORNIA

Bases	**Forts**
Oakland	Hunter Liggett
Los Alamitos	Irwin
Depots	Ord
Sharpe	**Presidios**
Sierra	Monterey
Sacramento	San Francisco
Camps	**Plants**
Roberts	Riverbank Army
Roberts Annex	Ammunition

12.15,90 Source: U.S. Department of Defense, *List of All Military Installations, Fiscal Year 1987*.

MAJOR NAVAL BASES IN CALIFORNIA

Main Stations/Bases	Marine Air Station
Alameda	El Toro
Long Beach	Camp Pendleton
Mare Island	Tustin
San Diego	**Naval Air Stations**
Treasure Island	Alameda
Naval Shipyards	Lemoore
Long Beach	Miramar
Mare Island	Moffett Field
Submarine Bases	North Island
San Diego	**Naval Postgraduate School**
Marine Bases	Monterey
Barstow	**Naval Weapons Stations**
Camp Pendleton	China Lake
29 Palms	Concord
Supply Center	Seal Beach
Oakland	**Amphibious Base**
San Diego	Coronado

12.16,90 Source: U.S. Department of Defense, *List of All Military Installations, Fiscal Year* 1987.

DEPARTMENT OF DEFENSE LAND IN CALIFORNIA

Branch	Acres
Navy	1,456,786
Army	911,601
Defense Agencies	448
Marine Corp.	855,704
Air Force	539,065
Total	**3,763,604**
Department of Defense Land as a % of Total	
Land in California	3.8%
Federal Land in California	8.3%
Department of Defense Land in the U.S.	13.3%

12.17,90 Source: Dept. of Defense, *List of Military Installations,* 1987.

CALIFORNIA READY RESERVE AND NATIONAL GUARD STRENGTH 1988		
Branch	**Troops***	**% of Total U.S. Strength**
Army		
Reserve	42,133	7.0%
National Guard	21,827	4.7%
Air Force		
Reserve	18,590	13.5%
National Guard	5,764	5.0%
Navy		
Reserve	32,334	13.9%
Marine Corps Reserve	10,446	12.2%
Total	**131,094**	**8.0%**

* Includes Selective Reserves, Individual Ready Reserves and Inactive National Guard.

12.18,90 Source: Department of Defense, *Official Guard and Reserve Manpower Strength and Statistics.*, FY 1988 Summary.

CALIFORNIA NATIONAL GUARD ARMY, 1989-90	
Authorized Strength	22,284
Company Sized Units	167
Detachment Sized Units	35
Armories	126
Maintenance Shops	40
Major Facilities	Camp San Luis Obispo Camp Roberts Los Alamitos Reserve Center
Budget* 1983-84	$11.5 million
1984-85	$12.9 million
1985-86	$13.7 million
1986-87	$14.1 million
1987-88	$14.2 million
1988-89	$14.3 million
1989-90	$15.0 million

* From the State of California General Fund.

12.19,90 Source: *Governor's Budget,* 1989-90.

CALIFORNIA NATIONAL GUARD AIR FORCE 1989-90	
Authorized Strength	6,090
Operational Units	
Air Defense	Fresno
Tactical Airlift	Van Nuys
Air Rescue	Moffett Field
Tactical Fighter	March A. F. Base
Communications	North Highlands
Communications	Van Nuys
Communications	Hayward
Communications	Sepulveda
Communications	Costa Mesa
Communications	San Diego
Communications	Ontario
Budget* 1981-82	$1.2 million
1982-83	$1.8 million
1983-84	$1.6 million
1984-85	$1.9 million
1985-86	$2.2 million
1986-87	$2.4 million
1987-88	$2.4 million
1988-89	$2.6 million
1989-90	$2.7 million

* From the State of California General Fund.
12.20,90 Source: *Governor's Budget*, 1989-90.

CALIFORNIA MILITARY DEPT. BUDGET (Including the California National Guard) (in millions)			
Year	California General Fund	Federal Funds	Total Budget
1981-82	$16.4	$8.4	$24.8
1982-83	$14.5	$11.4	$25.9
1983-84	$16.0	$9.8	$25.7
1984-85	$17.5	$13.8	$31.2
1985-86	$19.3	$12.5	$31.7
1986-87	$19.7	$15.7	$35.5
1987-88	$20.1	$18.0	$38.1
1988-89	$20.3	$23.3	$43.8
1989-90	$21.3	$24.3	$45.7

12.21,90 Source: *Governor's Budget*, 1989-90.

CIVIL DEFENSE AND EMERGENCY EXPENDITURES BY THE GOVERNOR'S OFFICE OF EMERGENCY SERVICES	
Year	**Expenditures**
1983-84	$93,826,000
1984-85	$70,322,000
1985-86	$41,836,000
1986-87	$68,335,000
1987-88	$44,600,000
1988-89	$71,975,000
1989-90	$75,383,000

12.22,90 Source: *Governor's Budget,* 1989-90

CALIFORNIA VETERANS	
	Number
Sex*	
Male	2,947,816
Female	149,505
Wartime Veterans	
World War I	14,000
World War II	1,017,000
Korean War	574,000
Vietnam Era	905,000
Peacetime Veterans	
1975 and later	211,000
Service Between	
Korean and Vietnam Wars	309,000
Other	43,000
Total	**2,844,000†**

* Based on 1980 U.S. Census Data.
† 10.4% of all U.S. Veterans live in California.
12.23,90 Source: U.S. Veterans Administration, *Annual Report,* 1988.

VETERANS UNEMPLOYMENT RATE					
	1984	**1985**	**1986**	**1987**	**1988**
All California Veterans	2.4%	4.8%	NA	3.7%	NA
Vietnam Era Veterans*	2.7%	4.8%	3.9%	3.1%	3.3%

* Males only.
12.24,90 Source: California Employment Development Department, unpublished data.

VA CEMETERIES IN CALIFORNIA			
City	**Phone**	**City**	**Phone**
Los Angeles	(213) 824-4311	San Diego	(619) 225-7447
Riverside	(714) 653-8417	San Francisco	(415) 561-2008

12.25,90 Source: California Department of Veterans Affairs, *1989 Directory*.

Labor and Employment

California's amazing performance in producing new jobs continues to delight just about everyone. So successful has the state been that economists are beginning to worry about a shortage of people to fill the new jobs, particularly in the San Francisco Bay Area, which has some of the lowest unemployment rates in the state. By early 1989, unemployment statewide had dropped to 4.5 percent, a twenty-year low. With job growth so vigorous in the state and with unemployment at record low levels, many economists expect that labor shortages will lead to higher-than-normal wage increases as employers bid up salaries to hold on to their existing employees and to attract new workers. Statewide in 1987 the average annual wage was $22,000.

Over the next twenty years, economists predict, the Los Angeles-Long Beach and the Anaheim-Santa Ana metropolitan areas will lead the nation in job growth. San Diego will be the eighth fastest growing area in new jobs, and San Jose will be tenth. Other areas expected to have high growth rates are Santa Rosa-Petaluma, Oxnard-Ventura, and Santa Cruz. A major problem for the future labor market in all of California, however, is the weakness of the K-12 education system. Many doubt that it can prepare a work force adequate to the needs of the next century.

What sectors of the economy have produced the new jobs? Since 1980, employment has increased in all sectors of the economy except mining: there are 200,000 more jobs in construction, 160,000 more in manufacturing, 40,000 more in transportation and utilities, 200,000 more in government, 200,000 more in finance and real estate, and 4,000 more in agriculture. During the 1980s retail and wholesale trade and services have been the areas of greatest job growth, adding 700,000 and 1 million new jobs, respectively. The state's economy has provided large numbers of jobs requiring a high level of skill as well as entry jobs requiring little skill for newcomers in the labor market.

Farmers worry that the new federal immigration law will sharply reduce the number of seasonal agricultural workers from Mexico. Job shortages in urban areas and nonagricultural jobs that offer higher pay may lure away existing farm laborers, further complicating the problems of the state's farmers at harvest time. All these factors may increase the pressure on California farmers to mechanize to forestall the shift of farm production to foreign locales, particularly Mexico, where labor costs remain low.

	Civilian Labor Force	Employed	Un-employed	Percent Un-employed	Percent in U.S. Unemployed
EMPLOYMENT AND UNEMPLOYMENT IN CALIFORNIA 1940-1989 (in thousands)					
Year					
1940	3,083	2,703	380	12.3%	14.6%
1950	4,552	4,202	350	7.7%	5.3%
1960	6,423	6,051	372	5.8%	5.5%
1970	8,157	7,566	591	7.3%	4.9%
1972	8,582	7,930	651	7.6%	5.6%
1974	9,195	8,525	670	7.3%	5.6%
1976	9,709	8,820	889	9.2%	7.7%
1978	10,911	10,137	775	7.1%	6.1%
1980	11,584	10,794	790	6.8%	7.1%
1982	12,178	10,967	1,210	9.9%	9.7%
1984	12,610	11,631	980	7.8%	7.5%
1986	13,365	12,473	892	6.7%	7.0%
1988	14,036	13,292	743	5.3%	5.5%
1989	14,120	13,480	640	4.5%	5.0%

* As of March 1989.

13.1,90 Source: California Employment Development Dept, *California Labor Market Bulletin*, and *Report to the Governor on Labor Market Conditions*.

	Unemployment Rate					
Metropolitan Area	1982*	1984*	1986*	1987*	1988*	1989†
UNEMPLOYMENT BY METROPOLITAN AREA						
Anaheim-Santa Ana-Garden Grove	7.2%	4.7%	4.0%	3.3%	3.0%	2.5%
Bakersfield	12.2%	12.2%	12.0%	10.5%	10.2%	11.4%
Fresno	13.8%	12.9%	12.3%	10.6%	10.6%	11.6%
Los Angeles-Long Beach	9.3%	7.9%	6.7%	5.9%	4.9%	3.7%
Modesto	18.3%	16.1%	14.1%	12.1%	11.9%	12.1%
Oakland	-	6.8%	5.8%	5.0%	4.6%	3.8%
Oxnard-Simi Valley-Ventura	10.5%	7.7%	6.9%	5.5%	5.3%	3.9%
Riverside-San Bernardino-Ontario	12.2%	7.9%	6.4%	5.7%	5.9%	4.7%
Sacramento	11.4%	8.1%	6.2%	5.6%	5.4%	4.8%
Salinas-Seaside-Monterey	11.6%	10.7%	10.3%	8.6%	8.3%	9.9%
San Diego	9.3%	6.0%	5.0%	4.5%	4.3%	3.3%
San Francisco	8.2%	5.3%	4.5%	3.9%	3.6%	3.0%
San Jose	7.5%	5.3%	5.8%	4.5%	4.0%	3.5%
Santa Barbara-Santa Maria-Lompoc	7.9%	5.9%	5.1%	4.7%	4.4%	4.1%
Santa Rosa-Petaluma	10.3%	6.5%	5.7%	4.8%	4.8%	4.4%
Stockton	16.1%	13.1%	11.6%	9.8%	9.7%	10.1%
Vallejo-Fairfield-Napa	10.8%	7.6%	6.5%	5.9%	5.5%	5.0%
Statewide	**9.9%**	**7.8%**	**6.7%**	**5.8%**	**5.3%**	**4.7%**

* Annual average. †March 1989 (not seasonally adjusted).

13.2,90 Source: California Employment Development Department Rept. 400-c, U.S. Dept. of Labor - Bureau of Labor Statistics, *Employment and Earnings*.

	Civilian Labor		Unemployment	
County	**Force**	**Employment**	**Number**	**Percent**
Alameda	672,400	642,800	29,600	4.4
Alpine	500	475	25	5.1
Amador	10,575	9,875	700	6.6
Butte	72,650	66,125	6,525	9.0
Calaveras	9,750	8,800	950	9.7
Colusa	7,875	6,950	925	11.7
Contra Costa	408,700	391,100	17,600	4.3
Del Norte	8,150	7,050	1,100	13.6
El Dorado	63,000	59,900	3,100	4.9
Fresno	305,600	273,700	32,500	10.6
Glenn	10,575	9,425	1,150	10.9
Humboldt	50,700	46,400	4,300	8.4
Imperial	45,500	34,850	10,650	23.4
Inyo	7,800	7,475	325	4.2
Kern	228,000	203,600	24,400	10.7
Kings	34,150	30,325	3,825	11.2
Lake	16,725	14,800	1,925	11.6
Lassen	9,625	8,625	1,000	10.3
Los Angeles	4,098,400	3,921,100	177,300	4.3
Madera	33,925	29,275	4,650	13.7
Marin	125,900	122,500	3,400	2.7
Mariposa	6,550	6,150	400	6.1
Mendocino	33,725	30,725	3,000	8.9
Merced	72,675	63,075	9,600	13.2
Modoc	4,150	3,750	400	9.8
Mono	5,200	4,950	250	4.6
Monterey	161,100	147,300	13,800	8.6
Napa	54,500	52,000	2,500	4.6
Nevada	29,700	27,850	1,850	6.2
Orange	1,359,600	1,318,700	40,900	3.0
Placer	77,400	73,400	4,000	5.2
Plumas	8,425	7,225	1,200	14.2
Riverside	410,000	384,900	25,100	6.1
Sacramento	507,100	481,800	25,300	5.0
San Benito	16,700	14,025	2,675	16.0
San Bernardino	540,900	512,200	28,700	5.3
San Diego	1,142,900	1,098,100	44,800	3.9
San Francisco	399,600	383,000	16,600	4.1
San Joaquin	193,600	173,800	19,800	10.2
San Luis Obispo	95,750	92,000	3,750	3.9
San Mateo	350,300	340,400	9,900	2.8
Santa Barbara	177,800	170,300	7,500	4.2
Santa Clara	834,900	801,800	33,100	4.0
Santa Cruz	131,800	120,800	11,000	8.3
Shasta	57,525	51,500	6,025	10.5
Sierra	1,325	1,125	200	15.9
Siskiyou	18,875	16,750	2,125	11.2
Solano	139,300	131,200	8,100	5.8
Sonoma	191,500	182,400	9,100	4.7
Stanislaus	152,000	131,200	20,800	13.7
Sutter	28,025	23,600	4,425	15.8
Tehama	17,850	16,000	1,850	10.4
Trinity	5,400	4,675	725	13.4
Tular	139,500	125,850	13,650	9.8
Tuolumne	17,825	16,325	1,500	8.4
Ventura	358,200	342,100	16,100	4.5
Yolo	70,400	65,800	4,600	6.6
Yuba	18,875	16,450	2,425	12.9
State Totals	**14,051,500**	**13,327,900**	**723,600**	**5.1**

* April.

13.3,90 Source: Cal. Employment Dev. Dept., *California Labor Market Bulletin*.

UNEMPLOYMENT RATES BY SEX, RACE AND AGE IN CALIFORNIA

Year	Male	Female	White	Non-white	His-panic	Black	Aged 16-19	Aged 25-64
1979	5.7%	7.0%	5.8%	9.4%	8.5%	NA	17.4%	4.3%
1980	6.7	6.8	6.1	11.6	9.8	15.1	18.2	4.8
1981	7.4	7.3	6.9	10.4	11.0	14.4	18.4	5.7
1982	10.2	9.6	9.4	12.7	15.3	16.4	23.4	8.1
1983	10.2	9.0	8.9	14.0	15.0	18.9	23.0	8.0
1984	7.5	7.5	7.2	10.7	11.4	14.1	18.7	6.2
1985	7.2	7.1	6.9	8.9	10.9	12.1	20.1	5.7
1986	6.7	6.7	6.3	8.9	10.5	12.8	18.0	5.3
1987	5.8	5.7	5.4	7.7	7.9	10.8	16.9	4.6
1988	5.4	5.1	5.0	7.1	7.3	10.3	15.7	4.1
1989*	5.2	5.1	4.8	7.2	7.1	10.6	13.2	4.1

* March data.

13.4,90   Source: California Economic Development Department, *Report to the Governor on Labor Market Conditions.*

LABOR PARTICIPATION* RATES CALIFORNIA AND THE NATION

Year	California			United States		
	Total	Male	Female	Total	Male	Female
1940	55.3	82.6	27.9	54.6	82.6	26.6
1950	55.6	83.6	29.1	55.0	81.5	29.6
1960	58.3	81.4	37.1	59.2	82.4	37.1
1970	58.4	76.6	42.2	60.4	79.7	43.3
1980	63.8	76.1	52.5	63.8	77.4	51.5
1986	66.4	77.3	56.2	65.3	76.3	55.3
1987	66.9	77.9	56.6	65.6	74.2	56.0
1988	67.3	78.3	57.0	65.9	74.2	56.6

* Civilians 16 years and over who are in the labor force.

13.5,90   Sources: U.S. Bureau of Labor Statistics, *Employment and Unemployment.*
U.S. Bureau of the Census Decennial Census; *Current Population Reports* & unpublished data and *U.S. Statistical Abstract.*

SECTION 13 NOTE

At the end of 1988, the San Francisco Bay Area had the lowest unemployment rate of any region in the state: 3.7 percent.

13.6,90

UNEMPLOYMENT HIGHEST AND LOWEST COUNTIES	
County	**Unemployment Rate***
Plumas	19.7%
Sierra	19.7%
Trinity	19.7%
Imperial	19.2%
Sutter	17.8%
San Benito	17.8%
Colusa	17.3%
Siskiyou	15.9%
Del Norte	15.2%
Merced	14.6%
State Average	**5.5%**
Contra Costa	4.4%
San Luis Obispo	4.3%
San Francisco	4.1%
San Diego	4.0%
Santa Clara	3.9%
Mono	3.3%
Orange	3.0%
San Mateo	2.9%
Marin	2.9%
Alpine	2.8%

* February 1989. Data was not seasonally adjusted.
13.7,90 California Employment Development Department, *Report to the Governor on Labor Market Conditions.*

REASONS FOR UNEMPLOYMENT IN CALIFORNIA*				
Year	Job Loser	Job Leaver	New Entrant to Job Market	Re-Entrant to Job Market
1979	47%	18%	11%	24%
1980	56%	12%	10%	27%
1981	52%	15%	10%	24%
1982	61%	11%	8%	19%
1983	63%	7%	9%	20%
1984	57%	10%	10%	24%
1985	54%	11%	9%	26%
1986	51%	12%	11%	27%
1987	55%	12%	11%	22%
1988	44%	18%	15%	23%
1989	53%	15%	11%	20%

* Based on March unemployment data.
13.8,90 Source: California Economic Development Department, *Report to the Governor on Labor Market Conditions.*

EMPLOYMENT OUTLOOK-SURVEY RESULTS*		
Cities/Counties	**Expand**	**Reduce**
Southern California		
Bakersfield	13%	3%
City of Industry	9%	6%
Corona	27%	0%
Los Angeles	27%	6%
Orange County	25%	8%
Oxnard/Ventura	46%	0%
Pasadena	40%	7%
Riverside	23%	0%
San Bernardino	17%	7%
San Diego	39%	8%
Santa Barbara	40%	10%
Thousand Oaks	33%	0%
Upland	21%	7%
Total for Southern California	**30%**	**5%**
Cities/Counties	**Expand**	**Reduce**
Northern California		
Concord	31%	3%
Daly City	33%	0%
Fremont	16%	3%
Fresno	43%	0%
Hayward	41%	0%
Modesto	50%	7%
Monterey County	30%	7%
Oakland	34%	10%
Sacramento	25%	15%
San Francisco	14%	10%
San Mateo	41%	7%
San Rafael	20%	0%
San Ramon	45%	0%
Santa Clara County	32%	12%
Santa Cruz	43%	0%
Santa Rosa	23%	7%
Stockton	19%	9%
Visalia	37%	9%
Walnut Creek	19%	0%
Total For Northern California	**30%**	**7%**
Statewide	**30%**	**6%**
Western U.S.	**31%**	**6%**
National	**30%**	**6%**

* This shows the percentage of employers in California cities who plan to expand or reduce the size of their workforce during the third quarter of 1989 (July-Sept.)
13.9.90 Source: Manpower, Inc.

EDUCATION LEVEL OF CALIFORNIA WORKERS BY METROPOLITAN AREA AND REGION,1988 PERCENTAGE			
Area	Less than High School Graduate	High School Graduate	College Graduate
Anaheim-Santa Ana	17%	53%	30%
Los Angeles	22	49	29
San Bernardino-Riverside	13	64	23
Sacramento	15	58	27
San Diego	13	55	32
San Jose	8	44	48
San Francisco-Oakland	10	47	43
Rest of the State	18	58	25
Region			
South Coast	15%	54%	31%
Los Angeles-Inland	20	52	28
Mid Coast	14	49	37
Bay Area	10	48	42
San Joaquin Valley	24	58	18
Sacramento Valley	15	59	25
Rest of the State	15	64	21

13.10,90 Source: California Department of Finance, State Census Data Center, *Current Population Survey, 1988.*

CALIFORNIA'S FASTEST GROWING OCCUPATIONS through 1995			
	Occupation	Number of New Jobs	Occupation
1	Salespersons-Retail	114,000	Paralegals
2	Cashiers	89,000	Computer Programmers
3	Waiters	78,000	Computer Equipment Repair
4	Gen. Managers, Top Execs.	77,000	Lawyers
5	Office Clerks	70,000	Computer Programmer Aides
6	Registered Nurses	67,000	Systems Analysts-Elect. Data
7	Secretaries	59,000	Agricultural Engineers
8	Bookkeeping Clerks	59,000	Legal Secretaries
9	Janitors	52,000	Podiatrists
10	Accountants, Auditors	48,000	Lecturers
11	Grade School Teachers	47,000	Electrical Engineers
12	Electrical Engineers	45,000	Physical Therapists
13	Food Prep. & Service Workers	45,000	Demonstrators, Promoters, Models
14	Non-Scientific Sales Reps.	39,000	Sports Instructors & Coaches
15	Food Prep. Workers	37,000	Hotel Desk Clerks
16	Computer Programmers	37,000	Medical Assistants
17	Maintenance, Repair Workers	36,000	Social Welfare Service Aides
18	Watch Guards	35,000	Parking Lot Attendants
19	Lawyers	29,000	Bio, Agricul., Food Technology
20	Gardeners	29,000	Employee Interviewers

The "% Growth of New Jobs" column values:

Occupation	% Growth of New Jobs
Paralegals	122%
Computer Programmers	73%
Computer Equipment Repair	72%
Lawyers	69%
Computer Programmer Aides	65%
Systems Analysts-Elect. Data	63%
Agricultural Engineers	63%
Legal Secretaries	62%
Podiatrists	61%
Lecturers	61%
Electrical Engineers	55%
Physical Therapists	55%
Demonstrators, Promoters, Models	54%
Sports Instructors & Coaches	54%
Hotel Desk Clerks	53%
Medical Assistants	53%
Social Welfare Service Aides	53%
Parking Lot Attendants	53%
Bio, Agricul., Food Technology	52%
Employee Interviewers	52%

13.11,90 Source: California Employment Development Dept., *Projections of Employment 1985-1995 by Industry and Occupation, 1988.*

CALIFORNIA METROPOLITAN AREAS ESTIMATED EMPLOYMENT CHANGES 1988-2010		
Rank in U.S. in Employment Growth	**Metropolitan Area**	**Estimated Employment Growth**
1	Los Angeles-Long Beach	1,045,000
2	Anaheim-Santa Ana	852,000
8	San Diego	491,000
10	San Jose	465,000
18	San Francisco	322,000
21	Oakland	286,000
22	Riverside-San Bernardino	278,000
25	Sacramento	272,000
56	Oxnard-Ventura	128,000
64	Fresno	97,000
70	Santa Rosa-Petaluma	90,000
82	Bakersfield	78,000
85	Santa Barbara-Lompoc	75,000
96	Vallejo-Fairfield-Napa	59,000
101	Salinas-Seaside-Monterey	56,000
112	Santa Cruz	48,000
125	Stockton	44,000
127	Modesto	42,000
140	Visalia-Tulare-Porterville	37,000
170	Chico	27,000
191	Redding	22,000
202	Merced	20,000
267	Yuba City	10,000

Note: Ranking includes 317 U.S. metropolitan areas.
13.12,90 Source: National Planning Association, *Regional Economic Growth in the U.S., Projections for 1988-2010 Report # 87R-1*

DURATION OF UNEMPLOYMENT (Percent of Unemployed)				
Year	**0-4 Weeks**	**15-14 Weeks**	**15-26 Weeks**	**27+ Weeks**
1985	46%	30%	12%	12%
1986	45%	32%	12%	11%
1987	42%	33%	14%	10%
1988	44%	31%	16%	10%
1989	55%	27%	10%	9%

13.13,90 Source: California Dept. of Commerce, *California Economic Report.*

UNEMPLOYMENT DATA (in thousands)							
	1980	1982	1984	1985	1986	1987	1988
Initial claims for unemployment insurance (weekly average)	58	73	54	62	59	53	51
Insured unemployment average weeks claimed	373	518	343	390	390	339	321

13.14,90 Source: California Dept. of Finance, *California Economic Indicators.*

AGRICULTURAL AND NONAGRICULTURAL WAGE AND SALARY EMPLOYMENT BY INDUSTRY IN CALIFORNIA 1940-1989 (in thousands)							
Industry	1940	1950	1960	1970	1980	1988	1989*
Mining	40.0	32.2	30.6	31.4	43.5	42	41
Construction	92.1	235.0	294.8	303.0	428.3	575	616
Manufacturing							
Aerospace	NA	NA	422.5	466.3	632.6	760	754
All Durable	NA	NA	NA	NA	NA	1,443	1,456
Nondurable	NA	NA	NA	NA	NA	688	709
All Manufacturing	440.2	759.7	1,317.0	1,558.0	2,018.0	2,131	2,165
Transportation and Public Utilities	190.3	307.1	356.9	459.1	546.3	579	587
Trade							
Wholesale	NA	NA	NA	NA	NA	708	733†
Retail	NA	NA	NA	NA	NA	2,101	2,183†
All Trade	524.2	783.2	1,068.0	1,529.0	2,267.0	2,809	2,916
Finance, Insurance and Real Estate	98.3	142.1	243.6	374.5	623.1	808	822
Services	280.4	416.8	711.7	1,266.0	2,159.0	3,047	3,170
Government							
Federal	NA	NA	NA	NA	331.0	352	362†
State and Local	NA	NA	NA	NA	1,437.0	1,598	1,656†
All Government	266.3	533.3	874.0	1,425.0	1,764.0	1,950	2,018
Subtotal	1,932.0	3,209.0	4,896.0	6,946.0	9,849.0	11,940	12,336
Agricultural	NA	NA	NA	NA	NA	294	280
Total	NA	NA	NA	NA	NA	12,234	12,616

* March. † December.

13.15,90 Source: *Economic Report of the Governor*; California Employment Development Department *Annual Planning Information* 1984-1985; and *Report to the Governor on Labor Market Conditions.*

Industry	1940	1950	1960	1970	1980	1986	1988	1989
NONAGRICULTURAL WAGE AND SALARY EMPLOYMENT BY INDUSTRY IN CALIFORNIA, 1940-1989 Percentage Distribution								
Mining	2.0%	1.0%	0.6%	0.5%	0.4%	0.4%	0.4%	0.3%
Construction	5.0%	7.0%	6.0%	4.4%	4.5%	4.3%	4.8%	5.0%
Manufacturing	23.0%	24.0%	26.9%	22.4%	20.4%	18.8%	17.8%	17.6%
Transportation & Public Utilities	10.0%	10.0%	7.3%	6.6%	5.5%	4.3%	4.8%	4.8%
Trade	27.0%	24.0%	21.8%	22.0%	23.0%	24.0%	23.5%	23.6%
Finance, Insurance and Real Estate	5.0%	4.0%	5.0%	5.4%	6.3%	6.8%	6.8%	6.7%
Services	15.0%	13.0%	14.5%	18.2%	21.9%	24.2%	25.5%	25.7%
Government	14.0%	17.0%	17.9%	20.5%	17.9%	16.4%	16.3%	16.4%
Total	**100%**	**100%**	**100%**	**100%**	**100%**	**100%**	**100%**	**100%**

Note: Totals may not add due to rounding.
13.16,90 Source: 1983 *Economic Report of the Governor*; California Employment Development Department *Annual Planning Information 1985-86;* and *California Labor Market Bulletin,* March 1989. Percentages calculated by the editor.

Year	Agricultural Production	Agricultural Services*	Total Wage and Salary Employment
AGRICULTURAL EMPLOYMENT IN CALIFORNIA 1972-1988 (in thousands)			
1972	208.3	59.8	268.1
1973	222.4	66.6	288.9
1974	236.9	71.2	308.1
1975	243.7	72.0	315.7
1976	248.2	75.3	323.5
1977	241.7	72.9	314.7
1978	245.1	78.9	323.9
1979	253.6	85.0	338.6
1980	261.9	90.3	352.3
1981	258.6	95.8	354.4
1983	250.3	97.1	347.3
1985	232.7	102.7	335.4
1986	220.0	105.6	327.6
1987	227.2	117.8	345.0
1988	235.5	125.1	360.6

* Agricultural services include forestry, but exclude veterinary, other animal, and landscape and horicultural services.
13.17,90 Source: *Economic Report of the Governor.*

MANUFACTURING EMPLOYMENT IN CALIFORNIA 1981-1989 (in thousands)				
	1981	1987	1988	1989
Non-durable Goods				
Food and Kindred Products	187.0	171.0	176.0	182.0
Textile Mill Products	13.7	16.3	16.7	16.9
Apparel and other Textiles	108.0	126.0	126.0	128.0
Paper and Allied Products	38.5	41.1	41.1	41.1
Printing and Publishing	125.0	152.0	160.0	166.0
Chemicals and Allied Products	68.3	67.8	72.7	74.6
Petroleum and Coal Products	31.0	27.3	28.1	28.8
Rubber and Plastics	65.1	70.7	72.3	73.6
Leather and Leather Products	12.0	6.9	6.4	6.5
Total Non-durable Goods	**648.0**	**680.0**	**699.0**	**717.0**
Durable Goods				
Lumber and Wood Products	57.1	66.2	67.7	68.0
Furniture and Fixtures	55.0	63.0	62.1	62.4
Stone, Clay and Glass Products	56.7	53.7	56.8	58.2
Primary Metal Industries	54.7	42.0	43.7	44.4
Fabricated Metal Products	152.0	134.0	136.0	136.0
Non-Electrical Machinery	234.0	212.0	217.0	224.0
Electrical Equipment	351.0	397.0	400.0	389.0
Transportation Equipment	278.0	310.0	312.0	313.0
Instruments	103.0	113.0	118.0	121.0
Miscellaneous Manufacturing	41.5	35.8	36.5	38.0
Total Durable Goods	**1,384.0**	**1,427.0**	**1,449.0**	**1,454.0**
Total Manufacturing Employment	**2,032.0**	**2,108.0**	**2,148.0**	**2,171.0**

13.18,90 Source: *Economic Report of the Governor.*

CALIFORNIA STATE GOVERNMENT EMPLOYEES 1975-1989					
Year	Civil Service	Exempt and other	State Colleges	Univ. of California	Total
1975-1976	119,866	1,786	32,384	52,356	206,392
1976-1977	121,676	2,140	32,997	56,984	213,797
1977-1978	126,873	2,432	33,778	58,168	221,251
1978-1979	126,282	2,512	33,470	56,267	218,531
1979-1980	128,202	2,569	33,089	56,332	220,192
1980-1981	131,708	2,763	33,838	57,228	225,537
1981-1982	132,503	3,021	33,838	59,451	228,813
1982-1983	131,914	2,872	33,875	59,624	228,489
1983-1984	131,026	3,047	33,407	59,009	226,695
1984-1985	136,974	3,207	32,462	57,902	229,845
1985-1986	137,777	3,220	32,219	57,652	229,641
1986-1987	137,693	3,280	33,660	58,294	232,927
1987-1988*	147,414	3,410	33,573	58,771	243,168
1988-1989*	153,870	4,230	34,540	59,293	251,933

* Estimate.

13.19,90 Source: *Cal. Statistical Abstract* and Dept. of Finance, unpublished data.

	TOTAL GOVERNMENT FULL-TIME EQUIVALENT EMPLOYMENT IN CALIFORNIA AND OTHER STATES			
State	Number of State & Local Government Employees per 10,000 Residents	Rank	State & Local Government Employees' Average Monthly Pay	Rank
Alaska	758	1	$3,306	1
New York	628	3	$2,430	4
Oregon	520	18	$1,827	18
Texas	500	26	$2,042	29
Michigan	485	34	$2,337	5
Arizona	481	37	$1,968	6
California	**463**	**42**	**$2,404**	**2**
Florida	454	45	$2,725	21
U.S. Average	497	-	$2,089	-

Note: California had 1,112,574 (72%) full-time and 424,102 (28%) part-time employees.

13.20,90 Source: U.S. Bureau of the Census, *Public Employment in 1987.*

	FEDERAL, STATE and LOCAL GOVERNMENT EMPLOYMENT (in thousands)						
Year	Federal	State Education	State Non Education	Special District	County	City	Local Education
1986	346	154	178	92	233	198	647
1987	344	159	184	95	239	202	664
1988	353	157	196	97	247	214	651
1989	364	162	503	100	255	224	676

13.21,90 Source: Cal. Employment Dev. Dept., *California Labor Market Bulletin.*

STATE GOVERNMENT EMPLOYEES IN CALIFORNIA, 1951-1988	
Year	Government Employees per 100,000 in Population
1950-51	5.7
1960-61	7.3
1970-71	9.1
1980-81	9.5
1987-88	8.6

13.22,90 Source: *Governors Budget Summary, 1989-90* Schedule S.

	UNION MEMBERS IN CALIFORNIA 1951-1987			
	Union Members		Union Members in Manufacturing	
Year	Number†	% of Nonfarm Wage and Salary Workers††	% of All Wage and Salary Workers	% of Production and Related Workers
1951	1,443,100	40.8%	53.1%	69.4%
1961	1,737,000	34.5%	40.4%	62.0%
1971	2,135,100	30.7%	38.7%	59.6%
1981	2,230,000	22.0%	25.4%	41.0%
1983	2,076,700	20.6%	23.3%	39.5%
1985	2,152,700	20.1%	21.3%	NA
1987	2,240,200	19.1%	21.9%	NA

† July.
†† Does not include employers, own account workers, unpaid family workers, domestic servants, and agricultural workers. Union workers in agriculture are not included when determining percent of unionization.
13.23,90 Source: California Department of Industrial Relations, *Union Labor in California,* 1983, and unpublished data.

	NUMBER OF CALIFORNIA UNION LOCALS AND THEIR MEMBERSHIP RANKED BY NUMBER OF MEMBERS, 1987*			
	Union Locals		Union Members	
Membership	Number	Percent of Total	Number	Percent of Total
Under 50	797	28.0%	17,500	0.8%
50-99	368	12.9	26,900	1.2
100-199	424	14.9	60,200	2.7
200-299	210	7.4	47,700	2.1
300-399	145	5.1	49,300	2.2
400-499	113	4.0	49,600	2.2
500-999	317	11.1	219,900	9.8
1,000-1,999	211	7.4	290,500	13.0
2,000-4,999	177	6.2	34,700	23.9
5,000-9,999	53	1.9	343,800	15.3
10,000-14,999	13	0.5	168,000	7.5
15,000-19,999	5	0.2	86,600	3.9
20,000 or More	11	0.4	345,500	15.4
Total	2,844	100.0%	2,240,200	100.0%

* Data as of July, 1987.
13.24,90 Source: California Department of Industrial Relations, unpublished data.

UNION MEMBERSHIP IN CALIFORNIA AS A PERCENT OF NONFARM WAGE AND SALARY EMPLOYMENT, BY INDUSTRY* 1979-1987

Industry	Union Members as Percent of Nonfarm Wage and Salary Employment†		
	July 1979	July 1985	July 1987
Manufacturing	27.6%	21.3%	21.9%
Food and Kindred Products	79.9	73.2	76.6
Textiles and Apparel	12.7	10.8	6.9
Lumber and Furniture	31.3	24.6	24.3
Paper and Allied Products	54.0	45.6	44.0
Printing and Publishing	23.2	16.5	21.1
Petroleum, Chemicals, and Rubber	15.7	10.3	9.4
Stone, Clay, and Glass Products	34.5	28.2	28.5
Metals, Electrical and Non-electrical Machinery	17.4	11.8	11.1
Transportation Equipment	40.0	32.1	33.7
Other Manufacturing Industries†	5.2	3.3	2.7
Nonmanufacturing	22.1	19.8	18.5
Construction	73.9	60.9	54.4
Transportation and Warehousing	63.7	49.4	45.6
Public Utilities	64.8	63.4	64.2
Wholesale and Retail Trade	18.5	11.5	11.4
Eating and Drinking Places, Hotels and Other lodging Places	14.1	8.8	6.7
Motion Picture Production and Distribution, Theaters, and other Entertainment	65.7	55.2	57.6
Miscellaneous Service Industries††	5.4	4.9	4.2
Government	18.8	23.6	26.3
Agriculture	*	*	9.6
Total	**23.3%**	**20.1%**	**19.1%**

* Does not include employers, own account workers, unpaid family workers, domestic and agricultural workers. Union workers in agriculture are not included when determining the percent of unionization.

† Includes leather and leather products, instruments and related products, and miscellaneous manufacturing industries.

†† Includes finance, insurance, and real estate; personal services such as laundering, cleaning and dyeing, barber and beauty shops etc.; business services; and professional, educational and related services.

13.25,90 Source: California Department of Industrial Relations, *Union Labor in California,* 1983 and unpublished data.

SECTION 13 NOTE
In 1988 the San Diego region had the fastest employment growth of any region in the state.

13.26,90

RANKING OF INTERNATIONAL UNIONS BY SIZE OF MEMBERSHIP IN CALIFORNIA 1979-1987					
	Rank by Number of California Members				
International Union	July 1979	July 1981	July 1983	July 1985	July 1987
Teamsters	1	1	1	1	1
United Food & Commercial Workers	2	2	2	3	3
Service Employees	3	3	3	2	2
Carpenters	4	4	4	4	5
Machinists	5	5	5	5	4
Communications Workers	6	7	6	6	6
Hotel & Restaurant Employees	7	6	7	8	11
Electrical Workers (IBEW)	8	8	8	7	7
Laborers	9	9	9	11	10
Operating Engineers	10	10	10	10	9
Actors and Artists	12	11	11	9	8
Automobile Workers	11	12	12	12	13
Fire Fighters	*	*	*	*	14
United Farm Workers	17	18	13	13	17
Plumbers	15	14	14	16	18
Painters	13	13	15	17	*
Letter Carriers	19	15	16	15	12
Teachers	16	16	17	14	16
Musicians	14	17	18	20	*
Theatrical & Stage Employees	20	19	19	*	20
American Postal Workers	*	*	20	19	19
Steelworkers	18	20	*	*	*
American Federation of State, County, and Municipal Employees	*	*	*	18	15

* Not in top 20.

13.27,90 Source: California Department of Industrial Relations, *Union Labor in California,* 1983 and unpublished data.

LABOR - PROMINENT CALIFORNIANS	
Harry Bridges	Harry Lundeberg
Caesar Chavez	Patrick McCarthy
Andrew Furuseth	James McNamara
John Henning	John McNamara
Dennis Kearney	Tom Mooney

13.28,90 Source: Pacific Data Resources

	EXTENT OF UNIONIZATION IN CALIFORNIA'S MAJOR METROPOLITAN AREAS 1981-1987			
	Union Members as a Percent of Nonfarm Wage and Salary Employment*			
Area	July 1981	July 1983	July 1985	July 1987
Anaheim-Santa Ana-Garden Grove	15.4%	15.0%	14.1%	11.8%
Bakersfield	20.4%	18.7%	19.6%	14.3%
Chico	23.9%	12.7%	NA	15.2%
Fresno	19.9%	18.1%	19.4%	14.6%
Los Angeles-Long Beach	22.7%	21.6%	20.6%	19.8%
Modesto	29.7%	28.2%	20.6%	21.9%
Oakland	NA	NA	30.5%	24.4%
Oxnard-Simi Valley-Ventura	13.6%	14.3%	15.3%	9.4%
Redding	18.9%	18.8%	NA	19.3%
Riverside-San Bernardino-Ontario	21.5%	22.6%	20.4%	13.4%
Sacramento	20.9%	18.6%	12.9%	22.2%
Salinas-Seaside-Monterey	25.2%	24.2%	25.7%	17.7%
San Diego	18.4%	17.0%	15.0%	11.3%
San Francisco†	29.4%	28.2%	23.9%	35.5%
San Jose	16.6%	15.2%	14.8%	14.7%
Santa Barbara-Santa Maria-Lompoc	18.8%	15.5%	13.8%	12.6%
Santa Cruz	26.6%	25.3%	NA	13.0%
Santa Rosa	17.9%	20.3%	18.4%	12.4%
Stockton	28.7%	29.2%	30.1%	21.7%
Vallejo-Fairfield-Napa	26.0%	25.5%	21.6%	13.8%
Visalia-Tulare-Porterville	14.9%	13.2%	NA	11.4%
Yuba City	23.4%	21.0%	NA	19.7%

* Excludes union workers in agriculture, who are not included when determining the percent of unionization.

† Included Oakland until 1985.

13.29,90 Source: California Department of Industrial Relations, *Union Labor in California,* and unpublished data. Calculations done by the Editor.

CALIFORNIA MINIMUM WAGE (Per Hour)			
Effective Date	Wage	Effective Date	Wage
1916	16¢	1964	$1.30
1918	21¢	1968	$1.65
1919	28¢	1974	$2.00
1920	33¢	1976	$2.50
1942-43	45-50¢	1978	$2.65
1947	65¢	1979	$2.90
1952	75¢	1980	$3.10
1957	$1.00	1981	$3.35
1963	$1.25	1988	$4.25

13.30,90 Source: California Industrial Welfare Commision (No longer in Existence).

UNION MEMBERSHIP BY COUNTIES, JULY 1987

County	Membership	County	Membership
Alameda	154,100	Placer	9,000
Alpine	500	Plumas	1,700
Amador	2,700	Riverside	49,000
Butte	9,600	Sacramento	101,600
Calaveras	1,500	San Benito	3,100
Colusa	600	San Bernardino	66,000
Contra Costa	67,200	San Diego	115,600
Del Norte	900	San Francisco	138,400
El Dorado	3,100	San Joaquin	37,100
Fresno	40,100	San Luis Obispo	10,700
Glenn	1,100	San Mateo	65,000
Humboldt	5,300	Santa Barbara	21,900
Imperial	5,300	Santa Clara	114,000
Inyo	800	Santa Cruz	15,300
Kern	29,900	Shasta	9,800
Kings	3,400	Sierra	700
Lake	1,900	Siskiyou	2,700
Lassen	1,200	Solano	17,500
Los Angeles	788,900	Sonoma	22,500
Madera	4,400	Stanislaus	29,900
Marin	21,100	Sutter	4,700
Mariposa	1,100	Tehama	1,900
Mendocino	5,300	Trinity	500
Merced	9,400	Tulare	13,300
Modoc	400	Tuolumne	1,900
Mono	900	Ventura	30,400
Monterey	26,400	Yolo	4,500
Napa	7,600	Yuba	4,200
Nevada	2,800		
Orange	149,800	**State Totals**	**2,240,200**

13.31,90 Source: Cal. Dept. of Indust. Rel., unpublished data, 1989.

WOMEN UNION MEMBERS IN CALIFORNIA
1950-1987

Year	Number	Percent Change from Previous Census Year	Percent of Total Membership
1950	257,400	NA	19%
1966	392,400	-	20%
1971*	469,700	1.7%	22%
1975	512,400	4.0%	24%
1981	633,000	-0.1%	28%
1983	596,000	-5.8%	29%
1985	660,200	10.7%	31%
1987	658,000	-0.3%	29%

* Union membership surveys were conducted annually prior to 1971 and have been conducted biennially since that year.

13.32,90 Source: Cal. Dept. of Indust. Rel., and unpublished data, 1989.

DISABLING WORK INJURIES AND ILLNESS UNDER CALIFORNIA WORKERS' COMPENSATION 1988
Detailed Industry by Nature of Injury

Industry	Fatal	Amputations	Burns and Scalds	Contusions, Crushing Injuries	Cuts, Punctures	Abrasions Scratches	Fractures	Strain, Sprain	Other Injuries	Occupational Illness	Nature Not Stated	Total
Agriculture, Forestry Fishing	28	74	228	1,812	3,720	1,310	2,190	8,666	264	1,484	2,004	21,752
Mining	6	14	68	196	166	92	280	644	22	126	86	1,694
Construction	66	108	1,076	3,990	10,032	3,302	7,030	19,812	880	1,750	3,926	51,906
Manufacturing	59	562	2,120	8,660	12,600	4,024	8,138	34,072	914	6,144	4,318	81,492
Transportation and Public Utilities	58	42	288	2,704	2,142	762	2,784	14,614	658	1,986	1,940	27,920
Wholesale Trade	32	42	268	2,714	2,662	766	2,602	12,938	408	996	1,592	24,988
Retail Trade	30	116	3,092	7,530	13,768	1,770	5,322	32,566	1,102	3,168	5,396	73,830
Finance, Insurance, Real Estate	10	8	106	814	972	238	1,008	4,308	288	1,550	896	10,188
Services	51	98	1,632	6,962	7,410	2,122	6,430	37,584	1,396	5,946	5,792	75,372

13.33,90 Source: California Department of Industrial Relations, *California Work Injuries and Illnesses, 1988.*

DISABLING WORK INJURIES, ILLNESSES AND FATALITIES UNDER CALIFORNIA WORKERS' COMPENSATION, 1988
Sector by Nature of Injury

Industry	Fatal	Amputations	Burns and Scalds	Contusions, Crushing Injuries	Cuts, Punctures	Abrasions Scratches	Fractures	Strain, Sprain	Other Injuries	Occupational Illness	Nature Not Stated	Total
Private Sector Total	333	1,064	8,878	35,322	53,472	14,386	35,784	165,204	5,932	23,150	25,950	369,142
State Government Total	NA	8	188	1,106	820	296	888	5,792	252	3,052	1,124	13,526
Local Government Total	NA	28	674	4,084	3,540	1,250	3,818	28,042	910	7,718	4,162	54,226
Grand Total	399	1,100	9,740	40,512	57,832	15,932	40,490	199,038	7,094	33,920	31,236	436,894

Note: (Totals exclude Fatalities)

13.34,90 Source: California Department of Industrial Relations, *California Work Injuries and Illnesses, 1988.*

WORK-RELATED FATALITIES, INJURIES, ILLNESSES AND COSTS				
Year	Fatalities	Injuries and Illnesses	Permanent Disabilities*	Total Incurred Losses (millions)
1943	698	152,000	NA	NA
1951	682	144,393	12,896	$74
1961	832	161,233	26,239	$206
1971	711	209,617	45,422	$441
1981	567	361,416	61,658	$1,509
1982	444	330,870	62,587	$1,726
1983	436	344,060	70,657	$2,360
1984	442	373,600	83,819	$2,905
1985	401	400,157	90,540	$3,120
1986	407	406,276	89,124	$2,880
1987	476	400,344	NA	NA
1988	399	436,894	NA	NA

* Leading to indemnity compensation.
13.35,90 Source: California Department of Industrial Relations, *California Work Injuries and Illnesses*.

AVERAGE WEEKLY EARNINGS AND HOURS						
	Earnings			Hours		
Year	Cal*	U.S.*	All U.S. Workers	Cal*	U.S.*	All U.S. Workers
1981	---	$318.00	$255.20	---	39.8	35.2
1982	$353.00	$330.26	$267.26	38.8	38.9	34.8
1983	$376.00	$354.08	$280.70	39.7	40.1	35.0
1984	$393.73	$374.03	$292.86	40.3	40.7	35.2
1985	$406.82	$385.97	$299.09	40.2	40.5	34.9
1986	$417.91	$396.01	$304.85	40.3	40.7	34.8
1987	$433.23	$406.31	$312.50	40.3	41.0	34.8
1988	$442.00	$417.99	$323.29	40.7	41.1	34.8

* Production workers on manufacturing payrolls.
13.36,90 Source: U.S. Dept. of Labor, Bureau of Labor Statistics-*Employment and Earnings*.

CALIFORNIA'S TOP PRIVATE EMPLOYERS*

Rank	Company	Headquarters	Number of Employees
1	Safeway Stores	Oakland	107,000
2	Lockheed Corporation	Burbank	87,800
3	Hewlett-Packard	Palo Alto	83,000
4	National Medical Enterprises	Los Angeles	80,900
5	Pacific Telesis	San Francisco	74,900
6	Pacific Bell	San Francisco	68,400
7	Lucky Stores	Dublin	67,000
8	Wicks Companies	Santa Monica	57,000
9	Chevron	San Francisco	56,500
10	Bank America Corporation	San Francisco	55,700
11	Litton Industries	Beverly Hills	55,000
11	Dennys	La Mirada	55,000
13	Northrop	Los Angeles	46,900
14	American Medical International	Los Angeles	45,000
15	Teledyne	Los Angeles	44,800
16	Occidental Petroleum	Los Angeles	43,000
17	Taco Bell	Irvine	40,000
18	Castle and Cooke	Los Angeles	35,000
19	Hilton Hotels	Beverly Hills	34,000
20	First Interstate Bancorp.	Los Angeles	33,500
21	Security Pacific	Los Angeles	32,300
22	Atlantic Richfield	Los Angeles	31,300
23	National Semiconductor	Santa Clara	30,800
24	Times Mirror	Los Angeles	30,500
25	Walt Disney	Burbank	30,000
26	Pacific Gas & Electric	San Francisco	29,000
27	Southern Pacific	San Francisco	28,200

* Corporations with headquarters in California.

13.37,90 Source: *Dun's Business Rankings*, 1989, and Pacific Data Resources.

SECTION 13 NOTE

Minimum wages in the states range from a low of $1.60 in Wyoming to a high of $4.25 in California and Connecticut.

13.38,90

Income and Wealth

Are today's Californians better off or worse off than they were ten, twenty, and thirty years ago? Despite a welter of seemingly conflicting statistics that are treated uncritically by most of the media, the evidence seems unequivocal that California families are better off now than in the past. U.S. Census Bureau data for median family income, adjusted for inflation, indicate that in 1987 the typical California family had an income 37 percent higher than in 1959, 8 percent higher than in 1969, and 5 percent higher than in 1979.

Overall California is the seventh wealthiest state in the nation in per capita income. Three of the top ten wealthiest metropolitan areas in the United States are in California: San Francisco, San Jose, and Anaheim-Santa Ana. In 1987 California also had the fastest growing metropolitan area in the country in per capita personal income: the Visalia-Tulare-Porterville area in that year experienced a 9.7 percent increase in annual income.

According to Claritas Partners research, California has 130,000 millionaires, although in the ratio of millionaires to the general population the state ranks only fourteenth in the United States. The wealthiest cities in California are exclusively in the greater Los Angeles area and the San Francisco Bay Area. The poorest cities tend to be in the agricultural areas of the San Joaquin Valley and in Imperial County, with a scattering in Los Angeles County. As growth spills over from the rapidly developing areas of the state where the cost of living is high, some of the poorer cities should experience a significant improvement in their per capita income.

Although the state's economy has grown rapidly since the 1982 recession, with a huge increase in the number of new jobs, poverty in the state declined only slightly from 1986 to 1988, from 9.2 to 8.2 percent for families with children and from 1.7 to 1.5 percent for families without children. Women heads of households with children had a poverty rate of 26.7 percent, unchanged from 1986. To some extent this poverty is inflicted by a young generation upon itself: young unmarried women who become pregnant and teenagers who drop out of high school often doom themselves to lives on the economic margins of society. These young parents and dropouts are responsible for much of the poverty in California. Unfortunately, there seem to be no clear remedies for the problem.

TOTAL AND PER CAPITA PERSONAL INCOME IN CALIFORNIA

Year	Total			Per Capita		
	Amount (in billions)	Percent Change from Prior Year	Amount	Percent Change from Prior Year	Percent of U.S. Average
1960	$44.2	-	$2,786	-	123.6%
1970†	$95.0	7.5%	$4,746	5.8%	117.2%
1975	$149.7	9.9%	$6,951	8.1%	114.5%
1980	$276.1	12.8%	$11,603	10.2%	117.0%
1981	$308.7	11.8%	$12,723	9.7%	116.2%
1982	$328.0	6.3%	$13,235	4.0%	115.3%
1983	$352.4	7.4%	$13,926	5.2%	115.1%
1984	$389.2	10.4%	$15,096	8.4%	115.1%
1985	$422.1	8.5%	$16,016	6.1%	115.3%
1986	$453.4	7.4%	$16,792	4.8%	115.0%
1987	$493.0	8.7%	$17,821	6.1%	115.1%
1988*	$534.2	8.4%	$18,866	5.9%	114.5%

* Estimated.   † Data revised after 1969.

14.1,90 Source: *Economic Report of the Governor.*

CALIFORNIA FAMILY INCOME BY RACE, 1988

Income	White	Asian and Other	Black	Hispanic	Total
$0-9,999	44%	11%	11%	34%	100%
$10-19,999	52%	7%	10%	31%	100%
$20-29,999	61%	6%	7%	26%	100%
$30-39,999	68%	7%	6%	18%	100%
$40-49,999	70%	9%	5%	16%	100%
$50-74,999	78%	9%	2%	10%	100%
$75,000+	82%	9%	3%	7%	100%
Median	**$38,600**	**$37,700**	**$22,800**	**$23,200**	**$34,000**

14.2,90 Source: California Department of Finance, California State Census Data Center, *Current Population Survey Report, March 1989.*

SECTION 14 NOTE

According to Claritas Partners, California leads the U.S. with 129,480 millionaires, but 13 states have more millionaires per 1,000 residents.

14.3,90

CALIFORNIA FAMILY INCOME BY RACE, 1988					
Income	White	Asian and Other	Black	Hispanic	Total
$0-9,999	6%	12%	16%	15%	9%
$10-19,999	14%	16%	28%	28%	18%
$20-29,999	15%	12%	19%	20%	16%
$30-39,999	17%	15%	16%	15%	16%
$40-49,999	13%	14%	10%	10%	12%
$50-74,999	21%	20%	7%	9%	18%
$75,000+	14%	12%	5%	4%	11%
	100%	100%	100%	100%	100%

14.4,90   Source: California Department of Finance, California State Census Data Center, *Current Population Survey Report, March 1989.*

TOTAL AND PER CAPITA PERSONAL INCOME BY COUNTY, 1987						
County	Total (millions)	Per Capita Amount	Rank	County	Total (millions)	Per Capita Amount	Rank
Alameda	22,960	18,774	8	Riverside	14,487	15,836	20
Alpine	17	14,220	30	Sacramento	15,349	16,238	16
Amador	354	13,979	33	San Benito	464	14,049	31
Butte	2,199	13,013	43	San Bernardino	17,456	14,496	27
Calaveras	356	11,989	52	San Diego	38,021	16,633	15
Colusa	221	14,950	22	San Francisco	17,159	23,174	3
Contra Costa	16,195	21,737	4	San Joaquin	6,109	13,774	38
Del Norte	214	11,085	57	San Luis Obispo	2,934	14,529	26
El Dorado	1,766	15,517	21	San Mateo	15,071	24,237	2
Fresno	8,690	14,545	25	Santa Barbara	6,446	18,909	7
Glenn	309	13,455	41	Santa Clara	30,437	21,510	5
Humboldt	1,617	14,224	29	Santa Cruz	3,881	17,507	13
Imperial	1,243	11,345	56	Shasta	1,878	13,849	35
Inyo	261	14,570	24	Sierra	48	14,044	32
Kern	7,020	13,914	34	Siskiyou	545	12,807	49
Kings	1,131	12,929	46	Solano	4,457	14,893	23
Lake	648	12,883	48	Sonoma	6,533	18,510	9
Lassen	301	11,490	55	Stanislaus	4,442	13,567	39
Los Angeles	151,919	17,863	12	Sutter	812	13,457	40
Madera	982	12,492	51	Tehama	533	11,692	53
Marin	6,872	30,181	1	Trinity	157	11,670	54
Mariposa	178	12,698	50	Tulare	3,781	12,958	44
Mendocino	1,037	13,836	36	Tuolumne	584	13,092	42
Merced	2,142	13,919	47	Ventura	11,393	18,133	11
Modoc	119	12,958	45	Yolo	2,082	16,179	17
Mono	148	16,040	19	Yuba	596	10,746	58
Monterey	5,538	16,141	18				
Napa	1,942	18,476	10	State Totals	493,547	17,841	---
Nevada	1,051	14,265	28	Metropolitan			
Orange	47,586	21,444	6	Portion	477,826	18,044	---
Placer	2,588	17,399	14	Non-Metropolitan			
Plumas	269	13,781	37	Portion	15,721	13,299	---

14.5,90 Source: U.S. Dept. of Commerce, Bureau of Economic Analysis, *Survey of Current Business.*

	Disposable Personal Income		Per Capita Disposable Income		Rank in U.S.
DISPOSABLE PERSONAL INCOME IN CALIFORNIA 1960-1988					
Year	Amount (millions)	Percent Change	Amount	Percent Change	
1960	38,551	-	2,429	-	NA
1961	40,875	6.0	2,478	2.0	NA
1962	44,022	7.7	2,579	4.1	NA
1963	47,103	7.0	2,666	3.4	NA
1964	51,957	10.3	2,862	7.4	NA
1965	55,584	7.0	2,991	4.5	NA
1966	60,093	8.1	3,187	6.6	NA
1967	64,452	7.3	3,361	5.5	NA
1968	69,774	8.3	3,598	7.1	NA
1969	75,674	8.5	3,839	6.7	NA
1970	82,712	9.3	4,131	7.6	NA
1971	88,578	7.1	4,354	5.4	NA
1972	94,949	7.2	4,613	5.9	NA
1973	106,005	11.6	5,080	10.1	NA
1974	118,249	11.6	5,585	9.9	NA
1975	131,533	11.2	6,107	9.3	NA
1976	145,806	10.9	6,647	8.8	NA
1977	161,575	10.8	7,229	8.8	NA
1978	184,885	14.4	8,095	12.0	NA
1979	209,087	13.1	8,991	11.1	NA
1980	235,003	12.4	9,875	9.8	3
1981	262,962	11.9	10,836	9.7	NA
1982	280,812	6.8	11,330	4.6	5
1983	303,927	8.2	12,009	6.0	4
1984	335,105	10.3	12,998	8.2	5
1985	361,501	7.9	13,715	5.5	5
1986	388,371	7.4	14,384	4.9	6
1987	419,322	8.0	15,162	5.4	6
1988	455,691	8.7	16,177	6.7	7

14.6,90 Source: U.S. Department of Commerce, Bureau of Economic Analysis, *Survey of Current Business.*

SECTION 14 NOTE
Twice as many of the nation's top holders of wealth live in California as in any other state. Texas is next, followed by New York.

14.7,90

MEDIAN FAMILY INCOME*					
County	Median Income	Rank	County	Median Income	Rank
Alameda	$21,973	8	Placer	$21,776	9
Alpine	$19,077	19	Plumas	$17,889	29
Amador	$19,157	18	Riverside	$18,885	21
Butte	$14,778	51	Sacramento	$20,039	13
Calaveras	$18,282	27	San Benito	$16,922	36
Colusa	$14,703	52	San Bernardino	$20,548	11
Contra Costa	$26,117	1	San Diego	$19,397	17
Del Norte	$13,850	55	San Francisco	$18,827	22
El Dorado	$19,845	14	San Joaquin	$17,263	32
Fresno	$14,689	53	San Luis Obispo	$18,382	26
Glenn	$14,984	50	San Mateo	$25,387	3
Humboldt	$15,926	43	Santa Barbara	$19,706	15
Imperial	$12,421	58	Santa Clara	$25,137	4
Inyo	$17,660	31	Santa Cruz	$18,421	25
Kern	$17,178	34	Shasta	$15,989	41
Kings	$15,797	44	Sierra	$18,489	24
Lake	$15,778	45	Siskiyou	$15,544	48
Lassen	$19,583	16	Solano	$23,485	5
Los Angeles	$18,714	23	Sonoma	$20,464	12
Madera	$15,574	47	Stanislaus	$16,619	38
Marin	$25,696	2	Sutter	$15,693	46
Mariposa	$16,126	39	Tehama	$15,443	49
Mendocino	$15,975	42	Trinity	$16,636	37
Merced	$14,518	54	Tulare	$13,530	56
Modoc	$16,066	40	Tuolumne	$17,719	30
Mono	$17,168	35	Ventura	$22,691	6
Monterey	$17,956	28	Yolo	$17,207	33
Napa	$21,054	10	Yuba	$13,383	57
Nevada	$19,034	20			
Orange	$22,580	7	State Median	$19,900	-

* Based on joint tax returns filed for 1987.
  14.8,90 Source: California Franchise Tax Board, news release, 1989.

STATES WITH LARGEST NUMBER OF INDIVIDUALS IN THE TOP 400 WEALTHIEST AMERICANS		
State	Number of Individuals	Average Wealth (millions)
New York	82	$577
California	62	$479
Texas	36	NA
Illinois	22	NA
Florida	18	NA

14.9,90 Source: *Forbes Magazine.*

MEDIAN HOUSEHOLD INCOME BY AGE OF HOUSEHOLDER AND REGION, 1988									
Metro Area	Age of Householder - Income by Age					House-holds	Families	Median Family Income	Median Household Income
	Under 35	35-44	45-54	55-64	65+				
Anaheim -
Santa Ana	$39,700	$46,900	$56,800	$52,400	$21,900	800,300	560,300	$41,800	$34,400
Los Angeles	$31,700	$42,700	$48,800	$40,700	$22,500	3,067,600	2,144,500	$33,400	$29,200
San Bernardino -
Riverside	$30,100	$40,100	$37,700	$41,400	$16,600	785,600	572,600	$33,800	$27,400
Sacramento	$26,100	$44,100	$41,900	$31,200	$22,700	540,300	327,400	$31,900	$23,800
San Diego	$33,200	$45,000	$47,500	$36,200	$26,100	803,200	556,800	$33,700	$30,400
San Jose	$45,600	$56,900	$62,400	$63,100	$29,200	519,500	358,900	$48,600	$40,000
San Francisco -
Oakland	$36,200	$42,200	$49,900	$48,700	$32,200	1,405,300	903,400	$38,900	$33,200
Rest of the State	$25,600	$35,300	$43,800	$32,300	$21,900	2,260,900	1,667,300	$28,600	$25,000
Region									
South Coast	$36,400	$46,000	$52,700	$43,600	$24,300	1,603,500	1,117,100	$37,200	$32,100
Los Angeles- Inland	$31,400	$42,100	$47,200	$40,900	$21,100	3,833,200	2,717,100	$33,500	$28,100
Mid-Coast	$31,800	$43,900	$57,600	$46,600	$25,600	560,500	417,600	$35,100	$31,900
Bay Area	$37,100	$45,400	$51,900	$48,900	$30,500	2,185,700	1,434,000	$40,500	$34,300
San Joaquin Valley	$23,100	$32,000	$39,900	$29,800	$17,900	816,900	615,200	$24,800	$22,300
Sacramento Valley	$26,100	$40,100	$41,300	$26,900	$23,600	786,700	518,800	$30,600	$23,100
Rest of the State	$23,300	$27,200	$44,700	$31,700	$18,500	376,300	271,400	$25,800	$23,600

14.10,90 Source: U.S. Dept. of Commerce, Bureau of Economic Analysis, BEA, 89-18.

TOTAL AND PER CAPITA PERSONAL INCOME IN CALIFORNIA, 1960-1988							
Total Personal Income (Amount in Billions)				Per Capita Personal Income (Amount in Dollars)			
Year	Cur-rent	% Change	Con-stant*	% Change	Cur-rent	% Change	Con-stant*	% Change
1960	$43	NA	NA	NA	NA	NA	NA	NA
1970	$95	121%	$213	NA	$4,776	NA	$10,617	NA
1975	$150	58%	$253	18.8%	NA	NA	NA	NA
1980	$276	84%	$319	26.1%	$11,603	NA	$13,398	26.2%
1981	$308	12.8%	$326	2.2%	$12,057	3.9%	$12,745	-4.9%
1982	$328	6.4%	$328	0.6%	$13,235	9.8%	$13,235	3.8%
1983	$354	7.9%	$340	3.7%	$13,984	5.7%	$13,433	1.5%
1984	$391	10.4%	$362	6.5%	$15,097	8.0%	$13,966	4.0%
1985	$423	8.4%	$378	4.4%	$16,036	6.2%	$14,343	2.7%
1986	$456	7.8%	$399	5.6%	$16,904	5.4%	$14,815	3.3%
1987	$494	8.3%	$413	3.5%	$17,846	5.6%	$14,934	0.8%
1988	$531	7.5%	$427	3.3%	$18,855	5.7%	$15,145	1.4%

* In 1982 dollars calculated by the editor using the U.S. Dept. of Commerce, Personal Consumption Deflator.

14.11,90 Source: U.S. Bureau of Economic Analysis, Survey of Current Business.

			CALIFORNIA AND THE UNITED STATES MEDIAN FAMILY INCOME 1959-1987				
			% Change	United States			
Year	In Current Dollars	In Constant 1982 Dollars*	in Constant Dollars	Current Dollars	Constant 1982 Dollars	% Change in Constant Dollars
1959	$6,726	$20,824	NA	NA	NA	NA
1969	10,828	$26,416	26.9%	$9,433	NA	NA
1979	21,169	$27,070	2.5%	$19,587	$30,669	-0.2%
1980	23,323	$26,932	-0.5%	$21,023	$28,996	-5.5%
1981	24,257	$25,642	-4.8%	$22,388	$27,977	-3.5%
1982	25,201	$25,201	-1.7%	$23,433	$27,591	-1.4%
1983	26,359	$25,321	0.5%	$24,674	$28,147	2.0%
1984	29,029	$26,854	6.1%	$26,433	$28,923	2.8%
1985	30,800	$27,599	2.8%	$27,735	$29,302	1.3%
1986	33,200	$29,046	5.2%	$29,498	$30,534	4.2%
1987	34,000	$28,452	-2.0%	$30,853	$30,853	1.0%

* Calculated using the National Personal Consumption Expenditure Deflater which is based on actual consumer purchases.

14.12,90 Source: California Department of Finance, unpublished data and U.S. Bureau of the Census, *Current Population Survey,* unpublished data and Series P60, No. 161.

			TOTAL AND PER CAPITA DISPOSABLE PERSONAL INCOME IN CALIFORNIA 1960-1988					
					Per Capita			
Year	Amount current dollars (billions)	% Change from prior year	Amount Constant dollars (billions)	% Change from prior year	Amount current dollars	% Change from prior year	Amount Constant dollars	% Change from prior year
1960	$38	NA	NA	NA	$2,372	NA	NA	NA
1965	$53	39%	NA	NA	$2,876	21%	NA	NA
1970	$78	47%	$182	NA	$3,880	35%	$9,044	NA
1975	$122	56%	$206	13.2%	$5,681	46%	$9,596	6.1%
1980	$231	92%	$270	31.1%	$9,845	73%	$11,378	18.6%
1981	$262	12.0%	$277	2.6%	$10,800	9.7%	$11,416	.3%
1982	$280	6.9%	$280	1.1%	$11,306	4.7%	$11,306	-1.0%
1983	$305	8.9%	$293	4.6%	$12,040	6.5%	$11,566	2.3%
1984	$336	10.2%	$311	6.1%	$13,032	8.2%	$12,055	4.2%
1985	$370	10.1%	$332	6.8%	$13,733	5.3%	$12,306	2.1%
1986	$389	5.1%	$340	2.4%	$14,409	4.9%	$12,606	2.4%
1987	$419	7.7%	$351	3.2%	$15,162	5.2%	$12,687	.6%
1988	$456	8.8%	$366	4.2%	$16,177	6.7%	$12,994	2.4%

* Constant dollar numbers calculated by the editor using the U.S. Dept of Commerce Personal Consumption Deflator.

Note: Disposable income is personal income left over after income taxes have been paid.

14.13,90 Source: U.S. Dept. of Commerce, Bureau of Economic Analysis, *Survey of Current Business, April, 1989.*

	In Current Dollars	Annual % Change in Current Dollars	% of U.S. GNP	In Constant 1982 Dollars	Annual % Change in 1982 Dollars
CALIFORNIA GROSS STATE PRODUCT, 1963-1991 (millions of dollars)					
Year					
1963	$65,905	-	-	$210,153	-
1964	$70,928	7.6%	11.0%	$220,848	5.1%
1965	$75,887	7.0%	NA	$229,125	3.7%
1966	$83,006	9.4%	NA	$240,495	5.0%
1967	$88,653	6.8%	11.0%	$245,762	2.2%
1968	$97,995	10.5%	NA	$257,843	4.9%
1969	$105,766	7.9%	NA	$264,621	2.6%
1970	$111,631	5.5%	NA	$263,933	-0.3%
1971	$119,192	6.8%	NA	$265,600	0.6%
1972	$132,199	10.9%	11.1%	$281,159	5.9%
1973	$146,473	10.8%	10.9%	$293,735	4.5%
1974	$160,979	9.9%	11.0%	$298,408	1.6%
1975	$179,858	11.7%	11.5%	$304,518	2.0%
1976	$201,536	12.1%	11.5%	$320,160	5.1%
1977	$227,590	12.9%	11.6%	$338,040	5.6%
1978	$260,296	14.4%	11.8%	$359,603	6.4%
1979	$293,600	12.8%	11.9%	$374,928	4.3%
1980	$325,171	10.8%	12.2%	$380,221	1.4%
1981	$354,905	9.1%	11.9%	$378,436	-0.5%
1982	$372,541	5.0%	12.0%	$372,541	-1.6%
1983	$408,216	9.6%	12.2%	$390,528	4.8%
1984	$456,874	11.9%	12.3%	$420,525	7.7%
1985	$496,850	8.7%	12.5%	$444,082	5.6%
1986	$533,816	7.4%	12.7%	$464,550	4.6%
1987*	-	-	NA	$485,900	4.6%
1988*	-	-	NA	$506,100	4.1%
1989*	-	-	NA	$520,500	2.9%
1990*	-	-	NA	$535,200	2.8%
1991*	-	-	NA	$557,300	4.1%

* Estimates.

14.14,90 Source: U.S. Department of Commerce, Bureau of Economic Analysis, *Survey of Current Business, May 1988 and California Commission on State Finance, Quarterly General Fund Forecast.*

NET NEW SAVINGS AT CALIFORNIA SAVINGS AND LOAN ASSOCIATIONS (in millions)	
Year	**New Savings**
1966-69	-$767
1970-79	$37,087
1980	$106
1981	-$5,815
1982	$1,281
1983	$29,205
1984	$28,355
1985	-$4,056
1986	$6,062
1987	$9,824
1988	$3,607

14.15,90 Source: *Economic Report of the Governor.*

AVERAGE ANNUAL PAY BY METROPOLITAN AREA 1987			
Area	Average Pay	Percent Increase from 1986	Rank among 317 Metropolitan areas
Anaheim-Santa Ana-Garden Grove	$22,994	5.2%	25
Bakersfield	$19,509	0.4%	132
Chico	$16,438	4.0%	285
Fresno	$16,818	4.8%	274
Los Angeles-Long Beach	$25,005	6.5%	11
Merced	$15,538	1.6%	305
Modesto	$17,934	3.0%	213
Oakland	$23,972	4.7%	18
Oxnard-Simi Valley-Ventura	$21,399	4.8%	49
Redding	$18,451	3.2%	191
Riverside-San Bernardino-Ontario	$19,301	6.5%	145
Sacramento	$21,047	4.1%	61
Salinas-Seaside-Monterey	$18,223	2.4%	202
San Diego	$21,051	4.5%	60
San Francisco	$26,594	3.9%	5
San Jose	$27,748	5.2%	4
Santa Barbara-Santa Maria-Lompoc	$20,389	3.6%	91
Santa Cruz	$17,959	5.3%	210
Santa Rosa-Petaluma	$19,601	2.9%	127
Stockton	$18,961	3.2%	165
Vallejo-Fairfield-Napa	$20,773	2.5%	74
Visalia-Tulare-Porterville	$15,164	3.8%	312
Yuba City	$16,398	1.8%	287
Average of All 317 U.S. Metropolitan Areas	**$21,724**	**4.6%**	

14.16,90 Source: U.S. Bureau of Labor Statistics, *Average Annual Pay in Metropolitan Areas,* Press Release 88-516,1988.

AVERAGE ANNUAL PAY IN CALIFORNIA AND THE UNITED STATES, 1987				
	California		United States	
Occupation	Average 1987 Annual Pay	Percent Change 1986-87	Average 1987 Annual Pay	Percent Change 1986-87
Private Industry	$22,721	5.0%	$20,620	4.4%
Mining	$35,606	-3.4%	$32,950	1.2%
Construction	$26,241	1.7%	$23,129	4.2%
Manufacturing	$27,910	2.9%	$25,668	3.2%
Transportation Communications & Public Utilities	$29,430	3.6%	$27,400	3.2%
Wholesale Trade	$27,431	4.0%	$26,033	4.9%
Retail Trade	$13,330	3.3%	$11,513	3.4%
Finance, Insurance & Real Estate	$29,187	9.9%	$25,991	7.2%
Services	$22,165	8.4%	$18,912	7.2%
Government	$25,218	5.0%	$22,063	4.6%
All Workers*	$23,100	5.0%	$20,855	4.5%

* Workers covered by unemployment insurance, or unemployment compensation for federal workers.
14.17,90 Source: U.S. Bureau of Labor Statistics, *Average Annual Pay by State and Industry*, 1987, Press Release 88-413.

CALIFORNIA AND THE U.S. POPULATION WITH INCOME BELOW THE POVERTY LEVEL*					
	Persons			Families	
	California		U.S.	California		U.S.
Year	Number (in millions)	Percent	Percent	Number (in thousands)	Percent	Percent
1959	2.2	14.4%	22.1%	461	11.6%	18.5%
1969	1.9	9.6%	12.3%	421	8.4%	10.7%
1979	2.6	11.3%	11.7%	513	8.6%	9.6%
1980	2.6	11.4%	13.0%	521	8.7%	10.3%
1982	NA	NA	15.0%	NA	NA	12.2%
1984	NA	NA	14.4%	NA	NA	11.6%
1985	NA	NA	14.0%	NA	NA	12.6%
1986	3.9	14.6%	13.6%	737	11.0%	10.9%
1987	3.4	12.7%	13.5%	660	9.6%	10.8%
1988	3.9	13.9%	NA	695	9.8%	NA

* Census data does not include a wide variety of Federal and State benefit programs such as food stamps, health care, and housing. When the cash equivalent of these programs is included in calculation poverty, the number of poor declines by 40 to 50 percent. The 1988 poverty level for a family of four was $12,091.
14.18,90 Source: U.S. Bureau of the Census, *State and Metropolitan Area Data Book, U.S. Statistical Abstract*; and California Employment Development Dept., Annual Planning Information, California Dept. of Finance, *Current Population Survey*.

FAMILY POVERTY IN CALIFORNIA METROPOLITAN/REGIONAL AREA, 1986 & 1988		
Metropolitan/ Regional Area	Percent of Families below Poverty	
	1986	1988
San Diego	11.3%	7.4%
Anaheim-Santa Ana	9.2%	5.0%
San Bernardino-Riverside	12.5%	11.2%
Los Angeles	12.6%	12.3%
San Jose	8.7%	4.4%
San Francisco-Oakland	6.7%	7.7%
Bay Area (1) (Region)	7.4%	7.7%
Sacramento	12.9%	8.5%
Sacramento Valley (2) (Region)	12.9%	8.9%
San Joaquin Valley (3) (Region)	12.3%	15.9%
Mid Coast (4) (Region)	11.2%	7.2%
South Coast (6) (Region)	21.0%	16.4%
Los Angeles-Inland (5) (Region)	10.1%	6.2%
Remainder of State (7)	12.5%	12.0%

1   Alameda, Contra Costa, Marin, Napa, San Francisco, San Mateo,
    Santa Clara, Solano, Sonoma.
2   Sacramento, Butte, El Dorado, Placer, Sutter, Yolo, Yuba.
3   Fresno, Kern, San Joaquin, Stanislaus, Tulare..
4   Monterey, Santa Barbara, Santa Cruz, Ventura.
5   Los Angeles, Riverside, San Bernardino.
6   Orange, San Diego
7   28 Counties
    14.19,90 Source: California Department of Finance, State Census
    Data Center, *Current Population Survey*, 1987 &1989.

POVERTY STATUS BY RACE/ETHNICITY AND AGE IN CALIFORNIA,1988				
Race/ Ethnicity	Number Above Poverty Level	Number Below Poverty Level	Total	Percent Below Poverty Level
White	15,659,800	1,295,300	16,955,100	7.6%
Hispanic	4,910,500	1,678,300	6,588,800	25.5%
Asian and Other	2,011,000	495,700	2,506,700	19.8%
Black	1,412,400	394,300	1,806,700	21.8%
Total	23,993,700	3,863,600	27,857,300	13.9%*
Age				
0-17	5,782,300	1,784,500	7,566,800	23.6%
Over 64	2,582,300	197,800	2,780,100	7.1%

*   In 1986 14.6% or the population was in poverty.
    14,20,90 Source: Cal. Dept. of Finance, State Census Data Center, 1986 *Current Population Survey*.

FAMILY POVERTY IN CALIFORNIA BY FAMILY TYPE, 1986 AND 1988 PERCENT OF FAMILIES IN POVERTY					
	Year	Married Couple	Male Householder	Female Householder	Total Families
Families with	1986	6.1%	3.2%	26.7%	9.2%
Children	1988	4.8%	5.9%	26.7%	8.2%
Families without	1986	1.5%	5.5%	1.5%	1.7%
Children	1988	1.4%	1.3%	2.3%	1.5%

14.21,90 Source: California Department of Finance, State Data Center, *Current Population Survey, 1988.*

CALIFORNIA'S WEALTHIEST AND POOREST METROPOLITAN AREAS						
California Rank	1987 U.S. Rank	1986 U.S. Rank	Metropolitan Area	Per Capita Personal Income	% Increase From 1986	% of U.S. Personal Income
1	2	2	San Francisco	$24,593	6.4%	159%
2	7	8	San Jose	$21,510	5.9%	139%
3	8	10	Anaheim-Santa Ana	$21,444	7.1%	139%
4	20	17	Oakland	$19,896	5.8%	129%
5	25	24	Santa Barbara-Santa Maria-Lompoc	$18,809	5.3%	122%
6	28	27	Santa Rosa-Petaluma	$18,510	5.4%	120%
7	32	34	Oxnard-Ventura	$18,133	6.8%	117%
8	34	38	Los Angeles-Long Beach	$17,863	6.8%	115%
9	41	42	Santa Cruz	$17,507	5.9%	113%
10	58	55	San Diego	$16,633	5.0%	107%
11	64	63	Sacramento	$16,300	5.7%	105%
12	70	69	Salinas-Monterey	$16,141	5.6%	104%
13	82	74	Vallejo-Fairfield-Napa	$15,854	4.9%	102%
14	117	115	Riverside-San Bernardino	$15,075	5.1%	97%
15	140	165	Fresno	$14,545	8.0%	94%
16	170	156	Bakersfield	$13,914	2.8%	90%
17	175	197	Redding	$13,849	7.9%	89%
18	179	181	Stockton	$13,774	5.6%	89%
19	193	198	Modesto	$13,567	5.8%	88%
20	228	238	Chico	$13,013	6.4%	84%
21	232	261	Visalia-Tulare-Porterville	$12,968	9.7%	84%
22	238	245	Merced	$12,919	7.1%	83%

14.22,90 Source: U.S. Department of Commerce, *Bureau of Economic Analysis*, BEA 89-18.

	SECTION 14 NOTE

The average age of Californians on the Forbes 400 list is 64; the divorce rate among them is 48%; their average number of children is 2.9. Twelve of them made their fortune in real estate, twelve in the media.

14.23,90

WEALTHIEST CALIFORNIANS							
U.S. Rank	Cal. Rank	Name	Business	Source of Wealth	Estimated Wealth (millions)	City	Age
10	1	David Packard	Computers	Self-made	$2,000	Los Altos Hills	76
11	2	Donald Bren	Real Estate	Self-made	$1,850	Newport Beach	56
14	3	Marvin Davis	Oil, Real Estate	Self-made	$1,600	Beverly Hills	63
27	4	Walter Annenberg	Publishing	Inheritance	$1,200	Rancho Mirage	80
35	5	Harold Simmons	Investments	Self-made	$1,100	Montecito	57
39	6	William Hewlett	Computers	Self-made	$1,000	Portola Valley	75
46	7	Kirk Kerkorian	Investments	Self-made	$950	Los Angeles	71
48	8	David Murdock	Investments	Self-made	$900	Bel Air	65
54	9	Michael Milken	Finance	Self-made	$800	Encino	42
58	10	Norton Simon	Conglomerates	Inheritance	$750	Los Angeles	81
59	11	George Randolph Hearst, Jr.	Publishing	Inheritance	$750	Los Angeles	61
59	11	Phoebe Hearst Cooke	Publishing	Inheritance	$750	San Francisco	61
59	11	David W. Hearst Jr.	Publishing	Inheritance	$750	Los Angeles	44
59	11	Millicent V. (Hearst) Baoudjakdji	Publishing	Inheritance	$750	Los Angeles	49
62	15	Helen Copley	Publishing	Inheritance	$750	La Jolla	65
63	16	Joan Kroc	Hamburgers	Inheritance	$745	La Jolla	60
82	17	Henry Singleton	Aerospace	Self-made	$590	Los Angeles	71
89	18	Alexander Spanos	Real Estate	Self-made	$550	Stockton	65
92	19	Melvin Simon	Shopping Centers	Self-made	$536	Beverly Hills	61
96	20	Robert Howard	Publishing	Self-made	$530	Rancho Santa Fe	64
107	21	Roy Disney	Entertainment	Inheritance	$500	Los Angeles	58
119	22	Gordon P. Getty	Oil	Inheritance	$450	San Francisco	54
127	23	M. Larry Lawrence	Real Estate	Self-made	$450	San Diego	62
132	24	Meshulam Riklis	Finance	Self-made	$440	Los Angeles	64
136	25	Guilford Glazer	Real Estate	Self-made	$430	Beverly Hills	67
144	26	Walter Shorestein	Real Estate	Self-made	$400	San Francisco	73
155	27	Stephen Bechtel, Sr.	Construction	Inheritance	$390	Oakland	88
155	27	Stephen Bechtel, Jr.	Construction	Inheritance	$390	San Francisco	63
157	29	Andrew Perenchio	Entertainment	Self-made	$390	Bel Air	57
158	30	Robert A. Lurie	Real Estate	Inheritance	$385	San Francisco	59
170	31	Gordon Moore	Computers	Self-made	$370	Santa Clara County	59
180	32	Nan Tucker McEvoy	Publishing	Inheritance	$350	San Francisco	69
182	33	Ernest Gallo	Wine	Self-made	$350	Modesto	79
182	33	Julio Gallo	Wine	Self-made	$350	Modesto	77
184	35	William Barron Hilton	Hotels	Inheritance	$350	Los Angeles	61
200	36	Robert E. Peterson	Publishing	Self-made	$340	Beverly Hills	62
202	37	Harry H. Hoiles	Publishing	Inheritance	$333	Santa Ana	72
202	37	Mary Jane Hoiles Hardie	Publishing	Inheritance	$333	Marysville	66
208	39	George Roberts	Finance	Self-made	$330	San Francisco	45
212	40	Lawrence J. Ellison	Software	Self-made	$330	Atherton	44
214	41	Sydney Mark Taper	Finance	Self-made	$325	Los Angeles	87
218	42	Howard Keck	Oil	Inheritance	$315	Los Angeles	75
220	43	Marshall Naify	Entertainment	Inheritance	$315	San Francisco	68
220	43	Robert Naify	Entertainment	Inheritance	$315	San Francisco	66
235	45	John E. Anderson	Beer	Self-made	$300	Bel Air	71
242	46	Armas Markkula	Computers	Self-made	$300	Woodside	46

14.24.1,90

U.S. Rank	Cal. Rank	Name	Business	Source of Wealth	Estimated Wealth (millions)	City	Age
			WEALTHIEST CALIFORNIANS				
237	47	Mervyn Griffin	Entertainment	Self-made	300	Beverly Hills	63
238	48	William Lyon	Real Estate	Self-made	300	Newport Beach	65
247	49	Lydia Kalmanovitz	Beer	Inheritance	280	Tuburon	83
248	50	Lloyd E. Cotson	Soap	Inheritance	280	Bel Air	59
249	51	Donald Fisher	Retail Stores	Self-made	280	San Francisco	60
252	52	Richard J. O'Neill	Real Estate	Inheritance	275	San Juan Capistrano	64
252	52	Alice O'Neill Avery	Real Estate	Inheritance	275	Los Angeles	71
272	54	John Arrillaga	Real Estate	Self-made	250	Palo Alto	50
272	54	Richard Taylor Peery	Real Estate	Self-made	250	Palo Alto	49
276	56	George L. Argyos	Real Estate	Self-made	250	Newport Beach	51
-	57	William Keck, III	Oil	Inheritance	245	Los Angeles	46
283	58	Max Palevsky	Computers	Self-made	240	Beverly Hills	64
286	59	Jack Tramiel	Computers	Self-made	240	Saratoga	60
287	60	Dorothy Green	Oil	Inheritance	240	Beverly Hills	80
292	61	David Geffen	Entertainment	Self-made	240	Malibu	45
303	62	Gene Autry	Baseball	Self-made	230	Los Angeles	81
310	63	Lew Wasserman	Entertainment	Self-made	225	Beverly Hills	75
311	64	Hugh Bancroft	Publishing	Inheritance	225	Newport Beach	39

14.24.2,90 Source: *Forbes Magazine.*

GREAT FAMILY FORTUNES IN CALIFORNIA	
Family	**Business**
Annenberg	Media (T.V. Guide)
Chandler	Newspapers (L.A. Times)
de Young	Newspapers (S.F. Chronicle)
Disney	Entertainment
Getly	Oil
Haas	Dry Goods (Levis)
Hearst	Newspapers (S.F. Examiner)
Hixon	Electronics (AMP Corp)
McClatchy	Newspapers (Bee Chain)
O'Neill	Real Estate (Mission Viejo)
Segerstrom	Real Estate (South Coast Plaza)
Schnitzer	Steel, Shipping
Swig	Real Estate (Fairmont Hotels)
Whittier	Oil (Belridge oil)

14.25,90 Source: *Forbes Magazine, Oct. 24, 1988.*

WEALTHIEST STATES IN THE U.S., 1988			
Rank	State	Average Per Capita Income	Average Annual % Change From 1982
1	Connecticut	$22,761	7.9%
2	New Jersey	$21,882	7.8%
3	Massachusetts	$20,701	8.4%
4	Alaska	$19,514	2.0%
5	Maryland	$19,314	7.2%
6	New York	$19,299	7.2%
7	New Hampshire	$19,016	8.6%
8	**California**	**$18,855**	**6.1%**
12	Nevada	$17,440	5.7%
27	Arizona	$14,887	6.3%
30	Oregon	$14,982	6.0%
	United States	$16,444	6.2%

14.26,90 Source: U.S. Commerce Department, Bureau of Economic Analysis, *Press Release BEA 89-14.*

CALIFORNIA'S WEALTHIEST CITIES			
Rank	City	County	Per Capita Income
1	Rolling Hills	Los Angeles	$56,149
2	Indian Wells	Riverside	$48,743
3	Hidden Hills	Los Angeles	$47,384
4	Belvadere	Marin	$41,062
5	Hillsborough	San Mateo	$37,147
6	Portola Valley	San Mateo	$36,269
7	Atherton	San Mateo	$34,915
8	Los Altos Hills	Santa Clara	$34,254
9	Woodside	San Mateo	$33,864
10	Beverly Hills	Los Angeles	$33,839
11	San Marino	Los Angeles	$33,050
12	Ross	Marin	$31,972
13	Sausalito	Marin	$31,766
14	Palos Verdes Estates	Los Angeles	$29,616
15	Rancho Mirage	Riverside	$29,191
16	Monte Sereno	Santa Clara	$27,850
17	Newport Beach	Orange	$28,712
18	Orinda	Contra Costa	$28,632
19	Tiburon	Marin	$27,657
20	Piedmont	Alameda	$27,502

Certain unincorporated areas such as Rancho Santa Fe in San Diego County and Marin Del Rey in Los Angeles County would be in the top 10 if they were cities.
14.27,90 Source: U.S. Bureau of the Census, *Current Population Estimates, Local Population Estimates, Series* P-26, No. 86-W-SC.

CALIFORNIA'S POOREST CITIES

Rank	City	County	Per Capita Income
1	Parlier	San Joaquin	$3,845
2	San Joaquin	San Joaquin	$3,988
3	Mendota	San Joaquin	$4,139
4	Orange Cove	San Joaquin	$4,270
5	McFarland	Kern	$4,305
6	Calexico	Imperial	$4,420
7	Cudahy	Los Angeles	$4,831
8	Woodlake	Tulare	$4,983
9	Bell Gardens	Los Angeles	$4,988
10	Farmersville	Tulare	$5,011
11	Calpatria	Imperial	$5,095
12	Livingston	Merced	$5,139
13	Arvin	Kern	$5,284
14	Westmorland	Imperial	$5,379
15	Coachella	Riverside	$5,572
16	Greenfield	Merced	$5,689
17	Delano	Kern	$5,739
18	Soledad	Monterey	$5,773
19	Huntington Park	Los Angeles	$5,886
20	Maywood	Los Angeles	$5,902

14.28,90 Source: U.S. Bureau of the Census, *Current Population Estimates*, *Local Population Estimates*, series P-26, No. 86-W-SC.

CALIFORNIA FAMILY INCOME BY NUMBER OF WORKERS IN FAMILY

Number of Workers	Percent of Families	Mean Income
None	14%	$18,900
One	28%	$30,700
Two	45%	$45,000
Three or more	13%	$59,400

14.29,90 Source: Cal. Dept. of Finance, State Census Data Center, *Current Population Survey*, 1988.

CALIFORNIA HOUSEHOLD INCOME BY AGE OF HOUSEHOLDER

Age	Number of Households (millions)	Percent of Households	Mean Income
Under 35	3.1	31%	$32,000
35-44	2.3	23%	$42,300
45-54	1.5	15%	$48,400
55-64	1.4	14%	$41,000
Over 65	1.8	18%	$23,800

14.30,90 Source: Cal. Dept. of Finance, State Census Data Center, *Current Population Survey*, 1988.

The Cost of Living

In the late 1980s inflation was less worrisome to Californians than it had been a decade earlier. By 1989, however, economists were beginning to worry that the state's tight labor markets might set off a wage-price spiral. Other factors that have recently affected the cost of living for Californians include the 1987-88 drought, which forced up the prices of agricultural products and raised electricity bills; the construction of an insufficient number of houses and apartments, which drove up the cost of shelter; and the rising price of oil. Oil prices rose for several reasons. First, OPEC supplied less oil to the market; second, the state of California pumped less domestic oil; and third, California became more dependent on Alaskan oil (43 percent of California's oil needs in 1988 were met by oil from Alaska) just as pumping in Alaska began to decline and as the major oil spill off the Alaska coast imposed new restraints and costs on the shipping of North Slope oil to the south. In the weeks immediately after the *Exxon Valdez* ran aground, spilling 240,000 barrels of oil, pump prices at California's gas stations increased by as much as thirty cents per gallon.

Natural gas prices declined slightly from 1986 to 1988, possibly because of an oversupply of gas that economists expect will soon disappear. Ample supplies coming in from Canada (filling 29 percent of the state's needs) may help to keep natural gas prices from rising too high, especially since the Canadians are willing to sell additional natural gas to the United States at long-term contract prices.

The huge increase in the state's population and the failure of the construction industry to keep pace with housing needs may be the most significant inflationary elements in California's future. Various factors have worked to discourage high levels of construction: rent-control laws, local slow-growth initiatives, higher local building fees, a shortage of available land, and high interest rates. Since these factors are unlikely to change in the near term, the housing shortage will continue and the state's housing prices will probably remain the highest in the nation.

Even the cost of in-home entertainment is accelerating rapidly. The average cost of a monthly subscription to cable television has increased by two-thirds since 1985. Since virtually all cable television systems are monopolies, few market mechanisms currently operate to hold down their price increases.

PURCHASING POWER OF THE DOLLAR (1967=$1.00)					
Year	United States	Calif.	Los Angeles-Long Beach	San Francisco-Oakland	San Diego
1950	1.27	1.45	1.43	1.50	NA
1960	1.07	1.13	1.13	1.14	NA
1967	1.00	1.00	1.00	1.00	1.00
1970	.91	.87	.87	.86	.87
1980	.41	.40	.40	.40	.37
1981	.37	.36	.37	.36	.33
1982	.35	.34	.35	.33	.31
1983	.34	.34	.34	.33	.32
1984	.32	.32	.33	.31	.28
1985	.32	.31	.32	.30	.27
1986	.31	.30	.30	.29	.26
1987	.30	.28	.29	.28	.25
1989	.28	.27	.28	.27	.24*

* Second half of 1988.

15.1,90 Source: U.S. Bureau of Labor Statistics Monthly Press Release - Consumer Price Indexes, and the California Dept. of Industrial Relations, unpublished data.

CONSUMER PRICE INDEX, SELECTED AREAS: ANNUAL AVERAGES, 1950-1989 (1982-84=100)					
Year	United States	California	Los Angeles-Anaheim-Riverside	San Francisco-Oakland-San Jose	San Diego
1950	24.1	22.8	23.7	22.0	NA
1960	29.6	29.2	30.0	28.6	NA
1970	38.8	37.9	38.7	37.7	34.1
1980	82.4	82.4	83.7	80.4	79.4
1981	90.9	91.4	91.9	90.8	90.1
1982	96.5	97.3	97.3	97.6	96.2
1983	99.6	98.9	99.1	98.4	99.0
1984	103.9	103.8	103.6	104.0	104.8
1985	107.6	108.6	108.4	108.4	110.4
1986	109.6	112.0	111.9	111.6	113.5
1987	113.6	116.6	116.7	115.4	117.5
1988	118.3	121.9	122.1	120.5	125.0
1989*	124.1	128.2	128.7	126.2	128.9

* June.

15.2,90 Source: U.S. Department of Labor, Bureau of Labor Statistics.

	U.S. City Average (June 1989)		Los Angeles Long Beach Anaheim (June 1989)		San Francisco Oakland (June 1989)		San Diego (2nd Half 1988)	
CONSUMER PRICE INDEXES **ALL URBAN CONSUMERS** **BY EXPENDITURE CATEGORY, SELECTED AREAS** **(1982-1984=100)**								
Item	Index	Change from June 1988	Index	Change from June 1988	Index	Change from June 1988	Index	Change from June 1988
Food and Beverage	124.9	6.2	123.5	6.3	127.8	6.6	120.9	4.3
Food	125.0	6.3	123.0	6.5	128.6	6.5	121.1	4.4
At Home	124.3	7.3	123.4	6.2	128.9	7.8	117.5	3.0
Not At Home	127.1	4.6	123.0	7.0	129.1	5.0	125.8	6.0
Alcoholic Beverages	123.5	4.0	127.9	4.2	121.7	7.1	119.3	3.9
Housing	122.9	3.6	131.7	4.0	131.6	3.9	127.6	3.6
Shelter	132.3	4.5	139.7	5.0	138.9	4.8	139.8	4.4
Renter's Cost*	138.7	3.7	146.2	3.9	152.1	4.0	151.7	4.8
Fuel and Utilities	109.2	3.1	121.0	1.5	123.1	1.2	103.4	0.6
Household Furnishings	111.1	1.4	110.6	1.0	116.4	1.3	105.5	2.1
Apparel and Upkeep	117.8	2.8	120.3	3.8	103.5	3.8	119.7	8.5
Transportation	115.9	6.8	122.8	7.1	111.6	6.0	116.9	7.8
Private	115.0	7.0	121.1	6.7	111.2	6.7	115.4	7.2
Public	129.6	5.2	151.4	10.3	122.5	1.8	137.1	13.2
Medical Care	148.5	7.5	149.1	7.2	146.6	7.7	145.9	10.5
Medical Care Services	147.9	7.3	NA	NA	NA	NA	145.5	10.9
Entertainment	126.2	5.1	120.7	5.2	134.2	3.8	133.2	9.0
Other	146.3	8.0	152.9	10.6	151.5	9.4	143.1	8.0
All Items	124.1	5.2	128.7	5.5	126.2	5.1	125.0	5.7
Commodities	117.2	5.5	117.7	6.3	117.7	6.3	114.9	5.3
Services	131.6	4.9	138.6	4.8	134.1	4.4	134.5	5.7
Energy	99.0	8.8	107.0	11.5	112.0	11.2	88.2	0.9

* 1982 = 100.

15.3,90 Source: U.S. Department of Labor, Bureau of Labor Statistics, monthly press releases.

PERCENT CHANGE IN CONSUMER PRICE INDEX FOR ALL URBAN CONSUMERS, 1988-89	
Area	Percent Change*
Los Ange ¨Long Beach	5.5%
San Francisco-Oakland	5.1%
San Diego†	6.0%
California	**5.3%**
United States	**5.2%**

* June 1988-June 1989. † 1st half 1988-1st half 1989.
15.4,90 Source: U.S. Bureau of Labor Stat.-Consumer Price Indexes, Pacific Cities & U.S. Cal. Dept. of Indust. Relations.

AVERAGE MONTHLY RESIDENTIAL TELEPHONE BILL 1985-1989			
	Amount		
Company	1985	1987	1989
Pacific Telephone	$21.60	$25.44	$28.75
GTE California	NA	NA	$29.00

Note: Pacific Telephone and General Telephone serve over 90% of the California phone market. 15.5,90 Source: The respective phone companies.

AVERAGE RESIDENTIAL ELECTRICITY BILL					
Utility	Dec. 1981	Dec. 1984	Nov. 1985	Nov. 1986	Nov. 1988
Pacific Gas and Electric	$43.79	$38.11	$40.20	$37.77	$43.41
Sacramento Municipal Utility District	$20.98	$29.61	$33.21	$35.90	$48.57
Southern California Edison	$35.52	$33.87	$35.57	$37.39	$46.00
Los Angeles Department of Water and Power	$24.17	$30.52	$26.21	$27.32	$33.97
San Diego Gas and Electric	$42.67	$47.47	$49.56	$46.16	$44.42
Statewide*	**$37.26**	**$36.07**	**$37.32**	**$36.96**	**$43.45**

* Average weighted by number of customers in service areas.
15.6,90 Source: California Energy Commission, *Energy Watch*.

AVERAGE RESIDENTIAL NATURAL GAS BILL					
Utility	Dec. 1981	Nov. 1984	Nov. 1985	Nov. 1986	Nov. 1988
Pacific Gas and Electric	$31.97	$35.43	$30.99	$20.07	$21.72
Southern California Gas	$30.13	$31.41	$28.62	$23.22	$29.10
San Diego Gas and Electric	$21.58	$21.19	$16.88	$15.22	$16.14
Long Beach	$12.21	$14.90	$13.15	$13.29	$17.37
Statewide*	**$29.74**	**$31.92**	**$28.40**	**$22.02**	**$25.12**

* Average weighted by number of customers in service areas.
15.7,90 Source: California Energy Commission, *Energy Watch*.

Elections and Politics

The California political scene was rocked by scandal in 1989. Members of the state's assembly and senate were indicted for political dirty tricks and for taking bribes in an FBI sting operation. The mayor of Los Angeles was under investigation for taking money from financial institutions doing business with the city. The ultimate shocker, however, was the resignation under a cloud of California's powerful congressman from Fresno, Tony Coehlo. Coehlo had been minority whip in the U.S. House of Representatives and was expected to rise eventually to the position of Speaker. He abandoned his fast-track political career after the *Washington Post* linked him to junk-bond dealers, exposing his own financial schemes.

The political scandals of the late 1980s may prompt another paroxysm of political reform like the one that resulted in voters' approving Proposition 9, the Political Reform Act, in 1974. But Proposition 9 did not prevent the scandals of the 1980s, and it is an open question whether the political reforms of the late 1980s limiting certain types of election financing will do any better.

While Sacramento, Los Angeles, and Washington insiders wallowed in the ongoing saga of influence peddling, the voters for the most part ignored the turmoil and reelected virtually all congressional and state legislative incumbents. The absence of elective competition makes these legislative bodies seem like Yankee versions of the House of Lords, whose members take a seat and hold it for life.

Despite their having relatively safe seats in the legislature, the lawmakers seem unable to deal with many of the pressing problems facing the state, such as crime, traffic congestion, the high cost of housing, poor schools, or even the need for insurance reform.

Although by the late 1980s the Republicans were closing the voter-registration gap with the Democrats, they remained eleven points behind in the official registration figures. Polls, however, indicated that an equal number of the state's voters identified with each of the two political parties. This ostensible equality, however, did not translate into an equal number of legislative seats for Republicans and Democrats. Perhaps gerrymandering kept a Democratic lock on the state's legislature and congressional delegation. Or perhaps the Democrats were better fund-raisers or had a better farm system for recruiting electable candidates. For whatever reason, the 1980s in California ended as they began, with the party of Roosevelt, Kennedy, and Jerry Brown in the political driver's seat.

	VOTER REGISTRATION							
	1930		1940		1950		1960	
County	Total Reg.†	% Dem.*	Total Reg.	% Dem.	Total Reg.	% Dem.	Total Reg.	% Dem.
Alameda	232,712	17.0	326,525	56.7	404,702	59.9	469,239	62.0
Alpine	137	7.3	240	32.9	189	26.3	213	37.1
Amador	2,819	33.8	5,178	65.5	5,623	66.7	5,584	66.0
Butte	6,152	28.6	24,726	59.0	30,607	59.5	41,862	55.4
Calaveras	3,358	22.4	5,546	60.3	6,065	61.8	6,345	60.7
Colusa	4,327	39.2	5,762	59.7	4,957	60.5	5,627	60.6
Contra Costa	29,705	18.6	60,160	63.3	126,980	65.7	202,184	61.9
Del Norte	2,455	23.0	3,067	50.5	4,150	57.1	7,720	63.2
El Dorado	4,610	28.8	8,548	66.2	10,090	64.9	14,643	62.7
Fresno	52,814	32.9	87,805	70.2	124,011	70.1	152,615	68.5
Glenn	5,002	31.6	7,109	53.6	7,000	56.9	8,369	58.1
Humboldt	20,223	13.3	28,412	49.4	31,808	56.5	45,231	60.8
Imperial	14,195	35.9	20,662	64.4	18,290	62.1	24,342	63.8
Inyo	3,312	38.4	4,511	61.8	5,289	58.9	6,286	57.3
Kern	31,661	37.0	69,718	69.6	90,210	68.8	122,389	67.1
Kings	9,430	34.3	16,284	67.9	16,467	69.6	19,121	71.9
Lake	4,044	29.0	5,456	46.4	7,287	53.0	8,346	52.8
Lassen	5,295	33.8	8,132	67.5	7,873	70.5	6,945	70.1
Los Angeles	853,676	21.6	1,721,780	64.3	2,198,878	61.3	3,011,379	59.9
Madera	6,887	38.5	11,557	70.6	12,931	69.3	16,415	70.5
Marin	16,979	15.9	26,160	52.8	40,151	52.4	71,905	47.1
Mariposa	2,477	34.4	4,174	73.1	3,401	63.9	3,497	59.2
Mendocino	11,047	21.8	15,710	51.9	17,230	56.2	22,632	60.2
Merced	12,096	27.8	22,647	65.8	24,301	65.8	31,986	67.7
Modoc	2,794	37.4	4,698	59.6	4,670	61.3	4,100	60.6
Mono	846	19.6	1,490	56.0	1,292	52.3	1,616	48.7
Monterey	16,304	23.6	34,295	59.5	47,834	60.3	67,867	56.2
Napa	10,650	20.3	16,715	55.0	21,732	56.0	33,158	57.3
Nevada	5,858	21.5	11,770	62.9	11,183	59.2	11,943	55.0
Orange	50,304	22.3	81,951	54.5	103,612	49.2	322,880	50.1
Placer	10,031	27.8	16,034	66.8	20,557	65.6	27,400	64.7
Plumas	3,379	27.6	6,539	70.9	7,648	72.9	6,502	69.5
Riverside	27,002	21.2	54,313	54.2	78,686	53.5	136,183	53.0
Sacramento	52,579	24.2	93,299	67.6	127,099	65.6	223,031	64.2
San Benito	4,434	27.2	6,075	55.0	6,140	55.9	6,989	59.0
San Bernardino	50,238	25.9	88,079	60.3	130,055	60.2	220,174	60.2
San Diego	92,842	23.7	163,711	61.6	273,328	59.3	451,649	54.1
San Francisco	228,582	15.3	386,028	65.9	429,864	65.4	404,613	64.5
San Joaquin	37,153	19.9	63,919	61.7	78,042	61.6	105,341	61.9
San Luis Obispo	13,744	20.7	20,631	61.0	27,212	59.0	39,989	57.5
San Mateo	33,545	17.8	67,064	55.5	118,777	54.5	225,476	54.5
Santa Barbara	22,520	22.3	39,212	56.5	46,782	53.0	77,530	51.2
Santa Clara	59,639	18.5	100,142	54.0	126,889	54.0	279,280	54.5
Santa Cruz	14,403	18.9	27,769	55.0	35,494	54.0	47,441	51.0
Shasta	7,345	30.2	17,736	70.5	18,733	67.9	27,663	67.7
Sierra	1,377	27.9	2,057	63.7	1,638	60.4	1,532	60.8
Siskiyou	10,496	31.4	16,454	61.8	16,883	64.3	17,247	65.3
Solano	15,496	25.3	26,205	68.1	46,380	69.8	52,492	70.0
Sonoma	30,127	20.5	39,209	49.1	51,664	54.1	73,837	55.1
Stanislaus	40,766	22.5	52,382	60.4	52,382	60.4	70,110	38.9
Sutter	9,719	32.1	9,945	57.9	9,945	57.9	13,603	55.9
Tehama	8,535	30.8	9,160	56.0	9,160	44.0	12,734	60.1
Trinity	3,225	25.8	3,375	66.4	3,375	66.4	4,953	70.5
Tulare	50,156	31.4	58,926	64.5	58,926	64.5	63,070	61.4
Tuolumne	7,443	39.9	7,714	64.5	7,714	64.5	9,054	63.8
Ventura	33,625	27.0	44,934	62.5	44,934	62.4	82,483	61.5
Yolo	13,873	30.3	17,211	62.2	17,211	65.9	25,886	63.1
Yuba	4,958	27.6	9,782	66.3	10,506	65.9	11;927	66.2
State Totals	2,245,228	21.8	4,052,395	62.4	5,244,867	61.2	7,464,626	59.5

* Percent Democratic is the Democratic percentage of the two party (Democratic plus Republican) registration. † Reg. = Registered.
16.1.1,90 Source: Lee and Keith, *California Votes;* and California Secretary of State, *Report of Registration.*

	VOTER REGISTRATION					
	1970		1980		1989	
County	Total Registered	% Demo.*	Total Registered	% Demo.*	Total Registered	% Demo.*
Alameda	509,635	67	595,292	71	657,625	72
Alpine	384	42	723	54	731	49
Amador	6,591	63	12,575	62	15,069	56
Butte	47,692	51	84,877	54	94,203	51
Calaveras	7,398	56	12,895	57	16,964	51
Colusa	5,050	58	6,141	58	6,624	54
Contra Costa	261,358	59	358,881	60	448,985	58
Del Norte	6,591	62	9,398	61	10,529	59
El Dorado	19,390	56	48,367	57	66,536	50
Fresno	170,997	66	220,431	64	279,465	60
Glenn	7,932	57	10,065	57	10,426	52
Humboldt	44,328	60	63,836	63	65,394	65
Imperial	24,825	60	30,170	62	35,485	62
Inyo	7,947	54	10,044	50	9,791	45
Kern	132,441	61	165,890	59	217,698	52
Kings	21,471	66	25,787	64	31,687	60
Lake	11,496	55	21,223	61	26,545	60
Lassen	7,305	67	10,218	65	10,793	58
Los Angeles	3,116,095	60	3,262,932	64	3,631,310	61
Madera	16,422	65	25,501	62	34,483	58
Marin	102,003	49	134,417	57	140,707	60
Mariposa	3,483	52	6,808	66	8,322	52
Mendocino	22,225	59	36,598	63	40,727	63
Merced	33,443	66	47,909	66	57,171	63
Modoc	3,853	57	4,801	57	5,213	52
Mono	2,407	45	4,558	47	5,073	45
Monterey	82,257	55	113,971	58	138,019	58
Napa	38,617	57	55,881	58	58,882	57
Nevada	14,589	51	32,663	53	45,889	46
Orange	612,006	44	1,013,337	48	1,134,229	39
Placer	35,027	61	68,014	60	88,322	51
Plumas	6,481	66	10,377	62	10,832	57
Riverside	177,984	53	313,450	55	466,077	49
Sacramento	286,850	63	411,310	65	529,139	61
San Benito	7,296	60	9,030	59	14,322	57
San Bernardino	261,469	56	381,549	57	546,502	48
San Diego	563,168	50	948,705	53	1,184,457	46
San Francisco	372,032	69	407,982	75	401,506	78
San Joaquin	118,591	61	151,537	62	196,354	59
San Luis Obispo	46,182	53	88,967	52	109,867	47
San Mateo	266,424	57	301,887	61	322,301	60
Santa Barbara	113,762	51	167,997	56	183,071	50
Santa Clara	444,696	57	613,758	60	717,727	58
Santa Cruz	62,192	52	112,457	62	128,126	67
Shasta	35,185	63	62,267	61	67,370	52
Sierra	1,553	60	2,198	63	2,150	57
Siskiyou	15,829	62	21,410	61	23,137	58
Solano	62,359	69	103,861	69	142,299	63
Sonoma	98,655	55	161,425	60	208,436	62
Stanislaus	82,805	63	108,372	62	141,256	58
Sutter	17,410	52	23,316	54	26,353	45
Tehama	13,111	60	19,540	60	23,548	56
Trinity	4,281	63	7,215	61	7,756	57
Tulare	65,336	59	94,067	58	111,843	50
Tuolumne	11,146	59	20,730	60	25,485	56
Ventura	144,670	54	237,901	54	311,895	46
Yolo	38,159	64	64,289	64	73,225	63
Yuba	13,463	82	21,220	65	21,146	55
State Totals	8,706,347	58	11,361,020	61	13,389,077	56

* Percent Democratic is the Democratic percentage of the two party (Democratic plus Republican) registration.

16.1.2,90 Source: Lee and Keith, *California Votes;* and California Secretary of State, *Report of Registration.*

	POLITICAL TURNOUT							
	1930		1940		1950		1960	
County	% of Reg.* Voters	% of Eligible Adults	% of Reg.* Voters	% of Eligible Adults	% of Reg.* Voters	% of Eligible Adults	% of Reg.* Voters	% of Eligible Adults
Alameda	71.3	42.9	87.5	72.5	77.7	56.2	82.4	71.7
Alpine	94.5	40.7	**	85.5	**	88.5	93.4	89.0
Amador	51.2	29.7	89.4	73.1	97.1	68.9	94.8	84.2
Butte	73.0	45.8	86.5	65.1	72.2	55.1	81.7	71.8
Calaveras	81.6	54.8	94.9	71.0	93.1	73.3	94.5	81.1
Colusa	63.9	48.4	87.0	68.5	66.1	52.8	77.0	67.9
Contra Costa	59.5	41.1	88.6	74.6	69.8	51.8	87.1	77.3
Del Norte	80.9	65.4	95.6	72.9	77.8	61.1	77.4	64.2
El Dorado	79.2	51.7	91.5	67.8	92.4	67.6	79.9	68.5
Fresno	61.4	44.2	77.2	63.0	72.7	51.1	73.1	63.7
Glenn	72.7	51.8	89.3	72.0	72.5	57.6	80.5	71.9
Humboldt	71.2	49.1	90.7	71.2	71.1	54.4	75.3	65.4
Imperial	40.5	28.3	59.9	43.4	49.6	35.2	59.1	49.0
Inyo	77.5	58.0	85.5	63.6	67.7	49.9	84.9	74.2
Kern	63.5	36.9	83.2	62.8	66.1	47.7	74.6	65.0
Kings	64.9	49.2	77.2	59.6	61.2	46.2	69.1	60.8
Lake	83.9	68.2	96.2	74.7	90.0	68.1	86.7	75.3
Lassen	65.2	37.6	87.2	68.7	69.7	50.1	84.6	72.9
Los Angeles	55.4	32.5	85.3	70.6	75.0	54.3	78.6	69.6
Madera	70.4	50.0	82.7	62.3	61.6	47.0	72.2	63.0
Marin	56.4	47.5	66.1	57.7	67.4	55.6	78.5	73.0
Mariposa	**	44.0	**	76.9	94.5	68.5	99.6	85.6
Mendocino	71.6	58.5	79.1	64.1	63.1	47.4	73.1	61.9
Merced	56.5	37.1	78.6	59.4	58.5	43.7	63.6	55.9
Modoc	53.8	31.6	80.9	63.7	74.6	56.6	82.0	72.1
Mono	87.3	51.0	90.6	61.2	85.8	62.1	**	92.8
Monterey	45.9	31.5	68.7	54.6	58.4	42.6	58.2	51.6
Napa	62.8	45.5	76.4	59.8	66.2	50.3	76.7	67.3
Nevada	79.9	61.3	89.0	67.4	83.5	61.0	86.9	75.0
Orange	67.3	45.1	93.7	74.9	72.4	53.7	80.7	72.6
Placer	64.4	43.1	84.0	66.4	72.1	57.1	75.7	67.1
Plumas	59.3	35.7	82.1	60.1	87.9	66.0	90.9	76.6
Riverside	53.6	32.1	80.1	63.2	71.5	51.3	73.4	64.3
Sacramento	54.7	38.5	77.4	63.2	68.1	54.9	75.0	66.4
San Benito	64.4	37.0	81.1	66.1	67.7	50.3	77.0	66.5
San Bernardino	59.3	35.9	82.9	65.8	71.2	51.7	74.1	65.4
San Diego	64.7	41.8	80.8	63.9	74.4	52.6	75.1	66.4
San Francisco	48.1	33.4	78.3	64.0	73.4	53.3	76.1	65.5
San Joaquin	53.3	45.5	67.8	54.3	58.8	45.5	69.3	61.4
San Luis Obispo	71.1	52.6	91.8	72.0	79.5	57.8	78.7	66.0
San Mateo	64.6	43.7	83.8	72.0	74.9	57.6	83.2	75.4
Santa Barbara	52.4	31.7	81.7	66.8	70.9	52.8	75.2	67.3
Santa Clara	62.1	49.6	81.7	67.0	65.9	50.1	75.3	68.1
Santa Cruz	56.8	45.6	85.8	70.4	75.3	59.4	83.8	74.8
Shasta	79.9	58.9	91.2	66.6	81.5	59.1	79.4	70.9
Sierra	79.3	60.7	93.0	72.3	**	74.9	**	86.9
Siskiyou	64.3	46.0	85.7	64.4	83.5	64.0	84.5	72.8
Solano	55.3	43.5	74.7	61.5	69.6	51.7	66.3	58.7
Sonoma	72.6	52.3	80.8	67.5	74.2	57.4	81.0	71.2
Stanislaus	57.2	43.0	84.3	66.7	65.3	49.2	74.3	65.7
Sutter	68.5	48.8	81.4	62.4	61.5	49.2	70.2	62.5
Tehama	71.1	48.7	90.3	70.6	74.5	58.9	84.3	74.3
Trinity	80.7	62.9	**	79.8	96.3	70.1	85.1	64.5
Tulare	58.4	38.4	78.4	57.3	67.7	49.1	66.0	58.1
Tuolumne	77.0	50.2	97.1	74.2	89.7	69.2	95.7	80.6
Ventura	58.5	35.3	75.8	61.0	61.1	45.0	70.5	61.3
Yolo	53.6	37.4	74.9	59.6	65.3	48.8	67.1	59.4
Yuba	64.4	38.0	86.5	64.8	70.4	52.7	61.6	53.5
State Totals	58.1	37.4	82.9	67.6	72.7	53.3	77.3	68.2

* Reg.=Registered.
** The registration total in these counties is higher than the census report of total adults.
16.2.1,90 Source: Lee and Keith, *California Votes,* and California Secretary of State, *Statement of Vote.*

	1970		1984		1986		1988	
	% of Reg.* Voters	% of Eligible Adults	% of Reg.* Voters	% of Eligible Adults	% of Reg.* Voters	% of Eligible Adults	% of Reg.* Voters	% of Eligible Adults
County								
Alameda	75.3	56.9	74.1	62.0	58.3	46.0	71.1	55.4
Alpine	122.2	99.0	68.6	47.2	63.4	48.5	74.1	75.1
Amador	87.9	73.2	82.7	67.4	73.4	56.2	80.9	60.6
Butte	73.3	54.8	74.7	60.2	63.0	46.5	75.7	57.5
Calaveras	80.5	61.3	84.8	62.5	74.3	53.4	80.4	64.3
Colusa	66.5	53.4	81.0	58.4	71.1	49.2	76.9	50.8
Contra Costa	79.1	61.9	76.3	67.5	62.4	51.7	75.4	64.3
Del Norte	76.0	56.6	74.8	54.8	68.4	50.1	71.6	48.0
El Dorado	69.9	51.3	77.0	57.9	64.4	46.1	76.0	63.5
Fresno	71.0	53.6	73.3	53.8	55.9	39.2	67.1	48.4
Glenn	73.1	60.1	81.2	56.5	68.3	46.1	87.5	61.3
Humboldt	74.1	56.3	79.4	66.8	65.3	50.8	77.9	64.4
Imperial	62.1	46.3	72.0	48.3	56.7	38.0	68.1	46.4
Inyo	79.3	63.7	81.4	61.8	68.8	51.4	78.7	64.8
Kern	69.8	53.0	71.0	51.4	58.8	41.0	68.9	45.6
Kings	59.5	46.6	70.5	47.1	56.9	36.8	67.7	40.5
Lake	81.7	66.1	78.4	57.2	64.4	42.9	74.7	48.8
Lassen	79.6	61.6	84.2	47.5	72.1	40.7	80.1	50.6
Los Angeles	70.4	53.1	73.9	53.0	60.0	40.7	72.6	47.7
Madera	66.7	52.6	73.4	48.2	59.3	36.9	70.0	46.8
Marin	77.7	60.1	79.8	71.4	65.5	56.8	81.7	67.6
Mariposa	86.2	70.5	84.1	67.4	69.6	53.8	82.9	64.2
Mendocino	69.2	54.3	77.2	62.7	62.7	51.2	75.3	63.1
Merced	57.3	43.0	75.2	47.8	57.7	33.1	59.5	34.2
Modoc	81.2	63.6	81.6	63.6	65.9	52.3	78.7	67.2
Mono	93.3	72.9	71.6	50.6	53.4	37.5	75.2	68.1
Monterey	56.9	42.3	74.9	56.1	58.0	39.4	71.9	50.0
Napa	76.1	61.0	80.2	65.0	64.7	52.2	77.6	61.3
Nevada	83.1	65.7	80.2	64.0	69.4	54.3	82.2	70.6
Orange	74.0	56.5	78.3	61.0	60.3	45.7	76.6	59.7
Placer	73.7	60.0	74.1	63.8	62.5	51.2	77.1	68.8
Plumas	86.4	68.6	81.0	67.4	70.7	52.5	82.1	64.6
Riverside	63.2	52.1	75.7	55.9	56.4	42.7	69.7	51.8
Sacramento	76.6	62.3	76.1	62.6	61.6	49.6	72.5	60.3
San Benito	69.4	51.2	77.4	56.4	61.7	45.0	71.2	48.6
San Bernardino	65.0	48.1	73.0	51.2	55.4	36.9	70.0	49.8
San Diego	69.3	52.6	72.8	58.7	53.2	43.5	70.8	60.1
San Francisco	71.6	50.5	70.4	61.6	61.2	47.6	67.1	52.7
San Joaquin	67.6	53.7	75.7	54.0	57.5	39.4	69.6	44.7
San Luis Obispo	68.2	49.3	76.4	58.0	63.7	43.4	76.6	51.7
San Mateo	75.6	58.1	79.7	63.6	64.9	47.2	77.0	57.5
Santa Barbara	71.8	55.0	77.0	66.1	59.9	47.2	75.6	57.8
Santa Clara	71.8	55.4	73.7	56.2	56.2	39.8	73.0	54.0
Santa Cruz	77.3	58.8	77.8	65.0	63.8	48.7	79.9	64.0
Shasta	76.1	59.6	81.1	59.6	62.6	45.7	82.8	56.3
Sierra	97.9	84.8	78.8	77.6	68.4	60.6	79.4	69.6
Siskiyou	75.7	60.0	80.0	61.1	69.7	52.1	77.8	62.4
Solano	62.5	46.9	76.4	56.5	59.9	42.6	73.3	57.8
Sonoma	77.6	61.2	77.0	64.8	62.6	52.7	75.9	64.6
Stanislaus	71.2	56.7	75.1	49.2	55.1	37.8	68.5	46.3
Sutter	70.8	58.2	73.1	54.2	63.4	42.4	76.7	53.0
Tehama	73.1	59.3	78.1	60.8	66.5	47.1	76.4	55.5
Trinity	90.0	70.3	82.7	66.3	73.0	58.7	78.7	66.2
Tulare	60.1	45.3	72.0	47.7	59.0	35.5	68.9	42.6
Tuolumne	75.2	58.3	77.6	63.4	66.4	52.8	75.2	58.0
Ventura	69.1	52.8	77.5	61.6	59.0	47.0	75.6	62.8
Yolo	71.4	57.4	76.0	61.6	62.4	49.5	74.6	60.3
Yuba	53.6	40.0	69.4	51.3	57.9	37.0	70.2	46.4
State Totals	71.1	54.1	74.9	57.2	59.4	43.4	72.8	53.5

POLITICAL TURNOUT†

* Reg.=Registered.   † General Elections
16.2.2,90 Source: Lee and Keith, *California Votes*, and California Secretary of State, *Statement of Vote*.

VOTER REGISTRATION AND TURNOUT 1930-1989					
Percent of Registered Voters*				Turnout	
Year	D	R	Other	% of Registered Voters	% of Eligible Voters
1930	20.3	73.0	6.7	64.4	41.7
1940	59.7	36.0	4.3	81.4	78.3
1950	58.4	37.1	4.6	73.3	60.0
1960	57.5	39.2	3.3	88.3	68.8
1970	54.9	39.8	5.2	76.2	54.5
1980	53.2	34.7	12.1	77.2	57.0
1984	52.0	36.5	10.4	74.9	59.1
1986	50.8	38.3	10.9	59.4	43.4
1988	50.4	38.6	11.0	72.8	53.5
1989	50.3	38.8	10.9	–	–

* Prior to the General Election, except for 1989.

16.3,90 Source: Secretary of State, *Statement of Vote*, and *Report of Registration*.

CALIFORNIA VOTES IN PRESIDENTIAL ELECTIONS							
Year	California Winner	Party	Winner's % of Total Vote	Year	California Winner	Party	Winner's % of Total Vote
1852	Pierce	D	53.0%	1924	Coolidge	R	57.2%
1856	Buchanan	D	48.4%	1928	Hoover	R	63.9%
1860	Lincoln	R	32.3%	1932	Roosevelt	D	58.4%
1864	Lincoln	R	58.6%	1936	Roosevelt	D	67.0%
1868	Grant	R	50.2%	1940	Roosevelt	D	57.4%
1872	Grant	R	56.4%	1944	Roosevelt	D	56.5%
1876	Hayes	R	50.9%	1948	Truman	D	47.6%
1880	*Hancock*	D	48.9%	1952	Eisenhower	R	56.3%
1884	*Blaine*	R	52.0%	1956	Eisenhower	R	55.4%
1888	Harrison	R	49.9%	1960	*Nixon*	R	50.1%
1892	Cleveland	D	43.8%	1964	Johnson	D	59.1%
1896	McKinley	R	49.0%	1968	Nixon	R	47.8%
1900	McKinley	R	54.4%	1972	Nixon	R	55.0%
1904	Roosevelt	R	61.9%	1976	*Ford*	R	49.3%
1908	Taft	R	55.4%	1980	Reagan	R	52.7%
1912	*Roosevelt*	P*	57.6%	1984	Reagan	R	57.5%
1916	Wilson	D	46.6%	1988	Bush	R	51.1%
1920	Harding	R	66.2%				

Candidates in bold were elected. * Progressive

16.4,90 Source: Lee and Keith, *California Voter* and California Secretary of State, *Statement of Vote*.

VOTER TURNOUT* IN SELECTED STATES								
	Presidential Elections				Non-presidential Elections			
	1976	1980	1984	1988	1974	1978	1982	1986
California	50%	49%	56%	52%	46%	39%	41%	45%
Oregon	61%	61%	67%	64%	50%	48%	52%	65%
Arizona	46%	45%	54%	54%	39%	29%	34%	46%
Texas	46%	45%	54%	54%	21%	23%	26%	37%
Illinois	59%	58%	67%	67%	40%	37%	43%	47%
New York	51%	48%	58%	54%	44%	34%	36%	44%
United States	59%	59%	60%	57%	45%	46%	49%	46%

* Based on the total number of eligible adults.
16.5,90 Source: *U.S. Statistical Abstract* and U.S. Bureau of the Census, *Current Population Reports,* Series P-20.

1984 GENERAL ELECTION						
President and Vice-President						
County	Ronald Reagan George Bush (Republican)	Walter Mondale Geraldine Ferraro (Democratic)	County	Ronald Reagan George Bush (Republican)	Walter Mondale Geraldine Ferraro (Democratic)	
Alameda	192,408	282,041	Placer	38,035	21,294	
Alpine	264	194	Plumas	5,224	3,837	
Amador	6,986	4,188	Riverside	182,324	102,043	
Butte	45,381	25,421	Sacramento	204,922	159,128	
Calaveras	7,632	4,081	San Benito	5,695	3,554	
Colusa	3,388	1,725	San Bernardino	222,071	116,454	
Contra Costa	172,331	140,994	San Diego	502,344	257,029	
Del Norte	3,996	2,696	San Francisco	90,219	193,278	
El Dorado	27,583	14,312	San Joaquin	81,795	53,846	
Fresno	104,757	86,315	San Luis Obispo	49,035	26,946	
Glenn	6,020	2,488	San Mateo	135,185	122,268	
Humboldt	27,832	25,217	Santa Barbara	89,314	51,243	
Imperial	13,829	8,237	Santa Clara	288,638	229,865	
Inyo	5,863	2,360	Santa Cruz	41,652	49,091	
Kern	94,776	49,567	Shasta	33,041	19,298	
Kings	13,364	7,324	Sierra	1,078	781	
Lake	10,874	8,648	Siskiyou	10,544	7,130	
Lassen	5,352	3,254	Solano	51,678	41,982	
Los Angeles	1,424,113	1,158,912	Sonoma	76,447	71,295	
Madera	13,954	8,994	Stanislaus	55,665	37,459	
Marin	56,887	57,533	Sutter	14,477	5,535	
Mariposa	3,989	2,399	Tehama	11,586	6,527	
Mendocino	16,369	14,407	Trinity	3,544	2,218	
Merced	24,997	17,012	Tulare	51,066	28,065	
Modoc	2,995	1,219	Tuolumne	10,485	7,283	
Mono	2,659	962	Ventura	151,383	66,550	
Monterey	55,710	40,733	Yolo	24,329	25,879	
Napa	26,322	18,599	Yuba	9,780	5,339	
Nevada	19,809	11,198	State Totals	5,467,009	3,922,519	
Orange	635,013	206,272	Percent	57.5%	41.3%	

16.6,90 Source: California Secretary of State, *Statement of Vote*, November 6, 1984.

1988 PRESIDENTIAL ELECTION BY COUNTY		
County	Michael S. Dukakis Lloyd Bentsen Democratic	George Bush Dan Quayle Republican
Alameda	310,283	162,815
Alpine	230	306
Amador	5,197	6,893
Butte	30,406	40,143
Calaveras	5,674	7,640
Colusa	2,022	3,077
Contra Costa	169,411	158,652
Del Norte	3,587	3,714
El Dorado	19,801	30,021
Fresno	92,635	94,835
Glenn	2,894	4,944
Humboldt	29,781	21,460
Imperial	10,243	12,889
Inyo	2,653	5,042
Kern	55,083	90,550
Kings	9,142	12,118
Lake	9,828	9,366
Lassen	3,446	5,157
Los Angeles	1,372,352	1,239,716
Madera	10,642	13,255
Marin	69,394	46,855
Mariposa	2,998	3,768
Mendocino	17,152	12,979
Merced	20,105	21,717
Modoc	1,416	2,518
Mono	1,284	2,177
Monterey	48,998	50,022
Napa	22,283	23,235
Nevada	14,980	21,383
Orange	269,013	586,230
Placer	27,516	42,096
Plumas	4,251	4,603
Riverside	133,122	199,979
Sacramento	188,557	201,832
San Benito	4,559	5,578
San Bernardino	151,118	235,167
San Diego	333,264	523,143
San Francisco	201,887	72,503
San Joaquin	61,699	75,309
San Luis Obispo	35,667	46,613
San Mateo	141,859	109,261
Santa Barbara	63,586	77,524
Santa Clara	277,810	254,442
Santa Cruz	63,133	37,728
Shasta	21,171	32,402
Sierra	791	860
Siskiyou	8,365	9,056
Solano	54,344	50,314
Sonoma	91,262	67,725
Stanislaus	44,685	51,648
Sutter	6,557	14,100
Tehama	7,213	9,854
Trinity	2,518	3,267
Tulare	30,711	46,891
Tuolumne	8,717	10,646
Ventura	89,065	147,604
Yolo	30,429	22,358
Yuba	5,444	8,937
State Totals	**4,702,233**	**5,054,917**
Percent	**47.56%**	**51.13%**

16.7,90 Source: California Secretary of State, *Statement of Vote.*

CHARACTERISTICS OF CALIFORNIA VOTERS IN THE 1988 GENERAL ELECTION			
	Total Voters	Precinct Voters	Absentee Voters
Vote for President			
Bush-Quayle	51.1%	50%	58%
Dukakis-Bentsen	47.6%	49%	41%
Other	1.3%	1%	1%
Vote for U.S. Senate			
Wilson	52.8%	51%	67%
McCarthy	44.0%	46%	31%
Other	3.2%	3%	2%
Region			
Southern California	58%	59%	53%
Northern California	42%	41%	47%
Party Registration			
Democrat	*	*	49%
Republican	*	*	42%
Other	*	*	9%
Political Ideology			
Conservative	32%	30%	43%
Middle-of-the-road	47%	48%	37%
Liberal	21%	21%	20%
Age			
18-29	20%	22%	12%
30-39	25%	27%	15%
40-49	19%	18%	22%
50-59	13%	12%	16%
60 or older	23%	21%	35%
Sex			
Male	49%	48%	58%
Female	51%	52%	42%
Ethnicity			
White (non-Hispanic)	81%	80%	85%
Hispanic	7%	7%	8%
Black	8%	8%	5%
Asian/other	4%	5%	2%
Education			
High school graduate or less	25%	24%	24%
Some college	34%	34%	35%
College graduate	23%	24%	21%
Post graduate degree	18%	18%	19%
Annual Household Income			
Under $10,000	9%	10%	5%
$10,000-$29,999	29%	30%	28%
$30,000-$49,999	32%	31%	32%
$50,000 or more	30%	29%	35%

* Network exit polls did not ask party registration.
16.8,90 Source: The Field Institute, California Opinion Index, Dec., 1988.

CHARACTERISTICS OF THE CALIFORNIA VOTE FOR PRESIDENT AND U.S. SENATOR			
	Bush-Quayle	Dukakis-Bentsen	Wilson	McCarthy
Statewide	51.1%	47.6%	52.8%	44%
Region				
Los Angeles County	47%	52%	49%	49%
Other Southern Counties	62%	37%	63%	34%
San Francisco Bay Area	41%	58%	43%	54%
Other Northern Counties	52%	47%	53%	44%
Party*				
Democrats	13%	85%	18%	78%
Republicans	91%	8%	90%	8%
Others	46%	47%	47%	47%
Political Ideology				
Conservative	83%	16%	82%	14%
Middle-of-the-road	46%	52%	50%	47%
Liberal	14%	84%	17%	80%
Sex				
Male	54%	43%	57%	40%
Female	48%	51%	50%	47%
Age				
18-29	49%	49%	50%	44%
30-49	48%	50%	49%	48%
50-59	56%	42%	59%	38%
60 or older	52%	46%	56%	42%
Ethnicity				
White (non-Hispanic)	56%	42%	58%	39%
Hispanic	34%	65%	35%	61%
Black	13%	86%	16%	80%
Asian/other	47%	52%	47%	51%
Education				
High school graduate or less	53%	45%	52%	46%
Some college	52%	46%	54%	42%
College graduate	53%	45%	58%	39%
Post graduate degree	44%	55%	48%	49%
Annual Household Income				
Under $10,000	35%	63%	43%	53%
$10,000-$29,999	39%	59%	44%	52%
$30,000-$49,999	56%	42%	56%	41%
$50,000 or more	57%	41%	59%	38%

* Results by party combine party indentification findings from network exit polls for precinct voters and party registration findings from the California Poll's pre-election survey of absentee voters.

Note: Differences between the sum of the percentage vote for each category and 100% equal the proportion of voters choosing other candidates.

16.9,90 Source: The Field Institute, California Opinion Index, Dec., 1988.

PARTY IDENTIFICATION VOTER'S SELF-INDENTIFICATION	
Republican	**33%**
Democratic	**38%**
Other Party	0.7%
No Preference	4%
Don't Know	3%
Independent	23%

The question posed to a random sample of voters was "Do you think of yourself as a Republican, a Democrat, an Independent or what?" Official voter registration records show a higher percentage of Democrats than Republicans. The discrepancy between the Field Poll and official records may be explained in two ways. Democratic registration on the official reports is overstated due to the failure to remove Democrats who have died or moved. Many registered Democrats now think of themselves as Republicans but they have not changed their official registration.

16.10,90 Source: The California Poll, 1988 (July and Sept).

STATEWIDE REFERENDA 1884-1989					
		Compulsory Referenda 1			
Year	Total	Consti-tutional Amend-ments	Bond Measures	Peti-tion Refer-enda 2	Ad-visory Refer-enda 3
1884-1889	7	7	0	NA	0
1890-1899	30	28	2	NA	3
1900-1909	54	51	3	NA	1
1910-1919	93	83	10	11	1
1920-1929	71	68	3	11	0
1930-1939	88	85	3	11	3
1940-1949	74	72	2	1	0
1950-1959	75	72	3	1	0
1960-1969	83	68	15	0	0
1970-1979	115	94	21	0	0
1980-1989	89	48	41	4	0
Totals	**779**	**676**	**103**	**39**	**8**

1. Legislatively passed constitutional amendments or bond measures which must be approved by the voters.
2. Citizen sponsored measures to kill recently passed laws. Adopted in 1911.
3. Nonbinding measures placed on the ballot to evaluate the mood of the electorate.
   16.11,90 Source: California Secretary of State, *A Study of Ballot Measures, 1884-1986* and unpublished data.

CALIFORNIA BALLOT MEASURES, 1884-1989							
Proposed By				Passed By the Voters			
Decade	Legis-lature	Initia-tives and Refer-enda	Total Number	Legis-lative Pro-posals %	Initia-tives and Refer-enda %	Total Number	Total %
1880's	7	(1)	7	57%	(1)	4	57%
1890's	33	-	33	52%	-	17	52%
1900's	55	-	55	64%	-	35	64%
1910's	94	41	135	70%	27%	77	57%
1920's	71	46	117	70%	33%	65	56%
1930's	91	47	138	48%	30%	58	42%
1940's	75	21	96	64%	33%	55	57%
1950's	82	13	95	70%	38%	60	63%
1960's	87	9	96	68%	33%	62	65%
1970's	120	22	142	73%	32%	95	67%
1980's	91	48	139	87%	52%	104	75%

(1) The Initiative and Referenda were adopted in 1911.

16.12,90 Source: California Secretary of State, *A Study of Ballot Measures 1884-1986* and unpublished data.

ELECTED OFFICIALS IN CALIFORNIA	
2	U.S. Senators
45	Members of the U.S. House
12*	Statewide Officeholders
40	State Senators
80	Members of the State Assembly
7	State Supreme Court Judges
84	State County Appeals Judges
296	County Supervisors
2,262	Mayors and City Council Members
425	Community College Trustees
5,459	School Board Members
8,849	Special District Members
Total 19,279	(or 3.8% of U.S. elected officials)

* Includes 4 State Board of Equalization members and the Insurance Commissioner.

16.13,90 Source: U.S. Bureau of the Census, *1987 Census of Governments, Preliminary Report*, Cal. School Board Asso., unpublished data, Cal. Community College Trustees, *Directory 1989*, California Judicial Council, unpublished data.

LOBBYING EXPENDITURES IN SACRAMENTO 1979-1988

Year	Expenses	Change from Prior Year
1977-78	$49,640,650	NA
1979	$27,763,229	12% *
1980	$31,259,921	13%
1981-82	Not Available	NA
1983-84	$112,519,158	80% †
1985	$73,320,805	30% *
1986	$64,263,442	-12%
1987	$75,601,407	18%
1988	$82,896,801	10%

* Change from Average of prior 2 year period.
† Change from Average of this 2 year period.
Expenses include money spent to influence legislative and administrative (Executive Branch) activity.
16.14,90   Source: California Fair Political Practice Commission, *Report on Lobbying*.

LOBBYING EXPENSES IN SACRAMENTO BY TYPE OF LOBBYING ORGANIZATION, 1988

Organization	Percent
Business	51.9%
Public Employees	2.3%
Labor	1.6%
Agriculture	2.3%
Utilities	4.7%
Health & Health Related	10.3%
Legal	2.1%
Public & Private Education	7.2%
Government	11.1%
Miscellaneous	6.4%
Total	**100%**

16.15,90 Source: Cal. Fair Pol. Practices Comm., *Rept. on Lobbying*.

LOBBYISTS IN SACRAMENTO

	1983-1984	1985-1986	1987-1988	1989-1990
Number of Lobbyists	760	738	762	791
Number of Female Lobbyists	123	157	183	193
Number of Hispanic Lobbyists	17	30	22	25
Number of Black Lobbyists	10	16	20	19
Number of Asian Lobbyists	2	6	11	9

16.16,90   Source: California Secretary of State, *Lobbyist and Employer Registration Directory*.

NUMBER OF LOBBYISTS IN SACRAMENTO BY INTEREST

Interest Represented	Number of Lobbyists 1987	1989	Interest Represented	Number of Lobbyists 1987	1989
Agriculture	52	47	Labor Unions	23	25
Automotive Businesses	18	19	Legal	20	22
Business	153	153	Manufacturing/Industrial	95	130
Computer, Electronic and Aerospace	15	16	Oil and Gas	30	32
Conservation/Environment	19	19	Political Organizations	--	5
Construction	37	38	Professional/Trade	93	105
Education	135	131	Public Employees	24	30
Lodging/Restaurants	8	5	Public Utilities	23	26
Entertainment, Recreation	32	48	Real Estate	43	44
Food-related Businesses	16	17	Transportation	34	43
Government	116	127	Retail Merchandise	26	22
Health	144	157	Lobbying Firms	276	264
Insurance and Finance	81	93	Miscellaneous	313	262
			Total	**762***	**791**

* Some groups counted are in more than one category. Numbers calculated by the editor.
16.17,90 Source: Cal. Sec. of State, *Lobbyist and Employer Registration Directory*.

NUMBER OF LOBBYISTS IN SACRAMENTO, 1975-1989

Year	Number of Lobbyists	Number of Employers*	Year	Number of Lobbyists	Number of Employers*
1975	660	950	1982	616	1,090
1976	600	1,000	1983	745	1,260
1977	588	761	1984	760	1,415
1978	575	759	1985	738	1,320
1979	624	846	1987	762	1,089
1980	601	867	1989	791	1,353
1981	659	991			

* Employers of Lobbyists.
16.18,90 Source: California Secretary of State, Press Release, May 30 1985 and *Lobbyist and Employer Registration Directory*.

TOP TEN LOBBYING ORGANIZATIONS IN SACRAMENTO

Rank	Organization	Expenditures on Lobbying
1	California Manufacturers Association	$2,200,000
2	Metropolitan Water District of S. Cal.	$1,100,000
3	California Medical Association	$1,100,000
4	California Bankers Association	$973,072
5	RJR Nabisco	$737,277
6	Asso. of California Insurance Companies	$725,165
7	California Trial Lawyers	$698,530
8	California Cogeneration Council	$645,109
9	Anheuser Busch	$631,033
10	California Asso. of Realtors	$628,624

16.19,90 Source: Cal. Fair Pol. Practices Comm., *Report on Lobbying*.

MAJOR PARTY AND NON-PARTISAN ORGANIZATIONS

Democratic Party Headquarters 329 Bryant, #3C San Francisco, CA 94107 (415) 896-5503 State Chair: Edmund G. Brown, Jr. Contributors: 160,000 Annual Budget: $6.5 Million (213) 461-2456	California Republican Assembly 600 S. Lake #303 Pasadena 91106 (818) 795-9952 State Chair: William Hoge Members: 10,000 Clubs: 110 Annual Budget: 70,000
California Democratic Council 8124 West 3rd Street #207 Los Angeles, CA 90048 (213) 653-1091 State Chair: Bob Ferran Affiliated Clubs: 100 Club Members: 5,000 Annual Budget: Not Available	California Republican League P.O. Box 71777 Los Angeles, CA 90071 (408) 946-3728 State Chair: Reynold Schweickhardt Clubs: 18 Members: 2,000 Annual Budget: $10,000
Campaign California 227 Broadway Suite 301 Santa Monica, CA 90401 (213) 393-3701 State Chair: Tom Hayden Dues Paying Members: 50,000 Annual Budget: $2.0 million	United Republicans of California 530 Madre St. Pasadena, CA 91107 (818) 796-7787 State Vice-Chair: Marion Hurley Clubs: Not Available Members: Approximately 2,000 Annual Budget: Not Available
Campaign California (Admin. Office) 926 J St. #300 Sacramento, CA 95814 (916) 447-8950	Libertarian Pary Headquarters 2156 The Alameda Suite B San Jose, CA 95126 (800) 637-1776 State Chair: John Vernon Clubs: 20 Dues Paying Members: 1,5000 Annual Budget: $150,000
Republican Party State Headquarters 1228 N. Street, Suite 14 Sacramento, CA 95814 (916) 443-0967 State Chair: Frank Visco Contributors: 150,000 Annual Budget: $8.2 million	
S. Cal. Republican Party Headquarters 1903 W. Magnolia Blvd. Burbank, Ca 91506 (818) 841-5210	League of Women Voters 926 J St. Suite 1000 Sacramento, CA 95814 (916) 442-7215 President: Wagner Vallianos Members: 13,388 Annual Budget: $330,000
Cal. Federation of Republican Women 1225 8th St. Suite 500 Sacramento, CA 95814 (916) 442-4084 President: June Wallin Clubs: 285 Members: 30,000 Annual Budget Not Available	California Common Cause 636 S. Hobart Blvd., #226 Los Angeles, CA 90005 (213) 387-2017 Chair: John Phillips Members: 52,000 Annual Budget: $300,000

16.20,90 Source; Pacific Data Resources.

SECTION 16 NOTE

In the 1988 general election, 14 percent of the electorate voted by absentee ballot.

16.21,90

POLITICAL APPOINTMENTS				
Governor's Appointments				
Total appointive positions over a four-year term				2,700
Average number of appoinments per year*				900
Governor Deukmejian's appointments as of 6/9/89				6,643
Governor Jerry Brown's appointments over 8 years				6,866

	Appointments by			
	George Deukmejian		**Jerry Brown**	
	Number	**Percent**	**Number**	**Percent**
Total	6,643	---	6,866	---
Women	1,781	27%	1,964	29%
Hispanics	458	7%	585	9%
Blacks†	328	5%	450	7%
Asians	241	4%	297	4%
Native Americans	38	.6%	46	.7%
All Minorities	1,065	16%	1,378	20%
Judicial Appointments				
Total	737	---	800	---
Women	114	15%	131	16%
Hispanics	37	5%	71	9%
Blacks	26	4%	90	11%
Asians	29	4%	34	4%
Native Americans	2	.3%	1	.1%

* A large number of individuals leave their appointive posts before their term is over, giving the governor approximately 3,500 appointments during a four year term in office.

† The number of black appointees is understated since some appointees do not list their race on the governor's appointment forms.

16.22,90 Source: Office of the California Governor, Appointments Section, 1989.

POLITICAL APPOINTMENTS
Legislative Appointments

Speaker of the State Assembly
The Speaker has appointments to 184 State Boards, Committees, Commissions, and Councils for a total of 360 appointments.

State Senate Rules Committee
The five-member Rules Committee has appointments to 166 State Boards, Committees, Commissions, and Councils for a total of 458 appointments.

President Pro Tempore of the State Senate
The President Pro Tempore has appointments to 8 State Boards, Committees, Commissions, and Councils for a total of 14 appointments.

16.23,90 Source: Office of the Speaker of the California Assembly and Office of the California Senate President Pro Tempore.

POLITICAL CAMPAIGN CONSULTANTS

Polling		Management(cont.)	
Corey, Canapary,		Towsend and Company	Sacramento
Glanis Research	San Francisco	Nelson- Ralston-Robb	Costa Mesa
Decision Research	San Diego	Woodward-McDowell	Burlingame
Fairbank, Bregman &		**Campaign Media**	
Maullin	San Francisco	Cerrell Associates	Los Angeles
Research & Decisions	San Francisco	Doak, Shrum & Associates	Los Angeles
Arnold Steinberg		Robert Gouty Co. Inc.	Covina
and Associates	Sherman Oaks	Michael Kaye	Studio City
Survey Research Institute	La Fayette	Paul Kinney Productions	Sacramento
Direct Mail		Hal Larson	San Francisco
Below, Tobe and Associates	Marina Del Rey	Ray McNally	Sacramento
Berman-Di Agostino	Beverly Hills	First Tuesday	Santa Monica
Braun & Co.	Los Angeles	Zimmerman, Galanty	Santa Monica
Cerrell Associates	Los Angeles	**Ballot Measure Campaigns**	
Campaign Pathways	Modesto	Braun Campaigns	Los Angeles
Campaign Performance		PBN Company	San Francisco
Group	San Francisco	Solem/Loeb and Associates	San Francisco
Dolphin Group	Los Angeles	Warn, Claussen & Glaub	Los Angeles
Clint Riley	San Francisco	The Wessel Company	Los Angeles
Russo, Marsh & Associates	Sacramento	Winner/Wagner	
Voter Contact, California	San Francisco	and Associates	Los Angeles
General Campaign		Woodward & McDowell	Burlingame
Management		George Young	Culver City
Cerrell Associates	Los Angeles	**Legal Advice**	
Dolphin Group	Los Angeles	Bagatelos & Fadem	San Francisco
John Davies	Santa Barbara	Nielson, Merksamer & Hodgson	San Francisco
Jack Davis and Associates	San Francisco	Pillsbury, Madison & Sutro	San Francisco
Hoffenblum and Associates	Los Angeles	Reed & Davidson	Costa Mesa
Paul Kinney Productions	Sacramento	Olson, Connelly	Sacramento
McGuire, and Company	San Francisco	Manatt, Phelps, Rothenberg	Los Angeles and
Marathon Communications	Los Angeles	and Tunney	San Francisco
McElroy Communications	Sacramento	**Signature Collection**	
Moolrich Communications	Newport Beach	**for Ballot Measure**	
Clint Reilly	San Francisco	**Qualifications**	
Ross Communications	Sacramento	American Petition Consultants	Sacramento
Russo Marsh & Associates	Sacramento	Masterson & Wright	Bolinas
Spencer-Roberts		F.G. Kimball	Los Angeles
and Associates	Irvine		

16.24,90 Source: Pacific Data Resources; and Corey, Canapary and Galanis Research.

SECTION 16 NOTE

As of March, 1989, 12 California counties had more registered Republicans than Democrats. These counties are San Diego, Orange, Riverside, San Bernardino, Ventura, and Santa Barbara in Southern California and Alpine Inyo, Mono, Nevada, San Luis Obispo, and Sutter in Northern California. In the other 46 counties, Democrats outnumber Republicans.

16.25,90

POLITICAL CAMPAIGN GUIDEBOOKS AND AGENCIES

Practical Guidebooks

1) California Journal Guide to State and Federal Campaign Laws $1.95	4) California Journal Roster & Government Guide $1.95
2) California Journal Political Action Handbook $1.95	5) California Journal Legislative District Maps of California $1.95
3) California Journal Visitors Guide to Sacramento $1.95	

Agencies

California Fair Political Practices Commission (F.P.P.C.) 428 J Street, Suite 800 Sacramento, CA 95814 (916) 322-5901	Federal Election Commission (F.E.C.) 999 E Street, N.W. Washington D.C. 20463 (202) 376-5140 (800) 424-9530

The F.P.P.C. and the F.E.C. provide many helpful pamphlets to guide candidates, contributors, parties, groups, and political action committees through the thicket of campaign laws and regulations. Individuals running for county or local office should check with the county or city clerk to determine if local election laws will affect their campaigns.

16.26,90 Source: Pacific Data Resources.

CAMPAIGN SPENDING IN CALIFORNIA
1976-1988

Election	Expenditures (millions)			
	Assembly Candidates	Senate Candidates	Statewide Candidtates	Ballot Propositions
1976 Primary	$4.89	$2.17	-	$4.93
1976 General	$5.10	$2.60	-	$5.83
1978 Primary	$7.34	$2.32	$12.55	$4.48
1978 General	$7.49	$3.13	$11.22	$10.00
1980 Primary	$13.13	$3.60	-	$18.50
1980 General	$13.72.	$3.88	-	$4.53
1982 Primary	$14.69	$5.01	$11.81	$11.81
1982 General	$17.38	$6.92	$24.26	$24.26
1984 Primary	$14.53	$6.03	-	$1.39
1984 General	$16.22	$8.04	-	$32.39
1986 Primary	$23.20	$6.72	$20.83	$10.96
1986 General	$21.85	$12.33	$28.47	$22.55
1988 Primary	$26.85	$11.87	-	$10.58
1988 General	$30.33	$9.87	-	$129.10

16.27,90 Source: California Fair Political Practices Commission, periodic reports and *Overview of Receipts & Expenditures by Ballot Measure Committees, April 1988* and unpublished data.

GOVERNORS AND LIEUTENANT GOVERNORS OF CALIFORNIA

Governors			Lieutenant Governors		
Name	Party	Date Assumed Office	Name	Party	Date Assumed Office
Peter H. Burnett	ID	Dec. 20, 1849	John McDougal	ID	Dec. 20, 1849
John McDougal	ID	Jan. 9, 1851	David C. Broderick (Acting)	D	Jan. 9, 1851
John Bigler	D	Jan. 8, 1852	Samuel Purdy	D	Jan. 8,1852
J. Neely Johnson	Am	Jan. 9, 1856	Robert M. Anderson	Am	Jan. 9, 1856
John B. Weller	D	Jan. 8, 1858	John Walkup	D	Jan. 8, 1858
Milton S. Latham	LD	Jan. 9, 1860	John G. Downey	LD	Jan. 9, 1860
John G. Downey	LD	Jan. 14, 1860	Isaac N. Quinn (Acting)	D	Jan. 20, 1860
Leland Stanford	R	Jan. 10, 1862	Pablo de la Guerra (Acting)	D	Jan. 7, 1861
Fredrick F. Low	Un	Dec. 10, 1863	John F. Chellis	R	Jan. 10, 1862
Henry H. Haight	D	Dec. 5, 1867	T. N. Machin	Un	Dec. 10, 1863
Newton Booth	R	Dec. 8, 1871	William Holden	D	Dec. 5, 1867
Romualdo Pacheco	R	Feb. 27, 1875	Romualdo Pacheco	R	Dec. 8, 1871
Willian Irwin	D	Dec. 9, 1875	William Irwin (Acting)	D	Feb. 27, 1875
George C. Perkins	R	Jan. 8, 1880	James A. Johnson	D	Dec. 9, 1875
George Stoneman	D	Jan. 10, 1883	John Mansfield	R	Jan 8, 1880
Bartlett Washington	D	Jan.8, 1887	John Daggett	D	Jan. 10, 1883
Robert W. Waterman	R	Sept. 13, 1887	Robert W. Waterman	R	Jan. 8, 1887
Henry H. Markham	R	Jan. 8, 1891	Stephen M. White (Acting)	D	Sept. 13, 1887
James H. Budd	D	Jan. 11,1895	Jon B. Reddick	R	Jan. 8, 1891
Henry T. Gage	R	Jan. 3, 1899	Spencer G. Millard	R	Jan. 11, 1895
George C. Pardee	R	Jan. 6, 1903	William T. Jeter	D	Oct. 25, 1895
James N. Gillett	R	Jan. 8, 1907	Jacob H. Neff	R	Jan. 3, 1899
Hiram W. Johnson	R	Jan. 3, 1911	Alden Anderson	R	Jan. 6, 1903
Hiram W. Johnson	Pr	Jan. 5, 1915	Warren R. Porter	R	Jan. 8, 1907
William D. Stephens	R	Mar. 15, 1917	A. J. Wallace	R	Jan. 3, 1911
Friend Wm.Richardson	R	Jan. 9, 1923	John M. Eshleman	Pr	Jan. 5, 1915
Clement C. Young	R	Jan. 4, 1927	William D. Stephens	R	Jan. 22, 1916
James Rolph, Jr.	R	Jan. 6, 1931	Vacancy	-	-
Frank F. Merriam	R	Jan. 7, 1934	C. C. Young	R	Jan. 7, 1919
Culbert L Olson	D	Jan. 2, 1939	Buron Fitts	R	Jan. 4, 1927
Earl Warren	R	Jan. 4, 1943	H. L. Carnahan	R	Dec. 4, 1928
Goodwin J. Knight	R	Oct. 5, 1953	Frank F. Merriam	R	Jan. 6, 1931
Edmund G. Brown	D	Jan. 5, 1959	Vacancy	-	-
Ronald Reagan	R	Jan. 2, 1967	George J. Hatfield	R	Jan. 8, 1935
Edmund G. Brown, Jr.	D	Jan. 6, 1975	Ellis E. Patterson	D	Jan. 2, 1939
George Deukmejian	R	Jan. 3, 1983	Frederick F. Houser	R	Jan. 4, 1943
			Goodwin J. Knight	R	Jan. 6, 1947
			Harold J. Powers	R	Oct. 5, 1953
			Glenn M. Anderson	D	Jon. 5, 1959
			Robert H. Finch	R	Jan. 2, 1967
			Ed Reinecke	R	Jan. 21, 1969
			John L. Harmer	R	Oct. 4, 1974
			Mervyn M. Dymally	D	Jan.6, 1975
			Mike Curb	R	Jan. 8, 1979
			Leo McCarthy	D	Jan. 3, 1983

Note: Am-American, LD-Lecompton Democratic, Pr-Progressive, D-Democratic, R-Republican, ID-Independent Democratic, Un-Union.
16.28,90 Source: Pacific Data Resources.

SECTION 16 NOTE

In 1988 more initiatives (18) qualified for the statewide ballot than in any statewide election year since 1914.

16.29,90

ADDRESSES OF MAJOR STATEWIDE OFFICIALS

Governor George Deukmejian (R)
State Capitol
Sacramento, CA. 95814
(916) 445-2841

Lieutenant Governor Leo T. McCarthy (D)
State Capitol
Sacracmento, CA 95814
(916) 445-8994

Secretary of State March Fong Eu (D)
1230 J Street
Sacramento, CA. 95814
(916) 445-6371

State Controller Gray Davis (D)
300 Capitol Mall
Sacramento, CA 95814
(916) 445-2636

State Treasurer Thomas Hayes (R)
915 Capitol Mall
Sacramento, CA 95814
(916) 445-5316

Attorney General John Van de Kamp (D)
1515 K Street
Sacramento, CA. 95814
(916) 324-5437

Superintendent of Public Instruction Bill Honig (*)
721 Capitol Mall
Sacramento, CA. 95814
(916) 445-4338

* Non-partisan.
16.30,90 Source: Pacific Data Resources.

CALIFORNIA'S MOST REPUBLICAN AND DEMOCRATIC COUNTIES			
Highest Republican Registration		**Highest Democratic Registration**	
County	**Percent**	**County**	**Percent**
Orange	55	San Francisco	65
Sutter	51	Alameda	63
Inyo	49	Humboldt	59
Ventura	48	Santa Cruz	59
San Diego	47	Merced	57

16.31,90 Source: California Secretary of State, *Report of Registration.*

GOVERNOR'S CABINET		
Name	**Address**	**Phone**
Michael R. Frost Chief of Staff	State Capitol Governor's Office	(916) 445-5106
Henry J. Voss Director, Dept. of Food and Agriculture	State Capitol 1220 N Street Sacramento 95814	(961) 445-7126
Joe Sandoval Secretary, Youth and Adult Correctional Agency	1100 11th Street Sacramento 95814	(916) 323-6001
Shirley Chilton Secretary, State and Consumer Services Agency	915 Capitol Mall 2nd Floor Sacramento 95814	(916) 445-1935
Jesse Huff Director of Finance	State Capitol Room 1145	(916) 445-4141
Ronald T. Rinaldi Director, Dept. of Industrial Relations	1121 L Street Suite 307 Sacramento 95814	(916) 324-4163
Jananne Sharpless Secretary for Environmental Affairs	1102 Q Street Sacramento 95814	(916) 322-5840
Cliff Allenby Secretary, Health and Welfare Agency	1600 Ninth Street Sacramento 95814	(916) 445-6951
Gordan Van Vleck Secretary, Resources Agency	1416 Ninth Street Sacramento 95184	(916) 445-5656
John Geoghegan Secretary for Business, Transportation and Housing Agency	1120 N Street Sacramento 95814	(916) 445-1332

16.32,90 Source: Pacific Data Resources.

NUMBER OF LEGISLATIVE STAFF		
Year	**State Senate**	**State Assembly**
1970	451	NA
1980	580	NA
1984	817	1,139
1985	797	1,194
1986	850	1,241
1987	909	1,279
1988	945	1,419

16.33,90 Source: Senate and Assembly Rules Committees.

Statewide Officals

Governor
George Deukemejian (R)

U.S. Senator
Alan Cranston(D)

U.S. Senator
Pete Wilson (R)

Lt. Governor
Leo McCarthy (D)

Attorney General
John Van de Kamp (D)

**Secretary of State
March Fong Eu (D)**

**Controller
Gray Davis (D)**

**Supt. of Public Intruction
Bill Honig (non-partisan)**

**State Treasurer
Thomas Hayes (R)**

POLITICAL IDEOLOGY OF ADULTS	
Conservative	
Strong Conservative	17%
Not-so-strong Conservative	14%
Total Conservative	**31%**
Middle-of-the-road	
Lean Conservative	5%
Genuine Middle-of-the-road	39%
Lean Liberal	4%
Total Middle-of-the-road	**48%**
Liberal	
Not-so-strong-liberal	7%
Strong Liberal	11%
Total Liberal	**18%**
No Ideological Self-Identification or No Opinion	4%

Note: Because of rounding, totals equal more than 100%.
16.34,90 Source: The California Poll, 1988.

COMPOSITION OF THE CALIFORNIA STATE LEGISLATURE AND CONGRESSIONAL DELEGATION BY PARTY 1961-1990								
	Senate			Assembly		U.S. Senate		Congress	
Year	D	R	I	D	R	D	R	D	R
1961-62	30	10		47	33	1	1	16	14
1963-64	27	13		52	28	1	1	24	14
1965-66	27	13		49	31	0	2	23	15
1967-68	21	19		42	38	0	2	21	17
1969-70	20	20		39	41	1	1	21	17
1971-72	21	19		43	37	2	0	20	18
1973-74	21	19		49	31	2	0	23	20
1975-76	25	15		55	25	2	0	28	15
1977-78	26	14		57	23	1	1	29	14
1979-80	25	14	*	50	30	1	1	26	17
1981-82	23	17		48	32	1	1	22	21
1983-84	25	14	1	48	32	1	1	28	17
1985-86	25	15		47	33	1	1	27	18
1987-88	24	15	1	44	36	1	1	27	18
1989-90	24	15	1	47	33	1	1	27	18

* 1 vacancy.
16.35,90 Source: *U.S. Statistical Abstract* and California Secretary of State, *Statement of Vote.*

SECTION 16 NOTE
Two Republican presidential candidates have been former U.S. senators from California: John C. Fremont and Richard Nixon.

16.36,90

CALIFORNIA CONGRESSIONAL DELEGATION			
U.S. Senators			
Name	Party	District Office	District Phone
Alan Cranston	D	1390 Market, #918 San Francisco 94102	415-556-8440
		5757 W. Century Blvd., Suite 620; Los Angeles 90045	213-215-2186
		880 Front St., #5-S-31; San Diego 92188	619-557-5014
Pete Wilson	R	2040 Ferry Blvd., #2040; San Francisco 94102	415-556-4307
		11111 Santa Monica Blvd., #915; Los Angeles 90025	213-209-6765
		410 B St., Suite 2209; San Diego 92101	619-557-5257
		1130 East O St., Fresno 93721	509-487-5727
		4590 MacArthur Blvd., #220; Newport Beach 92660	714-756-8820
Members of the House of Representatives			
Name	Party	District Office	District Phone
Glenn M. Anderson	D	300 Long Beach Blvd.; Long Beach 90801	213-437-7665
Jim Bates	D	3850 College Ave. #221; San Diego 92115	619-287-8851
Anthony Beilenson	D	11000 Wilshire Blvd., Suite 14223; Los Angeles 90024	213-209-7801
Howard Berman	D	14600 Rosco Blvd., #506; Panorama City 91402	818-891-0543
Douglas Bosco	D	777 Sonoma Ave., No. 329; Santa Rosa 95404	707-576-1466
Barbara Boxer	D	3301 Kerner Blvd.; San Rafael 94901	415-457-7272
George E. Brown, Jr.	D	657 N. La Cadena Dr.; Colton 92324	714-825-2472
Tom Campbell	R	599 N. Mathida Ave., #105; Sunnyvale 94086	408-245-4835
Christopher Cox	R	180 Newport Center Dr., #240; Newport Beach 92660	714-644-4040
William Dannemeyer	R	1235 N. Harbor Blvd., Suite 100; Fullerton 92632	714-992-0141
Ronald V. Dellums	D	201 13th St., Room 105; Oakland 94617	415-763-0370
Julian Dixon	D	5100 W. Gold Leaf Dr.; Inglewood 90056	213-678-5424
Robert Dornan	R	12387 Lewis St. #203; Garden Grove 92640	714-971-9292
David Dreier	R	112 N. 2nd Ave.; Covina 91723	818-339-9078
Mervyn Dymally	D	322 W. Compton Blvd., Compton 90220	213-632-4318
Don Edwards	D	1042 W. Hedding St., #100; San Jose 95126	408-247-1711
Vic Fazio	D	2525 Natomas Park Dr., #330; Sacramento 95833	916-978-4381
Elton Gallegly	R	20 N. Westlake Blvd., #207; Thousand Oaks 91362	805-496-4700
Augustus Hawkins	D	4509 S. Broadway; Los Angeles 90037	213-233-0733
Wally Herger	R	20 Declaration Dr., Room B; Chico 95926	916-893-8363
Duncan Hunter	R	366 S. Pierce; El Cajon 92020	619-579-3001
Robert Lagomarsino	R	5740 Ralston St.; Ventura 93003	805-642-2200
Tom Lantos	D	520 S. El Camino Real, #800; San Mateo 94402	415-342-0300
Richard Lehman	D	2115 Kern St., Suite 210; Fresno 93721	209-487-5760
Mel Levine	D	5250 W. Century Blvd., #447; Los Angeles 90045	213-410-9415
Jerry Lewis	R	1826 Orange Tree Lane, #104; Redlands 92374	714-792-5901
Bill Lowery	R	880 Front St., #6S-15; San Diego 92188	619-231-0957
Matthew G. Martinez	D	1712 W. Beverly Blvd, Suite 201; Montebello 90640	213-722-7731
Robert Matsui	D	650 Capitol Mall, #8058; Sacramento 95814	916-551-2846
Al McCandless	R	6529 Riverside Ave., #165; Riverside 92506	714-682-7127
George Miller	D	367 Civic Dr., #14; Pleasant Hill 94523	415-687-3260
Norman Mineta	D	1245 S. Winchester Blvd., #310; San Jose 95128	408-984-6045
Carlos J. Moorhead	R	420 N. Brand Blvd., Room 304; Glendale 91203	818-247-8445
Ron Packard	D	2121 Palomar Airport Rd., #105; Carlsbad 92009	619-438-0443
Leon Panetta	D	380 Alvarado; Monterey 93940	408-649-3555
Charles Pashayan	R	1702 E. Bullard, No. 103; Fresno 93710	209-487-5500
Nancy Pelosi	D	450 Golden Gate Ave., Rm 13470; San Francisco 94102	415-556-4862
Dana Rohrbacher	R	2733 Pacific Coast Hwy, #306; Torrance 90505	213-325-0668
Edward R. Roybal	D	300 N. Los Angeles St., Room 7106; Los Angeles 90012	213-894-4870
Norman Shumway	R	1150 W. Robinhood #1A; Stockton 95207	209-957-7773
Fortney (Pete) Stark	D	22300 Foothill Blvd. #1029; Hayward 94541	415-635-1092
William Thomas	R	4100 Truxton, #220; Bakersfield 93309	805-327-3611
Esteban Torres	D	8819 Whittier Blvd., #101; Pico Rivera 90660	213-695-0702
Henry A. Waxman	D	8425 West 3rd St.; Los Angeles 90048	213-651-1040

The Congressional Switchboard is (202) 224-3121. Mailing addresses: Senators, U.S. Senate, Washington, D.C. 20510; House Members, U.S. House of Representatives, Washington D.C. 20510.
16.37,90 Source: Pacific Data Resources.

CALIFORNIA STATE SENATE

Name	Party*	District Office	District Phone
Alfred E. Alquist	D	100 Paseo de San Antonio, Suite #209; San Jose 95113	408-286-8318
Ruben S. Ayala	D	515 N. Arrowhead Ave., Rm. 100; San Bernardino 92401	714-884-3165
Marian Bergeson	R	140 Newport Center Dr., #120; Newport Beach 92660	714-640-1137
Robert G. Beverly	R	1611 S. Pacific Coast Hwy; Redondo Beach 90277	213-540-1611
Daniel Boatwright	D	1035 Detroit Ave., Rm. 200; Concord 94518	415-689-1973
William Campbell	R	1661 Hanover Rd.; City of Industry 91748	818-964-1443
William A. Craven	R	2121 Palomar Airport Rd. Rm. 100; Carlsbad 92008	619-438-3814
Ed Davis	R	11145 Tampa Ave., No. 21B; Northridge 91326	818-368-1171
Wadie Deddeh	D	430 Davidson St., Chula Vista 92010	619-427-7080
Ralph C. Dills	D	16921 S. Western Ave., Rm 201; Gardena 90247	213-324-4969
John Doolittle	R	720 Sunrise Ave., Suite 110D; Roseville 95678	916-969-8232
John Garamendi	D	31 E. Channel St., Rm 440; Stockton 95202	209-948-7930
Cecil Green	D	12631 E. Imperial Hwy, #A-120; Santa Fe Springs 90670	213-929-0016
Bill Greene	D	9300 S. Broadway; Los Angeles 90003	213-620-5600
Leroy F. Greene	D	P.O. Box 254646; Sacramento 95825	916-481-6540
Gary Hart	D	1216 State St., Rm 507; Santa Barbara 93101	805-966-1766
Barry Keene	D	631 Tennessee St.; Vallejo 94590	707-648-4080
Quentin Kopp	I	363 El Camino Real, Rm. 205; S. San Francisco 94080	415-952-5666
Bill Leonard	R	400 N. Mountain, #109; Upland 91786	714-946-4889
Bill Lockyer	D	22300 Foothill Blvd., Suite 415; Hayward 94541	415-582-8800
Ken Maddy	R	3475 W. Shaw Ave., #105; Fresno 93711	209-445-5567
Milton Marks	R	350 McAllister St., Rm. 2045; San Francisco 94102	415-557-1437
Dan McCorquodale	D	4 North Second St., #590; San Jose 95113	408-277-1470
Henry Mello	D	1200 Aguajito Rd.; Monterey 93940	408-373-0773
Joseph B. Montoya	D	11001 Valley Mall; El Monte 91731	818-575-6956
Rebecca Q. Morgan	R	830 Menlo Ave., Suite 200; Menlo Park 94025	415-321-1451
Jim Nielsen	R	1074 East Ave., Suite N; Chico 95926	916-343-3546
Nicholas C. Petris	D	1111 Jackson St., Rm. 7016; Oakland 94607	415-464-1333
Robert B. Presley	D	3600 Lime, Rm. 111; Riverside 92501	714-782-4111
Alan Robbins	D	6150 Van Nuys Blvd., Suite 400; Van Nuys 91401	818-901-5555
David A. Roberti	D	3800 Barham Blvd., Suite 218; Hollywood 90068	213-876-5200
Don Rogers	R	1326 H St.; Bakersfield 93301	805-395-2927
Herschel Rosenthal	D	1950 Sawtelle Blvd., Suite 210; Los Angeles 90025	213-479-5588
Edward Royce	R	1661 N. Raymond Ave., No. 211; Anaheim 92801	714-871-0270
Newton R. Russell	R	401 N. Brand Blvd.; Glendale 91203	818-247-7021
John Seymour	R	2150 Town Centre Pl., Suite 205; Anaheim 92806	714-385-1700
Larry Stirling	R	7777 Alvarado Rd., #377; La Mesa 92041	619-237-7777
Art Torres	D	107 S. Broadway, #2105; Los Angeles 90012	213-620-2529
Rose Ann Vuich	D	120 W. Tulare; Dinuba 93618	209-591-5005
Diane Watson	D	4401 Crenshaw Blvd., Suite 300; Los Angeles 90043	213-295-6655

* Party Affiliation, I=Independent.
16.38,90 Source: Secretary of the Senate.

SECTION 16 NOTE

In 1859, California Supreme Court Chief Justice David fought a duel with U.S. Senator David Broderick at Lake Merced in San Francisco. Broderick was mortally wounded and died shortly after the duel at Haskell House on the grounds of Fort Mason.

16.39,90

SECTION 16 NOTE

From 1960 to 1976 absentee voting in California was between 3.9% and 4.5% of the voting population. In 1980, it jumped to 6.3%, in 1984 to 9.3% and in 1988 to 14.1%.

16.40,90

		CALIFORNIA STATE ASSEMBLY	
Name	Party	District Office	District Phone
Lucille Roybal-Allard	D	5261 E. Beverly Blvd; Los Angeles 90022	213-721-5557
Doris Allen	R	5911 Cerritos Ave; Cyprus 90630	714-821-1500
Rusty Areias	D	140 Central, Rm 203; Salinas 93901	408-422-4344
Charles Bader	R	203 W. G St.; Ontario 91762	714-983-6011
William Baker	R	1801 N. California Blvd., Suite 103; Walnut Creek 94596	415-932-2537
Tom Bane	D	5430 Van Nuys Blvd., Suite 206; Van Nuys 91401	818-986-8090
Tom Bates	D	1414 Walnut St., Suite 9; Berkeley 94709	415-540-3176
Carol Bentley	R	2755 Navajo Rd., El Cajon 92020	619-464-7204
Bruce Bronzan	D	2115 Kern St., Suite 250; Fresno 93721	209-445-5532
Dennis Brown	R	1945 Palo Verde, Suite 203; Long Beach 90815	213-493-5514
Willie L. Brown, Jr.	D	350 McAllister, Rm. 5046; San Francisco 94102	415-557-1784
John Burton	D	350 McAllister, Rm 1064; San Francisco 94102	415-557-2253
Charles Calderon	D	1712 W. Beverly Blvd., Suite 202; Montebello 90640	214-721-2904
Robert Campbell	D	2901 MacDonald Ave.; Richmond 94804	415-237-8171
Peter R. Chacon	D	1129 G St., San Diego 92101	619-232-2405
Chris Chandler	R	1227 Bridge St., Suite E; Yuba City 95991	916-673-2201
Steve Clute	D	3600 Lime St., No. 410; Riverside 92501	714-782-3222
Gary Condit	D	950 10th St., Suite 8; Modesto 95354	209-576-6211
Lloyd Connelly	D	2705 K St., No. 6-A; Sacramento 95816	916-443-1183
Dominic Cortese	D	100 Paseo de San Antonio, #300; San Jose 95113	408-269-6500
Jim Costa	D	1111 Fulton Mall, Suite 914; Fresno 93721	209-264-3078
Delaine Eastin	D	39245 Liberty St., Suite D-8; Fremont 94538	415-791-2151
Gerald R. Eaves	D	224 N. Riverside Ave., Suite A; Rialto 92376	714-820-1902
Dave Elder	D	245 W. Broadway, Room 300; Long Beach 90802	213-590-5009
Bob Epple	D	8221 E. 3rd , Suite 206; Downey 90241	213-929-1796
Sam Farr	D	1200 Aguajito; Monterey 93940	408-646-1980
Gerald Felando	R	3838 Carson St., Suite 110; Torrance 90503	213-540-2123
Gil Ferguson	R	4667 MacArthur Blvd., No. 305; Newport Beach 92660	714-756-0665
William Filante	R	30 N. San Pedro Rd., Suite 135; San Rafael 94903	415-479-4920
Richard E. Floyd	D	16921 S. Western Ave., Suite 101; Gardena 90247	213-516-4037
Robert C. Frazee	R	3088 Pio Pico, Suite 200; Carlsbad 92008	619-434-1749
Terry Friedman	D	14144 Ventura Blvd., Suite 100; Sherman Oaks 91423	818-501-8991
Nolan Frizzelle	R	17195 Newhope St., Suite 201; Fountain Valley	714-662-5503
Tom Hannigan	D	844 Union Ave., Suite A; Fairfield 94533	707-429-2383
Bev Hansen	R	50 Santa Rosa Ave., Suite 301; Santa Rosa 95401	707-546-4500
Elihu Harris	D	1111 Jackson St., Rm 5027; Oakland 94607	415-464-0339
Trice Harvey	R	2222 E St., Suite 2; Bakersfield 93301	805-324-3300
Dan Hauser	D	50 D St., Rm. 450; Santa Rosa 95404	707-576-2526
Tom Hayden	D	227 Broadway, Suite 300; Santa Monica 90401	213-373-2717

16.41.1,90 Source: Clerk of the Assembly.

SECTION 16 NOTE

In November 1914 the statewide election ballot had the largest number of measures ever put before California voters: 48. The November 1922 ballot had the second largest number, 30, and the November 1988 ballot the third largest number, 29.

16.42,90

SECTION 16 NOTE

According to the California Secretary of State, California had 25,414 election or polling precincts in 1988.

16.43,90

		CALIFORNIA STATE ASSEMBLY	
Name	**Party**	**District Office**	**District Phone**
Frank Hill	R	15111 E. Whittier Blvd., No. 385; Whittier 90603	213-945.7681
Teresa P. Hughes	D	3375 S. Hoover Ave., Suite F; Los Angeles 90007	213-747-7451
Philip Isenberg	D	1215 15th St., Suite 102; Sacramento 95814	916-324-4676
Ross Johnson	R	1501 N. Harbor Blvd., Suite 201; Fullerton 92635	714-738-5853
Pat Johnston	D	31 E. Channel St., No. 306; Stockton 95202	209-948-7479
Bill Jones	R	2929 W. Main St., Suite J; Visalia 93291	209-734-1182
Richard Katz	R	9140 Van Nuys Blvd., No 109; Panorama City 91402	818-894-3671
David Kelley	R	6840 Indiana, Suite 150; Riverside 92506	714-369-6644
Lucy Killea	D	2550 Fifth Ave., Suite 152; San Diego 92103	619-232-2046
Johan Klehs	D	2450 Washington Ave., Suite 270; San Leandro 94577	415-464-0847
Marian LaFollette	R	11145 Tampa Ave., Suite 17A; Northridge 91326	818-368-3838
Bill Lancaster	R	145 East Badillo; Covina 91723	818-332-6271
Ted Lempert	D	1650 Borel Pl., Suite 229; San Mateo 94402	415-571-9521
Tim Leslie	R	1098 Melody Lane, Suite 301; Roseville 95678	916-969-3660
John R. Lewis	R	1940 N. Tustin, Suite 102; Orange 92665	714-998-0980
Burt Margolin	D	8425 W. 3rd. St., Suite 406; Los Angeles 90048	213-655-9750
Tom McClintock	R	350 N. Lantana, Suite 222; Camarillo 93010	805-987-9797
Sunny Mojonnier	R	3368 Governor Dr., Suite C; San Diego 92122	619-457-5775
Gwen Moore	D	3683 Crenshaw Blvd., 5th Floor; Los Angeles 90016	213-292-0605
Richard Mountjoy	R	206 South First St.; Arcadia 91006	818-446-3134
Willard Murray	D	16444 S. Paramount Blvd., #100; Paramount 90723	213-516-4144
Patrick J. Nolan	R	143 S. Glendale Ave., Suite 208; Glendale 91205	818-240-6330
Jack O'Connell	D	127 El Paseo; Santa Barbara 93101	805-699-2296
Steve Peace	D	430 Davidson St., Suite B; Chula Vista 92010	619-426-1617
Richard Polanco	D	110 North Ave., No 56; Los Angeles 90042	213-255-7111
Curt Pringle	R	12822 Garden Grove, Suite A; Garden Grove 92643	714-895-4334
Byron Sher	D	785 Castro St.; Mountain View 94041	415-961-6031
Charles Quackenbush	R	456 El Paseo de Saratoga; San Jose 95130	408-446-4144
Michael Roos	D	625 S. New Hampshire; Los Angeles 90005	213-386-8042
Eric Seastrand	R	523 Higuera St.; San Luis Obispo 93401	805-549-3381
Jackie Speier	D	220 S. Spruce Ave., Suite 101; S. San Francisco 94080	415-871-4100
Stan Statham	R	429 Redcliff Dr., Suite 200; Redding 96002	916-223-6300
Sally Tanner	D	11100 Valley Blvd., Suite 106; El Monte 91731	818-442-9100
Curtis R. Tucker Jr.	D	1 Manchester Blvd., Inglewood 90306	213-415-6400
John Vasconcellos	D	100 Paseo de San Antonio, No. 106; San Jose 95113	408-288-7515
Maxine Waters	D	7900 S. Central Ave.; Los Angeles 90001	213-582-7371
Norman Waters	D	250 Main St,; Placerville 95667	916-626-4954
Paul Woodruff	R	300 E. State St.; Redlands 92373	714-798-0337
Cathie Wright	R	250 E. Easy St., Suite 7; Simi Valley 93065	805-522-2920
Phil Wyman	R	5393 Truxton Ave., Bakersfield 93309	805-395-2673

16.41.2,90 Source: Clerk of the Assembly.

SECTION 16 NOTE

The only statewide election in which voters passed all the ballot proposals put before them took place in November 1910 (12 of 12 passes).

16.44,90

SECTION 16 NOTE

The only statewide election in which voters rejected all the ballot proposals put before them took place in October 1915 (0 of 11 passed).

16.45,90

SALARIES OF MAJOR CALIFORNIA PUBLIC OFFICIALS
1989

Statewide Officers

Governor	$89,300	California Supreme Court:	
Lt. Governor	$72,500	Chief Justice	$115,013
Attorney General	$77,500	Associate Justice	$109,677
Secretary of State	$72,500	California Appeals Court	$97,003
Treasurer	$72,500	California Superior Court	$84,765
Controller	$72,500	California Municipal Court	$77,409
Superintendent of		U.S. Circuit Court of Appeal	$95,000
Public Instruction	$72,500	U.S. Federal District Court	$89,500

Congressional Delegation

U.S. Senator	$89,500	**U.S. Representative**	$89,500

State Legislature

State Senator		State Assemblyman	
Salary	$40,816*	Salary	$40,816*
Per diem	$88††	*Per diem*	$88††

County Supervisors: Illustrative Examples

Alpine County	$10,872	Orange County	$65,800
Alameda County	$39,926	Riverside County	$50,688
Del Norte County	$16,860	Sacramento County	$40,752
Kern County	$52,536	San Diego County	$61,712
Los Angeles	$84,753	San Francisco County	$23,928
Modoc County	$9,696	Tulare County	$28,928

*   Effective December 5, 1988.

††   The tax-free *per diem* allowance, paid for each day the legislature is in session, totals approximately $18,000 per year. Legislators also receive a state car and gasoline and telephone credit cards.

16.46,90 Source: Pacific Data Resources and Alameda County Taxpayers Association, *Salary Survey*, 1989.

SECTION 16 NOTE

Back in the 1860s Mono County officials were embarrassed to discover that the county seat, Aurora, was in the state of Nevada. The county seat was moved to its current location, Bridgeport, in 1864.

16.47,90

COUNTY SEATS			
County	County Seat	County	County Seat
Alameda	Oakland	Orange	Santa Ana
Alpine	Markleeville	Placer	Auburn
Amador	Jackson	Plumas	Quincy
Butte	Oroville	Riverside	Riverside
Calaveras	San Andreas	Sacramento	Sacramento
Colusa	Colusa	San Benito	Hollister
Contra Costa	Martinez	San Bernardino	San Bernardino
Del Norte	Crescent City	San Diego	San Diego
El Dorado	Placerville	San Francisco	San Francisco
Fresno	Fresno	San Joaquin	Stockton
Glenn	Willows	San Luis Obispo	San Luis Obispo
Humboldt	Eureka	San Mateo	Redwood City
Imperial	El Centro	Santa Barbara	Santa Barbara
Inyo	Independence	Santa Clara	San Jose
Kern	Bakersfield	Santa Cruz	Santa Cruz
Kings	Hanford	Shasta	Redding
Lake	Lakeport	Sierra	Downieville
Lassen	Susanville	Siskiyou	Yreka
Los Angeles	Los Angeles	Solano	Fairfield
Madera	Madera	Sonoma	Santa Rosa
Marin	San Rafael	Stanislaus	Modesto
Mariposa	Mariposa	Sutter	Yuba City
Mendocino	Ukiah	Tehama	Red Bluff
Merced	Merced	Trinity	Weaverville
Modoc	Alturas	Tulare	Visalia
Mono	Bridgeport	Tuolumne	Sonora
Monterey	Salinas	Ventura	Ventura
Napa	Napa	Yolo	Woodland
Nevada	Nevada City	Yuba	Marysville

16.48,90 Source: Pacific Data Resources.

SECTION 16 NOTE
In the June 1988 primary election, Proposition 74, a transportation bond issue, lost by 541 votes out of 5.3 million ballots cast. This was the closest ballot-measure contest since 1915, when Proposition 4, a judicial term issue, lost by 514 votes. The tightest ballot-measure contest was in 1905, when a proposal on pay for state officers passed by 2 votes.

16.49,90

SECTION 16 NOTE
No effort to recall a statewide officeholder in California has ever qualified for the state's ballot.

16.50,90

COUNTY SUPERVISORS BY COUNTY AND PARTY

Alameda	**Glenn**	**Marin**
Edward R. Campbell (D)	Joanne Overton (R)	Bob Roumiguiere (R)
Charles Santana (D)	George A. Edwards (R)	Harold Brown, Jr. (D)
Don Perata (D)	Dick Mudd (R)	Al Aramburu (R)
Mary King (D)	Daniel Cooper (R)	Gary Giacomini (R)
Warren Widener (D)	Jim Mann (R)	Robert Stockwell (R)
Alpine	**Humboldt**	**Mariposa**
Donald Jardine (R)	Stan Dixon (D)	Arthur Baggett (R)
John Brissenden (D)	Harry Pritchard (R)	Sally Punte (D)
Claudia Ann Wade (D)	Wesley Chesbro (D)	Eric Erickson (R)
Eric V. Jung (D)	Bonnie Neeley (R)	Leroy Randanovich (R)
John A. Bennett (S)	Anna Sparks (R)	Gertrude Taber (R)
Amador	**Imperial**	**Mendocino**
John C. Begovich (D)	Luis M. Legaspi (R)	Marilyn Butcher (R)
Edward T. Bamert II (D)	Bill Cole (R)	Nelson Redding (D)
Timothy R. Davenport (D)	James M. Bucher (R)	James (Jim) C. Eddie (R)
Steve Martin (R)	Abe Seabolt (D)	Liz Henry (D)
Gale R. Cuneo (D)	Jeanne Vogel (R)	Norman de Vall (D)
Butte	**Inyo**	**Merced**
Haskel A. McInturf (D)	H.B. Irwin (R)	Wyatt Davenport (R)
Jane Dolan (D)	Robert H. Campbell (R)	Ann Klinger (D)
Karen Vercruse (R)	Larry Calkins (R)	Michael Bogna, Jr. (R)
Edward C. McLaughlin (R)	Keith Bright (R)	Dean Peterson (R)
Leonard V. Fulton (D)	Paul Payne (R)	Anthony Whitehurst (R)
Calaveras	**Kern**	**Modoc**
Michael Dell'Orto (R)	Roy A. Ashburn (R)	John H. Schreiber (D)
Thomas A. Taylor (D)	Ben Austin (R)	Melvin L. Anderson (D)
Robert Harris (D)	Pauline Larwood (R)	Don E. Polson (R)
Tom Tryon (L)	Karl Hettinger (R)	M.W. Jones (D)
David J. Silveria (D)	Mary K. Shell (R)	John L. Coulson (R)
Colusa	**Kings**	**Mono**
James Kalfsbeek (D)	Leslie K. Brown (R)	Robert Stanford (R)
Mr. W.D. Mills (R)	Joe Hammond (D)	Dan Paranick (R)
Kay Nordyke (R)	Dom Faruzzi (R)	Don Rake (R)
William R. Waite (R)	Nick Kinney (R)	William Reid (R)
David G. Womble (R)	Abel J. Meirelles (R)	Andrea Lawrence (S)
Contra Costa	**Lake**	**Monterey**
Tom Powers (D)	Voris Brumfield (R)	Marc Del Piero (R)
Nancy C. Fahden (D)	Gary D. Lambert (R)	Barbara Shipnuck (D)
Robert I. Schroder (R)	Walter C. Wilcox (D)	Dusan Petrovic (D)
Sunne Wright McPeak (D)	Karan Mackey (D)	Sam Karas (D)
Tom Torlakson (D)	L.D. Franklin (D)	Karin S. Kaufman (D)
Del Norte	**Lassen**	**Napa**
Helga Burns (R)	Hughes de Martimprey (R)	Bob White (R)
Ray Thompson (D)	James Chapman (D)	Fred Negri (R)
Joyce Crockett (R)	John R. Gaither (R)	Mel Varrelman (D)
Glenn Smedley (R)	Gary Lemke (R)	Paul Battisti (D)
Mark Mellet (D)	Helen M. Williams (R)	John Mikolajcik (R)
El Dorado	**Los Angeles**	**Nevada**
Robert Dorr (R)	Peter E. Schabarum (R)	Todd Juvinall (R)
Patricia Lowe (R)	Kenneth Hahn (D)	James Callaghan (R)
James R. Sweeney (D)	Edmund D. Edelman (D)	Jim Weir (D)
Ray Thompson (D)	Deane Dana (R)	Bill Schultz (R)
John Cefalu (R)	Michael D. Antonovich (R)	Mr. G. B. Tucker (D)
Fresno	**Madera**	**Orange**
Deran Koligian (R)	Rick Jensen (D)	Roger R. Stanton (R)
Sharan Levy (R)	Alfred Ginsburg (R)	Harriett Wieder (R)
Doug Vagim (R)	Gail Hanhart McIntyre (D)	Gaddi Vasquez (R)
A. Vernon Conrad (D)	Jess Lopez (D)	Don Roth (R)
Judy Andreen (R)	Harry Baker (R)	Thomas F. Riley (R)

Note: "D" is Democratic, "L" is Libertarian, "R" is Republican, and "S" is decline to state.
16.51.1,90 Source: California Republican Party, and Pacific Data Resources.

COUNTY SUPERVISORS BY COUNTY AND PARTY

Placer
Robert P. Mahan (D)
Alex Ferriera (D)
George Beland (D)
Susan Hogg (R)
Mike Fluty (R)

Plumas
Jim Smith (R)
John Schramel (D)
Donald A. Woodhall (R)
Joyce F. Scroggs (D)
Bill Coates (R)

Riverside
Walt P. Abraham (D)
Melba Dunlap (D)
Kay Ceniceros (D)
Patricia Larson (R)
A. Norton Younglove (R)

Sacramento
Grantland Johnson (D)
Illa Collin (D)
Sandra R. Smoley (R)
Jim Streng (R)
Toby Johnson (D)

San Benito
Richard Scagliotti (R)
Ruth Kessler (D)
Rita M. Bowling (D)
Curtis Graves (R)
Mike R. Graves (D)

San Bernardino
Marsha Turoci (R)
John Mikels (R)
Barbara Cram Riordan (R)
Larry Walker (R)
Robert L. Hammock (R)

San Diego
Brian P. Bilbray (R)
George F. Bailey (R)
Susan Golding (R)
Leon L. Williams (D)
John MacDonald (R)

San Francisco
Angela Alioto (D)
Harry Britt (D)
Jim Gonzalez (D)
Terrance Hallinan (D)
Richard Hongisto (D)
Tom Hsieh (D)
Willie B. Kennedy (D)
Bill Maher (D)
Wendy Nelder (D)
Nancy G. Walker (D)
Doris Ward (D

San Joaquin
William Sousa (R)
Doug Wilhoit (R)
Ed Simas (R)
George Barber (R)
Evelyn L. Costa (R)

San Luis Obispo
Harry Ovitt (R)
William Coy (R)
Evelyn Delany (D)
James Johnson (R)
David Blakely (D)

San Mateo
Mary Griffin (R)
Tom Huening (R)
Anna Eshoo (D)
Tom Nolan (D)
William J. Schumacher (D)

Santa Barbara
Gloria Ochoa (D)
Tom Rogers (R)
Willima B. Wallace (D)
Dianne Owens (D)
Toru Miyoshi (R)

Santa Clara
Suzanne B. Wilson (D)
Zoe Lofgren (D)
Ron Gonzales (D)
Rodney J. Diridon (D)
Dianne McKenna (D)

Santa Cruz
Janet K. Beautz (R)
Robley Levy (D)
Gary A. Patton (D)
Sherry Mehl (R)
Fred Keeley (D)

Shasta
John Reit (R)
Bob Bosworth (R)
Frances Lynn Sullivan (D)
Molly Wilson (R)
Pete Peters (R)

Sierra
Donald McIntosh (D)
Nevada "Babe" Lewis (D)
Jerry McCaffrey (D)
Donald Bowling (R)
S. Craig McHenry (D)

Siskiyou
Norma Frey (R)
Ivan Young (R)
Roger Zwanziger (R)
Patti Jackson (D)
George R. Thackeray (R)

Solano
Osby Davis (D)
Lee Simmons (D)
Sam Caddle (R)
Don Pippo (D)
Ms. Jan Stewart (R)

Sonoma
Janet Nicholas (R)
James Harberson (R)
Tim Smith (D)
Nick Esposti (R)
Ernest Carpenter (D)

Stanisluas
Ms. Pat Paul (D)
Rolland C. Starn (R)
Nick Blom (R)
Raymond Clark Simon (R)
Sal Cannella (R)

Sutter
Larry Montna (R)
Joseph A. Benatar (R)
Tom Pfeffer (R)
Ron Southard (R)
Barbara LeVake (R)

Tehama
Vance Wood (R)
Phil Gunsauls (R)
Floyd Hicks (R)
Bill Floumoy (D)
Burton Bundy (R)

Trinity
Stan Plowman (D)
Mr. Dee Potter (R)
Arnold Whitridge (D)
Howard G. Myrick (D)
Patricia G. Mortensen (D)

Tulare
Clyde Gould (D)
John Conway (D)
Delores E. Mangine (R)
LeRoy Swiney (R)
Gary Reed (R)

Toulumne
Larry A. Rotelli (D)
Gregory Hurt (R)
Nell Farr (D)
Norman Tergeson (R)
Charles H. Walker (D)

Ventura
Susan K. Lacey (D)
Madge Schaefer (D)
Maggie Erickson (D)
James Dougherty (D)
John K. Flynn (D)

Yolo
Clark H. Cameron (D)
Helen R. Thomson (D)
George P. DeMars (D)
Betsy A. Marchand (D)
Cowles Mast (R)

Yuba
George Deveraux (R)
Thomas Belza (R)
Bill Harper (R)
Michelle Mathews (R)
J.E. McGill (D)

Note: "D" is Democratic, "L" is Libertarian, "R" is Republican, and "S" is decline to state.
16.51.2,90 Source: California Republican Party and Pacific Data Resources.

COUNTY SUPERVISORS' PARTY AFFILIATIONS

Of the 296 California Supervisors,
160 (54%) are registered Republicans,
133 (45%) are Democrats,
1 is a Libertarian,
and 2 are Decline to State.

16.52,90 Source: California Republican Party and Pacific Data Resources.

CALIFORNIA POLITICIANS

Leone Baxter	John McCone
Tom Bradley	Richard Nixon
David C. Broderick	Romualdo Pacheco
Pat Brown	Wilson Riles
Willie Brown	Ronald Reagan
Ralph Bunche	Abraham Ruef
Phil Burton	Artie Samish
Paul Gann	Upton Sinclair
S. I. Hayakawa	Dr. Francis Townsend
John R. Haynes	Earl Warren
Herbert Hoover	Clem Whitaker
Howard Jarvis	Jesse Unruh
Hiram Johnson	Sam Yorty
Dennis Kearney	

16.53,90 Source: Pacific Data Resources.

FEDERAL CONVICTIONS OF CORRUPT PUBLIC OFFICIALS, CALIFORNIA & THE U.S.

Year	California	United States	California as a % of U.S.
1977	10	301	3%
1978	6	273	2%
1979	15	314	5%
1980	12	310	4%
1981	18	400	5%
1982	12	422	3%
1983	23	714	3%
1984	88	945	9%
1985	88	756	12%
1986	83	802	10%
1987	77	826	9%
1988	72	1,065	7%
Total	**504**	**5,061**	**10%**

16.54,90 Source: U.S. Department of Justice, Public Integrity Section, *Annual Report to Congress*.

Banking and Finance

The world of institutional high finance in California is still beset by difficulties to match its tantalizing opportunities. After Texas, California had the highest number of savings and loan associations on the federal government's worst-one hundred list. The "thrift" crisis in California peaked with a run on the huge Stockton-based American Savings and Loan Association. American was eventually "saved" when it was acquired by the Bass Group of Fort Worth.

The major California banks are also feeling some strain. Their loans to Latin American countries, many of them unlikely to be repaid, continue to hang over them. The threat will be intensified on July 1, 1991, when interstate banking barriers drop and East Coast banks will be free to dip into the state's $400-billion base of deposits. California bankers are already feeling the competitive squeeze from foreign banks, particularly Japanese banks, which are assuming a commanding presence in the state's banking market. Seven of the top fifteen California banks are now Japanese.

The state's supercharged economy that has attracted Japanese bankers is also attracting the new-style American capitalist--the venture capitalist. Since California's economy is expanding far faster than that of any other state, venture capital is pouring in to finance a wide variety of high- and low-tech enterprises in the state. In 1987, according to the business magazine *Venture Economics,* $1.5 billion in venture capital was placed in California, 39 percent of all the venture capital in the United States. Established companies such as W. R. Grace and McKesson as well as newcomers such as Apple Computer have leapt into the venture-capital business. These companies offer entrepreneurs technical advice and marketing assistance as well as cash. A few banks and savings and loan associations are also placing a small portion of their resources into the venture-capital pool.

The passage of Proposition 103 by the voters in the November 1988 election came as a shock to California insurers. This proposition, much of it upheld by the California Supreme Court, mandates a 20 percent cut in automobile, property, and casualty insurance rates. Proposition 103 was a revolt of the yuppies, who resented high premiums for their two- and three-car families. The initiative did particularly well in upscale sections of the San Francisco Bay Area, where hefty premiums on new BMWs and Volvos were squeezing the upper middle class.

In the past, insurance rates in California were restrained to some extent by marketplace competition. Because the California Supreme Court has held that insurance companies must receive a fair rate of return, automobile insurance rates in the state may actually increase because of Proposition 103.

THE FOURTEEN LARGEST BANKS IN CALIFORNIA

Rank* in State	Rank* in U.S.	Bank Name	Head Office	Deposits (billions)	Equity Capital (billions)	Assets (billions)	Asset Rank in U.S.
1	2	Bank of America (n) †	San Francisco	$69.6	$3.6	$82.9	2
2	6	Security Pacific National (n)	Los Angeles	$36.1	$2.2	$48.9	8
3	7	Wells Fargo Bank (n)	San Francisco	$35.1	$2.6	$43.7	9
4	16	First Interstate of California (s)	Los Angeles	$16.6	$0.87	$20.5	18
5	22	Union Bank (s)	Los Angeles	$11.9	$0.82	$15.0	26
6	68	Sanwa Bank of California (s)	San Francisco	$5.1	$0.38	$6.4	81
7	72	Bank of California (n)	San Francisco	$4.9	$0.33	$6.9	69
8	101	City National Bank (n)	Beverly Hills	$3.5	$0.23	$4.3	113
9	106	Sumitomo Bank of California (s)	San Francisco	$3.3	$0.18	$3.7	133
10	177	Imperial Bank (s)	Los Angeles	$2.0	$0.14	$2.3	191
11	236	Mitsui Manufacturers Bank (s)	Los Angeles	$1.4	$0.12	$1.6	261
12	248	Bank of the West (s)	San Francisco	$1.4	$0.12	$1.7	249
13	257	San Diego Trust & Savings Bank (s)	San Diego	$1.3	$0.09	$1.4	293
14	283	Westamerica Bank (n)	San Rafael	$1.1	$0.07	NA	NA

* Rank in deposits. † An (n) indicates a federally-chartered national bank; an (s) a state-chartered one.

17.1.90 Source: *American Banker, 1989.* Used by permission.

CALIFORNIA BANK ASSETS AND LOANS*
1940-1988
(in millions)

	Assets			Loans		
Year	State Banks	National Banks	All Banks	State Banks	National Banks	All Banks
1940	NA	NA	$4,939	NA	NA	$1,862
1950	NA	NA	$15,193	NA	NA	$5,809
1960	NA	NA	$26,893	NA	NA	$14,079
1970	$13,344	$45,938	$59,282	$7,280	$25,370	$32,649
1979	$44,608	$115,365	$159,973	$26,747	$73,672	$100,420
1980	$50,966	$124,839	$175,805	$30,353	$81,051	$111,404
1981	$58,835	$140,533	$199,368	$35,985	$90,539	$126,525
1982	$63,537	$152,815	$216,352	$39,473	$100,504	$139,977
1983	$67,503	$160,362	$227,865	$41,640	$107,157	$148,797
1984	$69,849	$145,661	$215,511	$45,974	$107,947	$153,921
1985	$83,914	$210,393	$294,307	$55,002	$145,547	$200,549
1986	$94,338	$198,329	$292,667	$61,237	$142,132	$203,369
1987	$93,586	$189,245	$282,831	$62,773	$136,740	$199,514
1988	$94,492	$202,714	$297,206	$61,116	$146,860	$207,976

* Domestic subsidiaries of insured commercial banks. All data as of Dec. 31 for the year in question. 17.2,90 Source: *California Statistical Abstract*; California Banking Dept., unpublished data; U.S. Compt. of the Currency, *Quarterly Call Reports*.

CALIFORNIA BANK DEPOSITS*
1940-1988
(in millions)

	Transaction/Demand Deposits			Time/Non-transaction Deposits		
Year	State Banks	National Banks	All Banks	State Banks	National Banks	All Banks
1940	NA	NA	$2,052	NA	NA	$2,356
1950	NA	NA	$8,124	NA	NA	$5,895
1960	NA	NA	$12,954	NA	NA	$11,385
1970	$5,116	$15,741	$20,857	$6,097	$23,098	$29,196
1979	$14,818	$30,167	$44,985	$21,961	$55,083	$77,044
1980	$15,671	$29,308	$44,979	$25,499	$66,854	$92,354
1981	$15,402	$27,275	$42,676	$30,830	$78,802	$109,632
1982	$15,045	$25,381	$40,426	$35,007	$89,476	$124,484
1983	$17,001	$28,543	$45,544	$37,303	$95,833	$133,137
1984	$21,009	$38,395	$59,404	$37,592	$86,900	$124,491
1985	$21,504	$33,661	$55,166	$45,286	$94,226	$139,512
1986	$33,709	$51,097	$84,807	$43,294	$79,859	$123,153
1987	$22,221	$45,391	$67,612	$54,826	$108,852	$163,408
1988	$24,083	$49,209	$71,430	$54,886	$112,949	$167,775

* Domestic subsidiaries of insured commercial banks. All data as of Dec. 31 for the year in question. 17.3,90 Source: *California Statistical Abstract*; California Banking Dept., unpublished data; U.S. Compt. of the Currency, *Quarterly Call Reports*.

NUMBER OF CALIFORNIA BANKS AND BANK BRANCHES*
1970-1988

Year	Number of Banks State Banks	Number of Banks National Banks	Number with Branches State Banks	Number with Branches National Banks	Number of Branches State Banks	Number of Branches National Banks	Total Offices State Banks	Total Offices National Banks
1970	84	60	66	52	626	2,371	710	2,431
1979	200	42	146	29	1,339	2,762	1,539	2,804
1980	233	48	155	29	1,495	2,784	1,728	2,832
1981	252	60	177	28	1,673	2,804	1,925	2,864
1982	264	97	190	33	1,727	2,779	1,991	2,876
1983	273	123	201	44	1,734	2,962	2,007	3,012
1984	286	158	200	64	1,652	2,861	1,938	3,222
1985	285	171	214	72	1,682	2,795	1,967	2,956
1986	287	169	NA	76	1,686	2,640	1,973	2,711
1987	279	173	NA	NA	1,704	2,617	1,983	NA
1988	270	167	NA	NA	1,623	2,593	1,893	NA

* Domestic subsidiaries of insured commercial banks. All data as of Dec. 31 for the year in question.

17.4,90 Source: *California Statistical Abstract*; California Banking Dept., unpublished data; U.S. Compt. of the Currency, *Quarterly Call Reports*.

CALIFORNIA BANK LOANS BY SELECTED CATEGORIES*
1970-1988
(in millions)

Year	Residential Real Estate Loans 1 to 4 Family Properties	Residential Real Estate Loans Multifamily Properties	Other Real Estate	Commercial and Industrial Loans	Loans to Individuals	Total Loans and Leases
1970	$6,547†	NA	$3,044	$12,976	$3,480	$31,946
1979	$23,988	$941	$14,152	$30,261	$22,080	$128,042
1980	$27,733	$1,023	$17,749	$33,895	$22,049	$141,617
1981	$29,795	$1,133	$21,363	$39,502	$21,982	$161,591
1982	$30,649	$1,064	$21,962	$46,275	$22,034	$173,945
1983	$31,704	$1,222	$21,939	$48,845	$23,900	$178,622
1984	$32,355	$1,387	$24,070	$49,011	$28,814	$195,767
1985	$33,672	$1,439	$28,457	$49,297	$33,455	$203,879
1986	$32,353	$2,129	$32,410	$53,538	$32,451	$203,366
1987	$32,961	$1,838	$36,910	$50,237	$30,519	$199,514
1988	$38,589	$1,956	$41,124	$55,651	$31,982	$210,389

* Domestic Subsidiaries of insured commercial banks. † Residential Real Estate.
Note: All data as of December 31 for the year in question.

17.5,90 Source: *California Statistical Abstract;* California Banking Dept., unpublished data; U.S. Compt. of the Currency, *Quarterly Call Reports*.

	Deposits*	Foreign	Foreign	
Bank	**(in billions)**	**Ownership**	**Owner**	**Nationality**
Bank of America	$69.6	None		
Security Pacific	$36.1	None		
Wells Fargo Bank	$35.1	None		
First Interstate	$16.6	None		
Union Bank	$11.9	100%	Bank of Tokyo	Japan
Sanwa Bank	$5.1	100%	Sanwa Bank	Japan
Bank of California	$3.6	100%	Mitsubishi Bank	Japan
City National Bank	$3.5	None		
Sumitomo Bank	$3.3	100%	Sumitomo Bank	Japan
Imperial Bank	$2.0	None		

EXTENT OF FOREIGN CONTROL OVER CALIFORNIA'S TEN LARGEST BANKS

* As of December 31, 1988.
17.6,90 Source: California Banking Department and unpublished data.

THE FIVE LARGEST STATE BANKS IN CALIFORNIA

California Rank	National Rank	Bank	Assets (billions)
1	18	First Interstate	$20.5
2	26	Union Bank	$15.0
3	82	Sanwa Bank California	$6.4
4	133	Sumitomo	$3.7
5	191	Mitsui	$1.6

THE FIVE LARGEST NATIONAL BANKS IN CALIFORNIA

California Rank	National Rank	Bank	Assets (billions)
1	2	Bank of America	$82.9
2	8	Security Pacific	$48.9
3	9	Wells Fargo	$43.7
4	69	Bank of California	$6.9
5	113	City National Bank	$4.3

* National and State Ranking Based on assets.
17.7,90 Source: *American Banker*.

SECTION 17 NOTE

In 1988 California had 446 pawnbrokers, according to the California Dept. of Justice which regulates them. The state also has 2,225 registered secondhand dealers. Secondhand dealers must hold goods for 30 days before they can be sold.

17.8,90

NEW BANKS, BANK MERGERS AND BANK CLOSURES

	National Banks			State Banks		
Year	New Banks	Bank Mergers	Bank Closures & Failures	New Banks	Bank Mergers	Bank Closures & Failures
1982	30	0	1	22	7	1
1983	46	1	2	17	7	4
1984	27	1	1	31	4	5
1985	16	2	1	6	2	6
1986	6	1	5	5	3	2
1987	8	4	2	4	6	5
1988	5	5	1	2	14	1

17.9,90 Source: Federal Deposit Insurance Corporation, unpublished data and California Supt. of Banks, *Annual Report* and unpublished data.

AUTOMATED TELLER MACHINES

California Rank	National Rank	Bank	Number of A.T.M.s
1	2	Bank of America	1,400
2	3	First Interstate	1,328
3	4	Wells Fargo	1,229
4	5	Security Pacific	1,073
5	17	California First	362

17.10,90 Source: American Banker, *Top Numbers* 1989.

VENTURE CAPITAL IN CALIFORNIA AND THE UNITED STATES 1986-1988

	Number of Firms			New Capital Raised (millions)				Venture Capital Under Management (billions)		
			Cal. as a %	California			Cal as a %			Cal. as a %
Year	Cal.	U.S.	of US.	North-ern	South-ern	U.S.	of U.S.	Cal.	U.S.	of U.S.
1986	198	597	33%	$465	$52	$3,400	15%	NA	NA	NA
1987	202	755	27%	$1,044	$112	$4,404	26%	$8.7	$29.0	30%
1988	197	797	25%	$688	$110	$2,942	27%	$8.1	$31.0	26%

17.11,90 Source: *Venture Capital Journal*, 1989.

SECTION 17 NOTE

Japanese banks in California hold 25 percent of the banking assets in the state and 9 percent of all U.S. banking assets.

17.12,90

THE TWENTY LARGEST CALIFORNIA SAVINGS AND LOAN ASSOCIATIONS*

Rank in State	Rank in U.S.	Name	Head Office	Total Deposits (billions)	Assets (billions)	Net Worth (billions)	Net Worth as a % of Assets
1	1	Home Savings of America	Irwindale	$29.6	$40.9	$2.4	5.9%
2	2	Great Western Bank	Beverly Hills	$21.7	$30.8	$1.5	4.7%
3	3	California Federal S&L	Los Angeles	$18.8	$25.9	$1.3	5.0%
4	4	Glendale Federal S&L	Glendale	$15.3	$24.3	$1.3	5.3%
5	5	First Nationwide Bank	San Francisco	$14.8	$26.1	$1.3	5.1%
6	6	American Savings Bank	Stockton	$13.4	$15.4	$0.6	3.9%
7	8	Home Federal S&L of San Diego	San Diego	$11.6	$16.2	$1.2	7.2%
8	9	Great American First Savings Bank	San Diego	$10.8	$16.1	$0.8	4.9%
9	11	World Savings Federal S & L	Oakland	$10.1	$16.4	$1.0	6.2%
10	12	Coast Savings & Loan	Los Angeles	$8.8	$12.9	$1.0	8.0%
11	16	Imperial Savings Association	San Diego	$8.3	$12.3	$0.4	3.5%
12	18	Columbia Savings & Loan	Beverly Hills	$8.1	$11.8	$0.8	6.7%
13	19	Gibraltar Savings	Beverly Hills	$7.6	$13.4	$0.3	2.2%
14	30	Citicorp Savings Federal S & L	San Francisco	$4.7	$6.9	$1.0	13.7%
15	33	Lincoln Savings & Loan	Irvine	$4.4	$5.5	$0.3	4.6%
16	49	Sears Savings Bank	Glendale	$3.4	$4.8	$0.3	6.3%
17	52	Far West Savings & Loan	Newport Beach	$3.3	$4.8	$0.1	3.0%
18	57	Homestead Savings Federal S & L	Millbrae	$3.2	$5.8	$0.2	3.7%
19	63	Western Federal S&L	Marina Del Rey	$3.1	$4.5	$0.2	3.9%
20	64	Fidelity Federal S&L	Glendale	$3.1	$4.6	$0.2	4.4%

* Data as of December 31, 1988.
17,13,90 Source: *American Banker*, May 26, 1989.

Dec. 31	Number of Assoc- iations	Total Assets	Mortgage Loans Held	Refi- nancing Mortgages	Mortgages Foreclosed	Total Mortgage Loans Made
SELECTED BALANCE SHEET DATA FOR ALL INSURED SAVINGS AND LOAN ASSOCIATIONS, CALIFORNIA 1970-1988 (in millions of dollars)						
1970	225	$32,792	$23,308	NA	NA	$3,517
1971	207	36,934	31,965	NA	NA	NA
1972	182	42,866	37,204	NA	NA	NA
1973	176	47,149	41,103	NA	NA	NA
1974	175	50,789	43,799	NA	NA	NA
1975	169	58,009	49,077	NA	NA	10,689
1976	164	69,141	58,566	NA	NA	NA
1977	165	83,311	70,741	NA	NA	NA
1978	170	95,518	80,768	NA	NA	NA
1979	179	109,937	92,512	NA	NA	NA
1980	195	120,536	98,196	NA	NA	16,074
1981	187	137,883	107,866	NA	NA	10,504
1982	171	153,424	105,927	NA	NA	14,082
1983	181	193,566	132,297	NA	NA	42,594
1984	202	251,162	170,046	$17,319	$1,455	56,024
1985	219	273,157	182,628	16,368	2,048	56,444
1986	216	309,272	192,338	32,916	2,639	84,949
1987	206	346,291	212,699	33,492	3,585	91,422
1988	193	395,511	229,960	25,357	2,888	100,459

17.14.1,90 Source: Federal Home Loan Bank Board, Office of Economic Research, Unpublished Summary Statistics and *California Statistical Abstract*.

NUMBER OF NEW, MERGED, AND FAILED SAVINGS AND LOAN ASSOCIATIONS 1982-1988

Year	New	Acquisitions and Mergers	Closures or Failures
1982	18	34	NA
1983	17	0	1
1984	20	5	1
1985	20	0	0
1986	7	8	3
1987	0	9	2
1988	0	11	5

17.15,90 Source: Federal Home Loan Bank, *Annual Reports*.

SELECTED BALANCE SHEET DATA FOR ALL INSURED SAVINGS AND LOAN ASSOCIATIONS, CALIFORNIA 1970-1988 (in millions of dollars)

Dec. 31	Cash and Investment Securities*	Net New Savings	Total Savings	Delin- quent Loans	Net Income	Total Net Worth
1970	$2,498	$115	$25,043	NA	NA	$2,396
1971	2,842	NA	30,043	NA	NA	2,608
1972	3,258	NA	35,658	NA	NA	2,935
1973	2,984	NA	37,836	NA	NA	3,282
1974	3,384	NA	39,359	NA	NA	3,487
1975	4,755	5,565	47,146	NA	NA	3,716
1976	5,442	7,218	57,102	NA	NA	4,221
1977	6,592	6,480	66,918	NA	NA	4,961
1978	7,754	4,180	74,896	NA	NA	5,809
1979	7,921	4,814	84,166	NA	NA	6,634
1980	10,016	107	89,693	NA	NA	6,871
1981	13,018	-5,815	96,163	NA	NA	6,081
1982	16,799	1,281	108,712	NA	NA	5,884
1983	23,290	29,205	188,761	NA	NA	8,396
1984	29,545	28,355	189,788	3,006	-177	9,088
1985	32,466	-4,056	199,907	5,316	879	11,692
1986	36,604	6,062	218,132	6,536	891	13,513
1987	39,662	9,824	239,780	6,480	116	14,178
1988	41,090	3,607	258,726	5,712	716	18,553

* Investment securities are the total of liquid assets (exclusive of cash) as defined by Board Regulations, and other investment securities. Included are U.S. Government obligations, Federal agency securities, State and local government securities, time deposits at banks and miscellaneous securities, except FHLB stock.

17.14.2,90   Source: Federal Home Loan Bank Board, Office of Economic Research, Unpublished Summary Statistics and *California Statistical Abstract.*

SECTION 17 NOTE

In California 2 million items are pawned annually. Pawnbrokers with large inventories have $2 million in loans outstanding at any given time.

17.16,90

SECTION 17 NOTE

Approximately 250 (56 percent) of the state's 446 pawnbrokers belong to the Collateral Loan Association.

17.17,90

			FEDERALLY CHARTERED CREDIT UNIONS IN CALIFORNIA, 1940-1988		
Year	Number of Credit Unions	Number of Members	Total Assets (billions)	Shares/ Savings (billions)	Total Loans Outstanding (billions)
1940	258	93,450	$.002	$.007	$.006
1950	382	212,754	$.088	$.043	$.037
1960	1,014	787,450	$0.69	$0.34	$0.31
1970	1,249	1,655,307	$1.4	$1.2	$1.1
1980	1,056	3,672,304	$6.3	$5.7	$4.3
1981	979	3,746,696	$6.3	$5.7	$4.3
1982	905	3,863,511	$7.3	$6.6	$4.4
1983	850	3,973,973	$8.7	$8.0	$5.2
1984	813	3,991,110	$9.8	$8.9	$6.4
1985	790	4,171,234	$12.3	$11.3	$7.5
1986	766	4,307,160	$15.2	$14.0	$8.9
1987	742	4,603,968	$17.1	$15.7	$10.7
1988	712	5,059,752	$18.6	$17.0	$12.3

17.18,90 Source: Credit Union National Association, unpublished data, 1988.

			STATE CHARTERED CREDIT UNIONS IN CALIFORNIA, 1960-1988				
Year	Number of Credit Unions	Number of Members	Total Assets (thou- sands)	Shares (thou- sands)	Total Loans Outstanding (thousands)	Real Estate Loans Outstanding (thousands)	Net Profit* (thou- sands)
1960	568	573,548	$304,885	$263,793	$266,374	$41,676	NA
1970	631	1,139,372	998,764	868,721	858,839	101,161	NA
1975	587	1,341,288	1,935,507	1,710,369	1,621,089	224,553	NA
1980	478	1,973,513	3,798,533	3,189,679	2,977,642	615,902	NA
1981	450	1,975,104	3,794,317	3,221,836	3,011,722	655,907	$307,913
1982	417	1,921,032	3,788,929	3,351,392	2,710,921	607,421	312,327
1983	397	2,040,746	4,761,669	4,258,249	3,286,588	650,527	372,201
1984	376	2,010,832	5,439,894	4,885,542	4,101,413	855,287	454,289
1985	360	2,074,771	6,384,522	5,854,804	4,602,221	983,565	495,465
1986	345	2,122,970	7,699,129	7,094,105	5,286,139	1,374,214	526,035
1987	326	2,137,891	8,108,128	7,439,497	5,801,524	1,844,562	528,305
1988	306	2,244,916	8,925,000	8,170,000	6,566,000	2,355,322	575,837

* Before dividends paid to members.

17.19,90 California Department of Corporations, *Credit Union Newsletter*.

LICENSED INSURANCE COMPANIES				
Location	1976	1986	1987	1988
California Companies	177	241	249	253
Non-California Companies	907	1,168	1,173	1,206
Total	1,084	1,409	1,422	1,459

17.20,90 Source: California Insurance Commissioner, *Annual Report* and unpublished data.

DIRECT INSURANCE PREMIUMS DOLLAR VALUE (in billions)	
1972	$9.1
1974	$10.5
1976	$14.5
1978	$19.0
1980	$22.2
1981	$23.5
1982	$25.2
1983	$27.8
1984	$31.6
1985	$38.2
1986	$44.6
1987	$49.5

17.21,90 Source: California Insurance Commissioner, *Annual Reports*.

TEN LARGEST* FIRE AND CASUALTY INSURANCE COMPANIES			
	Taxable Premium Income (in millions)		
Company	1987	1985	1983
State Farm Mutual Auto	$1,604	$1,298	$902
Allstate	$1,380	$995	$794
State Compensation Fund	$1,221	$514	$292
State Farm Fire & Casualty	$1,014	$728	$475
Farmers Insurance	$949	$841	$604
California State Automobile Association	$945	$656	$447
Auto Club of Southern California	$800	$643	$619
National Union Fire Insurance	$748	NA	NA
Fireman's Fund	$663	$506	$267
Aetna Casualty & Surety	$612	$413	$256
Total Top Ten	$9,936	$7,049	NA

* Based on taxable premium income. Note: In 1987, the taxable premium income for all 602 Fire & Casualty Insurers was $28.7 billion. In 1985, the total was $21.2 billion.
17.22,90 Source: California State Board of Equalization, *Annual Reports*.

SECTION 17 NOTE
In ranking the largest banks in the world by assets, *American Banker* ranks Bank of America 49, Security Pacific 89, Great Western 119, First Interstate 174, and First Nationwide 189.

17.23,90

TEN LARGEST* LIFE INSURANCE COMPANIES

Company	Taxable Premium Income, 1987 (in millions)
Prudential	$1,196
New York Life	$529
Metropolitan Life	$480
Aetna Life	$478
Travelers Insurance	$426
Transamerica Occidental Life	$367
Pacific Mutual Life	$349
Provident Life	$321
Equitable Life	$301
Executive Life	$273
Total Top Ten	**$4.7**

* Based on taxable premium income. Note: Taxable premium income for all Life Insurers was $14.9 billion in 1987.

17.24,90 Source: California State Board of Equalization, *Annual Report.*

LIFE AND DISABILITY INSURERS-ASSETS, LIABILITIES, CAPITAL/SURPLUS 1987 (in millions)

Insurers	Total Assets	Total Liabilities and Reserves	Capital and/or Surplus
California Insurers	$44,516	$41,029	$3,487
California Fraternal Insurers	$54	$38	$16
Total	**$44,570**	**$41,067**	**$3,503**
Non-California Insurers	$970,923	$914,363	$56,570
Non-California Fraternal Insurers	$19,291	$17,182	$2,069
Total	**$990,183**	**$931,545**	**$58,639**
Grand Total	**$1,034,753**	**$972,612**	**$62,142**

17.25,90 Source: California Insurance Commissioner, *Annual Report 1987.*

SECTION 17 NOTE

In 1987, according to Sheshonoff Information Services, 4.39 percent of the loans of California banks were nonperforming. By 1988 that percentage had dropped to 3.14.

17.26,90

SECTION 17 NOTE

As of March 31, 1989, according to the Federal Home Loan Bank Board, 38 of the 189 savings and loans in California did not have enough capital to meet the new federal guidelines.

17.27,90

INSURANCE COMPANIES - NEW COMPANIES, MERGERS, CLOSURES, WITHDRAWALS & LIQUIDATIONS,				
Year	Companies in Liquidation & Conservation	New Companies	Mergers and Consolidations	Withdrawals
1978	NA	39	30	13
1981	NA	76	13	3
1983	NA	104	8	1
1984	NA	46	9	6
1985	19	40	16	1
1986	11	39	8	6
1987	12	50	14	3

17.28,90 Source: California Insurance Commissioner, *Annual Reports.*

INSURANCE COMPANIES - NEW COMPANIES, MERGERS, CLOSURES, WITHDRAWALS & LIQUIDATIONS,				
Year	Companies in Liquidation & Conservation	New Companies	Mergers and Consolidations	Withdrawals
1978	NA	39	30	13
1981	NA	76	13	3
1983	NA	104	8	1
1984	NA	46	9	6
1985	19	40	16	1
1986	11	39	8	6
1987	12	50	14	3

17.29,90 Source: California Insurance Commissioner, *Annual Reports.*

SECTION 17 NOTE
Approximately 18 percent of California homeowners now have earthquake insurance, up from 6 percent in 1984. 70 percent of the nation's earthquake insurance is written in California.

17.30,90

AVERAGE AUTO INSURANCE PREMIUMS				
	1983		1987	
State	**Rank in Nation**	**Average Premium**	**Rank in Nation**	**Average Premium**
California*	8	$374	3	$623
New York	2	$422	8	$584
New Jersey	1	$521	2	$635
Massachusetts	3	$417	1	$656
Nevada	5	$388	5	$600
Arizona	12	$354	4	$602
Oregon	20	$302	27	$435
South Dakota	50	$209	50	$295

* Some of California drivers in high risk areas of Los Angeles pay $2,000 to $3,000 annually for auto insurance. 10-20% of California drivers are uninsured.

17.31,90 Source: A.M. Best Insurance Management Report, 1989, and the Insurance Information Institute.

LIFE INSURANCE IN FORCE IN CALIFORNIA				
	Number of Policies (millions)	**% of U.S.**	**Amount of Insurance (billions)**	**% of U.S.**
Ordinary	10.7	7%	$451	11%
Group	13.7	10%	$333	11%
Industrial	1.3	3%	$1.0	4%
Credit	4.1	5%	$14.0	6%
Total	**29.7**	**8%**	**$800**	**11%**

17.32,90 Source: American Council of Life Insurance, *1988 Life Insurance Fact Book.*

REPORTABLE INCOME* OF CALIFORNIA FINANCIAL INSTITUTIONS (in millions)				
Year	**Banks**	**Savings and Loans†**	**Investment and Insurance**	**Real Estate**
1980	$1,072	$177	$334	$957
1981	$931	-$627	$39	$494
1982	$631	-$1,250	-$354	-$1,123
1983	$998	-$300	$354	$177
1984	$761	-$57	-$112	$870
1985	$374	$550	$760	-$115
1986	$1,019	$1,259	$2,624	$2,697

† Savings and Loans and Other Financials.

17.33,90 Source: California Franchise Tax Board, *Annual Report.*

REAL ESTATE TITLE INSURERS-ASSETS AND LEABILITIES AS OF DECEMBER 31, 1987 AND UNDERWRITING AND INVESTMENT RESULTS FOR 1987
(in millions)

Name of Insurer	Total Assets	Total Liabilities	Total Capital and/or Surplus	Under-writing Gain or Loss	Net Investment Gain or Loss	Net Surplus Changes	In California Direct Premiums Earned	Direct Losses Incurred
California Real Estate Title Insurers	$846	$383	$463	-$22	$91	$18	$526	$67
Non-California Real Estate Title Insurers	$1,104	$708	$396	$18	$91	$14	$340	$28
Grand Total	**$1,950**	**$1,092**	**$858**	**-$4**	**$181**	**$32**	**$866**	**$95**

17.34,90 Source: California Insurance Commissioner, *Annual Report 1987.*

FIRE, MARINE, CASUALTY AND MISCELLANEOUS INSURERS ASSETS AND LIABILITIES AS OF DECEMBER 31, 1987 AND INVESTMENT RESULTS FOR 1987
(in billions)

Name of Insurer	Total Assets	Total Liabilities	Total Capital and/or Surplus	Under-writing Gain or Loss	Net Investment Gain or Loss	Net Surplus Changes	In California Direct Premiums Earned	Direct Losses Incurred
California Insurers	$40.6	$31.4	$9.2	-$1.2	$2.9	$0.8	$12.5	$8.3
Non-California Insurers	$334.0	$242.6	$91.3	-$5.4	$20.9	$8.7	$16.2	$11.5
Nonprofit California Hospital Service Plan	$0.8	$0.7	$0.1	-$0.17	$0.11	$0.08	$2.4	$2.3
Grand Total	**$375.4**	**$274.7**	**$100.7**	**-$6.7**	**$23.9**	**$9.3**	**$31.1**	**$22.0**

17.35,90 Source: California Insurance Commissioner, *Annual Report 1987.*

TOP TEN CALIFORNIA MORTGAGE COMPANIES

California Rank	National Rank	Company	Location	Loans Services (billions)
1	8	Metmor Financial	Los Angeles	$13.2
2	11	Weyerhaeuser Mortgage	Los Angeles	$11.3
3	12	Shearson Lehman Mortgage	Irvine	$11.1
4	17	First Interstate Mortgage	Pasadena	$9.0
5	20	Countrywide Funding Corp.	Pasadena	$8.8
6	24	Imco Realty Services	Santa Rosa	$7.1
7	26	GlenFed Mortgage	Irvine	$6.3
8	49	Coldwell Banker Real Estate Fin. Ser.	El Segundo	$3.6
9	55	Meritor Mortgage	Orange	$3.3
10	58	Bowest Corp.	La Jolla	$3.2

17.36,90 Source: American Banker, *Top Numbers* 1989.

SECTION 17 NOTE

The first financial institution in the U.S. to offer bank credit cards was the Bank of America. The year was 1958.

17.37,90

SECTION 17 NOTE

The average California household has $79,400 in life insurance. The national average is $82,000.

17.38,90

SECTION 17 NOTE

From 1982 to 1987 auto insurance premiums in California rose by 74 percent, a rate exceeded in 14 other states.

17.39,90

SECTION 17 NOTE

In 1987 Californians purchased $121 billion in ordinary life insurance, or 12 percent of the national total.

17.40,90

SECTION 17 NOTE

In 1987 a total of 374 companies were writing auto insurance in California.

17.41,90

Business

California's dominant position in American business was increasingly obvious as the 1980s came to a close. In 1987 New York was still the home base for more large multinational manufacturing firms than California. By 1989, however, California had 150 such firms to only 130 for New York. Although 68 of the firms on the Fortune 500 list still have their headquarters in New York, compared with 41 in California, California has twice as many medium-sized and fast-growing companies as the Empire State.

According to improved export statistics, California as of 1987 was exporting more goods to European Common Market countries than to Japan. Although the state continues to export less to Europe than to Asian countries in general, Europe was responsible for a full 25 percent of California's foreign trade in 1987. This fact will probably lead California to establish additional trade offices in Europe (we now have only one--in London). The state is considering operating some foreign trade offices in cooperation with other large states that have an interest in the European marketplace. California's trade with China amounts to only 1.3 percent of the state's exports; with China's political instability that figure is unlikely to rise noticeably in the near future. One feature of California's foreign trade that is masked by the official trade statistics is the state's buoyant trade with Canada. Officially 9.3 percent of our trade is with our northern neighbor, but trade experts say that the actual figure is higher since some California products shipped to Canada--food, for example--are not counted as U.S. exports by customs agents.

California Business magazine, which provides a variety of useful lists and studies of the state's economy, has developed a particularly interesting list that names the one hundred fastest-growing companies in California. It offers a good indication of those businesses that will play important roles in the state's economic future. Firms in the computer hardware and software business are prominent on the list, as are biotechnology and health-care technology firms. This list seems to confirm that California's economic future, like its recent past, will be high-tech oriented.

					1988
Rank in State	*Fortune 500* **Rank**	**Name**	**Headquarters**	**Principal Activity**	**Gross Revenue* (billions)**
1	11	Chevron	San Francisco	Petroleum Products	$28.9
2	14	Occidental Petroleum	Los Angeles	Petroleum Products	$19.4
3	17	Atlantic Richfield	Los Angeles	Petroleum Products	$18.3
4	33	Lockheed	Burbank	Aerospace	$10.6
5	3(1)	Bank America	San Francisco	Banking	$10.2
6	47	Unocal	Los Angeles	Petroleum Products	$10.1
7	39	Hewlett-Packard	Palo Alto	Computer Systems	$9.8
8	6(2)	Pacific Telesis Group	San Francisco	Public Utility	$9.5
9	5(1)	Security Pacific	Los Angeles	Banking	$8.5
10	14(5)	Transamerica	San Francisco	Insurance & Finance	$7.9
11	4(6)	McKesson	San Francisco	Chemicals, Drugs, Liquor	$7.3
12	15(2)	Southern California Edison	Rosemead	Public Utility	$6.3
13	8(1)	First Interstate Bancorp	Los Angeles	Banking	$5.9
14	NA	Pacific Enterprises	Los Angeles	Diversified Industries	$5.9
15	75	Northrop	Los Angeles	Aerospace	$5.8
16	8(6)	Fluor	Irvine	Engineering/Construction	$5.1
17	105	Teledyne	Los Angeles	Diversified Industries	$4.6
18	11(1)	Wells Fargo	San Francisco	Banking	$4.6
19	96	Litton Industries	Beverly Hills	Diversified Industries	$4.5
20	24(4)	Price Club	San Diego	Membership Retail	$4.2
21	114	Apple Computer	Cupertino	Personal Computers	$4.1
22	1(3)	H.F. Ahmanson	Los Angeles	Savings & Loan	$3.5
23	20(6)	Bergen Brunswig	Orange	Pharmaceutical Products	$3.5
24	21(6)	Walt Disney	Burbank	Entertainment	$3.4
25	138	Times Mirror	Los Angeles	News Media	$3.3

TOP 25 PUBLICLY HELD CORPORATIONS IN CALIFORNIA

(1) Rank among the *Fortune* 100 largest Commercial Banks. (2) Rank among the *Fortune* 50 largest Utilities. (3) Rank among the *Fortune* 50 largest Savings Institutions. (4) Rank among the *Fortune* 50 largest Retailing Companies. (5) Rank among the *Fortune* 500 largest Diversified Financial Companies. (6) Rank among the *Fortune* 500 largest Diversified Service Companies.

Note: Some corporations Which are large enough to be listed, such as the Bechtel Construction Company; American Stores, and Safeway, are not included because they are privately held.

18.1,90 Source: *California Business Magazine,* May 1989. Permission to reprint by *California Business,* all rights reserved. Consult *California Business magazine for detailed information on the 500 largest corporations in California.*

CALIFORNIA CORPORATIONS

In California as of February 29, 1989:

There were 532,191 active domestic corporations (436,892 with stock and 95,299 without stock.)(nonprofit)

There were 43,478 active foreign corporations (41,816 with stock and 1,662 without stock.)(nonprofit)

There were 1,337,411 total corporations, including inactive and suspended corporations.

18.2,90 Source: California Secretary of State, Corporate Division, unpublished data.

CALIFORNIA GROSS STATE PRODUCT BY SECTOR, 1963-86 (in billions of current dollars)							
	1963	**1970**	**1975**	**1980**	**1982**	**1984**	**1986**
Agriculture, Forestry, and Fisheries	$2.2	$3.1	$6.1	$10.9	$10.9	$11.5	$11.3
Mining	0.9	1.0	2.1	6.0	7.7	7.7	5.9
Construction	3.8	5.4	8.2	16.3	15.3	20.0	23.9
Manufacturing	14.7	21.8	32.4	59.0	71.3	88.7	97.7
Transportation, Commun- ications, and Utilities	5.5	9.5	14.7	24.6	29.7	36.7	41.9
Wholesale Trade	4.5	7.4	13.1	23.3	25.9	33.2	38.7
Retail Trade	7.0	11.9	18.5	32.2	38.4	47.1	55.2
Finance, Insurance, and Real Estate	10.7	19.0	32.4	60.8	60.7	74.4	93.8
Services	8.4	15.8	26.3	53.5	66.8	85.1	103.4
Total Private Industries	57.6	94.9	154	287	327	404	472
Fed. Gov't.-Civilian	1.7	3.3	4.7	7.1	8.3	9.7	10.7
Fed. Gov't.-Military	1.5	3.1	4.1	5.7	7.6	8.6	9.4
State and Local Gov't.	5.1	10.4	17.0	25.7	30.1	34.6	41.9
Total Gov't.	8.3	16.7	25.8	38.4	46.0	52.9	62.0
Total- All Sectors	**$65.9**	**$111**	**$180**	**$325**	**$373**	**$457**	**$534**

18.3,90 Source: U.S. Dept. of Commerce, *Survey of Current Business*, May, 1988.

CALIFORNIA GROSS STATE PRODUCT, PERCENTAGE CONTRIBUTION OF EACH SECTOR 1963-1986								
	1963	**1965**	**1970**	**1975**	**1980**	**1982**	**1984**	**1986**
Farms	2.9	2.7	2.2	2.7	2.6	2.2	1.8	1.5
Agricultural Services, Forestry, Fisheries	0.5	0.5	0.5	0.7	0.7	0.7	0.7	0.6
Mining	1.4	1.1	0.9	1.2	1.9	2.1	1.7	1.1
Construction	5.8	5.5	4.9	4.6	5.0	4.1	4.3	4.5
Manufacturing	22.3	21.3	19.5	18.0	18.2	19.1	19.4	18.3
Durables	14.6	13.6	12.3	11.2	12.2	12.5	13.1	12.4
Non-Durables	7.7	7.7	7.2	6.8	5.9	6.6	6.3	5.9
Transportation and Public Utilities	8.3	8.5	8.5	8.2	7.6	8.0	8.0	7.9
Wholesale Trade	6.8	6.8	6.6	7.3	7.2	7.0	7.3	7.3
Retail Trade	10.6	10.9	10.6	10.3	9.9	10.3	10.3	10.3
Finance, Insurance and Real Estate	16.2	16.4	17.0	18.0	18.7	16.3	16.3	17.6
Services	12.8	13.3	14.2	14.6	16.5	17.9	18.6	19.4
Total Private Sector	**87.4**	**87.1**	**85.0**	**85.7**	**88.2**	**87.7**	**88.4**	**88.4**
Federal Gov't Civilian	2.6	2.6	2.9	2.6	2.2	2.2	2.1	2.0
Federal Gov't Military	2.3	2.2	2.7	2.3	1.7	2.0	1.9	1.8
State & Local Gov't	7.7	8.1	9.3	9.4	7.9	8.1	7.6	7.8
Total Government	**12.6**	**12.9**	**15.0**	**14.3**	**11.8**	**12.3**	**11.6**	**11.6**
Total All Sectors	**100**	**100**	**100**	**100**	**100**	**100**	**100**	**100**

18.4,90 Source: U.S. Dept. of Commerce, *Survey of Current Business, May 1988.*

NEW BUSINESS INCORPORATIONS			
Year	California	United States	California as a % of U.S.
1980	56,272	534,000	10.5%
1981	58,854	582,000	10.1%
1982	53,698	567,000	9.3%
1983	55,108	600,400	9.1%
1984	60,952	634,991	9.6%
1985	61,160	668,904	9.1%
1986	67,184	702,101	9.6%
1987	59,697	685,572	8.7%
1988	56,400	684,109	8.2%

18.5,90 Source: Cal. Dept. of Finance, *Cal. Economic Indicators*; Dun & Bradstreet Corporation, *Monthly New Business Incorporation Report*; and phone conversation with Dun & Bradstreet.

CORPORATE INCOME FROM CALIFORNIA OPERATIONS 1940-1986							
	Number of Corporations				Corporate Income (in millions)		
Year	With Net Income	With Net Loss	No Income or Loss	Total	Net Income	Net Loss	Total
1940	11,987	14,981	NA	26,968	$483	NA	NA
1950	21,987	11,560	8,830	42,377	$2,432	$168	$2,264
1960	56,987	28,843	15,351	101,081	$4,182	$665	$3,517
1970	81,340	44,318	19,694	145,352	$6,711	$2,326	$4,386
1975	106,213	53,965	17,487	177,665	$11,672	$3,309	$8,362
1980	165,183	86,482	23,838	275,493	$25,825	$5,171	$20,654
1981	172,122	101,398	25,695	299,215	$24,214	$7,847	$16,367
1982	175,054	120,964	30,246	326,264	$22,828	$12,083	$10,745
1983	184,408	125,149	27,614	337,165	$26,628	$10,143	$16,485
1984	208,566	149,831	39,456	397,854	$31,742	$12,393	$19,349
1985	207,388	139,408	41,448	388,244	$34,308	$13,188	$21,120
1986	216,677	149,684	48,241	414,602	$40,043	$14,586	$25,457

18.6,90 Source: California Franchise Tax Board, *Annual Reports*.

SECTION 18 NOTE
According to the ECONOMIST magazine, by the year 2000 California is likely to be the fourth leading economic power in the world, surpassed only by the U.S., Japan, and the Soviet Union.

18.7,90

NEW INDUSTRIAL EXPANSIONS AND NEW LOCATIONS IN CALIFORNIA BY YEAR		
Year	Expansions and Locations	Ranking in U.S.
1984	416	1
1985	638	1
1986	448	3
1987	264	1
1988	313	2
Total	2,079	

18.8,90 Source: California Department of Commerce, Office of Business Development, unpublished data.

CALIFORNIA BUSINESS FAILURES AND LIABILITIES 1970-1988				
	Failures		Liabilities	
Year	Number	As a % of All U.S. Failures	Amount	As a % of All U.S. Liabilities
1970	2,216	21%	265,703,000	21%
1971	1,803	17%	278,257,000	18%
1972	1,501	16%	207,661,000	16%
1973	1,677	18%	300,411,000	18%
1974	1,721	17%	360,212,000	17%
1975	1,667	15%	469,569,000	15%
1976	1,278	13%	335,106,000	13%
1977	1,133	14%	313,744,000	14%
1978	1,029	16%	298,841,000	16%
1979	1,162	15%	428,442,000	15%
1980	1,849	16%	521,735,000	16%
1981	2,849	17%	897,743,000	17%
1982	3,673	15%	3,805,800,000	15%
1983	4,423	14%	2,581,805,000	NA
1984	10,434	20%	6,341,029,964	22%
1985	10,296	18%	5,111,461,903	14%
1986	10,243	17%	6,083,528,335	14%
1987	9,957	16%	5,106,613,378	15%
1988	9,178	16%	5,685,738,341	16%

18.9,90 Source: The Dun and Bradstreet Corp., Economic Analysis Dept., *Failure Report* and unpublished data .

SECTION 18 NOTE
If San Diego County were a separate country, its economy would rank as the thirty-third strongest in the world.

18.10,90

District	1987 Total Filings	1987 Business Filings	1987 Nonbusiness Filings	1988 Total Filings	1988 Business Filings	1988 Nonbusiness Filings
Northern	19,348	3,075	16,273	19,546	2,532	17,014
Eastern	15,117	2,888	12,229	16,321	2,152	14,169
Central	49,288	4,875	44,413	50,629	3,119	47,510
Southern	8,991	928	8,063	9,858	675	9,183

BANKRUPTCY CASES FILED IN FEDERAL COURTS IN CALIFORNIA, 1987-1988

18.11,90 Source: U.S. Administrative Office of the Courts, *Annual Report*.

STOCK SHAREHOLDERS AND STOCKBROKERS

	California	New York	U.S.
Shareholders*	6,006,000	4,954,000	47,040,000
Stockbrokers†	10,639	15,562	86,121
Brokerage Sales Offices†	623	607	6,690

* Latest data as of June 30, 1985.
† Latest data as of December 31, 1987.
  Note: California has 12.7% of the shareholders in the United States.
  18.12,90 Source: New York Stock Exchange Research Department, 1989.

STOCK SALES ON THE PACIFIC STOCK EXHANGE

Year	Shares Traded
1970	178 million
1980	531 milion
1982	814 million
1983	1.097 billion
1984	1.010 billion
1985	1.362 billion
1986	1.786 billion
1987	2.540 billion
1988	1.522 billion

18.13,90 Source: Pacific Stock Exchange, Records Department, 1989.

SECTION 18 NOTE

The value of the underground economy in California is probably at least 10 percent of the value of the regular economy. The state's economy is thus even healthier than official statistics indicate. In addition, personal income and savings in the state are probably higher and unemployment lower than government data suggest.

18.14,90

SECTION 18 NOTE

Japanese investment during the 1980s created 70,000 new jobs in California.

18.15,90

NUMBER OF HOTEL-MOTEL ROOMS, OCCUPANCY RATE
AND AVERAGE ROOM RATES

	Number of Hotels & Motels	Number of Rooms	Occu-pancy Rates	12/88 Daily Rates*
Far North†	137	4,215	66%	$60.70
N. Bay(Napa, Sonoma, Marin)	270	8,786	59%	NA
Shasta-Cascade	107	4,160	69%	NA
San Francisco	160	25,487	71%	$106.54
San Mateo	84	10,285	69%	$61.19
South Bay(Santa Clara, Santa Cruz)	185	17,337	65%	$57.37
East Bay††	109	12,570	66%	$66.47
Sacramento Area	50	7,237	68%	$50.97
N. Central Valley	29	1,203	67%	NA
Lodi to Merced Area	48	4,022	71%	NA
Fresno-Visalia	75	7,003	61%	$45.32
Bakersfield	83	6,398	57%	NA
Gold Country	75	2,713	75%	NA
Tahoe Area	81	4,454	55%	NA
Other High Sierras	72	3,695	71%	NA
Monterey Peninsula	172	9,214	73%	$105.37
Central Coast	164	6,858	66%	NA
Northern California	1,901	135,637	NA	$87.45
Santa Barbara-Solvang	127	8,680	75%	NA
S. Fernando Valley & Canyon Country	76	7,667	76%	NA
West Los Angeles	71	9,357	74%	NA
L.A. Airport Area	55	12,905	77%	NA
South Bay	97	9,423	74%	NA
S. Gabriel Valley-Interstate 5 Corridor	122	10,809	70%	NA
Downtown L.A.	32	7,546	69%	NA
Mid-Wilshire, Hollywood	34	3,821	70%	NA
Ventura County	57	5,680	71%	NA
Greater Los Angeles	544	67,208	73%	$72.50
Orange County Airport Area	57	10,609	63%	NA
Central Orange County-Disneyland	61	13,409	75%	NA
North Orange County	29	3,729	67%	NA
South Orange County	29	2,903	65%	NA
Orange County	176	30,650	69%	$68.40
N. San Diego County	75	5,737	69%	NA
South Bay	46	2,648	72%	NA
Central San Diego	116	19,779	71%	NA
E. San Diego County	59	2,534	75%	NA
San Diego County	296	30,698	71%	$77.05
Eastern Deserts	92	4,850	68%	NA
Desert Resorts-Palm Springs	96	12,088	59%	NA
San Bernardino-Ontario	78	6,359	67%	NA
Riverside-Corona	58	3,221	63%	NA
State-wide	3,368	299,291	69%	NA

* For full service hotels and motels. † Del Norte, Humboldt, Mendocino.
†† Alameda, Contra Costa, City of Vallejo. 18.16,90 Source: Pannell Kerr Forster, *The Californias-California Lodging Industry Forecast, 1988.*

DISTILLERIES AND WINERIES IN CALIFORNIA

Brandy Distilleries	24
Distilled Spirits	16
Still Licensees	55
Wineries	705

18.17,90 Source: California Department of Alcoholic Beverage Control, 1989 unpublished data.

BREWERIES IN CALIFORNIA

Company	City
Major Breweries*	
Anheuser Busch	Fairfield
Anheuser Busch	Los Angeles
Miller Brewing	Irwindale
Stroh	Van Nuys
Microbreweries†	
Alpine Village	Torrance
Anchor	San Francisco
Angeles	Chatsworth
Asian American Brewing	Chico
Devil Mountain Brewery	Walnut Creek
Firestone-Fletcher	Los Olivos
Golden Pacific	Emeryville
Local Brewing	San Luis Obispo
Mendocino	Hopland
Nevada City	Nevada City
San Francisco Brewing	San Francisco
Santa Cruz Brewing	Santa Cruz
Saxton	Chico
Sierra Nevada	Chico
Stanilaus Brewing	Modesto
Thousand Oaks	Berkeley
Truckee Brewing	Truckee
Under the Oaks	Ojai
Xcelsior(ACME)	Santa Rosa

*   Over 60,000 barrels production per year.
†   Under 60,000 barrels production per year.
18.18,90 Source: California Department of Alcoholic Beverage Control, unpublished data and Association of Brewers, unpublished data, 1989.

SECTION 18 NOTE

The 2,650,000 small businesses in California employ 55 percent of the state's workers.

18.19,90

BREWERIES IN CALIFORNIA
(Micro Breweries)

Brewpubs	City	Brewpubs	City
Anderson Valley	Boonville	Marin	Larkspur
Biers Brasserie	San Jose	Monterey	Monterey
Bison	Berkeley	Napa Valley	Calistoga
Brewpub on the Green	Fremont	North Coast	Ft. Bragg
Buffalo Bills	Hayward	Old Columbia	San Diego
Butterfield	Fresno	Pacific Coast	Oakland
City of Angeles	Santa Monica	Rubicon	Sacramento
Crown City	Pasadena	San Andreas	Hollister
Dead Cat Alley	Woodland	San Francisco	San Francisco
Devil Mountain	Walnut Creek	Santa Cruz	Santa Cruz
Emery Pub	Emeryville	Seabright	Santa Cruz
Golden Gate	Berkeley	Seacliff Cafe	San Francisco
Gordon-Biersch	Palo Alto	SLO Brewing	San Luis Obispo
Gorky's Cafe	Los Angeles	Tied House Cafe	Mountain View
Grapevine	Lebec	Triple Rock	Berkeley
Hogshead	Sacramento	Truckee	Truckee
Humboldt	Arcata	Willett's	Napa
Kelmers	Santa Rosa	Winechester	San Jose
Mammoth Lakes	Mammoth Lakes		

18.20,90 Source: California Department of Alcoholic Beverage Control, unpublished data and Association of Brewers, unpublished data.

TOTAL TAXABLE SALES IN CALIFORNIA
1960-1988
(in millions)

Year	Taxable Sales
1960	$23,361
1970	$43,223
1972	$53,714
1974	$68,071
1976	$83,822
1978	$113,468
1980	$142,759
1982	$154,553
1984	$194,014
1986	$217,465
1987	$231,870
1988	$251,078

18.21,90 Source: *Economic Report of the Governor.*

	Total Sales (in billions)			Per Capita Sales	
Year	California	U.S.	California as a Percent of All U.S.	California	U.S.
1979	$87	$897	9.7%	$3,904	$3,993
1980	$94	$957	9.8%	$3,963	$4,212
1981	$102	$1,039	9.8%	$4,197	$4,523
1982	$102	$1,069	9.5%	$4,130	$4,609
1983	$113	$1,168	9.7%	$4,503	$4,987
1984	$127	$1,283	9.9%	$4,913†	$5,424
1985	$136	$1,367	9.9%	$5,155†	$5,727
1986	$142	$1,438	9.9%	$5,259†	$5,962
1987	$150	$1,511	9.9%	$5,433†	$6,202
1988	$163	NA	NA	$5,740†	NA

TOTAL TAXABLE* RETAIL SALES IN CALIFORNIA AND THE UNITED STATES, 1979-1988

* California figures exclude tax-exempt retail sales of food for home consumsuption and prescription medicines. † Calculated by the Editor.

18.22,90 Source: *U.S. Statistical Abstract* and *Economic Report of the Governor.*

BUSINESS - PROMINANT CALIFORNIANS

Gene Autry - Baseball	Allan Lockheed - Aircraft
Steven Bechtel - Construction	Issac Magnin - Retail Stores
Victor Bergeron - Restaurants	William Matson - Shipping
Jack Kent Cooke - Sports	Fritz Maytag - Brewing
Charles Crocker - Railroads	John Mackay - Mining, Banking
Al Davis - Football	Carver Mead - Computer Chips
Walt Disney - Amusement Parks, Film	John Northrop - Aircraft
Edward Doheny - Oil	William O'Brien - Mining, Banking
Peter Donahue - Natural Gas	Walter O'Malley - Baseball
Donald Douglas - Aircraft	David Packard - Computers
Edwin T. Earl - Refrigerated R.R. Cars	William C. Ralston - Banking
Max Factor - Cosmetics	T. Claude Ryan - Aircraft
James Fair - Mining, Banking	Walter Shorenstein - Real Estate
Charles Finley - Baseball	Francis Smith - Trollies
James C. Flood - Banker	Claus Spreckels - Sugar
A.P. Giannini - Banker	Leland Stanford - Railroads
Frank Havens - Trollies	Horace Stoneham- Baseball
William Hewlett - Computers	Levi Strauss - Dry Goods
Mark Hopkins - Railroads	Samuel Taylor - 1st Paper Mill
Howard Hughes - Aerospace	Gaylord Wilshire - Agriculture,
Collis Huntington - Railroads	Real Estate
Steven Jobs - Apple Computers	Stephen Wozniak - Apple Computers
Henry Kaiser - Construction, Ship Building	Anthony Zellerbach - Paper Products
William G. Kerchoff - Hydroelectric Power	Robert Noyce - Computers
Walter Knott - Amusement Park	Harris Weinstock - Dept. Stores
Ray Kroc - McDonalds	

18.23,90 Source: Pacific Data Resources.

CALIFORNIA'S MAJOR INTERNATIONAL TRADING PARTNERS BY REGION AND COUNTRY
1987

Region and Major Trading Partners (Ranked in Order)	Percent of California Trade 1987
Asia Japan Korea Taiwan Singapore Hong Kong	59.0%
Europe United Kingdom West Germany France Netherlands	22.0%
Latin America Mexico Brazil Venezuela	7.0%
Australia-Oceania Australia New Zealand	8.0%
Canada	1.5%
Middle East	1.0%
Africa	0.5%

18.24,90   Source: *Economic Report of the Governor, 1989*   and California Dept. of Finance unpublished data.

SECTION 18 NOTE

According to ECONOMIC AND BUSINESS OUTLOOK, published by the Bank of America, although California's economy is only 16 percent as large as Japan's, it is 45 percent larger than that of Mainland China, Asia's second-largest economy.

18.25,90

SECTION 18 NOTE

In 1987, according to CALIFORNIA BUSINESS magazine, 40 percent of the state's fastest growing companies were in the computer industry.

18.26,90

CALIFORNIA'S INTERNATIONAL TRADING PATTERNS BY VALUE OF TRADE, 1982-1987 (in billions of dollars)

Nation	Imports to California			Nation	Exports* from California 1987
	1982	1986	1987		
Japan	$12.9	$31.6	$32.1	Japan	$4.9
Taiwan	3.1	7.9	10.1	Canada	2.6
South Korea	2.0	5.1	6.9	United Kingdom	2.0
Hong Kong	1.6	3.0	3.4	Mexico	2.0
West Germany	1.6	3.3	3.6	West Germany	1.9
Mexico	NA	2.0	2.5	Singapore	1.4
Singapore	0.8	2.1	3.0	South Korea	1.4
Malaysia	NA	1.4	1.7	Taiwan	1.3
Indonesia	NA	0.6	0.7	France	1.2
United Kingdom	NA	1.2	1.4	Malaysia	0.9
Canada	NA	1.1	1.1	Netherlands	0.9
Australia	0.3	0.6	0.8	Australia	0.8
Italy	NA	NA	1.2	Hong Kong	0.7

* Starting with 1987, export data includes only products made in California. Prior to 1987 exports included all products shipped through California's ports.
18.27,90 Source: Security Pacific National Bank, International Trade Databank, and *Economic Report of the Governor.*

CALIFORNIA FOREIGN TRADE, 1960-1987 (in millions)

Year	Imports*	Exports*	Foreign Trade Deficit
1960	$1,250	$1,388	-$138
1965	1,916	1,519	397
1970	4,408	4,245	163
1975	11,715	10,340	1,375
1976	15,300	11,525	-3,775
1977	19,113	12,186	-6,927
1978	21,496	14,934	-6,562
1979	24,929	20,303	-4,626
1980	29,414	26,794	-2,619
1981	31,690	29,990	-1,700
1982	32,583	29,120	-3,463
1983	37,900	29,400	-8,500
1984	49,270	32,203	-17,067
1985	61,600	32,400	-29,200
1986	69,900	32,800	-37,000
1987	78,500	39,700	-38,800

* Imports to and Exports from the U.S. through California Customs Districts. These numbers exaggerate actual California imports and exports.
18.28,90 Source: Security Pacific National Bank, International Trade Databank, and *Economic Report of the Governor.*

MAJOR CALIFORNIA IMPORTS AND EXPORTS, 1985 and 1987
Imports Into California

Product	Value (billions)		
	1987	1986	1985
Electrical Machinery and Equipment	$18.1	$16.7	$15.5
Motor Vehicles and Equipment	$14.5	$13.3	$10.9
Machinery and Mechanical Equipment	$4.6	$4.3	$3.9
Office Machines & Computers	$9.6	$7.6	$5.1
Wearing Apparel	$4.8	$4.2	$3.6
Petroleum & Natural Gas	$1.0	$1.0	$1.6
Opticals, Scientific Instruments & Photographic Equipment	$2.5	$2.5	$1.9
Rubber & Plastics, Sporting Goods, Office Supplies & Jewelry	$5.7	$4.8	$3.9
Other	$27.3	$23.1	$20.3
Total Imports	**$78.5**	**$69.9**	**$61.6**

Exports from California

Product	Value (in billions)
	1987
Machinery and Mechanical Equipment	$7.0
Electrical Machinery and Equipment	$6.6
Aircraft and Spacecraft	$3.5
Opticals, Scientific Instruments & Photographic Equipment	$1.9
Food Crops & Meat	$1.4
Food Products	$1.2
Chemicals	$1.1
Other	$5.1
Total Exports	**$27.8**

Note: Import data is based on all shipments through California customs districts and is considerably higher than actual imports into California. Exports reflect accurate state of origin data.

18.29,90 Source: Security Pacific National Bank, *International Trade Databank* and *Economic Report of the Governor*.

SECTION 18 NOTE

The state of California now has trade and investment offices in Tokyo, London, and Mexico City to help California businesses sell their products abroad and to help foreigners invest in California.

18.30,90

ANNUAL VALUE OF DIRECT FOREIGN INVESTMENTS OF PLANT, PROPERTY AND EQUIPMENT CALIFORNIA, OTHER STATES, AND THE U.S. INVESTMENT BY STATES
(Billions of Dollars)

Year	California	New York	Texas	Ohio	Illinois	California as a % of U.S.
1982	$2.1	$1.9	$2.6	$0.3	$0.7	15%
1983	$2.3	$1.5	$0.8	$0.1	$0.1	23%
1984	$3.8	$1.1	$2.2	$0.7	$0.8	17%
1985	$6.2	$1.0	$3.0	$0.5	$1.9	30%
1986	$3.3	$11.7	$3.7	$1.2	$1.9	9%
1987	$5.3	$14.1	$1.0	$10.2	$1.6	9%

18.31,90 Source: U.S. Dept. of Commerce, International Trade Administration, *Foreign Direct Investment in the U.S., Annual Report.*

VALUE OF PROPERTY, PLANT, AND EQUIPMENT HELD BY FOREIGN - OWNED FIRMS

Country	Number of Affiliates with Property, Plant & Equipment in California		Gross Book Value of Property, Plant, & Equipment in California	
	Number	% of U.S.	$Million	% of U.S.
Canada	243	18.4	5,977	8.2
Europe	1,048	20.8	19,884	11.2
France	122	25.3	900	5.0
Germany	174	13.3	1,228	5.5
Netherlands	70	15.8	NA	NA
United Kingdom	337	31.0	4,655	7.8
Japan	459	50.9	5,261	23.6
Australia, New Zealand	55	39.6	672	6.9
Latin America	129	11.8	1,242	11.1
Middle East	115	21.4	1,985	15.7
Other - Africa, Asia, and Pacific	279	49.1	1,898	18.3
Total	**2,341**	**24.2%**	**37,017**	**11.6%**

18.32,90 Source: U.S. Bureau of Economic analysis, *Foreign Direct Investment in the United States, Operations of U.S. Affiliates, of Foreign Companies, Preliminary 1986 estimates.*

SECTION 18 NOTE

According to a Dun and Bradstreet study, 460,400 companies in California have fewer than 10 employees.

18.33,90

DIRECT FOREIGN INVESTMENTS OF PLANT, PROPERTY AND EQUIPMENT IN CALIFORNIA AND THE U.S.		
Year	Number of Investments California	Percent of Total U.S. Investments
1976	31	16%
1977	27	6
1978	103	15
1979	134	13
1980	184	15
1981	149	12
1982	120	13
1983	114	15
1984	155	17
1985	147	16
1986	178	17
1987	244	18
Total	**1,586**	**15%**

18.34,90 Source: U.S. Bureau of Economic Analysis, *Foreign Direct Investment in the United States, Operations of U.S. Affiliates of Foreign Companies, 1984 Preliminary Estimates*, and Dept. of Commerce, International Trade Administration, *Direct Foreign Investment in the U.S., 1988*.

EMPLOYEES WORKING IN CALIFORNIA FOR FOREIGN-OWNED FIRMS		
Country	Employment in California	
	Number of Jobs	Percent of U.S.
Canada	33,907	5.6
Europe	149,629	8.3
France	16,707	8.7
Germany	20,141	6.6
Netherlands	24,793	9.6
United Kingdom	53,029	8.3
Japan	60,044*	27.7
Australia, New Zealand	12,828	15.0
Latin America	12,336	9.3
Middle East	5,831	11.8
Other - Africa, Asia, and Pacific	7,754	20.7
Total	**284,496**	**9.6%**

* According to the Japan Business Association of California, Japanese companies in California employed 77,610 workers in 1987.

Note: 48% of the employment in foreign-owned firms in California is in manufacturing.

18.35,90 Source: U.S. Bureau of Economic Analysis, *Foreign Direct Investment in the United States, Operations of U.S. Affiliates of Foreign Companies, 1986 Preliminary Estimates*.

TOP FIVE STATES IN THE U.S. IN VALUE OF PROPERTY, PLANT AND EQUIPMENT OF FOREIGN-OWNED FIRMS		
State	Value of Investment (Billions)	Percent of Foreign Investment in U.S.
Texas	$40.3	13
California	**$37.0**	**12**
New York	$18.0	6
Alaska	$15.1	5
Louisiana	$13.6	4

* 24% of the Foreign Investment in California is in manufacturing plant and equipment and 28% is in real estate.

18.36,90 Source: U.S. Department of Commerce, Bureau of Economic Analysis, *Foreign Direct Investment in the United States, Operations of U.S. Affiliates of Foreign Companies, Preliminary 1986 Estimates.*

SECTION 18 NOTE
Until 1987, the only export-import data available for California included all the U.S. trade handled by California's customs districts. These data which did not indicate the state of origin for exports, exaggerated the dollar amount of the state's trade. The actual value of California's exports in 1987, for example, was $27.8 billion, not $39.7 billion, a figure that includes all shipments through the state.

18.37,90

FASTEST GROWING COMPANIES IN THE UNITED STATES, 1982-1988				
Rank	State	Number of Companies 1982-86	Rank	Number of Companies 1988
1	California	28	1	27
2	New York	11	4	5
3	Massachusetts	9	3	9
4	Texas	8	4	5
5	Florida	6	2	10

The fastest growing California companies tend to be in electronics, biotechnology, or medical technology.

18.38,90 Source: *INC. Magazine.*

Communications and Media

California as the nation's publishing capital? No, it hasn't happened yet. The Golden State is unlikely to displace New York as the country's leader in publishing, but California is the home of the magazine with the second largest circulation in the country as of 1988: *Modern Maturity,* with a circulation of 15.8 million,is published in Lakewood (Los Angeles County). And in the past few years some of the East Coast's publishing giants such as the *Wall Street Journal* and the *New York Times* have entered the California market with West Coast editions printed in California.

On a far less exalted plane, California is also home to Larry Flynt's magazine *Hustler*, although its high-flying days seem long past.

Every year several new magazines make their debut. One of the more interesting California start-ups is *Trips,* the San Francisco-based travel magazine that was started by one of the founders of the Banana Republic chain of stores.

California built its reputation as the nation's communications center on the movie and television entertainment industry, which has its home in the state. Back in the 1920s, Hollywood produced 90 percent of the world's movies, and moviemaking was the nation's fifth largest industry. Although that kind of world monopoly has ended, California is still the leading movie-producing state in the country, responsible for 211 out of the 383 films made in the United States in 1988. This dominance has stirred up the fast-track merger-and-acquisitions crowd, attracting buyers for successful Hollywood companies from New York and around the world. In 1989 Warner Communications merged with Lorimar television production and again just a few months later with Time, Inc., to create the largest media and entertainment conglomerate in the world. Eager to get into the tinsel-town profit picture, Australian interests bought MGM-United Artists and 20th-Century Fox, the British picked up Mary Tyler Moore (MTM) Entertainment, and the Italians acquired one of the top ten movie producers, Cannon. As the merger and buy-out dust settles, a new picture of a media industry increasingly controlled by diversified communications giants emerges. No seer has yet predicted how these radical changes will affect California's traditionally predominant role in the U.S. entertainment business.

		Newsstands and	
Year	Bookstores	News Dealers	Total
Number			
1972	1,107	NA	NA
1977	1,714	515	2,229
1981	1,009	146	1,155
1982	1,160	168	1,328
1984	1,286	130	1,416
1986	1,296	127	1,423
Annual Sales (in millions)			
1972	$146.0	NA	NA
1977	$266.0	$43	$310
Annual Payroll (in millions)			
1982	$65.3	$6.8	$72.2
1984	$83.2	$5.7	$89.0
1986	$96.2	$7.2	$103.4
Employees			
1986	11,689	825	12,514

NUMBER, SALES, AND ANNUAL PAYROLL OF BOOKSTORES, NEWS DEALERS AND NEWSSTANDS IN CALIFORNIA, SELECTED YEARS

19.1,90 Source: U.S. Bureau of the Census, *Census of Retail Trade*, 1972 and 1977; U.S. Bureau of the Census, *County Business Patterns, California*.

CALIFORNIA NEWSPAPERS* AND THEIR CIRCULATION

	1970		1981		1986		1988	
	Number	Percent of U.S. Total	Number	Percent of U.S. Total	Number	Percent of U.S. Total	Number	Percent of U.S. Total
Morning Dailies	22	7%	29	7%	42	9%	47	9%
Evening Dailies	104	7%	95	7%	76	6%	73	6%
Total Daily Papers	126	7%	124	7%	115	7%	118	7%
Sunday Papers	38	6%	50	7%	59	7%	61	7%
Circulation (millions)†								
Morning Dailies	2.4	9%	3.4	11%	4.2*	12%	4.7	12%
Evening Dailies	3.3	9%	2.7	8%	1.9*	7%	1.7	7%
Total Daily Circulation	5.7	9%	6.0	10%	6.1*	10%	6.4	10%
Sunday	4.8	10%	5.6	10%	6.0	10%	6.3	11%

† As of September 30, 1987.
* There is an additional daily circulation of 1,100,000 from AM papers with PM editions and PM papers with AM editions.
Note: California has 112 college and university papers.
19.2,90 Source: *Editor and Publisher Yearbooks*. Used by permission.

Circulation*	Newspaper	Circulation	Newspaper
	CALIFORNIA DAILY NEWSPAPERS		
7,040	Alameda Times Star	9,070	Oroville Mercury Register
6,620	Anaheim Bulletin	13,715	Oxnard Press Courier
58,423	Antelope Valley Press	38,539	Palm Springs Desert Sun
15,211	Anitoch Daily Ledger	47,982	Palo Alto Peninsula Times Trib.
12,765	Auburn Journal	37,825	Pasadena Star News
82,248	Bakersfiled Californian	5,588	Paso Robles Daily Press
3,500	Banning Record Gazette	9,707	Petaluma Argus-Courier
8,100	Barstow Desert Dispatch	6,577	Pittsburg Post-Dispatch
5,629	Brawley News	37,464	Pomona Progress Bulletin
	Burbank Daily Review	13,744	Porterville Recorder
10,690	Camarillo Daily News	8,573	Red Bluff Daily News
28,435	Chico Enterprise Record	36,655	Redding Record Searchlight
3,322	Colusa Sun-Herald	10,212	Redlands Daily Facts
30,000	Contra costa Independent	8,000	Ridgecrest Daily Independent
85,945	Contra Costa Times	140,941	Riverside Press-Enterprise
2,300	Corning Daily Observer	15,200	Roseville Press Tribune
6,500	Corona Daily Indpendent	251,120	Sacramento Bee
	Daily Bruin	83,272	Sacramento Union
	Daily Californian	23,473	Salinas Californian
	Daily Nexus	86,316	San Bernardino Sun
10,300	Davis Daily Enterprise	8,494	San Clemente Daily Sun-Post
	Downey Southeast News	8,930	San Diego Transcript
	& Champion	122,094	San Diego Tribune
20,567	El Cajon Daily Californian	269,190	San Diego Union
11,427	El Centro Imperial Valley Press	556,196	San Francisco Chronicle
43,820	Escondido Times Advocate	135,444	San Francisco Examiner
21,945	Eureka Times Standard	5,500	San Francisco Recorder
19,963	Fairfield Daily Republic	59,877	San Gabriel Valley Daily Trib.
3,600	Fontana Herald News	277,010	San Jose Mercury News
29,565	Fremont Argus	31,323	San Luis Obispo Telegram Trib.
144,384	Fresno Bee	44,506	San Mateo Times
41,519	Fullerton Daily News Tribune	15,544	San Pedro News Pilot
	Gilroy Dispatch	51,750	Santa Barbara News Press
21,170	Glendale News Press	27,387	Santa Cruz Sentinel
15,218	Grass Valley Union	20,256	Santa Maria Times
14,270	Hanford Sentinel		Santa Monica Evening Outlook
45,160	Hayward Daily Review		Santa Paula Daily Chronicle
	Hement News	84,736	Santa Rosa Press Democrat
5,276†	Hollister Evening Free Lance	16,498	Simi Valley Enterprise
22,136	Hollywood Reporter		Sonora Union Democrat
7,405	Indio Daily News	54,456	Stockton Record
5,025	La Habra-Brea Daily Star Progress		Taft Daily Midway Driller
16,169	Lodi News-Sentinel	12,519	Tahoe Daily Tibune
9,609	Lompoc Record	23,619	Thousand Oaks News Chronicle
129,457	Long Beach Press		Torrance Daily Breeze
21,000	Los Angeles Daily Journal	8,847	Tracy Press
183,402	Los Angeles Daily News	31,243	Tri-Valley Herald (Dublin)
238,392	Los Angeles Herald Examiner	9,378	Tulare Advance-Register
97,810	Los Angeles Investor's Daily	10,055	Turlock Daily Jounral
87,552	La Opinion	9,826	Ukiah Daily Journal
1,119,840	Los Angeles Times	16,314	Vacaville Reporter
8,764	Madera Daily Tribune	27,315	Vallejo Times Herald
37,588	Marin County Independent Journal	22,632	Variety
15,000	Martinez News Gazette	49,333	Ventura County Star-Free Press
24,255	Merced Sun-Star	25,797	Victor Valley Daily Press
79,058	Modesto Bee	22,594	Visalia Times-Delta
34,047	Monterey Peninsula Herald	8,200	Visa Morning Press
20,775	Napa Register	402,317	Wall Street Journal
142,456	Oakland Tribune	14,436	Watsonville Register-Pajornian
35,610	Oceanside Blade-Tribune	33,295	West County Times
45,926	Ontario Daily Report	17,253	Whittier Daily News
17,402	Orange Coast Daily Pilot	2,392	Willows Journal
	Orange County Bulletin	11,501	Woodland Daily Democrat
344,965	Orange County Register	6,000	Yreka-Siskiyou Daily News
2,136	Orland Press Register	25,020	Yuba-Sutter Appeal Democrat

* Total weekday circulation.   † As of 3/31/87.
19.3,90 Source: California Newspaper Asso. & Pacific Data Resources; Circulation: Audit Bureau of Circulations' *FAS-FAX Report*, Mar. 31, 1989 and National Research Bureau, *The Working Press of the Nation, 1989.*

\multicolumn{4}{c}{**TOP FOURTEEN CALIFORNIA NEWSPAPERS**}			
Rank	**Newspaper**	**Circulation (thousands)**	**National Rank**
1	Los Angeles Times	1,113	4
2	San Francisco Chronicle	568	13
3	Orange County Register	317	25
4	San Jose Mercury-News	269	34
5	San Diego Union	251	38
6	Sacramento Bee	242	40
7	Los Angeles Herald-Examiner	239	41
8	Los Angeles Daily News	159	68
9	Oakland Tribune	148	75
10	San Francisco Examiner	144	78
11	Fresno Bee	140	79
12	Riverside Press-Enterprise	138	84
13	Long Beach Press-Telegram	126	89
14	San Diego Tribune	123	93

19.4,90 Source: *Editor and Publisher International Yearbook*, 1988. Used by permission.

\multicolumn{6}{c}{**NUMBER OF PUBLISHERS IN CALIFORNIA**}					
	1970	**1980**	**1982**	**1984**	**1986**
Books	138	263	354	386	315
Periodicals	272	386	401	452	492
Newspapers	506	631	633	699	793
Miscellaneous	184	237	258	284	276
Total	**1,100**	**1,517**	**1,646**	**1,821**	**1,876**

19.5,90 Source: U.S. Bureau of the Census, *County Business Patterns.*

\multicolumn{2}{c}{**NUMBER OF OUTDOOR ADVERTISING BUSINESSES IN CALIFORNIA 1975-1986**}	
Year	**Number**
1975	65
1980	58
1981	64
1982	79
1984	82
1986	72

19.6,90 Source: U.S. Bureau of the Census, *County Business Patterns, California.*

NUMBER, SALES, AND ANNUAL PAYROLL OF RADIO AND TELEVISION AND RECORD STORES IN CALIFORNIA, SELECTED YEARS			
Year	Radio and Television Stores	Independent Music Stores	Total
Number			
1972	NA	NA	3,262
1977	2,623	1,650	4,273
1981	1,743	1,110	2,853
1982	2,157	1,119	3,276
1984	2,817	1,121	3,938
1986	3,119	1,198	4,317
Annual Sales (in thousands)			
1972	NA	NA	$571,978
1977	$797,007	$435,033	$1,232,040
Annual Payroll (in thousands)			
1982	NA	$69,498	NA
1984	$290,212	$83,902	$374,114
1986	$381,152	$107,880	$489,032
Employment			
1986	21,925	10,569	32,494

19.7,90 Source: U.S. Bureau of the Census, *Census of Retail Trade*, 1972 and 1977; U.S. Bureau of the Census, *Country Business Patterns, California.*

NUMBER OF COMMERCIAL RADIO STATIONS IN CALIFORNIA				
Year	AM Stations	FM Stations	National Public Radio	Total
1970	NA	NA	NA	**315**
1980	NA	NA	NA	**456**
1984	238	286	14*	**524**
1986	253	364	15*	**617**
1989	276	410	16*	**686**

* Counted in the AM/FM totals.
19.8,90 Source: U.S. Federal Communications Commission, *AM/FM Financial Data,* 1980; FCC Annual Reports, California Broadcasters' Association, *Broadcasting, Cable Yearbook.* For a comprehensive listing of TV and radio stations, frequencies, format and ownership see *The Working Press of the Nation,* published by the National Research Bureau.

SECTION 19 NOTE
KCBS in San Francisco claims to be the world's first broadcasting station. Its call letters when it began service in 1909 were FN.

19.9,90

NUMBER OF TELEVISION STATIONS IN CALIFORNIA

Year	Commerical Stations	Public Stations	Total
1975	52	13	65
1983	55	13	68
1985	61	14	75
1987	67	14	81
1989	75	16	91

19.10,90 Source: Newspaper television listings.

NATIONAL PUBLIC RADIO STATIONS

City	Station	Frequency
Arcata	KHSU(FM)	90.5
Bakersfield	KPRX(FM)	89.1
Chico	KCHO(FM)	91.1
Fresno	KVPR(FM)	89.3
Northridge	KCSN(FM)	88.5
Pasadena	KPCC(FM)	89.3
Sacramento	KXPR(FM)	90.9
San Bernardino	KVCR(FM)	91.9
San Diego	KPBS(FM)	89.5
San Francisco	KALW(FM)	91.7
San Francisco	KQED(FM)	88.5
San Luis Obispo	KCBX(FM)	90.1
San Mateo	KCSM(FM)	91.1
Santa Cruz	KUSP(FM)	88.9
Santa Monica	KCRW(FM)	89.9
Stockton	KUOP(FM)	91.3

19.11,90 Source: National Public Radio, *Member Stations*, 1988.

CABLE/SUBSCRIPTION TELEVISION IN CALIFORNIA
1978-1989

Year	Number of Companies	Number of Communities Served	Number of Subscribers	Total Revenues	Average Monthly Subscription Charge
1978	168	479	1,700,764	$33,504,972	$7.34
1980	174	462	2,952,052	$73,719,339	$8.10
1985	75	900	3,400,000	$500,000,000	$9.35
1987	77	990	4,000,000	$900,000,000	$14.00
1989	80	1,152	4,500,000	$1,000,000,000	$15.50

19.12,90 Source: U.S. Federal Communications Commission, *Annual Report*, FY 1979 and 1981; California Cable Television Association, 1989.

CALIFORNIA TELEVISION STATIONS, 1989

City and Station	Broadcast Channel	Network Affiliation	City and Station	Broadcast Channel	Network Affiliation
Anaheim			**Riverside**		
KDOC	56	IND	KSLD	62	E
Arcata			**Rohnert Park**		
KREQ	23	FOX	KRCB	22	D
Bakersfield			**Sacramento**		
KGET	17	NBC	KCRA	3	NBC
KERO	23	CBS	KVIE	6	E
KBAK	29	ABC	KXTV	10	CBS
Barstow			KOVR	13	ABC
KVVT	64	IND	KRBK	31	IND
Chico			KXTL	40	FOX
KHSL	12	CBS	**Salinas**		
KCPM	24	NBC	KSBW	8	NBC
Concord			KCBA	35	FOX
KFCB	42	IND	**San Bernardino**		
El Centro			KSCI	18	IND
KECY	9	CBS	KVCR	24	IND
Eureka			KAGL	30	E
KIEM	3	NBC	**San Diego**		
KVIQ	6	CBS	KETV	6	IND
KEET	13	E	KFMB	8	CBS
Fresno			KGTV	10	ABC
KMTF	18	E	KPBS	15	E
KSEE	24	NBC	KNSD	39	NBC
KFSN	30	ABC	KUSI	51	IND
KJEO	47	CBS	KTTY	69	IND
KAIL	53	IND	**San Francisco**		
Hanford			KRON	4	NBC
KFTV	21	SIN	KPIX	5	CBS
Huntington Beach			KGO	7	ABC
KOCE	50	E	KQED	9	E
Los Angeles			KDTV	14	SIN
KCBS	2	CBS	KOFY	20	IND
KNBC	4	NBC	KTSF	26	IND
KTLA	5	IND	KQEC	32	E
KABC	7	ABC	KWBB	38	IND
KHJ	9	IND	KBHK	44	IND
KTTV	11	FOX	**San Jose**		
KCOP	13	IND	KNTV	11	ABC
KWHY	22	IND	KICU	36	IND
KCET	28	E	KSTS	48	IND
KMEX	34	IND	KTEH	54	E
KVEA	52	IND	KLXV	65	IND
KLCS	58	E	**San Luis Obispo**		
KEEF	68	IND	KSBY	6	NBC
Modesto			**San Mateo**		
KCSO	19	SIN	KCSM	60	E
Monterey			**Sanger**		
KMST	46	CBS	KMSG	59	IND
KSMS	67	IND	**Santa Ana**		
Oakland			KTBN	40	IND
KTVU	2	FOX	**Santa Barbara**		
Oildale			KEYT	3	ABC
KDOB	45	IND	**Santa Maria**		
Ontario			KCOY	12	CBS
KHSC	46	IND	**Santa Rosa**		
Oxnard			KFTY	50	IND
KADY	63	IND	**Stockton**		
Palm Springs			KITL	64	IND
KMIR	36	NBC	**Vallejo**		
KESQ	42	ABC	KPST	66	IND
Redding			**Visalia**		
KRCR	7	ABC	KMPH	26	IND
KIXE	9	E	KNXT	49	E

Note: "E" is a Public or Educational TV Station.
19.13,90 Source: Newspaper station listings.

AVERAGE DAILY TIME SPENT WATCHING TELEVISION BY CALIFORNIANS

Time Watching TV	Percent of Californians
Less than 1 hour	11%
1 to 1.9 hours	16%
2 to 2.9 hours	26%
3 to 3.9 hours	20%
4 to 4.9 hours	12%
5 to 5.9 hours	7%
6 to 6.9 hours	4%
Over 7 hours	4%

19.14,90 Source: The California Poll, 1986.

NUMBER OF CALIFORNIA HOUSEHOLDS WITH TELEVISION SETS BY METROPOLITAN AREA
1988-89

California Rank	U.S. Rank	ADI Area*	Number of Households with T.V.	% of Cal. Households	% of U.S. Households
1	2	Los Angeles	4,807,700	47.7%	5.34%
2	5	San Francisco	2,164,100	21.5%	2.40%
3	21	Sacramento-Stockton	957,400	9.5%	1.06%
4	24	San Diego	836,300	8.3%	0.93%
5	62	Fresno-Visalia	419,900	4.2%	0.47%
6	111	Salinas-Monterey	205,600	2.0%	0.23%
7	112	Santa Barbara-Santa Maria-San Luis Obispo	202,000	2.0%	0.22%
8	143	Chico-Redding	150,600	1.5%	0.17%
9	145	Bakersfield	149,900	1.5%	0.17%
10	178	Palm Springs	66,200	0.7%	0.07%
11	181	El Centro-Yuma	62,500	0.6%	0.07%
12	187	Eureka	51,400	0.5%	0.06%
		Total	10,073,600	100.0%	11.19%

* ADI is the "Area of Dominant Influence" for home market commercial stations and satellite stations.

19.15,90 Source: Arbitron Ratings Company, *Arbitron Ratings-Television*, 1988-1989, Ethnic Population Book.

SECTION 19 NOTE

According to Survey Sampling of Fairfield, Connecticut, eight of the ten U.S. metropolitan areas with the largest percentages of unlisted phones are in California. In the L.A.-Long Beach area, 56 percent of phone numbers are unlisted, in Oakland 54 percent, in Fresno 53 percent, in San Jose 51 percent, in Sacramento 50 percent, in Riverside-San Bernardino 49 percent, in Bakersfield 49 percent, and in San Francisco 48 percent.

19.16,90

CABLE TV AND VCR (VIDEO CASSETTE RECORDER) PENETRATION BY CALIFORNIA MARKET, 1989				
Market	Number of Cable TV Households	% of Households with Cable	Number of Households with VCR	% of Households with VCR
Los Angeles	2,160,300	45%	3,380,300	70%
San Francisco	1,226,200	57%	1,653,800	76%
Sacramento-Stockton	471,200	49%	711,300	74%
San Diego	595,300	71%	632,600	76%
Fresno-Visalia	180,100	43%	303,200	72%
Salinas-Monterey	159,000	77%	158,000	77%
Santa Barbara-Santa Maria-San Luis Obispo	177,500	88%	146,900	73%
Chico-Redding	89,300	59%	95,500	63%
Bakersfield	110,700	74%	103,500	69%
Palm Springs	57,700	87%	47,900	72%
El Centro-Yuma	46,400	74%	40,900	65%
Eureka	41,700	81%	35,200	68%

19.17,90 Source: The Arbitron Company, Arbitron Feb. *1989 Cable Penetration Estimates and Feb. 1989 VCR Penetration Estimates* (used by permission).

NUMBER OF RECORD COMPANIES IN CALIFORNIA, 1986		
Number	Number of Employees	Annual Payroll (in millions)
122	2,525	$69

19.18, 90 Source: U.S. Bureau of the Census, *County Business Patterns, California. 1986.*

ADVERTISING AGENCIES IN CALIFORNIA Total Number, Employees, and Payroll, 1986		
Number	Number of Employees	Annual Payroll (millions)
1,116	13,113	$418

19.19,90 Source: U.S. Bureau of the Census, *County Business Patterns, California.*

U.S. FILM INDUSTRY REVENUES, 1987 ($ in millions)			
	U.S.	California	California as a % of U.S.
Feature Films	$3,934	$2,630	67%
Television Shows	$1,592	$1,393	88%
TV Commericals	$2,049	$650	32%
Total	$7,574	$4,673	62%

Note: According to the California Film Commission, approximately 118,000 people are directly employed in the state's film industry and another 116,000 receive indirect employment. 19.20,90 Source: Cal. Film Comm., *Economic Impact Study of the Film Industry in California, 1988.*

NUMBER, EMPLOYMENT, AND ANNUAL PAYROLL OF MOTION PICTURE COMPANIES IN CALIFORNIA, 1986			
Type	Number of Establishments	Number of Employees	Annual Payroll (in Millions)
Motion Picture Production			
For T.V.	955	23,377	$771
Except T.V.	569	34,101	$620
Allied Services	1,433	33,969	$811
Motion Picture Distribution			
Film Exchanges	136	3,876	$187
TV Film or Tape Distribution	82	1,818	$102
Allied Services	48	335	$310
Total*	**3,223**	**97,480**	**$2,501**

* Total includes other related employment, establishments, and payroll.

19.21, 90 Source: U.S. Census, *County Business Patterns, California, 1986.*

TOP FILM COMPANIES IN CALIFORNIA, 1988			
Rank	Company	Number of Pictures	Market Share (percent)
1	Buena Vista (Disney)	18	19.4%
2	Paramount	19	15.2%
3	Fox	14	11.6%
4	Warner Brothers	31	11.2%
5	MGM/UA	21	10.3%
6	Universal	20	9.8%
7	Orion	20	6.6%
8	Tri-Star	17	5.8%
9	Columbia	19	3.5%
10	New Line	10	1.9%
11	Cannon	17	1.1%
12	Vestron	18	0.7%

19.22,90 Source: *Variety* Jan. 25-31, 1989.

FEATURE FILMS MADE IN CALIFORNIA AND RIVAL STATES				
	Number of Films			
	1985	1986	1987	1988
California	**95**	**161**	**190**	**211**
New York	NA	62	65	62
North Carolina	NA	14	14	11
Texas	NA	12	11	11
Florida	NA	NA	15	17
New Jersey	NA	NA	5	12
Total	**NA**	**NA**	**360**	**383**

19.23,90 Source: California Government Film Office, *Year End Report.*

Energy

California's long-term energy picture is cloudy. The state's internal production of oil and natural gas is declining, making us more dependent on Alaskan and foreign oil supplies. After the huge oil spill off the Alaska coast in 1988 the reliability of the flow of oil from Alaska was called into question.

California's indeterminate quantities of offshore oil and gas, which could help to bridge the energy gap until more nonfossil-fuel sources of energy become available, may never be fully exploited because of intense opposition from the state's potent environmental lobby. While the state's demand for energy increases substantially each year, environmentalists mount fierce, effective opposition to virtually any method of producing energy. They oppose new generating plants that use nuclear and fossil-fuel energy and campaign against even the more benign sources of energy, such as hydroelectricity. Environmentalists and anglers along with local NIMBYs (who want development, perhaps, but "Not in My Backyard") have spent years fighting off or delaying geothermal projects to produce electricity in Mono County and in the Geysers area of Sonoma and Lake counties.

What has saved the day for California is that other states in the West and our Canadian neighbors have large natural gas and electricity surpluses and are happy to sell those surpluses to the state.

One bright innovation in California energy production is the anticipated construction of a $125-million solar power plant near Palmdale. This privately developed photovoltaic facility will be seven times larger than the largest solar plant now in existence. It will produce fifty megawatts of power, one-twentieth of the power of a nuclear plant, and will supply the electricity needs of 25,000 homes.

California has not made a maximum commitment to energy conservation to reduce the demand for energy itself. Millions of houses and businesses are still poorly insulated and use energy-wasting appliances and equipment. Significant energy savings could be achieved, however, if public entities, business, and individuals make a concerted effort.

MAJOR SOURCES OF CALIFORNIA ENERGY, 1986

Source	Trillion BTU's	Percent of Total Energy
Petroleum	3,709	56.5%
Natural Gas	1,679	25.6%
Hydropower	422	6.4%
Nuclear	297	4.5%
Geothermal	210	3.2%
Coal	195	3.0%
Total	**6,562**	**100%**

20.1,90 Source: Cal. Energy Commission, *Biennial Fuels Report Appendices, 1987*.

MAJOR USES OF CALIFORNIA ENERGY, 1986

Use	Trillion BTU's	Percent of Total Energy
Transportation	2,810	49.8%
Commercial	487	8.6%
Residential	699	12.4%
Industrial and Other Uses	1,643	29.1%
Total	**5,639**	**100%**

20.2,90   Source: California Energy Commission, *Biennial Fuels Report Appendices, 1987*.

SOURCES OF ENERGY BY SECTOR OF THE CALIFORNIA ECONOMY, 1986

Source	Industrial and Commercial	Residential	Transportation
Petroleum	41%	3%	100%*
Natural Gas	36%	68%	-
Electricity	22%	29%	-
Coal	1%	-	-
Total	**100%**	**100%**	**100%**

*   Transportation receives a negligible amount of energy from other sources.
   20.3,90 Source: California Energy Commission, *Biennial Report 1987*.

SECTION 20 NOTE

California has over 16,000 electricity-generating windmills.
20.4,90

LARGEST ENERGY-CONSUMING STATES
RANKED BY CONSUMPTION
1980-1986

		Fuel and Electrical Energy Consumption (trillion BTU)						
	1980		1982		1984		1986	
State	Rank	Con-sumption	Rank	Con-sumption	Rank	Con-sumption	Rank	Con-sumption
Texas	1	8,432	1	7,971	1	8,685	1	8,780
California	2	6,433	2	5,913	2	6,322	2	6,471
Pennsylvania	3	3,918	-		-		-	
Ohio	4	3,864	3	3,549	4	3,630	3	3,553
New York	5	3,856	4	3,456	5	3,485	4	3,397
Illinois	-	3,789	5	3,337	3	3,660	5	3,357
Largest Five States	26,500		24,226		25,782		25,558	
Total United States	75,944		70,756		74,045		74,255	

20.5,90 Source: *U.S. Statistical Abstract, 1987.* Although California is the number two state, nationally, in energy consumption, it is a very low per capita energy-using state, ranking 42 of the 50 states.

CALIFORNIA ELECTRICITY GENERATION

Year	Installed Capacity million kw	Percent of U.S. Capacity	Production billion kw	Percent U.S. Production	Sales billion kw	Percent of U.S. Sales
1970	28.5	7.9%	123.8	7.6%	118.6	8.5%
1975	33.7	6.6%	125.4	6.5%	143.4	8.3%
1978	37.1	6.2%	139.9	6.1%	160.0	7.9%
1979	37.5	6.3%	152.0	6.8%	167.3	8.0%
1980	37.8	6.2%	140.3	6.1%	164.9	7.9%
1982	38.8	5.8%	118.3	5.3%	165.8	7.9%
1983	39.8	6.0%	117.7	5.1%	165.2	7.7%
1984	41.9	6.2%	121.1	5.0%	175.1	7.7%
1985	45.1	6.5%	127.8	5.2%	178.8	7.7%
1986	45.0	6.4%	121.9	4.9%	184.6	7.9%
1987	45.4	6.3%	130.3	5.1%	190.3	7.8%

20.6,90 Source: *U.S. Statistical Abstract* and U.S. Energy Info. Admin., *Electric Power Annual and Electric Power Monthly.*

CALIFORNIA INVESTOR-OWNED UTILITIES
RATES & NATIONAL RANKING

	Rate (cents per k/wh)	Nat. Rank Among Most Expensive in U.S.
P.G.&E.	9.08¢	24th
SCE	8.78¢	29th
SDG&E	11.17¢	8th
National Average	6.90¢	

P.G.& E. - Pacific Gas and Electricity; SCE - Southern California Edison; SDG&E- San Diego Gas and Electric

20.7,90 Source: *Energy Users News, 1/11/88.*

CALIFORNIA ELECTRICITY GENERATING POWER PLANTS, 1986 Number of Plants and Capacity (in Megawatts)				
	Operational	Under Construction	Proposed	Total
Oil and Gas	241(26,531)	18(646)	92(4,430)	351(31,606)
Hydroelectric	305(11,782)	*	160(1,084)	465(12,866)
Coal	2(160)	0	1(100)	3(260)
Nuclear	3(5,280)	0	0	3(5,280)
Cogeneration	227(2,110)	23(685)	144(5,462)	394(8,257)
Geothermal	28(1,817)	7(550)	18(506)	53(2,873)
Wind	88(710)	38(943)	101(2,106)	227(3,759)
Biomass and Waste	84(574)	22(376)	112(1,954)	218(2,903)
Solar	15(121)	4(46)	5(199)	24(366)
Total†	769(47,067)	90(2,578)	502(10,714)	1,361(60,360)

* Included in Operational category.
† Cogeneration data included in Oil and Gas or Biomass totals.
  20.8,90 Source: Cal Energy Commission, *1986 Electricity Report.*

MAJOR SOURCES OF CALIFORNIA ELECTRICITY, 1987		
Source	Trillion BTU	Percent of Total
Natural Gas	431	24%
Hydropower	260	14%
Coal	398	22%
Nuclear	359	20%
Geothermal	265	15%
Heavy Oil	0	0%
Distillate	2	*
Wind	6	*
Biomass	73	4%
Solar	6	*
Total	1,800	100%

* Less than 1%.
  Hydropower's contribution to electricity generation varies greatly depending on season and rainfall.
  20.9,90 Source: California Energy Commission, *Electricity Report, 1988.*

MAJOR USES OF CALIFORNIA ELECTRICITY, 1987		
Use	Trillion BTU	Percent of Total
Conversion Loss	1,085	60%
Transmission Loss	50	3%
Commercial	230	13%
Residential	206	11%
Industruial and Other Uses	229	13%
Total	1,800	100%

20.10,90 Source: California Energy Commission, *Electricity Report, 1988.*

NUCLEAR POWER 1988		
	Percent of Electricity from Nuclear Plants	Nuclear Reactors in Operation
California	20%	5
United States	18%	107

Note: California has six nuclear power plants at three locations. The Rancho Seco plant near Sacramento has been plagued with severe operating problems and was permanently shut down by a vote of the residents of the utility district.
20.11,90 Source: *U.S. Statistical Abstract*, Cal Energy Commission unpublished data.

LIKELY ELECTRICITY GENERATING CAPACITY 1997	
Energy Source	Percent of Capacity*
Oil and Natural Gas†	39%
Hydropower	17%
Nuclear	12%
Out-of-State Purchases	9%
Cogeneration	8%
Coal	7%
Geothermal	4%
Wind, Biomass, Municipal Solid Waste and Solar	4%
Total	100%

* Excludes Out-of-State Purchases.
† 20.12,90 Source: Cal. Energy Commission, *Electricity Report, 1988.*

POTENTIAL HYDROELCTRIC SITES AND POWER	
Potential Hydroelectric Dam Sites	148
	Megawatts
Potential power installed by the year 1994	1,257
Potential power installed by the year 2002	1,400

20.13,90 Source: Cal. Energy Commission, *1983 Biennial Report.*

SECTION 20 NOTE
California produces 90 percent of all the electricity in the world generated by wind energy.

20.14,90

PRIVATELY OWNED ELECTRIC UTILITIES

C.P. National Corporation
Pacific Gas and Electric Company
Pacific Power and Light Company
San Diego Gas and Electric Company
Sierra Pacific Power Company
Southern California Edison Company

CONSUMER OWNED ELECTRIC UTILITIES

	Utility (Date Established)	Customers	Population
1	Alameda (1887)	30,191	75,232
2	Anaheim (1895)	93,568	237,506
3	Azusa (1898)	12,185	35,916
4	Banning (1895)	6,315	17,500
5	Biggs (1904)	588	1,459
6	Burbank (1913)	44,274	84,625
7	Colton (1897)	11,900	31,800
8	Glendale (1909)	75,300	159,000
9	Gridley (1910)	1,400	4,235
10	Hayfork Valley PUD (1987)	724	2,000
11	Healdsburg (1900)	4,840	8,275
12	Imperial Irrigation District (1936)	63,300	162,221
13	Lassen MUD (1987)	12,000	25,000
14	Lodi (1910)	20,248	45,800
15	Lompoc (1923)	12,824	31,000
16	Los Angeles Water & Power (1925)	1,320,818	3,311,500
17	Modesto Irrigation District (1923)	76,647	166,000
18	Needles (1983)	2,400	5,091
19	Palo Alto (1898)	26,992	55,556
20	Pasadena (1906)	54,868	130,600
21	Redding (1921)	26,665	52,745
22	Riverside (1911)	79,350	199,000
23	Roseville (1912)	14,621	30,500
24	Sacramento MUD (1947)	423,171	914,000
25	Santa Clara (1895)	40,664	90,052
26	Shasta Dam PUD (1948)	3,700	13,200
27	Trinity County PUD (1982)	1,650	3,000
28	Truckee-Donner PUD (1927)	6,463	15,000
29	Turlock Irrigation District (1923)	50,000	125,000
30	Ukiah (1897)	6,126	12,950
31	Vernon (1923)	2,097	2,097
	Subtotal	**2,627,964**	**6,117,210**

RURAL ELECTRIC COMPANIES

1	Anza Electric Corp	2,211	5,616
2	Plumas-Sierra Rural Electric Corp	4,500	11,430
3	Surprise Valley Electrification	4,400	11,176
4	Valley Electric Assn., Inc.	4,700	11,938
	Subtotal	**15,811**	**40,160**
	Total	**2,643,745**	**6,157,370**

20.15,90   Source: California State Board of Equalization, *Annual Report,* and California Municipal Utilities Association, unpublished data, 1989.

ACUTAL AND PROJECTED PEAK LOAD FOR ELECTRICITY IN CALIFORNIA BY UTILITY SERVICE AREA 1985-2007					
	Peak Demand (in megawatts)				Annual Growth Rate 1985-1999 (percent)
Area*	1985†	1992	1999	2007	
P.G. and E.	15,380	16,709	19,717	23,278	1.8%
S.M.U.D.	1,851	2,117	2,435	2,896	2.0%
S.C.E.	14,812	17,337	20,528	24,339	2.4%
L.A.D.W.P.	4,778	5,537	6,197	7,168	1.9%
S.D.G. and E.	2,384	3,062	3,614	4,311	3.0%
B.G.P.	691	794	864	960	1.6%
D.W.R.	709	744	852	948	1.3%
Other	596	747	826	902	2.4%
Statewide	41,201	47,047	55,033	64,802	2.1%

* The California Energy Commission forecast divides the state into nine planning areas based on utility service areas. They are:
Pacific Gas and Electric (P.G. and E.); Sacramento Municipal Utility District (S.M.U.D.); Southern California Edison (S.C.E.); Los Angeles Department of Water and Power (L.A.D.W.P.);
San Diego Gas and Electric Company (S.D.G. and E.); Anaheim Public Utilities Department (Anaheim);
Burbank, Glendale, and Pasadena (B.G.P.); California Department of Water Resources (D.W.R.); and other Regions (Other).
† Actual peak load, all other years are estimates.
20.16,90 Source: California Energy Commission, Electricity Report, 1988.

PROJECTED NEED FOR ELECTRICAL GENERATING CAPACITY AND ELECTRICAL ENERGY IN CALIFORNIA BY UTITLITY SERVICE AREA 1988-2007			
Planning Area	1988 New Capacity Needed (in Megawatts)	1999 New Capacity Needed (in Megawatts)	2007 New Capacity Needed (in Megawatts)
No. Cal.	16	4,296	9,029
So. Cal. Edison	None	3,823	7,901
L.A.D.W.P./ B.G.P.	None	820	2,200
S.D.G.& E.	198	1,376	2,294

20.17,90 Source: California Energy Commission, *Electricity Report, 1988.*

CALIFORNIA TRANSPORTATION FUEL DEMAND 1986	
Auto, Light Trucks	52%
Heavy Trucks	15%
Aircraft	15%
Ships	15%
Rail	2%
Mass Transit	1%
Total	**100%**

20.18,90 Source: California Energy Commission, *Energy Development Report, Aug. 1988.*

CALIFORNIA AND OTHER STATES PETROLEUM PRODUCTION (millions of barrels)				
State	**1981**	**1983**	**1985**	**1987**
Texas	945	903	889	761
Alaska	587	626	666	716
Louisiana	449	480	508	437
California*	**385**	**405**	**424**	**365**
Oklahoma	154	159	163	134
Wyoming	131	118	129	115

* California produced 12.3% of U.S. petroleum in 1981, 12.8%in 1983, 13% in 1985, 12.0% in 1987.
20.19,90 Source: *U.S. Statistical Abstract.*

SOURCES* OF OIL FOR CALIFORNIA						
Supplier	**1976**	**1981**	**1986**	**1988**	**1997†**	**2005†**
California	53%	50%	57%	52%	68%	55%
Alaska	7%	41%	37%	43%	25%	20%
Foreign	40%	9%	6%	5%	7%	25%
Total	**100%**	**100%**	**100%**	**100%**	**100%**	**100%**

* California exports negligible quantities of oil. †   Projected.
20.20,90 Source: California Energy Commission, *Biennial Report, 1988.*

PROVEN OIL RESERVES (in billions of barrels)		
California	5.2	(19% of U.S. Total)
United States	27.3	

20.21,90 Source: California Department of Conservation, Division of Oil and Gas, *Annual Report, 1987.*

SOURCES OF NATURAL GAS FOR CALIFORNIA				
	1987		1997	
Supplier	1,000 Cubic Feet, per day	Percent of Total	1,000 Cubic Feet, per day	Percent of Total
California	916	22%	1,009	21%
Southwestern U.S.	2,184	53%	2,017	43%
Canada	957	23%	1,217	26%
Rocky Mountains	43	1%	487	10%
Total	**4,100**	**100%**	**4,730**	**100%**

20.22,90 Source: California Energy Commission, *Biennial Report, Appendices 1987.*

MAJOR USES OF CALIFORNIA NATURAL GAS		
Use	Amount (MMCF)	Percent of Natural Gas Use
Industrial	1,440	28%
Commercial	499	10%
Electricity Generation	1,563	31%
Residential	1,309	26%
Cogeneration	50	1%
Thermal Enhanced Oil Recovery	204	4%
Total	**5,065**	**100%**

20.23,90   Source: Cal. Energy Commission, Biennial Fuels Report, Appendices, 1986.

CALIFORNIA AND OTHER STATES NATURAL GAS PRODUCTION (billions of cubic feet)					
State	Rank	1981	1983	1985	1987
Texas	1	7,010	5,913	6,012	6,061
Lousiana	2	6,773	5,288	5,146	5,096
Oklahoma	3	2,019	1,730	1,788	1,987
New Mexico	4	1,123	890	896	818
Wyoming	5	549	427	497	441
California*	**6**	**338**	**396**	**494**	**428**
Kansas	7	640	438	513	395

* California produced 1.7% of U.S. natural gas in 1981, 2.4% in 1983, 2.9% in 1985, and 2.5% in 1987.

20.24,90 Source: *U.S. Statistical Abstract.*

PROVEN NATURAL GAS RESERVES (in trillions of cubic feet)		
California	4.5	(2.4% of U.S. Total)
United States	187.2	

20.25,90 Sources: *U.S. Statistical Abstract;* California Department of Conservation, Division of Oil and Gas, *Annual Report, 1987.*

SECTION 20 NOTE

California has 24 operating geothermal power plants producing a total of 1,800 megawatts of electricity. More geothermal power is produced in California than in any other location in the world.

20.26,90

SECTION 20 NOTE

California wind energy saves California utilities over three million barrels of oil per year.

20.27,90

SECTION 20 NOTE

Wind energy in California is produced at three main sites: the Altamont Pass, in Alameda County; the Tehachapi Pass, north of Los Angeles; and the San Georgonio Pass, east of Los Angeles.

20.28,90

SECTION 20 NOTE

Arco Solar Company in Chatsworth, California, produces about 30 percent of the photovoltaic cells produced in the world.

20.29,90

SECTION 20 NOTE

The Chrovar Corporation will build the largest (50-megawatt) solar photovoltaic power plant in the nation near Los Angeles.

20.30,90

SECTION 20 NOTE

By late 1989, California should have 3 operating solid waste-to-energy plants with 2,250 tons per day capacity. These plants will generate 48 MW of power.

20.31,90

The Ames Research Center 40 by 80 foot wind tunnel in Mountain View. Photo Courtesy of NASA.

The AX-5 hard space suit being tested at the Ames Neutral Buoyancy Test Facility in
Mountain View. Photo Courtesy of NASA.

Science and Technology

High-tech innovations are springing up so fast and in so many places in California that just keeping track of them would be a full-time job for a team of experts.

University of California researchers at the Berkeley Sensor and Activator Center are continuing their astonishing development of microscopic motors and tools, which are expected to have a revolutionary influence on both medicine and manufacturing during the decades ahead.

The long-awaited evolution of the biotechnology industry from research to the commercial manufacturing of pharmaceuticals is about to occur. California biotech leaders such as Cetus, Chiron, Genentech, and Amgen have or soon will have new drugs in the marketplace that are expected to generate big profits. These profits, for the first time, will give the industry an infusion of internally generated capital and will allow venture capitalists to pursue other promising avenues for investment. The Industrial Biotechnology Association predicts that biotechnology sales, currently $600 million annually, will rise to almost $30 billion by the end of the decade. Since most of the major biotech companies in the United States are based in California, the state should see a large share of the profits from these sales accrue to businesses within its borders.

One cloud overshadowing biotechnology is the problem of delays as federal agencies such as the Environmental Protection Agency (EPA) and the Food and Drug Administration (FDA) drag their feet in testing new products for safety and effectiveness and approving their sale. The U.S. Patent Office has also developed a backlog of requests, resulting in delays of five to six years in the granting of patents for as many as 7,000 new biotechnology products.

California's attractiveness as a high-technology research center has brought foreign companies to the state to participate in the research and to share the benefits of the new products. Sony Corporation, for example, has established a new research facility in San Jose that will focus on developments in high-definition television.

OBLIGATED FEDERAL FUNDS FOR RESEARCH AND DEVELOPMENT BY GRANTING AGENCY CALIFORNIA AND UNITED STATES 1985 and 1987 (in millions)			
Granting Agency	California	Total U.S.	California as a Percent of All U.S.
Dept. of Agriculture			
1985	$56	$933	6%
1987	$56	$940	6%
Dept. of Commerce			
1985	$14	$397	4%
1987	$34	$402	9%
Dept. of Defense			
1985	$7,704	$29,700	26%
1987	$10,446	$35,084	30%
Dept. of Energy			
1985	$1,079	$4,964	22%
1987	$944	$4,754	20%
Dept of Health and Human Services			
1985	$635	$5,408	12%
1987	$778	$6,570	12%
Interior Dept.			
1985	$30	$390	8%
1977	$28	$404	7%
Dept. of Transportation			
1985	$73	$401	18%
1987	$20	$324	6%
Environmental Protection Agency			
1985	$25	$320	8%
1987	$20	$348	6%
National Aeronautics and Space Administration			
1985	$959	$3,320	29%
1987	$1,142	$3,770	30%
National Science Foundation			
1985	$193	$1,342	14%
1987	$203	$1,469	14%
Total			
1985	$10,768	$47,176	23%
1987	$13,671	$54,066	25%

21.1,90 Source: National Science Foundation, *Federal Funds for Research and Development.*

OBLIGATED FEDERAL FUNDS FOR RESEARCH AND DEVELOPMENT BY RECIPIENT CALIFORNIA AND UNITED STATES 1983-1987 (in millions)			
Recipient Agency	California	Total U.S.	California as a Percent of All U.S.
Federal Agencies			
1983	1,143	10,211	11%
1985	1,177	12,553	10%
1987	2,011	12,974	16%
Private Industry			
1983	5,191	18,471	28%
1985	7,119	23,636	30%
1987	8,576	26,683	32%
Universities and Colleges			
1983	1,641	7,074	23%
1985	2,058	8,657	24%
1987	1,084	7,195	15%
Non-profit Institutions			
1983	444	1,691	26%
1985	398	2,228	18%
1987	252	1,580	16%
State and Local Government			
1983	20	180	11%
1985	14	101	14%
1987	17	138	12%
Total			
1983	8,440	37,628	22%
1985	10,768	47,176	23%
1987	13,671	54,066	25%

21.2,90 Source: National Science Foundation, *Federal Funds for Research and Development..*

SECTION 21 NOTE
Scientists of the University of California's Lawrence Berkeley Lab have for the first time photographed a strand of DNA. The photo image was magnified 1 million times by a scanning tunneling microscope.

21.3,90

			California as a Percent
Year	California	Total U.S.	of all U.S.

EXPENDITURES ON RESEARCH AND DEVELOPMENT AT UNIVERSITIES AND COLLEGES BY FUNDING SOURCES CALIFORNIA AND UNITED STATES 1983-1987 (in millions)

Year	California	Total U.S.	California as a Percent of all U.S.
Federal Government			
1983	$727	$4,960	15%
1985	$877	$5,898	15%
1987	$1,063	$7,230	15%
State and Local Government			
1983	$21	$599	4%
1985	$15	$655	2%
1987	$37	$1,003	4%
Industry			
1983	$15	$370	4%
1985	$18	$529	3%
1987	$72	$764	9%
Institutional Funds			
1983	$176	$1,231	14%
1985	$216	$1,577	14%
1987	$290	$2,110	14%
All Other Sources			
1983	$84	$585	14%
1985	$105	$693	15%
1987	$90	$824	11%
Total			
1983	$1,023	$7,745	13%
1985*	$1,231	$9,352	13%
1987	$1,552	$11,931	13%

* Starting in 1985, data apply only to doctoral degree granting institutions.
21.4,90 Source: National Science Foundation, *Academic Science/Engineering: Research and Development Funds.*

SECTION 21 NOTE

The National Aeronautic and Space Administration's Ames Research Center in Mountain View has the world's largest wind tunnel. Full-sized planes can be tested in it.

21.5,90

			California as a Percent of All U.S.
EXPENDITURES ON RESEARCH AND DEVELOPMENT AT UNIVERSITIES AND COLLEGES CALIFORNIA AND UNITED STATES 1970-1987 (in millions)			
Year	**California**	**Total U.S.**	
1970	$245	$2,334	11%
1972	$324	$2,530	13%
1978	$585	$4,536	13%
1980	$784	$6,060	13%
1981	$891	$6,818	13%
1982	$947	$7,261	13%
1983	$1,023	$7,745	13%
1985*	$1,231	$9,352	13%
1987	$1,552	$11,931	13%

* Starting in 1985, data apply only to doctoral degree granting institutions.
21.6,90 Source: National Science Foundation, *Academic Science/Engineering: Research and Development Funds.*

			California as a percent of All U.S.
EXPENDITURES ON RESEARCH AND DEVELOPMENT AT UNIVERSITIES AND COLLEGES BY FIELD OF RESEARCH CALIFORNIA AND UNITED STATES 1987* (in millions)			
Field	**California**	**Total U.S.**	
Engineering	194	1,864	10%
Physical Sciences	219	1,353	16%
Environmental Sciences	121	808	15%
Mathematics and Computer Science	71	542	13%
Life Sciences	866	6,436	13%
Psychology	28	185	15%
Social Sciences	45	478	9%
Other Sciences	7	265	3%
Total	**$1,552**	**$11,931**	**13%**

* Starting in 1985, data apply only to doctoral degree granting institutions.
21.7,90 Source: National Science Foundation, *Academic Science/Engineering: Research and Development Funds.*

LEADING ACADEMIC DEPARTMENTS IN SCIENCE

Department	School	National Ranking*	Department	School	National Ranking*
Chemistry	Cal. Tech.	1	Electrical	U.C. Berkeley	2
	U.C. Berkeley	2	Engineering	Stanford	3
	Stanford	6		U.C.L.A	5
	U.C.L.A.	8		U.S.C.	6
				Cal. Tech.	9
Computer	Stanford	1			
Science	U.C. Berkeley	4	Mechanical	Stanford	2
	U.C.L.A.	8	Engineering	U.C. Berkeley	3
				Cal. Tech.	4
Geoscience	Cal. Tech.	1			
	U.C.L.A.	3	Biochemistry	Stanford	3
	Stanford	6		U.C. Berkeley	4
	U.C. Berkeley	9		U.C. San Francisco	8
Mathematics	U.C. Berkeley	2	Botany	U.C. Davis	1
	Stanford	6		U.C. Berkeley	3
				U.C. Riverside	7
Physics	Cal. Tech.	1		U.C.L.A.	9
	U.C. Berkeley	3			
	Stanford	8	Cellular &	Cal. Tech.	1
			Molecular	U.C. San Diego	7
Statistics-	U.C. Berkeley	1	Biology	U.C. Berkeley	8
Biostatistics	Stanford	2			
			Microbiology	U.C. San Diego	3
Chemical	Cal. Tech.	6		U.C.L.A.	8
Engineering	U.C. Berkeley	4			
	Stanford	5	Physiology	U.C. San Francisco	1
				U.C.L.A	5
Civil	U.C. Berkeley	1			
Engineering	Cal. Tech.	4	Zoology	U.C. Berkeley	1
	Stanford	6		U.C. DAvis	3
				U.C.L.A	5

* Rankings are based on reputational evaluations by faculty on the quality of the individual departments.

21.8,90 Source: Conference Board of Associations of Research Councils.

DOCTORAL SCIENTISTS AND ENGINEERS, 1987

Field	California	United States	California as a Percent of the U.S.
Engineers	11,397	71,126	16%
Physical Scientists	8,918	75,753	12%
Mathematicians	1,604	17,788	9%
Computer Scientists	3,415	18,626	18%
Environmental Scientists	2,812	18,985	15%
Life Scientists	13,199	117,453	11%
Psychologists	8,426	59,432	14%
Economists	1,607	19,580	8%
Social Scientists	6,137	52,695	12%
Total	**57,515**	**451,438**	**13%**

21.9,90 Source: Nat, Sci, Found. *Characteristics of Doctoral Sci. and Engr. in the U.S.*

SCIENTISTS AND ENGINEERS EMPLOYED AT DOCTORATE-GRANTING INSTITUTIONS, 1985

Field	California	United States	California as a Percent of the U.S.
Engineers	2,374	27,929	9%
Physical Scientists	2,141	20,699	10%
Mathematicians and Computer Scientists	962	20,298	5%
Environmental Scientists	905	7,453	12%
Life Scientists	12,735	135,102	9%
Psychologists	940	11,013	9%
Social Scientists	1,894	29,443	6%
Total	**21,951**	**251,237**	**9%**

21.10,90 Source: Nat. Science Found., *Academic Sci. and Engr., Sci. & Engineers.*

SCIENCE AND ENGINEERING GRADUATE STUDENTS IN DOCTORATE GRANTING INSTITUTIONS IN CALIFORNIA

Field	Number of Students
Engineering	14,368
Physical Sciences	3,254
Mathematics	1,610
Computer Sciences	2,396
Environmental Sciences	1,307
Life Sciences	8,215
Psychology	4,591
Social Sciences	6,973
Total	**42,714**

21.11,90 Source: National Science Foundation, Academic Science/ Engineering: *Graduate Enrollment and Support, Fall 1986.*

SCIENCE AND ENGINEERING GRADUATE STUDENTS IN DOCTORATE-GRANTING INSTITUTIONS

Year	California	United States	California as a Percent of the U.S.
1983	40,009	358,262	12%
1985	41,973	371,950	11%
1987	42,943	388,681	11%

21.12,90 Source: National Science Foundation *Academic Science Engineering Resources.*

NUMBER OF ENGINEERS AND SCIENTISTS EMPLOYED IN CALIFORNIA AND UNITED STATES
1980-1986

Year	California	Total U.S.	California as a Percent of All U.S.
Engineers			
1980	204,400	1,497,000	14%
1982	283,100	1,847,200	15%
1984	359,600	2,214,100	16%
1986	375,500	2,440,100	15%
Scientists			
1980	185,600	1,613,900	12%
1982	171,300	1,405,700	12%
1984	214,500	1,781,400	12%
1986	257,900	2,186,300	12%

21.13,90 Source: National Science Foundation, *U.S. Scientists and Engineers.*

SPERM BANKS

Name	Location
Southern California Cryobank	Westwood
Repository for Germinal Choice	Escondido
Tyler Medical Clinic	Los Angeles
Zygen Laboratory	Tarzana
California Cryobank	Berkeley
Life Bank	Manhattan Beach
Pacific Women's Health Services	San Francisco
Sperm Bank inc./Fertility Center	Santa Ana
Sperm Bank of California	Oakland
Northern California Cryobank	Carmichael

21.14,90 Source: Pacific Data Resources, 1989 and the American Association of Tissue Banks.

COMPUTER, ELECTRONICS AND INFORMATION TECHNOLOGY COMPANIES		
State	Number of Companies	Percent of Companies in U.S.
California	**5,588**	**23%**
New York	3,095	13%
Massachusetts	1,746	7%
Texas	1,400	6%
Total U.S.	**24,300**	**100%**

21.15,90 Source: American Electronics Asso., unpublished data, March 1989.

COMPUTER, ELECTRONICS AND INFORMATION TECHNOLOGY COMPANIES IN CALIFORNIA				
Year	Number of Companies	Percent of Companies in U.S.	Number Employed	Percent of Jobs in U.S.
1982	3,526	34%	485,000	NA
1983	3,900	34%	578,000	NA
1984	4,451	33%	592,000	NA
1986	5,010	23%	586,000	23%
1989	5,588	23%	590,000	22%

Note: Numbers are incomplete and subject to constant updating.
21.16,90 Source: American Electronics Association, unpublished data.

PATENTS ISSUED TO CALIFORNIANS			
Year	Patents Issued to Californians	% of Patents Issued to U.S. Residents	% of Patents Issued to U.S. Residents and Foreigners
1979	4,839	14.1%	8.7%
1980	5,335	14.0%	8.7%
1981	6,038	14.0%	8.5%
1982	5,481	14.0%	8.4%
1983	4,841	13.8%	8.1%
1984	5,808	13.8%	8.1%
1985	5,942	13.9%	7.9%
1986	5,983	14.1%	7.8%
1987	6,973	14.7%	7.9%
1988	6,875	15.4%	8.2%

21.17,90 Source: U.S. Dept. of Commerce, Patent and Trademark Office, *Annual Report.*

CALIFORNIA BIOTECHNOLOGY FIRMS, 1987

Company	Location	Company	Location
Aalto Biotechniques	**Esondido**	Calzyme	San Luis Obispo
Advanced Biotechnology		Cetus	Emeryville
Associates	San Francisco	Chemicon, International	Los Angeles
Advanced Genetic		Chiron Corp.	Emeryville
Sciences	Oakland	Clinetics	Tustin
Advanced Genetics		Clonal Research	Newport Beach
Research	Oakland	Clontech	Palo Alto
Agouron Institute	La Jolla	Codon Corporation	S. San Francisco
Allergy Immunotech	Newport Beach	Collagen	Palo Alto
Alpha Therapeutics	Los Angeles	Cooper Development	Menlo Park
Alza Corporation	Palo Alto	Creative Biomolecules	S. San Francisco
American Biogenetics	Irvine	Cryschem	Riverside
American Bionetics	Hayward	Cutter Labs	Emeryville
American Qualex	La Mirada	Cytoculture	San Francisco
Amgen	Thousand Oaks	Cytotech	San Diego
Antibodies Inc.	Davis	**Dako Corporation**	**Santa Barbara**
Applied Biosystems	Foster City	Diagnostic Products Corp.	Los Angeles
Arco Plant Cell Research	Dublin	Dionex	Sunnyvale
Astra Scientific	San Jose	DNAX Limited	Palo Alto
Bachem	**Torrance**	Dohrmann/Rosemount	
Bechtel	San Francisco	Analytic Div.	Santa Clara
Becton Dickinson	Mt. View	**E-Y Laboratories**	**San Mateo**
Beckman Instruments	Fullerton	Eantech	Mt. View
Berkeley Antibody	Berkeley	Earl-Clay Labs	Novato
Billups-Rothenberg	Del Mar	Engenics	Menlo Park
Bio-Con	Bakersfield	Enzyme System Products	Dublin
Bio-Genex	San Ramon	Escagen	San Carlos
Bio-Rad Laboratories	Richmond	**Fermentec**	**Los Altos**
Bio-Response	Hayward	Fluor Corporation	Irvine
Bioaccess	San Francisco	**Gametrics**	**Sausalito**
Biogrowth	Richmond	Gen-Probe	San Diego
Biomedia	Foster City	Genencor	S. San Francisco
Bioprobe	Tustin	Genentech	S. San Francisco
Biosystems	Foster City	Genetic Replication	
Bisearch	San Rafael	Technology	Newport Beach
Breit Labs	West Sacramento	Genta	San Diego
J. Brooks Labs	San Diego	Gilead	Foster City
BTX	San Diego	**Hana Bioglogics**	**Berkeley**
Cal. Integrated		Henkel Research	Santa Rosa
Diagnostics	**Berkeley**	Herd Technology	Chino
Calbiochem	La Jolla	Hybritech (E. Lilly)	San Diego
Calgene	Davis	Hytech Biomedical	Berkeley
California Biotechnology	Mountain View	**ICN Bio Medicals**	**Costa Mesa**

21.18.1,90

CALIFORNIA BIOTECHNOLOGY FIRMS, 1987

Company	Location	Company	Location
IDEC	Mt. View	Phytotec	Torrance
IDETEK	San Bruno	Plant Gene Expression	Albany
Immunetek		Plant Genetics	Davis
Pharmaceuticals	San Diego	Protein Design Labs	Palo Alto
Immuno Concepts	Sacramento	**Quindel**	**La Jolla**
Infergene	Benicia	**Replicon**	**San Francisco**
Ingene	Santa Monica	Research & Diagnostic	
Institute for Bio.		Antibodies	Emeryville
Research & Devel.	Newport Beach	**Salk Institute Biotech**	**La Jolla**
Intek Diagnostics	Brulingame	Salutar	Sunnyvale
Intelligenetics	Palo Alto	Sandoz	Palo Alto
International Enzymes	Fallbrook	Scripps Labs	San Diego
International Genetic		Senetek	Mt. View
Engineering	Santa Monica	Sensor Diagnostics	Irvine
Irvine Scientific	Santa Ana	The Seperations Group	Hesperia
Isis Pharmaceutical	Carlsbad	Sepragen	San Leandro
Johnson & Johnson		Setec	Livermore
Biotech Center	**San Diego**	Sibia	San Diego
JR Scientific	Woodland	Spectrum Laboratories	Los Angeles
Lee Biomolecular		Stratagene	La Jolla
Research Labs	**San Diego**	Sungene	Palo Alto
Lipsome Technology	Menlo Park	Symbiotics Corp.	San Diego
Locus Biosystems	San Francisco	Syncor	Chatsworth
Lucky Biotech	Emeryville	Syntex Research	Palo Alto
Mast Immunosystems	**Mt. View**	Sythetic Genetics	San Diego
Medi-Physics	Emeryville	Syntro	San Diego
Microgen	Laguna Hills	Syva	Palo Alto
Microgenics	Concord	**Tago**	**Burlingame**
Molecular Biosystems	San Diego	Techniclone	Santa Ana
Monoclonal Antibodies	Mt. View	3-M Diagnostics	Santa Clara
Multiple Peptide Systems	La Jolla	Tissue-Growth Corp.	Richmond
Mycogen	San Diego	Triton Biosciences	Alameda
Neurex	**Mt.View**	**Vector**	**Burlingame**
NIE Plant Tissue	San Mateo	Viratek	Costa Mesa
Northview Pacific Labs	Berkeley	Vestar	San Dimas
NUNC, Inc.	Newbury Park	**Wedgewood Technologies**	**San Carlos**
Ocean Genetics	**Santa Cruz**	**Xoma**	**Berkeley**
Peninsula Labs	**Belmont**	**Zoecon**	**Palo Alto**
Phytogen Crop.	Pasadena	Zymed	S. San Francisco

21.18.2,90 Source: Unpublished lists form various biotechnology firms, U.S. Department of Commerce, unpublished biotechnology data base and California Department of Commerce, unpublished data and U.C. Berkeley, City and Regional Planning Institute.

SECTION 21 NOTE

John Young (U.S. Navy) of San Francisco is the only Californian to have walked on the moon.

21.19,90

SPACE PROGRAM FACILITIES IN CALIFORNIA

Military Facilities
Vandenburg Air Force Base
Edwards Air Force Base
Los Angeles Air Force Station
Sunnyvale Air Force Station
Port Hueneme Naval Air Station
Fort Irwin Army Base

National Aeronautics and Space Administration (NASA) Facilities
Ames Research Lab, Mountain View
Jet Propulsion Laboratory, Pasadena
Dryden Flight Research Facility, Edwards AF Base

Research Institutes
RAND Corporation, Santa Monica
Aerospace Corporation, El Segundo

University-Related Space Research Programs
U.C. Berkeley, Space Sciences Laboratory
California Institute of Technology, Jet Propulsion Laboratory
Stanford Center for Space Sciences and Astrophysics
U.C. San Diego Center for Astrophysics and Space Sciences

Major Space Shuttle Contractors
Rockwell International, Anaheim
Aerojet General, Sacramento
General Dynamics, San Diego
Ford Aerospace, Palo Alto
Lockheed, Sunnyvale
McDonnell Douglas, Huntington Beach
TRW, Redondo Beach
Hughes Aircraft, Torrance

21.20,90 Source: NASA, 1989 phone update.

CALIFORNIA AEROSPACE EMPLOYMENT AND SPENDING, 1987

Industry	Employment Thousands	% of U.S. Jobs	Defense Purchases as a % of Sales (1986)	Total Federal Purchases as a % of Sales	Exports as a % of Sales
Electronic Components	147.6	23.2	3.4%	4.8%	19.2%
Office Computing & Accounting Machines	103.9	22.6	2.6%	NA	15.8%
Communications Equipment	177.6	28.9	16.9%	18.6%	6.7%
Aircraft & Parts	177.9	25.7	46.7%	48.3%	25.1%
Missiles & Space Vehicles	79.3	37.7	NA	85.1%	11.5%
Measuring & Controlling Instruments	54.2	22.8	4.3%	8.4%	19.9%
Engineering & Scientific Instruments	7.1	8.5	13.6%	16.6%	13.1%

21.21,90 Source: California Commission on State Finance, *Impact of Federal Expenditures on California, Spring 1988.*

SECTION 21 NOTE

Californians have a total of 3 million personal computers; 25 percent of computer owners in the state also have modems.
21.22,90

MAJOR CALIFORNIA THINK TANKS

Center for the Study of Democratic Institutions	Santa Barbara
Hoover Institution on War, Revolution and Peace	Stanford
Institute for Contemporary Studies	San Francisco
Institute for Civil Justice (RAND)	Santa Monica
Pacific Institute for Public Policy Research	San Francisco
Pan Heuristics	Los Angeles
Polaris	San Francisco
RAND Corporation	Santa Monica
Reason	Santa Barbara
Sequoia Institute	Sacramento
SRI International	Menlo Park
World Research	San Diego

21.23,90 Source: Pacific Data Resources.

SECTION 21 NOTE

Spending by the Defense Department and related federal agencies is a dominant factor in such parts of the aerospace industry as aircraft and missile production. Other components of the industry are not dependent on federal spending but are linked to other factors, such as exports and capital expenditures by business, both of which are expected to rise in the next few years.

21.24,90

SCIENTISTS/ SCHOLARS/ INVENTORS - PROMINENT CALIFORNIANS

Louis Alvarez - Physics	Robert Millikan - Physics
Lyman Byce - Inventor	Linus Pauling - Chemistry
Owen Chamberlain - Physics	R. Langley Porter - Psychiatry
George Davidson - Surveyor & Astronomer	Burt Rutan - Aircraft Designer
Lee DeForest - Inventor	Jonas Salk - Medicine
Gerard Debreu - Economics	Glenn Seaborg - Chemistry
Robert Goddard - Rocketry	Emilio Segre - Physics
David Starr Jordan - 1st President of Stanford	William Shockley - Physics
Alfred L. Kroeber - Anthropology	Robert Gordon Sproul - U.C. President
Ernest Lawrence - Physics	Paul Taylor - Economics
Edwin McMillan - Physics	Edward Teller - Physics
	Theodore Von Karman - Physics, Engineer

21.25,90 Source: Pacific Data Resources.

MOUNTAIN PASSES

Hazelview

Fandango
Cedar
Black Butte
Adin

Hatchet Mt.
Buckhorn
Wildwood
Noble
Fredonyer
Deer Creek

Mendocino
Jarbo
Ridgewood
Beckwourth
Yuba
Truckee
Henness
Donner

N

0 20 40 60 80 100
miles

Echo
Luther
Carson
Monitor
Ebbetts
Sonora
Devils Gate
Conway
Tioga

Kaiser
Pacheco
Mono
Westgard

Panoche
Cherry Gap
Kearsarge

Daylight

Townes

Cottonwood
La Cuesta
La Panza
Jubilee
Salsberry
Ibex

Mountain
Walker

Tehachapi

Gaviota
Pine Mt
Tejon
San Marcos
Casitas
South

San Fernando
Cajon
Lobecks
Cahuenga

San Gorgonio

The Narrows
San Carlos
Warners
Sweeney

© 1974 by the University of Oklahoma Press

Historical Atlas of California, 1974. University of Oklahoma Press. Reprinted by permission.

Land Transportation

Recent federal data confirm what thousands of Californians who commute by automobile have long suspected--that commute traffic in this state is the worst in the nation. As of 1988 the nine most congested highway interchanges in the country are all in California: six in Los Angeles County, two in Orange County, and one in Alameda County. Relief will not be soon in coming. No major new freeways are planned for the big metropolitan areas, although minor improvements and projects to widen existing freeways are under way.

If relief is to come, it will be from a more efficient use of existing freeways, staggered work hours, bans on truck traffic during rush hours, and a greater public use of mass transit. Many transit planners had hoped and even expected that massive freeway congestion would encourage drivers to switch to mass transit. This has not occurred. The use of mass transit actually declined from the early to the late 1980s. And we can only wait and see whether new construction and the expansion of heavy- and light-rail projects in San Diego, Los Angeles, San Jose, the San Francisco Bay Area, and Sacramento will reverse this disturbing trend.

California, unlike states in the East, was built around the automobile. Many mass transit systems simply do not go where enough people work, shop, or live. Thus the average Californian still relies on an automobile for transit.

With large increases in the number of cars on the road, the number of traffic fatalities has also risen during the past few decades. Driving, however, is generally much safer now than it was in the past because cars are built with passenger safety in mind and because more automobile occupants use seat belts. The overall road fatality rate in the state has dropped by almost 60 percent in the past two decades, and the fatality rate on rural roads, though higher than the overall rate, has dropped 70 percent over the past four decades.

Greater attention to the problems of drinking and driving and approval by the courts of random police checks for drunken drivers have also helped to make California's roads safer than they have ever been.

MILES OF PUBLIC ROADS IN EACH COUNTY, 1987							
		State Highways				State Roads Other Than State Highways	National Roads not Overlapping State or Local Systems
Counties	Total	Total	Outside Cities	Inside Cities	County Roads	City Streets	State Highways	Systems
Alameda	3,244	209	28	181	498	2,536	2	-
Alpine	394	83	83	-	134	-	4	173
Amador	584	127	127	-	402	53	1	1
Butte	2,293	181	155	26	1,379	318	23	391
Calaveras	1,431	150	150	-	688	16	39	538
Colusa	909	115	115	-	737	39	2	16
Contra Costa	2,784	112	22	90	761	1,834	75	2
Del Norte	671	91	91	-	298	18	26	238
El Dorado	1,590	173	147	25	1,005	160	175	78
Fresno	6,580	519	457	62	3,631	1,734	29	667
Glenn	1,112	110	110	-	866	49	-	86
Humboldt	2,158	334	306	28	1,198	253	52	321
Imperial	3,272	402	380	22	2,596	241	16	18
Inyo	2,401	424	424	-	1,127	11	-	839
Kern	5,859	867	787	80	3,334	1,536	12	111
Kings	1,371	157	151	6	987	226	-	1
Lake	1,082	136	136	-	620	191	39	97
Lassen	1,978	304	300	4	944	28	-	702
Los Angeles	21,357	903	250	653	3,627	16,054	155	617
Madera	2,191	131	121	9	1,564	160	-	336
Marin	1,216	91	50	40	412	566	65	83
Mariposa	1,057	117	117	-	560	-	-	380
Mendocino	2,033	380	370	10	1,014	98	395	145
Merced	2,397	255	229	27	1,774	341	27	-
Modoc	1,530	178	178	-	991	34	-	327
Mono	1,612	315	315	-	669	50	9	570
Monterey	2,335	289	244	45	1,275	563	40	167
Napa	826	112	94	18	467	236	9	2
Nevada	1,120	130	123	7	698	52	24	216
Orange	5,638	243	27	216	794	4,516	13	73
Placer	1,724	156	133	23	981	326	9	252
Plumas	1,779	182	182	-	659	21	16	901
Riverside	6,957	690	525	166	2,779	3,034	35	419
Sacramento	3,899	224	124	100	2,432	1,237	6	-
San Benito	839	91	82	8	440	58	242	8
San Bernardino	8,946	1,215	940	275	4,257	3,009	32	433
San Diego	8,440	583	312	271	1,851	4,722	813	470
San Francisco	893	34	-	34	-	850	4*	5
San Joaquin	3,061	261	217	44	1,745	1,038	17	-
San Luis Obispo	2,232	366	311	55	1,258	459	50	100
San Mateo	2,008	213	80	133	320	1,453	23	-
Santa Barbara	1,857	303	227	76	901	532	32	91
Santa Clara	4,479	243	87	156	726	3,323	187	-
Santa Cruz	1,112	124	41	82	601	273	115	-
Shasta	2,842	312	260	52	1,233	307	116	875
Sierra	861	98	98	-	389	5	-	369
Siskiyou	2,324	350	339	11	1,368	147	-	460
Solano	1,557	159	93	67	627	769	2	-
Sonoma	2,495	238	188	50	1,446	718	92	1
Stanislaus	2,572	181	146	35	1,590	798	4	-
Sutter	1,026	84	74	10	854	89	-	-
Tehama	1,733	207	198	9	1,098	87	2	339
Trinity	1,799	202	202	-	725	-	-	872
Tulare	4,595	353	306	47	3,152	596	31	464
Tuolumne	1,217	151	151	-	599	23	2	441
Ventura	2,534	272	168	104	542	1,562	76	83
Yolo	1,343	179	153	27	828	336	-	-
Yuba	789	65	51	14	586	67	-	71
State Totals	158,932	15,166	11,770	3,396	69,033	57,748	3,137	13,848

* Includes 2.0 miles for the Golden Gate Bridge.

22.1,90 Source: California Dept. of Transportation, Div. of Highways & Programming, Systems Engineering Branch, March, 1989.

Bridge	Year Opened	Cost (millions)	Total Length in Miles	Suspension (major span) Length (Feet) Miles	Cantilever (major span) Length (Feet) Miles	Tower Height	Type of Structure	Average Daily Traffic 1988*	Vertical Clearance (Feet)
				CALIFORNIA TOLL BRIDGES					
Golden Gate	1937	$35	1.2	(4,200)	NA	746	Suspension	111,723	220
SF-Oakland Bay Bridge	1936	$77	8.4	(2,310)	(1,400)	526	Suspension Tunnel	118,973	220*
San Mateo-Hayward	1967	$70	6.8	1.8	5	NA	Steel Plate Girder & Concrete Trestle	32,647	135
Dunbarton	1982	$50	1.6	(340)	NA	NA	Steel Box Girder Prestressed Concrete Approach Spans	20,655	85
Richmond-San Rafael	1956	$66	5.5	NA	(1,070)	325	Cantilever Truss	21,823	185
Antioch (Nejedly)	1978	$41	1.8	(460)	-	-	Steel Plate Girder	4,371	135
Carquinez (old)	1927	$8	0.8	NA	(1,100)	314	Steel		148
Carquinez (new)	1958	$32	0.8	NA	(1,100)	314	Cantilever	48,889	148
Benicia-Martinez	1962	$25	1.2	(528)	NA	NA	Deck Truss	38,105	138
Vincent Thomas	1973	$26	1.1	(1,500)	NA	365	Suspension	14,439	185
San Diego-Coronado	1969	$47	2.1	(660)	NA	NA	Steel Box Girder	25,262	194

* One way traffic.

22.2,90 Source: Cal. Dept. of Transportation, Office of Toll Bridge & Commute Management, *1987-88 Annual Financial Report State Owned Toll Bridges;* Golden Gate Bridge Auth., unpublished data.

REGISTERED MOTOR VEHICLES 1970-2005

Year	Autos	Trucks	Trailers	Motor-cycles	First Time Regis-trations†	Total
1970	10,004,155	1,758,685	1,299,716	561,621	873,862	13,624,177
1980	13,161,470	3,435,732	2,209,203	737,774	960,708	19,544,179
1981	13,095,045	3,404,991	1,794,002	731,310	920,149	19,025,348
1982	13,292,130	3,512,284	1,742,781	678,174	1,111,481	19,225,369
1986	14,187,278	3,842,543	1,407,227	661,395	1,991,406	20,098,349
1987	15,559,586	4,712,921	-	674,742	-	23,125,884
1988	15,279,088	4,156,125	1,521,131	614,533	1,962,230	21,570,877
1995*	15,640,000	4,929,600	2,643,100	1,109,500	-	24,322,200
2000*	16,863,800	5,502,000	2,930,900	1,236,400	-	26,533,600
2005*	18,044,300	6,068,900	3,216,600	1,363,200	-	28,693,000

* Projections. † Not included in totals.

22.3,90 Source: Dept. of Motor Vehicles, Rept. No. 48, and Budget Sec., unpublished data.

SECTION 22 NOTE

The first automobile-airplane combination, the Waterman Studebaker, was produced in Santa Monica in 1937.

22.4,90

NUMBER OF MOTOR VEHICLES BY COUNTY, 1988

County	Autos	Trucks	Trailers	Motorcycles	Total
Alameda	723,670	183,540	70,082	29,412	1,006,518
Alpine	609	299	119	35	1,062
Amador	16,609	9,805	4,337	999	31,750
Butte	98,730	43,108	24,425	5,559	171,322
Calaveras	18,939	11,043	5,515	1,071	35,568
Colusa	8,745	6,051	3,212	334	18,342
Contra Costa	491,053	117,755	50,673	20,105	679,586
Del Norte	10,127	5,281	2,884	416	18,708
El Dorado	73,705	33,288	15,397	3,673	125,063
Fresno	298,379	129,901	52,775	12,537	493,592
Glenn	13,316	8,428	5,101	623	27,468
Humboldt	62,883	32,257	14,986	3,182	113,308
Imperial	57,491	25,965	10,483	1,845	95,784
Inyo	11,068	6,716	3,647	839	22,270
Kern	249,556	120,310	51,616	14,151	435,533
Kings	41,021	18,880	7,546	2,275	69,722
Lake	31,322	15,099	9,798	1,980	58,199
Lassen	12,363	8,042	4,483	853	25,741
Los Angeles	4,789,229	1,055,784	312,783	160,103	6,317,899
Madera	41,766	22,561	10,468	2,054	76,849
Marin	164,326	32,205	10,326	6,724	213,581
Mariposa	8,609	5,065	2,424	596	16,744
Mendocino	43,590	24,607	10,047	2,682	80,926
Merced	81,676	36,644	15,388	3,521	137,229
Modoc	4,447	3,677	1,903	209	10,236
Mono	5,511	3,091	1,542	394	10,538
Monterey	189,640	55,427	19,329	6,359	270,755
Napa	63,836	23,702	11,633	3,190	102,361
Nevada	49,560	23,004	11,306	2,687	86,557
Orange	1,470,193	331,951	105,873	54,749	1,962,766
Placer	102,435	43,225	21,613	5,075	172,348
Plumas	11,956	7,139	4,073	750	23,917
Riverside	533,250	187,806	78,683	23,380	823,119
Sacramento	553,589	164,512	118,349	22,208	858,658
San Benito	18,002	8,578	3,273	747	30,600
San Bernardino	666,027	241,202	93,541	32,416	1,033,186
San Diego	1,350,814	358,609	106,081	53,624	1,869,128
San Francisco	335,536	75,196	31,885	17,354	459,971
San Joaquin	233,635	90,951	45,288	9,731	379,505
San Luis Obispo	120,428	47,671	21,759	6,587	196,445
San Mateo	472,766	95,446	45,621	15,027	628,860
Santa Barbara	220,486	65,020	21,941	11,195	318,642
Santa Clara	948,383	211,421	73,510	36,257	1,259,571
Santa Cruz	142,114	45,345	14,285	6,999	208,743
Shasta	81,317	42,816	27,095	3,999	155,227
Sierra	1,891	1,237	581	112	3,821
Siskiyou	24,193	16,001	8,336	1,258	49,788
Solano	172,635	51,455	21,446	8,192	253,728
Sonoma	222,701	81,449	33,545	9,912	347,607
Stanislaus	184,714	77,782	37,904	8,261	308,661
Sutter	34,500	16,262	8,304	1,536	60,602
Tehama	24,935	14,746	8,612	1,379	49,672
Trinity	7,229	4,712	2,904	602	15,447
Tulare	139,992	68,521	28,330	7,537	244,380
Tuolumne	27,445	14,658	7,335	1,579	51,017
Ventura	395,754	113,325	37,218	18,317	564,614
Yolo	70,477	33,075	25,834	3,137	132,523
Yuba	29,583	13,550	6,928	1,552	51,613
Out of State	114,384	44,323	47,759	2,485	208,951
State Totals	**16,373,140**	**5,069,422**	**2,291,910**	**654,365**	**24,388,837**
Percentage	**67.13%**	**20.79%**	**9.40%**	**2.68%**	**100.00%**

Note: There were also 356,226 registered vehicles in the state which were exempt from license fees.

22.5,90 Source: Department of Motor Vehicles, Budget Section, unpublished data.

NUMBER OF CURRENTLY REGISTERED* CALIFORNIA MOTOR VEHICLES BY YEAR FIRST SOLD

Year First Sold	Automobiles	Motorcycles	Commercial Vehicles
Through 1954	72,174	2,378	32,801
1955-1963	206,257	3,669	121,776
1964	85,162	1,374	36,107
1965	114,335	1,929	41,031
1966	120,750	2,274	40,303
1967	125,896	2,885	38,803
1968	153,029	4,201	52,912
1969	177,779	6,944	62,897
1970	184,859	10,049	65,085
1971	227,579	9,762	74,547
1972	279,225	9,862	103,412
1973	327,952	11,550	117,287
1974	290,883	12,331	98,513
1975	321,427	12,903	97,102
1976	464,603	15,904	129,473
1977	653,208	21,162	169,964
1978	774,314	21,889	195,072
1979	777,343	34,974	200,597
1980	717,430	33,626	168,246
1981	744,589	34,135	159,885
1982	751,528	34,639	179,439
1983	944,705	44,490	220,504
1984	1,113,435	50,982	298,748
1985	1,270,110	56,501	360,134
1986	1,385,591	56,143	373,149
1987	1,324,205	55,366	353,139
1988	1,489,307	50,909	366,583
Total	**15,097,675**	**602,831**	**4,157,509**

22.6,90 Source: California Department of Motor Vehicles, Budget Section Forecasting Unit, unpublished data, 1989.

DRIVERS USING LAP & SHOULDER BELTS, 1988

Atlanta	35%	New York	23%
Boston	29%	Phoenix	52%
Chicago	21%	San Diego	51%
Dallas	66%	San Francisco	55%
Los Angeles	48%	Seattle	60%
Miami	41%		

Note: In 1986, 57% of California drivers said they used seat belts all the time and another 20% said they wore seat belts most of the time.

22.7,90 Source: National Highway Traffic Safety Administration, unpublished data and the California Poll.

County	1970	1980	1985	1987	1988
DRIVERS' LICENSES BY COUNTY					
Alameda	606,600	735,800	796,800	831,300	836,500
Alpine	300	800	800	800	1,200
Amador	7,600	13,800	17,400	18,800	19,300
Butte	63,900	100,900	114,300	119,700	122,200
Calaveras	8,400	14,900	18,400	20,700	21,800
Colusa	7,300	9,100	10,100	10,600	10,800
Contra Costa	347,700	465,800	517,000	545,300	554,900
Del Norte	10,100	12,800	13,000	13,300	13,700
El Dorado	29,900	64,200	76,400	83,900	87,700
Fresno	234,800	320,400	347,200	364,300	373,000
Glenn	12,000	15,000	16,200	16,400	16,700
Humboldt	63,900	82,300	79,400	81,100	81,700
Imperial	41,100	53,900	57,900	61,300	64,000
Inyo	9,900	13,900	14,200	14,200	14,200
Kern	196,600	254,200	291,800	309,700	317,500
Kings	34,800	43,600	48,400	50,200	50,800
Lake	13,500	27,400	33,800	35,700	36,200
Lassen	10,000	15,700	16,400	17,200	17,300
Los Angeles	4,116,400	4,741,400	5,140,200	5,404,200	5,450,900
Madera	23,800	37,800	45,600	48,900	50,500
Marin	130,100	168,600	176,600	181,400	182,100
Mariposa	3,600	8,500	9,600	10,300	10,700
Mendocino	31,100	47,600	52,200	54,300	55,200
Merced	57,500	78,700	90,400	95,100	97,300
Modoc	4,700	5,800	6,300	6,200	6,200
Mono	2,200	6,000	6,600	6,700	6,900
Monterey	129,900	179,900	200,900	211,200	213,300
Napa	48,300	64,700	69,700	72,200	73,700
Nevada	16,900	36,700	48,900	53,900	56,400
Orange	866,600	1,386,900	1,569,500	1,675,200	1,705,000
Placer	47,200	90,400	105,400	115,700	120,700
Plumas	8,700	13,200	14,000	14,900	15,100
Riverside	269,700	437,000	535,900	610,700	651,900
Sacramento	380,600	536,700	605,800	649,100	663,800
San Benito	10,400	15,000	18,400	20,400	21,500
San Bernardino	388,200	568,800	679,200	768,800	812,900
San Diego	745,900	1,251,300	1,425,800	1,558,500	1,611,700
San Francisco	339,600	401,900	437,300	455,800	456,500
San Joaquin	170,800	223,100	252,000	271,300	276,300
San Luis Obispo	61,500	105,500	125,900	137,600	142,300
San Mateo	353,200	422,600	454,400	467,400	468,100
Santa Barbara	158,000	213,100	237,200	249,200	250,900
Santa Clara	631,800	904,900	998,500	1,044,500	1,053,200
Santa Cruz	78,700	131,600	147,200	155,800	158,900
Shasta	51,100	84,900	93,000	98,100	100,500
Sierra	1,500	2,500	2,500	2,500	2,500
Siskiyou	23,400	31,300	32,000	32,400	32,700
Solano	96,200	152,600	175,900	191,900	199,200
Sonoma	124,400	206,400	237,800	255,200	262,500
Stanislaus	118,100	171,900	194,000	211,100	218,600
Sutter	26,700	36,700	39,000	40,700	41,300
Tehama	17,500	25,700	29,000	30,500	31,300
Trinity	4,200	8,100	9,100	9,400	9,900
Tulare	102,500	142,700	161,000	168,700	172,500
Tuolumne	13,500	24,000	29,000	31,400	32,700
Ventura	214,500	351,600	411,500	443,300	454,000
Yolo	53,900	75,400	82,600	87,100	88,900
Yuba	24,700	33,500	34,400	35,700	36,000
State Totals	**11,646,000**	**15,669,000**	**17,452,900**	**18,571,800**	**18,934,100**

22.8,90 Source: Dept. of Motor Vehicles Budget Section, April 1989.

CALIFORNIA MOTOR VEHICLE REGISTRATIONS 1900-1960				
Year	Registrations		Year	Registrations
1900	780		1940	2,824,907
1910	44,120		1950	4,667,293
1920	604,187		1960	7,878,659
1930	2,069,095			

22.9,90 Sourcee: Federal Highway Administration, *Highway Statistics - Summary to 1975.*

DRIVERS' LICENSES, BY SEX	
Sex	Licenses
Male	10,014,524
Female	8,919,623
Total	18,934,147

22.10,90 Source: Cal. Department of Motor Vehicles, unpublished data, 1989.

DRIVER'S LICENSES, BY AGE	
Age	Percent of All Driver's Licenses
16-19	4.7%
20-24	10.6%
25-29	13.6%
30-34	13.5%
35-39	12.0%
40-44	10.1%
45-49	7.6%
50-54	6.1%
55-59	5.4%
60-64	5.2%
65-69	4.6%
70-74	3.2%
75-79	2.0%
80-84	1.0%
85-89	0.3%
90-99	0.1%
Total	100.0%

22.11,90 Source: California Department of Motor Vehicles, unpublished data, 1989.

MILES TRAVELLED ON STATE HIGHWAYS
1981-1988
(in billions)

Year	Miles Driven	Percent Change from Previous Year
1981*	91.4	-
1982*	92.4	1.1%
1983*	96.7	4.3%
1984*	103.3	6.8%
1985*	107.9	4.4%
1986*	114.2	5.8%
1987*	119.9	5.0%
1988*	128.3	7.1%

* 12 month period April through March.
22.12,90 Source: Cal. Energy Commission, *Energy Watch 1989*.

CALIFORNIA MOUNTAIN PASSES

Pass	Feet	Road
Adin	5,173	Cal. 299
Antelope Summit	5,472	Cal. 139
Beckwourth	5,212	Cal. 70
Carson	8,573	Cal. 88
Cedar	6,305	Cal. 299
Conway	8,138	U.S. 395
Deadman	8,041	U.S. 395
Devil's Gate	7,519	U.S. 395
Donner	7,089	U.S. 80
Ebbetts	8,731	Cal. 4
Echo	7,377	U.S. 50
Fredonyer	5,748	Cal. 36
Luther	7,740	Cal. 89
Monitor	8,314	Cal. 89
Mountain	4,731	U.S.15
Sagehew	5,556	U.S. 395
Sonora	9,626	Cal. 108
Pacific Grade	8,050	Cal. 4
Tejon	4,183	U.S. 5
Tioga*	9,941	Cal. 120
Tehachapi	3,988	Cal. 58
Townes	4,956	Cal. 190
Sherwin	7,000	U.S. 395
Walker	5,250	Cal. 178
Yuba	6,701	Cal. 49

* Highest auto pass.
22.13,90 Source: Assorted maps.

CALIFORNIA GASOLINE USE 1978-1988		
Year	Per Driver (in gallons)	Total Statewide Consumption (in billions of gallons)
1978	NA	11.6
1980	702	11.3
1981	677	11.2
1982	657	11.0
1983	666	10.9
1984	673	11.4
1985	672	11.6
1986	670 *	12.1
1987	668 *	12.4
1988	676 *	12.8

* Calculated by Editor (gasoline use / number of licensed drivers).
22.14,90 Source: California Energy Commission, *Energy Watch, Jan/Feb 1989*, California State Board of Equalization, *Annual Report.*

GASOLINE TAXES, 1989	
Federal Tax	9¢ per gallon
California	9¢ per gallon

22.15,90 Source: *U.S. Statistical Abstract, State Board of Equalization, Annual Report.*

MOTOR VEHICLE TAXES		
Year	Vehicle Fuel Taxes* (in millions)	Vehicle Fees† (in millions)
1960	$337	$256
1970	$669	$499
1980	$853	$1,097
1982	$833	$1,373
1984	$1,213	$1,906
1985	$1,160	$2,137
1986	$1,194	$2,515
1987	$1,246	$2,693
1988	$1,280	$2,974
1989ƒ	$1,304	$3,160
1990ƒ	$1,330	$3,362

* Tax on gasoline, diesel, and liquified petroleum gas. ƒ Estimates
† Registration, weight, license & other fees.
22.16,90 Source: Economic Report of the Governor.

TEN BUSIEST HIGHWAY INTERCHANGES IN THE UNITED STATES

Rank	City/County	Freeway/Highway	Vehicles Per Day
1	*Los Angeles (West L.A.)*	Santa Monica/San Diego	513,000
2	*Los Angeles (East L.A.)*	Santa Monica/Golden State/Pomona/Hollywood	509,000
3	*Los Angeles (Central L.A.)*	Santa Monica/Harbor	502,500
4	*Sherman Oaks*	Ventura/San Diego	480,000
5	*Oakland*	Eastshore/MacArthur/Nimitz	455,000
6	*Carson*	Harbor/San Diego	444,000
7	*Orange*	Santa Ana/Garden Grove/Orange	441,000
8	*Cerritos*	Artesia/San Gabriel River	425,500
9	*Anaheim*	Orange/Riverside	421,000
10	Chicago	Interstate 55/94	420,000

* California freeways in italics.

22.17,90 Source: Federal Highway Administration, unpublished data, 1988.

CALIFORNIA COVERED BRIDGES

Name	River	County	City
Honey Run	Butte Creek	Butte	5 mi. E. of Chico
Berta's Ranch	Elk	Humboldt	5 mi. S. of Eureka
Zane's Ranch	Elk	Humboldt	6 mi. S. of Eureka
Wawona	Merced, S. Fork	Mariposa	Wawona
Bridgeport	Yuba, S. Fork	Nevada	Bridgeport
Glen Canyon	Branci Forte Creek	Santa Cruz	2 mi. N.E. of Santa Cruz
Felton	San Lorenzo Creek	Santa Cruz	1 mi. E. of Felton
Paradise Park	San Lorenzo Creek	Santa Cruz	3 mi. N. of Santa Cruz
Sawyer's Bar	Salmon, Little N. Fork	Siskiyou	4 mi. W. of Sawyer's Bar
Knight's Ferry	Stanislaus	Stanislaus	Knight's Ferry
Freeman's Crossing	Oregon Creek	Yuba	3 mi. N. of N. San Juan

22.18,90 Source: Cal. State Auto Asso., Motorland Magazine July-Aug. 1985; S. Griswold Morley, *The Covered Bridges of California, 1938;* and *Covered Bridges of the West (1963).*

10 MOST FREQUENTLY STOLEN VEHICLES, 1988

Rank	Year	Make/Model
1	1988	Hyundai/Excel
2	1983	Toyota/Celica
3	1977	Toyota/Celica
4	1986	Toyota/MR2
5	1977	Toyota/Corolla
6	1976	Toyota/Corolla
7	1982	Toyota/ Celica
8	1978	Toyota/Corolla
9	1984	Toyota/ Celica
10	1978	Datsun/210

22.19,90 Source: California Highway Patrol, unpublished data.

California Rank	National Rank	City	Auto Thefts	California Rank	National Rank	City	Auto Thefts
		AUTO THEFT IN CALIFORNIA'S MAJOR CITIES					
1	10	San Diego	24,126	19	61	Anaheim	2,658
2	11	Chula Vista	2,769	20	65	Glendale	1,630
3	24	Inglewood	1,846	21	69	Stockton	1,906
4	25	Los Angeles	57,331	22	77	Riverside	2,072
5	26	Sacramento	5,611	23	78	Pasadena	1,313
6	30	Oakland	5,943	24	84	Fullerton	1,032
7	32	San Bernardino	2,379	25	87	Torrance	1,263
8	34	Santa Ana	3,834	26	89	Orange	908
9	35	West Covina	1,558	27	95	Bakersfield	1,148
10	37	El Monte	1,508	28	105	Concord	721
11	39	Fresno	4,231	29	109	Modesto	877
12	40	Long Beach	5,881	30	118	Hayward	614
13	48	San Francisco	9,578	31	121	Santa Rosa	565
14	51	Berkeley	1,302	32	122	San Jose	4,039
15	52	Pomona	1,379	33	131	Oxnard	681
16	54	Garden Grove	1,593	34	137	Huntington Beach	924
17	55	Ontario	1,392	35	164	Sunnyvale	408
18	56	Oceanside	1,176	36	170	Fremont	531

Note: Ranks are based on thefts per 100,000 residents.
22.20,90 Source: Federal Bureau of Investigation, *Uniform Crime Reports, 1987.*

Year	To California	Percent of Total Federal Funds
	FEDERAL HIGHWAY TRUST FUNDS (in millions)	
1970	$503	11.1%
1980	$502	5.5%
1981	$556	6.3%
1982	$492	6.5%
1983	$526	6.2%
1984	$688	7.1%
1985	$926	7.7%
1986	$855	6.1%
1987	$794	6.3%
1988	$904	6.5%

22.21,90 Source: U.S. Statistical Abstract ; U.S. Dept. of the Treasury, *Federal Aid to States, Fiscal Year 1982 (Revised Edition)*; and U.S. Bureau of the Census, *Federal Expenditures by State for Fiscal Year 1989.*

SECTION 22 NOTE

Between 1933 and 1987 traffic deaths per million miles of travel in California declined from 15.1 to 2.4.

22.22,90

FATALITIES AND INJURIES IN MOTOR VEHICLE TRAFFIC ACCIDENTS

Vehicle Type	Killed 1970	Killed 1987	Killed 1988	Injured 1970	Injured 1987	Injured 1988
Passenger Car	4,740	2,677	2,585	231,224	238,107	236,863
Motorcycle/Scooter/ Moped	447	744	603	16,918	25,401	21,556
Pickup or Panel Truck	785	837	844	24,716	55,015	57,030
Truck	505	97	90	8,510	3,399	3,680
School Bus	9	2	0	315	984	695
Other Bus	28	7	2	806	1,424	1,195
Emergency Vehicles	24	4	7	1,386	1,464	1,508
Bicycle	93	139	138	6,405	16,461	15,870
Pedestrians	819	975	1,084	13,001	17,647	17,695
Other	59	18	28	2,869	782	853
Total	**6,720**	**5,500**	**5,381**	**293,149**	**360,699**	**356,945**

22.23,90   Source: California Highway Patrol, *Annual Reports of Fatal and Injury Motor Vehicle Traffic Accidents.*

FATALITIES AND INJURIES IN MOTOR VEHICLE TRAFFIC ACCIDENTS BY AGE OF VICTIM, 1988

Age	Killed Number	Killed Percent	Injured Number	Injured Percent
0-4	146	3%	8,169	2%
5-14	239	5%	27,605	8%
15-24	1,486	28%	117,763	33%
25-34	1,228	23%	88,449	25%
35-44	717	13%	49,594	14%
45-54	373	7%	25,301	7%
55-64	365	7%	17,382	5%
65 or Over	692	13%	18,291	5%
Unkown	135	3%	4,391	1%
Totals	**5,381**	**100%**	**356,945**	**100%**

22.24,90   Source: California Highway Patrol , *Annual Report of Fatal and Injury Motor Vehicle Traffic Accidents.*

FATALITIES AND INJURIES IN ALCOHOL-RELATED MOTOR VEHICLE TRAFFIC ACCIDENTS, 1983-1988

	1983 Killed	1983 Injured	1985 Killed	1985 Injured	1987 Killed	1987 Injured	1988 Killed	1988 Injured
Number	2,386	66,909	2,412	66,667	2,754	68,816	2,510	65,033
% Accidents Alcohol- Related	52%	23%	49%	21%	50%	19%	47%	18%

22.25,90 Source: California Highway Patrol *Annual Reports of Fatal and Injury Motor Vehicle Traffic Accidents.*

TRAFFIC DEATHS-U.S. AND CALIFORNIA		
Year	U.S.	California
1981	49,301	5,170
1982	43,990	4,609
1983	42,600	4,571
1984	44,175	4,999
1985	45,700	4,933
1986	47,800	5,222
1987	46,390	5,500
1988	46,900	5,381

22.26,90 Source: California Highway Patrol upublished data; *U.S. Statistical Abstract*, U.S. National Highway Traffic Safety Administration, unpublished data.

CALIFORNIA STATE HIGHWAY FATALITIES						
	Fatalities			Rates per 100 million vehicle miles		
Year	Rural Roads	Urban Roads	Total	Rural Roads	Urban Roads	Total
1947	1,302	NA	NA	11.55	NA	NA
1957	1,474	NA	NA	8.64	NA	NA
1967	1,426	756	2,182	6.57	2.47	4.28
1977	1,089	849	1,938	4.39	1.52	2.40
1987	1,170	1,067	2,237	3.58	1.20	1.84

22.27,90 Source: California Dept. of Transportation, Division of Highways & Programming, Office of Highways, *Assembly of Statistical Reports, 1987*.

SCHOOL BUS ACCIDENTS BY TYPE OF BUS 1987 and 1988								
	Number of Buses		Miles Driven (in millions)		Number of Accidents		Accidents per million miles	
Bus Owner	1987	1988	1987	1988	1987	1988	1987	1988
Public School	13,555	13,250	169.6	171.8	1,345	1,479	7.9	8.6
Private School	1,337	1,227	12.4	10.7	97	76	7.8	7.1
Contractor	6,761	6,162	108.3	96.3	999	1,108	9.2	11.5
Total	**21,653**	**20,639**	**290.3**	**278.7**	**2,441**	**2,663**	**8.4**	**9.6**

22.28,90 Source: California Highway Patrol, *Information Bulletin*, 1987 and 1988.

SECTION 22 NOTE
The Bridgeport covered bridge (243 feet long) near Grass Valley is the longest single-span covered bridge in the U.S. It is also the oldest such bridge in the West in continuous service.

22.29,90

SECTION 22 NOTE
At least 33 covered bridges in the state have been destroyed since 1900.

22.30,90

SCHOOL BUS ACCIDENTS					
	1982-83	1984-85	1985-86	1986-87	1987-88
Accidents					
Fatal	3	3	4	6	4
Injury	295	387	419	455	482
Property Damage	1,179	1,347	1,714	1,980	2,177
Total Accidents	**1,477**	**1,737**	**2,137**	**2,441**	**2,663**
Pupil Passengers					
Killed	1	0	1	0	0
Severely Injured	8	11	0	4	0
Moderately Injured	97	148	103	103	96
Complained of Pain	177	427	277	523	467
Total Injured	**283**	**586**	**380**	**630**	**563**
Pupil Pedestrians					
Killed	0	0	1	0	0
Severely Injured	0	0	0	1	1
Moderately Injured	3	6	2	5	0
Complained of Pain	1	0	4	2	3
Total Injured	**4**	**6**	**6**	**8**	**4**
Total Number of School Buses	**19,099**	**19,179**	**19,773**	**21,653**	**20,639**
Total Mileage Driven (in millions)	**246**	**262**	**275**	**290**	**279**

22.31,90   Source: California Highway Patrol, *Information Bulletin.*

ACCIDENTS AT RAILROAD GRADE CROSSINGS				
Year	Accidents	Killed	Injuries	Casualties per 10,000 Registered Vehicles
1920	NA	104	260	6.0
1940	NA	159	661	2.7
1960	NA	133	631	0.8
1970	913	73	408	0.3
1980	409	27	119	0.1
1981	392	29	133	0.1
1982	312	31	105	0.1
1983	291	12	81	0.1
1984	289	26	101	0.1
1985	353	23	104	0.1
1986	249	27	58	0.04
1987	269	19	85	NA

22.32,90 Source: California Public Utilities Commission, *Annual Report of Railroad Accidents.*

RAILROAD ACCIDENTS			
Year	Accidents	Accidents Involving Hazardous Materials	Hazardous Materials Released
1978	364	23	4
1979	271	16	4
1980	361	35	2
1981	284	30	3
1982	249	27	1
1983	286	31	1
1984	257	24	3
1985	197	20	3
1986	132	17	1
1987	89	12	0

22.33, 90 Source: California Public Utilities Commission, *Annual Report of Railroad Accidents.*

RAILROAD EMPLOYMENT 1970-1989					
State	1970	1980	1985	1987	1989*
California	39,420	30,395	23,200	19,720	18,500
New York	35,860	25,327	18,900	18,043	17,400
Illinois	59,120	38,004	29,100	22,241	22,900
Texas	28,760	29,311	22,900	19,691	17,900
Pennsylvania	50,260	34,291	23,400	17,663	21,100
Arizona	3,660	3,219	3,400	2,742	2,800
Oregon	8,990	6,456	4,600	3,980	3,600
Nevada	1,820	1,840	1,300	885	1,000
Total U.S.	610,300	488,340	371,600	287,617	300,000

* Estimated.

Note: California has 6.9% of U.S. railroad employees.

22.34,90 Source: Association of American Railroads Yearbook of Railroad Facts, and Railroad Retirement Board, unpublished data.

MILES OF RAILROAD TRACK IN CALIFORNIA AND SELECTED STATES 1980-1987						
	1950	1980	1982	1985	1986	1987
California	7,533	6,862	6,476	6,438	6,287	6,267
New York	7,493	4,605	4,281	3,565	3,453	3,408
Illinois	11,643	10,672	9,639	8,380	7,960	7,584
Texas	15,611	13,313	13,011	12,853	12,802	12,683
Pennsylvania	9,695	7,197	6,761	5,232	5,113	4,900
Arizona	2,197	1,865	1,801	1,757	1,698	1,692
Oregon	3,217	2,944	2,941	2,889	2,865	2,848
Nevada	1,650	1,564	1,492	1,451	1,451	1,440
U.S. Total	223,500	183,077	171,178	159,360	154,657	146,584

Note: California has 4.3% of the railroad track mileage in the U.S.

22.35,90 Source: Association of American Railroads, *Yearbook of Railroad Facts.*

CALIFORNIA RAILROADS AND ASSESED VALUATION

Railroad Companies	Valuation (in thousands)
Alameda Belt Line	$7,896
Almanor Railroad Co.	$136
Amador Central Railroad Co.	$3,913
Atchison, Topeka, & Santa Fe Railroad Co.	$507,381
Burlington Northern, Inc.	$5,971
California Western Railroad (Mendocino Coast Railroad)	$1,496
Central California Traction Co.	$53,361
Eureka Southern Railroad Co.	$3,370
Lake County, Oregon Railroad Co.	$374
Los Angeles Junction Railway Co.	$17,152
McCloud River Railroad Co.	$14,345
Modesto and Empire Traction Co.	$17,668
Napa Valley Railroad (Napa Valley Wine Train)	$4,861
Northwestern Pacific Railroad Co.	$29,052
Oakland Terminal Railway	$731
Parr Terminal Railway	$531
Port Railroads Inc.	$71
Quincy Railroad Co.	$408
San Diego & Imperial Valley Railroad Co.	$2,082
San Diego and Arizona Eastern Railway Co.	$704
Santa Cruz, Big Tree & Pacific Railroad Co.	$680
Santa Maria Valley Railroad Co.	$2,863
Sierrra Railroad Co.	$1,058
Southern Pacific Transportation Co.	$1,323,285
Stockton Terminal and Eastern Railroad	$7,873
Sunset Railway Co.	$702
Trona Railway Co.	$17,112
Union Pacific Corporation	$278,636
Ventura County Railway Co.	$2,428
Visalia Electric Railroad Co.	$849
Yreka Western Railroad Co.	$1,085
Total for Railroad Companies	**$2,257,354**

22.36,90 Source: State Board of Equalization, *Annual Report 1987-88*.

CALIFORNIA MASS TRANSIT

Year	Passengers	Revenue Vehicle Miles (in millions)
1982-83	1,101,000,000	325
1983-84	1,176,000,000	329
1984-85	1,167,000,000	335
1985-86	1,103,000,000	334
1986-87	1,079,000,000	339
1987-88	1,110,000,000	344

22.37,90 Source: California State Controller, *Financial Transactions concerning Transit Operations and Non-Transit Claimants*.

MASS TRANSIT DISTRICTS	
Jurisdiction Providing Transit Services	Number
Counties	39
Cities	144
Transit Districts	49
Consolidated Transportation Service Agency	9
Total	**241**

22.38,90 Source: California State Controller, *Annual Report 1987-88 Transit Operators & Non-Transit Claimants*.

LAND TRANSPORTATION EMPLOYMENT & BUSINESSES			
Type of Employment	Number of Companies	Number of Employees 1986	Annual Payroll (millions)
Local and Intercity Passenger Transit	991	26,275	$384
Trucking	8,086	113,572	$2,561
Transportation Services	5,690	46,548	$876
California Department of Transportation	NA	16,651*	NA

* 1989.
22.39,90 Source: U.S. Bureau of the Census, *County Business Patterns, California*, and California Governor's Budget.

TRANSPORTATION SECTOR ESTABLISHMENTS AND INCOME		
Year	Establishments	Net Income* (in millions)
1979	4,195	$151
1980	4,373	$201
1981	4,567	$178
1982	5,375	-$110
1983	5,489	$672
1984	6,232	$481
1985	8,080	$344
1986	6,157	$140

* Subject to state taxation.
22.40,90 Source: *Economic Report of the Governor*.

CRUDE OIL PIPELINES IN CALIFORNIA		
Type	Miles	Capacity (barrels per day)
Trunk Lines	4,800	932,000
Gathering Lines	2,700	NA

Note: Trunk lines are large diameter pipelines. Gathering lines are smaller diameter pipelines that feed oil from the fields to the trunk lines.
22.41,90 Source: California Energy Commission, *Annual Petroleum Review*, 1982, and telephone update, 1989.

REFINED OIL (PRODUCT) PIPELINES IN CALIFORNIA		
	Miles	Capacity (barrels per day)
All Pipelines	1,680	916,000

22.42,90 Source: California Energy Commission, *Annual Petroleum Review*, 1982, and telephone update, 1989

NATURAL GAS PIPELINES IN CALIFORNIA	
Company	Miles of Pipeline
Pacific Gas and Electric	
Transmission Lines	5,300
Distribution Lines	32,600
Total	**37,900**
Southern California Gas Company	
Transmission and Storage Lines	3,353
Distribution Lines	38,926
Total	**42,279**
San Diego Gas and Electric Company	
Transmission Lines	133
Distribution Lines	5,832
Service Lines	1,799
Total	**7,764**

22.43,90 Source: The respective utility companies, 1989.

SECTION 22 NOTE
While the number of mass transit passengers in California has been unchanged for almost a decade, the annual cost of operating the state's mass transit has risen from $927 million to $1.8 billion. So it costs twice as much to move the same number of riders as it did a decade ago.

22.44,90

SECTION 22 NOTE
The most likely time to be in an auto accident where someone is injured is Friday afternoon between 5 and 6 P.M.

22.45,90

Air and Water Transportation

Two of the top four shipping ports in the United States are now in California: Los Angeles-Long Beach and Oakland. Los Angeles-Long Beach, the leading port in the United States, has expanded its lead over New York during the 1980s. The port of Oakland, however, has seen its market share slip significantly during the past two decades. In 1970, some 47 percent of the container shipments on the West Coast came through Oakland. That figure is now down to 17 percent (for Los Angeles-Long Beach it is 37 percent). Oakland has lost some share of the market because it has failed to modernize its equipment to compete with Seattle and Los Angeles.

Oakland faces the additional problem of silt buildup in its shipping lanes and the consequent need for periodic dredging so that the new and larger container vessels can use the port. In the past dredging was a fairly routine matter. More recently, however, Oakland's desire to widen and deepen its shipping channels has been thwarted by a coalition of individuals concerned about the effects of dredging on fishing and on the environment. The coalition's goals range from preventing the dumping of dredged mud at specific sites to ending all dredging. These goals are based largely on environmentalists' fears that dredging will stir up contaminants on the floor of San Francisco Bay.

Another threat to any port's long-term health is the possibility that its real estate will be appropriated for uses unconnected to the shipping business. This has happened in San Francisco, where wharf space is now being used primarily for tourist attractions such as Fisherman's Wharf and Pier 39. San Francisco's Port Authority reaps large rents from Fisherman's Wharf, the state's second largest tourist attraction, but few ships now dock on the San Francisco side of the bay. Oakland, in the face of similar pressures to develop its port and airport land, appears to be yielding. Backers of the port say that Oakland should puts its money and effort into modernizing its port facility and retaining its share of the market. If Oakland follows San Francisco's lead and emphasizes tourism instead, Los Angeles-Long Beach will most likely pick up the slack and become an even more dominant Pacific port.

VESSELS ARRIVING AT MAJOR PORTS 1981-1988					
	Number of Ships			Percent of Total		
City	1981	1987	1988	1981	1987	1988
Los Angeles-Long Beach	7,343	7,106	7,076	16.3%	19.0%	19.0%
New York-New Jersey	6,544	5,580	5,310	14.6	15.0	14.1
Houston	5,592	4,789	4,750	12.1	13.0	12.9
New Orleans	5,086	3,681	3,661	11.3	9.8	9.8
Oakland-San Francisco	3,781	3,662	3,675	8.4	9.8	9.8
Philadelphia	3,483	2,959	3,041	7.8	8.0	8.1
Hampton Roads	3,703	2,738	2,953	8.3	7.3	7.9
Baltimore	3,751	2,738	2,766	8.4	7.3	7.3
Columbia River	2,006	2,010	2,302	4.5	5.4	6.2
Seattle/Puget Sound	2,634	1,200	980	5.9	3.2	2.6
Boston	1,081	793	881	2.4	2.1	2.3
Total	45,014	37,379	37,395	100.0%	100.0%	100.0%

23.1,90 Source: Maritime Association of the Port of New York, unpublished data, 1989.

SHIPPING VESSELS - ARRIVALS						
	Los Angeles		San Francisco and Oakland		San Diego	
	1986	1988	1986	1988	1986	1988
Number - Foreign Flag	6,050	5,785	2,549	2,551	274	332
Percent - Foreign Flag	86%	82%	69%	69%	95%	98%
Number - Cargo	5,403	5,111	2,265	2,164	222†	91
Percent - Cargo	77%	72%	62%	59%	77%	27%
Number - Tankers	1,147	1,213	1,041	1,001	4	1
Percent - Tankers	16%	17%	28%	27%	1%	.3%
Number - Passenger	304	339	77	37	NA	127
Percent - Passenger	4%	5%	2%	1%	NA	37%
Number - Seagoing Barges	202	413	NA	NA	101††	122
Percent - Seagoing Barges	3%	6%	NA	NA	NA	36%
Number - Miscellaneous	NA	199	23	152	61	NA
Percent - Misscellaneous	NA	3%	1%	4%	21%	NA
Number - Auto Carriers	42	512	258	306	NA	0
Percent - Auto Carriers	0.6%	7%	7%	8%	NA	0%
Total Number of Vessels	7,056	7,076	3,669	3,671	287*	340

*   Another 781 vessels, mostly tuna boats, arrived in San Diego.
†   Includes passenger ships.
††   Not included in calculating foreign flag or major shipping arrivals.
    23.2,90 Source: Los Angeles, San Diego, & San Francisco Marine Exchanges.

SECTION 23 NOTE
The seventh-largest oil spill in the U.S. took place in San Francisco Bay on October 31, 1984, when a Puerto Rican tanker spilled 2 million gallons of oil.

23.3,90

SHIPPING VESSEL - ARRIVALS BY FLAGS, 1988			
Oakland/San Francisco		**Los Angeles/Long Beach**	
Country	Ships	Country	Ships
U.S.	1,120	Panama	1,517
Panama	674	U.S.	1,291
Liberia	347	Liberia	717
Japan	251	Japan	482
West Germany	156	Britain	254
Denmark	133	Philippines	237
Britain	113	Greece	236
Singapore	104	Cypress	209
South Korea	93	Bahamas	205
Norway	53	South Korea	196
		Taiwan	190
		West Germany	132

23.4,90 Source: Los Angeles & San Francisco Marine Exchanges.

BOATING FACILITIES								
County	Boat Facilities	Boat Storage			County	Boat Facilities	Boat Storage	
		Berths	Moorings	Dry Storage			Berths	Moorings	Dry Storage

County	Boat Facilities	Berths	Moorings	Dry Storage	County	Boat Facilities	Berths	Moorings	Dry Storage
Alameda	43	6,491	21	806	Plumas	30	694	28	25
Alpine	4	15	10	-	Riverside	28	421	300	760
Amador	9	302	58	160	Sacramento	54	3,759	73	606
Butte	16	516	296	80	San Benito	NA	NA	NA	NA
Calaveras	6	127	62	98	San Bernardino	37	2,185	1,155	821
Colusa	6	240	-	-	San Diego	83	8,133	303	782
Contra Costa	81	7,091	20	2,513	San Francisco	16	2,093	68	40
Del Norte	21	1,905	265	40	San Joaquin	37	3,525	50	428
El Dorado	21	1,143	260	94	San Luis Obispo	19	752	274	188
Fresno	26	1,882	61	79	San Mateo	12	3,412	204	500
Glenn	6	38	-	-	Santa Barbara	8	1,177	6	280
Humboldt	21	530	406	-	Santa Clara	12	489	10	130
Imperial	22	350	130	112	Santa Cruz	9	960	100	330
Inyo	5	10	16	-	Shasta	44	2,079	490	85
Kern	17	210	185	40	Sierra	5	-	-	-
Kings	NA	NA	NA	NA	Siskiyou	12	57	40	45
Lake	132	1,174	480	470	Solano	28	1,826	53	360
Lassen	4	100	4	25	Sonoma	18	715	10	181
Los Angeles	93	17,321	1,361	1,624	Stanislaus	9	40	10	-
Madera	12	80	65	-	Sutter	5	256	90	50
Marin	37	4,266	135	537	Tehama	17	195	16	60
Mariposa	6	132	246	110	Trinity	17	413	160	60
Mendocino	9	552	155	125	Tulare	8	543	-	-
Merced	6	51	-	-	Tuolumne	9	758	355	58
Modoc	9	-	-	-	Ventura	25	4,783	5	859
Mono	23	539	37	132	Yolo	12	148	-	150
Monterey	11	1,498	212	175	Yuba	7	178	112	40
Napa	15	1,483	24	600	State Totals	1,310	98,467	8,761	17,871
Nevada	13	179	107	9	S.F. Bay Area*	202	24,276	502	4,079
Orange	50	10,367	113	2,328	Delta †	142	10,778	166	2,298
Placer	25	284	120	866	South Coast ƒ	251	40,604	1,782	5,603

* Includes Sonoma, Napa, Marin, San Francisco, Alameda, San Mateo, Santa Clara counties & parts of Solano & Contra Costa counties.

† Includes San Joaquin County & parts of Solano, Contra Costa & Sacramento counties.

ƒ Includes Ventura, Los Angeles, Orange & San Diego counties.

23.5,90 Source: Cal. Resources Agency, Dept. of Boating and Waterways-*Inventory of California Boating Facilities* 1987.

BOATS	
Registered Boats*	
Year	Number of Boats
1981	576,166
1982	586,190
1983	548,895
1985	515,097
1986	679,880
1987	711,193
1988	737,143
Boat Characteristics	
Under 16 feet	354,546
16 - 25 feet	330,975
26 - 39 feet	42,163
40 - 65 feet	6,684
Over 65 feet	449
Wood	38,954
Plastic	485,166
Aluminum	148,848
Steel	3,746
Metal	167,031
Concrete	NA
Other	38,060
Inboard	53,061
Outboard	361,254
Inboard/Outboard	141,564
Auxiliary Sail	24,535
Sailboat	47,511
Rowboat	9,844
Canoe	1,236
Other Hand Propelled	6,979
Jet	69,575
Other	19,262

* 97% of the registered boats are pleasure boats.
23.6,90 Source: California Department of Motor Vehicles, unpublished data, 1989.

NUMBER OF EMPLOYEES IN AIR AND WATER TRANSPORTATION* IN CALIFORNIA, 1981-1986		
Year	Air Transportation	Water Transportation
1981	74,300	20,600
1982	68,595	22,775
1984	66,461	22,302
1986	74,385	20,996

* Includes employees in air and water transportation services.
23.7,90 Source: U.S. Bureau of the Census, *County Business Patterns, California.*

NUMBER OF ESTABLISHMENTS AND ANNUAL PAYROLL OF AIR AND WATER TRANSPORTATION BUSINESSES IN CALIFORNIA 1980-1986				
	Air Transportation		Water Transportation	
Year	Number	Payroll (in millions)	Number	Payroll (in millions)
1980	719	$1,965	510	$481
1981	764	$2,095	482	$514
1982	833	$2,080	499	$611
1984	998	$2,151	543	$760
1986	1,038	$2,419	535	$804

23.8,90 Source: U.S. Bureau of the Census, *County Business Patterns, California.*

U.S. COAST GUARD IN CALIFORNIA, 1988	
	11th C.G. District
Personnel	
Officers	NA
Enlisted	NA
Total Military	**1,723**
Civilians	77
Reserve Military	2,700
Auxilery	3,927
Ships	
Cutters (378-foot)	4
Medium Cutters (180-210-foot)	2
95-110-foot Patrol	2
Buoy Tenders	2
82-foot Patrol	14
Boats	
(under 65 feet)	81
Aircraft	
Fixed Wing	7
Helicopters	13
Search and Rescue Missions	
Total	4,959
Lives Lost	164
Lives Saved	308
Persons Assisted	10,118
Property Assisted (millions)	$201
Property Loss (millions)	$20.6
Coast Guard Auxiliary	
Boats	614
Aircraft	54
Navigational Aids (lighthouses, buoys, etc., for which U.S.C.G.is responsible)	1,700

23.9,90 Source: U.S. Coast Guard, 11th Districts Command, unpublished data.

CALIFORNIA AIRPORTS

	1947	1982	1984	1987	1989
Public Use	347	296	289	283	269
Private Use (inventory)	---	747	77	775	745
Pivate Use (exempt)	---	500*	529*	529*	606
Heliports	---	297	339	406	427
Stolports	---	3	0	3	1
Seaplane Bases	---	17	7	12	9
Total Airports and Helipads	---	**1,840**	**1,931**	**1,993**	**2,057**

* Estimate.

23.10,90 Source: California Department of Transportation - Division of Aeronautics; unpublished data, and FAA *Statistical Handbook of Aviation.*

CALIFORNIA AIRPORTS, PAVED AND LIGHTED

Paved Airports		Unpaved Airports		Ownership	
Lighted	Not Lighted	Lighted	Not Lighted	Public	Private
255	387	14	253	316	593

23.11,90 Source: FAA *Statistical Handbook of Aviation, 1987.*

NUMBER OF CALIFORNIA AIRPORTS WITH SCHEDULED AIRLINE SERVICE

	Number	
Type of Service	1987	1989
Major Carriers (Jet Aircraft Service)	19	18
Prior to Deregulation	27	27
Commuter Carriers	23	20
Total	**42**	**38**

23.12,90 Source: FAA *Statistical Handbook of Aviation,* and California Department of Transportation, Division of Aeronautics, unpublished data, 1989.

NUMBER OF SCHEDULED AIRLINE COMPANIES OPERATING IN CALIFORNIA*

	1987	1989
Major Domestic Carriers	27	20
Major Foreign Carriers	40	37
Commuter Carriers (Regionals)	11	4

* Cargo carriers are included among major & commuter carriers.

23.13,90 Source: California Department of Transportation, Division of Aeronautics, unpublished data, 1989.

SECTION 23 NOTE

California has more air shows annually than any other state.

23.14,90

AIR PASSENGER TRAFFIC IN CALIFORNIA AIRPORTS 1972-1988	
Year	Number of Passengers*
1972	51,837,195
1976	64,361,802
1978	81,403,197
1980	77,739,663
1981	75,433,650
1982	76,600,000
1983	83,300,000
1984	88,000,000
1985	95,727,660
1986	101,790,050
1987	115,298,974
1988	116,100,143

* Passenger counts are inflated by approximately 30% since intrastate traffic is counted twice, at the point of departure and the point of arrival.
23.15,90 Source: *FAA Statistical Handbook of Aviation, 1981*, and California Department of Transportation, *Division of Aeronautics, Travel and Related Factors in California*, and unpublished data.

AIR PASSENGER TRAFFIC BY MAJOR AIRPORTS (in millions)					
	1970	1980	1985	1987	1988
Los Angeles International	20.1	33.0	36.7	44.9	44.4
San Francisco	14.7	22.2	25.0	29.8	30.5
San Diego	3.9	5.1	7.9	9.4	10.7
San Jose	1.9*	2.9	4.7	5.7	5.7
Ontario	0.9	2.0	3.7	4.6	4.8
John Wayne (Orange County)	0.9	2.4	3.3	4.6	4.5
Oakland	2.1	2.4	4.1	4.0	3.8
Sacramento	1.5*	2.3	2.9	3.8	3.8
Burbank	1.4	1.9	2.9	3.2	3.0
Long Beach	---	---	1.1	1.2	1.2
Fresno	---	---	0.8	1.0	0.9
Palm Springs	---	---	0.6	0.8	0.8
Santa Barbara	---	---	0.5	0.7	0.6
Monterey	---	---	0.4	0.6	0.5

* Estimate.
Note: These 14 airports handle 95% of California air passenger traffic.
23.16,90 Source: *FAA Statistical Handbook of Aviation*, and California Dept. of Transportation, Division of Aeronautics, unpublished data.

CALIFORNIA AIRPORTS-CARRIER AIRCRAFT DEPARTURES, PASSENGER AND FREIGHT, 1987

	Domestic Aircraft Departures	International Aircraft Departures	Total Departures
Total Aircraft	664,723	7,464	672,187
Enplaned Passengers	50,255,192	1,130,598	51,385,790
Freight*	564,904	25,679	590,583
Express Freight*	308	NA	308
Priority U.S. Mail*	141,513	4,713	146,226
Non-priority U.S. Mail*	4,329	579	4,907
Foreign Mail*	10.9	17.3	28.2

* Freight & mail in revenue tons.
23.17,90 Source: *FAA Airport of Activity Statistics*, 1987.

GENERAL AVIATION AIRCRAFT AT CALIFORNIA AIRPORTS

Year	Public Use	Private Use*	Total
1970	19,261	1,030	20,291
1980	31,227	1,644	32,871
1981	31,595	1,663	33,258
1982	31,824	1,674	33,498
1983	NA	NA	29,236
1985	NA	NA	29,392
1987	NA	NA	30,982

* Estimate.   23.18,90 Source: *FAA Statistical Handbook of Aviation*, 1987.

GENERAL AVIATION ACTIVITY AT FAA OPERATED AIRPORTS IN CALIFORNIA

Rank	City	Number of Aircraft Operations*
1	Van Nuys	485,367
2	Santa Ana	436,408
3	Long Beach	419,907
4	Oakland	274,440

* Non-local itinerant operations.
23.19,90 Source: *FAA Statistical Handbook of Aviation*, 1987.

PILOT REPORTED NEAR MIDAIR COLLISIONS IN CALIFORNIA AIRSPACE, 1986-1989

Year	Near Midair Collisions	% of U.S. Incidents
1986	203	24%
1987	261	25%
1988	170	24%
1989*	23	19%

* 1st quarter.   23.20,90 Source: Federal Aviation Administration, *Safety Statistical Handbook*.

	AIRCRAFT ACCIDENTS IN CALIFORNIA					
	General Aviation			Commercial Aviation		
Year	Accidents	Fatalities	Serious Injuries	Accidents	Fatalities	Serious Injuries
1964	647	203	69	6	47	0
1970	587	171	74	13	9	4
1975	468	187	80	14	22	5
1980	455	198	81	14	3	7
1985	314	129	78	10	1	6
1986	305	195	56	8	5	7
1987	295	134	62	14	47	2
1988	306	131	67	7	8	6

23.21,90 Source: U.S. National Transportation Safety Board, unpublished data.

ACTIVE CERTIFICATED PILOTS IN CALIFORNIA BY CATEGORY					
Category	1981	1983	1985	1987	Percentage of 1987 U.S. Totals
Student Pilots	24,893	19,962	20,960	19,662	13.5%
Private Pilots	49,918	47,795	47,735	45,541	15.1%
Commercial Pilots	24,006	22,657	21,790	20,043	14.0%
Airline Pilots	10,575	10,625	10,994	11,916	13.1%
Flight Instructors	7,998	8,388	7,827	7,870	13.0%
Helicopter, Glider, Blimp and Other Pilots	2,457	2,786	2,894	2,940	16.6%
Total Pilots	111,849	103,825	104,373	100,102	14.3%

23.22,90 Source: *FAA Statistical Handbook of Aviation*, 1987.

ACTIVE CERTIFICATED PILOTS IN CALIFORNIA, BY YEAR	
Year	Number
1977	107,188
1979	117,038
1980	121,305
1981	111,849
1983	103,825
1985	104,373
1987	100,102

23.23,90 Source: *FAA Statistical Handbook of Aviation*, 1987.

SECTION 23 NOTE

The first nonstop flight across the U.S. was from Roosevelt
Field on Long Island to San Diego's Rockwell Field. The
two pilots were Army Air Sevice Lieutenants Oakky Kelly
and John Macready. The flight of 2,470 miles was completed
in 27 hours. The plane landed on May 3, 1923.

23.24,90

SECTION 23 NOTE

In 1989 there was only one publicly held airline based in California:
Westair (United Express), headquartered in San Francisco.

23.25,90

SECTION 23 NOTE

The second largest aircraft leasing company in the world is the
International Lease Finance Corporation in Beverly Hills.

23.26,90

Agriculture

After enduring three dry years, California farmers in early 1989 were bracing for a difficult growing season. The U.S. Bureau of Reclamation had threatened up to a 50-percent cut in irrigation water to its agricultural customers. State water cuts could have been as high as 60 percent. These cuts would have meant either that many crops could not be planted or that expensive well water would have been used to sustain the crops in many areas. Heavy rains in March 1989, however, rewrote the dire scenarios: the planting season was normal, with most of the federal Central Valley Project water customers getting their customary allocations.

As if California's farmers did not have enough to worry about from the weather, increased foreign competition from Mexico, Chile, Western Europe, and New Zealand has been cutting into California's share of the U.S. market. With domestic sales lagging, California farmers will be forced to look to overseas markets to sustain themselves. Currently about 25 percent of the state's farmland is planted with crops for export; the value of these exports has grown by 30 percent in the past two years--to about $3.7 billion. Exports, however, still lag behind those for the record year 1981, when they reached $4.2 billion. Japan continues as our leading buyer of farm products, consuming 29 percent of what we export--as much as all of Europe.

Periodic pesticide scares have created a renewed interest in organic farming, that is, agriculture in which farmers use either fewer synthetic chemicals and fertilizers or none at all. Until recently organic farming was limited to a relatively small core of health-food faddists. But mainstream farming entities such as Castle and Cooke and Sunkist are finding that consumers are increasingly interested in farm products free of chemicals. Although only 1 percent of produce is currently grown organically, some experts see this market growing to as much as 10 percent in the next few years.

Specialty agriculture in California is meeting with greater success as cooks--both in restaurants and at home--become more adventurous. Although relatively few farmers now cultivate baby vegetables, radicchio, purple potatoes, orange cauliflower, or edible flowers, this niche market is expanding rapidly, attracting mainstream farmers who see its potential for profits.

Not to be outdone by the state's dirt farmers, poultry producers in the Central Valley have put Modesto on the map as the nation's squab capital: Modesto produces 400,000 of the edible pigeons annually. California also produces a larger form of unusual poultry, the ostrich. The Circle M Ranch in Sonoma, the only ostrich ranch in the West, breeds this bird primarily for its hide and to a lesser extent for its feathers.

TOP 10 STATES IN CASH FARM RECEIPTS (in billions)				
	1985		1987	
State	**Rank**	**Receipts**	**Rank**	**Receipts**
California	**1**	**$14.0**	**1**	**$15.6**
Texas	2	$9.3	2	$9.2
Iowa	3	$9.2	3	$9.1
Nebraska	5	$7.2	4	$6.9
Illinois	4	$7.8	5	$6.2
Minnesota	6	$6.5	6	$5.7
Kansas	7	$5.7	7	$5.5
Wisconsin	8	$5.1	8	$5.2
Florida	9	$4.7	9	$5.1
Indiana	10	$4.6	11	$3.9
Total U.S.		**$142.1**		**$136.5**

24.1,90 Source: U.S. Department of Agriculture, *Economic Indicators of the Farm Sector, State Financial Summary.*

NUMBER OF FARMS, LAND IN FARMS AND SIZE OF FARM IN CALIFORNIA 1920-1988			
Year	**Number of Farms**	**Land in Farms (1,000 acres)**	**Average Size of Farm (acres)**
1920	117,670	29,400	250
1930	135,676	30,400	224
1940	132,658	30,500	230
1950*	137,030	36,600	267
1959	99,274	36,888	372
1969	77,875	35,772	459
1980†	80,000	33,900	424
1982	82,000	33,400	407
1984	78,000	33,000	423
1986	79,000	33,000	418
1988	78,000	33,000	417

* Old definition of farm: Places of 10 or more acres that had annual sales of agricultural products of $50 or more, and places of less than 10 acres that had annual sales of $250 or more.

† New definition of farm: Places with annual sales of agricultural products of $1,000 or more.

24.2,90 Source: California Department of Food and Agriculture, *California Agriculture,* 1988, and *U.S. Statistical Abstract.* Also, U.S. Bureau of the Census, *Census of Agriculture* and, U.S. Department of Agriculture, *Crop Production.*

	NUMBER OF FARMS, TOTAL LAND AREA, LAND IN FARMS, AND CROPLAND HARVESTED, BY COUNTY, 1987				
County	Number of Farms	Land in Farms (acres)	Average Size of Farm (acres)	% of Land Area in Farms	Crop Land Harvested (acres)
Alameda	692	241,276	349	51.2%	15,643
Alpine	8	6,987	873	1.5%	*
Amador	371	218,532	589	57.9%	5,749
Butte	2,030	494,530	244	46.9%	181,867
Calaveras	431	253,421	588	38.8%	1,987
Colusa	764	456,266	597	61.9%	214,297
Contra Costa	840	200,262	238	42.9%	30,267
Del Norte	84	13,139	156	2.0%	2,934
El Dorado	738	128,135	174	11.7%	3,632
Fresno	7,590	1,975,373	260	51.6%	1,010,151
Glenn	1,170	490,732	419	58.1%	181,890
Humboldt	890	616,267	692	26.9%	13,512
Imperial	804	542,958	675	20.3%	409,682
Inyo	94	219,816	2,338	3.4%	*
Kern	2,255	3,037,068	1,347	58.4%	746,185
Kings	1,204	702,173	583	78.8%	441,602
Lake	873	154,903	177	19.2%	23,336
Lassen	413	517,976	1,254	17.8%	63,614
Los Angeles	2,035	280,156	138	10.8%	37,102
Madera	1,746	757,263	434	55.2%	239,133
Marin	285	167,590	588	50.1%	4,123
Mariposa	255	236,709	928	25.4%	1,832
Mendocino	1,067	777,264	728	34.6%	26,299
Merced	3,048	1,049,302	344	84.3%	382,246
Modoc	495	729,023	1,473	28.0%	108,517
Mono	76	72,900	959	3.8%	8,871
Monterey	1,364	1,384,702	1,015	65.5%	214,053
Napa	1,197	258,197	216	54.2%	43,328
Nevada	386	56,179	146	9.1%	2,276
Orange	504	108,887	216	21.3%	18,888
Placer	1,233	168,223	136	18.6%	23,158
Plumas	109	88,132	809	5.4%	12,880
Riverside	3,874	491,150	127	10.6%	217,994
Sacramento	1,586	412,225	260	66.3%	115,478
San Benito	704	631,888	898	71.1%	50,154
San Bernardino	1,938	1,682,364	868	13.1%	39,642
San Diego	6,259	529,964	85	19.7%	82,419
San Francisco	5	*	*	*	10
San Joaquin	4,366	823,729	189	90.9%	457,638
San Luis Obispo	1,991	1,444,385	725	68.2%	123,171
San Mateo	330	63,511	192	22.2%	8,079
Santa Barbara	1,756	869,969	495	49.5%	91,383
Santa Clara	1,312	347,504	265	42.0%	28,725
Santa Cruz	813	55,205	68	19.3%	20,469
Shasta	899	377,352	420	15.6%	26,023
Sierra	46	51,352	1,116	8.4%	3,782
Siskiyou	765	669,385	875	16.7%	97,739
Solano	895	321,297	359	60.2%	117,395
Sonoma	3,039	549,539	181	53.5%	86,695
Stanislaus	4,630	719,845	155	74.7%	288,899
Sutter	1,438	355,973	248	92.4%	230,996
Tehama	1,420	1,104,584	778	58.4%	69,032
Trinity	133	104,010	782	5.1%	1,194
Tulare	5,911	1,410,172	239	45.8%	598,783
Tuolumne	271	121,119	447	8.5%	*
Ventura	2,120	328,960	155	27.6%	107,269
Yolo	1,011	505,597	500	77.9%	277,071
Yuba	654	222,748	341	54.4%	62,361
State Totals	83,217	30,598,178	368	30.6%	7,676,287

* Withheld to avoid disclosing data for individual farms.

24.3,90 Source: U.S. Department of Commerce, Bureau of the Census, *1987 U.S. Census of Agriculture.*

NUMBER OF FARMS AND LAND IN FARMS
1981-1988

Year	Number of Farms*		California as a % of U.S.	Land in Farms (in million acres)		California as a % of U.S.
	California	U.S.		California	U.S.	
1981	83,000	2,435,810	3.4%	33.6	1,044	3.3%
1982	82,000	2,241,000	3.6%	33.4	987	3.3%
1984	78,000	2,333,000	3.3%	33.0	1,020	3.2%
1985	79,000	2,285,000	3.5%	32.8	1,016	3.2%
1986	79,000	2,214,000	3.6%	33.0	1,007	3.3%
1988	78,000	2,159,000	3.6%	33.0	999	3.3%

* A farm is a place having annual sales of agricultural products of $1000 or more.

24.4,90 Source: California Department of Food and Agriculture, *California Agriculture* , and *U.S. Statistical Abstract*.

CALIFORNIA IRRIGATED AND HARVESTED FARMLAND IN ACRES*
1978-1987

Year	Total Cropland Harvested	Total Irrigated Land†
1978	8,908,961	8,568,886
1982	8,764,808	8,460,508
1987	7,676,287	7,596,091

* All farms with annual sales of agricultural products of $1,000 or more.

† Includes both cropland and pasture.

24.5,90 Source: U.S. Dept. of Commerce, Bureau of the Census, *U.S. Census of Agriculture*.

NUMBER OF CALIFORNIA FARMS BY SIZE GROUP
1920-1982

Year	Size in Acres							Total
	Under 10	10-49	50-179	180-499	500-999	1000-1999	2000-or More	
1920	16,697	49,093	NA	NA	5,052	4,906*	NA	117,670
1930	28,892	56,985	NA	NA	4,861	5,054*	NA	135,676
1940	31,546	54,467	25,869	10,960	4,551	5,265*	NA	132,658
1950	37,402	51,760	25,854	11,160	4,853	6,001*	NA	137,030
1959	24,110	34,570	20,195	9,922	4,464	2,821	3,192	99,274
1969	15,692	28,915	16,160	7,896	3,745	2,541	2,926	77,875
1978†	20,873	28,285	15,774	8,112	3,645	2,377	2,797	81,863
1982†	22,957	28,203	14,874	7,637	3,635	2,435	2,727	82,468

† All Farms with annual sales of $1,000 or more.   * 1,000 acres or more.

24.6,90 Source: U.S. Department of commerce, Bureau of the Census, *U.S. Census of Agriculture*.

LAND UTILIZATION IN CALIFORNIA, 1988 (in 1,000 acres)								
	Crop Land							
	Used for Crops*	Idle	Used only for Pasture	Grass-land Pasture**	Forest Land†	Special Use Areas	Other††	Total Land
California	9,579	642	1,345	22,580	37,043	13,827	15,015	100,031
U.S.	382,755	21,498	65,028	596,664	655,280	269,739	274,183	2,265,147
Calif. as a % of U.S.	2.5%	3.0%	2.1%	3.8%	5.7%	5.1%	5.5%	4.4%

  * Cropland harvested, crop failure, and cultivated summer fallow.
** Grassland and other nonforest pasture and range.
  † Excludes reserved forest land in parks and other special uses of land. Includes forested grazing land.
†† Includes rural transportation areas, Federal and State areas used primarily for recreation and wildlife purposes, military areas, farmsteads, and farm roads and lanes.
24.7,90 Source: *U.S. Agricultural Statistics, 1988.*

CALIFORNIA FARMLAND SOWN AND HARVESTED (in thousand acres)						
	Sown (Planted) Area			Harvested Area		
Year	California	All U.S.	California as a % of U.S.	California	All U.S.	California as a % of U.S.
1980	7,055	356,173	2.0%	6,662	340,535	2.0%
1981	7,322	364,771	2.0%	6,903	355,731	1.9%
1982	6,582	358,708	1.8%	6,185	349,644	1.8%
1983	5,207	309,536	1.7%	4,839	293,944	1.6%
1984	6,120	344,927	1.8%	5,740	335,644	1.7%
1985	6,021	342,224	1.8%	5,609	330,063	1.7%
1986	5,508	328,264	1.7%	5,091	312,578	1.6%
1987	5,431	305,101	1.8%	4,990	289,628	1.7%
1988	5,520	308,344	1.8%	5,075	290,077	1.7%

24.8,90 Source: u.S. Dep. of Agriculture, National Agricultural Statistics Service, *Annual Crop Production Summary-Acres Planted & Harvested, 1989.*

CALIFORNIA GRASS COVER TYPES AND OWNERSHIP (acres)							
	Bureau of Land Management	Other Public Ownership	U.S. Forest Service	Private	Total	Percent Private	Percent Public
Annual Grass	276,000	353,000	82,000	7,771,000	8,482,000	92%	8%
Perennial Grass	0	2,000	2,000	27,000	31,000	87%	13%
Fresh Wetland Wet Meadow	66,000	13,000	30,000	100,000	209,000	48%	52%
Total Grass	381,000	377,000	132,000	7,964,000	8,854,000	90%	10%

24.9,90 Source: California Department of Forestry, Forest Resource Assessment Program, prepublication data.

CALIFORNIA'S TWENTY LEADING FARM PRODUCTS			
	Commodity Ranking		
Farm Product	**1981**	**1986**	**1987**
Milk and Cream	1	1	1
Cattle and Calves	2	2	2
Grapes	4	3	3
Cotton	3	5	4
Nursery Products	6	4	5
Hay	5	6	6
Flowers and Foliage	9	7	7
Almonds	11	9	8
Lettuce	7	8	9
Oranges	14	12	10
Strawberries	18	11	11
Tomatoes, Processing	12	10	12
Chickens	15	14	13
Eggs, Chickens	10	13	14
Walnuts	NA	17	15
Sugar Beets	NA	19	16
Broccoli	23	15	17
Rice	13	32	18
Turkeys	20	16	19
Tomatoes, Fresh	NA	18	20

24.10,90 Source: California Dept. of Food and Agriculture, *California Agriculture,* 1987.

CROP AND LIVESTOCK COMMODITIES IN WHICH CALIFORNIA ACCOUNTS FOR MOST OF U.S. PRODUCTION 1987		
Alfalfa Seed	Green Lima Beans	Pistachios
Almonds	Hay	Plums
Apricots	Herbs	Pomegranates
Artichokes	Honeydew Melons	Prunes
Asparagus	Indoor Plants	Rabbits
Avocados	Kiwifruit	Raisins
Broccoli	Ladino Clover Seed	Safflower
Brussels Sprouts	Lemons	Spinach
Cantaloupes	Lettuce	Strawberries
Carrots	Nectarines	Sudan Grass
Casaba Melons	Nursery Products	Table Grapes
Cauliflower	Olives	Tomatoes, Processing
Celery	Onions	Turnips
Chinchillas	Oriental Vegetables	Vegetable & Flower Seeds
Crenshaw Melons	Parsley	Walnuts
Cut Flowers	Peaches	Wild Rice
Dates	Pears, Bartlett	Wine Grapes
Eggs	Persian Melons	Worms
Figs	Persimmons	
Garlic	Pigeons and Squabs	

24.11,90 Source: California Dept. of Food and Agriculture. *California Agriculture, 1987.*

Commodity	Rank in U.S. (10)	% of U.S. Prod- uction	Har- vested Acreage (1,000s)	Production (10) (short tons) (1,000s)	Value (2) ($1,000)	Rank in California (2) 1986	Rank in California (2) 1987	Leading Counties (2)
CALIFORNIA AGRICULTURAL COMMODITIES, 1987								
Alfalfa Seed	1	NA	67.0	20.3	43,784	45	43	Fresno Kings, Imperial
Almonds (Shelled)	1	100.0%	411.0	330.0	615,600	9	8	Kern, Stanislaus, Merced, San Joaquin, Fresno
Apples	4	6.2%	22.5	325.0	72,070	33	37	Kern, Santa Cruz, Sonoma, San Joaquin, Madera
Apricots	1	95.7%	22.0	110.0	33,451	52	46	Stanislaus, San Joaquin, San Benito, Kern, Merced
Asparagus	NA	NA	39.7	59.6	74,746	39	36	San Joaquin, River- side, Monterey, Imperial
Avocados	1	91.8%	75.0	278.0	93,686	21	33	San Diego, River- side, Santa Barbara, Ventura
Barley	8	2.9%	300.0	367.2	32,895	44	47	Siskiyou, Fresno, San Luis Obispo, Kern, Kings
Beans,dry	4	11.9%	168.0	155.9	84,186	35	34	Stanislaus, San Joaquin, Fresno, Sutter, Tulare
Broccoli	1	90.0%	107.6	516.5	212,562	15	17	Monterey, Santa Barbara, Fresno, Imperial, San Luis Obispo
Bushberries								
Boysenberries	NA	NA	0.5	1.7	2,364	67	67	Stanislaus, Fresno
Ollalieberries	NA	NA	0.2	0.8	1,275	69	68	Santa Cruz, Merced
Raspberries	NA	NA	0.4	1.7	5,324	60	62	Santa Cruz, Monterey
Carrots	1	50.1%	43.0	629.0	125,952	27	30	Kern Imperial, Monterey, Fresno
Desert	-	-	14.0	150.5	32,013	-	-	-
Other	-	-	29.0	478.5	93,939	-	-	-
Cauliflower	1	75.1%	51.1	281.1	147,156	25	25	Monterey, Santa Barbara, Imperial, Fresno, San Luis Obispo
Celery	1	71.3%	21.3	633.6	136,348	26	27	Ventura, Monterey, Santa Barbara
Central Coast	-	-	9.9	314.4	58,850	-	-	-
South Coast	-	-	11.4	319.2	77,498	-	-	-
Cherries, Sweet	3	21.3%	10.3	45.0	28,445	58	49	San Joaquin, Santa Clara, Stanislaus
Corn for Grain	23	0.4%	190.0	798.0	69,825	34	38	San Joaquin, Solano, Sacra- mento, Yolo, Kings

24.12.1,90 See part 5 for footnotes.

SECTION 24 NOTE
Fresno County produces more cotton than any other county in the U.S.

24.13,90

Commodity	Rank in U.S. (10)	% of U.S. Prod- uction	Har- vested Acreage (1,000s)	Production (10) (short tons) (1,000s)	Value (2) ($1,000)	Rank in California (2) 1986	Rank in California (2) 1987	Leading Counties (2)
CALIFORNIA AGRICULTURAL COMMODITIES, 1987								
Corn, Sweet	9	2.1%	16.0	76.0	20,216	49	53	Riverside, Ventura, Santa Clara, Contra Costa
Cotton	2	-	-	-	1,095,565	5	4	Fresno, Kern, Kings, Tulare
Lint	2	20.3%	1,140.9	717.9	992,479	-	-	
Seed	2	20.0%	-	1,151.8	103,086	-	-	
Cucumbers for Processing	3	9.8%	4.1	61.5	12,177	57	57	San Diego, San Joaquin, Santa Clara, Tulare, Ventura
Dates	1	100.0%	4.8	19.4	15,889	54	55	Riverside, Imperial
Figs	1	100.0%	18.1	49.4	15,313	56	56	Madera, Merced, Fresno
Flowers and Foliage (4) (5)	1	28.6%	-	-	632,465	7	7	San Diego, San Mateo, Monterey, Santa Barbara, Los Angeles
Grapefruit	2	14.4%	20.7	298.6	59,127	42	41	Riverside, San Diego, Kern, San Bernardino
Desert	-	-	9.2	134.4	23,488	-	-	-
Other	-	-	11.5	164.2	35,639	-	-	-
Grapes, All	1	88.5%	661.4	4,660.0	1,205,850(9)	3	3	Fresno, Tulare, Kern, Madera, Riverside
Raisin Type	-	-	274.5	2,200.0	504,660(9)	-	-	Fresno, Tulare, Kern, Madera
Table Type	-	-	82.8	510.0	217,260	-	-	Tulare, Riverside, Kern, Fresno, San Joaquin
Wine Type	-	-	304.1	1,950.0	483,930	-	-	Napa, Sonoma, San Joaquin, Madera, Fresno
Hay, Alfalfa and Other	1	6.0%	1,670.0	9,005.0	720,400	6	6	Imperial, Tulare, Kern, Fresno, Merced
Kiwifruit	1	100.0%	6.5	29.0	18,886	50	54	Butte, Tulare, Kern, Yuba, Sutter
Lemons	1	75.2%	48.3	817.0	152,890	20	24	Ventura, Kern, Riverside, Tulare, San Diego
Lettuce	1	67.9%	149.5	1,980.9	598,232	8	9	Monterey, Imperial, Fresno, Riverside, San Luis Obispo
Melons								
Cantaloupe	NA	NA	85.1	638.3	146,798	22	26	Imperial, Fresno, Merced, Riverside
Casaba & Santa Claus	NA	NA	2.5	22.5	4,860	62	64	Stanislaus, River-side
Crenshaw	NA	NA	1.2	9.3	3,478	65	66	Riverside, Stanislaus
Honeydew	1	77.1%	20.6	185.4	43,754	46	44	Imperial, Yolo, Fresno, Riverside
Persian	NA	NA	0.4	2.6	796	68	69	Fresno, Stanislaus, Kern

24.12.2,90 See part 5 for footnotes.

	Rank in U.S. (10)	% of U.S. Prod- uction	Har- vested Acreage (1,000s)	Production (10) (short tons) (1,000s)	Value (2) ($1,000)	Rank in California (2) 1986	1987	Leading Counties (2)
CALIFORNIA AGRICULTURAL COMMODITIES, 1987								
Commodity								
Mushrooms	2	18.2%	0.5	56.0	129,710	30	28	Monterey, Santa Clara
Nectarines	1	100.0%	23.1	191.0	65,545	38	39	Fresno, Tulare, Kern, Kings
Nursery Products (4) (6)	1	27.6%	-	-	831,042	4	5	San Diego, Los Angeles, Orange, Kern, Ventura
Oats	21	0.7%	40.0	44.8	5,040	64	63	Siskiyou, Merced, San Joaquin, Sonoma, Sacra- mento
Olives	1	100.0%	31.5	67.5	41,991	41	45	Tulare, Kern, Glenn, Butte, Tehama
Onions	1	29.4%	37.2	652.9	129,125	29	29	Imperial, Fresno, Kern, Los Angeles, San Joaquin
Oranges, All	2	32.1%	172.9	2,193.8	422,520	12	10	Tulare, Kern, Fresno, Ventura, Riverside
Navel & Misc.	-	-	106.0	1,293.8	242,840	-	-	Tulare, Kern, Fresno, Riverside, San Bernardino
Valencia	-	-	66.9	900.0	179,680	-	-	Tulare, Ventura, Kern, Riverside, San Diego
Peaches, All	1	60.5%	53.7	734.0	163,864	23	22	Fresno, Stanislaus, Tulare, Sutter, Merced
Clingstone	-	100.0%	28.8	478.5	95,612	-	-	Stanislaus, Sutter, Yuba, Merced, Butte
Freestone	-	34.7%	24.9	255.5	68,252	-	-	Fresno, Tulare, Kings
Pears, All	1	38.7%	23.1	337.0	64,794	40	40	Lake, Sacramento, Mendocino, Solano
Peppers, Chili	NA	NA	3.0	8.3	9,510	59	58	Monterey, Santa Clara
Pistachios	1	100.0%	40.3	16.6	45,477	37	42	Kern, Madera, Merced, Kings, Tulare
Plums	1	82.1%	39.2	245.0	75,361	31	35	Tulare, Fresno
Pomegranates	1	100.0%	3.4	18.5	5,631	61	61	Tulare, Fresno
Potatoes	8	4.9%	51.0	937.9	159,649	28	23	Kern, Riverside, Siskiyou, Modoc

24.12.3,90 See part 5 for footnotes.

CALIFORNIA HOUSEHOLDS OWNING PETS		
Animal	% of Households	Estimated Number of Pets
Dogs	38.7 - 46%	6 to 7.2 million
Cats	34.7 - 35%	8 million
Birds	8.9 - 10%	1 million
Horses	2.4 - 2.5%	260,000

24.14,90 Source: American Veterinary Medical Association, unpublished data, California Veterinary Medical Association, unpublished data, and Dr. Care Wise.

CALIFORNIA AGRICULTURAL COMMODITIES, 1987								
Commodity	Rank in U.S. (10)	% of U.S. Prod- uction	Har- vested Acreage (1,000s)	Production (10) (short tons) (1,000s)	Value (2) ($1,000)	Rank in California (2) 1986	1987	Leading Counties (2)
Prunes, Dried Basis	1	100.0%	75.4	228.0	166,440	36	21	Sutter, Butte, Yuba, Glenn, Tehama
Rice	2	20.4%	367.0	1,302.9	195,428(8)	32	18	Colusa, Butte, Sutter, Glenn, Yuba
Safflower	1	NA	106.0	122.0	26,962	48	51	Kings, Yolo, Fresno, Sacramento, Sutter
Sorghum Grain	18	0.2%	20.0	50.4	3,629	66	65	Kern, Tulare, Sutter, Glenn, Butte
Strawberries	1	74.1%	16.8	411.6	407,657	11	11	Monterey, Ventura, Santa Barbara, Santa Cruz, Orange
Fresh Market	1	77.4%	-	300.1	348,116	-	-	-
Processing	1	66.3%	-	111.5	59,541	-	-	-
Sugar Beets	2	21.7%	215.0	5,956.0	212,629(8)	19	16	Imperial, San Joaquin, Fresno, Merced, Solano
Sweetpotatoes	3	11.5%	6.6	67.7	27,601	53	50	Merced, Fresno
Tangerines, Manderins, Tangelos & Tangors	1	52.7%	8.5	83.6	25,327	51	52	Riverside, Kern, Tulare
Tomatoes	1	77.8%	242.6	7,113.4	560,728	-	-	-
Fresh Market	2	27.2%	28.6	410.9	177,346	18	20	Fresno, Monterey, San Diego, Merced, San Joaquin
Processing	1	88.2%	214.0	6,702.5	383,382	10	12	Fresno, Yolo, San Joaquin, Solano, Sutter
Walnuts	1	100.0%	180.3	247.0	234,650	17	15	San Joaquin, Tulare, Stanislaus, Butte, Sutter
Wheat	15	2.0%	537.0	1,248.3	117,249	24	31	Imperial, Kings, Kern, Solano, Yolo
Other Fruits & Nuts	-	-	-	-	33,515	-	-	-
Misc. Vegetables	-	-	185.7	1,590.0	645,000	-	-	-

24.12.4,90 See part 5 for footnotes.

LEADING FRESH VEGETABLE PRODUCING STATES 1988						
	Harvested Area		Production		Value	
Rank	State	Percent of Total	State	Percent of Total	State	Percent of Total
1	California	47.6%	California	54.2%	California	50.3%
2	Florida	12.7%	Florida	12.5%	Florida	16.7%
3	Arizona	5.8%	Arizona	6.3%	Arizona	9.2%
4	Michigan	4.8%	Texas	3.8%	Texas	3.2%
5	Texas	4.7%	Oregon	3.3%	New York	2.6%

24.15,90 Source: U.S. Department of Agriculture, *Vegetables: 1988 Summary*.

	Rank in U.S. (10)	% of U.S. Production (10)	Production (10) (1,000lbs.)	Value (2) ($1,000)	Rank in California (2) 1986	Rank in California (2) 1987	Leading Counties (1)
CALIFORNIA AGRICULTURAL COMMODITIES, 1987							
Commodity							
Cattle and Calves	7	5.0%	2,738,700	1,552,109	2	2	Imperial, Fresno, Tulare, Kings, Siskiyou
Chickens	9	5.0%	996,164	346,633	14	13	Merced, Stanislaus, Fresno
Broilers and Fryers	9	4.8%	921,764	341,053	-	-	-
Other	4	7.2%	74,400	5,580	-	-	-
Eggs, Chicken	1	11.5%	8,023(7)	307,548	13	14	Riverside, San Bernardino, Stanislaus, San Diego, San Joaquin
Hogs and Pigs	29	0.3%	54,562	31,680	47	48	Tulare, Merced, Stanislaus
Honey	4	7.3%	16,500	8,415	55	59	Imperial, Kings, Tulare, Fresno
Milk and Cream	2	12.7%	17,877,000	2,084,731	1	1	San Bernardino, Tulare, Stanislaus, Merced, Riverside
Sheep and Lambs	2	16.0%	131,438	94,663	43	32	Kern, Solano, Imperial, Merced
Turkeys	3	1'1.2%	545,700	180,081	16	19	Fresno, Madera, Stanislaus, Merced, Kings
Wool	3	9.4%	8,021	6,978	63	60	Kern, Imperial, Merced, Fresno
Other Livestock & Poultry	-	-	-	46,748	-	-	-

(1) Based on values published in tha Annual county Agricultural Commissioners' Reports.

(2) Based on value of quantity harvested for crops and on value of quantity marketed for livestock and poultry products.

(3) Share of U.S. production based on 1982 Census of Agriculture.

(4) Extracted from Agricultural Commissioners' Annual Crop Reports.

(5) Includes cut flowers, potted plants, foliage plants, bedding plants, and indoor decoratives.

(6) Includes trees, shrubs, vines, bulbs, turf, and cut Christmas trees, etc., not included in flowers and foliage category.

(7) Millions of eggs.

(8) The 1987 price and value are based on U.S. average price.

(9) In 1987, 15,000 acres were enrolled in the California Raisin Diversion Program (RID). These acres have been deducted form bearing acres for yield calculations.

(10) Based on quantity produced for crops and on quantity marketed for livestock and poultry products.

24.12.5,90 Source: California Department of Food and Agriculture, *California Agriculture*, 1987.

SECTION 24 NOTE

Ninety-five percent of U.S. wine exports come from California.

24.16,90

FRUIT AND NUT CROP SUMMARY 1987-1988						
	Bearing Acres		Tons Harvested* (thousands)		Value of Harvest	
Crop	1987	1988	1987	1988	1987	1988
Apples	22,500	22,500	325,000	275,000	$72,070	$85,800
Apricots	22,000	21,500	110,000	95,000	33,970	29,613
Avocados	75,000	74,700	278,000	178,000	93,964	199,360
Sweet Cherries	10,300	10,300	45,000	26,000	28,615	20,040
Dates	4,800	5,000	19,400	21,000	15,889	17,871
Figs	18,100	17,700	48,800	46,500	16,006	NA
Raisin Grapes	274,500	270,700	2,170,000	2,410,000	487,690	473,665
Table Grapes	82,800	84,100	540,000	700,000	235,040	189,010
Wine Grapes	304,100	298,900	1,950,000	2,130,000	483,930	555,065
All Grapes	661,400	653,700	4,660,000	5,240,000	1,206,660	1,217,740
Kiwi Fruit	6,500	6,700	29,000	31,000	18,886	22,989
Nectarines	23,100	23,600	191,000	200,000	65,545	78,861
Clingstone Peaches	28,800	28,300	460,000	507,500	90,100	109,620
Firestone Peaches	24,900	24,600	255,500	261,500	68,252	79,600
All Peaches	53,700	52,900	715,500	769,000	158,352	189,220
Olives	31,500	30,900	67,500	87,500	42,192	49,318
Bartlett Pears	21,700	20,700	325,000	292,000	57,058	69,308
Other Pears	1,400	1,700	12,000	11,000	7,736	5,281
All Pears	23,100	22,400	337,000	303,000	64,794	74,589
Plums	39,200	40,000	245,000	216,000	75,361	102,661
Pomegranates	3,400	3,400	18,500	15,000	5,617	NA
Dried Prunes	75,400	75,800	229,000	155,000	168,315	NA
In-Shell Almonds	411,000	406,000	660,000	580,000	648,000	589,575
Pecans	1,800	2,300	1,100	2,000	880	1,400
In-Shell Pistachios	40,300	44,500	33,100	92,000	47,419	103,400
Total Walnuts	175,200	174,200	247,000	200,000	243,048	NA
Desert Grapefruit	9,200	9,000	4,300	4,200	23,578	22,008
Other Grapefruit	11,500	11,600	5,000	4,700	32,673	33,396
All Grapefruit	20,700	20,600	9,300	8,900	56,251	55,404
Lemons	48,900	48,900	21,500	17,000	152,890	171,436
Navel Oranges	106,100	105,500	34,500	31,500	242,840	246,462
Valencia Oranges	66,900	66,500	23,400	27,300	191,284	211,984
All Oranges	173,000	172,000	57,900	58,800	434,124	458,446
Tangerines	8,600	8,200	2,230	2,090	25,697	32,297

* Thousands of boxes for all citrus.

24.17,90 Source: U.S. Department of Agriculture, *California Fruit and Nut Review.*

SECTION 24 NOTE

According to industry sources, the 8,000-acre San Bernabe Vineyard in Monterey County is the largest contiguous vineyard in the world that is held by one owner. The property is 13 miles long and 25 miles wide.

24.18,90

VEGETABLE CROP SUMMARY 1987-1988						
	Acres Harvested		Production in Hundredweight (thousands)		Value of Harvest (millions of dollars)	
Crop	1987	1988	1987	1988	1987	1988
Artichokes	11,126	NA	60,830	NA	$36.7	NA
Asparagus	39,700	40,100	1,191	1,163	74.7	$83.4
Broccoli	107,600	104,300	10,330	9,700	213	220
Bushberries	1,020	1,100	83	98	8.9	14.7
Cantaloupe	85,100	87,200	12,765	13,080	147	118
Carrots	43,000	46,000	12,580	13,498	126	158
Casaba and Santa Claus Melons	2,500	2,500	450	500	4.9	6
Cauliflower	51,100	48,900	5,621	5,135	147	136
Celery	21,300	22,300	12,671	11,873	136	131
Sweet Corn	16,000	18,000	1,520	1,620	20.2	24.9
Crenshaw	1,200	1,000	186	165	3.5	3.1
Honeydew	20,600	21,300	3,708	3,621	44.1	47.8
Lettuce	149,500	153,400	39,618	43,719	598	538
Mushrooms	495	501	1,078	1,126	106	110
Onions	37,200	35,000	13,058	13,661	129	86.6
Persian Melons	400	500	52	85	0.8	1.4
Potatoes	50,600	47,200	19,039	16,765	163	NA
Sweet Potatoes	6,600	6,900	1,353	1,311	27.6	NA
Strawberries	16,800	17,600	8,232	8,624	408	389
Tomatoes, Fresh	28,600	31,700	8,217	7,522	177	228
Tomatoes, Processing	214,000	226,100	6,702*	6,548*	383	386
Dried Chili Peppers	2,990	3,460	8,290†	9,840†	9.5	9.6
Cucumbers, Pickling	4,100	3,800	61,500	69,010	12.2	14.7
Misc. Vegetables	234,600	241,638	30,858	31,000	684	670
Total	**1,077,805**	**1,106,399**	**297,663**	**298,724**	**$3,433**	**$3,375**

* 1,000 tons   † Tons

24.19,90 Source: U.S. Department of Agriculture, *California Vegetable Review*, 1989.

AGRICULTURE/LAND - PROMINENT CALIFORNIANS	
J.G. Boswell - Corporate Farmer	Paul Mason - Wine
Luther Burbank - Horticulturalist	Henry Miller and Charles Lux - Ranching
Joseph Di Giorgio - Food Processing	Louis Martini - Wine
Edwin Earl - Refrigerated Rail Cars	Pietro C. Rossi - Wine
Alice Eastwood - Founded Cal. Botanical Club	E. Clarence Salyor - Corporate Farmer
Mark Fontana - Estab. Cal. Fruit Canners Asso.	Kate Sessions - Balboa Park Founder
Ernest and Julio Gallo - Wine	Jean Louis Vignes - Wine
Hugh Glenn - Wheat	Ernest Wente - Wine
Agoston Haraszthy - Wine	Herman Wente - Wine
James Irvine - Rancher	William Wolfskill - Citrus

24.20,90 Source: Pacific Data Resources.

FIELD CROP SUMMARY 1988			
Crop	Acres Harvested (thousands)	Metric Tons Harvested (thousands)	Value of Harvest (millions)
Wheat (grain)	460	1,145	139
Durum Wheat	59	NA	26
Barley	360	410	44
Oats	35	39	6.9
Corn (Grain)	187	759	85
Corn (Silage)	182	4,186	NA
Sorghum (Grain)	15	33.6	3.5
Sorghum (Silage)	4	78	NA
Rice	420	29,490	192
Cotton	1,335	2,850**	870
Cottonseed	NA	131	169
Dry Beans	150	2,894°	106
Potatoes	47	16,765°	163*
Sweet Potatoes	6.9	1,311°	28*
Safflower*	106	122	27
Sugar Beets	212	5,300	NA
Hay	1,680	8,652	813
Alfalfa Seed	69	35,611	42
Alfalfa Hay	1,100	7,260	NA

* 1987   **Bales
° cwt.

24.21,90 Source: California Department of Food and Agriculture, *Field Crop Review, 1989* and *California Vegetable Review, 1989*.

FOREIGN OWNED AGRICULTURAL LAND IN CALIFORNIA						
By Country of Owner						
	United Kingdom	Netherlands Antilles	Federal Republic of Germany	Canada	Netherlands	All Others	Total
% of Land	36%	11%	9%	5%	10%	30%	100%
Acres	329,799	101,350	79,747	43,103	89,547	279,134	922,680
By Type of Agricultural Land						
	Crop Land	Pasture	Forest	Other Agri-culture	Non Agri-culture	
% of Land	28%	28%	26%	11%	7%	100%
Acres	261,788	261,758	241,525	99,049	66,023	922,680

24.22,90 Source: U.S. Dept. of Agriculture, Economic Research Service, *Foreign Ownership of U.S. Agricultural Land Through Dec. 31, 1987*.

CALIFORNIA'S LEADING AGRICULTURAL COUNTIES BY TOTAL VALUE OF PRODUCTION* 1985-1987				
	1987		1985	
County	Rank	Value (thousands)	Rank	Value (thousands)
Fresno	1	$2,270,170	1	$2,113,840
Tulare	2	$1,606,162	2	$1,368,704
Kern	3	$1,379,921	3	$1,218,233
Monterey	4	$1,087,319	4	$971,817
Riverside	5	$970,741	5	$944,585
Merced	6	$942,482	6	$812,419
Stanislaus	7	$881,306	7	$772,299
Imperial	8	$805,815	8	$738,243
San Joaquin	9	$746,095	9	$699,407
Ventura	10	$669,273	11	$551,923
Kings	11	$640,178	12	$548,626
San Diego	12	$564,372	13	$545,528
San Bernardino	13	$549,937	10	$556,617
Madera	14	$421,133	15	$321,740
Santa Barbara	15	$381,663	14	$341,801
Los Angeles	16	$250,520	16	$293,223
San Luis Obispo	17	$247,811	19	$213,254
Orange	18	$245,086	17	$260,088
Sonoma	19	$227,069	20	$211,551
Sutter	20	$216,184	18	$255,476

* Does not include value of timber products.

24.23,90 Source: *California Agricultural Commissoners' Annual Crop Reports.*

CALIFORNIA LIVESTOCK, 1982-1988							
	Cows, Sheep and Hogs (in thousands)			Poultry (in millions)			
Year	All Cattle	Sheeps and Lambs	Hogs and Pigs	Chickens Sold	Broilers Produced	Chicks Hatched	Turkeys Produced
1982	5,000	1,210	160	21.7	167	NA	20.0
1983	4,900	1,115	160	18.0	172	NA	20.2
1984	5,000	1,115	155	21.5	175.4	458	19.7
1985	4,960	1,065	140	19.0	174.3	407	20.5
1986	5,000	1,065	145	19.7	184.8	424	21.9
1987	4,700	980	150	18.6	196.1	428	25.5
1988	4,600	1,015	130	19.2	212.2	368	26.5

24.24,90 Source: *U.S. Statisical Abstract*, Cal. Dept. of Food and Agriculture, *California Livestock Statistics*, U.S. Dept. of Agriculture, *Poultry and Egg Statistics.*

CALIFORNIA LIVESTOCK PRODUCTION AND INCOME 1973-1988					
Year	Production (million lbs.)	Marketings (million lbs.)	Average Price per 100 Pounds		Gross Income (in millions)
Cattle and Calves					
1973	1,899	2,788	$42.90*	$53.70†	$1,221
1981	1,757	2,200	$57.90	$60.20	$1,294
1982	1,850	2,721	$54.40	$55.70	$1,506
1983	1,698	2,482	$53.30	$57.10	$1,348
1984	1,896	2,718	$53.80	$56.30	$1,491
1985	1,743	2,556	$48.80	$55.80	$1,270
1986	1,783	2,814	$46.70	$53.70	$1,338
1987	1,803	2,349	$56.30	$71.60	$1,350
1988	2,094	2,591	$61.80	$82.70	$1,637
Sheep and Lambs					
1973	71	78	$14.20f	$35.30¥	$27
1981	64	74	$12.10	$37.90	$39
1982	79	106	$18.60	$54.50	$55
1983	77	85	$17.90	$56.40	$46
1984	79	93	$17.40	$59.70	$54
1985	73	83	$23.10	$68.30	$54
1986	74	93	$23.20	$68.60	$60
1987	83	108	$25.10	$74.90	$80
1988	74	98	$23.60	$70.30	$68
Hogs and Pigs					
1973	44	45	$37.70	-	$17
1981	61	61	$48.00	-	$31
1982	50	47	$58.20	-	$30
1983	56	54	$51.50	-	$30
1984	55	54	$49.70	-	$29
1985	51	47	$47.30	-	$24
1986	58	54	$52.20	-	$31
1987	55	55	$58.00		$34
1988	37	47	$47.00		$24
Total Meat Animals					
1973	2,015	2,911	-	-	$1,266
1981	1,883	2,337	-	-	$1,366
1982	1,980	2,876	-	-	$1,591
1983	1,792	2,510	-	-	$1,364
1984	2,029	2,865	-	-	$1,574
1985	1,867	2,686	-	-	$1,348
1986	1,915	2,961	-	-	$1,428
1987	1,940	2,512			$1,464
1988	2,204	2,736			$1,729

* Cattle. † Calves. f Sheep. ¥ Lambs.
24.25,90 Source: California Crop and Livestock Reporting Service, *California Livestock Statistics*.

LIVESTOCK ON FARMS AND RANCHES					
	California		All U.S.		California
Year	Number (thousands)	% Change from Previous Year	Number (thousands)	% Change from Previous year	as % of U.S.
Beef Cows					
1982	1,160	NA	39,139	NA	3.0%
1983	1,030	-11.0%	38,081	-3.0%	2.7%
1984	1,008	-0.8%	37,660	-1.1%	2.7%
1987	950	0.0%	33,910	0.8%	2.8%
1988	915	-3.4%	32,958	-2.8%	2.8%
1989	925	1.1%	33,669	2.2%	2.7%
Milk Cows					
1982	940	NA	11,012	NA	9.0%
1983	940	0.0%	11,066	0.0%	8.5%
1984	962	2.3%	11,140	0.7%	8.6%
1987	990	-3.9%	10,547	-5.6%	9.4%
1988	1,005	1.5%	10,307	-2.3%	9.8%
1989	1,025	2.0%	10,217	-0.8%	10.0%
Total Cattle and Calves					
1982	5,000	NA	115,604	NA	4.0%
1983	4,900	-2.0%	115,201	0.0%	4.3%
1984	5,000	2.0%	114,040	-1.0%	4.4%
1987	4,750	-5.0%	102,031	-3.3%	4.7%
1988	4,650	-2.1%	98,994	-3.0%	4.7%
1989	4,700	1.1%	99,484	0.5%	4.7%

24.26,90 Source: California Department of Food and Agriculture, *California Livestock Statistics.*

CALIFORNIA MILK PRODUCTION			
Year	Production (in million pounds)	% of U.S. Total	% Change from Previous Year
1980	13,577	NA	NA
1981	14,248	10.7%	4.9%
1982	14,528	NA	NA
1983	14,743	NA	NA
1984	15,278	10.6%	1.5%
1985	16,768	11.7%	9.8%
1986	17,235	12.0%	2.8%
1987	17,930	12.6%	4.0%
1988	18,769	12.9%	4.6%

24.27,90 Source: U.S.D.A. Economics and Statistics Service, *Dairy Outlook and Situation.*

CATTLE RUSTLING		
Year	Cattle Stolen or Slaughtered	Value
1986	2,336	$1,100,000
1987	1,776	$686,000
1988	2,464	$1,000,000

Note: By some estimates, 50% of all cattle rustling is not reported.
24.28,90 Source: Cal. Farm Bureau Federation, *Ag. Alert.*

CASH RECEIPTS FROM FARM MARKETING OF LIVESTOCK AND POULTRY COMMODITIES (in thousands of dollars)						
Commodity	1981	1983	1985	1986	1987	1988
Cattle and Calves	$1,275,645	$1,266,744	$1,090,949	$1,319,211	$1,331,433	$1,613,819
Sheep and Lambs	37,867	42,108	51,771	57,830	78,237	66,547
Hogs*	29,627	28,663	22,142	29,575	31,680	22,146
Wool	10,006	5,875	5,760	5,431	6,300	10,157
Turkeys*†	182,067	145,642	204,672	208,926	180,081	200,340
Farm Chickens*†	9,544	5,390	7,372	7,673	5,580	3,996
Commercial Broilers and Fryers*†	257,494	252,628	274,495	312,736	341,053	339,094
Chicken Eggs*†	398,300	371,417	335,500	347,362	307,548	297,786
Dairy Products	1,943,229	1,947,565	2,075,531	2,062,508	2,082,883	2,080,739
Honey	5,145	NA	NA	14,872	8,085	9,984
Other Livestock and Poultry	82,356	93,938	92,431	75,400	53,078	59,163
Total	$4,231,280	$4,159,970	$4,324,222	$4,435,313	$4,425,958	$4,703,771

* Marketings ending December 1.   † Cash receipts include value of home consumption.
24.29,90 Source: California Dept. of Food & Agriculture, *California Livestock Statistics*.

CALIFORNIA FARM INCOME AND EXPENSES 1978-1988								
	Cash Receipts		Gross Farm Income		Production Costs		Net Farm Income	
	Amount	%	Amount	%	Amount	%	Amount	%
Year	millions	Change	millions	Change	millions	Change	millions	Change
1978	$10,638	12.4%	$11,025	11.6%	$8,512	11.5%	$2,513	12.2%
1979	$12,899	21.3%	$13,447	22.0%	$10,155	19.3%	$3,292	31.0%
1980	$13,722	6.4%	$14,291	6.3%	$11,188	10.2%	$3,103	-5.8%
1981	$13,844	0.9%	$14,536	1.7%	$12,134	8.5%	$2,402	-22.6%
1982	$14,379	2.4%	$15,364	3.3%	$11,979	5.3%	$3,384	-3.4%
1983	$13,228	-8.0%	$14,495	-5.7%	$11,936	-0.3%	$2,558	-24.4%
1984	$14,418	9.0%	$16,082	10.9%	$12,179	2.0%	$3,903	52.6%
1985	$14,311	-0.7%	$15,738	-2.1%	$11,584	-4.9%	$4,154	6.4%
1986	$14,645	2.3%	$15,478	-1.7%	$10,860	-6.3%	$4,618	11.2%
1987	$15,522	6.0%	$16,786	8.5%	$11,105	2.2%	$5,482	23.0%
1988	$16,136	4.0%	NA	NA	NA	NA	NA	NA

24.30,90 Source: U.S. Department of Agriculture, *Economic Indicators of the Farm Sector, State Financial Summary, Annual*.

SECTION 24 NOTE
California cows are the most productive in the nation. The average California dairy cow gives 18,403 pounds of milk per year.

24.31,90

SECTION 24 NOTE
The only commercial snail ranch in the U.S., the Enfant Riant, is in Petaluma.

24.32,90

FARM REAL ESTATE VALUES

	Dollars per Acre		Index (1977=100)	
Year	California	U.S.*	California	U.S.*
1980	$1,426	$725	166	145
1981	$1,735	$795	201	158
1982	$1,905	$789	221	157
1983	$1,918	$788	223	148
1984	$1,918	$782	223	146
1985	$1,726	$679	201	128
1986	$1,571	$596	183	112
1987	$1,366	$547	159	103
1988	$1,341	$564	156	106

* Excluding Hawaii and Alaska.
24.33,90 Source: U.S. Dept. of Agric., *Agricultural Statistics.*

FARM REAL ESTATE DEBT*
(in billions)

Year	California	All U.S.	California as a % of U.S.
1965	$1.7	$18.9	9.0%
1970	$2.5	$30.5	8.3%
1975	$3.9	$46.3	8.4%
1980	$7.2	$95.8	7.5%
1981	$8.2	$105.8	7.8%
1982	$8.7	$110.0	7.9%
1983	$9.2	$112.6	8.2%
1984	$9.3	$111.6	8.3%
1985	$8.9	$105.4	8.4%
1986	$8.2	$95.8	8.6%
1987	$7.7	$87.4	8.8%

* Amount outstanding.
24.34,90 Source: U.S. Dept. of Agriculture, *Agricultural Statistics*, and *Economic Indicators of the Farm Sector, State Financial Summary, Annual.*

FARM NON-REAL ESTATE DEBT
(in billions)

Year	California	All U.S.	California as a % of U.S.
1983	$8.4	$92.7	9.1%
1984	$8.3	$92.0	9.0%
1985	$7.4	$82.2	9.0%
1986	$6.0	$71.0	8.5%
1987	$5.5	$65.9	8.3%

24.35,90 Source: U.S. Dept. of Agriculture, *Agricultural Statistics*, and *Economic Indicators of the Farm Sector, State Financial Summary, Annual.*

HOLDERS OF CALIFORNIA FARM REAL ESTATE DEBT, 1987		
Creditor	Amount (in billions)	Percent of Debt
Federal Land Banks	$3.3	43%
Farmers Home Administration	0.2	3%
Insurance Companies	1.9	25%
Commercial Banks	0.7	9%
Individuals and Other	1.6	21%
Total	**$7.7**	**100%**

24.36,90 Source: U.S. Department of Agriculture, Economics Research Service, *Agricultural Statistics* and *Economic Indicators of the Farm Sector, State Financial Summary, Annual.*

VALUE OF LAND AND BUILDINGS, ASSETS, DEBT AND INCOME OF CALIFORNIA FARMS, 1980-1988								
	Value of Land and Buildings		Farm Income				Debt to Assets Ratio	Income to Debt Ratio
Year	Per Acre	Total (billions)	Gross (billions)	Net (billions)	Assets	Debt		
1980	$1,424	$48.3	$14.8	$4.1	NA	NA	20.9%	NA
1982	$1,905	$64.2	$15.6	$3.7	$76.5	$15.6	20.4%	NA
1983	$1,918	$63.7	$14.5	$2.6	$75.3	$17.6	23.4%	14.9%
1984	$1,918	$63.3	$16.1	$3.9	$68.9	$17.6	25.5%	22.2%
1985	$1,726	$56.8	$15.7	$4.2	$63.6	$16.3	25.6%	24.6%
1986	$1,571	$51.5	$15.5	$4.6	$56.9	$14.3	25.0%	30.3%
1987	$1,366	$44.8	$16.8	$5.7	$56.2	$13.2	23.5%	41.4%
1988	$1,421	$46.2	NA	NA	NA	NA	NA	NA

24.37,90 Source: U.S. Department of Agriculture, Economic Research Service, *Agricultural Statistics and Economic Indicators of the Farm Sector, State Financial Summary, Annual* and unpublished data.

WINE INVENTORIES (millions of gallons)							
	1973	1980	1982	1984	1985	1986	1987
Table Wine							
California	299	504	596	538	539	518	501
United States	321	534	631	578	574	555	540
Dessert Wine							
California	82	58	49	44	42	38	35
United States	92	69	57	51	49	45	42
Sparkling Wine							
California	5.3	5.7	9.7	13.5	11.8	13.6	10.9
United States	8.5	9.3	13.1	16.4	14.4	16.3	14.0
All Wine							
California	394	575	661	603	602	582	558
United States	431	620	708	654	648	630	609

24.38,90 Source: *Wines & Vines Magazine.*

WINE PRODUCTION*
(millions of gallons)

Year	California	New York	Total U.S.	California as a % of the U.S.
1980	439	36	486	90%
1981	385	35	433	89%
1982	514	29	556	92%
1983	385	30	428	90%
1984	398	28	441	90%
1985	415	24	454	91%
1986	439	29	485	91%
1987	391	34	440	89%

* Wine removed from from fermenters.
24.39,90 Source: *Wines & Vines* Magazine.

WINERIES IN CALIFORNIA AND THE NATION

Year	California	Total U.S.	California as a % of the U.S.
1970	316	571	55%
1980	422	781	54%
1983	552	1,000	55%
1985	623	1,123	55%
1986	739	1,455	51%
1989	669	1,217	55%

24.40,90 Source: *Wines & Vines* Magazine and U.S. Dept. of Alcohol, Tobacco, and Firearms, unpublished data.

CALIFORNIA'S LARGEST WINERIES

Rank	Winery	Storage Capacity (millions of gallons)	Rank	Winery	Storage Capacity (millions of gallons)
1	E&J Gallo	330	11	Sebastiani	13
2	Guild	60	12	Robt. Mondavi	12
3	The Beverage Source	55	13	Wine World	7.7
4	Vie-Del	50	14	Oak Ridge	7.3
5	The Wine Group	44	15	Charles Krug	6.0
6	JFJ Bronco	42	16	ASV Wines	5.3
7	Golden State Vintners	37	17	F. Korbel	5.3
8	Christian Brothers	37	18	Delano Growers	5.0
9	Delicato Vineyards	37	19	Fetzer	5.0
10	Guimarra Vineyards	17	20	Wente	4.0

24.41,90 Source: *Wines & Vines Magazine.*

PER CAPITA WINE CONSUMPTION

State	Rank	State	Rank
District of Columbia	1	Kentucky	47
Nevada	2	Utah	48
California	3	West Virginia	49
Washington	4	Arkansas	50
Vermont	5	Mississippi	51

24.42,90 Source: *Wines & Vines* Magazine.

CALIFORNIA CHAMPAGNE AND SPARKLING WINE PRODUCERS

Adler Fels Winery	Geyser Peak Winery	Pesenti Winery
Almaden Vineyards	Guild Wineries & Distilleries	Piper Sonoma
S. Anderson Vineyards	Handley Cellars	Martin Ray
Beaulieu Vineyards	Hop Kiln Winery	Roederer U.S., Inc.
JFJ Bronco Winery	Iron Horse Vineyards	Rosenblum Cellars
Chateau De Baun	Jepson	Salamandre Wine Cellars
Chateau St. Jean	F. Korbel & Brothers	San Pasqual Vineyards
The Christian Brothers	Hanns Kornell	Scharffenberger Cellars
Congress Springs Vineyards	Thomas Kruse Winery	Schramsberg Vineyards
Crystal Valley Cellars	Domaine M. Marion	Sebastiani Vineyards
John Culberstson Winery	Mark West Vineyards	Tijsseling Vineyards
Domaine Chandon	Paul Masson Vineyards	Tonio Conti
Maison Deutz	Mirassou	Tribaut Devavry, Inc.
Estrella River Winery	Mount Palomar Winery	Ventana Vineyards Winery
J. Filippi Vintage Co.	Nevada City Winery	Weibel Champagne Vineyards
Filsinger Vineyard & Winery	Nicasio Vineyards	Wente Brothers
Franzia Brothers Winery	North Bay Cellars	Windsor Vineyards
Freixenet Sonoma Caves	Oceania Cellars	York Mountain Winery
E&J Gallo	Parsons Creek	

24.43 Source: *Wines & Vines Magazine.*

SECTION 24 NOTE

California's per person wine consumption rose from 3.99 gallons in 1977 to 4.59 gallons in 1987.

24.44,90

SECTION 24 NOTE

It takes 4 .5 pounds of grapes to produce 1 pound of raisins.

24.45,90

SECTION 24 NOTE

According to the California Department of Industrial Relations, 9.6 percent of the state's farm workers are unionized.

24.46,90

ALL GRAPES (EXCLUDING ROOTSTOCK): ACREAGE BEARING, AND NONBEARING, AND TOTAL, BY COUNTY, CALIFORNIA, 1988 (in acres)			
County	Bearing	Nonbearing	Total
Alameda	1,236	559	1,795
Amador	1,536	100	1,636
Butte	232	0	232
Calaveras	175	1	176
Colusa	110	438	548
Contra Costa	760	15	775
El Dorado	489	9	498
Fresno	203,849	3,203	207,052
Glenn	958	300	1,258
Humboldt	4	0	4
Kern	75,463	3,717	79,180
Kings	3,858	213	4,071
Lake	2,434	231	2,665
Los Angeles	4	0	4
Madera	80,234	1,333	81,567
Marin	11	0	11
Mariposa	22	20	42
Mendocino	10,628	1,205	11,833
Merced	16,136	689	16,825
Monterey	23,456	4,407	27,863
Napa	29,382	2,784	32,166
Nevada	120	60	180
Placer	108	4	112
Riverside	20,938	949	21,887
Sacramento	2,862	543	3,405
San Benito	1,568	23	1,591
San Bernardino	1,688	780	2,468
San Diego	168	14	182
San Joaquin	46,330	5,486	51,816
San Luis Obispo	6,405	1,020	7,425
San Mateo	44	9	53
Santa Barbara	7,797	1,516	9,313
Santa Clara	1,076	13	1,089
Santa Cruz	123	22	145
Shasta	36	0	36
Solano	1,003	218	1,221
Sonoma	28,484	3,076	31,560
Stanislaus	15,962	434	16,396
Sutter	22	0	22
Tehama	152	0	152
Trinity	5	0	5
Tulare	67,191	3,120	70,311
Ventura	1	0	1
Yolo	1,271	387	1,658
Yuba	354	5	359
State Total	654,685	36,903	691,588

24.47,90 Source: California Crop & Livestock Reporting Service, *California Grape Acreage, 1988.*

CALIFORNIA GRAPE ACREAGE

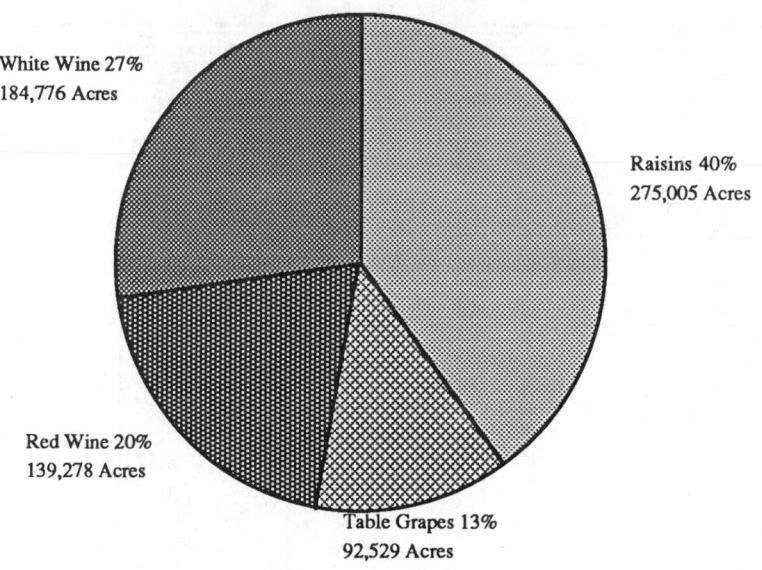

White Wine 27%
184,776 Acres

Raisins 40%
275,005 Acres

Red Wine 20%
139,278 Acres

Table Grapes 13%
92,529 Acres

24.48,90 Source: California Crop and Livestock Reporting Service, California Grape Acreage, 1988.

SECTION 24 NOTE

A California farmer provides food and fiber for 114 people, a Soviet farmer for 11, and a Japanese farmer for 3.

24.49,90

SECTION 24 NOTE

Some tomato gourmets believe that the Weimar tomato, grown at Weimar (Placer County), is the best tasting-tomato grown in the state.

24.50,90

SECTION 24 NOTE

Move over Italy. California now has the world's largest mozzarella cheese plant, in Lemoore. It will process 2.5 million pounds of milk a day.

24.51,90

WINE GRAPES FOR CRUSHING				
	Total Tons Crushed		Dollars per Ton	
Type and Variety	1987	1988	1987	1988
White				
Burger	25,766	30,856	$174	$170
Chardonnay	101,336	115,404	$922	$1,122
Chenin Blanc	290,692	306,013	$172	$181
Emerald Riesling	15,716	18,172	$147	$152
Feher Szagos	104	49	$115	$115
Flora	195	325	$1,044	$678
Folle Blanche	320	361	$0	$238
French Colombard	619,684	702,090	$144	$139
Gewurztraminer	12,054	10,617	$410	$453
Gray Reisling	8,455	6,721	$180	$276
Green Hungarian	1,990	1,900	$255	$254
Kleinberger	11	10	$500	$650
Malvasia Bianca	10,538	19,324	$188	$190
Muscat Blanc/M Canelli	7,437	8,535	$267	$258
Muscat Orange	211	154	$286	$326
Palomino/G Chasselas	11,346	14,590	$125	$119
Pedro Ximenes	2	0	$0	$0
Pinot Blanc	6,325	6,207	$490	$690
Sauvignon Blanc	58,911	58,448	$414	$474
Sauvingnon Mosque	94	104	$396	$430
Sauvingnon Vert	387	562	$219	$308
Scheurebe	0	9	$0	$0
Semillon	14,092	14,815	$254	$289
St. Emlion (Ugni Blanc)	6,968	6,000	$136	$137
Sylvaner	1,419	1,834	$210	$207
Symphony	74	620	$436	$389
White Riesling	25,368	23,606	$363	$418
Other White	3,812	8,830	$130	$92
Total White	**1,223,310**	**1,356,160**	**$226**	**$238**
Red				
Aleatico	300	433	$112	$108
Alicante Bouschet	683	3,449	$145	$156
Barbera	74,245	94,733	$142	$167
Black Malvoisie	87	386	$134	$141
Cabernet Franc	2,156	2,864	$963	$1,046
Cabernet Sauvignon	64,616	72,782	$631	$822
Carignane	72,281	90,499	$159	$202

24.52,90 Source: California Depts of Food and Agriculture, *Final Grape Crush Report, 1988 Crop.*

SECTION 24 NOTE
The typical Californian consumes 96 quarts of milk, 9.5 quarts of skim milk, 1.6 quarts of half and half, and 3.2 quarts of yogurt per year.

24.53,90

WINE GRAPES FOR CRUSHING				
	Total Tons Crushed		Dollars Per Ton	
Type and Variety	1987	1988	1987	1988
Red(cont.)				
Carmine	182	264	$153	$209
Carnelian	7,615	11,086	$125	$152
Centurian	6,048	6,720	$130	$157
Charbono	186	225	$477	$579
Early Burgundy	512	609	$294	$356
Gamay (Napa)	11,434	10,582	$247	$341
Gamay Beaujolais	4,985	3,000	$348	$575
Grand Noir	8	0	$125	$0
Granache	108,117	97,461	$130	$156
Grignolino	74	73	$0	$0
Malbec	338	260	$268	$234
Mataro	287	315	$344	$490
Merlot	6,782	7,654	$767	$886
Meunier	371	434	$746	$728
Mission	6,215	7,459	$129	$163
Muscat Hamburg	71	117	$389	$286
Nebbiolo	38	86	$379	$472
Petite Sirah	11,467	16,709	$334	$394
Petite Verdot	41	43	$992	$1,065
Pfeffer Cabernet	28	36	$397	$716
Pinot Noir	29,766	28,221	$573	$688
Pinot St. George	226	106	$220	$182
Refosco/Mondeuse	26	65	$377	$404
Royalty	5,647	6,169	$125	$176
Rubired	51,270	62,356	$127	$175
Ruby Cabernet	43,315	55,096	$131	$173
Salvador	6,299	6,894	$125	$173
Sangioveto	2	8	$0	$900
Souzao	60	116	$171	$186
St. Macaire	206	295	$137	$175
Syrah/ French Syrah-Shiraz	295	394	$461	$558
Tinta Cao	5	14	$582	$724
Tinta Madeira	399	332	$136	$150
Touriga	18	22	$507	$600
Valdepenas	1,712	1,314	$136	$175
Verdelho	1	7	$419	$600
Zinfandel	143,349	170,091	$480	$817
Other Red	4,871	3,669	$126	$186
Total Red	**666,635**	**760,444**	**$288**	**$409**
Total Wine	**1,889,945**	**2,116,604**	**$247**	**$297**
Total All Varieties*	**2,486,631**	**2,840,630**	**$221**	**$260**

* Including Wine, Raisin and Table Grapes.

24.54,90 Source: California Dept. of Food and Agriculture, *Final Grape Crush Report, 1988.*

| | | Value | | Percent |
| | 1987 | (in millions) | | Change |
Commodity	Rank	1986	1987	from 1986
VALUE OF CALIFORNIA AGRICULTURAL EXPORTS 1986-1987				
Cotton Lint	1	$433	$620	43%
Almonds	2	$420	$465	11%
Grapes	3	$246	$296	20%
Oranges	4	$197	$181	-8%
Walnuts	5	$95	$120	27%
Beef	6	$101	$110	9%
Prunes	7	$73	$88	21%
Lemons	8	$78	$75	-4%
Rice	9	$55	$72	31%
Wheat	10	$24	$69	183%
Strawberries	11	$55	$63	14%
Alfalfa	12	$83	$59	-29%
Vegetable Seeds	13	$47	$51	7%
Peaches	14	$46	$44	-4%
Tomatoes	15	$36	$42	16%
Melons	16	$18	$41	134%
Lettuce	17	$36	$41	15%
Plums	18	$24	$40	66%
Flowers and Nursery	19	$29	$32	12%
Dairy	20	$24	$31	29%
Onions	21	$28	$28	0%
Dry Beans	22	$27	$26	-2%
Sweet Cherries	23	NA	$24	NA
Grapefruit	24	$29	$24	-20%
Avocadoes	25	$14	$23	67%
Total		**$2,838**	**$3,337**	**18%**

24.55,90   Source: California Department of Food and Agriculture, *Exports of Agricultural Commodities Produced in California.*

SECTION 24 NOTE

One-third of the cropland in California produces crops for export.

24.56,90

SECTION 24 NOTE

According to the NEW YORK TIMES, the Nestle-owned Carnation Company has recently spent $80 million building the world's largest ice cream factory in Bakersfield. The factory will produce 35 million gallons of ice cream and 325 different products annually with a 150-person crew.

24.57,90

CALIFORNIA'S MOST HEAVILY USED PESTICIDES

Pesticide	Millions of Pounds	Pesticide	Millions of Pounds
Calcium Hydroxide	19.3	Petroleum Distillates	7.4
Calcium Hypochlorite	4.0	Petroleum Distillates, Aromatic	2.6
Chlorine	118.9	Petroleum Hydrocarbons	8.2
Chloropicrin	3.3	Petroleum Oil, unclassified	27.5
Coal Tar Neutral Oils &		Phosphoric Acid	3.1
Coal Tar Acid Combinations	2.6	Pine Oil	5.2
Copper Hydroxide	3.6	Propargite	3.0
Copper Sulfate (Pentahydrate)	5.8	Sodium Bisulfate	3.3
Cryolite	4.2	Soduim Chlorate	13.0
Dicofol	3.9	Sodium Hypochlorite	52.8
Ethylene Oxide	2.1	Sulfur	125.0
Glyphosate, Isopropylamine Salt	3.6	Sulfur Dioxide	2.3
Hydrogen Chloride	18.8	Sulfuric Acid	2.8
Isopropyl Alcohol	2.0	Trichloro-S-Triazinetrione	9.4
Malathion	5.8	Trisodium Phosphate	2.6
Metam-Sodiam	3.4	Ziram	2.5
Methyl Bromide	13.7	1,3 Dichloropropene	15.8
Mineral Oil	3.8		
Oxyfluorfen	3.0	**Total All Pesticides**	**586.3**

24.58,90 Source: California Dept. of Food and Agriculture, Division of Pest Management, *Report of Pesticides Sold in California for 1987.*

SECTION 24 NOTE

According to the AG ALERT newspaper, the orange was introduced into California in 1769, but the first orange grove was not planted until 1804 at the San Gabriel Mission.

24.59,90

SECTION 24 NOTE

The world's largest chocolate truffle made its appearance at Macy's in San Francisco on March 23, 1987.

24.60,90

SECTION 24 NOTE

In 1879, Lyman Byce invented the egg incubator, setting Petaluma on its course toward becoming the "egg basket of the world."

24.61,90

PESTICIDE USE IN CALIFORNIA BY COUNTY 1984-1987 (in thousands of pounds)							
County	1984	1985	1987	County	1984	1985	1987
Alameda	302	315	201	Placer	172	154	215
Alpine	---*	---*	3	Plumas	9	3	21
Amador	18	16	14	Riverside	1,730	1,867	2,054
Butte	1,656	1,280	1,746	Sacramento	878	707	1,103
Calaveras	9	38	12	San Benito	262	163	164
Colusa	1,535	1,529	1,742	San Bernardino	262	407	357
Contra Costa	280	299	187	San Diego	814	1,072	1,144
Del Norte	147	135	132	San Francisco	28	26	27
El Dorado	36	45	50	San Joaquin	6,355	6,167	6,620
Fresno	11,001	10,529	13,812	San Luis Obispo	712	721	1,281
Glenn	1,205	1,069	1,583	San Mateo	180	207	179
Humboldt	30	45	62	Santa Barbara	1,729	1,953	3,379
Imperial	5,350	5,188	5,318	Santa Clara	451	828	487
Inyo	6	6	5	Santa Cruz	977	893	1,083
Kern	9,170	8,548	10,728	Shasta	212	302	245
Kings	3,570	3,486	3,106	Sierra	3	3	2
Lake	24	44	84	Siskiyou	249	177	225
Lassen	216	188	226	Solano	1,809	1,823	1,619
Los Angeles	1,536	2,385	2,658	Sonoma	418	592	492
Madera	1,895	1,753	2,627	Stanislaus	2,726	2,687	3,191
Marin	29	96	39	Sutter	1,624	1,523	2,243
Mariposa	5	4	3	Tehama	299	266	232
Mendocino	139	129	140	Trinity	---*	32	2
Merced	3,526	3,323	4,623	Tulare	4,526	4,142	4,497
Modoc	137	324	172	Tuolumne	12	12	10
Mono	3	1	11	Ventura	1,960	1,831	2,301
Monterey	4,977	4,421	5,595	Yolo	2,551	2,071	3,239
Napa	493	389	603	Yuba	476	463	531
Nevada	26	20	22				
Orange	951	1,219	1,441	**State Total**	79,697	77,913	93,888

* Less than 1,000 pounds.

24.62,90 Source: California Department of Food and Agriculture, *Pesticide Use Report, Annual*.

Cotton Ginnings		
Year	**Millions of Running Bales†** California	U.S.	California as a % of U.S.
1984	2.8	12.5	23%
1985	3.0	13.0	23%
1986	2.2	9.4	23%
1987	2.9	14.4	20%
1988	2.8	15.0	18%

† Bale=approximately 496 pounds.

24.63,90 Source: U.S. Bureau of the Census, *Cotton Ginnings Reports A10 87-13,88-13, and A20-88-5*.

SECTION 24 NOTE
California strawberry growers average 23 tons of fruit per acre. Growers in other states average 3 tons per acre.

24.64,90

SECTION 24 NOTE

The University of California at Davis runs the Sustainable
Agriculture Research and Education program. Its purpose
is to help grow crops with fewer chemicals and less water.

24.65,90

SECTION 24 NOTE

According to the Cal-Farm Insurance Company, avocado stealing
and cattle rustling are the two most serious agricultural crimes.

24.66,90

SECTION 24 NOTE

Sixty percent of the world's almonds are grown in California.

24.67,90

SECTION 24 NOTE

The California Farm Bureau has a membership of 99,300.

24.68,90

SECTION 24 NOTE

Eight of the top ten agricultural counties in the U.S. are in California.

24.69,90

SECTION 24 NOTE

Just over 32 percent of California's land is farm land.

24.70,90

SECTION 24 NOTE

As of 1988, San Francisco had only one remaining commercial
farm. The 3-acre site may be converted to housing.

24.71,90

SECTION 24 NOTE

Jockey shorts are made exclusively from San Joaquin Valley Acala cotton.

24.72,90

The IRA. J. Chrisman Wind Gap Pumping Plant for the California Water Project. Photo Courtesy of the California Department of Water Resources.

A California Orchard. Photo Courtesy of the California Farm Bureau Federation.

Forestry

California's booming economy and moderate interest rates have led to a robust residential and commercial construction industry. This, in turn, has led to a strong demand for timber and wood products. As a result, the California timber harvest is at a twenty-year high. In California during 1986, a total of 4.6 billion board feet of timber, worth $670 million, was harvested. With this harvest California ranked second only to Washington, the leading timber state in the nation.

Over the past thirty years the timber harvest on private lands has declined while the harvest on public lands has increased. This change has made timber companies subject to the policy shifts of federal and state forestry agencies, shifts that can affect the availability and price of government-owned timber.

The economic boom that is fueling the demand for timber has also led to a modest increase in employment in the timber-products industry and other related industries, the economic mainstay of several rural counties in the state. Employment in these industries is at its highest point in two decades; this increase has come about despite the introduction of labor-saving equipment in California's lumber mills.

Although currently somewhat more timber is harvested in the state each year than is replanted, the California Department of Forestry expects that this practice will be reversed in the early twenty-first century and that the state's timber inventory will increase substantially through the middle of the next century.

Because of low rainfall in the late 1980s, the number of forest fires in the state increased by 15 percent over the average for the mid-1980s. The severity of the recent fires has also been much greater than usual. In 1987, for example, 873,000 acres burned, more than three times the average acreage burned annually.

The future success of the timber industry in California and the Pacific Northwest may depend on long-term agreements between the timber industry and environmentalists, who want to end the cutting of old-growth timber and severely limit the cutting of new growth to mitigate environmental damage. Without such agreements, environmentalists' lawsuits to delay the cutting of timber on public and private lands could plunge the industry into an extended recession.

LAND AREA BY USE OR MAJOR VEGETATION TYPE CALIFORNIA		
Land Use or Vegetation Type	Thousand acres	Percent
Forest:		
Productive forest	17,944	17.9%
Unproductive forest	22,216	22.2%
Total forest	**40,160**	**40.1%**
Non-forest:		
Coastal sagebrush	2,300	2.3%
Inland sagebrush	3,800	3.8%
Desert	23,900	23.9%
Grassland	12,000	12.0%
Riparian, marsh, tidelands	700	0.7%
Barren	1,800	1.8%
Agriculture	11,000	11.0%
Urban, industrial, roads, and other	4,390	4.4%
Total non-forest	**59,890**	**59.9%**
All types	**100,050**	**100.0%**

25.1,90 Source: U.S. Forest Service: Pacific Northwest Forest and Range Experiment Station, *California Forests: Trends, Problems and Opportunities (Resource Bulletin PNW-89), 1985.*

TIMBER ACREAGE IN CALIFORNIA AND THE U.S. (thousand acres)	Total Land Area	Forest Land				
		Total	Com-mercial	Productive Reserved	Productive Deferred*	Other Forest
California	99,773	39,381	16,712	2,940	268	19,729
Total U.S.	2,257,578	731,377	483,311	34,536	4,626	213,532

* 1982 data.

25.2,90 Source: U.S. Forest Service, *An Analysis of the Timber Situation in the U.S., 1952-2040, 1989.*

FOREST LAND-OWNERSHIP, SAWTIMBER AND GROWING STOCK	Total forest and (1,000 acres)	Commercial Timberland Ownership (1,000 acres)				Sawtimber Net Volume		Growing Stock, Net Volume	
		Total	Federally owned or managed	State, county, munic-ipal	Private	Total (mil. bd. ft.)	Softwood (mil. bd. ft.)	Total (mil. cu. ft.)	Softwood (mil. cu. ft.)
California	39,381	16,712	9,150	107	7,455	311,966	289,174	53,711	46,307
Total U.S.	727,921	483,072	102,295	33,722	347,055	2,823,246	2,025,957	754,916	449,977

25.3,90 Source: U.S. Forest Service, *An Analysis of the Timber Situation in the U.S.,1952-2040, 1989.*

County	United States Forest Service	Public non-Nat'l Forest	Forest Industry	Farmer and Misc. Private	Total Private	Total all Owner-ships	TPZ*
Alpine	69	1	-	14	14	84	5
Amador	26	3	23	33	56	85	28
Butte	116	12	120	107	227	355	161
Calaveras	66	7	66	71	137	210	71
Colusa	23	-	1	8	9	32	-
Del Norte	231	1	100	62	162	394	146
El Dorado	301	7	119	119	238	546	166
Fresno	290	1	3	29	32	323	18
Glenn	79	-	18	6	24	103	31
Humboldt	273	124	541	616	1,157	1,554	974
Inyo	-	2	-	2	2	4	-
Kern	87	3	-	26	26	116	-
Lake	108	11	8	56	64	183	23
Lassen	376	24	94	215	309	709	312
Los Angeles	27	-	-	-	-	27	-
Madera	213	-	5	21	26	239	4
Marin	-	-	-	16	16	16	-
Mariposa	100	2	1	40	41	143	6
Mendocino	114	127	487	613	1,100	1,341	857
Modoc	339	5	36	185	221	565	185
Mono	162	1	-	7	7	170	-
Monterey	22	1	-	28	28	51	-
Napa	-	1	1	25	26	27	-
Nevada	130	14	5	192	197	341	85
Placer	238	11	63	111	174	423	126
Plumas	959	4	138	159	297	1,260	219
Riverside	21	1	-	2	2	24	-
San Bernardino	94	-	-	5	5	99	-
San Diego	12	5	-	4	4	21	-
San Luis Obispo	-	-	1	5	6	6	-
San Mateo	-	2	8	53	61	63	31
Santa Clara	-	1	-	31	31	32	-
Santa Cruz	-	2	7	122	129	131	65
Shasta	407	37	265	473	738	1,182	647
Sierra	346	2	27	66	93	441	77
Siskiyou	1,396	20	230	468	698	2,114	571
Sonoma	-	11	33	280	313	324	82
Sutter	-	-	1	3	4	4	-
Tehama	189	3	195	39	234	426	240
Trinity	672	39	98	272	370	1,081	291
Tulare	373	16	-	16	16	405	7
Tuolumne	358	7	60	50	110	475	75
Ventura	29	-	-	1	1	30	-
Yolo	-	-	1	4	5	5	-
Yuba	36	2	5	44	49	87	31
State Totals	**8,282**	**510**	**2,760**	**4,699**	**7,459**	**16,251**	**5,534**

Title: AREA OF CALIFORNIA COMMERCIAL FOREST LAND BY COUNTY AND OWNERSHIP 1986 (thousand acres)

* Timber Preserve Zone-Under the Control of the State Board of Equalization.
25.4.90 Source: U.S. Forest Service, *Pacific Northwest Forest and Range Experiment Station*, 1985 and *California Forests: Trends, Problems & Opportunities*, and Cal. Dept. of Forestry, Forest & Rangeland Assessment Program, 1986

									Public			Private		

COMMERCIAL TIMBERLAND IN CALIFORNIA
(1,000 acres)

		Federal						County	Private		
Year	Total public	Total Federal	National Forest	Bureau of Land Management	Other	Indian	State	and municipal	Total Private	Forest Industry	Total farmer & other private
1952	9,075	8,730	8,372	318	40	144	193	8	8,052	2,167	5,885
1962	9,430	9,244	8,918	286	40	114	67	5	7,768	2,445	5,323
1970	9,448	9,236	8,935	244	39	109	79	24	7,633	2,671	4,962
1977	8,675	8,434	8,168	226	40	135	79	27	7,628	2,687	4,941
1987	9,257	9,051	8,742	300	9	99	95	12	7,455	2,757	4,698

25.5,90 Source: U.S. Forest Service, *An Analysis of the Timber Situation in the U.S., 1952-2040, 1989.*

NET VOLUME OF SAWTIMBER IN CALIFORNIA
1987

Species	Volume (million cubic feet)
Softwoods	
Douglas Fir	12,701
Incense Cedar	2,365
True Firs	12,690
Ponderosa and Jeffrey Pine	8,695
Redwood	5,114
Spruce	50
Sugar Pine	3,031
Other Pines	1,180
Western Hemlock	42
Other Softwoods	441
Total softwoods	**46,309**
Hardwoods	
Oak	5,728
Cottonwood & Aspen	20
Red Alder	133
Other Hardwoods	1,588
Total Hardwoods	**7,469**
Total-all species	**53,778**

25.6,90 Source: U.S. Forest Service, *An Analysis of the Timber Situation in the U.S., 1952-2040, 1989.*

SECTION 25 NOTE

Almost 12 percent of California land has been set aside in reserves where timbering and commercial activity are limited or prohibited.

25.7,90

CALIFORNIA FOREST, GRASS, SHRUB AND DESERT LAND LOST TO URBAN AND AGRICULTURAL USES, 1950-1980						
Type of Land	Land converted to Urban uses (acres)	%	Land Converted to Agricultural Uses (acres)	%	Total Land Converted	%
Conifer Forest	158,000	15%	62,000	2%	220,000	5%
Hardwood						
Hardwood Grassland	136,000	13%	481,000	13%	617,000	13%
Shrubland	293,000	28%	419,000	11%	712,000	15%
Grassland	283,000	27%	2,711,000	72%	2,994,000	62%
Desert	182,000	17%	118,000	3%	300,000	6%
Total	**1,052,000**	**100%**	**3,791,000**	**100%**	**4,843,000**	**100%**

25.8,90 Source: California Department of Forestry: Forest and Range Land Assessment Program, *California's Forests and Rangelands*, 1988.

CALIFORNIA HARDWOOD GROWING STOCK		
Species	Volume (million cubic feet)	Percent
California Black Oak	2,531	20.2%
Canyon Live Oak	2,033	16.2
Tan Oak	1,938	15.5
Pacific Madrone	1,517	12.1
Blue Oak	1,113	8.9
Coast Live Oak	881	7.0
Oregon White Oak	600	4.9
Interior Live Oak	553	4.4
California Laurel	427	3.4
Eucalyptus	231	1.8
Valley Oak	198	1.6
Alder	167	1.3
Other	346	1.5
Total	**12,535**	**100%**

Note: 3 percent of U.S. timberland (productive forest) hardwood growing stock is in California.

25.9,90 Source: U.S. Forest Sevice, Pacific Northwest Research Station, *The Hardwoods of California's Timberlands, Woodlands, and Savannas*, 1988.

SECTION 25 NOTE
The California Department of Forestry expects 2 million acres of forest land to be converted to urban and agricultural uses between 1980 and 2010.

25.10,90

SECTION 25 NOTE
By some accounts, the tallest tree in the world is a 367-foot monster in California's Redwood National Park.

25.11,90

| LAND COVER TYPES BY VEGETATION CLASS ||
Vegetation Type	Acres (in thousands)
Conifer	**23,013**
Closed-Cone Pine/Cypress	78
Ponderosa Pine	2,651
Mixed Conifer	9,268
Douglas Fir	1,772
Redwood	1,570
Red Fir	1,906
Jeffrey-Pine	700
Lodgepole Pine	752
Subalpine Conifer	228
Pinyon-Juniper	1,463
Juniper	1,469
Montane Hardwood-Conifer	1,156
Hardwood	**9,547**
Montane Hardwood	2,049
Valley-Foothill Hardwood	7,363
Valley Riparian	49
Montane Riparian	86
Shrub	**19,151**
Coastscrub	2,507
Chamise-Redshank Chaparral	4,808
Mixed Chaparral	2,954
Montane Chaparral	1,039
Alpine Dwarf Shrub	206
Sagebrush	6,549
Bitterbrush	581
Low Sagebrush	507
Grass	**9,557**
Annual Grass	8,653
Perennial Grass	90
Fresh Emergent Wetland	576
Wet Medow	238
Desert	**21,278**
Alkali Scrub	1,299
Other Desert	19,979
Alpine Barrren and Rock	**2,120**
Total Forest and Rangeland	**84,666**

25.12,90 Source: California Dept. of Forestry, *FRRAP Information and Analysis System.*

SECTION 25 NOTE
In 1988, the timber harvest from national forest land in California was 2,195,074 thousand board feet, valued at $233 million.

25.13,90

State	1972	1976	1980	1981	1983	1985	1986	1987
LUMBER PRODUCTION IN LEADING STATES 1972-1987 (million Board feet)								
Oregon	7,943	7,335	5,784	5,115	6,579	7,211	8,149	8,846
California	**5,376**	**4,824**	**3,768**	**3,224**	**3,574**	**4,168**	**4,865**	**5,408**
Washington	3,749	3,661	3,161	3,243	3,821	3,419	4,132	4,645
Idaho	1,851	1,908	1,391	1,319	1,657	1,676	1,876	2,016
Montana	1,311	1,197	983	1,032	1,316	1,445	1,563	1,640
Alabama	1,406	1,275	1,104	NA	1,567	1,838	2,064	2,084
Arkansas	1,482	1,320	1,424	NA	1,382	1,376	1,360	1,449
North Carolina	1,218	1,177	1,116	NA	1,505	1,411	1,608	1,674
Georgia	1,286	1,251	1,121	NA	2,018	1,923	2,349	2,428
Mississippi	1,158	1,146	1,102	NA	1,614	1,565	1,922	2,136

25.14,90 Source: U.S. Bureau of the Census, *Current Industrial Reports, Lumber Production and Mill Stocks, Series MA-2T,* and Western Wood Products Association, *Statistical Yearbook of the Western Lumber Industry.*

	Public	Private		Value
CALIFORNIA TIMBER HARVESTS (millions of board feet)				
Year	Lands	Lands	Total	(millions)
1955	1,087	4,928	6,015	NA
1960	1,438	3,699	5,137	NA
1965	1,056	3,215	5,217	NA
1970	1,942	2,642	4,566	NA
1975	1,622	2,712	4,334	NA
1980	1,228	1,863	3,091	NA
1981	950	1,722	2,672	$493
1982	818	1,510	2,319	NA
1983	1,468	1,890	3,358	NA
1984	1,417	2,093	3,510	$425
1985	1,613	2,172	3,786	$397
1986	1,786	2,313	4,099	$452
1987	1,849	2,582	4,431	$577
1988	2,027	2,598	4,625	$669

25.15,90 Source: California State Board of Equalization, Timber Tax Division, unpublished data.

SECTION 25 NOTE
According to the California Dept. of Forestry, clearcutting accounted for 38% of the timber harvest on U.S. Forest Service land in 1986. This was up from 12% in 1984. On private land, clearcutting accounted for only 8% of the harvest.

25.16,90

CALIFORNIA TIMBER HARVEST BY COUNTY, 1988					
County	Board Feet*	Value†	County	Board Feet*	Value†
Alameda	-	$58	Orange	-	$49
Alpine	9.6	$334	Placer	120.2	$18,042
Amador	31.6	$3,496	Plumas	215.2	$36,247
Butte	146.4	$23,109	Riverside	-	$131
Calaveras	99.3	$11,818	Sacramento	-	$55
Colusa	6.5	$1,241	San Benito	-	$7
Contra Costa	-	$39	San Bernardino	1.4	$124
Del Norte	191.9	$42,496	San Diego	-	$137
El Dorado	217.4	$22,415	San Francisco	-	
Fresno	81.3	$6,106	San Joaquin	-	$24
Glenn	29.2	$4,661	San Luis Obispo	-	$22
Humboldt	742.7	$139,916	San Mateo	14.6	$2,071
Imperial	-		Santa Barbara	-	$24
Inyo	-		Santa Clara	2.3	$367
Kern	19.0	$1,253	Santa Cruz	15.2	$2,041
Kings	-		Shasta	267.1	$40,200
Lake	42.3	$4,106	Sierra	205.5	$19,904
Lassen	124.5	$25,456	Siskiyou	584.4	$74,438
Los Angeles	-	$201	Solano	-	$28
Madera	62.1	$6,633	Sonoma	37.9	$4,776
Marin	-	$2	Stanislaus	-	$18
Mariposa	86.2	$9,373	Sutter	-	
Mendocino	474.5	$58,609	Tehama	159.8	$27,327
Merced	-	$22	Trinity	319.8	$43,356
Modoc	47.9	$9,664	Tulare	36.5	$3,019
Mono	7.0	$918	Tuolumne	135.0	$12,645
Monterey	-	$36	Ventura	-	$191
Napa	1.8	$187	Yolo	-	$40
Nevada	72.2	$8,961	Yuba	17.5	$2,762
			State Totals	4,625	$669,155

* (Millions of board feet) Board feet is the quantity of timber cut and scaled.
† Value of the timber in thousands of dollars immediately berore cutting.
  25.17,90 Source: Cal. State Bd. of Equalization, Timber Tax Div., unpublished data.

FOREST FIRES 1984-1988										
Agency Responsible for Area	Number of Fires					Acres Burned (in thousands)				
	1984	1985	1986	1987	1988	1984	1985	1986	1987	1988
California Dept. of Forestry	7,830	7,238	7,149	8,062	8,121	104	223	54	87	191
U.S. Forest Service	2,744	2,069	1,915	3,664	3,421	41	271	29	710	54
National Park Service	172	152	115	280	246	15	3	4	14	8
U.S. Bureau of Land Management	261	107	308	430	493	48	16	10	20	34
Contract Counties*	NA	NA	NA	1,040	1,009	NA	NA	NA	42	58
Total	NA	NA	NA	13,476	13,290	NA	NA	NA	873	345
5 Year Average (1983-87)	NA	NA	NA	NA	11,726	NA	NA	NA	NA	279

* Kern, Los Angeles, Marin, Orange, Santa Barbara and Ventura counties contract with the California Dept. of Forestry to control fires in their counties.
25.18,90 Source: California Dept. of Forestry, 1989, U.S. Forest Service, *Annual Fire Report*, U.S. Park Service and U.S. Bureau of Land Management, unpublished data.

CALIFORNIA TIMBER HARVEST, 1988				
Product **Softwood Sawlogs**	**Board Feet***	**Percent**	**Value†**	**Percent**
Ponderosa Pine	940,600,000	20.3%	195,357,000	29.2%
Sugar Pine	357,100,000	7.7%	83,578,000	12.5%
Fir	1,146,100,000	24.8%	68,284,000	10.2%
Douglas Fir	1,193,000,000	25.8%	127,729,000	19.1%
Incense Cedar	133,200,000	2.9%	9,191,000	1.4%
Redwood	779,200,000	16.8%	175,309,000	26.2%
Miscellaneous Species	76,200,000	1.7%	6,170,000	0.9%
Subtotal for Sawlogs	**4,625,400,000**	**100.0%**	**665,618,000**	**99.5%**
Miscellaneous Products	470,000		3,537,000	0.5%
Total	**4,625,800,000**	**100.0%**	**669,155,000**	**100.0%**

*   Board feet is the quantity of timber cut and scaled.

†   Value of the timber immediately before cutting.

25.19,90   Source: California State Board of Equalization, Timber Tax Division, unpublished data.

EMPLOYMENT IN FOREST PRODUCTS INDUSTRIES IN CALIFORNIA 1971-1989 (in thousands)			
Year	**Lumber and Wood** **Products**	**Paper and Allied** **Products**	**Total**
1971	50.5	35.5	86.0
1972	52.4	37.9	90.3
1973	54.1	36.1	90.2
1974	50.9	37.3	88.2
1975	52.8	34.5	87.3
1976	59.9	36.7	96.6
1977	66.6	37.6	104.2
1978	69.9	37.2	107.1
1979	68.7	39.1	107.8
1980	62.6	38.7	101.3
1981	57.9	38.7	96.6
1982	46.2	37.5	83.7
1983	50.2	37.3	87.5
1984	55.4	39.1	94.5
1985	55.9	39.8	95.7
1986	59.5	39.6	99.0
1987	66.2	41.3	107.5
1988*	66.4	41.1	107.5
1989*	68.2	41.4	109.6

*   Data as of April.

25.20,90 Source: Cal. Department of Employment, *Report to the Governor on Labor Market Conditions*.

CALIFORNIA* SAWMILLS, 1986

Source of Timber
Company-owned	39.8%
Federal	39.0%
Other	21.2%

Species Cut
Douglas Fir & Larch	29.3%
Ponderosa Pine	17.8%
Hem-Fir	22.6%
Redwood	20.9%
Sugar Pine	5.4%
Incense Cedar	3.8%
Other	0.2%

Degree of Processing
Kiln Dried	41.1%
Air Dried	4.0%
Green	54.9%

Finish
Rough	28.1%
Surfaced	71.9%

Mode of Transportation
Rail	15.7%
Truck	82.1%
Water	2.2%

Principal Markets
California	71.6%
Other West	12.8%
Midwest	5.2%
Northeast	2.7%
South Central	3.8%
Southeast	2.9%
Export	1.0%

Distribution Channels
Direct to User	5.2%
Direct to Retailer	6.7%
Wholesaler	62.0%
Company-owned Distribution Yard	3.3%
To Factory for Further Manufacturing	22.8%

* Nevada forestry is included in the data but is a very small percent of the totals.

25.21,90 Source: Western Wood Products Association, *Statistical Yearbook of the Western Lumber Industry, 1987.*

SECTION 25 NOTE

Of the 20 largest timber producers in the U.S. and Canada, only 1, Sierra Pacific Industries, is headquartered in California. It is ranked 12.

25.22,90

CALIFORNIA* FOREST PRODUCTS PROFILE				
Total commercial Forest Land (acres)†				**16,437,300**
Commercial Forest Land Ownership				
Federal				51.7%
Indian				0.8%
Other				0.7%
Government				
Private				46.8%
Total volume of Sawtimber (millions of feet)†				**256,957,100**
Sawtimber Ownership				
Public	64.1%	Private		35.9%
Lumber Production and Wholesale Value				
1975		4,153,000 Million feet		$808,800,000
1977		5,052,000		$1,358,900,000
1979		4,639,000		$1,611,300,000
1980		3,768,000		$1,186,200,000
1981		3,224,000		$1,015,500,000
1982		2,987,000		$804,100,000
1983		3,574,000		$1,124,900,000
1984		3,891,000		$1,160,700,000
1985		4,168,000		$1,216,000,000
1986		4,865,000		$1,441,300,000
1987		5,408,000		$1,706,800,000
Employment	**1984**	**1985**	**1986**	**1987**
Lumber and Wood Products,				
except Furniture	55,100	56,300	60,100	64,900
Logging, Sawmills, Planing Mills	20,900	20,400	20,900	21,300
Millwork, Plywood, and Related				
Products	16,900	18,400	20,900	24,200

* Nevada forestry is included in the data but is only a very small part of the totals.

† As of January 1, 1977.

25.23,90 Source: Western Wood Products Association, *Statistical Yearbook of the Western Lumber Industry, 1987.*

SECTION 25 NOTE
Grazing takes place on 17.9 million acres of private land in California and on 23 million acres of public land.

25.24,90

SECTION 25 NOTE
In 1988, California had 13 pulp mills, 33 paper mills, 13 assorted pulp and paper mills, and 75 rag and paper stock dealers.

25.25,90

SECTION 25 NOTE
Grazing takes place on 17.9 million acres of private land in California and on 23 million acres of public land.

25.26,90

		TIMBER SOLD ON PUBLICLY OWNED OR MANAGED LANDS IN CALIFORNIA (millions of board feet)			
Year	Forest Service	Bureau of Land Management	Bureau of Indian Affairs	State of California	Total
1983	1,787	8.9	3.0	31.5	1,830
1984	1,490	13.1	3.6	33.5	1,541
1985	1,608	16.6	4.3	27.2	1,657
1986	1,472	20.4	81.5	31.3	1,605
1987	1,628	19.7	10.0	40.3	1,698

25.27,90 Source: U.S. Forest Service, *Production, Prices, Employment and Trade in Northwest Forest Industries,* Quarterly.

	TIMBER INVENTORY, HARVEST AND GROWTH PROJECTIONS (MBF) FOR CALIFORNIA 1980-2060		
Period	Inventory (average MBF)	Harvest (ave. annual MBF)	Growth (ave. annual MBF)
1980-1990	212,763,657	3,910,034	3,746,957
1990-2000	211,428,303	3,922,569	3,667,211
2000-2010	210,481,808	3,700,242	3,803,856
2010-2020	214,145,838	3,341,362	4,130,885
2020-2030	223,401,603	3,264,001	4,349,170
2030-2040	234,906,961	3,242,764	4,458,730
2040-2050	247,404,493	3,208,342	4,491,881
2050-2060	253,822,253	3,227,225	NA

25.28,90 Source: California Dept. of Forestry, *FRRAP Information and Analysis System.*

	CALIFORNIA FOREST INVENTORY AND NET GROWTH, 1982-1984			
	Hardwoods (million cubic ft.)		Softwoods (million board feet-Scribner)	
	Standing Inventory	Net Growth	Standing Inventory	Net Growth
National Forest	2,401	66	170,384	1,891
Other Public Forest	555	16	6,501	146
Forest Industry	1,377	46	38,692	1,077
Other Industry	432	12	15,090	381
Non-Industrial Private Forest	2,927	83	32,966	874
Total	**7,692**	**144**	**263,633**	**4,369**

25.29,90 Source: California Department of Forestry, Forest Resource Analysis Program, unpublished data, 1987.

Fisheries

How are California's ocean fisheries doing? Compared with what? Compared with the 1976 glory catch of 917 million pounds, the 1988 catch of 496 million pounds is paltry. But the 1988 catch was the best since 1984. Whether the ocean catch can keep up with the rising consumer demand for fish in California is uncertain. Fisheries experts worry that coastal pollution, the reduction of spawning sites that results when dams are built, and overfishing by both U.S. and foreign fishing fleets have seriously diminished the potential of the oceans to provide all the fish consumers want.

The fishing business may also be in for a regulatory shock in the next few years: a number of health experts are advocating that fish in the wholesale market be subjected to the same kind of inspection for wholesomeness that meat and poultry regularly undergo. Fish is not currently inspected, and a few catches reach the market with higher bacteria levels than are desirable. The logistical difficulties of inspecting fish from thousands of individual ships, however, may be beyond the ability of even an ambitious and activist regulatory agency to overcome.

The real potential for providing large quantities of fish for California's fish eaters will probably come from inland and marine fisheries--the so-called fish farms. Currently there are fifty-two marine or saltwater aquaculturists registered with the California Department of Fish and Game. There are also 306 freshwater aquaculturists in the state. San Bernardino and Riverside counties have more fish farms than any other California counties. Catfish and trout are now the most popular fish-farm products, but researchers are working on the commercial production of shellfish, sturgeon, and other varieties of fish.

The new fish farmers are a far cry from their predecessors. Modern fish farmers often have college degrees--even advanced degrees--in marine biology as well as business experience. Modern fish farmers are also often backed by individual and corporate investors with deep pockets and the fortitude to continue providing support until the enterprise achieves commercial levels of production. Visionaries in the aquaculture business foresee a time not too far hence when the bulk of our fish, shrimp, lobster, abalone, and oysters come from fish farms, with only supplementary supplies from the oceans.

CALIFORNIA FISHERIES
1987 AND 1988 LANDINGS

Species	1987 $ Value (1,000)	1987 Pounds (1,000)	1988 $ Value (1,000)	1988 Pounds (1,000)
Abalone	$2,476	763	$1,995	557
California Baracuda	$105	113	$113	138
Anchovy†	$253	3,064	$379	3,345
Bonito	$2,405	11,140	$1,695	8,682
Clams	$17	38	$16	22
Ling Cod	$742	1,859	$780	1,929
Dungeness Crab	$9,741	6,857	$14,810	11,262
Rock Crab	$1,480	1,567	$1,205	1,243
Croaker	$340	913	$410	1,083
Flounder	$109	311	$138	345
Groundfish/ Rockfish	$11,909	30,143	$9,990	25,856
Halibut	$2,676	1,950	$2,555	1,149
Pacific Herring	$5,812	18,563	$5,662	19,032
Spiny Lobster	$2,144	450	$3,306	625
Mackerel	$8,260	120,695	$8,989	123,074
Salmon	$25,622	9,302	$41,906	14,752
Pacific Sardine	$63	969	$158	2,620
Sea Urchin	$13,694	46,062	$18,344	49,472
Shark	$2,419	2,604	$1,985	1,763
Shrimp/ Prawn	$6,668	8,507	$6,062	11,799
Sole	$10,754	30,760	$8,660	24,358
Squid	$4,103	44,057	$7,941	80,777
Swordfish	$11,152	2,741	$9,537	2,443
Tuna	$73,779	70,027	$42,094	66,893
All Others	$8,409	29,927	$9,967	36,854
Total	**$205,132**	**443,382**	**$198,697**	**490,073**

† Includes bait landings and prices estimated by National Marine Fisheries Service.
26.1,90 Source: California Department of Fish and Game, unpublished data.

QUANTITY AND VALUE OF CALIFORNIA CATCH
(Catch in millions of pounds; Value in millions of dollars)

	1960	1965	1970	1974	1978	1980	1982	1984	1985	1986	1987	1988
Catch	541	458	703	685	722	804	695	459	363	387	443	496
Value	50	51	86	140	228	353	241	177	133	139	205	199

26.2,90 Source: National Marine Fisheries Service, *Fishery Statistics of the United States,* and *Fisheries of the United States,* annual.

CALIFORNIA FISHING DISTRICTS AND PORTS	
District 1: San Diego Area San Diego Imperial Beach Mission Bay Oceanside	**District 4: Monterey Area** Monterey Moss Landing Santa Cruz
District 2: Los Angeles Area Los Angeles San Pedro Dana Harbor Long Beach Malibu Redondo Beach Santa Monica	**District 5: San Francisco Area** San Francisco Princeton Half Moon Bay Bodega Bay
District 3: Santa Barbara Area Santa Barbara Oxnard Port Hueneme Morro Bay Ventura Avilla Beach	**District 6: Eureka Area** Eureka Fort Bragg Crescent City

26.3,90 Source: California Department of Fish and Game, unpublished data.

CALIFORNIA COMMERCIAL FISHERIES LANDINGS BY PORT					
	Millions of Pounds				
Port	**1984**	**1985**	**1986**	**1987**	**1988**
San Diego	NA	6.4	NA	NA	4.6
Los Angeles	237	150	187	203	232

Port Hueneme,
  Oxnard
  & Ventura
	9.4	20	31	42	55

Santa Barbara	10	11	14	NA	NA
San Francisco Area	22	31	26	27	25
Bodega Bay	NA	6.9	8.5	13	14
Crescent City	16	20	21	23	36
Eureka	23	29	19	29	27
Fort Bragg	13	16	18	26	31
Monterey	30	18	16	16	14

26.4,90 Source: National Oceanic and Atmospheric Administration, *Fisheries of the U.S.*, 1988 and unpublished data.

SECTION 25 NOTE
California coastal kelp (actually algae) grow up to 200 feet long and increase by as much as 2 feet per day.

26.5,90

FISHING BOATS AND EMPLOYMENT		
Year	Number of Commercial Fishing Boats	Number of Commercial Fishermen
1981	8,400	18,852
1985	8,767	16,794
1989	8,000	14,844

26.6,90 Source: National Marine Fisheries Service Southwest Region, *Commercial Fishery Statistics,* 1984, and Cal. Dept. of Fish & Game, Licenses Section, unpublished data.

EMPLOYMENT IN FISH PROCESSING AND WHOLESALING				
Year	Number of Processing Plants	Employment	Number of Wholesaling Establishments	Employment
1981	68	9,500	59	654
1983	82	7,460	57	523
1985	70	4,606	64	873
1987	55	3,627	50	1,384

26.7,90 Source: National Marine Fisheries Service, *Processed Fishery Products, Annual Summary.*

VALUE OF PROCESSED FISH PRODUCTS CALIFORNIA 1981-1986 (in millions)	
1981	$822.7
1983	$603.4
1985	$261.9
1986	$267.2

26.8,90 Source: National Marine Fisheries Services, *Processed Fishery Products, Annual Summary.*

CALIFORNIA FISH PLANTS, 1984-1988			
Type of Plant	1984	1986	1988
Canned Fish Products	9	5	6
Industrial Fish Products	8	7	6
Fish Fillets and Steaks	34	29	27

26.9,90 Source: National Marine Fisheries Services, *Fisheries of the United States, Annual.*

CALIFORNIA FISHERMEN'S UNIONS AND LABOR ORGANIZATIONS

Fishermen and Allied Workers Union, Local 33, ILWU 150 W. 7th St. Stuite 105 San Pedro, CA 90731, (213) 833-1391 Members: 100 Boats: 9 Species: Tuna, Squid, Mackerel, Bonito	Fishermen's Union of American-Pacific and Caribbean Area, Affiliated with Seafares's International AFL-CIO P.O. Box 2227 Monterey, Ca 93940, (408) 375-3126 Members: 125 Boats: 16 Species: Squid, Anchovy, Mackerel, Herring
Fishermen's Union of American-Pacific and Caribbean Area, Affiliated with Seafarer's International AFL/CIO 529 West 9th Street San Pedro, CA 90731 (213) 833-3571 Members: 235 Boats: 9 Species: Mackerel, Bonito, Tuna, Squid, Bluefin, Yellowfin, Sardenes	Fishermen's Union of American-Pacific and Caribbean Area, Affiliated with Seafarer's International AFL/CIO 1809 Main St. (State H.Q.) San Diego, CA 92113 (619) 239-5184 Members: 300 Boats: 5 Species: Tuna, Mackerel, Bonito, Anchovy, Squid, Albacore, Bluefin

26.10,90 Source: The respective unions, 1989.

FISHING LICENSES AND ANGLING STAMPS*

Year	Fishing Licenses	Angling Stamps
1970-1971	2,286,195	3,545,528
1975-1976	2,251,081	3,270,994
1980-1981	2,464,463	3,850,488
1981-1982	2,539,946	3,907,456
1982-1983	2,529,593	4,380,343
1983-1984	2,434,223	4,223,464
1984-1985	2,450,992	1,205,746
1985-1986	2,363,704	1,142,737
1986-1987	2,218,298	1,096,468

* Licenses are for ocean fishing; stamps are for inland fishing.
26.11,90 Source: California Department of Fish and Game, License Section, unpublished data, and *California Statistical Abstract*.

SECTION 26 NOTE

According to Bob Lea of the California Deptartment of Fish and Game, from 1926 to 1989 sharks attacked and killed seven people off the California coast. During the same period, 63 shark attacks were reported, less than 10 percent of them in the waters off Southern California.

26.12,90

ANNUAL CATCHES OF THE CALIFORNIA COMMERCIAL PASSENGER FISHING VESSEL FLEET 1984-1988

Species	Number of Fish Caught			
	1984	1986	1987	1988*
Barracuda, Calif.	67,414	85,043	157,913	139,750
Bass, giant sea	NA	74	45	NA
Bass, kelp & sand	359,383	422,095	734,323	729,805
Bass, striped	13,524	8,572	8,858	9,337
Bonito, Pacific	377,678	325,565	517,523	244,842
Cabezon	1,759	4,285	4,773	5,314
Croaker	4,659	14,195	4,785	125,528
Flatfish, unspec.	11,896	12,606	10,311	16,225
Halfmoon	24,429	61,952	32,296	80,000
Halibut, Calif.	3,209	7,697	7,560	11,501
Jacksmelt	262	318	60	341
Ling Cod	23,797	24,682	42,504	63,393
Mackerel, jack	13,261	4,380	3,056	21,251
Mackerel, Pacific	604,324	596,586	517,166	470,854
Marlin	287	42	168	134
Rockfish, unspec.	2,012,684	1,760,446	1,698,523	1,851,137
Rockfish, Cowcod	3,105	584	511	1,421
Sablefish	568	7,420	3,375	2,803
Salmon	71,471	88,572	126,202	112,788
Sanddab	1,576	5,142	514	2,539
Seabass, white	973	1,342	616	2,358
Sculpin	46,539	70,725	59,125	127,774
Shark	1,416	2,047	1,943	2,594
Sheephead, Calif.	38,522	34,119	21,072	30,898
Sole, Petrale	159	27	58	33
Sturgeon, unspec.	530	944	418	332
Tuna, Albacore	211,285	26,610	7,046	559
Tuna, Bluefin	2,834	671	1,859	313
Tuna, Skipjack	30,357	2,098	8,181	1,888
Tuna, Yellowfin	8,648	5,439	14,794	20,065
Wahoo	4,807	3,723	3,087	2,208
Whitefish, ocean	64,291	71,499	34,967	56,849
Yellowtail	96,081	40,899	58,537	66,447
Total no. of Fish	**4,172,393**	**3,970,415**	**4,102,852**	**4,203,038**
Total Anglers	**701,737**	**645,590**	**678,594**	**689,380**
No. of Reporting Boats	**323**	**298**	**287**	**308**

* Preliminary 26.13,90 Source: Cal. Dept of Fish and Game, Marine Resources Division, *Preliminary Report of Fish Caught by the Commercial Passenger Fishing Boat Fleet.*

SECTION 26 NOTE

The biggest blue fin Pacific tuna ever caught was a 625-pounder netted off the Santa Barbara Channel Islands in November 1988. The giant tuna, which was 94 pounds heavier than the largest tuna previously caught in the Pacific, was brought in by a tuna boat called the PIONEER.

26.14,90

Mining and Minerals

James Wilson Marshall, who set off the 1849 Gold Rush when he found gold at Sutter's Mill, near Placerville, would be more than a bit surprised to see that the industry that sprang up out of his discovery has had a major resurgence in the 1980s. With the incentive of $400-an-ounce prices on the commodities exchanges and large capital investments from both U.S. and Canadian mining companies, old pits have been reopened and old slag heaps combed for the precious metal. Gold production soared from 38,000 to 440,000 troy ounces between 1983 and 1988. Although gold mining has not provided broad opportunities for employment, it has added a few hundred positions in rural California, where jobs that pay well are often hard to find.

One entire segment of the mining industry is likely to disappear in the near future. The federal government has banned the use of asbestos in insulation and most other products. This ban will hurt California more than other asbestos-producing states because we have been the nation's number one asbestos-mining state. But because asbestos mining is a hazardous occupation, the closing of the mines, even as it eliminates a number of mining jobs, may lengthen the life span of the miners involved.

The bulk of California's mining jobs have been in the oil and gas industries, which have been declining since high oil prices dropped in the early 1980s. The output of both oil and gas is down from the production peaks of those years. The state continues to use up its existing reserves, and no significant new oil and gas reserves have been discovered. The only area where significant new reserves may be found is in the lands off the coast. Memories of the 1970 Santa Barbara oil spill and the more recent *Exxon Valdez* spill in Alaska, however, have generated fierce opposition to even exploratory offshore drilling. Although some such drilling is likely to occur in the 1990s, there is no certainty that new offshore oil fields would be opened for production.

Responding to an ever-increasing number of cars on the road and the need to refine more heavy oil, California's oil refiners are spending billions of dollars to upgrade and expand their refineries. Tough federal EPA guidelines for air pollution control in the Los Angeles area, if enforced, may eventually lead to a decline in oil-refining activities in the Los Angeles basin unless the oil companies can drastically cut emissions levels associated with the refining process.

CALIFORNIA MINERAL PRODUCTION 1987-1988				
	1987		1988*	
Product	Quantity	Value (thousands)	Quantity	Value (thousands)
Fuel Minerals				
Petroleum(million barrels)	397	$4,698,000	388	$3,551,000
Natural gas(billion cubic feet)	427	$1,005,600	409	NA
Nonfuel Minerals				
Asbestos	W	W	11,000	$5,000
Boron Minerals (thousand short tons)	NA	$475,092	624	$420,900
Portland Cement (thousand short tons)	9,937	$593,859	10,600	$648,400
Clays† (thousand short tons)	2,296	$33,045	2,470	$37,164
Gem Stones	NA	$3,367	NA	$3,365
Gold (recoverable content of ores, troy ounces)	602,605	$269,937	729,272	$320,150
Gypsum (thousand short tons)	1,468	$11,719	1,316	$10,505
Lime (thousand short tons)	465	$25,745	473	$26,190
Mercury (76lb. Flasks)	3	NA	NA	NA
Pumice (shousand short tons)	42	$1,539	44	$1,668
Constuction Sand & Gravel (thousand short tons)	141,600††	561,300††	134,800	$726,800
Industrial Sand & Gravel (thousand short tons)	2,241	$41,472	2,445	$42,000
Silver (recoverable content of ores, thousand troy ounces)	122	$854	133	$871
Crushed Stone (thousand short tons)	44,315	$186,501	45,900	$266,700
Dimension Stone (thousand short tons)	33	$4,554	42	$5,991
Talc & Prophyllite (thousand short tons)	42	$922	NA	NA
Other Minerals	NA	$342,298	NA	$335,648
Total	**NA**	**$2,551,285**	**NA**	**$2,851,352**

* Preliminary. † Excludes fire clay, which is included in "Other Minerals." †† Estimated.
NA = not available; W = withheld to avoid disclosing company proprietary data.
27.1,90 Source: California Department of Conservation, Division of Oil and Gas, *73rd Annual Report, 1989 California Oil & Gas Production Statistics and new Well Operations Preliminary Report;* and United States Bureau of Mines, *State Mineral Summaries.*

SECTION 27 NOTE
The largest gold nugget ever found in California was the 54-troy-pound Willard nugget (also called the Dogtown or Magalia nugget). It was found at Magalia (Butte County) in 1859.

27.2,90

NUMBER OF MINES AND MINING CLAIMS IN CALIFORNIA	
Operating Mines	
Type	**Number**
Surface	553
Underground	34
Total	**587**
As of the end of fiscal 1988 212,729 mining claims in California had been accepted for recording, 59,322 had been voided, 93 claims patented, and 153,314 were unpatented.	

27.3,90 Sources: U.S. Bureau of Land Management, *Public Land Statistics*, 1988; U.S. Mine Safety and Health Administration, unpublished data, December 31, 1988.

NONFUEL MINERAL PRODUCTION IN CALIFORNIA 1985 (By County)	
County	**Minerals Produced, In Order of Value**
Alameda	Salt, Stone (crushed), clay
Amador	Industrial sand, clay, stone (crushed)
Calaveras	Asbestos, talc, stone (crushed)
Colusa	Stone (crushed)
Contra Costa	Stone (crushed), industrial sand, clay
Del Norte	Stone (crushed), gold
El Dorado	Stone (crushed)
Fresno	Gold Stone (dimension), stone (crushed), clay, silver
Glenn	Lime, stone (crushed)
Humboldt	Stone (crushed)
Imperial	Gypsum, gold, stone (crushed), lime, silver
Inyo	Boron, tungsten, stone (crushed), talc, perlite, clays, molybdenum, pumice, copper, stone (dimension), gold
Kern	Boron, cement, clays, stone (crushed), gypsum, stone (dimension)
Kings	Gypsum
Lake	Stone (crushed)
Lassen	Diatomite, stone (crushed)
Los Angeles	Stone (crushed), clay, stone (dimension)
Madera	Tungsten, stone (dimension), pumice stone (crushed)
Marin	Stone (crushed), clay
Mariposa	Stone (dimension & crushed)
Modoc	Stone (crushed), peat
Mono	Pumice, clay, gold, silver, talc, stone (crushed)
Monterey	Magnesium, stone (crushed), sand (industrial)
Napa	Gold, stone (crushed), salt, silver, stone (dimension)
Nevada	Clay, stone (crushed)
Orange	Clay, sand (industrial), feldspar, stone (crushed)
Placer	Clay, stone (crushed & and dimension)

27.4.1,90

County	Minerals Produced, In Order of Value
	NONFUEL MINERAL PRODUCTION IN CALIFORNIA **1985** **(By County)**
Plumas	Gold, Stone (dimension & crushed)
Riverside	Cement, stone (crushed), iron ore, clay, gypsum, sand (industrial)
Sacramento	Clay
San Benito	Stone (crushed), asbestos, clay
San Bernardino	Cement, sodium carbonate, boron, stone (crushed), rare earths, sodium sulfate, potassium salts, calcium chloride, salt, clay, gold, iron ore, talc, cement, feldspar, silver, gypsum
San Diego	Sand (industrial), stone (dimension & crushed), feldspar, salt
San Joaquin	Gold, Silver
San Luis Obispo	Stone (crushed), gypsum, stone (dimension)
San Mateo	Magnesium compounds, salt, stone (crushed)
Santa Barbara	Diatomite, lime, stone (dimension & crushed)
Santa Clara	Cement, stone (crushed)
Santa Cruz	Cement, stone (crushed), sand (industrial), clay, peat
Shasta	Cement, stone (crushed), clay
Sierra	Gold
Siskiyou	Gold, silver, stone (crushed), pumice
Solano	Stone (crushed)
Sonoma	Stone (crushed)
Stanislaus	Gold, silver
Sutter	Clay
Tehama	Stone (crushed)
Trinity	Stone (crushed)
Tulare	Stone (crushed)
Tuolumne	Stone (crushed)
Ventura	Sand (industrial), clay, stone (crushed), gypsum
Yuba	Clay
Undistributed	Sand & Gravel, gem stones

27.4.2,90 Source: U.S. Bureau of Mines, *Minerals Yearbook, 1989.*

SECTION 27 NOTE
According to the historian J. S. Holliday, 8,000 gold seekers came to California in 1848, followed by 89,000 in 1849 and 85,000 in 1850.

27.5,90

SECTION 27 NOTE
Gold has been commercially mined in 47 of California's 58 counties.

27.6,90

CALIFORNIA'S RANK AMONG THE FIFTY STATES AS A PRODUCER OF MINERALS			
Mineral	**Rank**	**Mineral**	**Rank**
Fuels		**Nonmetallic Metals (cont.)**	
Petroleum	4	Feldspar	4
		Gypsum	7
Metals		Gypsum, Calcined	2
Rare Earth Metals	1	Magnesium Compounds	2
Tungsten Ore	1	Perlite	3
		Potassium Salts	2
Nonmetallic Minerals		Pumice	3
Asbestos	1	Construction Sand	1
Boron	1	Industrial Sand	3
Calcium Chloride	2	Natural Sodium Carbonate	2
Diatomite	1	Sodium Sulfate	1
		Wallastonite	2

27.7,90 Source: U.S. Bureau of Mines, *Minerals Yearbook*, 1986.

MINING ESTABLISHMENTS AND PAYROLL					
Number of Establishments		**Annual Payroll (in millions of dollars)**		**Number of Employees**	
1984	**1986**	**1984**	**1986**	**1984**	**1986**
Oil and Gas 1,037	968	$852	$730	28,917	26,964
Bituminous coal and lignite 16	13	NA	NA	43	20-99
Metals 117	97	42	NA	1,419	*
Nonmetallic 320	301	$234	$253	7,549	7,662
Administrative and Auxiliary 78	73	$518	$527	26,530	10,789
Total Mining 1,568	**1,452**	**$1,647**	**$1,550**	**64,458**	**46,435-48,013**

*   1,000-2,499.   27.8,90 Source: U.S. Bureau of the Census, *County Business Patterns-Cal.*

STRATEGIC MATERIALS STORED IN CALIFORNIA	
Counties	**Material***
Lassen Riverside Monterey San Francisco San Joaquin	Refractory Bauxite 5,814 (ST), Metallurgical Chromite ore 113,840 (ST), Refractory Chromite 30,809 (ST), High Carbon Ferrochrome 589 (ST), Low Carbon Ferrochrome 4,951 (ST), Iodine 302 (ST), Lead 24,562 (ST), Manganese ore 25,113 (ST), Platinum-Irridium 6,288 (T.O.), Platinum-Paladium 200,483 (T.O.), Platinum 84,406 (T.O.), Rutile 1,198 (ST), Silver 84,989,231 (T.O) Tin 15,599 (ST), Titanium Sponge 4,637 (S.T.), Tungsten 852 (ST), Tungsten Metal Powder 60 (ST), Tungsten Ores & Concentrates 103 (ST), Zinc 1,835 (S.T.)

*   Precise location of materials by county cannot be released for security reasons.
    (ST) is short tons, (T.O.) is troy ounces.
    27.9,90 Source: U.S. Gen. Serv. Admin., Federal Property Resources Service, .

	California			United States		
MINERAL PRODUCTION VALUE **1940-1988** **(millions of dollars)**						
Year	Fuel	Nonfuel	Total	Fuel	Nonfuel	Total
1940	$228	$115	$343	$2,659	$1,539	$4,198
1950	774	282	1,056	8,681	3,174	11,855
1960	NA	NA	1,422	12,142	5,890	18,032
1970	NA	NA	1,900	20,153	9,637	29,790
1975	NA	NA	3,153	47,505	14,761	62,266
1979	4,862	1,770	6,632	82,889	23,968	106,857
1980	8,611	1,886	10,497	118,747	25,108	143,855
1981	11,264	1,975	13,239	162,639	25,173	187,812
1983	10,215	1,764	11,979	147,644	21,134	168,778
1985	10,039	2,095	12,134	144,330	23,232	166,809
1986	5,993	2,269	8,262	93,393	23,452	116,845
1987	5,704	2,551	8,255	97,110	26,346	123,456
1988	NA	2,851	NA	88,480	30,460	118,940

27.10,90 Source: U.S. Energy Information Administration, *Annual Energy Review, Natural Gas Annual, and Report 182*, U.S. Bureau of Mines, *Mineral Commodity Survey*, and *U.S. Statistical Abstract*.

CAVE EXPLORING IN CALIFORNIA

Illustrative Caves Open to the Public

Northern California	Southern California
Lava Beds National Monument	Mojave Desert-Mitchell Caverns
Lake Shasta Caverns	Sequoia Natl. Park-Crystal Cave
San Andreas-California Caverns	
Boyden Cavern-East of Fresno	

CAVE EXPLORING (SPELUNKING) CLUBS

Northern California	Southern California
Mother Lode Grotto (916) 756-4137 or (209) 267-0696	Southern California Grotto (818) 248-6546 or (213) 255-9446
San Francisco Bay Chapter (408) 427-0638 or (408) 287-0890	Waldo Brothers Grotto (818) 285-4228 or (213) 866-9449

27.11,90 Source: National Speleological Society.

CALIFORNIA OIL AND GAS FACTS, 1987	
General Statistics	
Total land area of California	101,563,520 acres
Total land area productive for oil and gas	417,746 acres (0.42%)
Counties with oil and/or gas production	30
First year of commercial production	1876
Crude Oil Production	
Counties producing crude oil	17
Active oil fields	242†
Wells producing crude oil in December, 1987	46,516*
Average daily production of crude oil per well on december 31, 1987	23.2 bbl
Year of greatest crude oil production	1985
Crude oil produced in record year	423.9 million bbl**
Crude oil produced in 1987	397 million bbl**
Cumulative crude oil production as of December 31, 1987	21.7 billion bbl
† Includes 7 active federal OCS fields. Carpinteria offshore field is situated in both state and federal waters. * Includes 362 federal OCS producing wells. ** Includes federal OCS production.	
Natural Gas Production	
Active dry gas fields	103
Dry gas wells producing in December, 1987	1,294
Year of greatest natural gas production (total gas)	1968
Natural gas produced in record year*	714.9 billion cu. ft.
Natural gas produced in 1987	427† billion cu. ft.
Cumulative natural gas production as of December 31, 1987	32.1 trillion cu. ft.
* Includes both associated and nonassociated gas. Includes federal OCS production, which was 1.6 billion cu. ft. † Includes federal OCS production. (1 field)	
Offshore (State and Federal)	
Percent of state crude oil production	15.50%
State offshore lease production	30.3 million bbl
Federal offshore lease production (OCS)	31.1 million bbl
Total	**61.4 million bbl**
Percent of total state natural gas production	13.60%
State offshore lease production	13.0 billion cu. ft.
Federal offshore lease production	45.1 billion cu. ft.
Total	**58.1 billion cu. ft.**

27.12,90 Source: California Department of Conservation, division of Oil & Gas, *73rd Annual Report*, 1987.

SECTION 27 NOTE
As of December 31, 1988, California's refinery and bulk terminal stocks of selected petroleum products were as follows (in thousands of barrels): (1) leaded gasoline, 42,412; (2) unleaded gasoline, 107,384; (3) kerosene, 1,636; (4) distillate fuel oil, 70,094; and (5) residual fuel oil, 60,458.

27.13,90

CALIFORNIA OIL AND GAS FACTS	
1987	
Exploration and Development	
Onshore	
Deepest oil well (not producing): Total depth: 18,876 feet Year completed: 1975 Producing interval: 17,610-18,060 feet Field: Semitropic County: Kern Operator: Tenneco Oil Company	**Deepest oil well (producing in 1987):** Total depth: 14,680 feet Year completed: 1982 Producing interval: 14,528-14,540 feet Field: Rio Viejo County: Kern Operator: Koch Exploration Company
Deepest gas well (not producing): Total depth: 11,402 feet Year completed: 1966 Producing interval: 11,064-11,444 feet Field: Clarksburg Gas County: Yolo Operator: Occidental Petroleum Corp.	**Deepest gas well (producing in 1987):** Total depth: 12,576 Year completed: 1978 Producing interval: 10,800-12,574 feet Field: Cal Canal Gas County: Kern Operator: Occidental Petroleum
Deepest dry hole: Total depth: 22,711 feet Year drilled: 1974 County: Kern Operator: Tenneco Oil Company	**Deepest well** Total depth: 24,426 feet Year completed: 1987 County: Kern Operator: Bechtel Petroleum
First well drilled to find oil: 1861 in Humboldt County	
Offshore	
Deepest oil well*: Total depth: 14,236 feet Year completed: 1956 Producing interval: 12,551-13,927 feet Field: Montalvo Offshore Area County: Ventura Operator: Chevron U.S.A. Inc.	**Deepest gas well:** Total depth: 12,589 feet Year completed: 1985 Producing interval: 11,135-11,365 feet Field: Molino Offshore Gas County: Santa Barbara Operator: Shell Western
Deepest dry hole*: Total depth: 17,180 feet Year drilled: 1966 County: Ventura Operator: Chevron U.S.A. Inc.	

* Drilled from an onshore location.
27.14,90 Source: California Dept. of Conservation-Division of Oil & Gas, *73rd Annual Report*, 1987.

PROVEN OIL RESERVES*		
(billions of barrels)		
California	5.2	(19.0% of U.S. total)
United States	27.3	

* As of December 31, 1987.
27.15,90 Source: California Department of Conservation, Division of Oil and Gas, *73rd Annual Report*, 1987, and United States Energy Information Administration, Reserves and Natural Gas Division and U.S. *Statistical Abstract*.

CRUDE PETROLEUM AND NATURAL GAS PRODUCTION 1966-1988		
Year	California	United States
Petroleum Production (in millions of barrels)		
1966-1970, average	365	3,292
1971-1975, average	337	3,306
1976-1980, average	346	3,085
1981-1988, average	403	3,145
1975	322	3,057
1979	352	3,121
1980	347	3,146
1981	385	3,129
1982	402	3,157
1983	405	3,171
1984	412	3,241
1985	424	3,274
1986	408	3,164
1987	397	3,047
1988	388	2,975
Natural Gas Marketed Production (in billion cubic feet)		
1966-1970, average	683	19,464
1971-1975, average	447	21,876
1976-1980, average	307	20,161
1981-1988, average	433	17,585
1975	318	20,109
1979	248	19,663
1980	311	20,379
1981	381	19,960
1982	384	18,520
1983	415	16,822
1984	476*	18,230
1985	494	17,198
1986	477	16,737
1987	427	16,536
1988	409	16,675

* Total production, which is 4-5% higher than marketed production.
27.16,90 Source: U.S. Statistical Abstract and U.S. Energy Information Administration,
Monthly Energy Review, 1989.

SECTION 27 NOTE
According to the California Division of Mines and Geology, California has 805 active mines.

27.17,90

	PRODUCING WELLS AND PRODUCTION OF OIL AND GAS BY COUNTY, 1987					
	Number of Wells				Oil Produc- tion (bbl)	Total Gas Production (mcf)
	Oil		Gas			
County	Produc- ing	Shut- in	Produc- ing	Shut- in		
Alameda	5	6	0	0	19,540	0
Butte	0	0	10	10	0	639,818
Colusa	0	0	203	26	0	23,225,274
Contra Costa	39	11	54	23	114,507	3,927,160
Fresno	2,601	1,859	5	3	12,315,105	3,619,187
Glenn	0	0	166	35	0	12,434,707
Humboldt	0	0	35	1	0	3,085,541
Kern	35,308	12,242	130	70	255,458,962	164,649,269
Kings	142	191	0	17	382,742	1,642,450
Los Angeles	5,377	3,420	10	14	50,500,625	21,327,359
Madera	0	0	18	30	0	1,170,895
Merced	0	0	1	0	0	84,461
Monterey	635	789	0	0	4,972,299	880
Orange	2,995	1,504	0	0	14,105,024	5,256,173
Riverside	18	3	1	0	19,540	6,984
Sacramento	0	0	124	39	0	14,048,239
San Benito	44	10	0	9	34,479	1,356
San Bernardino	40	10	0	0	41,618	2,777
San Joaquin	0	0	110	23	0	23,312,055
San Luis Obispo	342	171	0	0	1,125,709	943,749
San Mateo	26	13	0	0	16,687	1,195
Santa Barbara	1,463	1,767	21	15	11,590,989	12,120,557
Santa Clara	4	16	0	0	4,936	8,118
Solano	0	1	244	70	0	36,724,565
Sonoma	0	1	1	8	0	72,360
Sutter	0	0	212	36	0	21,590,423
Tehama	0	0	66	17	0	3,446,670
Tulare	56	42	4	1	60,735	14,110
Ventura	2,491	1,183	0	8	15,170,793	15,570,842
Yolo	0	0	105	51	0	13,290,773
Total	51,586	23,239	1,520	526	365,934,296	382,217,947

Note: Data does not include federal offshore oil production.

27.18,90 Source: California Dept. of Conservation, Division of Oil and Gas, *73rd Annual Report, 1987.*

PROVEN NATURAL GAS RESERVES* (trillions of cubic feet)		
California	4.5	(2.4% of U.S. total)
United States	187.2	

* As of December 31, 1987.

27.19,90 Source: California Department of Conservation, Division of Oil and Gas, *73rd Annual Report*, 1987, and United States Energy Information Administration, Reserves and Natural Gas Division and *U.S. Statistical Abstract.*

FIFTEEN LARGEST OIL PRODUCERS IN CALIFORNIA, 1987		
Rank	**Producer**	**Oil Production (thousand bbl)**
1	Shell Western E & P	85,902
2	Texaco, Inc.	48,492
3	Bechtel Petroleum Operations, Inc.	40,654
4	Chevron U.S.A., Inc.	40,057
5	Mobil Oil Corporation	22,127
6	THUMS Long Beach Company	20,953
7	Santa Fe Energy Company	16,320
8	Tenneco Oil Company	16,177
9	Union Oil Company of California	15,835
10	Sun Oil Company	10,732
11	ARCO Oil and Gas Company	6,980
12	Celeron Oil & Gas Company	4,716
13	Union Pacific Resources Company	2,994
14	Exxon Corporation	2,731
15	Berry Petroleum Company	2,517

Note: does not include federal offshore production.
27.20,90 Source: California Dept. of Conservation, division of Oil and Gas, *73rd Annual Report, 1987.*

FIFTEEN LARGEST GAS PRODUCERS IN CALIFORNIA, 1987		
Rank	**Producer**	**Net Gas Production (million cubic feet)**
1	Bechtel Petroleum Operations Inc.	67,378
2	Chevron U.S.A. Inc.	39,122
3	Shell Western E & P, Inc.	36,176
4	Union Oil Company of California	24,360
5	Amerada Hess Corporation	23,219
6	Texaco, Inc.	22,414
7	Mobile Oil Corporation	11,983
8	Marathon Oil Company	10,395
9	ARCO Oil and Gas Company	9,805
10	TXO Production Corporation	8,514
11	Tenneco Oil Company	7,778
12	Celeron Oil & Gas Company	7,503
13	Exxon Corporation	5,624
14	Conoco Inc.	5,102
15	Graham Royalty	4,727

Note: Does not include federal offshore production.
27.21,90 Source: California Dept. of Conservation, Division of Oil and Gas, 73rd Annual Report, 1987.

TOP THREE OIL AND GAS PRODUCING COUNTIES, 1987

	Oil			Gas	
Rank	County	% of State Production*	Rank	County	% of State Production*
1	Kern	73%	1	Kern	43%
2	Los Angeles	14%	2	Solano	10%
3	Ventura	4%	3	San Joaquin	6%

* Does not include federal offshore production.

27.22,90 Source: Cal. Dept. of Conserv., Div. of Oil & Gas *73rd Annual Report.*

CALIFORNIA'S GIANT OIL FIELDS

Field	County	Producing Wells	Cumulative Production*	Estimated Reserve*	Year Discovered
Wilmington	Los Angeles	2,055	2,261,472	526,686	1932
Midway-Sunset	Kern	9,875	1,821,712	430,645	1894
Kern River	Kern	7,220	1,158,042	789,674	1899
Huntington Beach	Orange	998	1,060,187	77,874	1920
Long Beach	Los Angeles	415	907,115	20,313	1921
Ventura	Ventura	570	887,658	103,367	1919
Elk Hills	Kern	1,217	854,146	618,999	1911
Coalinga	Fresno	2,343	743,996	162,399	1890
Buena Vista	San Luis Obispo	1,035	645,722	39,939	1909
Belridge, South	Kern	6,161	616,000	494,942	1911

* In millions of barrels.

27.23,90 Source: Cal. Dept. of Conserv., Div. of Oil & Gas *73rd Annual Report.*

CALIFORNIA OIL AND GAS LEASES AND PRODUCTION ON THE CONTINENTAL SHELF, 1979-1988

Year	Number of Federal Leases	Federal Acreage (in thousands)	Oil Production (in million bbl) State Land	Oil Production (in million bbl) Federal Land	Gas Production (in billion cu. ft.) State Land	Gas Production (in billion cu. ft.) Federal Land
1979	148	789	NA	11.1	NA	3.0
1980	142	761	NA	10.2	NA	3.0
1981	150	795	39.2	14.0	13.5	6.0
1982	184	967	NA	28.4	NA	10.7
1983	199	715	39.7	30.5	13.8	16.0
1984	NA	NA	39.5	30.7	13.8	39.1
1985	315	81	39.5	69.1	19.5	71.9
1986	NA	NA	34.6	28.7	18.3	48.0
1987	NA	NA	30.3	31.1	13.0	45.1
1988	305	73	28.3	31.8	10.7	40.7

27.24,90 Source: U.S. Bur. of Land Mgmt., *Pub. Land Stat.*, annual, and Cal. Dept. of Conserv., Div. of Oil and Gas, *Cal. Oil and Gas Prod. Stat. and New Well Operations.*

NEW WELL OPERATIONS IN CALIFORNIA*
1980-1988

Year	Exploratory	Development	Service
1980	354	2,620	686
1981	463	3,151	747
1982	256	2,253	408
1983	205	2,564	460
1984	322	3,601	769
1985	362	3,311	545
1986	146	2,193	430
1987	191	2,506	489
1988†	190	2,030	480

* Notices filed.   † Preliminary

27.25,90 Source: California Energy Commission, *Annual Petroleum Review*, 1982, and California Dept. of Conservation Division of Oil and Gas, 1988 *California Oil and Gas Production, Statistics and New Well Operations.*

CALIFORNIA REFINERY CRUDE OIL RECEIPTS
1988
(thousands of barrels per day)

Source	Amount	Percent
Domestic*	997	50%
Alaskan	864	44%
Foreign	115	6%
Total	1,975	100%

* 99% of the domestic oil used in California is from California sources.

27.26,90 Source: California Energy Commission, *Quarterly Oil Reports, Dec. 1988.*

CALIFORNIA PETROLEUM REFINERIES, 1989

	Number	Distillation Capacity*
Operating	31	2,206,200
Idle	1	29,100
Total	32	2,235,300

* Barrels per day.

27.27,90 Source: U.S. Energy Information Administration, *Petroleum Supply Annual 1988, Volume 1.*

SECTION 27 NOTE

Benitoite, the state gem, is named for San Benito County, where it was first found. Gem-quality benitoite is found only in California.

27.28,90

MAJOR OIL COMPANIES' SHARES OF THE CALIFORNIA GASOLINE MARKET 1978-1988						
Company	1978	1981	1983	1985	1986	1988
Arco	11.1%	10.8%	14.3%	15.7%	16.5%	18.3%
Chevron	16.3%	18.0%	15.4%	15.2%	15.4%	15.7%
Shell	14.3%	13.5%	14.0%	14.0%	13.8%	14.4%
Unocal	11.2%	11.2%	12.3%	13.2%	13.0%	12.2%
Mobil	8.0%	7.8%	7.6%	8.1%	7.7%	7.2%
Texaco	6.9%	6.4%	5.8%	3.6%	7.4%	6.2%
Exxon	4.6%	5.9%	4.8%	5.1%	6.3%	5.5%
Tosco	6.0%	6.4%	5.1%	4.9%	4.3%	4.3%
Union Pacific	NA	NA	NA	NA	NA	2.9%
Golden West	NA	NA	*	3.3%	2.8%	2.7%
Beacon	2.0%	2.1%	2.4%	2.7%	2.5%	2.2%
Wickland	*	*	1.5%	2.0%	2.5%	1.8%

* Under 1.0%

27.29,90 Source: California State Board of Equalization, *Annual Report*.

OIL COMPANY PROFITS BEFORE INCOME TAXES (in millions)							
Company	1977	1981	1983	1985	1986	1987	1988
Arco	$968	$2,940	$1,548	$1,299	$604	$1,214	$1,583
Chevron	$1,758	NA	$1,590	$1,547	$694	$1,007	$1,768
Exxon	$8,086	NA	$4,985	$4,845	$5,350	$4,841	$5,260
Mobil	NA	$6,855	$1,501	$1,548	$1,405	$1,264	$2,018
Phillips	NA	NA	NA	NA	NA	$35	$650
Shell	$1,286	$3,018	$1,633	$1,650	$882	$1,268	$1,172
Texaco	$1,975	NA	$1,233	$1,233	$725	-$4,296	$1,304
Unocal	$605	$1,422	$626	$325	$176	$470	$480

27.30,90 Source: California Energy Commission, *Quarterly Oil Reports*.

STATE TIDELANDS OIL REVENUE*	
Year	Revenue (in millions)
1982-83	368
1983-84	335
1984-85	490
1985-86	421
1986-87	99
1987-88	210
1988-89†	77
1989-90†	52

* These revenues are dedicated to capital outlay projects. † Estimates Note: In the Budget this revenue is now called "State Lands Royalties."

27.31,90 Source: Governor's Budget and Cal. Dept. of Finance, unpublished data.

CALIFORNIA MINING EMPLOYMENT (in thousands)*				
Year	Fuel	Metal	Nonmetal	Total
1972	19.7	1.6	7.8	29.2
1976	25.0	2.1	7.5	34.7
1980	33.4	2.2	7.9	43.5
1981	39.4	2.5	7.3	49.2
1982	41.9	1.9	6.6	50.4
1983	40.1	1.7	6.3	48.1
1984	41.7	1.6	6.7	50.0
1985	41.8	1.7	7.1	50.6
1986†	38.2	1.9	6.7	46.8
1987†	30.0	2.2	6.6	38.8
1988†	33.4	2.1	6.9	42.4
1989†	32.3	2.2	7.0	41.5

* Annual average except for 1986 - 1989.
† March data, seasonally adjusted.
27.32,90 Source: California Employment Development Department, *California Labor Market Bulletin*, and *Report to the Governor on Labor Market Conditions*, April 1989.

MINING INJURIES AND ACCIDENTS IN CALIFORNIA 1987				
Nature of Work Injury or Illness	Oil and Gas Extraction	Metal Mining	Nonmetallic Mining and Quarrying	All Mining
Amputations	6	0	4	10
Burns and Scalds	42	4	8	54
Contusions and Crushing	158	8	36	202
Cuts and Punctures	122	4	40	166
Abrasions	48	0	26	74
Fractures	260	18	44	322
Strains and Sprains	408	22	134	564
Other	22	2	10	34
Occupational Illness	122	8	14	144
Unknown	110	6	42	158
Total	**1,298**	**72**	**358**	**1,728**

27.33,90 Source: California Department of Industrial Relations, Division of Labor Statistics and Research, *California Work Injuries and Illnesses*, 1987.

SECTION 27 NOTE
Borax was first produced commercially in the U.S. at Borax Lake (Lake County) in 1884.

27.34,90

AVERAGE ANNUAL PAY IN MINING					
	California			United States	
Year	Amount	% Change from Prior Year		Amount	% Change from Prior Year
1981	$25,386	---		$23,037	---
1982	$28,662	12.9%		$25,723	11.7%
1983	$32,573	13.6%		$28,808	12.0%
1984	$34,298	5.3%		$30,157	4.7%
1985	$35,223	2.7%		$31,326	3.9%
1986	$36,857	4.6%		$32,546	3.9%
1987	$35,606	-3.4%		$32,950	1.2%

27.35,90 Source: U.S. Department of Labor, Bureau of Labor Statistics News Release, *Average Annual Pay by State & Industry*.

CALIFORNIA STATE TAXES PAID FROM MINERAL PRODUCTION (in millions of dollars)			
Year	Oil and Gas Production	Metal Mining	Nometallic Mining
1980	$295.8	$1.20	$7.6
1981	$242.6	$0.54	$8.0
1982	$206.7	NA	$6.7*
1983	$211.2	$0.24	$3.1
1984	$182.3	$0.10	$7.0
1985	$140.0	$0.06	$10.0
1986	$128.0	NA	$104.0*
1987	-$58.0	NA	$190.0*

* Includes taxes for metal mining.
27.36,90 Source: California Franchise Tax Board, unpublished data.

SECTION 27 NOTE
The most ancient rocks in Yosemite National Park are 500 million years old.

27.37,90

SECTION 27 NOTE
Fossilized ichthyosaurs (Fish-like reptiles) have been found in Shasta, Kern, and San Joaquin counties. Some of these fossils are up to 140 million years old.

27.38,90

SECTION 27 NOTE
The famous twenty-mule teams used to haul borax out of Death Valley actually had 18 mules and 2 horses. The horses were used for their strength and obedience.

27.39,90

Construction and Housing

Although California has a justifiable reputation as the most expensive state in which to buy a home, there are ways to find affordable housing in the state. Housing costs, for example, are much lower than average in certain areas of the state--the Palm Springs-Lower Desert area, the Sacramento area, most of the Central Valley, and most of Northern California north of the San Francisco Bay Area. Even in the high-priced areas of Los Angeles, Orange County, San Diego, and San Francisco there are neighborhoods where housing prices are well below the regional average.

The California Association of Realtors prepares official statistics on housing prices based on the sales of single-family detached houses. The data, acquired from a sample of 40 percent of the local realty boards in the state, comprise figures for 50 percent of the home sales statewide. Some of the boards that do not report to the association, however, represent areas of the state where mostly lower-priced houses are sold.

Typically, the statistics for home sales exclude new-home sales, which make up one-third of the residential sales in the state. New homes often sell for considerably less than existing houses in California. Also missing from some home price averages are figures for transactions in which the buyer and seller do not negotiate through a realtor. Because such sales do not include the payment of a commission, it is reasonable to assume that the home prices agreed upon might be lower than the average.

Home-price statistics are similarly incomplete for condominiums because some regional home-price averages do not include figures for condominium sales. Since condominium prices are usually far lower than those for single-family detached houses, many more Californians can afford this housing option. To illustrate, in 1988 the median price of a condominium in the state was only $122,750, compared with $165,600 for a detached house. At the median price, only 26 percent of households could afford a detached house, but 41 percent could afford a condominium.

Renters determined to join the ranks of home owners even though they lack the savings or income to buy a condominium or a house, can always consider the option of mobile-home ownership. As of 1989 there were 480,000 mobile homes in the state, with more in Riverside County, 64,611, than in any other county in California. Those who buy a mobile home should make sure it is bolted to its foundation or braced so that it will not tip over in an earthquake.

	California				United States			
		NUMBER OF SALES AND MEDIAN SALE PRICE OF EXISTING (USED) SINGLE-FAMILY HOMES, 1970-1988						
Year	Number of Sales	% Change from Prior Year	Median Sale Price	% Change from Prior Year	Number of Sales	% Change from Prior Year	Median Sale Price	% Change from Prior Year
1970	265,669	NA	$24,300	1.7%	1,612,000	NA	$23,000	5.5%
1971	360,730	36.8%	$26,500	9.1%	2,018,000	25.2%	$24,800	7.8%
1972	425,513	18.0%	$28,400	7.2%	2,252,000	11.6%	$26,700	7.7%
1973	405,120	-4.8%	$31,000	9.2%	2,334,000	3.6%	$28,900	8.2%
1974	401,342	-0.9%	$34,100	12.3%	2,272,000	-2.7%	$32,000	10.3%
1975	454,572	13.3%	$41,000	18.1%	2,476,000	9.0%	$35,300	10.3%
1976	559,105	23.0%	$47,910	16.9%	3,064,000	23.7%	$38,100	7.9%
1977	573,244	2.5%	$61,360	28.1%	3,650,000	19.1%	$42,900	12.5%
1978	604,953	5.5%	$69,800	13.8%	3,986,000	9.2%	$48,700	13.5%
1979	584,185	-3.4%	$82,880	18.7%	3,827,000	-4.0%	$55,600	9.7%
1980	465,186	-20.4%	$98,040	18.3%	2,973,000	-22.3%	$62,200	11.9%
1981	332,969	-28.4%	$106,040	8.2%	2,419,000	-18.6%	$66,400	6.3%
1982	233,810	-29.8%	$110,020	3.8%	1,990,000	-17.7%	$67,700	2.0%
1983	343,200	46.8%	$112,592	2.3%	2,719,000	36.6%	$70,300	3.7%
1984	382,090	11.3%	$112,472	-0.1%	2,868,000	5.5%	$72,400	3.0%
1985	407,240	6.6%	$117,930	4.9%	3,215,000	12.1%	$75,500	4.3%
1986	484,570	19.0%	$131,530	11.5%	3,565,000	10.9%	$80,300	6.4%
1987	512,477	5.8%	$139,821	6.3%	3,526,000	-1.1%	$85,600	6.6%
1988	562,759	9.8%	$165,602	18.4%	3,594,000	1.9%	$89,300	4.3%

28.1,90 Source: California Association of Realtors and National Association of Realtors, unpublished data.

HOUSING AFFORDABILITY CALIFORNIA AND UNITED STATES 1977-1988

Year	Minimum Income Needed to Afford a Medium-priced Home		Percent of Households Able to Afford a Medium-priced Home	
	California	All U.S.	California	All U.S.
1977	$16,500	$11,560	45%	57%
1978	$21,320	$15,240	36%	50%
1979	$31,240	$19,960	24%	42%
1980	$40,640	$26,160	17%	33%
1981	$45,560	$29,520	18%	33%
1982	$39,000	$24,640	29%	46%
1983	$39,360	$24,440	31%	49%
1984	$45,040	$29,360	29%	43%
1985	$43,489	$27,842	28%	42%
1986	$43,767	$26,720	31%	47%
1987	$43,403	$27,113	32%	49%
1988	$51,444	$28,360	26%	48%

28.2,90 Source: California Association of Realtors, unpublished data.

CONDOMINIUM SALES AND AFFORDABILITY						
Year	Sales	Median Price	% Price Change From Prior Year	% of Single Family Houses	Minimum Income Needed to Afford a Medium Priced Condo	% of Households Able to Afford a Medium Priced Condo
1982	39,500	$108,900		16.9%	NA	NA
1983	53,200	$112,400	3.2%	15.5%	NA	NA
1984	54,200	$109,100	-2.9%	14.2%	NA	NA
1985	61,100	$110,900	1.7%	15.1%	NA	NA
1986	84,000	$108,320	-2.3%	17.2%	NA	NA
1987	99,300	$112,280	3.7%	19.4%	$34,854	44%
1988	134,500	$122,750	9.3%	23.9%	$38,132	41%

Based on a Survey of 33 market areas of California. This list is only of resales of used condominiums.
28.3,90 Source: California Association of Realtors, *California Real Estate Trends*.

ANNUAL INCOME DISTRIBUTION OF BUYERS OF EXISTING (USED) HOMES				
Income	1985	1986	1987	1988
Less than $20,000	3.6%	3.8%	1.6%	1.1%
$20,000 to $29,999	7.5%	7.6%	10.0%	5.7%
$30,000 to $39,999	23.2%	22.4%	18.6%	13.1%
$40,000 to $49,999	17.0%	21.3%	21.7%	18.4%
$50,000 to $59,999	9.4%	9.0%	9.0%	14.3%
$60,000 to $74,999	21.8%	18.4%	18.8%	20.0%
$75,000 to $99,999	7.6%	9.2%	8.2%	12.0%
$100,000 or more	9.9%	8.3%	11.2%	15.4%
Median	$48,000	$48,000	$48,000	$55,000

28.4,90 Source: California Association of Realtors, *1988 Housing Finance Survey*.

UNSOLD HOUSING INVENTORY* (in months)					
Houses		Condominiums	Houses		Condominiums
Year	Months	Months	Year	Months	Months
1982	23	31	1986	9	19
1983	16	28	1987	6	10
1984	11	22	1988	5	7
1985	10	23			

*   The number of months it would take to deplete the supply of houses on the market.
    28.5,90 Source: California Association of Realtors., *California Real Estate Trends*.

HOME SALES BY PRICE, 1989

Price Brackets	% of Monthly Totals
0-$39,999	0.8%
$40,000-$79,999	6.8%
$80,000-$119,999	13.1%
$120,000-159,999	16.1%
$160,000-$199,999	15.7%
$200,000-$249,999	16.4%
$250,000 and over	31.2%

Bedrooms In Home and Median Price*		
2 or less	21.7%	$127,763*
3	50.5%	$163,050*
4 or more	27.7%	$244,895

* December 1988.
28.6,90 Source: California Asso. of Realtors, *California Real Estate Trends, Feb. 1989.*

MEDIAN SELLING PRICES OF EXISTING (USED) SINGLE-FAMILY HOMES BY REGION OF CALIFORNIA, 1987-1989

Region	1987		1988		1989*	
	Price (Dollars)	% Change from Prior Year	Price (Dollars)	% Change from Prior Year	Price (Dollars)	% Change from Prior Year†
Los Angeles	$147,667	8.3%	$180,081	22.%	$201,024	12%
Orange County	$169,277	13.%	$211,402	24.9%	$237,887	13%
Palm Springs- Lower Desert	$95,714	8.8%	$97,952	2.3%	$109,193	11%
Riverside- San Bernardino	$96,149	4.4%	$106,706	11.%	$116,053	9%
Ventura	$159,047	11.9%	$204,286	28.4%	NA	NA
Santa Barbara	$149,084	- 2.6%	$204,984	37.5%	$199,443	- 3%
San Diego	$129,160	9.%	$147,788	14.4%	$163,941	11%
San Francisco	$171,315	6.3%	$206,463	20.4%	$243,997	18%
Santa Clara	$151,500	6.7%	$182,000	20.%	$217,500	20%
Monterey	$161,787	10.7%	$185,658	14.8%	$215,066	16%
Northern Wine Country	$118,107	7.3%	$131,299	11.2%	$142,321	8%
Northern California	$66,862	1.7%	$73,110	9.3%	$77,499	6%
Sacramento Sub-region	$87,456	5.5%	$94,379	7.9%	$100,256	6%
Central Valley	$82,151	6.6%	$86,945	5.8%	$89,516	3%

* 1st Quarter. † Change from 1988 median annual price.
28.7,90 Source: California Asociation of Realtors, *California Real Estate Trends Newsletter* and press releases, San Jose Real Estate Board, unpublished data.

MOST EXPENSIVE MEDIAN PURCHASE PRICE FOR HOMES IN U.S. 1988*	
Metropolitan Area	**Median Home Price**
1 **Orange County**	**$231,000**
2 **San Francisco Bay Area**	**$228,000**
3 Honolulu	$225,000
4 **San Jose**	**$196,000**
5 **Los Angeles**	**$191,000**
6 Boston	$183,000
7 New York	$179,000
8 Hartford	$165,000
9 **San Diego**	**$157,000**

* Fourth Quarter.
28.8,90 Source: National Association of Realtors, Press Release.

HOUSEHOLD TYPES AND AGES OF BUYERS OF EXISTING (USED) HOMES				
Household Type	**1985**	**1986**	**1987**	**1988**
Married Couple-Dependents	46.6%	43.9%	41.9%	40.9%
Married Couple-No Dependents	26.9%	26.8%	26.0%	27.5%
Single Male	11.9%	12.4%	13.8%	12.2%
Single Female	8.7%	10.9%	11.5%	12.2%
2 or More Unrelated Individuals	4.0%	4.3%	4.9%	4.8%
% Retired	2.8%	6.4%	6.0%	6.9%
Ages				
24 years or less	2.2%	2.5%	2.8%	2.8%
25 to 34 years	36.4%	32.8%	30.8%	32.1%
35 to 44 years	35.4%	36.5%	38.8%	35.6%
45 to 54 years	14.6%	16.3%	15.5%	17.1%
55 years or more	11.4%	11.9%	12.1%	12.4%
Median Age	35 years	36 years	37 years	36 years
Reason for Buying				
Tired of Renting	32.3%	29.3%	28.5%	25.0%
Desired Larger Home	*	23.8%	18.5%	18.1%
Desired Smaller Home	*	2.6%	2.5%	3.5%
Desired Better Location	*	16.8%	16.0%	16.9%
Changed Jobs	14.6%	9.7%	12.1%	9.5%
Investment/Tax Considerations	4.1%	9.3%	6.5%	9.6%
Divorce/Death/Retirement	6.4%	4.8%	5.2%	6.2%
Other	14.6%	4.2%	13.4%	11.2%

28.9,90 Source: California Association of Realtors, *1988 Housing Finance Survey*.

CHARACTERISTICS OF FIRST-TIME VS. REPEAT BUYERS OF EXISTING (USED) HOMES, 1988

Demographic Characteristics	First-Time Buyers	Repeat Buyers
Proportion of all Buyers	42.9%	57.1%
Median Age	31 Years	40 Years
Median Annual Income	$48,000	$60,000
Married Couple Households	67.0%	68.3%
Buyer Households with 2 Incomes	56.8%	45.6%
Median Number of Years in Previous Residence	2 Years	4.5 Years
Type of Property Purchased		
Size (median square footage)	1,399	1,700
Median Sales Price	$139,900	$178,200
Number of Bedrooms		
2 or fewer	29.9%	18.2%
3	53.2%	50.4%
4 or more	16.9%	31.4%
Single-family home	84.8%	82.5%
Condominium	14.3%	16.7%
Mortgage Financing Characteristics		
Median Loan-to-Value Ratio	89.7%	79.4%
Median Debt-to-Income Ratio (P & I)	23.8%	22.0%
Type of Mortgage:		
Fixed-Rate	39.0%	38.7%
ARM	58.4%	59.2%
FHA/VA	21.7%	11.3%

28.10,90 Source: California Association of Realtors, *1988 Housing Finance Survey.*

PERCENTAGE OF SALES BY NUMBER OF BEDROOMS 1978-1988

Year	Two Bedrooms	Three Bedrooms	Four or More Bedrooms
1978	20.3%	53.9%	25.8%
1979	19.5%	53.1%	27.4%
1980	21.1%	51.7%	27.2%
1981	20.7%	51.4%	27.9%
1982	20.2%	50.4%	29.4%
1983	19.4%	51.5%	29.1%
1984	19.3%	51.1%	29.6%
1985	18.9%	51.9%	29.2%
1986	18.7%	51.1%	30.2%
1987	19.3%	50.9%	29.9%
1988	19.0%	51.2%	29.8%

28.11,90 Source: California Asso. of Realtors, *California Real Estate Trends.*

MAJOR HOUSEHOLD TYPES

United States   California

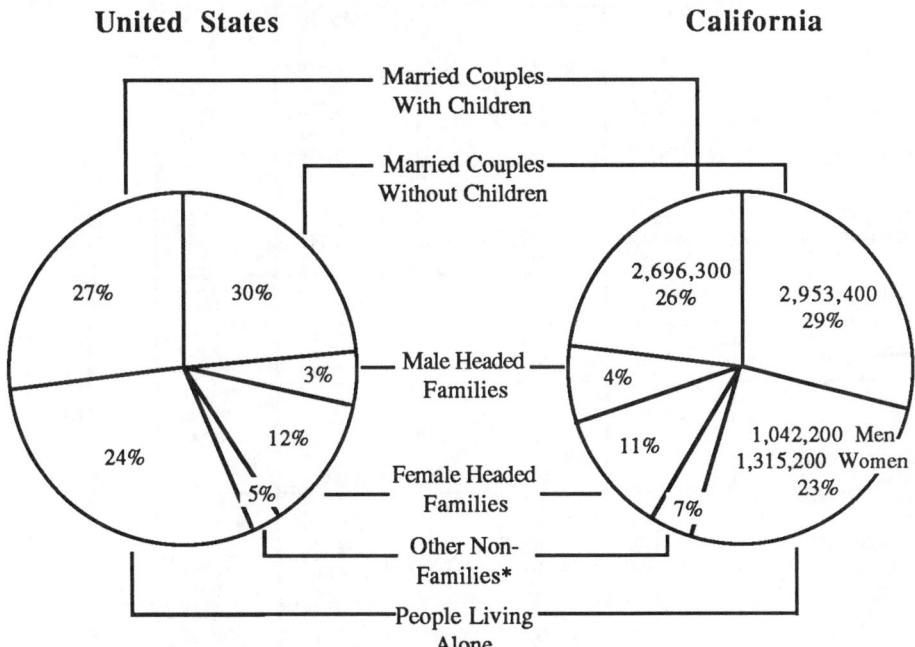

* Other Non-Families are unmarried couples or roommates.
28.12,90 Source: U.S. Bureau of the Census, Current Population Survey.

TOP FIFTEEN HOME BUILDERS IN CALIFORNIA, 1988				
Rank in State	Rank in U.S.	Firm	Location	Number of Housing Units Built
1	12	Lewis Homes	Upland	4,731
2	13	William Lyon Co.	Newport Beach	4,581
3	17	A.G. Spanos	Stockton	3,569
4	18	Anden Group	Sherman Oaks	3,443
5	20	Kaufman and Broad	Los Angeles	3,400
6	22	Robertson Homes	Stockton	3,070
7	25	Citation	Tustin	2,900
8	28	Presley	Irvine	2,603
9	33	Watt Industries	Santa Monica	2,320
10	37	The Lusk Co.	Irvine	2,168
11	41	Calmark	Los Angeles	1,854
12	42	J.L. Construction	Carlsbad	1,840
13	44	Homestead Land Dev.	Burlingame	1,782
14	47	Standard Pacific	Costa Mesa	1,756
15	48	Barnett-Rang	Stockton	1,690

Note: Cal. has 29 of the top 100 U.S. firms. 28.13,90 Source: *Prof. Builder Mag.*

CALIFORNIA HOUSING, 1989						
		Apartments			Single	All Housing
County	Total Units	2 to 4 Units	5 or more Units	Mobile Homes	Family Housing	Percent Vacant
Alameda	500,620	58,725	140,637	5,786	295,472	3.34
Alpine	1,221	112	344	53	712	63.14
Amador	12,300	572	742	1,006	9,980	19.60
Butte	75,726	6,749	10,221	11,493	47,263	7.46
Calaveras	18,827	891	591	2,438	14,907	35.33
Colusa	6,123	367	642	559	4,555	11.63
Contra Costa	306,458	22,989	55,407	6,294	327,577	3.60
Del Norte	8,892	501	693	2,296	5,402	11.50
El Dorado	58,842	3,262	4,824	3,772	46,984	23.22
Fresno	236,405	20,909	51,432	10,831	153,233	8.03
Glenn	9,755	672	999	1,312	6,772	9.04
Humboldt	50,022	5,317	5,021	5,385	34,299	7.94
Imperial	36,500	3,058	5,989	5,224	22,229	9.34
Inyo	9,359	525	1,026	3,018	4,790	18.22
Kern	197,819	19,067	26,403	21,290	131,059	8.11
Kings	31,562	2,736	4,115	2,038	22,673	7.92
Lake	28,706	1,131	1,775	9,702	16,098	26.05
Lassen	10,844	580	1,102	2,822	6,140	18.78
Los Angeles	3,131,076	209,812	1,187,725	46,450	1,687,089	3.73
Madera	31,340	1,855	2,804	2,908	23,723	14.66
Marin	100,088	10,097	21,295	1,728	66,968	2.91
Mariposa	7,974	308	606	2,207	4,853	32.73
Mendocino	34,132	3,102	3,759	4,812	22,459	14.30
Merced	58,998	5,257	8,179	4,181	41,361	7.41
Modoc	4,590	188	287	1,092	3,023	20.37
Mono	10,316	1,097	4,303	785	4,131	59.04
Monterey	118,809	10,895	28,050	5,275	74,589	5.84
Napa	44,825	3,259	5,660	4,629	31,277	7.57
Nevada	35,163	1,854	2,083	3,132	27,694	15.99
Orange	851,516	84,059	230,176	26,685	510,586	3.13
Placer	73,233	4,394	8,103	4,323	56,413	18.11
Plumas	11,627	550	1,051	1,720	8,306	29.66
Riverside	439,620	26,123	66,018	64,611	282,868	17.58
Sacramento	406,945	36,067	94,000	12,456	264,422	5.65
San Benito	12,068	1,163	1,323	902	8,680	5.98
San Bernardino	527,686	34,145	86,151	34,036	373,354	14.63
San Diego	921,940	76,094	283,775	40,264	521,807	4.90
San Francisco	327,274	72,453	142,694	243	111,884	4.26
San Joaquin	165,014	13,090	29,989	7,193	114,742	6.62
San Luis Obispo	87,077	8,371	12,180	9,642	56,884	10.24
San Mateo	250,530	18,279	69,695	2,840	159,716	3.16
Santa Barbara	132,918	13,031	32,188	6,838	86,861	4.38
Santa Clara	531,534	47,210	131,133	16,879	336,312	2.90
Santa Cruz	91,439	9,183	14,646	6,069	61,541	9.28
Shasta	60,248	3,783	6,972	11,695	37,798	10.99
Sierra	2,097	125	142	220	1,610	32.76
Siskiyou	20,998	1,230	1,759	3,675	14,324	15.81
Solano	112,223	9,620	18,492	3,691	80,420	2.85
Sonoma	154,948	12,130	21,316	9,812	111,690	6.33
Stanislaus	129,955	9,589	17,741	7,658	94,967	6.26
Sutter	23,779	2,168	4,332	1,578	15,701	6.85
Tehama	20,592	1,458	1,828	5,047	12,259	12.27
Trinity	7,355	368	457	1,850	4,680	27.14
Tulare	104,581	7,624	10,622	8,726	77,609	8.25
Tuolumne	24,596	1,091	1,053	4,269	18,183	32.42
Ventura	222,302	15,110	37,891	9,808	159,443	3.80
Yolo	52,750	4,142	14,443	3,020	31,145	3.60
Yuba	22,087	1,759	3,787	3,140	13,401	9.55
State Totals	10,966,024	910,306	2,920,681	481,408	6,653,629	6.20

28.14,90 Source: California Dept. of Finance, Population Research Unit, *Report E-5, 1989.*

NEW RESIDENTIAL CONSTRUCTION: UNITS AND VALUATION BY COUNTY, 1988					
	New Residential Construction				Residential Alterations and Additions
	Single Dwellings		Multiple Dwellings		
County	Units	Value (thousands)	Units	Value (thousands)	Number of Permits	Value (thousands)
Alameda	$3,810	$451,363	$2,685	$130,013	$11,066	$121,710
Alpine	18	2,264	0	0	0	0
Amador	266	22,694	12	647	136	1,944
Butte	1,200	95,851	173	8,561	1,343	7,902
Calaveras	566	56,755	47	1,793	243	3,030
Colusa	68	3,307	4	202	200	789
Contra Costa	5,853	615,451	2,171	99,677	7,794	62,576
Del Norte	83	6,956	62	2,753	78	219
El Dorado	2,019	208,136	331	15,017	964	11,817
Fresno	3,248	259,174	883	30,907	1,724	14,377
Glenn	51	3,738	7	215	129	979
Humboldt	481	31,718	179	5,303	828	6,640
Imperial	440	32,268	150	5,485	757	4,825
Inyo	31	3,813	0	0	57	775
Kern	2,864	231,638	294	20,604	1,553	14,296
Kings	415	36,187	206	11,578	525	2,840
Lake	284	22,153	54	1,605	447	3,458
Lassen	127	7,324	9	267	152	1,554
Los Angeles	17,408	2,193,992	31,543	1,797,762	69,369	876,657
Madera	669	36,719	151	4,772	234	2,484
Marin	944	119,425	389	22,542	2,870	47,753
Mariposa	169	12,194	2	66	36	666
Mendocino	316	24,284	111	3,955	410	4,428
Merced	955	74,938	386	16,478	895	5,203
Modoc	9	843	0	0	98	518
Mono	52	5,428	30	1,071	39	566
Monterey	1,084	129,698	418	21,154	2,256	31,348
Napa	859	91,449	115	3,475	1,963	16,801
Nevada	1,204	120,388	220	13,067	737	8,623
Orange	11,288	1,613,592	11,864	675,237	22,149	186,980
Placer	3,071	335,956	852	36,392	1,254	13,331
Plumas	256	17,505	0	0	163	541
Riverside	28,199	2,769,534	5,531	269,623	7,481	56,634
Sacramento	8,289	913,258	3,424	151,958	9,676	58,034
San Benito	473	47,624	34	1,507	84	934
San Bernardino	14,830	1,391,349	3,591	159,070	11,412	76,341
San Diego	15,081	2,355,735	14,277	928,578	9,341	175,569
San Francisco	157	26,527	1,774	148,826	11,021	116,043
San Joaquin	3,294	311,072	789	36,748	2,331	17,702
San Luis Obispo	2,250	238,799	225	14,487	960	12,046
San Mateo	1,430	249,231	989	86,331	9,247	115,652
Santa Barbara	1,071	148,375	261	14,539	1,736	33,726
Santa Clara	3,690	486,249	2,800	129,159	7,649	135,538
Santa Cruz	835	112,517	263	18,397	1,075	23,408
Shasta	1,138	76,677	261	9,132	701	6,514
Sierra	22	1,835	0	0	32	222
Siskiyou	162	12,399	23	813	232	2,468
Solano	4,423	449,549	732	34,213	2,836	16,841
Sonoma	3,858	394,570	816	31,041	2,192	24,856
Stanislaus	4,376	330,252	618	22,262	1,457	9,340
Sutter	239	22,398	92	3,218	347	1,969
Tehama	126	10,721	25	1,554	281	3,074
Trinity	56	2,445	56	1,793	77	667
Tulare	1,298	88,460	223	5,840	1,484	12,316
Tuolumne	543	26,153	43	1,564	320	2,556
Ventura	3,675	514,642	1,479	102,485	4,784	40,746
Yolo	787	68,203	228	14,610	454	5,404
Yuba	109	9,517	99	2,640	286	2,009
State Totals	160,519	17,925,290	92,001	5,120,982	217,965	2,406,242

28.15,90 Source: Economic Sciences Corporation (Berkeley) *California Permit Activity, Annual Summary.*

VALUE OF NEW RESIDENTIAL CONSTRUCTION BY COUNTY (in thousands of dollars)				
County	1972	1983	1985	1987	1988
Alameda	$231,157	$470,501	$562,474	$869,396	$703,086
Alpine	182	840	8,595	1,408	2,264
Amador	8,059	13,978	19,724	31,889	25,285
Butte	20,932	71,592	83,339	118,226	112,315
Calaveras	9,535	36,600	36,318	68,376	61,578
Colusa	764	5,241	2,607	5,219	4,298
Contra Costa	201,333	432,288	579,866	671,900	777,704
Del Norte	1,044	6,766	3,174	25,214	9,928
El Dorado	35,169	69,875	95,909	195,918	234,970
Fresno	94,139	240,600	256,918	278,096	304,458
Glenn	2,483	3,449	4,963	4,813	4,932
Humboldt	10,711	25,115	26,170	35,842	43,661
Imperial	13,482	18,526	26,659	26,884	42,579
Inyo	3,098	5,412	3,502	5,682	4,587
Kern	57,718	278,811	277,908	295,968	266,538
Kings	8,359	50,837	39,601	33,973	50,605
Lake	6,034	26,110	28,603	38,827	27,216
Lassen	1,080	4,948	5,880	10,877	9,145
Los Angeles	1,073,972	2,306,031	4,070,730	5,084,299	4,868,412
Madera	6,203	27,473	36,484	42,398	43,975
Marin	77,235	107,864	105,102	172,335	189,720
Mariposa	1,343	7,916	7,916	10,049	12,926
Mendocino	11,226	23,020	32,673	60,355	32,667
Merced	24,664	74,368	58,572	77,262	96,618
Modoc	845	2,919	1,212	1,116	1,360
Mono	14,409	413	NA	8,360	7,065
Monterey	78,526	113,303	177,595	170,263	182,200
Napa	28,918	72,441	70,528	75,164	111,725
Nevada	14,997	35,236	55,438	112,667	142,078
Orange	741,244	861,532	1,421,776	1,926,778	2,475,809
Placer	45,851	114,867	145,854	274,041	385,679
Plumas	2,595	16,736	11,422	13,965	18,046
Riverside	197,318	840,218	1,079,388	1,544,462	3,095,790
Sacramento	181,856	447,274	908,727	818,629	1,123,249
San Benito	2,951	15,993	33,285	30,644	50,065
San Bernardino	170,013	770,098	1,333,347	1,592,144	1,626,760
San Diego	735,552	1,423,652	2,514,979	2,811,480	3,459,881
San Francisco	105,829	175,188	246,939	344,207	291,397
San Joaquin	55,939	205,289	212,872	235,431	365,522
San Luis Obispo	44,195	178,984	254,327	216,216	265,332
San Mateo	168,583	163,774	244,230	382,505	451,214
Santa Barbara	73,346	164,152	225,969	227,363	196,640
Santa Clara	288,244	497,493	712,107	718,922	750,946
Santa Cruz	68,130	97,337	108,071	160,872	154,321
Shasta	16,893	48,502	23,290	82,870	92,323
Sierra	239	583	NA	2,140	2,057
Siskiyou	4,183	12,240	13,436	17,580	15,680
Solano	55,664	133,466	238,297	301,248	500,603
Sonoma	99,093	218,547	284,821	301,533	450,467
Stanislaus	54,920	96,783	183,286	244,212	361,853
Sutter	8,302	18,206	26,779	42,932	27,585
Tehama	5,291	17,134	28,344	24,891	15,349
Trinity	1,257	3,166	3,055	3,608	4,905
Tulare	38,646	104,256	96,316	124,023	106,616
Tuolumne	10,049	17,699	21,839	27,554	30,273
Ventura	144,806	271,842	471,503	517,312	657,873
Yolo	33,346	48,838	61,672	86,547	88,217
Yuba	5,430	14,741	14,845	17,961	14,167
State Totals	5,397,379	11,511,046	17,599,232	21,625,145	25,452,514

28.16,90 Source: Economic Sciences Corporation (Berkeley) *California Permit Activity, Annual Summary.*

VALUE OF NEW NON-RESIDENTIAL CONSTRUCTION BY COUNTY, 1988 (in thousands of dollars)				
County	New Commercial Valuation	New Industrial Valuation	New Other Valuation	Non-Residential Alterations and Additions	Total Non-Residential Valuation
Alameda	$195,936	$62,656	$26,507	$204,863	$489,963
Alpine	$72	$0	$0	$0	$72
Amador	$1,428	$592	$2,066	$359	$4,444
Butte	$40,414	$54	$13,406	$8,135	$62,010
Calaveras	$1,232	$4,241	$4,261	$1,401	$11,135
Colusa	$500	$0	$2,169	$1,780	$4,449
Contra Costa	$98,398	$13,032	$29,333	$72,979	$213,742
Del Norte	$1,961	$0	$4,630	$1,601	$8,191
El Dorado	$20,402	$3,205	$9,191	$5,333	$38,131
Fresno	$62,630	$57,236	$96,459	$44,597	$260,921
Glenn	$468	$326	$1,693	$1,023	$3,509
Humboldt	$11,216	$1,397	$4,507	$4,051	$21,171
Imperial	$3,655	$50,825	$64,609	$2,618	$121,707
Inyo	$664	$150	$609	$1,513	$2,936
Kern	$103,711	$8,415	$75,290	$35,638	$223,054
Kings	$8,716	$1,853	$6,353	$3,510	$20,432
Lake	$1,365	$2,167	$29,832	$1,270	$34,633
Lassen	$1,874	$7,536	$1,544	$445	$11,400
Los Angeles	$2,190,133	$457,499	$410,458	$1,378,346	$4,436,435
Madera	$3,010	$2,977	$22,478	$7,482	$36,046
Marin	$27,621	$1,037	$4,646	$24,161	$57,434
Mariposa	$12,842	$0	$1,722	$774	$15,337
Mendocino	$3,055	$2,096	$4,954	$3,318	$13,424
Merced	$7,101	$16,525	$17,663	$6,265	$47,554
Modoc	$61	$0	$711	$243	$1,015
Mono	$711	$0	$618	$644	$1,973
Monterey	$33,316	$5,096	$15,479	$24,069	$77,961
Napa	$4,721	$16,110	$8,030	$14,893	$43,755
Nevada	$11,702	$1,386	$8,374	$1,817	$23,279
Orange	$830,343	$134,413	$134,656	$396,913	$1,496,326
Placer	$32,857	$26,273	$17,188	$12,863	$89,181
Plumas	$2,779	$1,954	$2,683	$135	$7,551
Riverside	$239,206	$102,314	$126,982	$58,999	$527,500
Sacramento	$305,455	$32,983	$56,351	$165,716	$560,505
San Benito	$1,811	$1,330	$380	$373	$3,894
San Bernardino	$312,891	$261,875	$71,893	$115,308	$761,967
San Diego	$678,760	$116,958	$143,528	$276,380	$1,215,626
San Francisco	$235,475	$9,145	$20,970	$313,259	$578,848
San Joaquin	$45,042	$25,135	$23,751	$27,608	$121,535
San Luis Obispo	$20,504	$9,092	$13,164	$10,463	$53,224
San Mateo	$74,390	$7,416	$13,926	$144,857	$240,589
Santa Barbara	$39,476	$11,623	$14,974	$26,758	$92,832
Santa Clara	$151,055	$94,940	$62,950	$399,201	$708,146
Santa Cruz	$24,922	$1,984	$7,159	$22,267	$56,333
Shasta	$19,538	$2,338	$10,221	$4,953	$37,050
Sierra	$69	$0	$129	$199	$397
Siskiyou	$600	$1,975	$3,733	$1,118	$7,426
Solano	$41,979	$15,538	$7,246	$12,283	$77,046
Sonoma	$58,587	$8,763	$20,082	$24,835	$112,268
Stanislaus	$44,761	$40,824	$20,716	$24,873	$131,174
Sutter	$7,951	$14,119	$6,802	$3,582	$32,454
Tehama	$1,592	$564	$6,754	$1,080	$9,989
Trinity	$239	$163	$341	$114	$857
Tulare	$10,129	$3,243	$15,080	$12,983	$41,434
Tuolumne	$2,827	$268	$2,840	$210	$6,145
Ventura	$96,882	$69,472	$50,106	$49,692	$266,152
Yolo	$18,828	$1,123	$3,914	$6,175	$30,039
Yuba	$1,494	$370	$2,410	$1,869	$6,141
State Totals	$6,149,355	$1,712,606	$1,728,618	$3,968,195	$13,558,774

28.17,90 Source: Economic Sciences Corporation (Berkeley) *California Permit Activity, Annual Summary.*

TOTAL BUILDING VALUATION* BY COUNTY, 1982-1988 (in thousands of dollars)					
County	1982	1984	1986	1987	1988
Alameda	$728,086	$1,234,762	$1,210,299	$1,416,302	$1,193,049
Alpine	2,229	1,022	1,157	1,408	2,337
Amador	14,902	24,291	29,198	36,496	29,729
Butte	79,248	116,426	117,001	164,070	174,324
Calaveras	35,528	40,425	54,099	76,642	72,713
Colusa	15,185	5,353	4,290	8,013	8,747
Contra Costa	419,752	853,564	1,133,685	971,126	991,447
Del Norte	6,519	5,554	5,538	29,465	18,119
El Dorado	88,172	96,327	161,280	219,000	273,100
Fresno	200,105	387,924	406,600	407,622	565,379
Glenn	8,764	19,728	6,771	7,581	8,441
Humboldt	33,771	63,911	27,168	63,849	64,831
Imperial	30,854	47,483	81,524	186,218	164,285
Inyo	11,280	8,997	8,587	10,495	7,523
Kern	400,344	496,502	536,004	504,091	489,592
Kings	29,113	56,360	60,758	46,538	71,036
Lake	44,882	40,630	42,022	72,273	61,849
Lassen	14,197	12,406	15,201	13,899	20,544
Los Angeles	4,128,522	6,609,063	9,108,588	9,088,672	9,304,847
Madera	30,189	45,266	48,743	69,964	80,022
Marin	114,514	189,541	154,728	220,417	247,184
Mariposa	6,661	11,671	15,581	12,361	28,263
Mendocino	28,664	47,747	58,494	77,893	46,091
Merced	67,972	76,633	113,865	116,854	144,172
Modoc	5,068	3,929	2,576	2,168	2,375
Mono	16,926	N A	0	11,043	9,038
Monterey	138,035	238,857	273,969	250,051	260,161
Napa	81,495	122,832	106,452	123,918	155,480
Nevada	43,324	54,203	133,371	132,061	165,357
Orange	1,178,945	2,259,313	3,286,156	3,294,097	3,972,135
Placer	105,628	214,568	201,623	340,621	474,860
Plumas	14,052	19,403	17,580	16,829	25,597
Riverside	619,721	1,774,403	2,197,327	2,063,778	3,623,290
Sacramento	498,051	1,099,058	1,309,422	1,246,171	1,683,755
San Benito	18,165	29,623	35,531	36,917	53,960
San Bernardino	656,471	1,560,798	2,823,590	2,304,436	2,388,727
San Diego	1,130,631	2,938,236	4,597,991	3,947,312	4,675,507
San Francisco	1,044,123	674,381	880,860	700,747	870,245
San Joaquin	223,856	344,667	361,944	352,618	487,057
San Luis Obispo	125,207	278,937	275,607	280,877	318,555
San Mateo	291,763	410,255	722,481	695,972	691,803
Santa Barbara	165,542	283,687	308,590	325,991	289,472
Santa Clara	838,412	1,727,878	1,493,858	1,490,690	1,459,092
Santa Cruz	151,543	150,535	128,889	218,423	210,654
Shasta	68,917	62,590	58,893	107,731	129,373
Sierra	2,168	N A	2,059	2,734	2,454
Siskiyou	15,153	12,987	17,637	22,208	23,106
Solano	117,302	185,374	416,002	356,451	577,649
Sonoma	166,750	392,504	437,501	463,257	562,735
Stanislaus	110,413	192,629	503,940	390,569	493,027
Sutter	26,667	32,539	49,576	54,693	60,039
Tehama	23,085	34,602	24,828	34,947	25,339
Trinity	5,120	5,196	4,680	4,770	5,762
Tulare	93,472	136,375	193,737	194,453	148,050
Tuolumne	22,610	34,009	63,269	32,843	36,417
Ventura	295,749	619,151	1,026,069	710,487	924,025
Yolo	49,623	85,269	128,535	124,742	118,256
Yuba	25,773	16,245	27,773	24,956	20,308
State Totals	14,909,273	26,486,619	35,513,499	34,180,809	39,011,288

28.18,90 Source: Economic Sciences Corporation (Berkeley) *California Permit Activity, Annual Summary.*

			Additions &	
Year	Commercial	Industrial	Other	Alterations	Total

Year	Commercial	Industrial	Other	Additions & Alterations	Total
1963	$734,878	$198,932	$708,507	$280,024	$1,922,338
1970	1,089,054	288,077	674,969	491,669	2,543,764
1973	1,349,105	717,549	826,827	337,156	3,230,637
1980†	3,274,076	1,276,735	1,202,940	1,716,358	7,470,108
1981	4,034,262	1,484,011	1,308,224	2,079,348	8,905,845
1982	4,159,933	1,045,014	1,398,106	2,095,323	8,698,376
1983	4,456,664	1,312,568	1,478,114	2,663,477	9,910,803
1984	5,643,180	2,020,359	1,561,724	2,747,846	11,973,109
1985	6,235,954	1,956,566	1,800,293	3,324,965	13,317,778
1986	5,780,519	2,135,479	1,886,448	3,392,460	13,194,906
1987	5,554,884	1,764,065	1,642,449	3,594,267	12,555,665
1988	6,149,355	1,712,606	1,728,618	3,968,195	13,558,774

CALIFORNIA BUILDING PERMIT ACTIVITY NONRESIDENTIAL VALUATION BY SELECTED TYPES OF CONSTRUCTION, 1963-1988 (thousands of dollars)

† Prior to 1980 all additions and alterations of $100,000 or over were recorded as new construction in either the commercial, industrial or other category.

28.19,90 Source: Security Pacific Bank, *California Construction Trends* and *California Building Permit Activity*, Economic Sciences Corp. (Berkeley), Calif. *Building Permit Activity, Annual Summary*.

CALIFORNIA SKYSCRAPERS

Building	Height (feet)	(stories)		Height (feet)	(stories)
Los Angeles			**Sacramento**		
Library Tower*	1,017	73	Renaissance Tower	NA	28
First Interstate Bank	858	62	**San Francisco**		
Wells Fargo Bank	750	53			
Security Pacific Bank	743	55	Transamerica Pyramid	853	48
Arco Towers	699	52	Bank of America	778	52
Bank of America	699	52	101 California Street	600	48
San Diego			California Center	600	47
Symphony Towers	429	34	5 Fremont Center	600	43
Emerald Shapery	400	30	**Oakland**		
First Interstate Bank	398	23			
California First Bank	388	24	Ordway Building	404	28
First National Bank	379	27	Kaiser Center	390	28
Meridian Condominiums	371	27	Lake Merritt Plaza	371	27
Imperial Bank	355	24	Kaiser Engr. Building	336	25
Wells Fargo Bank	348	20	Clorox Building	330	24
Orange County			**Berkeley**		
Century Tower, Costa Mesa	NA	21	Sather Tower (Campanile) U.S. Berkeley	307	NA

* To be completed in 1990.

28.20,90 Source: Pacific Data Resources.

RENTAL HOUSING COSTS 2 BEDROOM APARTMENT-AVERAGE† COST 1988	
County/Area	**Cost**
San Jose Area	$700
Santa Clara	$739
San Mateo	$795
Santa Cruz	$645
San Francisco	$950
Marin	$800
Contra Costa	$590
Sonoma	$550
Solano	$448
Oakland Area	$630
So. Alameda County	$640
Orange	$699*
Riverside-San Bernardino Area	$519**
San Fernando Valley Area	$640
San Diego	$612
Los Angeles (City)	$776
Sacramento	$463

* Apartments over two years old. ** Riverside, Western San Bernardino county, Upper Desert, San Gabriel. † For an unfurnished apartment.
28.21,90 Source: California Apartment Association, unpublished data; The Bay Area Council, unpublished data.

PROFILE OF CALIFORNIA LANDLORDS				
Median Age	49 years	**Occupation**		
Sex (Male)	63%	Manager or Professional	58%	
Race		Not in Labor Force	23%	
White	94%	Technical, Sales	8%	
Black	1%	Service	7%	
Hispanic	3%	Operators, Laborers	4%	
Asian	2%	**Family Income**		
Married	82%	$0 - $24,999	21%	
Education		$25,000 - $49,999	46%	
High School or less	31%	$50,000 +	34%	
Junior College	14%	**Religion**		
College	32%	Protestant	55%	
Advanced Degree	22%	Catholic	21%	
Party		None	19%	
Republican	68%	Jewish	3%	
Democrat	22%	**Units Owned**		
Ideology		0-3	24%	
Conservative	77%	4-7	27%	
Liberal	9%	8-29	35%	
		30 +	13%	

28.22,90 Source: California Apartment Association, unpublished data.

RENT CONTROL IN CALIFORNIA 1989		
Jurisdiction	Coverage	How Adopted
Alameda (City and County)	Mobilehomes Only	Ordinance
Arroyo Grande	Mobilehomes Only	Ordinance
Atascadero	Mobilehomes Only	Initiative
Beaumont	Mobilehomes Only	Ordinance
Benicia	Mobilehomes Only	Ordinance
Berkeley	All Units	Initiative
Beverly Hills	All Units	Ordinance
Calistoga	Mobilehomes Only	Ordinance
Camarillo	Mobilehomes Only	Ordinance
Campbell	Mobilehomes Only	Ordinance
Capitola	Mobilehomes Only	Ordinance
Carpinteria	Mobilehomes Only	Ordinance
Carson	Mobilehomes Only	Ordinance
Cathedral City	Mobilehomes Only	Initiative
Chino	Mobilehomes Only	Initiative
Cloverdale	Mobilehomes Only	Ordinance
Clovis	Mobilehomes Only	Ordinance
Cotati	All Units	Initiative
Daly City	Mobilehomes Only	Ordinance
Delano	Mobilehomes Only	Initiative
East Palo Alto	All Units	Ordinance
Fairfield	Mobilehomes Only	Ordinance
Fontana	Mobilehomes Only	Ordinance
Hayward	All Units	Ordinance
Hemet	Mobilehomes Only	Initiative
Indio	Mobilehomes Only	Initiative
Lancaster	Mobilehomes Only	Ordinance
La Verne	Mobilehomes Only	Ordinance
Lompoc	Mobilehomes Only	Ordinance
Los Angeles	All Units	Ordinance
Los Gatos	All Units	Ordinance
Merced	Mobilehomes Only	Ordinance
Montclair	Mobilehomes Only	Ordinance
Moorpark	Mobilehomes Only	Ordinance
Moreno Valley	Mobilehomes Only	Ordinance
Morgan Hill	Mobilehomes Only	Ordinance
Oakland	All Units	Ordinance
Oxnard	Mobilehomes Only	Ordinance
Palmdale	Mobilehomes Only	Ordinance
Palm Desert	Mobilehomes Only	Ordinance
Palm Springs	All Units	Ordinance
Pismo Beach	Mobilehomes Only	Ordinance
Rancho Mirage	Mobilehomes Only	Ordinance
Redlands	Mobilehomes Only	Ordinance
Rialto	Mobilehomes Only	Ordinance
Riverside County	Mobilehomes Only	Ordinance
Rocklin	Mobilehomes Only	Ordinance
Rohnert Park	Mobilehomes Only	Initiative
San Francisco	All Units	Ordinance
San Jose	All Units	Ordinance
San Juan Capistrano	Mobilehomes Only	Ordinance
San Luis Obispo (City)	Mobilehomes Only	Ordinance
San Luis Obispo (County)	Mobilehomes Only	Initiative
San Marcos	Mobilehomes Only	Ordinance
Santa Barbara (City and County)	Mobilehomes Only	Ordinance
Santa Cruz County	Mobilehomes Only	Ordinance
Santa Monica	All Units	Initiative
Scotts Valley	Mobilehomes Only	Ordinance
Simi Valley	Mobilehomes Only	Ordinance
Thousand Oaks	All Units	Ordinance
Union City	Mobilehomes Only	Ordinance
Upland	Mobilehomes Only	Ordinance
Vacaville	Mobilehomes Only	Ordinance
Vallejo	Mobilehomes Only	Ordinance
Ventura (City and County)	Mobilehomes Only	Ordinance
West Covina	Mobilehomes Only	Ordinance
West Hollywood	All Units	Ordinance
Westlake Village	Mobilehomes Only	Ordinance

28.23,90 Source: California Association of Realtors, 1989, unpublished data.

REAL ESTATE BROKER AND REAL ESTATE SALESPERSON LICENSES ISSUED							
Licenses Issued	1980	1982	1984	1985	1986	1987	1988
Original Broker	11,437	8,387	4,875	6,818	8,840	4,635	7,024
Original Salesperson	37,583	15,106	16,076	24,542	35,832	28,049	27,979
Broker Renewal	16,996	19,125	19,799	19,503	20,717	18,778	20,257
Salesperson Renewal	31,524	29,658	30,183	24,284	22,940	24,919	25,568

28.24,90 Source: State of California, Dept. of Real Estate, unpublished data.

AVAILABLE AND VACANT SPACE AS A PERCENT OF TOTAL OFFICE SPACE						
			Fourth Quarter Rate			
			1988†			
	1980	1984	Down-town Areas	Sub-urban Areas	Indus-trial Areas	Total
Los Angeles	0.2	16.7	13.5	NA	NA	15.4
Orange County*	NA	13.9	NA	NA	NA	22.2
San Diego	3.7	23.4	10.1	23.8	NA	21.2
Southern California	NA	NA	NA	NA	6.4	NA
Oakland-East Bay	NA	19.1	18.7	23.4	NA	22.4
Sacramento	1.1	23.4	5.7	18.4	NA	15.4
San Francisco	0.1	17.9	13.2	18.4	NA	15.3
San Jose	NA	15.7	20.1	15.9	NA	16.8
Northern and Central California	NA	NA	NA	NA	7.0	NA
United States Average	4.1	17.2	16.2	21.5	6.0	19.7

*   No downtown.   † December 1988.
    28.25,90 Source: Dept. of Finance, *California Economic Indicators*.

SECTION 28 NOTE CALIFORNIA'S SEVEN MANMADE WONDERS
Carmel Mission
Disneyland
Golden Gate Bridge
Hearst Castle
Highway 1
Oroville Dam
The Watts Towers

28.26,90

CALIFORNIA AVERAGE YEARLY EFFECTIVE MORTGAGE INTEREST RATES

Year	Rate
1980	12.95%
1981	15.12%
1982	15.38%
1983	12.85%
1984	12.49%
1985	11.74%
1986	10.25%
1987	9.28%
1988	9.31%

28.27,90   Source: California Asso. of Realtors, *California Real Estate Trends.*

SOURCES OF NEWLY ORIGINATED FIRST MORTGAGES

Source	1983	1984	1985	1986	1987	1988
Savings & Loans	46.0%	55.4%	47.6%	47.3%	58.7%	47.3%
Commercial Banks	5.2%	4.8%	6.6%	5.1%	6.0%	9.4%
Mortgage Bankers	34.6%	30.2%	39.5%	44.3%	33.0%	41.1%
Sellers	11.8%	6.4%	3.2%	1.4%	0.7%	0.6%
Others	2.4%	3.1%	3.2%	2.0%	1.5%	1.6%

28.28,90 Source: California Association of Realtors, *1988 Housing Finance Survey.*

CALIFORNIA DELINQUENCY RATES OF 1- TO 4- UNIT RESIDENTIAL MORTGAGE LOANS, SEASONALLY ADJUSTED
(Percent of Loans)

End of 4th Qtr.	All Loans	Conventional Loans	VA Loans	All FHA Loans
1980	5.00	3.14	5.44	6.35
1981	5.18	3.13	5.60	6.61
1982	5.70	3.18	6.18	7.14
1983	5.95	4.52	6.38	7.57
1984	5.79	4.44	6.49	7.12
1985	5.30	4.21	5.88	6.25
1986	4.56	2.79	5.82	6.24
1987	2.80	1.50	3.80	4.10
1988	2.70	1.50	3.80	4.20
1989*	3.30	1.60	5.00	5.30

* First Quarter
Note: Delinquency refers to loans with installments past due thirty days or more. As of the first quarter of 1987, the ALL LOANS default rate in California was 1.2 points below the national average.
28.29,90 Source: Mortgage Bankers Association, *National Delinquency Survey.*

CALIFORNIA ARCHITECTS*	
Gregory Ain - Residences	Cliff May - The California Ranch House
John Bakewell - S.F. City Hall	Bernard Maybeck - Residences, Churches
Arthur Brown, Jr. - Coit Tower S.F.	John McLaren - Golden Gate Park
Page Brown - Ferry Bldg. S.F.	Charles Moore - Sea Ranch
Bernard J.S. Cahill - Columbarium S.F.	Julia Morgan - Hearst Castle
Ernest Coxhead - Churches & Residences	Richard Nuetra - Residences
Gardiner Dailey - Residences, BART Hq. - Oakland	Frederick Law Olmsted - U.C. Berkeley Landscaping
Charles A. Ellis - Golden Gate Bridge	William Pereira - Transamerica Pyramid
Frank Gehry - Residences	Willis Polk - Hallidie Bldg. (S.F.) & Residences
Irving Gill - Residences	Simon Rodia - Watts Towers
Charles and Henry Greene - Residences	R.M. Schindler - Residences
Lawerence Halprin - Levi's Plaza, Sea Ranch	Paul Revere Williams - Residences, Office Bldgs.
John Galen Howard - U.C. Berkeley Campanile	Frank Lloyd Wright - Marin Civic Center
John Jehde - Shopping Malls	William W. Wurster - Ghirardelli Square S.F.
Philip Johnson - Crystal Cathedral - Garden Grove	
Lewis Hobart - Grace Cathedral S.F.	

* Including non-Californians who have done important work in California.
28.30,90 Source: Pacific Data Resources.

JAPANESE REAL ESTATE INVESTMENTS, 1988		
Metropolitan Area	**Millions of Dollars**	**% of U.S. Total**
Los Angeles	$3,049	18%
San Francisco/		
Oakland	$740	5%
Anaheim	$506	3%
San Diego	$421	3%
Statewide Total	**$5,620**	**34%**

• In 1987 the Japanese invested $2,980,000,000 in California real estate or 23% of its U.S. real estate investments.
28.31,90 Source: Kenneth Leventhal & Co.

BUILDERS/ENGINEERS - PROMINENT CALIFORNIANS	
George Chaffey	Henry Huntington - Mass Transit
-Built 1st hydro electric plant in Cal.	Theodore D. Judah - Transcontinental Railroad
-Opened 1st electricly lighted house in Cal.	Abbott Kinney - Founder of Venice
-Organized 1st private water company.	Daniel A. McMillan Jr. - Geothermal Energy
Charles Crocker - Transcontinental Railroad	William Mulholland - Owens Valley Water
Andrew Hallidie - Cable Car	Michael M. O'Shaughnessy
Mark Hopkins - Transcontinental Railroad	-Hetch Hetchy Water System
Collis P. Huntington	Leland Stanford - Transcontinental Railroad
-Transcontinental Railroad	Joseph B. Strauss - Golden Gate Bridge

28.32,90 Source: Pacific Data Resources.

The Stealth Bomber. Manufactured in Southern California by the Northrop Corporation.

STATE BOUNDARIES

Major, 1868-1870
212 miles

LAT. 40° 59' 54.65" N
LONG 124° 12' 28.31" W

LAT 41° 59' 41.36" N
LONG 119° 59' 55.60" W

Von Schmidt, 1873
222 miles

N

0 20 40 60 80 100
miles

Sacramento
(since 1854)

Vallejo
(1851-53)

Benicia
(1853)

San Jose
(1849-1851)

Geographic Center

Monterey
(first capital)

U.S. Coast & Geodetic Survey, 1893-96, 1898-99
405 miles

Mt Whitney
14,495' above sea level

Badwater
282' below sea level

Northern

Southern

LAT 35° 00' 12.46" N
LONG 114° 38' 03.31" W

● State Capitals
+ Highest and lowest points
- - - Proposed division of State in 1859

LAT 32° 32' 03.82" N
LONG 117° 07' 18.84" W

LAT 32° 43' 07.29" N
LONG 114° 43' 07.35" W

U.S.C. & G.S. 1964

140 miles

Weller, Gray, Emory, 1849-50: Barlow, 1891-96

© 1974 by the University of Oklahoma Press

Historical Atlas of California, 1974. University of Oklahoma Press. Reprinted by permission.

Manufacturers

One of the more vigorous elements of the California economy during the past two decades has been manufacturing. As of early 1989 almost 2.2 million Californians earned their living in manufacturing businesses, making California by far the leading manufacturing state in the nation. While most of the other major manufacturing states have lost manufacturing jobs over the past two decades, California has gained over 400,000 such jobs. Furthermore, in the past decade manufacturing's share of the California gross state product has increased. Two-thirds of the state's manufacturing workers produce such durable goods as machinery, electrical equipment, and transportation equipment.

According to studies by the Bank of America and the Bank of Japan, U.S. manufacturing productivity increased by an average of 3.7 percent per year from 1980 to 1986, a rate only slightly lower than that of Japan and equal to that of West Germany. Manufacturing productivity in California, however, increased by an average of 4.7 percent per year during the same period. This gain in the state's manufacturing productivity should signal an increase in both its percentage of the total output of U.S. manufactured goods and its share of the world export market.

Gains in productivity alone do not guarantee that the state's exports of manufactured goods will grow. James Vaughn, the director of the state's Asian Office of Trade and Investment in Tokyo, has criticized California's manufacturers, particularly its high-tech manufacturers, for failing to look to Japan for sales and for failing to invest in Japan. California's manufacturers, Vaughn asserts, spend too much money on lobbying in Washington and not enough on marketing research in Japan.

Foreign investment in California, by contrast, seems to be quite buoyant. Japan's NEC Corporation plans a major expansion of its semiconductor plant in Roseville, and South Korea's Pohang Iron and Steel Company has invested $400,000 to modernize the old U.S. Steel plant in Pittsburg (Contra Costa County). The Pohang plant will be operated jointly with U.S. Steel (USX) and will employ 1,200 workers.

While most manufacturers are satisfied to locate in California, those in the nine-county San Francisco Bay Area appear to have soured on further expansions in their home territory. High payroll costs, the lack of affordable housing, and hostile public attitudes toward business have prompted manufacturers to look to the Central Valley and even outside the state for sites on which to expand.

CALIFORNIA'S TWENTY-FIVE LARGEST PUBLICLY HELD INDUSTRIAL MANUFACTURING* COMPANIES 1988				
California 500 Rank	Rank† in State	Name	Revenues (billions)	Net Income (in millions)
1	1	Chevron	28.9	1,768
2	2	Occidental Petroleum	19.4	302
3	3	Atlantic Richfield	18.3	1,583
4	4	Lockheed	10.6	624
6	5	Unocal	10.1	480
7	6	Hewlett-Packard	9.8	816
11	7	McKesson	7.3	95
15	8	Northrup	5.8	104
17	9	Teledyne	4.6	392
19	10	Litton Industries	4.5	167
21	11	Apple Computer	4.1	400
23	12	Bergen Brunswig	3.5	33
31	13	Intel	2.9	453
35	14	National Semiconductor	2.5	63
43	15	Amdahl	1.8	223
46	16	Avery International	1.6	78
49	17	Fleetwood Enterprises	1.4	48
53	18	Syntex	1.3	297
54	19	Seagate Technology	1.3	77
55	20	Clorox	1.3	133
58	21	Varian Associates	1.2	28
61	22	Tosco Petroleum	1.1	90
62	23	Advanced Micro Devices	1.1	19
63	24	Raychem	1.1	125
64	25	Potlatch	1.1	112

* Some companies are involved in manufacturing and nonmanufacturing endeavors.

† Ranking only of manufacturing firms.

29.1,90 Source: *California Business Magazine,* May 1989. Permission to reprint by *California Business,* all rights reserved. Consult *California Business Magazine* for detailed information on the 500 largest corporations in California.

SECTION 29 NOTE
Three of the nation's top five computer chip (semiconductor) manufacturers are located in California: Intel (1), National Semiconductor (4), and Advanced Micro Devices (5).

29.2,90

SECTION 29 NOTE
California is the home to 2,081 microcomputer producers and suppliers, 29 percent of the nation's total.

29.3,90

			WAGE AND SALARY WORKERS IN CALIFORNIA, 1940-1987 (in thousands)	
Year	Total Workers*	Manufacturing Workers	Manufacturing Workers as a % of the Work Force	Production Workers as a % of all California Manufacturing Workers
1940	1,932	440	23%	NA
1950	3,209	760	24%	NA
1960	4,896	1,317	27%	NA
1970	6,946	1,558	22%	NA
1972	NA	NA	NA	66%
1977	8,600	1,738	20%	65%
1980	9,849	2,018	20%	NA
1981	9,985	2,032	20%	NA
1982	9,810	1,958	20%	60%
1983	9,966	1,949	20%	60%
1984	10,574	2,066	20%	60%
1985	10,979	2,076	19%	59%
1986	11,258	2,070	18%	58%
1987	11,679	2,108	18%	NA
1988	12,075	2,148	18%	NA
1989†	12,363	2,165	18%	NA

* Nonagricultural employment. Data seasonally adjusted. † April.
29.4,90 Source: California Employment Development Department, unpublished data; *Annual Planning Information, California 1986-87;* and *Report to the Governor on Labor Market Conditions.*

	AVERAGE WEEKLY EARNINGS AND HOURS WORKED BY PRODUCTION AND RELATED WORKERS IN MANUFACTURING CALIFORNIA AND UNITED STATES, 1960-1988					
	California			United States		
Year	Average Weekly Earnings	Average Hourly Earnings	Average Hours per Week	Average Weekly Earnings	Average Hourly Earnings	Average Hours per Week
1960	104.28	2.62	39.8	89.72	2.26	39.7
1970	150.48	3.80	39.6	133.33	3.35	39.8
1980	304.15	7.70	39.5	288.62	7.27	39.7
1981	338.98	8.56	39.6	318.00	7.99	39.8
1982	362.21	9.24	39.2	330.65	8.50	38.9
1983	380.80	9.52	40.0	354.08	8.83	40.1
1984	393.73	9.77	40.3	374.03	9.19	40.7
1985	406.82	10.12	40.2	385.97	9.53	40.5
1986	417.51	10.36	40.3	396.01	9.73	40.7
1987	433.23	10.75	40.3	406.31	9.91	41.0
1988	442.00	10.86	40.7	417.99	10.17	41.1

29.5,90 Source: U.S. Dept. of Labor, Bureau of Labor Statistics, *Employment and Earnings.*

CALIFORNIA MANUFACTURING FIRMS REPORTING NET INCOME SUBJECT TO STATE TAXATION BY INDUSTRY*
1985 and 1986

	1985			
	Corporations Reporting Net Income Subject to State Taxation		All Reporting Corporations	
Industry	Number	Net Income (in thousands)	Number	Net Income Less Net Loss (in thousands)
Beverages, Food, and Kindred Products	1,048	$927,795	1,942	$700,616
Textile-mill Products	52	$17,481	383	$8,728
Apparel and Products Made from Fabric	1,074	$206,119	1,943	$116,122
Wood Products (except Furniture)	1,306	$324,452	1,783	$297,284
Furniture and Fixtures	840	$169,878	1,847	$45,655
Paper and Allied Products	221	$86,888	545	-$61,480
Printing, Publishing, and Allied Industries	2,353	$663,943	4,384	$570,233
Chemicals and Allied Products	1,733	$914,387	2,713	$651,170
Petroleum, Coal and Rubber Products	499	$299,384	658	$101,891
Stone, Clay, and Glass Products	421	$159,950	916	$150,723
Primary Metals	383	$203,261	490	$58,586
Electric Machinery and Equipment	2,557	$2,408,919	5,039	$883,360
Transportation Equipment	849	$2,224,647	1,740	$2,103,299
Other Equipment	2,161	$402,611	3,223	$267,299
Precision Equipment	565	$679,563	1,199	$634,425
Other Fabricated Metal Products	3,782	$565,394	5,664	$213,416
Other Manufacturing	1,940	$465,296	4,212	$212,142
Total Manufacturing	**21,784**	**$10,719,968**	**38,691**	**$6,953,439**

* Net income of manufacturing firms which is subject to Federal taxation is 2 to 20 times greater than income subject to state taxation.
29.6.1,90 Source: California Franchise Tax Board, *Annual Report*.

SECTION 29 NOTE
California, according to ELECTRONIC BUSINESS magazine, has 41 of the 100 fastest-growing electronic companies in the nation, more than any other state. Massachusetts, with 14, follows.

29.7,90

CALIFORNIA MANUFACTURING FIRMS REPORTING NET INCOME SUBJECT TO STATE TAXATION BY INDUSTRY* 1985 and 1986				
	1986			
	Corporations Reporting Net Income Subject to State Taxation		**All Reporting Corporations**	
Industry	**Number**	**Net Income (in thousands)**	**Number**	**Net Income Less Net Loss (in thousands)**
Beverages, Food, and Kindred Products	1,283	$1,294,089	2,514	$940,160
Textile-mill Products	235	$66,200	369	$49,804
Apparel and Products Made from Fabric	1,303	$1,293,294	2,425	$1,206,666
Wood Products (except Furniture)	797	$255,288	1,364	$205,545
Furniture and Fixtures	797	$149,627	1,391	$106,847
Paper and Allied Products	477	$172,871	969	$133,000
Printing, Publishing, and Allied Industries	2,612	$1,259,535	4,918	$1,070,527
Chemicals and Allied Products	1,262	$1,355,604	2,261	$1,164,559
Petroleum, Coal and Rubber Products	1,027	$705,196	2,051	$192,107
Stone, Clay, and Glass Products	595	$333,473	1,069	$287,486
Primary Metals	303	$88,770	560	-$44,859
Electric Machinery and Equimpment	2,723	$2,686,161	5,956	$1,200,331
Transportation Equipment	796	$1,843,306	1,608	$1,628,612
Other Equipment	1,560	$468,461	3,047	$241,656
Precision Equipment	720	$295,758	1,511	$119,684
Other Fabricated Metal Products	4,336	$844,340	7,305	$620,477
Other Manufacturing	2,022	$554,133	4,312	$268,626
Total Manufacturing	**22,848**	**$13,666,106**	**43,630**	**$9,391,228**

* Net income of manufacturing firms which is subject to Federal taxation is 2 to 20 times greater than income subject to state taxation.

29.6.2,90 Source: California Franchise Tax Board, *Annual Report*.

SECTION 29 NOTE
California's pharmaceutical industry employs 23,000 people and is concentrated in Los Angeles, Santa Clara, Orange, Alameda, and San Mateo counties.

29.8,90

NET INCOME OF CALIFORNIA MANUFACTURING CORPORATIONS

Year	Number of Corporations Reporting Net Income	Net Income (in billions)	Manufacturing Corporation Income as a Percent of Total Corporate Income
1980	20,210	$8.2	32%
1981	20,534	$7.9	33%
1982	17,871	$6.8	30%
1983	18,754	$8.7	32%
1984	21,815	$11.2	35%
1985	21,784	$10.7	31%
1986	22,848	$13.7	34%

29.9,90 Source: California Franchise Tax Board, *Annual Report.*

AEROSPACE EMPLOYMENT, 1960-1988
(in thousands)

Year	Total Aerospace	Office Computing and Accounting Machines	Radio and TV Receiving Equipment	Communication Equipment	Electronic Components & Accessories	Aircraft and Parts	Guided Missiles and Space Vehicles	Measuring and Controlling Instruments
1960	422.5	23.3	9.9	92.2	29.1	181.4	68.4	18.2
1970	466.3	58.3	15.1	102.9	53.0	148.3	64.5	24.3
1980	632.6	97.9	17.6	137.3	124.2	151.0	58.6	46.0
1981	647.1	98.4	17.3	146.5	126.1	147.9	62.7	48.2
1982	658.3	103.0	14.9	157.2	131.0	137.3	66.4	47.6
1983	672.0	109.9	13.5	158.7	139.8	133.3	69.3	47.5
1984	730.0	117.9	13.7	167.2	165.3	141.1	73.8	51.1
1985	753.7	111.4	13.6	179.1	160.8	156.7	78.1	54.1
1986	752.0	107.2	14.0	179.5	148.6	167.4	81.0	54.3
1987	752.2	105.8	14.5	174.3	150.4	171.6	81.1	54.5
1988	760.3	107.8	15.1	168.7	157.6	172.3	81.2	57.7

29.10,90 Source: *Economic Report of the Governor.*

CALIFORNIA'S MAJOR BRANDY PRODUCERS

Distiller	1988 Brandy Shipped (thousands of gallons)	% of Brandy Shipments
Gallo	5,360	53.0%
Christian Brothers	2,698	26.0%
Korbel	943	9.0%
Paul Mason	558	5.0%
Beverage Source	289	3.0%
East-Side	113	1.0%
Heublein/Almaden	99	1.0%
Busch	80	0.8%
Guild	47	0.5%
Total Production	**10,188**	**100.0%**

Note: In 1987 Brandy Shipments were up 7% from 1986, in 1988 down 8% from 1987. 29.11,90 Source: *Wines and Vines Magazine* and Gomberg, Fredrickson & Associates.

ALCOHOL PRODUCTION AND SALES IN CALIFORNIA			
(in millions of gallons)			
Year and Beverage	Produced and Sold in California	Produced and Sold Outside California	Imported and Sold in California	Total Production
Beer				
1980	267.5	142.4	NA	410.0
1981	282.6	148.8	NA	431.4
1982	384.6	185.8	NA	570.5
1983	411.1	208.5	201.1	619.6
1984	429.8	219.8	198.1	649.6
1985	434.7	227.0	184.2	661.7
1986	452.5	226.4	196.5	679.0
1987	452.9	240.5	209.5	693.4
1988	453.2	215.9	203.4	674.0
Sparkling Wine				
1980	6.5	15.4	NA	21.9
1981	7.2	16.9	NA	24.1
1982	7.8	17.9	NA	25.6
1983	9.0	19.3	1.4	28.3
1984	8.7	19.7	2.0	28.4
1985	8.9	13.9	2.2	22.8
1986	9.2	18.1	2.0	27.2
1987	8.2	17.5	2.1	25.7
1988	7.9	16.3	1.9	24.4
Wine (less than 14% Alcohol)				
1980	81.3	196.5	NA	277.9
1981	82.7	214.7	NA	297.4
1982	84.4	214.7	NA	299.1
1983	87.4	212.5	10.4	299.9
1984	89.3	224.5	9.4	313.8
1985	98.5	234.4	9.7	332.9
1986	102.5	262.0	8.4	364.5
1987	99.8	266.4	7.7	366.2
1988	93.4	243.3	5.7	334.6
Wine (more than 14% Alcohol)				
1980	7.7	32.4	NA	40.1
1981	7.5	29.4	NA	37.0
1982	7.5	28.3	NA	35.8
1983	7.5	27.6	1.0	35.1
1984	6.6	25.2	1.0	31.8
1985	6.9	24.5	1.2	31.4
1986	7.0	23.9	1.5	30.9
1987	7.5	24.7	1.7	32.2
1988	7.3	21.5	1.4	28.8

29.12,90 Source: *Wines & Vines Magazine*, July issue and California State Board of Equalization, unpublished computer report ABSTI-01.

MULTINATIONAL MANUFACTURING COMPANIES CALIFORNIA AND SELECTED STATES*, 1988		
State	**Number of Companies**	**% of U.S. Companies**
California	**150**	**15%**
New York	130	13%
Illinois	85	9%
Ohio	70	7%
Massachusetts	61	6%
Pennsylvania	59	6%

* Firms with sales of $100 million or more. New York leads the U.S. with multinational manufacturing firms with sales of $1 billion or more. New York has 44 such firms while California is second with 24. As recently as 1987, New York led California 123 to 108 in firms with sales of $100 million or more.

29.13,90 Source: The Conference Board, *Where the Multinationals Are - Key Company Directory, 1989.*

MANUFACTURING: CALIFORNIA AND THE NATION 1967-86									
	Estab- lish- ments	% of U.S.	Pay- roll *	% of U.S.	Value Added †	% of U.S.	Value of Ship- ments *	% of U.S.	Capi- tal Expendi- tures *	% of U.S.
1964	32,201**	10.3%	$10	9.3%	$18	8.7%	$38	8.3%	$1.0	7.8%
1967	31,962	10.3%	$13	9.5%	$23	8.9%	$47	8.4%	$1.5	7.1%
1972	35,699	11.1%	$15	8.9%	$31	8.8%	$63	8.3%	$1.6	6.8%
1977	45,289	12.6%	$25	9.3%	$55	9.4%	$121	8.9%	$3.4	7.1%
1982	47,625	13.3%	$43	11.2%	$94	11.5%	$200	10.2%	$8.4	11.3%
1985	NA	NA	$51	11.6%	$111	11.1%	$227	10.0%	$9.1	11.0%
1986	NA	NA	$52	11.6%	$113	10.9%	$225	9.9%	$8.1	10.6%

*   Billions
†   In billions by manufacturing.
** 1963

29.14,90 Source: U.S. Bureau of the Census, *Census of Manufacturers, 1967, 72, 77, 82* and *Annual Census of Manufacturers.*

SECTION 29 NOTE
California is second only to New York in the production of wearing apparel and in the number of individuals employed in the apparel industry.

29.15,90

SECTION 29 NOTE
From 1982 to 1989 California has increased its share of U.S. manufacturing workers from 10.5% to 11.0%

29.16,90

Culture

For decades California has been the reputed pop culture capital of the nation, if not the world. That reputation was secured initially by the state's dominance of the motion-picture industry. Then in the fifties Los Angeles began to dominate television's entertainment programming, which in turn had an incalculable effect on the nation's popular culture. Whether via Johnny Carson's late-night show or Disney's family programs, the message came from--and was often about--California. In recent years the development of the record and music-video business has increased the state's influence over middle- and low-brow culture. Television's network news programs and commentary, however, as well as public television's major productions still come from the East Coast, as do most of the nation's important newspapers, news weeklies, and high-brow journals of opinion and culture.

Although California is better known for movie stars and rock musicians than for writers, in fact the state has long been home to serious writers of both fiction and nonfiction. Earlier in the century Jack London lived here, along with Upton Sinclair, Dashiell Hammett, John Steinbeck, William Saroyan, and Ray Bradbury. More recently, prominent writers at home in California include Joan Didion, Maxine Hong Kingston, Alice Walker, Ishmael Reed, John Gregory Dunne, and Joseph Wambaugh.

Although the detective novel did not originate in California, writers like Hammett, Wambaugh, Raymond Chandler, and Ross McDonald have given their readers a distinctive sense of the state's places and moods. We are still waiting for the great California novel--or waiting to recognize it if it has already been written. Perhaps it will be a multigenerational saga focusing on the transformation of the landscape as the state emerged from rural innocence into a flawed but energetic multi-ethnic giant. Movie and music-video rights are pending.

Lacking royal patronage or, for the most part, government subsidies, the arts in the United States have developed nonetheless, often under the sponsorship of wealthy business patrons. As California's great industrial wealth has grown in the twentieth century, its museums, symphonies, opera companies, choral groups, and dance companies have begun to flourish. Because California's wealthier citizens seem as willing as their counterparts in the East and the Midwest to subsidize all these traditional elements of high culture, California's cultural institutions should increasingly take their rank among the nation's best.

CONDENSED CALIFORNIA HISTORY

1542	Sept. 28	Juan Rodriguez Cabrillo sails into San Diego Harbor.
1579	June 15	Sir Francis Drake sails into Drake's Bay (Marin County).
1769	Apr. 11	First permanent Spanish colony established in California at San Diego.
	July 16	First of the 21 Californian missions dedicated in San Diego by Father Junipero Serra.
1774	March 16	First overland journey to California by Europeans led by Jaun Bautista de Anza.
1775	Aug. 16	Monterey becomes the capital of California.
1796	Oct. 29	First American ship, the Otter, sails into California waters in Monterey Bay.
1810	Sept. 16	Mexican rebellion against Spain begins.
1812	Sept. 10	Russians establish fur trading post at Fort Ross (Sonoma County).
1816	Jan. 15	Thomas Doak becomes first American settler in California.
1821	Sept.	Spain grants independence to Mexico.
1822	Nov. 9	First provincial legislature meets in Monterey.
1826	Nov. 27	Jedediah Smith completes first overland trip by Americans to California.
1830		California non-Indian population set at 4,256.
1833	Aug. 17	Mexican government secularizes the missions.
1831-1836		California revolt against the government of Mexico.
1836	Nov. 8	The free and sovereign state of Alta California established (for 8 months).
1840		John Sutter builds Sutter's Fort in Sacramento Valley.
1841	Nov. 4	First American wagon train, the Bidwell-Bartleson party, arrives in California.
1842	Oct. 9	Commodore Thomas Jones, believing U.S. and Mexico are at war, seizes Monterey and raises the U.S. flag. Realizing this error, Jones leaves Monterey two days later.
1844-1845		California revolt forces Mexican governor Micheltorena out of the state.
1846	June 14	Americans seize Gen. Vallejo at Sonoma; proclaim "Bear Flag" California Republic.
1846	July 7	Commodore John Sloat sails into Monterey Bay and claims California for U.S.
1846-1847		Donner party trapped in Sierra snows.
1847		California non-Indian population set at 15,000.
1847	Jan. 8-9	American victory at battle of La Mesa ends 1846-1847 war with California.
1848	Jan. 24	James Marshall discovers gold at Sutter's Mill.
1848	Feb. 2	In treaty of Guadalupe Hidalgo, Mexico cedes California to U.S.
1849	Oct. 18	California's first playhouse, The Eagle Theater, opens in Sacramento.
1849	Nov. 13	First California constitution ratified.
1849	Nov. 13	Peter Burnett elected first governor of California.
1850		California population is 92,597.
1850	Sept. 9	California admitted to the union as the thirty-first state.
1854	Feb. 25	Sacramento becomes the State Capital.
1861	Oct. 24	First transcontinental telegraph line connected.
1868	Mar. 23	University of California founded.
1869	May 10	First transcontinental railroad completed.
1873	June	Modoc War, the last Indian war in California.
1906	Apr. 18	San Francisco earthquake.
1911	Jan. 3	Hiram Johnson inaugurated as Governor.
1911	Apr. 3	Initiative, Referendum and Recall approved.
1913		Los Angeles Aqueduct from the Owens Valley completed.
1913		California Alien Land Law passed.
1914	Aug. 1	Panama Canal opened.
1915	Feb. 20	Panama-Pacific International Exposition opens in San Francisco.
1919		Hearst Castle erected.
1921-1954		Simon Rodia constructs Watts Towers.
1924		Immigration Act passes Congress to limit Asian immigration.
1932	July	Olympic Games held in Los Angeles.
1936	Nov.	San Francisco-Oakland Bay Bridge opens.
1937	May	Golden Gate Bridge opens.
1942	Feb. 19	President Roosevelt orders internment of Japanese-Americans in California.
1945		United Nations founded in San Francisco.
1956		Republican National Convention held in San Francisco.
1957		Brooklyn Dodgers move to Los Angeles; New York Giants move to San Francisco.
1957		California Water Plan adopted.
1960		Winter Olympics held in Squaw Valley.
1960		Democratic National Convention held in Los Angeles.
1964		California becomes the most populous state in the nation.
1964		Republican national convention held in San Francisco.
1965	Aug.	Watts Riots.
1984		Democratic National Convention held in San Francisco.
1984		Olympic Games held in Los Angeles.

30.1,90 Source: Pacific Data Resources.

COUNTY MUSEUMS, GARDENS, ZOOS, AND PLACES OF GENERAL AND HISTORICAL INTEREST

Alameda County

Albany
Golden Gate Fields Racetrack
Berkeley
Judah Magnes Jewish Museum
Lowie Museum of Anthropology
Lawrence Hall of Science
Municipal Rose Garden
Pacific Film Archive
University Art Museum
University Botanical Garden
Fremont
Ardenwood Historic Farm
Mission San Jose de Guadalupe
Hayward
Historical Society Museum
Japanese Gardens
McConaghy Estate
Sulphur Creek Park Nature Center
and Museum
Livermore
Lawrence Livermore Laboratory
Visitor Center
Oakland
Jack London Square
Knowland Zoo
Oakland Museum
Pleasanton
Amador-Livermore Valley
Historical Society Museum
Rapids Waterslide
San Leandro
Casa Peralta
Sunol
Pacific Locomotive Association
Railroad

Amador County

Jackson
Amador County Museum
Fiddletown
Chinese Museum

Butte County

Gridley
Grey Lodge Bird Museum
Oroville
Chinese Temple
Feather River Hatchery
Lott Home
Oroville Dam

Calaveras County

Angels Camp
Angels Camp Museum
Murphys
Old Timer's Museum
San Andreas
Calaveras Caverns
Calaveras County Museum

Colusa County

Williams
Sacramento Valley Museum

Contra Costa County

Danville
Behring Auto Museum
Eugene O'Neill House
Martinez
John Muir National Historic Site
Pittsburg
Pittsburg Historical Society Museum
Richmond
Richmond Art Center
Walnut Creek
Alexander Lindsay Junior Museum

Del Norte County

Crescent City
Battery Point Lighthouse Museum
Del Norte County Historical
Society Museum
McNulty Pioneer Memorial Home
Rellim Demonstration Forest
Undersea Gardens
Klamath
Trees of Mystery Park

COUNTY MUSEUMS, GARDENS, ZOOS, AND PLACES OF GENERAL AND HISTORICAL INTEREST

El Dorado County
Coloma
Marshall Gold Discovery Museum
Lake Tahoe
Vikingsholm
Lake Cruises
Placerville
El Dorado County
Historical Museum
Gold Bug Mine
South Lake Tahoe
Log Cabin Museum

Fresno County
Coalinga
R.C. Baker Memorial Museum
Fresno
The Discovery Center
Forestiere Underground Gardens
Fresno Arts Museum
Kearney Mansion
Metropolitan Museum of Art,
History& Science
Meux Museum
Roeding Park Zoo
Sun Maid Raisin Tour
Woodward Park
Sequoia National Park
Sequoia and Kings Canyon
National Park Museum

Humboldt County
Arcata
Azalea Reserve
Eureka
The Carson Mansion
Clarke Memorial Museum
Ferndale
Ferndale Museum
Scotia
Pacific Lumber Company Museum

Imperial County
Brawley
Imperial Sand Dunes

Inyo County
Big Pine
Bristlecone Pine Forest
Death Valley
Amargosa Opera House
Death Valley Museum
Scotty's Castle
Bishop
Laws Railroad Museum
Independence
Eastern California Museum

Kern County
Bakersfield
California Living Museum
Cunningham Memorial
Art Gallery
Kern County Museum
and Pioneer Village
Delano
Delano Heritage Park Museum
Lebec
Fort Tejon State Historic
Park and Museum
Porterville
Porterville Historical Museum
Randsburg
Desert Museum
Ridgecrest
Maturango Museum of
Indian Wells Valley
Rosamund
Burton's Gold Mine
and Museum
Taft
West Kern Oil Museum

Kings County
Hanford
China Alley
Carnegie Museum

Lake County
Lakeport
Lake County Museum

Lassen County
Hat Creek
Subway Cave

COUNTY MUSEUMS, GARDENS, ZOOS, AND PLACES OF GENERAL AND HISTORICAL INTEREST

Lassen County (cont.)

Susanville
Lassen County Historical
Society Museum
Roop's Fort

Los Angeles County

Alhambra
Alhambra Historical
Society History Room

Arcadia
Los Angeles State
and County Arboretum
Santa Anita Raceway

Avalon
Catalina Island Museum
Wrigley Memorial and Botanical
Garden

Azusa
Azusa Historical Society Museum

Burbank
Burbank Studio Tour
NBC Studio Tour

Calabasas
Leonis Adobe

Canoga Park
Orcutt Horticultural Center

Claremont
Rancho Santa Ana Botanic Garden
ALF Museum of Life

Covina
Firehouse Museum

Downey
Downey Historical Society Museum
Room
Downey Museum of Art

Duarte
Duarte Historical Museum

El Monte
El Monte Historical Museum
Whittier Narrows Nature Center

Encino
Los Encinos State Historical Park
Museum

Glendale
Brand Library and Art Center
Forest Lawn Memorial Park

Glendora
Glendora Historical Society Museum

Hacienda Heights
Dibble Museum
Rowland Museum

Industry
Workman & Temple Homestead

Inglewood
English Brass Rubbing Center
The Forum
Hollywood Park Racetrack

La Canada-Flintridge
Descanso Gardens
Mt. Wilson Observatory

La Mirada
Neff Home

Lancaster
Antelope Valley Indian Museum
NASA Flight Research Facility

Lomita
Kuska Museum
Lomita Railroad Museum

Long Beach
General Banning Home
El Dorado Nature Center and
Museum
La Casa De Rancho Los Cerritos
Long Beach Museum of Art
R.M.S. Queen Mary
Rancho Los Alamitos
Spruce Goose

Los Angeles
ABC Television Center
Amateur Athletic Foundation Sports
Museum
Avila Adobe
Cabrillo Beach Marine Museum
California Afro-American Museum
California Museum of Science and
Industry

COUNTY MUSEUMS, GARDENS, ZOOS, AND PLACES OF GENERAL AND HISTORICAL INTEREST

Los Angeles County (cont.)
Los Angeles (cont.)
CBS Television City
Chinatown
Citizens Savings Sports Museum
Dunbar Museum
El Pueblo De Los Angeles State
  Historical Park
Federal Archives
Goez Art Gallery
Griffith Observatory
Griffith Park
Heritage Square
History Center
Hollywood Bowl
Hollywood Memorial Park Cemetary
Hollywood Studio Museum
Hollywood Wax Museum
Junior Arts Center
KCET-TV Tour
L.A. Equestrian Center
Lawry's Kitchen & Plant Collection
  Center
Little Tokyo
Los Angeles Childrens Museum
Los Angeles County Museum of Art
Los Angeles Municipal Art Gallery
Los Angeles Zoo
Lummis Home
Mann's Chinese Theatre
Margaret Cavigga Quilt Collection
Military History Museum
Museum of Contemporary Art
Museum of Neon Art
Natural History Museum
Old Plaza Firehouse
Otis/Parsons Gallery
Page Museum of LaBrea Discoveries
Pico House
Rancho La Brea Tar Pits
Skirball Museum
Southwest Museum
Traveltown
Universal Studios Tour

Los Angeles County (cont.)
Los Angeles (cont.)
Watts (Rodia) Towers
Wells Fargo History Museum
Western Heritage Museum
Malibu
J. Paul Getty Museum
Marina del Rey
Fisherman's Village
Monrovia
George Anderson House
Montebello
Juan Matias Sanchez Adobe
Mount Wilson
Mount Wilson Observatory
Norwalk
Sproul Gilbert Museum
Newhall
Hart County Park Art Museum
Pacific Palisades
Will Rogers State Historic Park
Palos Verdes
Point Vincente Interpretive Center
South Coast Botanic Garden
Pasadena
Gamble House
Kidspace
Norton Simon Museum of Art
Pacific-Asia Museum
Pasadena Historical Society Museum
Rose Bowl
Pomona
Adobe De Palomares
Kellog Arabian Horse Center
La Casa Primera de Rancho San Jose
Rancho Palos Verdes
Palos Verdes Art Center
Redondo Beach
Redondo Pier
San Fernando
Lopez Adobe
Mission San Fernando Rey
  De Espana

30.2.4,90

COUNTY MUSEUMS, GARDENS, ZOOS, AND PLACES OF GENERAL AND HISTORICAL INTEREST

Los Angeles County (cont.)

San Dimas
Raging Waters

San Gabriel
Mission San Gabriel Arcangel

San Marino
The Old Mill
Huntington Library, Art Gallery and Gardens

San Pedro
L.A. Maritime Museum
Cabrillo Maritime Museum

Santa Catalina Island
Catalina Island Museum
Wrigley Memorial and Botanical Garden

Santa Fe Springs
Hathaway Museum

Santa Monica
Bob's Military Antiques and Wax Museum
Donald Douglas Museum
Hawkins Doll Museum
Heritage Museum
Santa Monica Pier

Sierra Madre
Richardson House

Signal Hill
Kid Mexico Museum

Universal City
Universal Studios

Valencia
California Institute of the Arts
Six Flags Magic Mountain Amusement Park

Van Nuys
General Motors Plant Tour
Tillman Water Plant & Japanese Garden

Walnut
William Rowland Ranch House

Whittier
Pio Pico Mansion

Madera County

Madera
Madera County Museum

Yosemite
Yosemite Collections

Marin County

Belvedere
Old St. Hillary's Church

Muir Beach
Slide Ranch

Novato
Marin Miwok Museum

Olema
Point Reyes National Seashore

Petaluma
California Co-op Creamery-Tour
Cheese Factory-Tours
Historical Library & Museum
Winners Circle Ranch

San Rafael
Marin County Historical Museum
Marin Wildlife Center
Mission San Rafael Arcangel

Sausalito
Corps of Engineers Bay Model

Stinson Beach
Audubon Canyon Ranch

Mariposa County

Fish Camp
Sugar Pine Railroad

Mariposa
Mariposa County History Center
State Mining & Mineral Museum

Coulterville
Magnolia Saloon

Mendocino County

Crescent City
Redwood National Park

Fort Bragg
Guest House Museum
Mendocino Coast Botanical Gardens
Skunk Railroad

COUNTY MUSEUMS, GARDENS, ZOOS, AND PLACES OF GENERAL AND HISTORICAL INTEREST

Mendocino County (cont.)
Little River
Pygmy Forest
Mendocino
Art Center
Ecological Staircase
Georgia Pacific Nursery
Kelly House Museum
Kwan Tia Temple
Piercy
Confusion Hill & Railroad
Point Arena
Lighthouse & Museum
Ukiah
Grace Hudson Museum
Held-Poage Memorial Home
Willits
Mendocino County Museum

Merced County
Atwater
Castle Air Force Base Museum
Yosemite Wildlife Museum
Los Banos
Ralph Milliken Museum

Modoc County
Alturas
Modoc National Wildlife Refuge
Modoc County Museum
Tule Lake
Lava Beds National Monument

Mono County
Bodie
Ghost Town
Bridgeport
Mono County Museum
Lee Vining
Mono Lake Tufa Reserve

Monterey County
Carmel
17-Mile Drive
Mission Carmel
Jolon
Mission San Antonio de Padua

Monterey County (cont.)
King City
Mission San Antonio
Monterey
Allen Knight Maritime Museum
Cannery Row
Colton Hall Museum and Jail
Dennis the Menace Playground
First Theater
Fisherman's Wharf
Fort Ord Museum
Monterey Bay Aquarium
Monterey Peninsula Museum of Art
Monterey State Historic Park
San Carlos Cathedral
Pacific Grove
Asilomar Conference Center
Pacific Grove Art Center
Pacific Grove Museum of Natural
History
Point Pinos Lighthouse
Salinas
First Mayor's House
Boronda Adobe History Center
Soledad
Mission Nuestra Senora de
La Soledad

Napa County
Calistoga
Baloon & Glider Rides
Old Faithful Geyser
Petrified Forest
Sharpsteen Museum
Sterling Vineyards
St. Helena
Napa County Museum
Silverado Museum
Winery Tours

Nevada County
Grass Valley
Empire Mine State Historic Park
Pelton Wheel Mining Museum

30.2.6,90

COUNTY MUSEUMS, GARDENS, ZOOS, AND PLACES OF GENERAL AND HISTORICAL INTEREST

Nevada County (cont.)
Nevada City
American Victorian Museum
Firehouse Museum
National Hotel
Malakof Diggins Park
Marsh House
Truckee
Emigrant Trail Museum

Orange County
Anaheim
Disneyland
Doll and Toy Museum
Museum of World Wars and Military
History
Buena Park
California Alligator Farm
Knott's Berry frarm
6 Flags Movieland Wax Museum
Whitaker-Jaynes House
Costa Mesa
Briggs Cunningham Auto Museum
Historical Society Museum
Diego Sepulveda Adobe
Corona del Mar
Sherman Gardens
Dana Point
Marine Institute
Fullerton
Muckenthaler Center
Museum of North Orange County
Garden Grove
Crystal Cathedral
Stanley House Museum
Irivine
Wild Rivers Amusement Park
Laguna Beach
Museum of Art
Laguna Hills
Lion Country Safari
La Habra
Children's Museum

Orange County (cont.)
Los Alamitos
Los Alamitos Museum
Los Alamitos Racetrack
Newport Beach
Newport Harbor Art Museum
Sherman Library & Gardens
Orange
Museum of Dentistry
Tucker Wildlife Sactuary
San Juan Capistrano
Mission San Juan Capistrano
O'Neil Museum
Santa Ana
Bowers Museum
Frank Tallman's Movieland of the
Air
Santa Ana Zoo
Tustin
Tustin Area Museum

Placer County
Auburn
Bernard Museum
Placer County Museum

Plumas County
Blairsden
Plumas Eureka State Park Museum
Quincy
Plumas County Museum
Portola
Portola Railroad Museum

Riverside County
Banning
Malki Museum
Beaumont
Dean Museum
Corona
Glen Ivy Hot Springs

30.2.7,90

COUNTY MUSEUMS, GARDENS, ZOOS, AND PLACES OF GENERAL AND HISTORICAL INTEREST

Riverside County (cont.)
Desert Hot Springs
Cabot's Old Indian Pueblo
& Museum
Palm Desert
The Living Desert Park
Palm Springs
Aerial Tramway
Moorten Botanic Garden
Oasis Waterpark
Palm Canyon
Palm Springs Desert Museum
Perris
Orange Empire Railroad Museum
Riverside
Castle Amusement Park
Evans' Early Home
Jurupea Mountains Cultural Center
March A.F. Base Museum
Riverside Art Center and Museum
Riverside Municipal Museum
Sherman Indian Museum
San Jacinto
San Jacinto Museum

Sacramento County
Folsom
The Old Powerhouse
Sacramento
Blue Diamond Almond Tour
California Railroad Museum
California State Fair and Exposition
California State Indian Museum
Crocker Art Gallery
Governor's Mansion
Old Sacramento State Historic Park
River City Queen
Sacramento City and County
Museum
Sacramento Science Center,
Planetarium and Junior Museum
Sacramento Zoo
State Capitol
Sutter's Fort
Towe Ford Museum
Waterworld U.S.A.

San Benito County
San Juan Bautista
Mission San Jan Bautista
San Juan Bautista State Historic Park
Paicines
Pinnacles National Monument
Natural History Museum

San Bernardino County
Barstow
Calico Ghost Town
Earlyman Digs
Mojave River Valley Museum
Solar One Solar Power Plant
Chino
Planes of Fame Museum
Yorba Slaughter Adobe
Lake Arrowhead
Santa's Village
Ontario
Museum of History & Art
Graber Olive House Tour
Rancho Cucamonga
John and Merced Rains Home
Redlands
Asistencia De San Gabriel
Lincoln Shrine
San Bernardino County Museum
Rialto
Rialto Historical Society Museum
San Bernardino
Rim of the World Highway
29 Palms
Historical Society Museum
Upland
Chaffey Communities Cultural
Center
Victorville
Roy Rogers and Dale Evans Museum
Yucaipa
Mousley Museum of Natural
Museum
Yucca Valley
Hi-Deserts Nature Museum

COUNTY MUSEUMS, GARDENS, ZOOS,
AND PLACES OF GENERAL AND HISTORICAL INTEREST

San Diego County

Carlsbad
Memorabilia
Chula Vista
Nature Center
Coronado
Hotel del Coronado
Encinitas
Quail Botanic Gardens
Escondido
Antique Gas & Steam Engine
Museum
Lawrence Welk Theater & Museum
Mount Palomar Observatory
San Diego Wild Animal Park
Julian
Eagle Mine
Pioneer Memorial Museum
La Jolla
Beach Caves
Children's Museum
Museum of Contemporary Art
Salk Institute
Scripps Aquarium-Museum
Underwater Ecological Reserve
Lakeside
Old La Mesa Depot Museum
National City
Museum of American Treasures
Oceanside
Landing Vehicle Museum
San Luis Rey Historical Mission
& Museum
Pala
Mission San Antonia De Pala
Pauma Valley
Sengme Oaks Water Park
Ramona
Woodward Museum
San Diego
Aero-Space Museum
Balboa Park
Cabrillo National Monument

San Diego County (cont.)

San Diego (cont.)
Derby Pendleton House
Firehouse Museum
Fleet Space Theater and Science
Center
Hall of Champions
Hall of Nations
Historical Museum of Old California
House of Pacific Relations
Maritime Museum
Mission San Diego
Model Railroad Museum
Museum of Art
Museum of Man
Museum of Photographic Arts
Museum of World Folk Art
Natural History Museum
Navy Ship Tours
Old Town State Historic Park
Paddle-wheel Showboat
San Diego Union Museum
San Diego Zoo
Seaport Village
Seaworld
Serra Museum
Timken Art Gallery
Villa Montezuma Museum
San Luis Rey
Mission San Luis Rey
San Pasqual
San Pasqual Battlefield
Santa Ysabel
Santa Ysabel Chapel

San Francisco County

San Francisco
Afro-American Historical Cultural
Society Museum
Alcatraz Island
Anchor Steam Beer Brewery
Asian Art Museum
California Academy of Sciences-
Natural History Museum

COUNTY MUSEUMS, GARDENS, ZOOS, AND PLACES OF GENERAL AND HISTORICAL INTEREST

San Francisco County (cont.)
San Francisco (cont.)
Cable Car Museum
California Palace of the Legion of
   Honor
California Pioneers Museum
The Cannery
Carosel Museum
Chevron World of Oil Museum
Chinatown
Chinese Historical Society Museum
Cliff House
Coit Tower
Dubley Herbarium
East-West Arts Gallery
The Exploratorium
Federal Reserve World of Economics
Fire Department Museum
Fisherman's Wharf
Fort Mason Center
Fort Point
Ghirardelli Square
Golden Gate National Recreation
   Area
Golden Gate Park
Guinness Museum of World Records
Haas-Lilienthal House
Hyde St. Pier
Japan Center
Japanese Tea Garden
Jeremiah O'Brian Liberty Ship
   Memorial
Jewish Community Museum
Josephine Randall Junior Museum
The Mexican Museum
M.H. de Young Museum
Mission Dolores de San Francisco
Morrison Planetarium
Musee Mechanique
Museo Italo Americano
Museum of Modern Art
Museum of Money
Museum of Photography

San Francisco County (cont.)
San Francisco (cont.)
Museum of Russian Culture
National Maritime Museum
Navy/Marine Corps Museum
North Beach Museum
Octagon House
The Old Mint Museum
Pacific Heritage Museum
Palace of Fine Arts
Pier 39
Presidio Army Museum
Ripley's Believe It or Not Museum
San Francisco Art Institute Gallery
San Francisco Zoo
Sherlock Holmes Collection
Ship Balclutha
Society of California Pioneers
   Museum
Steinhart Aquarium
Strybing Arboretum
Tattoo Art Museum
Treasure Island Museum
U.S.S. Pampanito - Submarine Tour
Wax Museum
Wells Fargo Museum
Whittier Mansion

San Joaquin County
Lodi
San Joaquin County Historical
   Museum
Manteca
Oakwood Water Theme Park
Stockton
Haggin Museum

San Luis Obispo County
Atascadero
Historical Society Museum
Treasure of El Camino Real
Morro Bay
State Park Museum of Natural
   History

COUNTY MUSEUMS, GARDENS, ZOOS,
AND PLACES OF GENERAL AND HISTORICAL INTEREST

San Luis Obispo County (cont.)
Paso Robles
  Moe's Doll Museum
San Luis Obispo
  Mission San Luis Obispo
  San Luis Obispo County Historical
    Museum
  Shakespere Press Museum
San Miguel
  Mission San Miguel
  Rios-Caledonia Adobe
San Simeon
  Hearst San Simeon State Historical
    Monument

San Mateo County
Belmont
  Ralston Hall
Menlo Park
  Allied Arts Guild
  Lane Publishing Tour
Pacifica
  Sanchez Adobe
Redwood City
  Lathrop House
San Bruno
  Federal Archives
San Mateo
  County Historical Museum
  Coyote Point Museum
Stanford
  Leland Stanford Jr. Museum
  Hoover Institution
Woodside
  Filoli Mansion
  Woodside Store

Santa Barbara County
Carpinteria
  Abbey Cactus and Succulent Nursery
  Carpinteria Valley Historical
    Museum
Goleta
  Stow House

Santa Barbara County (cont.)
Lompoc
  Mission La Purissima
  Lompoc Museum
  Fabing-McKay-Spanne House
Santa Barbara
  Botanic Garden
  Fernald House
  Historical Society Museum
  Mission Santa Barbara
  Museum of Art
  Museum of Natural History
  Old Spanish Days Carriage Museum
  Santa Barbara Zoo
  Stearn's Wharf
  Trussel Winchester Adobe
Santa Maria
  Santa Maria Historical Museum
Santa Ynez
  Santa Ynez Valley Historical
    Museum
Solvang
  Danish Architecture
  Mission Santa Ines

Santa Clara County
Cupertino
  De Anza College Planetarium
Gilroy
  Historical Museum
Los Altos Hills
  Foothill College Electronics
    Museum
Los Gatos
  Los Gatos Museum
  Youth Science-Discovery Center
Milpitas
  Splash Down Waterslide
Mountain View
  NASA-AMES Research Center
Palo Alto
  Barbie Doll Hall of Fame
  Palo Alto Cultural Center and Art
    Gallery
  Palo Alto Junior Museum

COUNTY MUSEUMS, GARDENS, ZOOS, AND PLACES OF GENERAL AND HISTORICAL INTEREST	
Santa Clara County (cont.)	**Shasta County (cont.)**
San Jose	**Fall River Mills**
Happy Hollow Park and Baby Zoo	Fort Crook Historical Museum
Japanese Friendship Garden	**Mount Shasta**
Lick Observatory	California Fish Hatchery
Municipal Rose Garden	**Redding**
Museum of Quilts & Textiles	Coleman Fish Hatchery
Raging Waters	Lake Shasta Caverns
Rosicrucian Egyptian Museum	Redding Museum and Art Center
Rosicrucian Science Museum	Shasta Dam
San Jose Historical Museum	Shasta Natural Science Museum
San Jose Museum of art	Waterworks Park
Winchester Mystery House	**Sierra County**
Youth Science Institute	**Downieville**
Santa Clara	Sierra County Museum
De Saisset Art Gallery	**Sierra City**
Great America	Kentucky Mine & Museum
Mission Santa Clara de Asis	**Siskiyou County**
Triton Museum of Art	**Doris**
Saratoga	Herman's House of Guns
Hakone Gardens	**Fort Jones**
Montalvo Center for the Arts	Fort Jones Museum
Sunnyvale	**Tulelake**
Sunnyvale Historical Museum	Lava Beds National Monument Museum
Santa Cruz County	**Yreka**
Big Basin	Blue Goose Railroad
Big Basin State Park	Siskiyou County Museum
Natural History Museum	**Solano County**
Felton	**Benicia**
Big Trees Narrow Gauge Railroad	Benicia Capitol State Historic Park
Santa Cruz	California Doll and Toy Museum
The Boardwalk	**Fairfield**
Long Marine Lab	Travis Air Museum
Mission Santa Cruz	**Suisun City**
Santa Cruz Art League Gallery	Western Railway Museum
Santa Cruz Big Trees & Pacific Railway	**Vacaville**
Santa Cruz County Historical Museum	Pena Adobe
	Vacaville Museum
Santa Cruz City Museum	Wooz Maze
Shasta County	**Vallejo**
Anderson	Naval Museum
Coleman Fish Hatchery	Marine World

30.2.12,90

COUNTY MUSEUMS, GARDENS, ZOOS, AND PLACES OF GENERAL AND HISTORICAL INTEREST	
Sonoma County	**Trinity County (cont.)**
Fort Ross	**Weaverville**
Fort Ross	Jackson Museum
Glen Ellen	Joss House State Historical Park
Jack London State Historic Park	**Tulare County**
Petaluma	**Porterville**
Petaluma Adobe	Porterville Museum
Santa Rosa	Zalud House
Coding Museum of Natural History	**Tulare**
Luther Burbank Memorial Garden	Reptile World
Sonoma County Museum	**Visalia**
Xcelsior Brewery	Tulare County Museum
Sonoma	**Tuolumne County**
Mission San Francisco Solano	**Columbia**
Sonoma Depot Museum	State Historic Park
Sonoma State Historic Park	**Jamestown**
Train Town	Railtown 1897 State Historic Park
Sonoma Valley Historical Society Museum	**Sonora**
	Tuolumne County Museum
Stanislaus County	**Vallecito**
Modesto	Moaning Cavern
Almond Growers Exchange Tour	**Ventura County**
McHenry Mansion	**Fillmore**
McHenry Museum of Art and History	Fillmore Historical Museum
Miller Horse & Buggy Ranch	**Ojai**
Orchard Waterslide	Historical Society Museum
Valley Museum of Natural History	**Oxnard**
Oakdale	Carnegie Art Museum
Hershey Tour	**Port Hueneme**
Sutter County	Civil Engineer Corps/Seabee Museum
Yuba City	Port Hueneme City Museum
Community Memorial Museum	**Santa Paula**
Tehama County	California Oil Museum
Red Bluff	**Simi Valley**
Kelly-Griggs House Museum	Strathearn Historical Park Museum
Salmon Ladder Viewing Area	**Thousand Oaks**
Tehama	Conejo Valley Art Museum
Tehama County Museum	Stagecoach Inn Museum
Trinity County	**Ventura**
Trinity Center	A.J. Comstock Fire Museum
Scott Museum of Trinity Center	Albinger Archaeological Museum

COUNTY MUSEUMS, GARDENS, ZOOS, AND PLACES OF GENERAL AND HISTORICAL INTEREST

Ventura County (cont.)	Yuba County
Ventura (cont.)	**Marysville**
Mission San Buenaventura	Bok Kai Chinese Temple
Olivas Adobe	Mary Aaron Memorial Museum
Ortega Adobe	**Yuba City**
Ventura County Historical Museum	Sutter Buttes
	Yolo County
	Davis
	University Arboretum

30.2.14,90 Sources: California Institute of Public Affairs, *California Museum Directory* (used by permission); California Historic Society; California Department of Parks and Recreation; and Pacific Data Resources.

* The California Museum Directory is the best source of information in this general area and should be consulted for detailed information on museum collections, addresses and hours.
* Many universities and colleges have specialized museums and centers on campus which are listed in the California Museum Directory.

CALIFORNIA SYMBOLS, SLOGANS AND SONGS

Nickname	The Golden State
Motto	Eureka (I Have Found It)
Colors	Blue & Gold
Animal	California Grizzly Bear
Bird	California Valley Quail
Fish	California Golden Trout
Flower	Golden Poppy
Fossil	Saber Toothed Cat
Gem	Benitoite
Insect	California Dog-Face Butterfly
Marine-Mammal	California Gray Whale
Mineral	Native Gold
Poet-Laureate	Charles Garrigus*
Reptile	California Desert Tortoise
Song	*I Love You, California*
Stone	Serpentine
Theatre	Pasadena Community Playhouse
Tree	California Redwood

* A former state legislator.

30.3,90 Source: The *California Blue Book* and Pacific Data Resources.

SECTION 30 NOTE

In response to Gertrude Stein's famous line about the vacuum in Oakland, a sculpture titled "There" has been installed near City Hall.

30.4,90

CALIFORNIA DANCE COMPANIES	
Name	**City**
Aman Folk Ensemble	Los Angeles
Avaz	Los Angeles
Big Flood	Los Angeles
Contraband	San Francisco
Dancers' Workshop	Mill Valley
Della Davidson & the Moving Company	San Francisco
Jazz Tap Ensemble	Los Angeles
Karpatok Hungarian Folk Ensemble	Calabasas
Lewitsky Dance Company	Los Angeles
Linda Vega's Danzas de Espana	Los Angeles
Lines Dance Company	San Francisco
L.A. Contemporary Dance Theatre	Los Angeles
Loretta Livingston & Dancers	Los Angeles
LTD/Unlimited	Los Angeles
Margaret Jenkins Dance Company	San Francisco
Mary Jane Eisenberg...Shale	Los Angeles
Lola Montez and Her Spanish Dancers	Burbank
Gloria Newman Dance Theatre	Orange
O.D.C.	San Francisco
Rudy Perez Performance Ensemble	Los Angeles
Sarah Elgart and Company	Los Angeles
Fred Strickler	Los Angeles
Tandy Beal and Company	Santa Cruz
Three's Company	San Diego

30.5,90 Source: Various dance connoisseurs.

PROFESSIONAL BALLET COMPANIES
Los Angeles Ballet
Joffrey Balley
Oakland Ballet
San Francisco Ballet

30.6,90 Source: Pacific Data Resources, unpublished data.

MUSIC - PROMINENT CALIFORNIANS	
Kurt H. Adler	Otto Klemperer
Dave Brubeck	Josef Krips
Alfred Hertz	Pierre Monteux
Al Jolson	Gerry Mulligan
Stan Kenton	

30.7,90 Source: Pacific Data Resources.

MAJOR CALIFORNIA THEATRE COMPANIES

Company/Theatre	City
American Conservatory Theatre	San Francisco
Berkeley Repertory Theatre	Berkeley
Berkeley Shakespeare Festival	Berkeley
California Theatre Center	Sunnyvale
El Teatro Campesino	San Juan Bautista
La Jolla Playhouse	La Jolla
Los Angeles Theatre Center	Los Angeles
Magic Theatre	San Francisco
Mark Taper Forum	Los Angeles
Old Globe	San Diego
Pacific Conservatory of the Performing Arts	Santa Maria
San Diego Repertory Theatre	San Diego
San Jose Repertory	San Jose
South Coast Repertory Company	Costa Mesa

30.8,90 Source: Pacific Data Resources.

CALIFORNIA OPERA COMPANIES

Company	City
Major Companies	
Los Angeles Opera	Los Angeles
San Francisco Opera Association	San Francisco
San Diego Opera Association	San Diego
Correspondent Companies*	
California Coast/Scholar Opera	Palo Alto
Desert Opera	Palmdale
Fullerton Civic Light Opera	Fullerton
Hidden Valley Opera	Carmel
Lamplighters	San Francisco
Long Beach Civic Light Opera	Long Beach
Long Beach Opera	Long Beach
Los Angeles Civic Light Opera	Los Angeles
Marin Opera Company	San Rafael
Oakland Opera	Oakland
Opera Pacific	Orange County
Opera San Jose	San Jose
Pocket Opera	San Francisco
Riverside Opera Association	Riverside
Sacramento Opera	Sacramento
San Jose Civic Light Opera	San Jose
San Jose Symphony/Opera	San Jose
West Bay Opera	Palo Alto
West Coast Opera Company	San Gabriel

* Companies with short seasons or relatively small budgets. See
Opera Guide for further information on California opera.
30.9,90 Source: Assorted opera connoisseurs.

SELECTED CALIFORNIA ORCHESTRAS

Orchesta	City
American Youth Orchestra	Los Angeles
Bakersfield Symphony Orchestra	Bakersfield
Bay Area Women's Philharmonic	San Francisco
Berkeley Symphony	Berkeley
Beverly Hills Symphony	Beverly Hills
Brentwood-Westwood Symphony Orchestra	Los Angeles
California Chamber Symphony	Los Angeles
Camellia Symphony	Sacramento
Chamber Orchestra of San Francisco	San Francisco
Claremont Symphony	Claremont
Diablo Symphony Orchestra	Walnut Creek
Fresno Philharmonic	Fresno
Garden Grove Symphony	Garden Grove
Glendale Chamber Orchestra	Glendale
Glendale Symphony Orchestra	Glendale
Inglewood Philharmonic Orchestra	Inglewood
Inland Empire Symphony	San Bernardino
Irvine Symphony	Irvine
Livermore-Amador Symphony	Livermore
Long Beach Symphony	Long Beach
Los Angeles Baroque Orchestra	Venice
Los Angeles Chamber Orchestra	Los Angeles
Los Angeles Mozart Orchestra	Sunland
Los Angeles Philharmonic Orchestra	Los Angeles
Los Angeles Pops Orchestra	Santa Monica
Marin Symphony Orchestra	San Rafael
Merced Symphony	Merced
Modesto Symphony	Modesto
Monterey County Symphony Orchestra	Carmel
Music Academy of the West Orchestra	Santa Barbara
Napa Valley Symphony Orchestra	Napa
New American Orchestra	Culver City
North Coast Symphony	Solana Beach
Orange County Pacific Symphony	Santa Ana
Paradise Symphony Orchestra	Paradise
Pasadena Symphony Orchestra	Pasadena
Peninsula Symphony Orchestra	Cupertino
Riverside Symphony	Riverside
Sacramento Symphony Orchestra	Sacramento
San Diego Chamber Orchestra	Rancho Santa Fe
San Diego Symphony Orchestra	San Diego
San Francisco Chamber Orchestra	San Francisco
San Francisco Symphony Orchestra	San Francisco
San Jose Symphony Orchestra	San Jose
Santa Barbara Symphony Orchestra	Santa Barbara
Santa Cruz Couty Symphony Orchestra	Santa Cruz
Santa Rosa Symphony Orchestra	Santa Rosa
Stockton Symphony	Stockton
Ventura County Symphony	Oxnard

30.10,90 Source: Association of California Symphony Orchestras.

CALIFORNIA CHOIRS AND CHORAL GROUPS

Name	City
Chanticleer	San Francisco
I Cantori	Los Angeles
Los Angeles Gay Men's Chorus	Los Angeles
Los Angles Jazz Choir	Woodland Hills
Los Angeles Master Chorale	Los Angeles
Masterworks Chorale	San Mateo
Orange County Master Chorale	Costa Mesa
Pacific Master Chorale	Santa Ana
Redlands Chorale	Redlands
Riverside Master Chorale	Riverside
Roger Wagner Chorale	Los Angeles
Sacramento Symphony Chorus	Sacramento
San Diego Chorale	San Diego
San Francisco Boys' Chorus	San Francisco
San Francisco Gay Men's Chorus	San Francisco
San Francisco Girls' Chorus	San Francisco
San Francisco Symphony Chorus	San Francisco
Santa Clara Chorale	San Jose
Schola Cantorum	Palo Alto
Valley Master Chorale	San Fernando Valley
Ventura Master Chorale	Ventura

30.11,90 Source: Assorted connoisseurs, 1989.

CULTURE AS A BUSINESS, OVERVIEW
1981-1986

Category	Year	Number of Establishments	Number of Employees	Annual Payroll (in millions)
Theatrical Producers	1981	660	9,929	191
and Services	1984	991	12,690	267
	1986	953	15,662	321
Bands, Orchestras,	1981	681	7,702	166
Actors, Entertainers	1984	1,065	9,667	236
and Groups	1986	1,010	9,746	282

30.12,90 Source: U.S. Bureau of the Census, *County Business Patterns, California*, 1981-86.

DANCE - PROMINENT CALIFORNIANS

Fred Astaire	Gene Kelly
Busby Berkeley	Lola Montez
Isadora Duncan	Ginger Rogers

30.13,90 Source: Pacific Data Resources.

CALIFORNIA MOTION PICTURE INDUSTRY OVERVIEW 1981-1986				
Activity	Year	Number of Establishments	Number of Employees	Annual Payroll (in millions)
Production and	1981	2,322	56,074	1,368
Allied Services	1984	3,688	62,317	1,917
	1986	4,696	97,185	2,447
Distribution and	1981	259	6,471	201
Allied Services	1984	333	6,807	277
	1986	293	6,108	301
Theaters Indoor	1981	758	11,414	75
	1984	830	11,265	84
	1986	744	12,863	90
Outdoor	1981	144	3,009	17
	1984	142	2,155	15
	1986	119	1,840	13
Total Theatres	1981	923	14,616	93
	1984	979	13,475	99
	1986	921	14,842	104

30.14,90 Source: U.S. Bureau of the Census, *County Business Patterns, Cal.*, 1981-86.

CALIFORNIA MOTION PICTURE THEATER SCREENS				
	Number of Screens*			
Type of Theater	1982	1984	1986	1988
Indoor	1,633	1,848	1,976	2,268
Drive-In	266	249	220	184
Total	**1,899**	**2,097**	**2,196**	**2,452**

* Some theaters have 2 or more screens. California has 10% of the indoor screens and 12% of the Drive-in screens in the nation.

30.15,90 Source: Motion Picture Asso. of America, unpublished data, 1989.

ARTISTS - PROMINENT CALIFORNIANS	
Ansel Adams - Photographer	Arnold Genthe - Photographer
Robert Aitken - Sculptor	Andrew Jackson Grayson - Painter
Robert Arneson - Sculptor	Dorothea Lange - Photographer
Albert Bierstadt - Painter	David Hockney - Painter
Elmer Bischoff - Painter	Robert Motherwell - Painter
Carl Borg - Photographer, Painter	Edward Moybridge - Photographer
Samual Brooks - Painter	Isanu Noguchi - Sculptor
Beniamino Bufano - Sculptor	Roger Sturtevant - Photographer
Alexander Calder - Sculptor	Edward Dewitt Taylor - Printer
Imogen Cunningham - Photographer	Edward Weston - Photographer

30.16,90 Source: Pacific Data Resources.

MAJOR CALIFORNIA PRIVATE ART COLLECTIONS		
Name	City	Type of Art
Margeret & Harry Anderson	San Francisco	Modern & Contemporary Art
David Bermant	Santa Barbara	Technological Art
Donald Bren	Newport Beach	20th Century U.S. Art
Edye Eli Broad	Los Angeles	Modern & Contemporary Art
Phoebe Cowles	San Francisco	European Still Lifes
Douglas Schoolfield Cramer	Bel Air	Contemporary Art
Doris & Peter Drucker	Claremont	Japanese Paintings
Jo Ann & Julian Ganz	Los Angeles	19th Century U.S. Art
David Giffen	Los Angeles	Modern Art
Dennis Hopper	Venice	Contemporary Art
Madonna	Los Angeles	Modern Paintings & Photographs
Steve Martin	Los Angeles	Modern Paintings
Jack Nicholson	Los Angeles	U.S. & European Art, Antiquities
Michael Ovitz	Los Angeles	Modern, Contemporary, African Art
Etsuko & Joe Price	Newport Beach	Japanese Art
Pia Zadora & Meshulam Riklis	Beverly Hills	Contemporary Art & Modern Masters
Joel Silver	Hollywood	Frank Lloyd Wright Art, Pottery
Steven Spielberg	Beverly Hills	Disney animation, Norman Rockwell Paintings
Barbara Streisand	Los Angeles	Arts & Crafts, and Frank Lloyd Wright Furniture
Fredrick Weisman	Los Angeles	Modern & Contemporary Art.
Marcia Weisman	Los Angeles	Modern & Contemporary Art
Abe Winter	Los Angeles	Judaica

30.17,90 Source: *Art and Antiques Magazine, 1989*.

SELECTED MAJOR CALIFORNIA ROCK BANDS AND PERFORMERS		
Bangles	Guns N Roses	Tom Petty
The Beach Boys	Van Halen	Pointer Sisters
Camper Van Beethoven	Herbie Hancock	Poisen
Blasters	Don Henley	Lionel Richie
Jackson Browne	Chris Isaak	Stan Ridgeway
The Call	Michael Jackson	Todd Rundgren
Club Nouveau	Huey Lewis and The News	Santana
Concrete Blond	Los Lobos	Boz Scaggs
Dynatones	Bobby McFerrin	Sea Hags
Sheila E.	Metallica	Starship
Faith No More	Mister Mister	The Tide
Fleetwood Mac	Joni Mitchell	Toto
John Fogerty	Eddie Money	Vain
Glenn Frey	Motley Crue	Stevie Wonder
Grateful Dead	NWA	Neil Young

31.18,90 Source: Assorted rock connaiseurs.

FRATERNAL AND SERVICE CLUBS IN CALIFORNIA				
Group or Club	Lodges, Posts, or Chapters	% of U.S. Chapters	Members	% of U.S. Members
American Legion	640	5%	121,000	5%
Eagles	115	6%	25,000	2%
Elks	190	8%	163,245	11%
Foresters	35	12%	206,988	26%
Kiwanis	629	7%	27,000	9%
Knights of Columbus	402	4%	49,800	3%
Lions	920	NA	32,150	6%
Masons	528	NA	156,000	NA
Moose	218	9%	96,000	7%
Native Sons of Golden West	98	-	12,825	-
Native Daughters of Golden West	157	-	11,500	-
Odd Fellows	241	5%	9,366	4%
Optimists	280	9%	10,500	9%
Rebeccas*	276	5%	19,640	7%
Rotary	628	9%	38,900	10%

* Associated with the Odd Fellows

30.19,90 Source: Club representatives and headquarters.

ASSORTED CALIFORNIA CELEBRITIES	
Joan Baez - Singer	Captain Jack - Indian
Allen Bakke - Civil Rights Plaintiff	Winnie Ruth Judd - Felon
Ralph Sonny Barger - Hell's Angel	Charles Manson - Felon
David Brower - Environmentalist	James Melton - Car Collector
Eldridge Cleaver - Political Radical	Helena Modjeska - Actress
Bing Crosby - Singer	John Muir - Naturalist
James Dean - Actor	Joaquin Murietta - Bandit
Angela Davis - Political Radical	Michael Murphy - Esalen Founder
Chuck Dederich - Synanon Founder	Huey Newton - Political Radical
Werner Erhard - EST Founder	Joshua Norton - Emperor
Bobby Fisher - Chess World Champion	Will Rodgers - Humorist
Rube Goldberg - Cartoonist	Mario Savio - Political Radical
Burnette Haskell - Founded the	Charles Schulz - Cartoonist
Kaweah Colony	Bobby Seale - Black Panther
Bob Hope - Actor	Robert Stroud - (Birdman of Alcatraz)
Ishi - Indian	

30.20,90 Source: Pacific Data Resources.

SECTION 30 NOTE
The Dorland Art Colony sits on 300 acres of mountainous terrain near Temucula in western Riverside County.

30.21,90

WRITERS/HISTORIANS - PROMINENT CALIFORNIANS

Maya Angelou	Oscar Lewis
Gertrude Antherton	Sinclair Lewis
Mary Austin	Jack London
Hubert Howe Bancroft - Historian	Charles Lummis - Historian
Ambrose Bierce	Thomas Mann
Ray Bradbury	Edwin Markham
Richard Brautigan	Carey McWilliams
Charles Bukowski	Kenneth Millar
Edgar Rice Burroughs	Henry Miller
James Cain	Scott Momaday
Raymond Chandler	John Muir
Richard Henry Dana - Historical Account	Frank Norris
William Heath Davis - Historian	Kathleen Norris
Joan Didion	Clifford Odets
John Gregory Dunne	Eugene O'Neill
John Fante	Harris Newmark - Historian
F. Scott Fitzgerald	Kenneth Rexroth
Earle Stanley Gardner	Richard Rodriguez
Theodor Seuss Geisel - Dr. Suess	Josiah Royce
Henry George	William Saroyan
Herb Gold	Bud Schulberg
Zane Grey	Sam Shepard
Dashiell Hammett	Henryk Sienkiewitz
Bret Harte	Upton Sinclair
Robert Heinlein	Lincoln Steffens
Eric Hoeffer	John Steinbeck
Theodore Hittell - Historian	George Stewart
Sidney Howard	Robert Louis Stevenson
L. Ron Hubbard	Mark Twain
Aldous Huxley	Dalton Trumbo
Clarence King	Alice Walker
Christopher Isherwood	Franklin Walker
Helen Hunt Jackson	Evelyn Waugh
Maxine Hong Kingston	Nathanael West
Jack Kerouac	Yvor Winters
Louis L'Amour	Dr. Felix Wierzbicki
Janet Lewis	Stewart Edward White

30.22,90 Source: Pacific Data Resources.

SECTION 30 NOTE

Since 1987 California has had the distinction of having the only state self-esteem panel in the nation. Don't you feel better already?

30.23,90

CALIFORNIA NOBEL PRIZE WINNERS* (part 1) 1919-1988		
Year	Laureate	Institution
Physics		
1923	Robert A. Millikan	California Institute of Technology
1936	Carl D. Anderson	California Institute of Technology
1939	Ernest O. Lawrence	University of California, Berkeley
1952	Felix Bloch	Stanford University
1955	Willis E. Lamb	Stanford University
1956	William Shockley	Stanford Universtiy
1959	Emilio G. Segrê	University of California, Berkeley
1959	Owen Chamberlain	University of California, Berkeley
1960	Donald A. Glaser	University of California, Berkeley
1961	Robert Hofstadter	Stanford University
1963	Maria Goeppert-Mayer	University of California, San Diego
1964	Charles Townes	University of California, Berkeley
1965	Richard P. Feynman	California Institute of Technology
1965	Julian Schwinger	Universiy of California, Los Angeles
1968	Luis W. Alvarez	University of California, Berkeley
1969	Murray Gell-Mann	California Institute of Technology
1970	Hannes Al Fuen	University of California, San Diego
1972	Robert Schrieffer	University of California, Santa Barbara
1976	Burton Richter	Stanford Linear Accelerator Center
1981	Arthur Schawlow	Stanford University
1983	William A. Fowler	California Institute of Technology
1988	Melvin Schwartz	Digital Pathways Corp.
Chemistry		
1945	John Northrop	University of California, Berkeley
1946	Wendell Stanley	University of California, Berkeley
1949	William F. Giauque	University of California, Berkeley
1951	Edwin M. McMillan	University of California, Berkeley
1951	Glenn T. Seaborg	University of California, Berkeley
1954	Linus C. Pauling	California Institute of Technology
1960	Willard F. Libby	University of California, Los Angeles
1961	Melvin Calvin	University of California, Berkeley
1962	Francis Crick	University of California, San Diego
1968	Robert Holley	University of California, San Diego
1974	Paul J. Flory	Stanford University
1980	Paul Berg	Stanford University
1983	Henry Taube	Stanford University
1986	Yuan T. Lee	University of California, Lawrence Berkeley Laboratory
1987	Donald J. Cram	University of California, Los Angeles

* Some individuals moved to California after winning the Nobel prize.
30.24.1,90 Source: Nobel Foundation Directory, 1982, and Pacific Data Resources.

CALIFORNIA NOBEL PRIZE WINNERS* (part 2) 1919-1988		
Year	Laureate	Institution
Physiology or Medicine		
1933	Thomas H. Morgan	California Institute of Technology
1958	George W. Beadle	California Institute of Technology
1959	Arthur Kornberg	Stanford University
1968	Robert W. Holley	The Salk Institute
1969	Max Delbruck	California Institute of Technology
1975	Renato Dulbecco	University of California, San Diego
1977	Roger Guillemin	The Salk Institute
1981	Roger Sperry	California Institute of Technology
Literature		
1962	John Steinbeck	
1980	Czeslaw Milosz	University of California, Berkeley
Peace		
1963	Linus C. Pauling	California Institute of Technology
Economics		
1972	Kenneth J. Arrow	Stanford University
1976	Milton Friedman	Hoover Institution
1983	Gerard Debreu	University of California, Berkeley

* Some individuals moved to California after winning the Nobel prize.
30.24.2,90 Source: Nobel Foundation Directory, 1982, and Pacific Data Resources.

POETS - PROMINENT CALIFORNIANS	
Leonard Bacon	Edwin Markham
James Broughton	Michael McClure
Ina Coolbrith	Josephine Miles
Henri Coulette	Joaquin Miller
Robert Creeley	Scott Momaday
Diane Diprima	Tillie Olsen
Robert Duncan	George Oppen
William Everson	Michael Palmer
Lawrence Ferlinghetti	Robert Pinsky
Kathleen Fraser	Kenneth Rexroth
Nora French	Edward Sill
Allen Ginsberg	Gary Snyder
Robert Hass	George Sterling
Robinson Jeffers	Charles Stoddard
Carolyn Kaiser	Len Welch
Janet Lewis	Philip Whelen

30.25,90 Source: Pacific Data Resources.

SECTION 30 NOTE

The first president to visit California was U. S. Grant in 1879. Grant had been stationed in the state in 1853 as an army officer at Fort Humboldt.
30.26,90

Religion

Unlike the early American colonies in New England, which were settled by Puritan divines and governed for decades with moral rigor, California was first settled heavily during the Gold Rush by hard-drinking, rowdy miners; camp followers; and aggressive land speculators and business entrepreneurs. If the white church steeple symbolized early New England, the mining camp or San Francisco saloon as easily characterized California after the Gold Rush.

Father Serra and the other Spanish missionaries who preceded the miners established in California the nucleus of city (pueblo) government with twenty-one missions from San Diego to Sonoma. Although these priests left behind a remarkable architectural record of the Catholic church's early dominance, the effects of Spanish Catholicism in California were neither as deep nor as pervasive as those of Puritanism in New England. And the influence of the mission priests was dissipated when, a few years before California joined the United States, the Mexican government confiscated church lands and secularized most of the missions.

Religion, however, is far from irrelevant to the lives of many Californians. Most inhabitants of the state indicate that they have a religious preference; only 18 percent are nonbelievers. Although the Catholic church is by far the largest single denomination in California (25 percent of the population), more people, 45 percent, consider themselves Protestants than adherents of any other broad persuasion. With the recent influx of immigrants from Asia and the Middle East, a variety of Islamic, Hindu, and Buddhist mosques and temples have appeared throughout the state, adding to what was already a highly diverse ecumenical mix.

With the issues of abortion, government funding for church-run childcare, and homosexual rights entering, even dominating, the political arena, the 1990s will probably see more lobbying by churches and church-related groups than in the past. Because religious groups have generally taken a low profile politically during the past few decades, their potential to influence legislation has not been fully tested.

RELIGIOUS DENOMINATIONS IN CALIFORNIA			
Denomination	Number of Churches	Adherents	% of Total State Adherents
Advent Christian Church	12	1,063*	-
African Methodist Episcopal Zion*	27	14,484	0.2
American Baptist Association	129	14,241	0.2
American Baptist USA	492	194,594*	2.4
American Lutheran Church	254	122,795	1.5
Apostolic Christian (Naz)	7	279*	-
Apostolic Lutheran	2	148*	-
Assemblies of God	864	189,577	2.5
Baptist General Conference	100	40,088*	0.5
Baptist Mission Assn.	18	2,733*	-
Berean Fundamental Church	3	221*	-
Brethren Church (Ashland)	3	312*	-
Brethren In Christ	13	1,105	-
Catholic	1,250	4,759,250	58.3
Christ Catholic Church	2	42	-
Christian & Missionary Alliance	87	14,991	0.2
Christian Brethren	58	6,100	0.1
Christian Church (Disciples)	185	50,177	0.6
Christian Churches & Churches in Christ	223	52,761*	0.6
Christian Methodist Episcopal	53	44,141*	0.5
Christian Reformed Church	45	15,097	0.2
Church of God (Abrahamic)	3	141*	-
Church of God (Anderson)	117	34,896	0.4
Church of God (Cleveland)	162	11,776*	0.1
Church of God (7th day)	13	570*	-
Church of God in Christ (Mennon)	3	685	-
Church of Jesus Christ (Bickerton)	7	338	-
Latter Day Saints	884	405,441	5.0
Church of Brethren	32	6,490*	0.1
Church of Lutheran Brethren	2	265	-
Church of the Lutheran Confession	2	187	-
Church of the Nazarene	372	82,071	1.0
Churches of Christ	676	88,415	1.1
Congregational Christian	33	16,589*	0.2
Conservative Baptist Assn.	162	52,325*	0.6
Conservative Congregational	9	6,474*	0.1
Cumberland Presbyterian	3	1,027	-
Episcopal	426	184,330	2.3
Estonian	2	780	-
Evangelical Covenant	64	14,593*	0.2
Evangelical Free Church	88	13,977*	0.2

* Total Adherents estimated from known number of communicant, confirmed full members.
  31.1.1,90 Source: Glenmary Research Center, *Churches and Church Membership in the U.S.*, 1980.

RELIGIOUS DENOMINATIONS IN CALIFORNIA			
Denomination	Number of Churches	Adherents	% of Total State Adherents
Evangelical Lutheran Association	2	399	-
Evangelical Lutheran Synod	4	285	-
Evangelical Mennonite Brethren	1	40	-
Evangelical Methodist	10	684*	-
Fire Baptized Holiness	4	48	-
Free Methodist	77	18,012	0.2
Friends-USA	65	9,910*	0.1
Gen. Church of the New Jerusalem	3	113*	-
Gen. Conf. of Mennonite Brethren	36	6,848*	0.1
Swedenborgian	6	571*	-
Grace Brethren	47	11,850*	0.1
International Foursquare Gospel	274	78,175*	1.0
Conservative Judaism	62	16,856*	0.2
Reform Judaism	68	59,683*	0.7
Latvian Evangelical Lutheran	5	1,214	-
Lutheran Church in America	208	82,637	1.0
Lutheran-Missouri Synod	376	148,292	1.8
Mennonite Church	9	806*	-
Mennonite General Conference	6	1,243	-
Metropolitan Community	29	7,180	0.1
Missionary Church	31	3,468	-
Moravian-North Province	4	912	-
North American Baptist Conference	13	7,310*	0.1
Open Bible Standard	33	8,470	0.1
Orthodox Presbyterian	23	2,201*	-
Pentecostal Holiness	48	2,496*	-
Presbyterian Church in America	7	338	-
Protestant Reformed	1	148	-
Reformed Church in America	36	30,778	0.4
Reformed Presbyterian-Evangelical	8	767	-
Reformed Presbyterian of N. America	4	236	-
Romanian Orthodox Church	1	1,024*	-
Salvation Army	66	21,105	0.3
Scientology	11	NA	NA
Seventh Day Adventist	429	148,561*	1.8
Seventh Day Baptist Gen. Conf.	4	552*	-
Southern Baptist Convention	937	392,451*	4.8
Syrian Orthodox	1	6,025*	0.1
Unitarian-Universalist	72	13,575*	0.2
United Churches of Christ	243	67,979*	0.8
United Methodist	714	290,720*	3.6
United Presbyterian	526	261,279*	3.2
Wisconsin Evangelical Lutheran Synod	41	7,096	0.1

* Total Adherents estimated from known number of communicant, confirmed full members.
31.1.2,90 Source: Glenmary Research Center, *Churches and Church Membership in the U.S.*, 1980.

RELIGION BY COUNTY				
County and Three Largest Churches	Number of Churches	Number of Adherents	Percent of Total Adherents	Percent of Total Population
Alameda	468	393,520	-	35.6
Catholic	55	249,745	63.5	22.6
LD Saints	34	17,339	4.4	1.6
So Bapt Conv	45	17,113	4.3	1.5
Alpine	2	70	-	6.4
Chr Chs & Chs Cr	1	59	84.3	5.4
Assemb of God	1	11	15.7	1.0
Amador	23	5,531	-	28.6
Catholic	6	3,150	57.0	16.3
LD Saints	2	608	11.0	3.1
Un Methodist	3	535	9.7	2.8
Butte	110	36,734	-	25.5
Catholic	8	9,773	26.6	6.8
LD Saints	12	5,444	15.1	3.9
So Bapt Conv	8	2,532	6.9	1.8
Calaveras	30	5,934	-	38.7
Catholic	6	2,680	45.2	12.9
LD Saints	2	893	15.0	4.3
Ch God (Ander)	1	675	11.4	3.3
Colusa	25	4,253	-	32.5
Catholic	7	1,850	44.5	14.5
Un Methodist	5	851	20.5	6.7
Assemb of God	4	286	6.9	2.2
Contra Costa	321	243,841	-	37.1
Catholic	35	140,354	57.6	21.4
LD Saints	27	15,058	6.2	2.3
So Bapt Conv	30	13,345	5.5	2.0
Del Norte	19	6,566	-	36.0
Catholic	3	2,356	35.9	12.9
LD Saints	3	1,113	17.0	6.1
S.D.A.	3	651	9.9	3.6
El Dorado	49	16,744	-	19.5
Catholic	5	6,500	38.8	7.6
LD Saints	5	2,410	14.4	2.8
S.D.A.	4	1,094	6.5	1.3
Fresno	392	202,696	-	39.4
Catholic	48	107,396	53.0	20.9
So Bapt Conv	34	14,599	7.2	2.8
Assemb of God	43	11,270	5.6	2.2
Glenn	33	9,265	-	43.4
Catholic	3	4,482	48.4	21.0
Amer Bapt USA	3	1,007	10.9	4.7
Un Methodist	2	640	6.9	3.6

31.2.1,90

RELIGION BY COUNTY				
County and Three Largest Churches	Number of Churches	Number of Adherents	Percent of Total Adherents	Percent of Total Population
Humboldt	130	33,318	-	30.8
Catholic	14	12,835	38.5	11.9
So Bapt Conv	16	3,320	10.0	3.1
LD Saints	6	2,059	6.2	1.9
Imperial	86	50,680	-	55.0
Catholic	13	36,871	72.8	40.0
So Bapt Conv	8	2,671	5.3	2.9
Assemb of God	10	1,845	3.6	2.0
Inyo	34	8,234	-	46.0
Catholic	8	4,179	50.8	23.4
LD Saints	2	685	8.3	3.8
Un Methodist	3	443	5.4	2.5
Kern	354	162,494	-	40.3
Catholic	32	79,888	49.2	19.8
So Bapt Conv	49	19,976	12.3	5.0
LD Saints	21	8,519	5.2	2.1
Kings	90	30,199	-	41.0
Catholic	7	15,607	51.7	21.1
GC Menn Br Chs	7	1,430	4.7	1.9
Assemb of God	8	1,287	4.3	1.7
Lake	50	9,348	-	25.7
Catholic	9	4,115	44.0	11.3
So Bapt Conv	5	837	9.0	2.3
Un Methodist	7	837	9.0	2.3
Lassen	28	4,711	-	21.7
Catholic	5	1,328	28.2	6.1
LD Saints	3	857	18.2	4.0
So Bapt Conv	4	720	15.3	3.3
Los Angeles	2,837	2,928,140	-	39.2
Catholic	262	1,904,617	65.0	25.5
LD Saints	220	96,962	3.3	1.3
So Bapt Conv	187	77,816	3.2	1.3
Madera	59	22,555	-	35.7
Catholic	6	11,491	50.9	18.2
Assemb of God	11	2,067	9.2	3.3
So Bapt Conv	7	1,886	8.4	3.0
Marin	106	60,306	-	27.0
Catholic	20	36,150	59.9	16.2
Episcopal	11	4,695	7.8	2.1
Un Pres Ch USA	16	4,187	6.9	1.9
Mariposa	17	1,790	-	16.1
Catholic	4	636	35.5	5.7
Un Methodist	3	263	14.7	2.4
S.D.A.	2	252	14.1	2.3

31.2.2,90

RELIGION BY COUNTY				
County and Three Largest Churches	Number of Churches	Number of Adherents	Percent of Total Adherents	Percent of Total Population
Mendocino	72	16,877	-	25.3
Catholic	9	6,145	36.4	9.2
So Bapt Conv	9	1,697	10.1	2.5
LD Saints	4	1,432	8.5	2.1
Merced	103	59,888	-	44.5
Catholic	15	39,182	65.4	29.1
So Bapt Conv	16	5,442	9.1	4.0
Un Methodist	5	2,224	3.7	1.7
Modoc	16	1,875	-	21.8
Catholic	2	558	29.8	6.5
Un C of Christ	5	387	20.6	4.5
LD Saints	2	252	13.4	2.9
Mono	11	638	-	7.4
Assemb of God	2	191	29.9	2.2
LD Saints	2	183	28.7	2.1
Luth-Mo Synod	1	84	13.2	1.0
Monterey	142	82,441	-	28.4
Catholic	19	46,212	56.1	15.9
So Bapt Conv	16	6,993	8.5	2.4
Un Pres Ch USA	8	3,442	5.1	1.4
Napa	58	35,049	-	35.3
Catholic	9	15,947	45.5	16.1
S.D.A.	7	6,067	17.3	6.1
So Bapt Conv	5	1,543	5.2	1.8
Nevada	37	10,351	-	20.0
Catholic	5	3,205	31.0	6.2
LD Saints	2	1,370	13.2	2.7
So Bapt Conv	3	992	9.6	1.9
Orange	617	620,464	-	32.1
Catholic	51	351,081	56.6	18.2
LD Saints	77	41,300	6.7	2.1
Un Pres Ch USA	30	26,291	4.2	1.4
Placer	88	32,095	-	27.4
Catholic	12	12,800	39.9	10.9
LD Saints	9	4,726	14.7	4.0
So Bapt Conv	12	2,700	8.4	2.3
Plumas	31	4,636	-	26.7
Catholic	5	1,940	41.8	11.2
Un Methodist	5	662	14.3	3.8
So Bapt Conv	4	629	13.6	3.6
Riverside	408	197,576	-	29.8
Catholic	34	87,237	44.2	13.1
So Bapt Conv	41	15,564	7.9	2.3
LD Saints	33	13,977	7.1	2.1

31.2.3,90

RELIGION BY COUNTY				
County and Three Largest Churches	Number of Churches	Number of Adherents	Percent of Total Adherents	Percent of Total Population
Sacramento	365	240,733	-	30.7
Catholic	35	111,038	46.1	14.2
LD Saints	38	20,597	8.6	2.6
So Bapt Conv	41	19,711	8.2	2.5
San Benito	16	6,783	-	27.1
Catholic	3	4,372	64.5	17.5
LD Saints	1	532	7.8	2.1
Assemb of God	4	520	7.7	2.1
San Bernardino	554	300,820	-	33.7
Catholic	55	148,335	49.3	16.6
So Bapt Conv	45	23,936	8.0	2.7
LD Saints	39	20,641	6.9	2.3
San Diego	752	555,244	-	29.8
Assemb of God	92	308,464	55.6	16.6
LD Saints	76	31,872	5.7	1.7
So Bapt Conv	58	28,411	5.1	1.5
San Francisco	254	208,142	-	30.7
Catholic	60	144,182	69.3	21.2
Episcopal	19	8,132	3.9	1.2
Reform Judaism	5	7,588	3.6	1.1
San Joaquin	225	138,137	-	39.8
Catholic	18	75,549	54.6	21.7
So Bapt Conv	21	6,405	4.6	1.8
Un Methodist	14	6,338	4.6	1.8
San Luis Obispo	117	44,225	-	28.5
Catholic	12	20,516	46.4	13.2
LD Saints	6	3,117	7.0	2.0
So Bapt Conv	8	2,434	5.5	1.6
San Mateo	226	194,241	-	34.0
Catholic	39	133,320	68.6	22.7
Un Pres Ch USA	11	8,411	4.3	1.4
Episcopal	15	8,322	4.3	1.4
Santa Barbara	147	104,107	-	34.9
Catholic	15	64,414	61.9	21.6
Un Pres Ch USA	11	5,382	5.2	1.8
LD Saints	13	4,932	4.7	1.7
Santa Clara	447	364,192	-	28.1
Catholic	53	202,958	55.7	15.7
LD Saints	49	24,926	6.8	1.9
Un Methodist	31	16,676	4.6	1.3
Santa Cruz	108	49,824	-	26.5
Catholic	12	23,176	46.5	12.3
Consrv Bapt	3	4,609	9.3	2.4
Assemb of God	14	2,632	5.3	1.4

31.2.4,90

RELIGION BY COUNTY				
County and Three Largest Churches	Number of Churches	Number of Adherents	Percent of Total Adherents	Percent of Total Population
Shasta	84	28,118	-	24.3
Catholic	10	9,685	34.4	8.4
LD Saints	10	3,997	14.2	3.5
So Bapt Conv	8	2,974	10.6	2.6
Sierra	11	775	-	25.2
Amer Bapt USA	1	266	34.3	8.7
Catholic	5	200	25.8	6.5
Assemb of God	2	141	18.2	4.6
Siskiyou	71	13,374	-	33.7
Catholic	14	5,815	43.5	14.6
So Bapt Conv	7	1,283	9.6	3.2
LD Saints	4	1,259	9.4	3.2
Solano	121	69,976	-	29.8
Catholic	10	34,006	48.6	14.5
So Bapt Conv	14	7,058	10.1	3.0
LD Saints	13	5,332	7.6	2.3
Sonoma	172	86,762	-	28.9
Catholic	21	47,789	55.1	15.9
LD Saints	15	5,845	6.7	1.9
So Bapt Conv	12	4,469	5.2	1.5
Stanislaus	198	89,429	-	33.6
Catholic	13	31,800	35.6	12.0
So Bapt Conv	20	7,517	8.4	2.8
Assemb of God	26	6,419	7.2	2.4
Sutter	34	15,548	-	29.8
Catholic	1	6,800	43.7	13.0
So Bapt Conv	4	1,967	12.7	3.8
LD Saints	4	1,320	8.5	2.5
Tehama	41	10,033	-	25.8
Catholic	3	3,270	32.6	8.4
Un Methodist	5	897	8.9	2.3
Assemb of God	3	179	6.8	1.7
Trinity	16	1,469	-	12.4
Catholic	3	412	28.0	3.5
LD Saints	1	264	18.0	2.2
S.D.A.	2	210	14.3	1.8
Tulare	242	99,393	-	40.4
Catholic	20	48,600	48.9	19.8
So Bapt Conv	22	6,749	6.8	2.7
Assemb of God	28	4,451	4.5	1.8
Tuolumne	30	6,492	-	19.1
Catholic	6	2,525	38.9	7.4
S.D.A.	1	577	8.9	1.7
So Bapt Conv	3	534	8.2	1.6

31.2.5,90

RELIGION BY COUNTY				
County and Three Largest Churches	Number of Churches	Number of Adherents	Percent of Total Adherents	Percent of Total Population
Ventura	238	185,076	-	34.9
Catholic	17	107,558	58.1	20.3
LD Saints	28	13,161	7.1	2.5
So Bapt Conv	16	9,383	5.1	1.8
Yolo	69	34,092	-	30.1
Catholic	11	20,080	58.9	17.7
Un Pres Ch USA	5	1,913	5.6	1.7
LD Saints	6	1,827	5.4	1.6
Yuba	37	12,042	-	24.2
Catholic	2	4,020	33.4	8.1
So Bapt Conv	5	2,108	17.5	4.2
LD Saints	3	1,038	8.6	2.1
State Totals	**11,421**	**8,157,906**	-	-

* Total Adherents estimated from known number of communicant, confirmed full members.

Abbreviations: Catholic=Roman Catholic Church; So Bapt Conv=Southern Baptist Convention; LD Saints=The Church of Jesus Christ of Latter -Day Saints; Un Pres Ch USA=The United Presbyterian Church in the U.S.A.; Assemb of God=Assemblies of God; S.D.A.=Seventh Day Adventists; Amer Bapt USA=American Baptist Churches in the U.S.A.; Episcopal=The Episcopal Church; Chr Chs & Chs Cr=Christian Churches and Churches of Christ; GC Menn Br C=General Conference of Mennonite Brethren Churches; Ch God (Ander)=Church of God (Anderson, Indiana); Luth-Mo Synod=The Lutheran Church, Missouri Synod; Un Methodist=The United Methodist Church; Consrv Bapt=Conservative Baptist Association of America.

31.2.6,90 Source: Glenmary Research Center, *Churches and Church Membership in the U.S.*, 1980.

CALIFORNIANS' RELIGIOUS PREFERENCES 1988	
Protestant	45%
Roman Catholic	25%
No Preference	18%
Other Faith	7%
Jewish	5%

31.3,90 Source: The California Poll, 1988.

INTENSITY OF CALIFORNIANS' RELIGIOUS COMMITMENT 1980	
Very Religious	22%
Fairly Religious	47%
Not Too Religious	22%
Not at All Religious	9%

31.4,90 Source: The California Poll, 1980.

PERCENT OF CALIFORNIANS WHO CONSIDER THEMSELVES TO BE BORN AGAIN CHRISTIANS 1988	
Yes	30%
No	70%

31.5,90 Source: The California Poll, 1988.

ASSESSED VALUE OF CHURCH AND RELIGIOUS EXEMPTIONS 1988-1989 (thousands of dollars)					
	Assessed Value of Exemptions			Assessed Value of Exemptions	
County	Church Property	Religious Property	County	Church Property	Religious Property
Alameda	$15,790	$159,535	Placer	$5,233	$26,268
Alpine	$39	-	Plumas	$855	$4,900
Amador	$157	$3,639	Rioverside	$1,769	$154,118
Butte	$99	$50,133	Sacramento	$65,609	$151,842
Calaveras	-	$7,075	San Benito	$224	$5,097
Colusa	$3,371	-	San Bernardino	$65,418	$152,516
Contra Costa	$2,405	$164,348	San Diego	$30,662	$308,535
Del Norte	$42	$5,355	San Francisco	$45,555	$129,771
El Dorado	$484	$18,955	San Joaquin	$1,795	$106,935
Fresno	$35,622	$95,646	San Luis Obispo	$5,922	$40,988
Glenn	$13	$7,518	San Mateo	$10,833	$106,592
Humboldt	$2,680	$17,302	Santa Barbara	$4,703	$75,219
Imperial	$384	$22,045	Santa Clara	$78,541	$194,169
Inyo	$2,180	$4,637	Santa Cruz	$36,173	-
Kern	$145,659	-	Shasta	$492	$41,908
Kings	$2,083	$15,442	Sierra	-	$1,151
Lake	$101	$9,510	Siskiyou	-	$10,005
Lassen	-	$5,500	Solano	$4,603	$31,961
Los Angeles	$68,878	$1,339,635	Sonoma	$6,880	$48,532
Madera	$81	$18,342	Stanislaus	$12,852	$94,419
Marin	$18,197	$26,812	Sutter	$463	$17,427
Mariposa	$214	$3,210	Tehama	$48	$10,529
Mendocino	$972	$8,905	Trinity	$71	$2,196
Merced	$5,100	$33,111	Tulare	$1,019	$69,557
Modoc	$8	$1,471	Tuolumne	$1,843	$10,243
Mono	$617	$2,362	Ventura	$26,391	$108,202
Monterey	$9,857	$44,577	Yolo	$1,613	$21,135
Napa	$6,042	$22,301	Yuba	-	$11,181
Nevada	$286	$11,719			
Orange	$23,318	$373,166	**State Totals**	**$754,245**	**$4,407,650**

*   Church and religious property tax exemptions are approximately 0.4% of the total gross assessed value of property in California.

31.6,90 Source: California State Board of Equalization, Annual Report, 1987-1988.

	Christian Schools			Catholic	Jewish	Other
	Number of Students					
County	1 - 2	3 - 10	11 or more	Schools	Schools	Religions
Alameda	7	7	47	46	1	0
Alpine	0	0	0	0	0	0
Amador	3	2	2	0	0	0
Butte	8	1	12	3	0	0
Calaveras	1	3	2	0	0	0
Colusa	1	1	0	1	0	0
Contra Costa	14	6	32	20	3	0
Del Norte	2	0	3	1	0	0
El Dorado	7	5	9	0	0	0
Fresno	6	3	26	8	0	0
Glenn	1	2	2	0	0	0
Humboldt	8	6	10	3	0	0
Imperial	2	1	5	4	0	0
Inyo	0	0	2	0	0	0
Kern	11	3	28	8	0	0
Kings	2	2	5	2	0	0
Lake	1	4	4	0	0	0
Lassen	5	1	3	0	0	0
Los Angeles	18	22	342	255	35	2
Madera	6	2	7	1	0	0
Marin	1	2	7	10	1	1
Mariposa	0	2	2	0	0	0
Mendocino	6	4	8	1	0	2
Merced	0	0	12	4	0	0
Modoc	1	2	1	0	0	0
Mono	2	0	1	0	0	0
Monterey	18	7	9	7	0	0
Napa	8	4	11	5	0	0
Nevada	16	2	6	1	0	0
Orange	24	17	98	45	4	2
Placer	27	8	7	2	0	0
Plumas	1	1	2	0	0	0
Riverside	51	28	64	14	1	0
Sacramento	41	12	41	28	1	1
San Benito	3	2	4	1	0	0
San Bernardino	110	35	78	20	0	0
San Diego	42	23	100	44	6	1
San Francisco	2	1	12	50	2	0
San Joaquin	13	6	19	9	0	0
San Luis Obispo	13	3	11	4	0	1
San Mateo	3	1	18	28	1	0
Santa Barbara	15	3	11	10	0	0
Santa Clara	40	16	47	38	1	1
Santa Cruz	11	5	8	6	0	0
Shasta	4	0	7	2	0	0
Sierra	1	0	0	0	0	0
Siskiyou	3	3	1	1	0	1
Solano	12	9	10	7	0	0
Sonoma	10	6	19	9	0	2
Stanislaus	8	5	21	7	0	0
Sutter	4	2	5	1	0	0
Tehama	2	0	2	2	0	0
Trinity	2	2	1	0	0	0
Tulare	5	4	15	3	0	0
Tuolumne	2	0	5	0	0	0
Ventura	17	12	37	14	0	1
Yolo	3	2	6	4	0	0
Yuba	1	3	2	1	0	0
State Totals	**625**	**303**	**1,249**	**730**	**56**	**15**

Note: 35% of the private schools in California are religiously affiliated but 83% of the students enrolled in private schools attended church-affiliated schools.

31.7,90 Source: Cal. Dept. of Ed., *California Private School Directory*, 1988-1989.

THE ELECTRONIC CHURCH
Religiously Oriented Television Stations

City	Station	Also consult cable TV listings in these cities	
Anaheim	KDOC (56)	Alpine	Oxnard
Barstow	KVVT (64)	Auburn	Palm Desert
Chico	VPN (3,6)	Bakersfield	Porterville
Concord	KFCB (42)	Berkeley	Poway
Corona	KVEA (52,57)	Bishop	Rancho San Diego
El Centro	KECY (9)	Boron	Riverbank
Eureka	KIEM (3)	Burlingame	Roseville
Fresno	KAIL (53)	Carlsbad	Rocklin
Fresno	KMSG (59)	Castro Valley	Sacramento
Fresno	KMPH (26)	Ceres	San Diego
Los Angeles	KMJ (9)	Chowchilla	Santa Ana
Los Angeles	KWHY (22)	Costa Mesa	Santa Maria
Modesto	KCSO (19)	Cypress	Santa Rosa
Morro Bay	KO9UF (9)	Davis	Seal Beach
Ontario	KIHS (46)	Desert Hot Springs	Sierra Madre
Palm Springs	KMIR (36)	Edwards AFB	Simi Valley
Placerville	K62BT (62)	El Monte	Torrance
Salinas	KCBA (35)	Eureka	Turlock
Salinas	KSBW (8)	Huntington Beach	Union City
San Bernardino	KAGL (30)	Lake Elsinore	Ventura
San Francisco	KTSF (26)	Lakewood	Watsonville
San Jose	KNTV (11)	Lomita	West Sacramento
San Jose	KLXV (65)	Los Angeles	Wilmington
San Luis Obispo	KSBY (6)	Marysville	
Santa Ana	KTBN (40)	Modesto	
Santa Maria	KO7TA (7)	Mountain View	
Santa Rosa	KFTY (50)	Mt. Shasta	
Vallejo	VPN (3)	Oakdale	
Visalia	KNXT (49)	Oceanside	

Note: Some stations may have religious broadcasts for as little as 3 hours per week.
31.8,90 Source: *The Directory of Religious Broadcating, 1989*; used by permission. See the *Directory* for addresses, phone numbers, and program content of religious broadcasting.

RELIGIOUSLY AFFILIATED HOSPITALS 1988

California had 60 hospitals operated by churches.

31.9,90 Source: American Hospital Association, *1988 Guide to the Health Care Field*. Copyright, used by permission.

THE ELECTRONIC CHURCH

Religiously Oriented Radio Stations

City	Station	City	Station
Anaheim	KPZE-AM 1190	Ontario	KNSE-AM 1510
Angwin	KCDS-FM 89.9	Oxnard	KDAR-FM 98.3
Arcadia	KMAX-FM 107.1	Palmdale	KAVC-FM 105.5
Avalon	KBRT-AM 740	Paradise	KKXX-AM 930
Bakersfield	KERI-AM 1180	Pasadena	KPPC-AM 1240
Bakersfield	KHIS-AM 800	Pomona	KTSJ-AM 1220
Bakersfield	KHIS-FM 96.5	Prunedale	KELM-FM 89.1
Calexico	KICO-AM 1490	Redding	KCIB-FM 99.3
Camarillo	KMRO-FM 90.3	Redding	KVIP-AM 540
Carmichael	KFIA-AM 710	Redding	KVIP-FM 98.1
Delano	KDNO-FM 98.5	Redlands	KUOR-FM 89.1
Dinuba	KRDU-AM 1130	Riverbank	KPLA-AM 770
El Cajon	KECR-FM 93.3	Riverside	KPRO-AM 1570
El Cajon	KMJC-AM 910	Riverside	KSGN-FM 89.7
Fields Landing	KKDV-AM 1390	Sacramento	KJAY-AM 1430
Fresno	KBIF-AM 900	Sacramento	KEBR-FM 100.5
Fresno	KIRV-AM 1510	San Bernardino	KLFF-AM 1240
Fresno	KTED-FM 96.7	San Clemente	KWVE-FM 107.9
Gonzales	KKMC-AM 880	San Diego	KPRZ-AM 1240
Holtville	KGBA-FM 100.1	San Francisco	KEAR-FM 106.9
Inglewood	KTYM-AM 1460	San Francisco	KEST-AM 1450
La Mirada	KBBK-AM 830	San Francisco	KFAX-AM 1100
Le Grand	KEFR-FM 89.9	San Francisco	KUSF-FM 90.3
Long Beach	KFRN-AM 1280	Santa Ana	KYMS-FM 106.3
Long Beach	KGER-AM 1390	Santa Maria	KGDP-AM 660
Los Angeles	KFSG-FM 96.3	Santa Rosa	KCLB-FM 91.9
Los Angeles	KXLU-FM 88.9	Stockton	KCJH-FM 90.1
Merced	KAMB-FM 101.5	1000 Palms	KPSL-AM 1010
Modesto	KCIV-FM 99.9	Ukiah	KPRA-FM 89.5
Moraga	KSMC-FM 89.7	Yucaipa	KLRD-FM 90.1
North Hollywood	KKLA-FM 99.5		

31.10,90 Source: *The Directory of Religious Broadcating, 1989*; used by permission. See the *Directory* for addresses, phone numbers, and program content of religious broadcasting.

RELIGION - PROMINENT CALIFORNIANS

L. Ron Hubbard	Aimee Semple McPherson
Jim Jones	Fr. Junipero Serra
Thomas Starr King	Katherine A. Tingley
Thomas Lake	Ellen G. White

31.11,90 Source: Pacific Data Resources.

ECUMENICAL GROUPS IN CALIFORNIA	
Name	**City**
Northern California Ecumenical Council	San Francisco
California Church Council, Office of State Affairs	Sacramento
Southern California Ecumenical Council	Los Angeles
Pacific and Asian American	
Center for Theology and Strategies (PACTS)	Berkeley
Council of Churches of Contra Costa County	Walnut Creek
Fresno Metropolitan Ministry	Fresno
South Coast Ecumenical Council	Long Beach
Ecumedia/Los Angeles	Los Angeles
Ecumenical Council of the Pasadena Area Churches	Pasadena
Pomona Valley Council of Churches	Pomona
San Fernando Valley Interfaith Council	Chatsworth
Interfaith Service Bureau	Sacramento
San Diego County Ecumenical Conference	San Diego
San Francisco Council of Churches	San Francisco
The Council of Churches of Santa Clara County	San Jose
Westside Ecumenical Conference	Santa Monica

31.12,90 Source: National Council of Churches of Christ, Office of Research, *Yearbook of American and Canadian Churches, 1988*. Used by permission.

CALIFORNIA CATHOLIC ARCHDIOCESES

Los Angeles-Archbishop Roger M. Mahoney
Subdioceses:

    Fresno-Bishop Joseph Madera
    Monterey - Bishop Thaddeus A. Shubsda
    Orange - Bishop Norman McFarland
    San Bernardino - Bishop Phillip F. Straling
    San Diego - Bishop Leo T. Maher

San Francisco Archbishop John Quinn
Subdioceses:

    Oakland - Bishop John S. Cummins
    Sacramento - Bishop Francis P. Quinn
    San Jose - Bishop R. Pierre Du Maine
    Santa Rosa - Bishop John T. Steinbock
    Stockton - Bishop Donald Montrose

31.13,90 Source: San Francisco Archdiocese, 1989.

SECTION 31 NOTE

According to the 1984 Statistical Profile of Black Catholics, 5.7% of California Blacks (103,000) are Catholic.

31.14,90

CATHOLIC CHURCH OVERVIEW, 1988						
Diocese	Parishes	Members	Priests	Brothers	Nuns	Deacons
Los Angeles	285	2,753,952	1,280	196	2,375	137
Fresno	86	311,664	163	14	182	2
Monterey	45	148,693	109	35	285	2
Orange	52	448,937	235	13	415	42
San Bernardino	95	360,993	230	20	202	59
San Diego	98	392,709	357	35	449	70
San Francisco	103	386,000	527	42	1,067	13
Oakland	87	440,110	372	90	515	53
Sacramento	95	290,835	252	45	273	59
San Jose	46	348,773	347	90	528	18
Santa Rosa	41	107,068	106	36	121	7
Stockton	31	147,272	78	6	71	16
Total, 1988	1,059	6,137,006	4,056	622	6,483	478
Total, 1984	1,039	5,469,475	4,202	704	6,956	364
Total, 1976	1,010	4,528,905	3,933	762	5,967	NA
Total, 1960	866	3,277,400	3,128	750	8,025	NA
California as a Percent of U.S. Totals						
1988	5.4%	11.5%	7.6%	8.8%	6.1%	5.6%
1986	5.5%	11.1%	7.6%	7.5%	5.9%	5.8%
1984	5.4%	10.4%	7.2%	9.3%	5.9%	5.4%

31.15,90 Source: *The Catholic Almanac,* Copyrighted. Used by permission of *Our Sunday Visitor.*

NUMBER OF CATHOLIC BAPTISMS AND CONVERSIONS						
	Baptisms			Conversions		
Year	California	U.S.	Percent of All U.S.	California	U.S.	Percent of All U.S.
1960	118,416	1,344,576	8.8%	19,099	146,212	13.1%
1976	115,076	894,992	12.9%	16,724	80,035	20.9%
1982	141,295	982,586	14.3%	7,839	92,861	8.4%
1984	144,503	975,017	14.8%	8,300	95,346	8.7%
1986	148,617	953,323	15.6%	7,860	87,996	8.9%
1988	139,002	937,947	14.8%	7,085	81,739	8.7%

31.16,90 Source: *The Catholic Almanac, 1988.* Copyrighted. Used by permission of *Our Sunday Visitor.*

CATHOLIC EDUCATION-UNIVERSITIES AND COLLEGES

	Number			Enrollment		
Year	California	U.S.	% of All U.S.	California	U.S.	% of All U.S.
1960	15	265	5.7%	14,757	302,906	4.9%
1976	13	245	5.3%	28,670	432,597	6.6%
1982	16	237	6.8%	32,924	533,086	6.2%
1984	16	239	6.7%	32,924	560,835	5.9%
1986	16	243	6.6%	32,649	545,461	6.0%
1988	15	233	6.4%	34,569	563,799	6.1%

31.17.1,90 Source: *The Catholic Almanac, 1988.* Copyrighted. Used by permission of *Our Sunday Visitor.*

CATHOLIC EDUCATION-HIGH SCHOOLS

	Number			Enrollment		
Year	California	U.S.	% of All U.S.	California	U.S.	% of All U.S.
1960	129	2,433	5.3%	55,711	844,299	6.6%
1976	131	1,616	8.1%	70,152	895,845	7.8%
1982	126	1,470	8.6%	76,756	833,902	9.2%
1984	124	1,456	8.5%	75,466	801,440	9.4%
1986	129	1,418	9.1%	74,223	766,744	9.7%
1988	127	1,391	9.1%	79,454	708,189	11.2%

31.17.2,90 Source: *The Catholic Almanac.* Copyrighted. Used by permission of *Our Sunday Visitor.*

CATHOLIC EDUCATION-GRADE SCHOOLS

	Number			Enrollment		
Year	California	U.S.	% of All U.S.	California	U.S.	% of All U.S.
1960	531	10,372	5.1%	248,947	4,285,896	5.8%
1976	606	8,484	7.1%	185,799	2,576,856	7.2%
1982	607	8,079	7.5%	187,003	2,333,469	8.0%
1984	606	8,009	7.6%	181,515	2,220,964	8.2%
1986	613	7,865	7.8%	177,986	2,099,379	8.5%
1988	603	7,659	7.8%	174,522	1,959,466	8.9%

31.17.3,90 Source: *The Catholic Almanac.* Copyrighted. Used by permission of *Our Sunday Visitor.*

MORMONS IN CALIFORNIA, 1985 -1988			
	1985	**1987**	**1988**
Stakes (Dioceses)	135	140	153
Wards (Congregations)	966	1,030	1,064
Branches (Small congregations)	132	131	128
Temples*	2	2	2
Bishops' Storehouses	12	10	10
Missions in California	10	11	11
Total Church Membership	**475,000**	**646,000**	**681,000**

* Oakland and Los Angeles.
Note: For more information on Mormons in California see *Deseret News Church Almanac* and Leo J. Muir, *A Century of Mormon Activities in California, 1952.*
31.18,90 Source: Latter Day Saints Church Office, Salt Lake City, unpublished data.

EPISCOPALIANS IN CALIFORNIA, 1988						
Diocese	Parishes	Clergy	Baptized Members	Baptisms	Communicants	Church School Pupils
California	87	349	31,385	868	23,619	6,421
El Camino Real	41	139	16,253	548	11,924	3,121
Los Angeles	149	359	76,921	1,905	54,269	11,162
Northern California	68	121	17,881	617	13,202	3,223
San Diego	45	130	21,217	604	15,932	4,128
San Joaquin	54	89	11,369	397	8,191	2,590
Total 1988	**444**	**1,187**	**175,026**	**4,939**	**127,137**	**30,645**
Total 1986	**438**	**1,295**	**194,358**	**5,798**	**134,909**	**30,515**
Total 1984	**432**	**1,132**	**198,348**	**N/A**	**N/A**	**32,464**

Seminary: Church of Divinity School of the Pacific, Berkeley.
School of Theology: Episcopal Theological School at Claremont, Claremont.
31.19,90 Source: *The Episcopal Church Annual*, 1988, Morehouse Barlow Co., publishers. Used by permission.

EPISCOPALIAN HIERARCHY IN CALIFORNIA PROVINCE VIII	
Diocese	**Bishop**
California	William E. Swing
El Camino Real	C. Shannon Mallory
Los Angeles	Frederick H. Borsch
Northern California	Lester Thompson III
San Diego	C. Brinkley Morton
San Joaquin	David M. Schofield

31.20,90 Source: California Diocese of the Episcopal Church, 1989.

AMERICAN BAPTIST CHURCHES IN CALIFORNIA, 1988		
Seminaries	1	(American Baptist Seminary of the West, Berkeley)
Colleges	1	(Redlands University)
Children's homes	1	(Children's Baptist Home of So. Calif., LA)
Number of churches	527	
Retirement homes	15	

31.21,90 Source: *Directory of American Baptist Churches in the U.S.A., 1988.*

SECTION 31 NOTE
According to the 1988 Yearbook of the Greek Orthodox Archdiocese of North and South America there are 36 Greek Orthodox and related parishes active in California. The Bishop of the San Francisco (Cal.) diocese is His Grace, Bishop Anthony.

31.22,90

MAJOR JEWISH FEDERATIONS & COMMUNITY COUNCILS	
City	**Group**
Fresno	Jewish Federation of Fresno
Long Beach	Jewish Community Federation of Greater Long Beach
Los Angeles	Jewish Federation-Council of Greater Los Angeles
Oakland	Jewish Federation of the Greater East Bay
Orange County	Jewish Federation of Orange County
Palm Springs	Jewish Welfare Federation of Palm Springs-Desert Area
Sacramento	Jewish Welfare Federation of Sacramento
San Diego	United Jewish Federation of San Diego County
San Francisco	United Jewish Welfare Federation of San Francisco/Marin
San Jose	United Jewish Federation of Greater San Jose
Santa Barbara	Santa Barbara Jewish Federation

31.23,90 Source: *American Jewish Yearbook, 1988* copyright, used by permission.

JEWS IN CALIFORNIA

	Number	Percent of Population
California	868,200	3.3%
United States	5,943,700	2.5%

31.24,90 Source: *American Jewish Yearbook, 1988*
copyright, used by permission.

LUTHERANS IN CALIFORNIA, 1988

Churches*	Pastors	Baptized Members	Commu- nicants	Sunday School Pupils	Total Contri- butions (millions)
380	378	144,394	108,604	33,937	52.3†

* Includes preaching stations which may not always be a church.
† 1987 data.
   31.25,90 Source: *The Lutheran 1989 Annual.*

CALIFORNIA MISSIONS

Name	City	Founded
San Diego De Alcalá	San Diego	July 16, 1769
San Carlos Borromeo De Carmelo	Carmel	June 3, 1770
San Antonio De Padua	near King City	July 14, 1771
San Gabriel Arcángel	Los Angeles	Sept. 1, 1772
San Luis Obispo De Tolosa	San Luis Obispo	Sept. 8, 1771
San Francisco De Asis	San Francisco	June 29, 1776
San Juan Capistrano	San Juan Capistrano	Nov. 1, 1776
Santa Clara de Asis	Santa Clara	Jan. 12, 1777
San Buenaventura	Ventura	Mar. 31, 1782
Santa Barbara	Santa Barbara	Dec. 4, 1786
La Purísima Conceptión	near Lompoc	Dec. 8, 1787
Santa Cruz	Santa Cruz	Aug. 28, 1791
Nuestra Señora De La Soledad	near Soledad	Oct. 9, 1791
San Jose	near Fremont	June 11, 1797
San Juan Bautista	San Juan Bautista	June 24, 1797
San Miguel Arcángel	near Paso Robles	June 25, 1797
San Fernando Rey De España	near San Fernando	Sept. 8, 1797
San Luis Rey De Francia	Oceanside	June 13, 1798
Santa Inés	Solvang	Sept. 17, 1804
San Rafael Arcángel	San Rafael	Dec. 14, 1817
San Francisco Solano	Sonoma	July 4, 1823

31.26,90 Source: Pacific Data Resources.
For a brief Historical and photograhic survey of the missions see *The California Missions* published by Sunset Books.

DEPARTMENTS OF RELIGION OR RELIGIOUS STUDIES

Ambassador College	Occidental College
Bethany Bible College	Pepperdine University
Biola College	Pomona College
California State University, Bakersfield	San Diego State University
California State University, Chico	School of Theology at Claremont
California State University, Dominguez Hills	Southern California College
	St. Albert's College
	St. Mary's College
California State University, Fullerton	St. Patrick's College
California State University, Long Beach	Stanford University
California State University, Los Angeles	University of California, Berkeley
California State University, Northridge	University of California, Davis
California State University, San Diego	University of California, Irvine
California State University, San Jose	University of California, Los Angeles
Chapman College	University of California, Riverside
Graduate Theological Union	University of California, San Diego
Holy Names College	University of California, Santa Barbara
Immaculate Heart College	University of Judaism
John F. Kennedy University	University of San Diego
La Verne College	University of San Francisco
Loma Linda University	University of Santa Clara
Los Angeles Baptist College	University of Southern California
Loyola Marymount University	University of the Pacific
Marymount College	Westmont College
Mount St. Mary's College	Whittier College

Note: For a comprehensive list of departments of Religion or Religious Studies see Council of Societies for the Study of Religion, *Directory of Departments and Programs of Religious Studies in North America, 1987.*
31.27,90 Sources: College catalogs; California State Departments of Education, *California Private Post-secondary Education Directory.*

Sports

Could any state's sports teams have done better than California's in the late 1980s? It seems unlikely. The San Francisco 49ers became professional football's team of the decade with their third Superbowl victory since 1981. Just to keep the fans in suspense, Joe Montana and Company waited until the last minute of the 1989 Superbowl game to secure a spectacular come-from-behind victory.

Not to be outdone by Northern California teams, the 1988 Los Angeles Dodgers won their second World Series since 1981 with a surprisingly easy series win over the Oakland A's. The Dodgers can also boast of another record of sorts. Their pitcher Orel Hershiser was the highest paid baseball player in the nation in 1989, earning almost $2.8 million for the year's work. Eddie Murray, the Dodgers' first baseman, was the nation's third-highest-paid baseball player, with an annual pay stub of more than $2.2 million.

The Los Angeles Kings hockey team pulled off a remarkable coup in obtaining from the Edmundton Oilers the superstar Wayne Gretzky. Gretzky took the Kings, perennial losers, to the 1989 play-offs. The Kings defeated the first-place Calgary team before being thrashed by the Oilers in the second round of the play-offs. The recent success of the Kings and the fame of such California skating wonders as Brian Boitano of Sunnyvale and Debi Thomas of San Jose, however, have not stimulated young Californians to become skaters: the number of skating rinks in the state continues to shrink.

Dennis Conner of San Diego recaptured the America's Cup in yachting, but if he held his own against the wind during the race, Conner had trouble afterward in the courts, which stripped him of his trophy. Despite this turmoil, San Diego is still hoping to be the site of the next America's Cup race.

College basketball in California continues to disappoint fans who remember the glory years at U.C.L.A. under John Wooten or U.C. Berkeley's heady moment of victory in the late 1950s. Now fans are surprised if a California team gets past the second round in the NCAA tournament. Both Fresno State and U.C.L.A. managed to win a post-season NIT tournament in the 1980s, but that is hardly the brass ring.

PROFESIONAL BASEBALL
(National League)

San Francisco Giants

Manager:	Roger Craig	Owner:	Bob Lurie
1989 Average Player Salary:	$522,074	Arena:	Candlestick Park, Capacity 58,000

Team Record

1981: 56 wins, 55 losses, .504 pct.
4th in Western Division

1982: 87 wins, 75 losses, .537 pct.
3rd in Western Division

1983: 79 wins, 83 losses, .487 pct.
5th in Western Division

1984: 66 wins, 96 losses, .407 pct.
6th in Western Division

1985: 62 wins, 100 losses, .383 pct.
6th in Western Division

1986: 83 wins, 79 losses, .512 pct.
3rd in Wstern Division

1987: 90 wins, 72 losses, .556 pct.
1st in Western Division

1988: 83 wins, 79 losses, .512 pct.
4th in Western Division

Attendance

1981: 632,276	1983: 1,251,530	1985: 818,697	1987: 1,917,863
1982: 1,200,948	1984: 1,001,545	1986: 1,528,748	1988: 1,786,482

Los Angeles Dodgers

Manager:	Tom Lasorda	Owner:	Peter O'Malley
1989 Average Player Salary:	$844,002	Arena:	Dodger Stadium, Capacity 56,000

Team Record

1981: 63 wins, 47 losses, .573 pct.
World Series Champions

1982: 88 wins, 74 losses, .543 pct.
2nd in Western Division

1983: 91 wins, 71 losses, .563 pct.
1st in Western Division

1984: 79 wins, 83 losses, .488 pct.
4th in Western Division

1985: 95 wins, 67 losses, .586 pct.
1st in Western Division

1986: 73 wins, 89 losses, .451 pct.
5th in Western Division

1987: 73 wins, 89 losses, .451 pct.
4th in Western Division

1988: 94 wins, 67 losses, .584 pct.
World Series Champions

Attendance

1981: 2,381,292	1983: 3,510,313	1985: 3,264,593	1987: 2,797,409
1982: 3,608,881	1984: 3,134,824	1986: 3,023,208	1988: 2,980,262

San Diego Padres

Manager:	Jack McKeon	Owner:	Joan Kroc
1988 Average Player Salary:	$540,705	Arena:	Jack Murphy Stadium, Capacity 59,021

Team Record

1981: 41 wins, 69 losses, .373 pct.
6th in Western Division

1982: 81 wins, 81 losses, .500 pct.
4th in Western Division

1983: 81 wins, 81 losses, .500 pct.
4th in Western Division

1984: 92 wins, 70 losses, .568 pct.
1st in Western Division

1985: 83 wins, 79 losses, .512 pct.
3rd in Western Division

1986: 74 wins, 88 losses, .457 pct.
4th in Western Division

1987: 65 wins, 97 losses, .401 pct.
6th in Western Division

1988: 83 wins, 78 losses, .516 pct.
3rd in Western Division

Attendance

1981: 519,161	1983: 1,539,815	1985: 2,210,350	1987: 1,454,061
1982: 1,607,516	1984: 1,983,904	1986: 1,805,776	1988: 1,506,890

32.1.1,90 Source: Team Media Guides and Team Press Officials.

PROFESIONAL BASEBALL (American League)		
California Angels		
Manager:	Doug Rader	Owner: Gene Autry
1989 Average Player Salary:	$556,455	Arena: Aneheim Stadium, Capacity 64,573

Team Record

1981:	51 wins, 59 losses, .464 pct. 7th in Western Division	**1985:**	90 wins, 72 losses, .555 pct. 2nd in Western Division
1982:	93 wins, 69 losses, .547 pct. 1st in Western Division	**1986:**	92 wins, 70 losses, .568 pct. 1st in Western Division
1983:	70 wins, 92 losses, .431 pct. 5th in Western Division	**1987:**	75 wins, 87 losses, .463 pct. 6th in Western Division
1984:	81 wins, 81 losses, .500 pct. Tied for 2nd in Western Division	**1988:**	75 wins, 87 losses, .463 pct. 4th in Western Division

Attendance

1981: 1,441,543	1983: 2,555,061	1985: 2,567,427	1987: 2,696,299
1982: 2,807,360	1984: 2,402,997	1986: 2,655,892	1988: 2,340,925

Oakland Athletics		
Manager:	Tony LaRussa	Owners: Walter Haas
1989 Average Player Salary:	$533,000	Arena: Oakland Coliseum, Capacity 50,219

Team Record

1981:	64 wins, 45 losses, .538 pct. 1st in Western Division	**1985:**	77 wins, 85 losses, .475 pct. 4th in Western Division
1982:	68 wins, 94 losses, .420 pct. 4th in Western Division	**1986:**	76 wins, 86 losses, .469 pct. 3rd in Western Division
1983:	74 wins, 88 losses, .456 pct. 4th in Western Division	**1987:**	81 wins, 81 losses, .500 pct. 3rd in Western Division
1984:	77 wins, 85 losses, .475 pct. 4th in Western Division	**1988:**	104 wins, 58 losses, .642 pct. American League Champions

Attendance

1981: 1,304,052	1983: 1,294,942	1985: 1,334,609	1987: 1,678,921
1982: 1,735,489	1984: 1,565,559	1986: 1,314,646	1988: 2,287,335

32.1.2,90 Source: Team Media Guides and Team Press Officials.

GOLF COURSES IN CALIFORNIA	
Northern California	321
Southern California	374
Total	**695**

32.2,90 Source: California Office of Tourism.

PROFESSIONAL BASKETBALL
(National Basketball Association)

Team: Los Angeles Lakers

Coach: Pat Riley   Owner: Jerry Buss   Arena: The Forum, Capacity 17,505

Team Record

1981-82:	57 wins, 25 losses		**1985-86:**	62 wins, 20 losses
.695 pct.	NBA Champions		.756 pct.	1st in Pacific Div.
1982-83:	58 wins, 24 losses		**1986-87:**	65 wins, 17 losses
.707 pct.	NBA Runner-up		.793 pct.	NBA Champions
1983-84:	54 wins, 28 losses		**1987-88:**	62 wins, 20 losses
.659 pct.	NBA Runner-up		.756 pct.	NBA Champions
1984-85:	62 wins, 20 losses		**1988-89:**	57 wins, 25 losses
.756 pct.	NBA Champions		.695 pct.	NBA Runner-up

Attendance

1981-82:	605,367	1985-86:	689,905
1982-83:	644,000	1986-87:	681,707
1983-84:	794,522	1987-88:	714,477
1984-85:	598,392	1988-89:	717,347

Team: Los Angeles Clippers

Coach: Don Casey
Owner: Donald T. Sterling
Arena: Los Angeles Sports Arena, Capacity 15,371

Team Record

1981-82:	17 wins, 65 losses		**1985-86:**	32 wins, 50 losses
.207 pct.	Last in Pacific Div.		.390 pct.	3rd in Pacific Div.
1982-83:	25 wins, 65 losses		**1986-87:**	12 wins, 70 losses
.207 pct.	Last in Pacific Div.		.146 pct.	Last in Pacific Div.
1983-84:	30 wins, 52 losses		**1987-88:**	17 wins, 65 losses
.366 pct.	Last in Pacific Div.		.207 pct.	Last in Pacific Div.
1984-85:	31 wins, 51 losses		**1988-89:**	21 wins, 61 losses
.378 pct.	Tied for 4th in Pacific Div.		.256 pct.	Last in Pacific Div.

Attendance

1981-82:	224,571	1985-86:	341,614
1982-83:	193,693	1986-87:	316,140
1983-84:	228,710	1987-88:	359,674
1984-85:	384,119	1988-89:	439,343

Team: Golden State Warriors

Coach: Don Nelson   Owner: Jim Fitzgerald & Don Finnane   Arena: Oakland Coliseum Arena, Capacity 15,025

Team Record

1981-82:	45 wins, 37 losses		**1985-86:**	30 wins, 52 losses
.549 pct.	4th in 6 team Pacific Div.		.366 pct.	Tied for last in Pacific Div.
1982-83:	30 wins, 52 losses		**1986-87:**	42 wins, 40 losses
.366 pct.	5th in 6 team Pacific Div.		.512 pct.	3rd in 6 team Div.
1983-84:	37 wins, 45 losses		**1987-88:**	20 wins, 62 losses
.451 pct.	5th in 6 team Pacific Div.		.244 pct.	5th in 6 team Pacific Div.
1984-85:	22 wins, 60 losses		**1988-89:**	43 wins, 39 losses
.268 pct.	Tied for last in Pacific Div.		.524 pct.	4th in 7 team Pacific Div.

Attendance

1981-82:	401,646	1985-86:	401,195
1982-83:	341,246	1986-87:	427,252
1983-84:	348,500	1987-88:	465,356
1984-85:	299,300	1988-89:	587,820

Team: Sacramento Kings

Coach: Jerry Reynolds   Owner: Joseph Benvenuti & Greg Lukenbill   Arena: Arco Arena, Capacity 16,517

Team Record

1985-86:	37 wins, 45 losses		**1987-88:**	24 wins, 58 losses
.451 pct.	5th in 6 team Midwest Div.		.293 pct.	Last in Midwest Div.
1986-87:	29 wins, 53 losses		**1988-89:**	27 wins, 55 losses
.354 pct.	5th in 6 team Midwest Div.		.329 pct.	5th in 7 team Pacific Div.

Attendance

1985-86:	423,653	1987-88:	433,986
1986-87:	423,633	1988-89:	693,714

Note: The average NBA salary in 1989 was $600,000. Average team salaries are not available.
32.3,90 Source: Team Media Guides and Press Offices.

PROFESIONAL FOOTBALL
(National Football Conference)

Team: San Francisco Forty-Niners

Coach:	George Seifert
Owner:	Eddie DeBartolo
Arena:	Candlestick Park
	Capacity 61,185

Team Record:		
1981:	16 wins, 3 losses, .842 pct.	Super Bowl Champions
1982:	3 wins, 6 losses, .333 pct.	11th place in Conference
1983:	11 wins, 7 losses, .611 pct.	NFC Runner-up
1984:	18 wins, 1 loss, .947 pct.	Super Bowl Champions
1985:	10 wins, 6 losses, .625 pct.	2nd in NFC Western Division
1986:	10 wins, 5 losses, 1 tie, .625 pct.	NFC Western Division Champions
1987:	13 wins, 2 losses, .867 pct.	NFC Western Division Champions
1988:	10 wins, 6 losses, .625 pct.	Super Bowl Champions

Attendance:			
1981:	431,181	1985:	470,506
1982:	270,837	1986:	470,339
1983:	435,088	1987:	457,222
1984:	466,769	1988:	541,887

1988 Average Player Salary: $277,000

Team: Los Angeles Rams

Coach:	John Robinson
Owner:	Georgia Frontiere
Arena:	Anaheim Stadium
	Capacity 69,008

Team Record:		
1981:	6 wins, 10 losses, .375 pct.	3rd in NFC Western Division
1982:	2 wins, 7 losses, .222 pct.	Last in Conference
1983:	9 wins, 7 losses, .563 pct.	2nd in NFC Western Division
1984:	10 wins, 6 loss, .625 pct.	2nd in NFC Western Division
1985:	11 wins, 5 losses, .688 pct.	NFC Runner-up
1986:	10 wins, 6 losses, .625 pct.	2nd in NFC Western Division
1987:	6 wins, 9 losses, .400 pct.	3rd in Western Division
1988:	10 wins, 6 losses, .625 pct.	Tied for 1st in Western Division

Attendance:			
1981:	484,024	1985:	448,068
1982:	258,451	1986:	511,598
1983:	422,239	1987:	331,690
1984:	435,637	1988:	435,749

1988 Average Player Salary: $244,000

32.4.1,90 Source: Club Media Guides, Press Offices, and NFL Players Association, 1989.

PROFESIONAL FOOTBALL
(American Football Conference)

Team:	**San Diego Chargers**
Coach:	Dan Henning
Owner:	A.G. Spanos
Arena:	Jack Murphy Stadium
	Capacity 60,750

Team Record:		
1981:	10 wins, 6 losses, .625 pct.	
	Division Champions	
1982:	6 wins, 3 losses, .667 pct.	
	AFC Runner-up	
1983:	6 wins, 10 losses, .375 pct.	
	4th in Division	
1984:	7 wins, 9 loss, .438 pct.	
	Last in Division	
1985:	8 wins, 8 losses, .500 pct.	
	4th in Division	
1986:	4 wins, 12 losses, .250 pct.	
	Last in Division	
1987:	8 wins, 8 losses, .500 pct.	
	3rd in Division	
1988:	6 wins, 10 losses, .375 pct.	
	4th in Division	

Attendance:				
	1981:	411,661	1985:	415,626
	1982:	200,248	1986:	416,612
	1983:	368,844	1987:	331,676
	1984:	409,085	1988:	347,400

1988 Average Player Salary: $195,000

Team:	**Los Angeles Raiders**
Coach:	Mike Shanahan
Owner:	Al Davis
Arena:	Los Angeles Coliseum
	Capacity 92,488

Team Record:		
1981:	7 wins, 9 losses, .438 pct.	
	4th in Division	
1982:	8 wins, 1 loss, .889 pct.	
	Division Champions	
1983:	12 wins, 4 losses, .750 pct.	
	Super Bowl Champions	
1984:	11 wins, 5 losses, .688 pct.	
	3rd in Division	
1985:	12 wins, 4 losses, .750 pct.	
	Division Champions	
1986:	8 wins, 8 losses, .500 pct.	
	4th in Division	
1987:	5 wins, 10 losses, .333 pct.	
	4th in Division	
1988:	7 wins, 9 losses, .438 pct.	
	3rd in Division	

Attendance:				
	1981:	391,908	1985:	562,448
	1982:	226,976	1986:	560,080
	1983:	420,776	1987:	432,000
	1984:	550,171	1988:	456,000

1988 Average Player Salary: $298,000

32.4.2,90 Source: Club Media Guides, Press Offices, and NFL Players Association, 1989.

PROFESSIONAL SOCCER MAJOR INDOOR SOCCER LEAGUE	
Team:	**San Diego Sockers**
Coach: Owner:	Ron Newman Arena: San Diego Sports Arena Ron Fowler Capacity 12,888
Team Record:	**1982-83:** 32 wins, 16 losses, .667 pct. League Champions **1983-84:** Did not play in league **1984-85:** 37 wins, 11 losses, .771 pct. League Champions **1985-86:** 36 wins, 12 losses, .750 pct. League Champions **1986-87:** 27 wins, 25 losses, .519 pct. 3rd in West **1987-88:** 42 wins, 14 losses, .750 pct. League Champions **1988-89:** 27 wins, 21 losses, .563 pct. League Champions
Attendance:	1982-83: 205,470 1986-87: 253,434 1983-84: Not in league 1987-88: 251,901 1984-85: 230,263 1988-89: 201,956 1985-86: 229,935

32.5,90 Source: Team Press Office.

PROFESSIONAL HOCKEY (National Hockey League) (Campbell Conference) (Smythe Division)	
Team:	**Los Angeles Kings**
Coach: **Owners:** **Arena:**	Robbie Ftorek Average NHL Player Bruce McNall Salary: $188,000 The Forum Capacity 16,005
Team Record:	1981-82: 24 wins, 41 losses, 15 ties 1982-83: 27 wins, 41 losses, 12 ties 1983-84: 23 wins, 44 losses, 13 ties Last in the division 1984-85: 34 wins, 32 losses, 14 ties 4th in 5-team division 1985-86: 23 wins, 49 losses, 8 ties Last in the division 1986-87: 31 wins, 41 losses 8 ties 4th in 5-team division 1987-88: 30 wins, 42 losses, 7 ties 4th in 5-team division 1988-89: 43 wins, 31 losses, 7 ties 2nd in Smythe Division- Division runner-ups
Attendance:	1981-82: 430,062 1985-86: 409,240 1982-83: 464,670 1986-87: 425,769 1983-84: 419,725 1987-88: 466,677 1984-85: 471,789 1988-89: 595,000

32.6,90 Source: Team Media Guides and Press Offices and NHL Players' Association.

PROFESSIONAL TENNIS
(Team Tennis)

Team:	Los Angeles Strings
Players:	Roger Smith
	John Lloyd
	Ann Minter
	Lisa Gregory
Coach:	John Lloyd
Owner:	Jeanie Buss
Arena:	The Forum
	Capacity 18,000

Team Record:

1982:	3rd in 8 team league	**1986:**	5th in 8 team league
1983:	2nd in 8 team league	**1987:**	5th in 6 team league
1985:	6th in 8 team league	**1988:**	7th in 8 team league

Attendance:		1986:	7,672
1982:	15,829	1987:	6,808
1985:	7,968	1988:	7,800

Team:	Sacramento Capitols
Players:	Greg Holmes
	Molly Van Nostrand
	Sophie Amiach
	Robert Van'thof
Coach:	Larry Willens
Owners:	Ramsey Osborne & Bill Campbell
Arena:	Gold River Racket Club
	Capacity 2,200

Team Record:		**1987:**	4th in 6 team league
1986:	2nd in 8 team league	**1988:**	4th in 8 team league

Attendance:		1987:	4,900
1986:	13,600	1988:	10,500

Team:	Fresno Sun-Nets
Players:	Elly Hakami
	Sandy Callins
	Clinton Banducci
	Jean Fleurian
Coach:	Virginia Brown
Owner:	Al Geller
Arena:	Sierra Sport and Racquet Club
	Capacity 1,370

Team Record:	**1988:**	8th in 8 team league
Attendance:	1988:	5,000

Note: Due to the Olympics, Team Tennis only had a 1 week season in 1984. Attendance was 22,000 for the1984 season. Players do not receive salaries but play for prize money.
32.7,90 Source: Team Media Guides and U.S. Team Tennis League.

	Daily Attendance	Total Attendance	Amount Wagered (millions)
CALIFORNIA HORSE RACING			
MAJOR TRACKS AND RACE MEETINGS, 1987-1988			
Track			
Thoroughbred Meetings			
Santa Anita (Dec. 26, 1987-Apr. 25, 1988)	33,533	3,051,498	$647.9
Santa Anita (Oct. 5, 1988-Nov. 7, 1988)	27,071	730,925	$160.7
Hollywood Park (Apr. 27, 1988-July 25, 1988)	27,501	1,870,086	$417.9
Hollywood Park (Nov. 9, 1988-Dec. 24, 1988)	21,420	728,288	$172.0
Del Mar (July 27, 1988-Sept. 14, 1988)	32,944	1,416,574	$288.7
Golden Gate Fields (Jan. 26, 1988-June 26, 1988)	13,074	1,451,243	$283.5
Bay Meadows (Dec. 26, 1987-Jan. 24, 1988)	12,965	285,235	$55.3
Bay Meadows (Aug. 24, 1988-Dec. 24, 1988)	11,748	1,045,569	$203.8
Total	**21,813**	**10,579,418**	**$2,230**
Quarter House Meetings			
Bay Meadows (Feb. 5, 1988-Apr. 10, 1988)	4,411	167,618	$22.8
Los Alamitos (May 5, 1988-July 23, 1988)	4,869	282,416	$48.8
Los Alamitos (Aug. 16, 1988-Sept. 10, 1988)	4,504	90,072	$15.2
Los Alamitos (Sept. 13, 1988-Nov. 19, 1988)	4,986	249,285	$43.6
Total	**4,755**	**789,391**	**$130.4**
Harness Meetings			
Los Alamitos (Dec 31, 1987-Apr. 30, 1988)	2,813	247,505	$56.1
Los Alamitos (Nov. 25, 1988-Dec. 23, 1988)	2,703	56,757	$12.8
Sacramento (May 12, 1988-July 23, 1988)	3,319	142,707	$10.3
Total	**2,941**	**446,969**	**$79.3**
County Fair Race Meetings			
Alameda (Pleasanton) (June 28, 1988-July 10, 1988)	13,034	169,445	$27.4
Fresno (Fresno) (Oct. 4, 1988-Oct. 16, 1988)	4,194	54,526	$7.4
Humboldt (Ferndale) (Aug. 11, 1988-Aug 21, 1988)	4,455	44,550	$1.4
Los Angeles (Pomona) (Sept. 15, 1988-Oct. 2, 1988)	15,223	274,012	$55.6
Orange (Los Alamitos) (July 26, 1988-Aug. 13, 1988)	8,716	148,169	$25.0
Sacramento (State Fair) (Aug. 19, 1988-Sept. 5, 1988)	6,732	87,512	$10.9
San Joaquin (Stockton) (June 14, 1988-June 26, 1988)	4,627	60,151	$9.3
San Mateo (Bay Meadows) (Aug. 9, 1988-Aug. 21, 1988)	10,036	120,437	$23.1
Solano (Vallejo) (July 12, 1988-July 24, 1988)	10,149	131,942	$21.1
Sonoma (Santa Rosa) (July 26, 1988-Aug. 7, 1988)	13,052	169,679	$26.7
Total	**9,336**	**1,260,423**	**$207.8**
State Total	**13,941**	**13,076,201**	**$2,647**

32.8,90 Source: California Horse Racing Board, *Horse Racing California*,1988.

		HORSE RACING REVENUES TO CALIFORNIA STATE GOVERNMENT			
Year	Attendance (millions)	Revenues Recieved by the State (millions)	Amount Wagered (millions)	Revenue Received as a % of Amount Wagered	Payment to Winning Ticket Holders
1935	NA	$1.0	$24	4.1%	NA
1940	NA	$2.8	$70	4.0%	NA
1950	NA	$14.1	$278	5.1%	NA
1960	NA	$36.1	$481	7.5%	NA
1970	NA	$58.2	$792	7.4%	NA
1975	NA	$86.8	$1,188	7.3%	NA
1980	11.9	$127.6	$1,692	7.5%	NA
1981	12.7	$131.7	$1,932	6.8%	NA
1982	12.8	$129.5	$2,037	6.4%	NA
1983	12.8	$127.4	$2,039	6.3%	NA
1984	12.7	$141.7	$2,180	6.5%	NA
1985	12.3	$138.3	$2,022	6.8%	NA
1986	11.6	$138.7	$2,185	6.3%	NA
1987	11.7	$140.4	$2,219	6.3%	81.2%
1988	13.1	$146.4	$2,490	5.9%	81.2%

32.9,90 Source: California Horse Racing Board, Annual Reports.

SCOUTING IN CALIFORNIA			
Boy Scouts*		**Girl Scouts†**	
Career Awareness Explorer Scouts	113,903		
Explorer Scouts	45,135		
Varsity Scouts	16,560	Girl Scouts	**192,502**
Boy Scouts	86,348		
Cub Scouts	169,063		
Tiger Cubs	20,538		
Total	**451,547**		
Adult Leaders	103,662	Adult Leaders	76,906
Coucils	32	Councils	19

* As of Dec. 1988 10.7% of U.S. Boy Scouts. † As of 1988. 8.2% of U.S. Girl Scouts.

32.10,90 Source: Boy Scouts and Girl Scouts National Headquarters, unpublished data.

NATIONAL COLLEGIATE ATHLETIC ASSOCIATION MEN'S NATIONAL CHAMPIONS BY DIVISION			
1987-1988			
Sport	**Division I**	**Division II**	**Division III**
Baseball	**Stanford**	Florida Southern	Ithaca
Basketball	Kansas	Lowell	Ohio Wesleyan
Cross Country	Arkansas	Edinboro	North Central
Fencing	Columbia*	---	---
Football	Northeast La.**	Troy St.	Wagner
Golf	**UCLA**	Tampa	**C.S.U. Stanislaus**
Gymnastics	Nebraska*	---	---
Ice Hockey	Lake Superior St.	---	Wis.-River Falls
Lacrosse	Syracuse	---	Hobart
Rifle	West Va.†	---	---
Skiing	Utah†	---	---
Soccer	Clemson	Southern Conn. St.	N.C.-Greensboro
Swimming	Texas	**C.S.U. Bakersfield**	Kenyon
Tennis	**Stanford**	Chapman	Wash. & Lee
Track, Indoor	Arkansas	St. Augustine's Abilene Christian	Wis.-LaCrosse
Track, Outdoor	**UCLA**	Abilene Christian	Wis.-LaCrosse
Volleyball	**Southern Cal***	---	---
Water Polo	**U.C. Berkeley***	---	---
Wrestling	Arizona St.	North Dakota St.	St. Lawrence
1988-1989			
Sport	**Division I**	**Division II**	**Division III**
Baseball	Wichita State	**Cal. Poly-SLO**	N. Caro, Wesleyan
Basketball	Michigan	N. Caro. Central	Wisconsin, Whitewater
Cross Country	Wisc., Madison	Edinboro (Penn.)	Wisconsin, Oshkosh
Fencing	Columbia*	---	---
Football	Furman**	N. Dakota State	Ithaca College
Golf	Olkahoma	Columbus College	**C.S.U., Stanislaus**
Gymnastics	Illinois*	---	---
Ice Hockey	Harvard	---	Wisc., Stevens Point
Lacrosse	Syracuse	---	Hobart College
Rifle	West Virgina†	---	---
Skiing	Vermont†	---	---
Soccer	Indiana	Florida Tech.	**U.C. San Diego**
Swimming	Texas	**C.S.U., Bakersfield**	Kenyon
Tennis	**Stanford**	Hampton Univ.	**U.C. Santa Cruz**
Track, Indoor	Arkansas	St. Augustine's, N. Caro.	N. Cent. College, Ill.
Track, Outdoor	LSU	St. Augustine's, N. Caro.	N. Cent. College, Ill.
Volleyball	**UCLA***	---	---
Water Polo	**U.C. Berkeley***	---	---
Wrestling	Olkahoma State	Portland State	Ithaca

*   National Collegiate champion.   **   Division 1-AA champion.
†   Coeducational championship.
Note: C.S.U. = California State University.
32.11,90 Source: NCAA *Annual Reports.*

NATIONAL COLLEGIATE ATHLETIC ASSOCIATION WOMEN'S NATIONAL CHAMPIONS BY DIVISION			
1987-1988			
Sport	Division I	Division II	Division III
Basketball	Louisiana Tech	Hampton	Concordia-M'head
Cross Country	Oregon	**Cal Poly SLO**	Wisconsin, Oshkosh
Fencing	Wayne St.*	---	St. Thomas
Field Hockey	Maryland	---	---
Golf	Tulsa*	---	Bloomsburg
Gymnastics	Alabama*	---	---
Lacrosse	Temple	---	Trenton St.
Soccer	North Carolina*	---	Rochester
Softball	**UCLA**	**C.S.U. Bakersfield**	Central (Iowa)
Swimming	Texas	**C.S.U. Northridge**	Kenyon
Tennis	**Stanford**	SIU-Edwardsville	Mary Washington
Track, Indoor	Texas	Abilene Christian	Christopher Newport
Track, Outdoor	Louisiana St.	Abilene Christian	Christopher Newport
Volleyball	Hawaii	**C.S.U. Northridge**	U.C. San Diego
1988-1989			
Sport	Division I	Division II	Division III
Basketball	Tenn., Knoxville	Delta State	Elizabethtown College
Cross Country	Kentucky	**Cal. Poly-SLO**	Wisconsin, Oshkosh
Fencing	Wayne State	---	---
Field Hockey	Old Dominion	---	Trenton State
Golf	**San Jose State**	---	---
Gymnastics	Georgia	---	---
Lacrosse	Penn. State	---	Ursinus
Soccer	North Carolina	**C.S.U., Hayward**	William Smith College
Softball	**UCLA**	**C.S.U., Bakersfield**	Trenton State
Swimming	**Stanford**	**C.S.U., Northridge**	Kenyon
Tennis	**Stanford**	S. Ill. Edwardsville	**U.C. San Diego**
Track, Indoor	LSU	Abilene Christian	Christopher Newport
Track, Outdoor	LSU	**Cal. Poly-SLO**	Christopher Newport
Volleyball	Texas, Austin	Portland State	**U.C. San Diego**

* National Collegiate champion.   Note: C.S.U. = Cal. State University
32.12,90 Source: NCAA *Annual Reports.*

CALIFORNIA ICE SKATING RINKS

San Francisco Bay Area	Greater Los Angeles Area
Belmont Iceland (415) 592-0532	Burbank-Pickwick Ice Arena
Berkeley Iceland (415) 843-8800	(213) 846-0032
Cupertino Ice Capades (408) 446-2906	Costa Mesa-Ice Capades Chalet
Dublin Iceland (415) 829-4444	(714) 979-8880
San Francisco Ice Arena	Culver City Ice Rink
(415) 664-1408	(213) 398-5718
San Jose-Eastridge Ice Arena	Harbor City Olympic Ice Arena
(408) 238-0440	(213) 325-4474
San Mateo-Ice Capades Chalet	Lancaster Iceland ((805) 942-8127
(415) 574-1616	Newbury Park-Conejo Valley Ice Arena
Santa Rosa-Redwood Empire Ice Arena	(805) 498-6669
(707) 546-7147	N. Hollywood-Ice Capades Chalet
Redwood City Golden Gate Arena	(213) 985-5555
(415) 364-8090	Norwalk-Zero Temp Ice Rink
	(213) 921-5391
Sacramento	Paramount-Iceland (213) 633-1171
N. Sacramento Ice Land (916) 925-3121	Pasadena Ice Capades (213) 578-0800
	Rolling Hills Estates Ice Capades
Other	(213) 541-6630
Yosemite National Park Outdoor Rink	Van Nuys Iceland (213) 785-2171
(209) 372-1441	
	San Diego Area
Inland Empire	San Diego Mira Mesa House of Ice
Lake Arrowhead-Bluejay Ice Castle	(619) 271-4001
(714) 337-5283	San Diego Ice Capades (619) 452-9110

32.13,90 Source: Pacific Data Resources and Berkeley Iceland.

SECTION 33 NOTE

The nation's only professional roller-derby training school is in Hayward, California.

32.14,90

FAMOUS CALIFORNIA ATHLETES/COACHES

Baseball

Vida Blue	Sandy Koufax
Orlando Cepeda	Willie Mays
Joe Cronin	Willie McCovey
Joe Dimaggio	Jackie Robinson
Don Drysdale	Tom Seaver
Lefty Gomez	Duke Snyder
Catfish Hunter	Ted Williams
Jackie Jensen	

Football

Frank Albert	Joe Montana
George Blanda	Jim Plunkett
John Brodie	O. J. Simpson
Mike Garrett	Y. A. Tittle
Elroy Hirsch	

Basketball

Rick Barry	Hank Luisetti
Elgin Baylor	Bill Russell
Wilt Chamberlain	Bill Sharman
Kareem Abdul-Jabbar	Bill Walton
Magic Johnson	Jerry West

Track

Charles Dumas	Charles Paddock
Lee Evans	Bob Richards
Bob Mathias	Bob Seagren
Parry O'Brien	Cornelius Warmerdam

Swimming

Matt Biondi	Don Schollander
Sammy Lee	Mark Spitz
Pat McCormick	Chris Von Saltza
Debbie Meyer	Johnny Weissmuller

Golf

Billy Casper	Ken Venturi
Gene Littler	Mickey Wright

Tennis

Tracy Austin	Billy Jean King
Pauline Betz	Jack Kramer
Don Budge	Alice Marble
May Bundy	Dennis Ralston
Maureen Connolly	Bobby Riggs
Pancho Gonzales	Ellsworth Vines
Hazel Hotchkiss	Helen Wills
Helen Jacobs	

Yachting

Dennis Conner

Horse Racing

Willie Shoemaker

Ice Skating

Brian Boitano	
Peggy Fleming	Charlie Tickner

Boxing

Henry Armstrong	George Foreman
Max Baer	James Jeffries
James J. Corbett	Archie Moore

Olympics

Avery Brundage	Peter Uberroth

Coaches & Owners & Officials

George Allen	John Madden
Walter Alston	Billy Martin
Jerry Buss	Pete Newell
Jack Kent Cooke	Bill Walsh
Charlie Finley	John Wooten

32.15,90 Source: Pacific Data Resources.

Consumers

California's consumers eager to find bargains and willing to put up with a low-overhead sales environment have been flocking to discount warehouses in recent years. The big enchilada of warehouse discounters is Price Club, based in San Diego, with $3.3 billion in sales per year from its thirty-nine stores. Because big cities often lack the space for the necessary 100,000-square-foot warehouses and the acres of accompanying parking lots, the discount warehouse idea has not caught on as much in the large cities of the East and the Midwest as in the West. If Price Club continues its spectacular growth rate, it will soon begin to threaten a variety of established high-overhead retail outlets, including department and specialty stores.

Other companies have picked up on the warehouse sales concept and have established themselves in California as Price Club's competitors. These are Costco, based in Seattle, and Pace stores, based in Denver. In addition, some specialized warehouse sales businesses have sprung up, focusing on particular niches in the market. Home Club specializes in building materials; the Office Club and Arvey's offer discounted office supplies; the Sports Club stocks athletic equipment. Of course, all the low-overhead volume discounters do not succeed. Liquor Barn, which was successful under the control of Safeway, filed for bankruptcy after it was acquired by a British conglomerate.

Where can consumers find out about bargain outlets? Newspapers occasionally run stories on local stores that are factory outlets or specialize in discounted merchandise. And several books are now available that list these merchandisers and describe their wares to help shoppers find bargains in Southern California or in the San Francisco Bay Area.

Consumer activists were shocked and saddened at the demise of the Consumers' Co-ops based in Berkeley and Palo Alto. The Berkeley Co-op chain was the largest of its kind in the nation. A combination of poor management, high salaries, an overambitious expansion plan, theft, and ideological rigidity forced the Co-op into bankruptcy in 1988.

On the state level, consumerism is flexing its muscles, having successfully supported the initiatives Proposition 65 (toxic products labeling) and Proposition 103 (insurance rate regulation). The success of these initiative campaigns may encourage the support of other proposals for statewide regulation under the rubric of consumerism.

PRIVATE AND QUASI-PUBLIC CONSUMER GROUPS IN CALIFORNIA	
California Consumer Affairs Association (CCAA)* C/o David Ball Marin County Dist. Atty. Office Hall of Justice, Rm. 181 San Rafael, CA 94903 (415) 499-6482	Consumer Federation of California Dr. Regene Mitchell P.O. Box 20630 Los Angeles, 90006 (213) 381-5611 (714) 891-2141
California Public Interest Research Groups (CalPIRG) University of California, Berkeley University of California, Santa Barbara University of California, Santa Cruz University of California, Los Angeles (916) 448-4516 (619) 279-5553 (415) 644-3454 (213) 278-9244	Consumer's Union 1535 Mission St. San Francisco, CA 94103 (415) 431-6747
Consumer Action 693 Mission St. San Francisco, CA 94105 (415) 777-9635	Golden State Mobile Home Owners League P.O. Box 876 Garden Grove, CA 92642 1 (800) 888-1727
Toward Utility Rate Normalization (TURN) 693 Mission St., 8th Floor San Francisco, CA 94105 (415) 543-1576	

* The California Consumer Affairs Association is an umbrella organization of public and private groups.

33.1,90 Source: Pacific Data Resources.

BETTER BUSINESS BUREAUS IN CALIFORNIA			
County	Phone	County	Phone
Alameda, Contra Costa	(415) 839-5900	San Francisco and Northern	
Fresno, Madera, Merced	(209) 222-8111	Coastal Counties	(415) 775-3300
Kern, Kings, Inyo, Tulare	(805) 322-2074	San Joaquin and Central	
Los Angeles	(213) 383-0992	Valley Counties	(209) 948-4880
Orange	(714) 544-6942	San Mateo	(415) 347-1251
Sacramento and Northern		Santa Barbara, Ventura,	
Inland Counties	(916) 443-6843	San Luis Obispo	(805) 963-8657
San Bernardino, Riverside	(714) 825-7280	Santa Clara, Santa Cruz	(408) 978-8700
San Diego, Imperial	(619) 234-0966		

33.2,90 Source: U.S. Office of Consumer Affairs, *Consumer's Resource Handbook, 1988.*

STATE AND FEDERAL AGENCIES DEALING WITH CONSUMER COMPLAINTS		
Subject of Complaint	**Agency**	**Phone**
Accountants	State Board of Accountancy	(916) 920-7121
Acupuncturists	State Board of Medical Quality Assurance	(916) 924-2642
Adult Education	Adult Education Field Services	(916) 322-6535
Adulterated Food or Drugs	Department of Health Services	(916) 445-2263
Advertising (Food or Drugs)	Department of Health Services	(916) 445-2263
Advertising (Intrastate)	County District Attorney	
Advertising (Intrastate)	Federal Trade Commission	(213) 209-7575
		(415) 995-5220
Aging	California Dept. of Aging	(916) 322-5290
Agricultural Products	Department of Food and Agriculture	(916) 445-9386
AIDS	Department of Health and Human Services	(800) 342-AIDS
Air Conditioner Repair	Bureau of Electronic and Appliance Repair	(916) 445-4751
Airlines	U.S. Department of Transportation	
	Consumer Affairs Division	(202) 366-2220
Air Pollution	State Air Resources Board	(916) 322-2990
Alarm Companies	Bureau of Collection and Investigative Services	(916) 739-3028
Alcohol and Bars	Department of Alcoholic Beverage Control	(916) 445-6811
Ambulance (Billing)	Department of Consumer Affairs	(916) 445-1254
Ambulance Services (Safety)	Highway Patrol	(916) 445-1564
Appliance Repairs (Major)	Bureau of Electronic and Appliance Repair	(916) 445-4751
Architects	State Board of Architectural Examiners	(916) 445-3393
Asbestos	U.S. Environmental Protection Administration	(202) 382-3949
Auctioneers	Auctioneers Commission	(916) 324-5894
Audiologists	Board of Medical Quality Assurance	(916) 920-6388
Auto Advertising	Department of Motor Vehicles	(916) 732-0339
Auto Leasing	Office of the Attorney General	(800) 952-5225
Auto Odometer Fraud	Department of Motor Vehicles	(916) 732-0339
Auto Recalls	National Highway Traffic Safety Administration	(800) 424-9393
Auto Repairs	Bureau of Automotive Repair	(800) 952-5210
Auto Safety	National Highway Traffic Safety Administration	(800) 424-9393
Auto Sales (New)	New Motor Vehicle Board	(916) 445-1888
Auto Sales (Used)	Department of Motor Vehicles	(916) 732-0339
Auto Smog Devices	Bureau of Automotive Repair	(800) 952-5022
Bail Bond Agents	Department of Insurance	(415) 557-3646
Banks (National)	Comptroller of the Currency	(202) 287-4265
Banks (State)	State Banking Department	(415) 557-3535
Barbers	State Board of Barber Examiners	(916) 445-7008
Beds	Bureau of Home Furnishings	(916) 920-6951
Beauty Salons	Board of Cosmetology	(916) 445-7061
Blue Cross/Blue Shield	Health Care Financing Administration	(415) 556-0254
Blue Shield	Department of Corporations	(916) 324-9013
Boats	Department of Boating and Waterways	(916) 445-5684
Boat Repair	Department of Consumer Affairs	(916) 445-1254
Boat Safety	Coast Guard Hotline	(800) 368-5647
Bonds	U.S. Securities and Exchange Commission	(202) 272-7440
Bonds	Department of Corporations	(213) 736-2713
Boxing, Karate, Wrestling	State Athletic Commission	(916) 920-7300
Broadcasting	Federal Communications Commission	(202) 632-7048
Buses	Public Utilities Commission	(415) 557-2298
Business Taxes	State Board of Equalization	(916) 445-6464
Cable TV	Department of Consumer Affairs	(916) 445-1254
Carpet Sales	Department of Consumer Affairs	(916) 445-1254
Carpet Installing	Contractors State License Board	(916) 366-5153
Cancer	Department of Health and Human Services	(800) 4CA-NCER
Cars (Advertising)	Department of Motor Vehicles	(916) 732-7683

STATE AND FEDERAL AGENCIES DEALING WITH CONSUMER COMPLAINTS

Subject of Complaint	Agency	Phone
Cars (Repairs)	Bureau of Automotive Repair	(916) 366-5105
Cars (Safety)	National Highway Traffic Safety Administration	(800) 424-9393
Cars (Sales)	New Motor Vehicles Board	(916) 445-1888
Cemeteries	Cemetery Board	(916) 920-6078
Charities	Registry of Charitable Trusts	(916) 445-2021
Check Cashers	Department of Corporations	(213) 736-2776
Child Abuse	National Center on Child Abuse	(202) 245-0586
Child Car Seats		(800) CAR-SEAT
Child Care	Department of Social Services	(916) 324-4038
Child Support	Department of Social Services	(916) 323-8994
Child Support	U.S. Dept. of Health & Human Services	(202) 252-5377
Chiropractors	State Board of Chiropractic Examiners	(916) 445-3244
Civil Rights	Department of Fair Employment and Housing	(916) 739-4616
Collection Agencies	State Bureau of Collections and Investigative Services	(916) 739-3028
Commodity Options	Commodity Futures Trading Commission	(202) 254-3067
Computer (Home) Repair	Bureau of Electronic and Appliance Repair	(916) 445-4751
Co-ops	Department of Consumer Affairs	(916) 445-1254
Condominiums	Department of Real Estate	(916) 739-3684
Consumer Fraud (general)	Department of Consumer Services	(213) 620-4360
	Division of Consumer Services	(916) 445-1254
Consumer Products	U.S. Consumer Product Safety Commission	(800) 638-2772
Contests/Free Offers	Department of Justice	(800) 952-5225
Contractors	Contractor's State License Board	(916) 366-5153
Convalescent Homes	Department of Health Services	(916) 445-4171
Correspondence Courses	Department of Education	(916) 445-3427
Corporate Stock	Department of Corporations	(916) 445-7205
Cosmetics	Department of Health Services	(916) 445-4171
Cosmetologists	Board of Cosmetology	(916) 445-7061
Credit, Retail	Federal Trade Commission	(213) 209-7575
Credit Reporting	Federal Trade Commission	(213) 209-7575
Credit Unions (Federal)	National Credit Union Administration	(202) 682-9600
Credit Unions (State)	Department of Corporations	(916) 445-7205
Crematories	Cemetery Board	(916) 920-6078
Dance Studios	Department of Justice	(800) 952-5225
Deceptive Sales Practices	Department of Justice	(800) 952-5225
Dentists	State Board of Dental Examiners	(916) 920-7451
Dental Hygienists	State Board of Dental Examiners	(916) 920-7451
Detectives	Bureau of Collection and Investigative Services	(916) 739-3028
Disasters	Federal Emergency Management Agency	(202) 646-3615
Discrimination (Education)	U.S. Office of Civil Rights	(415) 227-8040
Discrimination (by employers)	U.S. Equal Employment Opportunity Commission	(415) 273-7588
Discrimination (Housing)	Department of Fair Employment and Housing	(916) 739-4616
Dishwasher Repair	Bureau of Electronic and Appliance Repair	(916) 445-4751
Doctors	Board of Medical Quality Assurance	(916) 920-6013
Drape Installation	Department of Consumer Affairs	(916) 445-1254
Driving Schools	Department of Motor Vehicles	(916) 732-0339
Drugs	Department of Health Services	(916) 445-4171
Drugs	U.S. Food and Drug Administration	(301) 443-3170
Drug Smuggling	U.S. Customs Service	(800) BE-ALERT
Dry Cleaners	Board of Fabric Care	(916) 445-4751
Dryer (Clothes) Repair	Bureau of Electronic and Appliance Repair	(916) 445-4751
Economic Development	Department of Commerce	(916) 322-5665

33.3.2,90

STATE AND FEDERAL AGENCIES DEALING WITH CONSUMER COMPLAINTS		
Subject of Complaint	**Agency**	**Phone**
Educational Psychologists	Board of Behavioral Science Examiners	(916) 445-4933
Electricians	Contractors State License Board	(916) 366-5153
Electricity (rates/service)	Public Utilities Commission	(415) 557-0647
Electrolysis (Hair Removal)	Board of Cosmetology	(916) 445-7061
Employment Agencies (Private)	Bureau of Personnel Services	(916) 920-6311
Energy Conservation	Department of Energy	(800) 428-2525
Engineers	Board of Registration for Professional Engineers	(916) 920-7466
Environmental Regulations	Environmental Protection Agency	(415) 974-8076
Escrow Companies	Department of of Corporations	(213) 736-2741
Explosives	U.S. Bureau of Alcohol, Tobacco, and Firearms	(800) 424-9555
Eyeglasses	Board of Medical Quality Assurance	(916) 924-2612
False Labels or Low Weights	Department of Food and Agriculture	(916) 445-9280 (714) 558-4196
Firearms	Bureau of Alcohol, Tobacco and Firearms	(202) 789-3175
Fire-related Problems	State Fire Marshall	(916) 424-7088
Fish and Game Code Violations	Department of Fish and Game	(916) 445-3531
Food	Department of Health Services	(916) 445-4171
Food	U.S. Food and Drug Administration	(301) 443-3170
Forests and Trees	Department of Forestry	(916) 445-9920
Foundations	Office of the Attorney General, Registry of Charitable Trusts	(916) 445-2021
Franchises	Department of Corporations	(916) 445-7205
Freight (Interstate)	Interstate Commerce Commission	(202) 275-7148
Freight (Intrastate)	Public Utilities Commission	(415) 557-0647
Funeral Directors	Board of Funeral Directors and Embalmers	(916) 445-2413
Furniture	Bureau of Home Furnishings	(916) 920-6951
Futures Trading	Commodity Futures Trading Commission	(202) 254-3067
Gas, Natural (rates/service)	Public Utilities Commission	(415) 557-0647
Geologists and Geophysicists	Board of Registration for Geologists and Geophysicists	(916) 445-1920
Guard Dog Companies	Bureau of Collection and Investigative Services	(916) 739-3028
Guide Dogs	Board of Guide Dogs for the Blind	(916) 445-9041
Handicapped Infants	Department of Health Services	(916) 322-4780
Handicapped Problems	Operator Services-U.S. Government TDD/TTY	(800) 855-1155
Health Care Financing	Health Care Financing Administration	(301) 966-3000
Health Care Plans	Department of Corporations	(916) 445-7205
Health Spas/Studios	Department of Consumer Affairs	(916) 445-1254
Hearing Aids	Board of Medical Quality Assurance	(916) 920-6377
Highway Accidents	California Highway Patrol	911
Highway Conditions	Caltrans	(916) 445-7623
Highway Emergencies	Caltrans	(916) 445-3887
Highways	Caltrans	(916) 445-4616
Horse Racing	California Horse Racing Board	(916) 920-7178
Hospital Care, Free	U.S. Health Care Financing Administration	(800) 638-0742
Hospitals	Department of Health Services	(916) 445-4171
Hotels/Motels	Department of Consumer Affairs	(916) 445-1254
Housing Discrimination	Department of Fair Employment and Housing	(916) 739-4616
Housing	Department of Housing and Community Development	(916) 445-4775
Immigration	U.S. Immigration and Naturalization Service	(703) 235-4055
Immigration Consultants	Department of Justice	(800) 952-5225
Imports	U.S. Customs Services	(800) USA-FAKE
Indoor Air	Department of Health Services	(415) 445-1967
Insurance	Department of Insurance	(800) 233-9045
Interior Designers	Department of Consumer Affairs	(916) 445-1254
Interstate Transportation	Interstate Commerce Commission	(202) 275-7148
Investment Counselors	Department of Corporations	(916) 445-7205

STATE AND FEDERAL AGENCIES DEALING WITH CONSUMER COMPLAINTS		
Subject of Complaint	**Agency**	**Phone**
Job Safety	Department of Industrial Relations	(415) 557-1946
Judges	Judicial Performance Commission	(415) 557-2503
Labor Standards	Department of Industrial Relations	(415) 557-0860
Landlord/Tenant	Department of Consumer Affairs	(916) 445-1254
Land Sales, Interstate	U.S. Dept. of Housing and Urban Develpment	(202) 755-0502
Landscape Architects	Board of Landscape Architects	(916) 445-4954
Lawyers	State Bar of California	(415) 561-8200
Loan Brokers	Department of Real Estate	(916) 739-3684
Loan Companies	Department of Corporations	(916) 445-7205
Locksmiths	Bureau of Collection and Investigative Services	(916) 738-3028
Lottery	State Lottery Commission	(916) 324-2025
Magazines	Magazine Action Line	(800) 645-9242
Mail (removing name from a sexually oriented mailing list)	Go to local Post Office and fill out Form 2201	
Mail (removing name from a list)	Direct Mail Marketing Association 6 East 43rd Street New York, NY 10017	
Mail (unordered merchandise)	U.S. Postal Inspector-Local Office	
Mail Fraud	U.S. Postal Inspector-Local Office	(202) 268-4267
Mail Order Companies	Department of Consumer Affairs	(916) 445-1254
Maritime Emergencies	U.S. Coast Guard (Business Hours Only)	(800) 368-5647 (415) 556-2103 (213) 499-5380
Marriage, Family and Child Counselors	State Board of Behavioral Science Examiners	(916) 445-4933
Massage Parlors	Department of Consumer Affairs	(916) 445-1254
Measurement Devices	County Office of Weights and Measurements	
Meat or Poultry	U.S. Department of Agriculture, Division of Food Safety	(800) 535-4555 (415) 273-7788
Medical and Radiological Devices	U.S. Food and Drug Administration	(415) 556-2062
Medi-Cal	Department of Health Services	(916) 445-4171
Medi-Care	U.S. Health Care Financing Administration	(301) 966-3000
Mental Hospitals	Department of Health Services	(916) 445-4171
Midwives	Board of Registered Nursing	(916) 322-3350
Mine Safety	Department of Labor	(703) 235-1452
Minority Business	Department of Commerce	(916) 322-1394
Mobile Homes	Department of Housing and Community Development	(800) 952-5275
Modeling Agencies	Bureau of Personnel Services	(916) 920-6311
Moving Companies (Interstate)	Interstate Commerce Commission	(202) 275-7148
(Intrastate)	Public Utilities Commission	(415) 557-0647
Notary Publics	Secretary of State	(916) 322-2577
Nurses, Registered	Board of Registered Nurses	(916) 322-3350
Nurses, Vocational	Board of Vocational Nurses	(916) 445-0793
Nursing Homes	Department of Health Services	(916) 445-4171
Occupational Safety and Health	Department of Industrial Relations	(916) 557-1946
Oil Drilling	Department of Conservation	(916) 445-9686
Ophthalmologists	Board of Medical Quality Assurance	(916) 347-4651
Opticians	Board of Medical Quality Assurance	(916) 347-4651
Optometrists	Board of Optometry	(916) 739-4131
Osteopaths	Board of Osteopathic Examiners	(916) 322-4306
Painters	Contractors State License Board	(916) 366-5153

33.3.4,90

	STATE AND FEDERAL AGENCIES DEALING WITH CONSUMER COMPLAINTS	
Subject of Complaint	**Agency**	**Phone**
Paramedics	County Health Department	
Parks (State)	Department of Parks and Recreation	(916) 445-6477
Passports	Department of State	(202) 647-0518
Patents and Trademarks	Department of Commerce	(703) 557-3341
Pawnbrokers	Department of Consumer Affairs	(916) 445-1254
Pensions	Pension Benefit Guaranty Corporation	(202) 778-8800
Personal Income Tax	See Taxes	
Personnel Agencies	Bureau of Personnel Services	(916) 920-6311
Pest Control	Structural Pest Control Board	(916) 924-2291
Pesticides	Department of Food and Agriculture	(916) 327-1409
Pesticides	Structural Pest Control Board	(916) 924-2291
Pharmacists	Board of Pharmacy	(916) 445-5014
Physical Therapists	Board of Medical Quality Assurance	(916) 920-6373
Plants, Infected	Department of Food and Agriculture	(916) 924-9280
Plumbers	Contractors State License Board	(916) 366-5153
Podiatrists	Board of Medical Quality Assurance	(916) 920-6347
Polygraph Examiners	Polygraph Examiners Board	(916) 739-3855
Pool Construction	Contractors State License Board	(916) 366-5153
Private Investigators	Bureau of Collection and Investigative Services	(916) 739-3028
Private Schools		
K-12	Department of Education	(916) 324-4934
Postsecondary	Office of Private Postsecondary Education	(916) 445-3427
Product Safety	U.S. Consumer Product Safety Commission	(800) 638-2772
Psychiatrists	Board of Medical Quality Assurance	(916) 920-6013
Public Pools	County Health Department	
Property Taxes	State Board of Equalization	(916) 445-4982
Property Taxes	Your County Assessor	
Pyramid Schemes	Department of Justice	(800) 952-5225
Psychiatric Technicians	Board of Psychiatric Technical Examiners	(916) 920-6013
Psychiatrists	Board of Medical Quality Assurance	(916) 920-6341
Psychologists	Board of Medical Quality Assurance	(916) 920-6383
Raffle Tickets	Department of Justice	(800) 952-5225
Rail Passenger Service	Amtrak	No Phone
	400 N. Capitol St., N.W.	Complaints
	Washington, D.C. 20001	
Railroad Safety	Federal Railroad Administration	(202) 366-0522
Real Estate Sales	Department of Real Estate	(916) 739-3684
Recreational Vehicles	Department of Motor Vehicles	(916) 732-0339
Refrigerator Repair	Bureau of Electronic and Appliance Repair	(916) 445-4751
Repair of Major		
Appliances	Bureau of Electronic and Appliance Repair	(916) 445-4751
Repossessors	Bureau of Collection and Investigative Services	(916) 739-3028
Restaurants	County Health Department	
Ride Sharing	Caltrans	(916) 445-4616
Roadside Hazards	California Highway Patrol	911
Roofers	Contractors State License Board	(916) 366-5153
Runaways	National Center on Child Abuse	(800) 621-4000
Sales Tax	Board of Equalization	(916) 445-6464
Savings and Loan		
Federal	Federal Home Loan Bank	(202) 906-6211
State	Department of Savings and Loan	(213) 736-2798
Satellite Dish Repair	Bureau of Electronic and Appliance Repair	(916) 445-4751
Securities Brokers	Department of Corporations	(916) 445-7205
Security Guards	Bureau of Collection and Investigative Services	(916) 739-3028
Service Stations	Department of Consumer Affairs	(916) 445-1254

33.3.5,90

STATE AND FEDERAL AGENCIES DEALING WITH CONSUMER COMPLAINTS		
Subject of Complaint	Agency	Phone
Shorthand Reporters	Certified Shorthand Reporters Board	(916) 445-5101
Small Business Development	Department of Commerce	(916) 324-1295
Smoke Detectors	State Fire Marshall	(916) 427-4161
Social Security	U.S. Social Security Administration	(916) 551-1000
Social Workers	State Board of Behavioral Science Examiners	(916) 445-4933
Solar Heating	Contractors' State License Board	(916) 366-5153
Speech Pathologists	Board of Medical Quality Assurance	(916) 920-6388
Stamps, Trading	Department of Corporations	(213) 736-2741
Stereo Repair	Bureau of Electronic and Appliance Repair	(916) 445-4751
Stocks	U.S. Securities and Exchange Commission	(202) 272-7440
Stove Repair	Bureau of Electronic and Appliance Repair	(916) 445-4751
2nd Surgical Opinions	U.S. Dept. of Health & Human Services	(800) 838-6833
Student Aid, Federal	U.S. Department of Education	(202) 732-3391
Surveyors	Board of Registration for Professional Engineers	(916) 920-7466
Talent Agencies	Division of Labor Standards Enforcement	(415) 557-0860
Tanning Salons	Department of Consumer Affairs	(916) 445-1254
Tax Preparers	Tax Preparer Program	(916) 324-4977
Taxes (Federal)	Internal Revenue Service (forms only)	(800) 424-3676
Taxes (State)	Franchise Tax Board	(916) 369-0500
		(800) 852-7050
		(Northern California)
		(800) 852-5711
		(Southern California)
Teachers	Your local school district	
Teaching Credentials, K-12	Commission for Teacher Preparation and Licensing	(916) 445-7254
Telephone	Federal Communications Commission	(202) 632-7553
Telephone	Public Utilities Commission	(415) 557-0647
Telephone (Intrastate)	Public Utilities Commission	(415) 557-0350
Telephone (Interstate)	Federal Communications Commission	(202) 632-7048
Television Advertising	Federal Communications Commission	(202) 632-7048
Television Programs	Federal Communications Commission	(202) 632-7048
Television Repair	Bureau of Electronic and Appliance Repair	(916) 445-4751
Telephone Solicitors	Direct Mail Marketing Program	
(Removing name from	Name Removal Program	
their lists)	6 East 43rd Street	
	New York, NY 10017-4609	
Thrift Companies	Department of Corporations	(213) 736-2741
Tire Chain Installers	Department of Transportation	
Highway 50		(916) 324-7312
Highway 80		(916) 265-4290
Tires	U.S. Department of Transportation	(800) 424-9393
Title Companies	Department of Insurance	(415) 557-3646
Tour Companies	Department of Consumer Affairs	(916) 445-1254
Towing Services	Department of Consumer Affairs	(916) 445-1254
Toxic Waste or Spills	Department of of Health Services National Response Center	(800) 424-8802
Toys	U.S. Consumer Product Safety Commission	(800) 638-2772
Transportation (Intrastate)	Public Utilities Commission	(415) 557-0647
Travel Agents	Department of Justice	(800) 952-5225
Tree Trimmers	Contractors State License Board	(916) 366-5153
Trucking Companies	Public Utilities Commission	(415) 557-0647
Truck Rental (Intrastate)	Public Utilities Commission	(415) 557-0647
Unemployment Benefits	Employment Development Department	(916) 445-8008
Unfair Business Practices	Federal Trade Commission	(213) 209-7575
Unsolicited Goods	Federal Trade Commission	(213) 209-7575
Upholstery	Bureau of Home Furnishings	(916) 920-6951
Utility Companies	Public Utilities Commission	(415) 557-3703
Veterans	Department of Veterans Affairs	(916) 323-5325
Veterans	U.S. Veterans Administration	(202) 233-3113

Subject of Complaint	Agency	Phone
STATE AND FEDERAL AGENCIES DEALING WITH CONSUMER COMPLAINTS		
Victim/Witness Assistance	Office of Criminal Justice Planning	(916) 324-9116
Veterinaries	Board of Examiners in Veterinary Medicine	(916) 920-7662
Video Recorder Repair	Bureau of Electronic and Appliance Repair	(916) 445-4751
Vocational Schools	Office of Private Postsecondary Education	(916) 445-3427
Washer (Clothes) Repair	Bureau of Electronic and Appliance Repair	(916) 445-4751
Water (rates/service)	Public Utilities Commission	(415) 557-0647
Water (taste/smell)	Department of Health Services	(916) 323-6111
Waterbeds	Bureau of Home Furnishings	(916) 920-6951
Weights and Measures	California Department of Food and Agriculture	(916) 366-5119
Weights and Measures	County Offices of Weights and Measures	
Williamson Act (Agricultural Land)	Department of Conservation	(916) 322-7683
Worker Complaints with Employers	Department of Industrial Relations	(415) 557-3356
Yacht and Ship Brokers	Department of Boating and Waterways, Yacht and Ship Broker Licensing	(916) 445-5684

Note: The California Dept. of Consumer Affairs, Division of Consumer Services, Complaint Assistance Unit acts as a clearinghouse and complaint referral service. Call (916) 445-0660 and 445-1254 between 10:00 a.m. and 3:00 p.m. For more detailed consumer complaint information see *Consumer Complaints,* published by the Dept. of Consumer Affairs.

33.3.7,90 Source: Cal. Dept. of Consumer Affairs, *Consumer Complaints: Resource and Referral Guide, 1987* and Pacific Data Resources update, 1989.

STATE LEGISLATIVE COMMITTEES DEALING WITH CONSUMER ISSUES

State Assembly
Government Efficiency and Consumer Protection
(916) 324-7440
Delaine Eastin, Chair

State Senate
Business and Professions
(916) 445-3435
Joseph Montoya, Chair

33.4,90 Source: Pacific Data Resources

FEDERAL AGENCIES DEALING WITH CONSUMER ISSUES

Department of Health & Human Services	(800) 336-4797
Department of Agriculture	(202) 447-8998
Consumer Products Safety Commission	(800) 638-2772
San Francisco	(415) 556-1816
Los Angeles	(213) 251-7464
Department of Commerce	(202) 377-5001
Department of Education	(202) 732-3679
Department of Energy	(800) 523-2929
Federal Communications Commission	(202) 632-7048
Federal Deposit Insurance Corporation	(800) 424-5488
Federal Trade Commission	
San Francisco	(415) 995-5220
Los Angeles	(213) 209-7575
Food and Drug Administration	(301) 443-3170
Department of the Interior	(202) 343-5521
Department of Labor	(202) 523-6060
Post Office	(202) 268-4267
Small Business Administration	(202) 653-6170
Securities and Exchange Commission	(202) 272-7440
U.S. Coast Guard	(800) 368-5647
Veterans Administration	(202) 233-3113

33.5,90 Source: U.S. Office of Consumer Affairs, *Consumer Resource Handbook, 1990.*

FEDERAL CONSUMER COMPLAINT/QUESTION HOT LINES

To report fraud, waste, and abuse in the U.S. Government	(800) 424-5454
To report fraud, waste, and abuse in the Defense Dept.	(800) 424-9098
To complain about unwholesome meat or poultry	(800) 535-4555
To complain about most household consumer products	(800) 638-2772
To complain about auto defects or repairs	(800) 424-9393
For information on hazardous waste	(800) 424-9346
For information on toxic substances	(202) 554-1404
To report toxic spills	(800) 424-8802

33.6,90 Source: The relevant Federal agencies.

FEDERAL LEGISLATIVE COMMITTEES DEALING WITH CONSUMER ISSUES	
U.S. House of Representatives	
Committee on Agriculture Subcommittee on Domestic Marketing Consumer Relations and Nutrition	(202) 225-1867
Committee on Banking, Finance and Urban Affairs Subcommittee on Consumer Affairs and Coinage	(202) 225-8872
Committee on Energy and Commerce Subcommittee on Commerce Consumer Protection and Competition Subcommittee on Health and the Environment	(202) 226-3160 (202) 225-4952
Committee on Government Operations Subcommittee on Commerce, Consumer and Monetary Affairs	(202) 225-4407
Select Committee on Aging Subcommittee on Housing and Consumer Interests	(202) 226-3344
U.S. Senate	
Committee on Banking, Housing and Urban Affairs Subcommittee on Consumer Affairs	(202) 224-7391
Committee on Commerce, Science and Transportation Subcommittee on Consumers	(202) 224-0415

33.7,90 Source: U.S. Congress.

FEDERAL INFORMATION CENTERS*	
Los Angeles	(213) 894-3800
Sacramento	(916) 978-4189
San Diego	(619) 557-6030
San Francisco	(415) 556-6600
Santa Ana	(714) 836-2386

* Federal Information Centers help citizens locate the specific Federal agencies which can assist with a given problem.
33.8,90 Source: Pacific Data Resources.

Department or Office	Telephone Number	For Calls Regarding
TOLL-FREE TELEPHONE NUMBERS OF CALIFORNIA'S STATE AGENCIES		
Air Resources Board	(800) 242-4450	Warranties on auto emission devices, automobile exhaust emissions, certification of out-of-state vehicles and Cal. emission standards for newly invented auto parts
Assistance Fund for Energy	(800) 343-7233	Energy loans
Attorney General	(800) 952-5225	Complaints and inquiries
Banking, State	(800) 622-0620	Complaints and inquiries about state banks
Cal. Conservation Corps	(800) 952-5627	General information
Consumer Affairs	(800) 952-5210	Vehicle repair problems and the Smog Check Program
	(916) 445-0660	Complaint Assistance
Energy Resources, Conservation, and Development Commission	(800) 433-4327	Conservation and low income Energy Assistance
	(800) 822-6228	General information
Fish and Game	(800) 952-5400	Secret witness number to report violations of hunting or fishing laws (eligible for rewards)
Franchise Tax Board	(800) 852-7050	Taxpayer information - Northern California
	(800) 852-5711	Southern California
Cal. Highway Patrol	911	To report accidents or drunk drivers
Housing and Community Development	(800) 852-5275	Complaints against mobile home dealers, and sales agents Registration of mobile homes
Parks and Recreation	(800) 444-PARK	Hearst Castle and California state campground reservations (Mistix)
Social Services	(800) 952-5253	General information, complaints or inquiries
Veteran Affairs	(800) 952-5626	Information on benefits
Waste Management Board	(800) 327-9886	Information on recycling
Water Resources	(800) 952-5530	Information about floods or to report floods

33.9,90 Source: Cal. Dep. of Consumer Affairs, *Consumer Complaints: Resource & Referral Guide, 1987,* and update by Editor, 1989.

LOCAL AGENCIES DEALING WITH CONSUMER ISSUES		
County Offices		
County	**Office**	**Phone**
Alameda	District Atty., Consumer & Environ. Prot. Div.	(415) 881-6150
Contra Costa	District Attorney-Special	(415) 646-4500
	Operations Division	ex. 4500
Fresno	District Attorney-Consumer Fraud Division	(209) 488-3156
Fresno	Community Development and Consumer Protection	(209) 488-3860
Kern	Deputy District Attorney-Consumer Unit	(805) 861-2421
Los Angeles	District Attorney-Consumer Protection Division	(213) 974-3970
Los Angeles	L.A. County Dept. of Consumer Affairs	(213) 974-1452
Madera	Weights and Measures Office	(209) 675-7809
Marin	District Attorney, Consumer Protection Division	(415) 499-6450
Mendocino	Deputy District Attorney-Consumer Division	(707) 463-4211
Monterey	Consumer Affairs	(408) 755-5073
Napa	Consumer Affairs Division	(707) 253-4211
Orange	District Attorney-Major Fraud	
	Consumer Protection Unit	(714) 541-7600
Riverside	District Attorney-Economic Crime Division	(714) 787-6372
Sacramento	Deputy District Attorney-Fraud Division	(916) 440-6174
San Diego	District Attorney-Consumer Fraud Division	(619) 531-4070
San Francisco	Assistant District Attorney-Consumer	
	Fraud Unit	(415) 552-6400
San Joaquin	Deputy District Attorney-Fraud Division	(209) 944-3811
San Luis Obispo	Consumer Fraud Department	(805) 549-5677
San Mateo	District Attorney-Fraud Unit	(415) 366-8221
Santa Barbara	Dep. District Atty.-Consumer Advocate Program	(805) 568-2300
Santa Clara	District Attorney-Consumer Fraud Unit	(408) 299-7435
Santa Clara	County Dept. of Consumer Affairs	(408) 299-4211
Santa Cruz	District Attorney-Division of Consumer Affairs	(408) 425-2054
Shasta	Consumers' Aid	(916) 221-0294
Solano	Deputy District Attorney-Consumer Affairs	(707) 429-6451
Sonoma	District Attorney-Consumer Affairs Division	(707) 527-3458
Stanislaus	Deputy District Attorney-Consumer Fraud Unit	(209) 571-5550
Ventura	Deputy District Attorney-Consumer Fraud Unit	(805) 654-3110
Yolo	Consumer Fraud Division	(916) 666-8180
City Offices		
City	**Office**	**Phone**
Los Angeles	Assistant City Attorney-Consumer	
	Protection Section	(213) 485-4515
San Diego	City Attorney-Consumer Fraud Unit	(619) 236-6007
Santa Monica	City Attorney-Consumer Fraud Division	(213) 458-8336

33.10,90   Source: California Department of Consumer Affairs, *Consumer Complaints: Resource and Referral Guide,* 1990 and update by Editor.

AUTO MAKERS' CUSTOMER RELATIONS	
Audi	(800) 822-AUDI
BMW	(415) 463-0690
	(213) 305-2913
Chrysler	(415) 463-0656
	(714) 870-4000
Fiat	(201) 393-4042
Ford	(714) 520-8300
	(408) 262-9110
General Motors	
Buick	(800) 521-7300
Cadillac	(313) 554-5536
Chevrolet	(800) 222-1020
Oldsmobile	(517) 377-5546
Pontiac	(800) 762-2737
GMC	(313) 456-4547
Honda	(213) 781-4565
Isuzu	(714) 770-2626
Jaguar	(415) 467-0625
Jeep/Eagle	(714) 855-3533
Mazda	(714) 380-7705
Mercedes-Benz	(415) 871-5125
	(213) 835-8315
Nissan (Datsun)	(714) 549-1277
	(415) 932-0550
Peugeot	(800) 345-5549
Porsche Audi	(702) 348-3154
Saab	(800) 255-9007
Subaru	(714) 951-6592
	(916) 371-7901
Toyota	(800) 331-4331
Volkswagen	(415) 463-1080
	(213) 390-8011
Volvo	(201) 768-4737
Yugo	(201) 825-4600

33.11,90 Source: U.S. Office of Consumer Affairs, Consumer's Resource Handbook, 1990.

Women

The year 1990 is shaping up as an interesting one politically for women in California. For the first time in California history there is a credible female candidate running for governor. Dianne Feinstein, the former mayor of San Francisco, is seeking the Democratic party's nomination. Candidates from Northern California are generally perceived to be at a disadvantage in statewide races, and Feinstein could find herself in this position if she wins the primary, but with 48 percent of the Democratic primary vote coming from Northern California, particularly from the San Francisco Bay Area, Feinstein has at least an even chance of being nominated. Some political observers had thought that Secretary of State March Fong Eu might try for the governor's seat or for a U.S. Senate seat, but she seems unwilling to risk her safe position in a bid for higher office.

Another possible female contender for statewide office in the near future is Mayor Maureen O'Connor of San Diego, who has worked her way up from the city council to her city's top slot. Senator Pete Wilson, a former mayor of San Diego, has shown that the mayor's office is not necessarily a dead end, and O'Connor may well decide to follow his lead.

Dianne Feinstein, March Fong Eu, and Maureen O'Connor have similar political advantages in running for higher office. All are personable and experienced, and each comes from a very wealthy family. In an era when political fund-raising and political action committee contributions are being described by the media as ethical gray areas, each of these women could spend millions of dollars of her own money to finance her campaign.

A recent Census Bureau study of businesses owned by women in California indicates that there are 396,000 such establishments, more than half of them in the services sector and most of them sole proprietorships, that is, businesses with no employees. California, with 14 percent of all the businesses in the nation owned by women (the state has 12 percent of the U.S. population), seems to be a hospitable environment for women entrepreneurs. The annual sales of businesses owned by women in California exceed $7 billion and their yearly payroll is more than $1.2 billion.

CALIFORNIA CHILD CARE RESOURCE AND REFERRAL PROGRAMS BY COUNTY

Alameda	Colusa
Action Alliance for Children 700 Broadway Ste. 300 Oakland, CA 94612 (415) 654-0535 Referral	Colusa County Supt. of Schools 146 Eleventh Street Colusa, CA 95932 (916) 458-7711
BANANAS 6501 Telegraph Avenue Oakland, CA 94609 (415) 658-6046 (415) 658-7101 Administration	**Contra Costa** Contra Costa Children's Council 3020 Grant Ave. Concord, CA 94520 (415) 676-KIDS Referral (415) 676-5442 Administration
4-C's of Alameda County* 1036 A St. 3rd Floor Hayward, CA 94541 (415) 790-0655 Referral (415) 582-2182 Administration	Contra Costa Children's Council 2075 Railroad Avenue Pittsburg, CA 94565 (415) 427-5437
4-C's of Alameda County* 35553 Fremont Blvd. Fremont, CA 94536 (415) 790-0656 Referral (415) 790-0658 Administration	Contra Costa Children's Council 3727 Barrett Avenue Richmond, CA 94805 (415) 233-5437
Resources for Family Development 1520 Catalina Court Livermore, CA 94550 (415) 455-5111 Referral	**Del Norte** Del Norte Child Care Council P.O. Box 1350 Crescent City, CA 95531 (707) 464-8311
Amador Mountain Family Service Agency 1001 Broadway, Suite 204 Jackson, CA 95642 (209) 223-1624	**El Dorado** CDI-Choices for Children P.O. Box 413 South Lake Tahoe, CA 95705 (916) 541-5848
Butte Valley Oak Children's Services 1024 Esplanade Chico, CA 95926 (916) 895-3509 Administration	Choices for Children 2716 Colma St. Placerville, CA 95667 (916) 626-8545
Calaveras Mountain Family Service Agency P.O. Box 919 134 East Charles Street San Andreas, CA 95249 (209) 754-1028	**Fresno** Central Valley Children's Services 841 North Fulton Fresno, CA 93728 (209) 264-0200

* 4-C's means Community Child Care Council.
34.1.1,90

CALIFORNIA CHILD CARE RESOURCE AND REFERRAL PROGRAMS BY COUNTY

Humboldt Humboldt Child Care Council 805 Seventh Street Eureka, CA 95501 (707) 444-8293 Administration	**Los Angeles (continued)** Connections for Children 612 Colorado Ave. Santa Monica, CA 90401 (213) 452-0283 Referral (213) 452-3325 Administration
Imperial Imperial County Child Development Services 1398 Sperber Road El Centro, CA 92243 (714) 339-6431	Pomona School Dist. 800 South Garey Ave. Pomona, CA 91766 (714) 623-1461
Kern Community College Dist. 2100 Chester Ave. Bakersfield, CA 93301 (805) 322-7633	Child Care Resource Center of the San Fernando Valley 14410 Sylvan Street, Room 116 Van Nuys, CA 91401 (818) 781-7099
Kings Kings County Community Action Organization 1222 W. Lacey Blvd. Hanford, CA 93230 (209) 582-4386 Administration	Children's Home Society 2727 West 6th St. Los Angeles, CA 90057 (213) 389-6750
Lake Rural Communities Child Care 934 South Forbes Street. Lakeport, CA 95453 (707) 263-4693	Child and Family Services 2406 Kent St. Los Angeles, CA 90026 (213) 413-0777
Rural Communities Child Care 14893 Lakeshore Dr. Clear Lake, CA 95457 (707) 994-4647	Crystal Stairs, Inc. P.O. Box 92240 Los Angeles, CA 90009 (213) 299-0199 Referral (213) 299-8998 Administration
Lassen Lassen Union High School Dist. 1324 Cornell Street. Susanville, CA 96130 (916) 257-9781	Equipoise 219 E. Bennett Avenue Compton, CA 90224 (213) 537-9016
Los Angeles Child Care Information Service 330 South Oak Knoll, Suite 22 Pasadena, CA 91101 (818) 796-4341 Referral (818) 796-4347 Administration	I&R Federation of L.A. County 3035 Tyler Avenue El Monte, CA 91731 (800) 242-4612

34.1.2,90

CALIFORNIA CHILD CARE RESOURCE AND REFERRAL PROGRAMS BY COUNTY

Los Angeles (continued) Mexican American Opportunity Foundation 6252 E. Telegraph Road Commerce, CA 90040 (818) 289-4511	**Mendocino (continued)** Parent/ Child Info Center 413 North State Ukiah, CA 95482 (707) 463-2579
Child Care and Human Services P.O. Box 6067 Alhambra, CA 91802 (818) 309-9117	**Merced** Children's Service Network 1701 N Street Merced, CA 95340 (209) 722-3804
Madera Madera County Action Committee 1200 West Maple St. Madera, CA 93637 (209) 673-5529	**Modoc** Modoc County Teach 110 West Carlos St. Alturas, CA 96101 (916) 233-5437
Marin Project Care for Children 828 Mission Ave. San Rafael, CA 94901 (415) 454-7951 Referral (415) 454-7959 Administration	**Monterey** Mexican American Opportunity Foundation 1021 Montana St. Salinas, CA 93905 (408) 757-0756
Mendocino N. Coast Opportunities Inc. 413A North State Street Ukiah, CA 95482 (707) 462-1954	**Napa** Rainbow Childcare Council 1801 Oak Street Napa, CA 94599 (707) 253-0366
Rural Communities Child Care 155 Cypress Fort Bragg, CA 95437 (707) 964-3080	**Nevada** Nevada County Community Services Council 256 Buena Vista St. # 210 Grass Valley, CA 95945 (916) 272-8866
Rural Communities Child Care 273 Franklin St. Willits, CA 95490 (707) 459-2019	Nevada County Community Services Council P.O. Box 3239 Truckee, CA 95734 (916) 587-5960

34.1.3,90

CALIFORNIA CHILD CARE RESOURCE AND REFERRAL PROGRAMS BY COUNTY

Orange Children's Home Society/DCS 1823 East 17th Street, Ste. 123 Santa Ana, CA 92701 (714) 543-2273	**San Diego** Childcare Resource Service Project of YMCA Human Development 7510 Clairemont Mesa Blvd. San Diego, CA 92111 (619) 275-7000
Placer Motherlode Childcare Assistance Network 3268 Penryn Rd., Suite 100 Loomis, CA 95650 (916) 624-5436 Referral	**San Francisco** California Child Care Resource and Referral Network 809 Lincoln San Francisco, CA 94122 (415) 661-1714
Plumas Plumas Rural Services P.O. Box 1079 Quincy, CA 95971 (916) 283-4453	Child Care Law Center 22 2nd St. 5th Floor San Francisco, CA 94105 (415) 495-5498
Riverside Coordinated Child Care Resource and Referral 3939 13th Street Riverside, CA 92502 (714) 788-6626 Referral	Children's Council of S.F. 1435 Market St. San Francisco, CA 94103 (415) 864-1881 Referral (415) 826-1130 Providers (415) 647-0778 Administration
Sacramento Child Action, Inc. 2103 Stockton Blvd., No. B Sacramento, CA 95817 (916) 453-1110	Children's Rights and Services 777 Stockton Street, Room 202 San Francisco, CA 94108 (415) 391-8993
San Benito Growth and Opportunity 321 San Filipe Rd. Hollister, CA 95023 (408) 637-9205	**San Joaquin** San Joaquin-Stockton Metro Ministry 1149 N. El Dorado Suite C Stockton, CA 95204 (209) 948-1552 Referral (209) 465-4611 Administration
San Bernardino Child Care Information Service 601 North E. Street San Bernardino, CA 92410 (714) 387-3111	**San Luis Obispo** San Luis Obispo-Economic Opportunity Commission 880 Industrial Way San Luis Obispo, CA 93401 (805) 544-4355

34.1.4,90

CALIFORNIA CHILD CARE RESOURCE AND REFERRAL PROGRAMS BY COUNTY

San Mateo San Mateo 4-C's* 1838 El Camino, Suite 214 Burlingame, CA 94010 (415) 692-6645 Referral (408) 692-6647 Administration	**Shasta** County Office of Education 1644 Magnolia Avenue Redding, CA 96001 (916) 244-4600
Santa Barbara Children's Resource Center/I and R 1124 Castillo Santa Barbara, CA 93101 (805) 962-8988 (805) 963-6631	**Siskiyou** Child Care Council P.O. Box 500 Weed, CA 96094 (916) 938-2748
Santa Clara 4-C's of Santa Clara* 160 East Virginia St. San Jose, CA 95112 (408) 947-0900	**Solano** Solano Family and Children's Council 746 N. Texas Street, Suite G Fairfield, CA 94533 (707) 442-2881
CDI-Choices for Children 901 Campisi Way, Suite 250 San Jose, CA 95008 (408) 725-1717	**Sonoma** 4-C's of Sonoma County 1212 College Ave. Santa Rosa, CA 95404 (707) 544-3170
Childcare Resource Center at Stanford 859 Escondido Road Stanford, CA 94305 (415) 723-2660	River Child Care Box 1060 Guerneville, CA 95446 (707) 887-1809 (707) 869-3613
Growth and Opportunity 16430 Monterey Road, Suite #2 Morgan Hill, CA 95037 (408) 779-9343	**Stanislaus** Child Care Resource and Referral 801 County Center Three Court Modesto, CA 95355 (209) 571-6575
Palo Alto Community Childcare 3990 Ventura Court Palo Alto, CA 94306 (415) 493-2361	**Sutter** Children's Home Society/DCS 670 Joy Way, No. C Yuba City, CA 95991 (916) 673-7503
Santa Cruz Child Development Resource Center 809 Bay Avenue Capitola, CA 95010 (408) 476-7140, ext. 282	**Trinity** Human Response Network P.O. Box 2370 Weaverville, CA 96093 (916) 623-2024

* 4-C's means Community Child Care Council.
34.1.5,90

CALIFORNIA CHILD CARE RESOURCE AND REFERRAL PROGRAMS BY COUNTY	
Tulare County Sup. of Schools 7000 Doe Ave., Suite C Visalia, CA 93291 (209) 651-3022	**Yolo** City of Davis 23 Russell Blvd. Davis, CA 95616 (916) 756-3747
Tuolumne Tuolumne County Resource and Referral 14326 Tuolumne Road Sonora, CA 95370-9727 (209) 533-0377	**Yuba** Children's Home Society/DCS 670 Joy Way, No. C Yuba City, CA 95991 (916) 673-7503
Ventura Child Development Resources 505 South A Street Oxnard, CA 93030 (805) 487-4931 (805) 486-3531	

34.1.6,90 Source: Cal. Dep. of Education, Child Development Division, 1989 and Pacific Data Resources.

FEMALE PILOTS IN CALIFORNIA	
Category	**Number**
Student Pilots	2,778
Private Pilots	3,158
Commercial Pilots	702
Airline Pilots	255
Flight Instructors	477
Helicopter, Glider, Blimp and other Pilots	195
Total Pilots	**7,088**

34.2,90 Source: *FAA Statistical Handbook of Aviation.*

LOCAL GOVERNMENT AGENCIES DEALING WITH WOMEN

County Commissions

County	Commission
Alameda	Commission on the Status of Women 401 Broadway; Oakland, CA 94607 (415) 268-2110
Contra Costa	Advisory Committee on the Employment and Economic Status of Women 2425 Bisso Lane, Suite 100; Concord, CA 94520 (415) 646-5391
El Dorado	c/o Barbara McCallum 901 H Street, Suite 310; Sacramento, CA 95814 (916) 444-7486
Fresno	Commission on the Status of Women 1028 N. Fulton St.; Fresno, CA 93728 (209) 264-4553
Humboldt	Commission on the Status of Women 825 5th St.; Eureka, CA 95501 (707) 839-1954
Los Angeles	Commission on the Status of Women 383 Hall of Administration 500 West Temple St.; Los Angeles, CA 90012 (213) 974-1455
Marin	Commission on the Status of Women Civic Center, Rm. 412; San Rafael, CA 94903 (415) 499-6195
Mendocino	Commission on the Status of Women c/o Courthouse; Ukiah, CA 95482 (707) 462-2948
Merced	Commission on the Status of Women 2222 M St.; Merced, CA 95340 (209) 385-6982
Monterey	Commission on the Status of Women 1000 South Main St., Suite 1000; Salinas, CA 93901 (408) 755-4499
Napa	Commission on the Status of Women PO Box 2191; Napa, CA 94558 (707) 255-7208 (after 5:30)
Orange	Commission on the Status of Women 1300 S. Grand, Bldg. B; Santa Ana, CA 92705 (714) 567-7474

34.3.1,90 Source: California State Commission on the Status of Women, 1989.

LOCAL GOVERNMENT AGENCIES DEALING WITH WOMEN (Cont.)	
County Commissions	
County	
Riverside	Advisory Committee on Women c/o Administration Office, 12th Fl. 4080 Lemon St.; Riverside, CA 92501-3651 (714) 787-2544
San Bernardino	Commission on the Status of Women 385 N. Arrowhead, 4th Floor; San Bernardino, CA 92415 (714) 387-4971
San Diego	Commission on the Status of Women 5555 Overland Ave., Bldg. 2, Rm. 135; San Diego, CA 92123 (619) 694-3211
San Francisco	Commission on the Status of Women 1095 Market St., Rm 409; San Francisco, CA 94103 (415) 558-3653; (TDD) 558-4901
San Mateo	Advisory Council on Women 300 Bradford St. Redwood City, CA 94063 (415) 363-4471
San Luis Obispo	Commission on the Status of Women PO Box 12928; San Luis Obispo, CA 93406 (805) 481-0698
Santa Barbara	Commission on the Status of Women 105 East Anapamu St., Rm. 403; Santa Barbara, CA 93101 (805) 568-3410
Santa Clara	Commission on the Status of Women 70 W. Hedding St., East Wing; San Jose, CA 95110 (408) 299-3131
Santa Cruz	Women's Commission 701 Ocean St., Rm. 214; Santa Cruz, CA 95060 (408) 425-2003
Sonoma	Commission on the Status of Women 2200 County Ctr. Dr., Suite F; Santa Rosa, CA 95403 (707) 527-2161
Stanislaus	Commission on the Status of Women PO Box 4254; Modesto, CA 95352 (209) 667-5115
Ventura	Commission for Women 505 Poli St.; Ventura, CA 93001 (805) 652-7611

34.3.2,90 Source: California State Commission on the Status of Women, 1989.

LOCAL GOVERNMENT AGENCIES DEALING WITH WOMEN (Cont.)	
City Commissions and Committees	
City	**Commission**
Berkeley	Commission on the Status of Women 2180 Milvia St.; Berkeley, CA 94704 (415) 644-6080
Compton	Commission on the Status of Women 205 Willowbrook Ave.; Compton, CA 90220 (213) 537-8000
Concord	Status of Women Committee 1950 Parkside Dr.; Concord, CA 94519 (415) 671-3170
Los Angeles	Commission on the Status of Women City Hall East 200 North Main St., Rm. 550; Los Angeles, CA 90012 (213) 485-6533
Pasadena	Commission on the Status of Women Pasadena City Hall 100 N. Garfield Ave., Rm. 321; Pasadena, CA 91109 (818) 405-4070
San Diego	Advisory Board on Women 202 "C" St., MS 10-A; San Diego, CA 92101 (619) 236-6330
Santa Monica	Commission on the Status of Women City Hall 1685 Main St.; Santa Monica, CA 90401 (213) 458-8246
Community Commissions	
Community	**Commission**
Sacramento Community	Commission for Women 1216 18th St.; Sacramento, CA 95814 (916) 448-2951
San Joaquin	Commission on the Status of Women 704 Diane Ave.; Stockton, CA 95207 (209) 447-7301

34.3.3,90 Source: California State Commission on the Status of Women, 1989.

SECTION 34 NOTE PRIVATE WOMEN'S ORGANIZATIONS
For information on private women's organizations contact: California Commission on the Status of Women 926 J Street, Rm. 1506 Sacramento, CA 95814 (916) 445-3173

34.4,90

CALIFORNIA RAPE CRISIS CENTERS BY CITY (COUNTY)

Auburn (Placer)
Rape Crisis Line
P.O. Box 9216
Auburn, CA 95604
C (916) 652-6658
B (916) 885-0443

Bakersfield (Kern)
Rape Hotline of Kern County
5604 Moonlight Way
Bakersfield, CA 93309
C (805) 324-7273 B 832-6941

Berkeley (Alameda)
U.C. Berkeley Rape Prevention Edu.
Building T-9, Room 201
Berkeley, CA 94720
B (415) 642-7310

Bishop (Inyo)
Wild Iris Women's Services
119 MacIver, Suite D
Bishop, CA 93514
C (619) 873-7384 B 873-6601

Camarillo (Ventura)
Ventura Rape Crisis Center
80 Wood Rd., Suite 304
Camarillo, CA 93010
C (805) 656-5225 B 987-0428

Chico (Butte)
Rape Crisis Intervention
P.O. Box 423 (114 N. 7th Ave.)
Chico, CA 95927
B (916) 891-1331 C 342-7273

Claremont (Los Angeles)
Sexual Assault Crisis Services Program
Project S.I.S.T.E.R.
P.O. Box 621
Claremont, CA 91711
C (714) 626-HELP B (714) 623-1619

Compton (Los Angeles)
YWCA Sexual Assault Crisis Center
509 E. Compton Blvd.
Compton, CA 90221
B (213) 636-1429

Concord (Contra Costa)
Rape Crisis Service of
    Central Contra Costa County
1760 Clayton Rd.
Concord, CA 94520
B (415) 680-8030 C 798-RAPE

Davis (Yolo)
Rape Prevention Education
U.C. Police Dept.
University of California
Davis, CA 95616
B (916) 752-3299

Douglas City (Trinity)
Family Crisis Line
P.O. Box 477
Douglas City, CA 96024
C (916) 623-4357 B 623-2024

El Centro (Imperial)
People Against Rape
120 N. Sixth Street
El Centro, CA 92243
C (619) 352-7273 B 352-7273

Escondido (San Diego)
Eye, Inc.
165 E. Lincoln Avenue
Escondido, CA 92026
C (619) 747-6281 B 747-6281

Eureka (Humboldt)
Humboldt Co. Rape Crisis Team
P.O. Box 543
Eureka, CA 95502
C (707) 445-2881 B 443-2737

Fairfield (Solano)
Rape Crisis Service of
    Upper Solano County
P.O. Box 368
Fairfield, CA 94533
C (707) 422-7273 B 422-7273

Fort Bragg (Mendocino)
CAARE Project, Inc.
461 N. Franklin Street
Fort Bragg, CA 95437
C (707) 964-HELP B 964-4055

34.5.1,90 C = Crisis line; B = Business phone.

CALIFORNIA RAPE CRISIS CENTERS BY CITY (COUNTY)

Fresno (Fresno) Rape Counseling Service of Fresno 4348 East Shields Fresno, CA 93726 C (209) 227-1800 or 227-RAPE	**Lancaster (Los Angeles)** Sexual Assault Response Antelope Valley Hospital Medical Center 1600 West Ave. J Lancaster, CA 93534 C (805) 945-3933 B 949-5566
Grass Valley (Placer) Domestic Violence Coalition Rape Intervention Program P.O. Box 484 Grass Valley, CA 95945 C (916) 272-3467 B 272-2046	**Livermore (Alameda)** Tri-Valley Haven for Women P.O. Box 2190 Livermore, CA 94550 C (415) 449-5842 B 449-5845
Hanford (Kings) Rape Crisis Program Kings County Community Action Organization 1222 W. Lacey Blvd. Hanford, CA 93230 C (209) 582-2968 B 582-4386	**Lompoc (Santa Barbara)** Lompoc Rape Crisis Center P.O. Box 148 Lompoc, CA 93438 C (805) 736-7273 B 736-8913
Hemet (Riverside) Center Against Sexual Assault P.O. Box 2564 Hemet, CA 92343 C (714) 652-8300 B 652-8300	**Long Beach (Los Angeles)** Long Beach Rape Hotline P.O. Box 14377 Long Beach, CA 90803 C (213) 597-2002 B 433-1337
Indio (Riverside) H.O.W. Foundation 82380 Miles Avenue, Suite 109 Indio, CA 92201 C (619) 345-5166 B 568-9071	**Los Angeles (Los Angeles)** Center for the Pacific Asian Family 543 N. Fairfax Ave., Room 108 Los Angeles, CA 90036 B (213) 653-4042
Irvine (Orange) Rape Prevention Center Women's Resource Center University of California Irvine, CA 92717 B (714) 856-7273	East Los Angeles Rape Hotline 133 North Sunol Drive P.O. Box 63245 Los Angeles, CA 90063 C (213) 262-0944 B 726-2201
La Jolla (San Diego) Rape Prevention Education Program University of California, San Diego Special Services Center B-009 La Jolla, CA 92093 C (619) 534-5793 B 534-5793	Response Center, Cedar- Sinai Medical Center 8730 Alden Dr. Los Angeles, CA 90048 C (213) 855-3506 B 855-3506
Lakeport (Lake) A.W.A.R.E. 120 N. Forbes St. Lakeport, CA 95453 C (707) 263-3577 B 263-0191	Los Angeles Commission on Assaults Against Women (Rape) 543 North Fairfax Los Angeles, CA 90036 C (213) 855-3506 B 655-4235

34.5.2,90 C = Crisis line; B = Business phone.

CALIFORNIA RAPE CRISIS CENTERS BY CITY (COUNTY)

Los Angeles (cont.)
Rosa Parks Sexual Assaults
  Crisis Center
3860 Martin Luther King Blvd., West
Suite 201
Los Angeles, CA 90062
B (213) 295-1999

Madera (Madera)
Rape and Sexual Assault Victim Services
131 B Yosemite Ave.
Madera, CA 93637
C (209) 661-7787 B 673-9173

Merced (Merced)
People Against Rape
P.O. Box 822
Merced, CA 95341
C (209) 722-4357 B 348-2232

Mission Viejo (Orange)
Family Crisis & Sexual Assault Hotline
27001 La Paz Rd., Suite 436 B
Mission Viejo, CA 92691
C (714) 770-HOPE
B (714) 859-1856

Modesto (Stanislaus)
Stanislaus Rape Task Force
1024 J Street, Room 211
Modesto, CA 95354
C (209) 527-5558 B (577-4344

Monterey (Monterey)
Rape Crisis Center of Monterey Peninsula
P.O. Box 2630
Monterey, CA 93940
C (408) 375-RAPE B 373-3955

Morgan Hill (Santa Clara)
South County Rape Crisis Service
16433 Monterey Road
P.O. Box 546
Morgan Hill, CA 95037
C (408) 779-2115 B 779-2113

Napa (Napa)
Napa Sexual Assault Victim
  Services Program
1700 Second Street, Suite 308
Napa, CA 94558
C (707) 252-6222 B 252-6222

Oakland (Alameda)
Bay Area Women Against Rape (BAWAR)
c/o YWCA
1515 Webster St., Room 406
Oakland, CA 94612
C (415) 845-7273
B (415) 465-3890

Highland Sexual Assault Center
1411 East 31st St.
Oakland, CA 94602
C (415) 548-0412 B 532-8055

National Action Against Rape
477 15th St., #200
Oakland, CA 94612
B (415) 452-0968

Orange (Orange)
Orange County
  Sexual Assault Network
172 N. Tustin, #205
Orange, CA 92667
C (714) 831-9110 B 538-7878

Palo Alto (Santa Clara)
Mid-Peninsula Rape Crisis Center
4161 Alma Street
Palo Alto, CA 94306
C (415) 493-7273 B 494-0972

Pasadena (Los Angeles)
YWCA Rape Hotline
70 N. Marengo
Pasadena, CA 91101
C (818) 793-3385 B 793-5171

Placerville (El Dorado)
El Dorado Women's Center
3133 Gilmore
Placerville, CA 95667
C (916) 626-1131 B 626-1450

Pittsburg (Contra Costa)
East Contra Costa County
Rape Crisis Unit
P.O. Box 1396
Pittsburg, CA 94565
C (415) 754-RAPE B 432-9838

34.5.3,90 C = Crisis line; B = Business phone.

CALIFORNIA RAPE CRISIS CENTERS BY CITY (COUNTY)

Redding (Shasta) Women's Refuge P.O. Box 4211 Redding, CA 96001 C (916) 244-0401 B 244-0401	**San Diego (cont.)** Child Sexual Abuse Treatment Program 6950 Levant St. San Diego, CA 92111 C (619) 694-5285 B 694-5285
Riverside (Riverside) Riverside Area Rape Hotline 2060 University Ave., #101 Riverside, CA 92507 C (714) 686-7273 B 686-7273	**San Francisco (San Francisco)** Center for Special Problems 1700 Jackson San Francisco, CA 94109 B (415) 558-4801 (Not a Crisis Center)
Rape Prevention Education Women's Resource Program University of California Riverside, CA 92521 B (714) 787-5000	San Francisco Women Against Rape 3543 18th Street San Francisco, CA 94110 C (415) 647-RAPE B (415) 861-2024
Sacramento (Sacramento) Sacramento Rape Crisis Center 1131 I Street Sacramento, CA 95814 C(916) 447-RAPE B 447-3223	San Francisco Sexual Trauma Service 995 Potrero San Francisco, CA 94110 C (415) 554-2970
Salinas (Monterey) Women's Crisis Center P.O. Box 1805 109 Central Avenue Salinas, CA 93902 C (408) 757-1001 B 757-1002	UCSF Rape Prevention Education University of California 1308 Third Avenue San Francisco, CA 94123 B (415) 476-5222
San Andreas (Calaveras) Calaveras Women's Crisis Line Box 623 San Andreas, CA 95249 C (209) 736-4011 B 754-1075	**San Jose (Santa Clara)** San Jose Rape Crisis Center c/o YWCA 375 South 3rd Street San Jose, CA 95112 C (408) 287-3000 B 295-4011
San Bernardino (San Bernardino) San Bernardino Sexual Assault Victim Services 1875 North "D" Street San Bernardino, CA 92405 C (800) 222-RAPE B (714) 883-8689	**San Luis Obispo (San Luis Obispo)** Rape Crisis Center/Victim Services P.O. Box 52 Courthouse Annex, Room 301 San Luis Obispo, CA 93406 C (805) 543-7273 B 549-5798
San Diego (San Diego) Rape Crisis Center for Women's Studies and Services 2467 "E" Street San Diego, CA 92102 C (619) 233-3088 B 233-8984	**San Luis Rey (San Diego)** Women's Resource Center P.O. Box 499 San Luis Rey, CA 92608 B (619) 757-3500

34.5.4,90 C = Crisis line; B = Business phone.

CALIFORNIA RAPE CRISIS CENTERS BY CITY (COUNTY)	
San Mateo (San Mateo) Rape Crisis Center 1811 Trousdale Dr. San Mateo, CA 94101 C (415) 877-8787 B 877-5604	**Santa Cruz (cont.)** Women's Crisis Center 1025 Center Street Santa Cruz, CA 95060 C (408) 429-1478 B 425-5525
San Pablo (Contra Costa) Rape Crisis Center of West Contra Costa County c/o Brookside Hospital 2000 Vale Road San Pablo, CA 94806 C (415) 236-7273 B 237-0113	**Santa Maria (Santa Barbara)** 1004 E. Main St. Suite A Santa Maria, CA 93454 C (805) 928-5818 B (805) 922-2994
San Rafael (Marin) Sexual Assault Counseling Services 24 H Street San Rafael, CA 94901 B (415) 453-2181	**Santa Monica (Los Angeles)** Rape Treatment Center 1225 15th Street Santa Monica, CA 90404 B (213) 391-4000
Santa Ana (Orange) Sexual Assault Victim Services Orange County Superior Court 700 Civic Center Dr., West Santa Ana, CA 92702 C (714) 957-2737 B 834-4317	**Santa Rosa (Sonoma)** Sonoma County Women Against Rape P.O. Box 1426 Santa Rosa, CA 95402 C (707) 545-7273 B 545-7270
Santa Barbara (Santa Barbara) Rape Prevention Education Women's Center University of California Santa Barbara, CA 92106 B (805) 961-3778	**Sonora (Tuolumne)** Sexual Assault Victim Services Program Mother Lode Women's Crisis Center P.O. Box 663 Sonora, CA 95370-0663 C (209) 532-4707 B 532-4746
Santa Barbara Rape Crisis Center 700 North Milpas Santa Barbara, CA 93103 C (805) 569-2255 B (805) 963-6832	**South Lake Tahoe (El Dorado)** South Lake Tahoe Women's Center P.O. Box 13111 South Lake Tahoe, CA 95702 B (916) 544-2118
Santa Cruz (Santa Cruz) Rape Prevention Education Health Center University of California Santa Cruz, CA 95064 B (408) 429-2721	**Stockton (San Joaquin)** County Sexual Assault Center 930 North Commerce Street Stockton, CA 95204 C (209) 465-4997 B (209) 941-2611
Santa Cruz Women Against Rape P.O. Box 711 Santa Cruz, CA 95061 C (408) 426-7273 B 426-7273	**Truckee (Nevada)** Domestic Violence Coalition P.O. Box 1200 Trukee, CA 95734 C (916) 546-3241 B 587-3101

34.5.5,90 C = Crisis line; B = Business phone.

CALIFORNIA RAPE CRISIS CENTERS BY CITY (COUNTY)	
Ukiah (Mendocino) Rape Crisis Services Project Sanctuary P.O. Box 995 Ukiah, CA 95482 C (707) 462-9196 B 462-7988	**Yreka (Siskiyou)** Siskiyou Sexual Assault Crisis Center P.O. Box 1354 Yreka, CA 96097 C (916) 842-3232 B 842-5096
Woodland (Yolo) Sexual Assault Center 933 Court St. Woodland, CA 95695 C (916) 662-1133 B 758-0540	**Yuba City (Sutter)** Casa de Esperanza P.O. Box 56 Yuba City, CA 95992 C (916) 674-2040 B 674-5400

C = Crisis line; B = Business phone.

34.5.6,90 Source: U.C. San Diego, Rape Prevention Education Program, unpublished data.

FEMALE OFFICIALS IN CALIFORNIA

Statewide Officials

Secretary of State
March Fong Eu

Governor's Staff
Scheduling Secretary-Sue Pedersen
Deputy Appointments Secretary
Bella Meese
Deputy Legislative Secretary
Maureen Higgins
Assistant to the Governor
Lorrie Barian
Director of Writing & Research
Sue Sims
Special Assistant for
Constituent Affairs-Peggy Bengs
Youthful Offender
Parole Board-Jaime S. Bailey

Major Statewide Appointees

Secretary State & Consumer Services Agency
Shirley Chilton

Regents of the University of California
Yvonne Brathwaite Burke
Vilma Martinez
Meredith Khachigian

Trustees of the California State Universities and Colleges
Marion Bagdasarian
Martha Fallgatter
Claudia H. Hampton
Marianthi Lansdale

Office of Administrative Law
Director-Linda S. Brewer

Dept. of Economic Opportunity
Director-Theresa Avillar Speake

Department of Aging
Director-Alice J. Gonzales

State Public Defender
Fern Laethem

Board of Corrections
Exec. Officer-Norma P. Lammers

California State Universities and Colleges Chancellor
W. Ann Reynolds

University of California Chancellor
Barbara Uehling-UCSB

California Film Office
Director-Lisa Rawlins

Dept. of Corporations
Director-Christine Bender

Dept. of Insurance
Commissioner-Roxani Gillespie

Environmental Affairs Agency
Secretary-Jan Sharpless

Commission on Economic Development
Exec. Director-Sue Johnson

Office of Tourism
Director-Florence Snyder

Public Employment Relations Board
Chair-Debbie Hesse

Dept. of Rehabilitation
Director-Cecie Fontanoza

Dept. of Social Services
Director-Linda McMahon

State Lands Commission
Exec. Officer-Claire Dedrick

Commission on the Status of Women
Exec. Director-Pat Towner

FEMALE OFFICIALS IN CALIFORNIA

Members of Congress
Barbara Boxer
Nancy Pelosi

Members of the State Senate
Marian Bergeson
Rebecca Morgan
Rose Ann Vuich
Diane Watson

Members of the State Assembly
Doris Allen
Lucile Roybal-Allard
Carol Bentley
Delaine Eastin
Bev Hansen
Teresa Hughes
Lucy Killea
Marian LaFollette
Sunny Mojonnier
Gwen Moore
Jackie Speier
Sally Tanner
Maxine Waters
Cathie Wright

County Supervisors
Mary King-Alameda
Anne Wade-Alpine
Jane Dolan-Butte
Karen Vercruse-Butte
Kay Nordyke-Colusa
Nancy C. Fahden-Contra Costa
Sunne Wright McPeak-Contra Costa
Helga Burns-Del Norte
Joyce Crockett-Del Norte
Patricia Lowe-El Dorado
Judy Andreen-Fresno
Sharon Levy-Fresno
Joanne Overton-Glenn
Bonnie Neely-Humboldt
Anna Sparks-Humboldt
Jeanne Vogel-Imperial
Pauline Larwood-Kern
Mary K. Shell-Kern
Voris Bromfield-Lake

Karan Mackey-Lake
Helen M. Williams-Lassen
Gail Hanhart-McIntyre-Madera
Sally S. Punte-Mariposa
Gertrude Taber-Mariposa
Liz Henry-Mendocino
Marilyn J. Butcher-Mendocino
Ann Klinger-Merced
Andrea Lawrence-Mono
Barbara Shipnuck-Monterey
Karin S. Kaufman-Monterey
Harriet Wieder-Orange
Susan Hogg-Placer
Joyce Scroggs-Plumas
Melba Dunlap-Riverside
Kay Ceniceros-Riverside
Patricia Larson-Riverside
Illa Collin-Sacramento
Sandra R. Smoley-Sacramento
Ruth Kesler-San Benito
Rita M. Bowling-San Benito
Marsha Turoci-San Bernardino
Barbara C. Riordan-San Bernardino
Susan Golding-San Diego
Angela Alioto-San Francisco
Willie B. Kennedy-San Francisco
Nancy G. Walker-San Francisco
Doris Ward-San Francisco
Wendy Nelder-San Francisco
Evelyn L. Costa-San Joaquin
Evelyn Delany-San Luis Obispo
Anna Eshoo-San Mateo
Mary Griffin-San Mateo
Gloria Ochoa-Santa Barbara
Diane Owens-Santa Barbara
Dianne McKenna-Santa Clara
Suzanne B. Wilson-Santa Clara
Zoe Lofgren-Santa Clara
Jan Beautz-Santa Cruz
Sherry Mehl-Santa Cruz
Frances Lynne Sullivan-Shasta
Molly Wilson-Shasta
Patti Jackson-Siskiyou
Norma Frey-Siskiyou
Jan Stewart-Solano

34.6.2,90

FEMALE OFFICIALS IN CALIFORNIA

Janet Nicholas-Sonoma
Pat Paul-Stanislaus
Barbara LeVake-Sutter
Patricia Garrett-Trinity
Delores E. Mangine-Tulare
Nell Farr-Tuolumne
Maggie Erickson-Ventura
Susan K. Lacey-Ventura
Madge Schaefer-Ventura
Mrs. Betsy A. Marchand-Yolo
Helen R. Tompson-Yolo
Mimi Matthews-Yuba

Judges

Federal
Hall, Cynthia-9th Circuit
Keep, Judith-S. Dist.
Marshall, Consuelo-Cent. Dist.
Nelson, Dorothy-9th Circuit
Patel, Marilyn-N. Dist.
Pfaelzer, Marianna-Cent. Dist.
Rymer, Pamela Ann-9th Circuit
Smith, Fern-N. Dist.
Stotler, Alicmarie H.-Cent. Dist.

Appellate Courts
Barry-Deal, Betty-1st Appellate District
Benke, Patricia-4th Appellate District
Lillie, Mildred-2nd Appellate District
Klein, Joan 2nd Appellate District
Sonnenshine, Sheila-4th Appellate District
Woods, Arleigh-2nd Appellate District

Superior Courts
Armstrong, Saundra B.-Alameda
Ashman, Judith M.-Los Angeles
Baird, Lourdes G.-Los Angeles
Baker, Valeri L.-Los Angeles
Bernstein, Florence-Los Angeles
Bond, Cecily-Sacramento
Brown, Nancy-Los Angeles
Chesney, Maxine-San Francisco
Chirlin, Judith-Los Angeles

Collins, Marie B.-Alameda
Connor, Jacqueline A.-Los Angeles
Cooper, Candace D.-Los Angeles
Cordell, LaDoris-Santa Clara
Croft, Janice C.-Los Angeles
Disco, Sally-Los Angeles
Dunbar, Rosemary-Los Angeles
Fieldhouse, Carol J.-Los Angeles
Flier, Madeleine-Los Angeles
Gamer, Barbara T.-San Diego
Girard, Dawn-Alameda
Godoy Perez, Ramona-Los Angeles
Goldin, Martha-Los Angeles
Grant, Isabella-San Francisco
Grignon, Margeret M.-Los Angeles
Gyemant, Ina-San Francisco
Hammes, Laura P.-San Diego
Hom Rose-Los Angeles
James, Ellen S.-Contra Costa
Janavs, Dzintra-Los Angeles
Johnson Melinda-Ventura
Johnson, Barbara J.-Los Angeles
Kemp, Margeret J.-San Mateo
Kozloski, Judith W.-San Mateo
Kutzner, Elizabeth Z.-San Diego
Lane, Barbara A.-Ventura
Marie-Victoire, Ollie-San Francisco
Martin, Bonnie Lee-Los Angeles
Matusinka, Jeane-Los Angeles
McConnell, Judith-San Diego
McLauglin, Linda Hodge-Orange
Miller, Carol J.-Sacramento
Moore, Eileen C.-Orange
Morrow, Dion-Los Angeles
Nichols, Leslie C.-Santa Clara
Parnell, Lorna-Los Angeles
Pate, Christine V.-San Diego
Pickard, Florence-Los Angeles
Pokras, Sheila-Los Angeles
Radin, Sara-Los Angeles
Revel, Marsha N.-Los Angeles
Rothschild, Frances-Los Angeles
Rutherford, Ann-Butte
Ryan, Judith-Orange
Savitt, Beverly Block-Marin

FEMALE OFFICIALS IN CALIFORNIA

Schempp, Darlene-Los Angeles
Soven, Abby-Los Angeles
Stevens, Lilian-Los Angeles
Stoltz, Kathryne A.-Los Angeles
Taber, Jacqueline-Alameda
Taylor, Meredith-Los Angeles
Todd, Kathryn Doi-Los Angeles
Vogel, Miriam T.-Los Angeles
Watai, Madge-Los Angeles
Watson, Nancy Belcher-Los Angeles
Wayne, Diane L.-Los Angeles
Weisberg, Jacqueline L.-Los Angeles
Zecher, Marilyn P.-Santa Clara

Municipal Courts
Abrams, Judith-Los Angeles
Altoon, Alice-Los Angeles
Andelson, Susan E.-Los Angeles
Anderson Margeret R.-Orange
Austin, Elvira-Los Angeles
Beason, Candace J.-Los Angeles
Beck, Barbara-Santa Barbara
Bemattre-Manoukian, Patricia-Santa Clara
Blackwell, Glenette-Los Angeles
Bobb, Alviva K.-Los Angeles
Brodie, Ellen-San Bernardino
Brosnahan, Carol-Alameda
Brown, Irma B.-Los Angeles
Burke, Barbara Lee-Los Angeles
Champagne, Judith L.-Los Angeles
Chavez, Victoria M.-Los Angeles
Cohen, Isabel-Los Angeles
Cole, Terry K.-Stanislaus
Collins, Patricia-Los Angeles
Comgan, Carol-Alameda
Conger, Julie-Alameda
Cowett, Patricia-San Diego
Days, Virginia-Santa Clara
Dreibelbis, Bessie-Contra Costa
Duffy-Lewis, Maureen-Los Angeles
Dunn, Leslie-Los Angeles
Elias, Betty-Orange
Essegian, Ruth-Los Angeles
Finlay, Susan-San Diego
Ford, Judith-Alameda

Gallagher, Catherine-Santa Clara
Geynup, Gayle Christine-Sonoma
Goldsmith, Christine-San Diego
Goodson, Carol-Los Angeles
Grignon, Margaret-Sacramento
Gubler, Marion-Los Angeles
Guy-Shell, Lisa-San Diego
Herrington, Gaye-Los Angeles
Hoffman, Marilyn-Los Angeles
Hoffman, Nancy-Santa Clara
Hora, Peggy-F.-Alameda
Huguenor, Susan D.-San Diego
Iles, Pamela Lee-Orange
Isacoff, Susan E.-Los Angeles
Isaeff, Marianne-San Bernardino
Jacobs-May, Jamie-Santa Clara
Kaneshiro, Gale E.-San Diego
Kennedy-Powell, Kathleen-Los Angeles
Kintner, Janet-San Diego
Kirakosian, Maral-Los Angeles
Kitching, Patti S.-Los Angeles
Knauf, Suzanne-San Diego
Kough, Ann-Los Angeles
Krott, Cheryl-Los Angeles
Lancet Miller, Linda E.-Orange
LaRue, Annette-Fresno
Lasater, Melinda J.-San Diego
Lewman, Bonnie-Alameda
Lytle, Alice-Sacramento
Marguiles, Sadra Lynn-Alameda
McBeth, Veronica S.-Los Angeles
McIntosh, Joan-Fresno
McIntyre-Poe, Janice-Riverside
McKay, Patti Jo-Los Angeles
Meirs, Barbara Ann-Los Angeles
Mettler, Sharon-Kern
Mitchell, Elvira-Los Angeles
Moreno, Tracy J.-Los Angeles
Morgan, Mary C.-San Francisco
Navarro, Rene-Santa Clara
Nomoto, Barbara Tam-Orange
O'Leary, Kathleene-Orange
O'Malley-Taylor, Lynn-Marin
Obera, Marion L.-Los Angeles
Ohanesian, Gail-Sacramento

FEMALE OFFICIALS IN CALIFORNIA

Parrilli, Joanne C.-Alameda
Person, Suzanne-Los Angeles
Petre, Donna-Yolo
Pichon, Rise-Yolo
Quinn, Linda-San Diego
Quon, Lillian L.-San Diego
Reilly, Joan T.-Orange
Rhine, Jennie-Alameda
Richli, Betty Ann-San Bernardino
Riggs, Elizabeth-San Diego
Rosenbaum, S. Patricia-San Diego
Shaw, Susanne S.-Orange
Shockley, Doris L.-Yolo
Shumsky, Rosemary-Los Angeles
Silver, Shari K.-Los Angeles
Silvers, Jessica P.-Los Angeles
Sing, Lilian Kwok-San Francisco
Smith, Sandra-San Joaquin
Soper, Elva-Los Angeles
Stein, Judith O.-Los Angeles

Sweet, Nancy-Sacramento
Takahashi, Irene-Contra Costa
Thomason, Jaquelyn-Orange
Thompson, Sandra-Los Angeles
Ure, Jane-Sacramento
Veron, Juaneita-Los Angeles
Von Beroldingen, Dorothy V.-San Francisco
Wagner, Marguerite L.-San Diego
Wasserman, Fumiko H.-Los Angeles
Waters, Mary Elizabeth-Los Angeles
Wetenkamp, Jean H.-Santa Clara
Wick, Diane E.-San Francisco
Wong Cerena-Sonoma
Zuniga, Barbara Ann-Contra Costa

Justice Courts
Doan, Glenda-Kings
Quinn, Vivian-Tuolumne

34.6.5,90

WOMEN OWNED BUSINESSES IN CALIFORNIA AND THE UNITED STATES

	All Firms (Number)	% of U.S.	Firms with Paid Employees	% of U.S.	Number of Employees	% of Cal. Total	% of U.S.	Annual Payroll*	% of Cal. Total	Annual Sales Receipts*	% of Cal. Total	% of U.S.
Agriculture, Forestry, Fishing, and Mining	4,142	9%	363	9%	1,367	1%	7%	$13	1%	$70	1%	4%
Construction	7,179	12%	1,061	8%	4,040	3%	7%	$53	4%	$238	4%	7%
Manufacturing	8,824	18%	1,574	15%	11,697	8%	13%	$118	9%	$474	7%	10%
Transportation, and Public Utilities	4,778	12%	1,001	12%	3,787	2%	10%	$48	4%	$320	5%	13%
Wholesale Trade	2,967	9%	678	8%	3,511	2%	7%	$49	4%	$580	8%	7%
Retail Trade	95,012	13%	13,183	11%	63,612	41%	12%	$395	32%	$2,948	42%	11%
Finance, Insurance, and Real Estate	41,343	16%	1,870	11%	6,146	4%	13%	$62	5%	$322	5%	11%
Services	202,511	14%	15,104	12%	59,105	38%	12%	$489	39%	$1,917	27%	14%
Other	29,538	11%	1,017	11%	2,103	1%	14%	$23	2%	$139	2%	13%
Total	396,294	14%	35,851	12%	155,368	100%	11%	$1,249	100%	$7,009	100%	11%

* Millions.
Note: Data is based on a 1982 survey by the Census Bureau.
34.7,90 Source: U.S. Bureau of the Census, *Women Owned Businesses, April 1986.*

FEMALE OFFICIALS IN CALIFORNIA WOMEN MAYORS OF CALIFORNIA CITIES			
City	**Mayor**	**City**	**Mayor**
Agoura Hills	Darlene McBane	Maywood	Rose Marie Busciglio
Anderson	Patricia A. Clarke	Menlo Park	Jan La Fetra
Angels Camp	Elizabeth P. Alford	Modesto	Carol Whiteside
Apple Valley	Heidi Larkin	Moorpark	Eloise Brown
Atascadero	Bonita Borgeson	Moreno Valley	Patty Goodwin
Auburn	Annabell McCord	Morro Bay	Rose Marie Sheetz
Benicia	Marilyn C. O'Rourke	Mountain View	Maryce Freelen
Berkeley	Loni Hancock	Newman	Janet Carlsen
Blue Lake	Gloria Thompson	Norwalk	Margret Nelson
Brentwood	Catherine Palmer	Novato	Christine Knight
Buena Park	Donna L. Chessen	Orinda	Bobbie Landers
Camarillo	Sandi Bush	Orland	Darlene Friesen
Campbell	Jeanette Watson	Petaluma	Patricia Hilligass
Carmel-by-the-Sea	Jean Grace	Piedmont	Susan Hill
Carson	Kay A. Calas	Placentia	Carol Downey
Claremont	Judy Wright	Pleasant Hill	Terri Williamson
Clayton	Ann Hall	Point Arena	Mary Cardwell
Clearlake	Caroline Constable	Pomona	Donna Smith
Coachella	Yolanda R. Coba	Portola Valley	Sue Crane
Coalinga	Sharon Wood	Red Bluff	Velma Trujillo
Colfax	Fern Chadd	Redlands	Carole Beswick
Commerce	Ruth Aldaco	Redondo Beach	Barabara J. Doerr
Concord	Collen Coll	Rocklin	Kathy Lund
Corning	JoAnn Landingham	Rolling Hills	Judy Murdoch
Coronado	Mary Herron	Sacramento	Anne Rudin
Corte Madera	Sandra Marker	San Bernardino	Evlyn Wilcox
Dana Point	Judy Curreri	San Carlos	Sally Mitchell
Danville	Beverly Lane	San Diego	Maureen O' Conner
Diamond Bar	Phyllis Papen	San Gabriel	Janis Cohen
East Palo Alto	Barbara Mouton	San Joaquin	Lenore Barnes
Encinitas	Anne Omsted	Santa Barbara	Shiela Lodge
Escondido	Doris Thurston	Santa Clarita	Janice H. Heidt
Fairfax	Wendy Baker	Santa Cruz	Mardi Wormhoudt
Ferndale	Kathryn R. Gilliland	Saratoga	Karen Anderson
Fillmore	Delores I. Day	Sausalito	Robin Sweeny
Fowler	Marcia Dennis	Sebastapol	Anne Magnie
Fullerton	Molly McClanahan	Shafter	Cathy Prout
Gilroy	Roberta H. Hughan	Signal Hill	Sara Hanlon
Glendora	Lois Shade	South San Francisco	Roberta C. Teglia
Half Moon Bay	Haomi Patridge	Stockton	Barbara Fass
Hawaiian Gardens	Kathleen Navejas	Tehama	Jeanne King
Hawthorne	Betty Ainsworth	Temple City	Mary Lou Swain
Hidden Hills	Kathleen M. Bartizal	Torrance	Katy Geissert
Imperial	Earnestine Wilson	Tustin	Ursula Kennedy
La Canada Flintridge	Joan C. Feehan	Ukiah	Colleen Henderson
Lafayette	Avon Wilson	Vista	Gloria E. McClellan
Lakewood	Jacqueline Rynerson	Walnut Creek	Evelyn Munn
Lawndale	Sarann Kruse	Watsonville	Betty Murphy
Loomis	Hazel M. Hineline	West Covina	Nancy Manners
Los Gatos	Joanne Benjamin	West Hollywood	Helen Albert
Maricopa	Sheila Hill	Wheatland	Karen Troxel
Marina	Valerie Kosorek	Woodside	Barbara Seitle

34.6.6,90

FEMALE OFFICIALS IN CALIFORNIA WOMEN CITY COUNCIL MEMBERS			
City	**Councilmember**	**City**	**Councilmember**
Adelanto	Charlotte Y. Foster	Blue Lake	Margie Caywood
Adelanto	Mary Scarpa	Blythe	Doris Morgan
Agoura Hills	Fran Pauley	Bradbury	Audrey Hon
Agoura Hills	Vicky Leary	Bradbury	Beatrice Lapisto-Kirtley
Alameda	Barbara Thomas	Bradbury	Audrey Chamberlain
Alameda	Lil Arnerich	Brawley	Orbia Hanks
Albany	Thelma Rubin	Brawley	Stella Mendoza
Alhambra	Barbara Messina	Brawley	Norma Saikhon
Amador	Susan Sandperl	Brea	Carrey Nelson
Amador	Susan Bragstad	Brea	Norma Arias Hicks
Anaheim	Miriam Kaywood	Brea	Clarice A. Blamer
Antioch	Barbara A. Price	Brentwood	Barbara J. Guise
Antioch	Cathryn R. Freitas	Brisbane	Susan Nielsen
Antioch	Mary Rocha	Buena Park	Rhonda J. McCune
Arcadia	Mary Young	Burbank	Mary Lou Howard
Arcata	Julie Fulkerson	Burbank	Mary E. Kelsey
Arcata	Thea Gast	Burlingame	Gloria W. Barton
Arroyo Grande	B'Ann Smith	Calexico	Amalia Katsigeanis
Arroyo Grande	Doris Olsen	California City	Lottie M. Walker
Arvin	Hilda Damron	Camarillo	Charlotte Craven
Arvin	Adalia Luevanos	Capitola	Stephanie Harlan
Atascadero	Marjorie R. Mackey	Carlsbad	Ann J. Kulchin
Atherton	Nanette Chapman	Carmel-by-the-Sea	Elinor Laiolo
Atwater	Leona Zimmerman	Carson	Sylvia L. Muise
Auburn	Mary Bunnell	Carson	Vera Robles DeWitt
Avalon	Irene L. Strubel	Cathedral City	Rena M. Murphy
Azusa	Jennie Avila	Cathedral City	Sarah E. DiGrandi
Bakersfield	Patricia DeMond	Ceres	Barbara Hinton
Baldwin Park	Bobbie Izell	Cerritos	Diana S. Needham
Baldwin Park	Julia S. McNeil	Cerritos	Ann Joynt
Baldwin Park	Bette L. Lowes	Chico	Mary Andrews
Banning	Barbara H. Sheldon	Chico	Georgie Willis
Barstow	Shirlee Hora	Chino	Eunice Ulloa
Beaumont	Ann Conners	Chowchilla	Kathy Horn
Bell Gardens	Letha Viles	Chula Vista	Gayle L. McCandliss
Benicia	Linda S. Temple	Claremont	Diann Ring
Berkeley	Ann Chandler	Clayton	Jeanne Musto
Berkeley	Maudelle Shirek	Clearlake	Vera Reed
Berkeley	Nancy Skinner	Cloverdale	Erlene Pell
Berkeley	Mary Wainwright	Cloverdale	Lillian Berg
Berkeley	Shirley Dean	Clovis	Peggy Bos
Beverly Hills	Vicki Reynolds	Coalinga	Jean Dakessian
Bishop	Jane Fisher	Colfax	Elizabeth Armando
Blue Lake	Bobbi Ricca	Colton	Connie Cisneros
Blue Lake	Adelene Jones	Compton	Jane D. Robbins

34.6.7,90

FEMALE OFFICIALS IN CALIFORNIA WOMEN CITY COUNCIL MEMBERS			
City	**Councilmember**	**City**	**Councilmember**
Compton	Maxcy D. Filer	Encinitas	Marjorie Gaines
Concord	Diane Longshore	Encinitas	Pamela Slater
Concord	June V. Bulman	Encinitas	Gail Hano
Corning	Helen M. Pitkin	Escalon	Lynn Gentry
Coronado	Lois Ewen	Escondido	Carla DeDominicis
Coronado	Ruth K. Schmidt	Fairfax	Carol Sherman
Corte Madera	Lucy Shuckin	Fairfield	Joy Pettygrove
Corte Madera	Carolyn Larson	Farmersville	Judy Barnes
Costa Mesa	Mary Hornbuckle	Firebaugh	Marcia Sablan
Costa Mesa	Sandra Genis	Folsom	Sara Myers
Cotati	Katherine Roberts	Fort Bragg	Mary C. Kendall
Cotati	Linda Shorey	Fort Jones	Janette Hancock
Culver City	Jozelle Smith	Fortuna	Arlene Werner
Cupertino	Barbara Rodgers	Fortuna	Doris Osburn
Cupertino	Barbara Koppel	Fountain Valley	Laurann Cook
Cypress	Cecilia L. Age	Fowler	Jane Bedrosian
Cypress	Margaret Arnold	Fresno	Karen Humphrey
Cypress	Gail H. Kerry	Galt	Marian O. Lawrence
Daly City	Jane Powell	Gardena	Gwen Duffy
Dana Point	Eileen Krause	Glendale	Ginger Bremberg
Dana Point	Ingid McGuire	Gonzales	Bertie Collins
Danville	Susanna Schlendorf	Grand Terrace	Barbara Pfennighausen
Danville	Millie Greenberg	Gridley	Susanne Ingram
Danville	Barbara Jagger	Guadalupe	Gloria Parlanti
Davis	Ann Evans	Gustine	Pat Rocha
Del Mar	Gay Hugo	Half Moon Bay	Helen Bedesem
Del Mar	Jacqueline Winterer	Hanford	Patricia Rapozo
Delano	June Fukawa	Hanford	Marcie Buford
Dinuba	Barbra Lankford	Hawaiian Gardens	Rosalie R. Sher
Dinuba	J.B. Westmoreland	Hawaiian Gardens	Lennie Wagner
Dorris	Cheri Addington	Hawthorne	Ginny M. Lambert
Dorris	Barbara Dent	Hayward	Shirley Campbell
Dos Palos	Peggy George	Hayward	Roberta Cooper
Downey	Diane P. Boggs	Hemet	Patricia L. Herron
Downey	Barbara J. Hayden	Hemet	Gaila Jennings
Duarte	Ginny Joyce	Hercules	Ann Earnest
Dublin	Georgean Vonheeder	Hermosa Beach	Etta Simpson
Dunsmuir	Maggie Lampitt	Hermosa Beach	June Williams
El Cajon	Beverly Miller	Hidden Hills	Colleen Hartman
El Cajon	Harriet M. Stockwell	Highland	Jody Scott
El Cajon	Joan Shoemaker	Highland	Laurie Tully
El Centro	Sedalia Sanders	Hillsborough	Jean Auer
El Cerrito	Jean Siri	Hollister	Mary Kuckenbaker
El Cerrito	W. Mae Ritz	Holtville	Linda Britschgi
Emeryville	Nora Davis	Huntington Beach	Ruth Finley

34.6.8,90

FEMALE OFFICIALS IN CALIFORNIA WOMEN CITY COUNCIL MEMBERS			
City	**Councilmember**	**City**	**Councilmember**
Huntington Beach	Grace Winchell	Los Angeles	Ruth Galanter
Huron	Oliva D. Cano	Loyalton	Kathryn Peterson
Imperial Beach	Tommie L. Schuette	Lynwood	Evelyn Wells
Inglewood	Ann A. Wilk	Madera	Margaret Medellin
Ione	Bonnie Randall	Mammoth Lakes	Barbara Campbell
Ione	Loretta Tillery	Manhattan Beach	Connie Sieber
Irvine	Sally Anne Sheridan	Manteca	Cynthia Tonkin
Irvine	Paula Werner	Marina	Joan Blake
Irwindale	Pat Mirauda	Martinez	Kathy Radke
Jackson	Marie C. Aiken	Martinez	Beverly McDowall
King City	Eleanor Dye	Marysville	Patti Peasley
Kingsburg	Sylvia S. Johnson	Maywood	Betty Lou Rogers
La Habra	Beth Graham	Mill Valley	Alison Ruedy
La Habra Heights	Judith Hathaway	Mill Valley	Kathleen Foote
La Mesa	Jerri Lopez	Mill Valley	Ruth Schneider
La Palma	Eva G.Miner	Millbrae	Janet Fogerty
La Quinta	Joyce Bosworth	Millbrae	Doris Morse
Lafayette	Gayle B. Uilkema	Mission Viejo	Victoria Jaffe
Laguna Beach	Martha Collison	Monrovia	Mary Wilcox
Laguna Beach	Lida Lenny	Montague	Trudi Soli
Laksport	Debbie Cole	Montague	Mary Lou Dunn
Lancaster	Lynn Harrison	Montague	Juel West
Larkspur	Karen Kunze	Montague	Helga Struckman
Larkspur	Joan Lubamersky	Montclair	Eloise (Dolly) Lewman
Lawndale	Carol Norman	Monte Sereno	Barbara F. Winckler
Lemon Grove	Lois M. Heiserman	Monte Sereno	Dorthea Bamford
Lemon Grove	Karen O'Rourke	Monterey	Ruth Vreeland
Lincoln	Roberta Babcock	Monterey	Theresa Canepa
Lindsay	Ellen Hendricks	Monterey Park	Patricia Reichenberger
Livermore	Ayn Wieskamp	Monterey Park	Judy Chu
Livermore	Cathie Brown	Monterey Park	Betty Couch
Livermore	Judy Bartoli	Moraga	Susan L. Noe
Lodi	Evelyn Olson	Moreno Valley	Judith Nieburger
Loma Linda	Ardyce Koobs	Moreno Valley	Cynthia Crothers
Lompoc	Christa Marks	Moreno Valley	Denise Lanning
Long Beach	Jan Hall	Morgan Hill	Lorraine Barke
Los Alamitos	Alice Jempsa	Morgan Hill	Linda English
Los Altos	Penelope Lave	Mountain View	Marilyn S. Perry
Los Altos	Margaret S. Bruno	Mountain View	Patricia Figueroa
Los Altos Hills	Mary van Tamelen	Mountain View	Dena Bonnell
Los Altos Hills	Barbara Tryon	Napa	Arlene Corsello
Los Altos Hills	Toni Casey	Needles	Marcia Albertson
Los Angeles	Joan Milke Flores	Nevada City	Glenda Zanone
Los Angeles	Joy Picus	Nevada City	Laurie Oberholtzer
Los Angeles	Gloria Molina	Newark	Shirley D. Sisk

34.6.9,90

FEMALE OFFICIALS IN CALIFORNIA WOMEN CITY COUNCIL MEMBERS			
City	Councilmember	City	Councilmember
Newark	Susan Johnson	Placerville	Kathi Lishman
Newport Beach	Ruthelyn Plummer	Pleasant Hill	Sherry M. Sterrett
Newport Beach	Evelyn Hart	Pleasanton	Karin Mohr
Newport Beach	Jean Hart	Point Arena	Anne N. Niven
Norwalk	Grace Napolitano	Pomona	Nell Soto
Oakdale	De Ann Isenberg	Portola	Julie Burton
Oakland	Aleta Cannon	Poway	Linda Brannon
Oakland	Mary Moore	Rancho Mirage	Anita Richmond
Oakland	Marge Gibson Haskell	Rancho Cucamonga	Deborah Brown
Oceanside	Lucy Chavez	Rancho Cucamonga	Pamela Wright
Oceanside	Melba Bishop	Rancho Palos Verdes	Jacki Bacharach
Ojai	Nina Shelley	Redding	Nancy K. Buffum
Ontario	Faye Myers Dastrup	Redlands	Barbara Wormser
Orange	Joanne Coontz	Redondo Beach	Kay Horrell
Orinda	Linda Knebel	Redwood City	Georgi La Berge
Orland	Kara Lazard	Redwood City	Judy Buchan
Oroville	Susan Sears	Rialto	Barbara J. Zupanic
Oroville	Irma Panevics	Richmond	LaVonne Niccolis
Oxnard	Dorothy S. Maron	Richmond	Rosemary Corbin
Oxnard	Ann Johs	Ridgecrest	Anna Maria Bergens
Pacific Grove	Susan Whitman	Ridgecrest	Florence S. Condos
Pacific Grove	Florence Schaefer	Rio Dell	Patricia Moranda
Pacifica	Ginny Silva Jaquith	Rio Vista	Grace Anderson
Palmdale	Janis C. Hamm	Rio Vista	Helen Madere
Palm Desert	Jean Benson	Ripon	Lorraine Hutchinson
Palm Springs	Sharon Apfelbaum	Riverside	Jean Mansfield
Palo Alto	Gail Woolley	Rocklin	Marie Huson
Palo Alto	Emily M. Renzel	Rohnert Park	Linda Spiro
Palo Alto	Betsy Bechtel	Rolling Hills	Gordana Swanson
Palo Alto	Ellen Fletcher	Rolling Hills	Ginny Leeuwenburgh
Palos Verdes Estates	Ruth Gralow	Rolling Hills Estates	Nell Mirels
Paradise	Lise A. Young	Ross	Anne Flemming
Paramount	Esther Caldwell	Sabastapool	Anne Magnie
Parlier	Nellie Rodriguez	Sacramento	Lynn Robie
Pasadena	Jess Hughston	Sacramento	Lyla Ferris
Pasadena	Loretta Glickman	Salinas	Phyllis Price-Meurer
Pasadena	Kathryn Nock	San Anselmo	Ann Walsh
Perris	Thelma Wilson	San Anselmo	Maria Zaharoff
Petaluma	Lynn C. Woolsey	San Bernardino	Esther Estrada
Piedmont	Katy Foulkes	San Bernardino	Valerie Pope-Ludlum
Pinole	Anna McCarty	San Bernardino	Norine Miller
Pinole	Lilian Ann Williams	San Bruno	Beverly Barnard
Pittsburg	Nancy Parent	San Clemente	Candace Haggard
Placentia	Maria Moreno	San Clemente	Holly Veale

34.6.10,90

	FEMALE OFFICIALS IN CALIFORNIA		
	WOMEN CITY COUNCIL MEMBERS		
City	Councilmember	City	Councilmember
San Diego	Gloria McColl	Santa Monica	Judy Abdo
San Diego	Judy McCarty	Santa Paula	Kay Wilson
San Diego	Maria Tortorelli	Santa Paula	Leslie Maland
San Francisco	Doris M. Ward	Santa Rosa	Naci Burton
San Francisco	Nancy G. Walker	Saratoga	Martha Clevenger
San Francisco	Wendy Nelder	Sausalito	Annete Rose
San Francisco	Willie B. Kennedy	Seal Beach	Edna Wilson
San Francisco	Angela Alioto	Seal Beach	Joyce A. Risner
San Gabriel	Jeanne A. Parish	Sierra Madre	Lisa Fowler
San Jose	Blanca Alvarado	Signal Hill	Jessie Blacksmith
San Jose	Iola Williams	Simi Valley	Ann H. Rock
San Jose	Lu Ryden	Simi Valley	Vicky Howard
San Jose	Nancy Ianni	Solana Beach	Margaret Schlesinger
San Jose	Patricia Sausedo	Solana Beach	Celine Olson
San Jose	Shirley Lewis	Solana Beach	Marion Dodson
San Jose	Susan Hammer	Solvang	Elaine Campbell
San Jose	Judy Stabile	Solvang	June S. Christensen
San Juan Bautista	Gladys Paradis	Sonoma	Jeanne M. Markson
San Juan Bautista	Anna Baccala	Sonoma	Phyllis Carter
San Leandro	Linda Perry	South Lake Tahoe	Neva Roberts
San Luis Obispo	Penny Rappa	South Pasadena	Evelyn Fierro
San Luis Obispo	Peg Pinard	Stanton	Martha V. Weishaupt
San Marcos	Pia Harris	Stockton	Catherine Linnerman
San Marino	Roesemary Simmons	Stockton	Loralee McGaughey
San Marino	Suzanne Crowell	Suisun City	Gertrude Lotz
San Mateo	Florence Rhoads	Suisun City	Jane Day
San Mateo	Jane Powell	Sunnyvale	Barabara Waldman
San Mateo	Jane Baker	Sunnyvale	Pat Castillo
San Pablo	Kathryn L. Carmignani	Susanville	Jacqueline K. Tripp
San Pablo	Marie H. Daniels	Tehachapi	Lavonne Booth
San Rafael	Dorothy L. Breiner	Tehama	Marie Carlson
San Rafael	Joan Thayer	Tehama	Janine Weston
San Ramon	Dianne Schinnerer	Tiburon	Fran Mayberry
San Ramon	Mary Lou Oliver	Torrance	Dee Hardison
Sand City	Ronda Lewis	Tracy	Dorothy Zanussi
Sanger	René Gonzalez	Tracy	Carol Shubert
Santa Ana	Patricia McGuigan	Trinidad	Jayne Hanlon
Santa Barbara	Jeanne Graffy	Tulare	Thelma J. Gomez
Santa Barbara	Harriet Miller	Union City	Jean Westgard
Santa Clara	Sue Lasher	Upland	Rosalie Kamansky
Santa Clara	Judy Nadler	Vallejo	Cynthia Kay
Santa Clarita	Jo Anne Darcy	Vallejo	Katherine A. Hoffman
Santa Cruz	Jane Yokoyama	Ventura	Nan Drake
Santa Fe Springs	Betty Wilson	Victorville	Jean De Blasis
Santa Monica	Christine Reed	Victorville	Peggy Sartor

34.6.11,90

| FEMALE OFFICIALS IN CALIFORNIA
WOMEN CITY COUNCIL MEMBERS | | | |
City	Councilmember	City	Councilmember
Visalia	Mary Louise Vivier	Westminster	Anita Huseth
Vista	Nancy Wade	Williams	Virginia Kizer
Vista	Jeanette M. Smith	Williams	Virginia L. Stranske
Walnut	Bertha Ashley	Woodland	Barbara Peyton
Walnut Creek	Gail Murray	Woodside	Jeanne Dickey
Walnut Creek	Gwen Regalia	Woodside	Elizabeth P. Alexander
Watsonville	Gwen Carroll	Woodside	Joan Stiff
Westlake Village	Berniece Bennett	Yountville	Carlee Leftwich
Westlake village	Bonnie Klove	Yountville	Cassandra Mitchell
Westminster	Joy L. Neugebauer	Yreka	Mary Lou Smith
Westminster	Lynn Gillespie		

34.6.12,90   Source: California League of Cities and the California Secretary of State, *California Roster*.

| FIRSTS FOR FEMALE POLITICIANS | | |
Position	Name	Elected
First women in the State Assembly	Esto Broughton (D)	1918
	Grace S. Dorris (R)	1918
	Elizabeth Hughes (R)	1918
	Anna L. Saylor (R)	1918
First Hispanic woman in the State Assembly	Gloria Molina (D)	1982
First Black woman in the State Assembly	Yvonne W. Brathwaite Burke (D)	1966
First Asian woman in the State Assembly	March Fong Eu (D)	1966
First woman in the State Senate	Rose Ann Vuich (D)	1976
First Black woman in the State Senate	Diane E. Watson (D)	1978
No Hispanic or Asian women have served in the State Senate		
First woman in Congress from California	Mae Ella Nolan (R)	1922
First Black woman in Congress from California	Yvonne W. Brathwaite Burke (D)	1972
No Hispanic or Asian women have served in Congress from California		
No Black or Hispanic women have been elected to statewide office		
First Asian Woman elected to statewide office	March Fong Eu (D) - Secretary of State	1974
First woman judge (Justice of the Peace in Palo Alto)	Isabel Charles	1916
First woman judge in the Municipal Court	Mary Wetmore (S.F.)	1930
First woman judge in the Superior Court	Theresa Meikle (S.F.)	1942
First woman Appeals Court judge	Annette Adams	1942
First woman on the California Supreme Court	Rose Bird	1977
First Asian woman on the California Supreme Court	Joyce L. Kennard	1989
First woman elected to statewide office	Ivy Baker Priest (R) - Treasurer	1966

34.8,90   Sources: James Driscoll, *California's Legislature; & Congressional Women - Their Recruitment, Treatment & Behavior*.

WOMEN'S SHELTERS BY COUNTY

Alameda County

A Safe Place
P.O. Box 275
Oakland, CA 94604
C (415) 536-SAFE
B (415) 444-7255

Berkeley's Women' Refuge (YWCA)
P.O. Box 3298
Berkeley, CA 94703
C (415) 849-2314
B (415) 658-7231

Emergency Shelter Program, Inc.
22430 Foothill Blvd.
Hayward, CA 94544
C (415) 786-1246
B (415) 581-5626

SAVE (Shelter Against
Violent Environments)
P.O. Box 8283
Fremont, CA 94537
C (415) 794-6055
B (415) 794-6055

Second Change Emergency Shelter
6330 Thornton
Newark, CA 94560
C (415) 792-4357

Tri-Valley Haven for Women
P.O. Box 2190
Livermore, CA 94550
C (415) 449-5842
B (415) 449-5845

Women Against Violence
Emergency Services (WAVES)
P.O. Box 1121
Berkeley, CA 94701
C (415) 540-5354
B (415) 540-5354

Amador County

Operation Care
120 Church St.
Jackson, CA 95642
(209) 223-2600

Butte County

Catalyst: Women's Advocates, Inc.
P.O. Box 4184
Chico, CA 95927
C (916) 895-8476
B (916) 343-7711

Calaveras County

Calaveras Women's Crisis Line
P.O. Box 623
San Andreas, CA 95249
C (209) 736-4011

Contra Costa County

Battered Women's Alternative
P.O. Box 6406
Concord, CA 94524
C (415) 930-8300
B (415) 676-2845

El Dorado County

El Dorado Women's Information Center
3133 Gilmore St.
Placerville, CA 95667
C (916) 626-1131
B (916) 626-1450

Womanspace, Unlimited
P.O. Box 13111
South Lake Tahoe, CA 95702
C (916) 544-4444
B (916) 544-2118

Fresno County

Good Samaritan Mission
1927 Young St.
Selma, CA 93662
C (209) 986-4648

Marjaree Mason Center (YWCA)
1600 M Street
Fresno, CA 93721
(209) 237-4701

Humboldt County

Humboldt Women for Shelter
P.O. Box 969
Eureka, CA 95501
C (707) 443-6042
B (707) 444-9255

34.9.1,90   C = 24 hour crisis number; B = Business phone.

WOMEN'S SHELTERS BY COUNTY

Imperial County
Womenhaven, Inc.
P.O. Box 2219
El Centro, CA 92244
C (619) 353-8530
B (619) 353-6922

Kern County
Alliance on Family Violence
P.O. Box 2054
Bakersfield, CA 93303
C (805) 327-1091
B (805) 322-0931

Kings County
Domestic Violence Prevention
Program
1222 W. Lacey Blvd.
Hanford, CA 93230
C (209) 582-2968
B (209) 582-4386

Lake County
A.W.A.R.E
P.O. Box 987
Lakeport, CA 95453
C (707) 263-3577
B (707) 263-8162

Lake County/Agape House
P.O. Box 542
Lakeport, CA 95453
C (707) 263-7233
B (707) 263-1516

Los Angeles County
1736 Projects
1736 Monterey Blvd.
Hermosa Beach, CA 90254
C (213) 379-3620
B (213) 372-5843

Carson Shelter
c/o Employment Readiness
Support Center
22015 S. Avalone Blvd.
Carson, CA 90745
C (213) 549-1375
B (213) 549-0137

Los Angeles County cont.
CSAC Bilingual Shelter for Women
(Chicana Service Action Center)
1264 W. First St.
Los Angeles, CA 90026
C (213) 268-7564
B (213) 268-7568

East Los Angeles Shelter
P.O. Box 23366
Los Angeles, CA 90023
C (213) 268-7564
B (213) 658-4042

Every Woman's Shelter/Nalina
543 Fairfax Ave., Rm. 408
Los Angeles, CA 90036
C (213) 653-4042
B (213) 653-4042

Good Shepherd Shelter
2561 Venice Blvd.
Los Angeles, CA 90019
(213) 737-6111

Haven Hills, Inc.
P.O. Box 260
Canoga Park, CA 91305
C (818) 887-6589
B (818) 998-7481

Haven House
P.O. Box 50007
Pasadena, CA 91105-0007
C (213) 681-2626
B (213) 681-5044

House of Ruth
P.O. Box 457
Claremont, CA 91711
C (714) 988-5559
B (714) 623-4364

Jenesse Center
P.O. Box 73837
Los Angeles, CA 90003
C (213) 290-2115
B (213) 751-1145

34.9.2,90 C = 24 hour crisis number; B = Business number.

WOMEN'S SHELTERS BY COUNTY

Los Angeles County cont.	Los Angeles County cont.
Pacific Asian Rape and Battering Line 543 N. Fairfax Ave., Rm 108-A Los Angeles, CA 90036 C (213) 653-4042	Women's & Children's Crisis Shelter P.O. Box 404 Whittier, CA 90608 C (213) 945-3937 B (213) 696-4551
Rainbow Shelter P.O. Box 1925 San Pedro, CA 90733 C (213) 547-9343 B (213) 548-5450	Womenshelter (YWCA) 853 Atlantic Avenue Long Beach, CA 90813 C (213) 437-4663 B (213) 491-5362
Sojourn House Ocean Park Community Center 254 Hill Street Santa Monica, CA 90405 C (213) 392-9896 B (213) 399-9239	Women's Crisis Center (Wings) P.O. Box 1464 West Covina, CA 91793 C (213) 967-0658 B (213) 331-0814

Los Angeles County cont.	Madera County
South Bay Coalition for Alternatives to Domestic Violence P.O. Box 7000-851 Redondo Beach, CA 90277 B (213) 372-9855	Shelter and Help in Emergency P.O. Box 503 Madera, CA 93639 C (209) 673-8776 B (209) 673-9174
Southern Cal. Coalition on Battered Women P.O. Box 5036 Santa Monica, CA 90405 (213) 578-1442	**Marin County** Marin Abused Women Services (YWCA) 1717 5th Avenue San Rafael, CA 94901 C (415) 924-6616 B (415) 457-2464
Su Casa P.O. Box 998 Artesia, CA 90701 C (213) 402-7081 B (213) 860-3921/924-2557	**Mendocino County** CAARE Project (Community Assistance in Assault & Rape Emergency) P.O. Box 764
Valley Oasis P.O. Box 4226 Lancaster, CA 93539 C (805) 945-6736 B (805) 945-5509	Fort Bragg, CA 95434 C (707) 964-4357 B (707) 964-4055

34.9.3,90 C = 24 hour crisis number; B = Business number.

WOMEN'S SHELTERS BY COUNTY

Mendocino County cont.

Project Sanctuary
P.O. Box 995
Ukiah, CA 95482
C (707) 462-7988/462-9196
B (707) 462-7862

Merced County

A Woman's Place
P.O. Box 822
Merced, CA 95341
C (209) 722-4357
B (209) 384-2232

Monterey County

Salinas Family Emergency Shelter
P.O. Box 3584
Salinas, CA 93912
C (408) 758-5769
C (408) 422-2201

Woman Against Domestic Violence
404 Camino El Estero
Monterey, CA 93940
C (408) 372-6300
B (408) 649-0834

Woman's Crisis Center of Salinas
P.O. Box 1805
Salinas, CA 93902
C (408) 757-1001
B (408) 757-1002

Napa County

Napa Emergency
Women's Service (NEWS)
P.O. Box 427
Napa, CA 94559
C (707) 255-6397

Volunteer Center
1303 Jefferson
Napa, CA 94559
C (707) 255-6397
B (707) 252-3687

Nevada County

Domestic Violence Coalition
P.O. Box 484
Grass Valley, CA 95945
C (916) 272-3467
B (916) 272-2045

Orange County

Human Options
P.O Box 445
South Laguna, CA 92677
C (714) 494-7017
B (714) 494-5367

Interval House
P.O. Box 3151
Seal Beach, CA 90740
C (213) 594-4555

Orange County Coalition
Against Domestic Violence
17421 Irvine Blvd.
Tustin, CA 92680
C (714) 638-5604
B (714) 838-7377

Women's Transitional Living Center
P.O. Box 6103
Orange, CA 92667-1103
C (714) 992-1931/992-1932
B (714) 992-1939

Placer County

Women's Center
P.O. Box 5462
Auburn, CA 95603
C (916) 652-6558
B (916) 885-0443

Riverside County

Horizon House
(Riverside County Coalition for
Alternatives to Domestic Violence)
P.O. Box 910
Riverside, CA 92502
C (714) 653-0829
B (714) 684-1720

34.9.4,90 C = 24 hour crisis number; B = Business number.

WOMEN'S SHELTERS BY COUNTY

Sacramento County	San Diego County cont.
WEAVE (Women Escaping A Violent Environment) P.O. Box 161356 Sacramento, CA 95816 C (916) 920-2952 B (916) 448-2321	Center of Women's Studies and Services 2467 E Street San Diego, CA 92102 C (619) 233-3088 B (619) 233-8984

Sacramento County

WEAVE (Women Escaping
A Violent Environment)
P.O. Box 161356
Sacramento, CA 95816
C (916) 920-2952
B (916) 448-2321

San Bernardino County

Desert Sanctuary, Haley House
P.O. Box 1781
Barstow, CA 92312-1781
C (619) 252-3441

Domestic Violence Project
15579 Eighth St.
Victorville, CA 92392
C (619) 245-4211
B (619) 241-0035

Doves, Inc.
P.O. Box 3646
Big Bear Lake, CA 92315
C (714) 866-5723
B (714) 866-8264

Option House
P.O. Box 970
San Bernardino, CA 92402
C (714) 825-8862
B (714) 381-3471

Unity Home
P.O. Box 1622
Joshua Tree, CA 92252
C (619) 366-9663
B (619) 366-8233

San Diego County

Battered Women's Services
Casa de Paz
P.O. Box 4007
San Diego, CA 92104
C (619) 234-3164
B (619) 234-3416

San Diego County cont.

Center of Women's Studies and Services
2467 E Street
San Diego, CA 92102
C (619) 233-3088
B (619) 233-8984

Women's Resource Center
P.O Box 499
San Luis Rey, CA 92058
C (619) 757-3500

San Francisco County

La Casa de los Madres
P.O. Box 27236
San Francisco, CA 94127
C (415) 469-7637
B (415) 469-7650

Rosalie House
c/o Vincent de Paul
1745 Folsom Street
San Francisco, CA 94110
C (415) 861-2566
B (415) 861-2566

Women, Inc. (Women Organized to
Make Abuse Non-existent)
2940 16th Street
San Francisco, CA 94103
C (415) 964-4722
B (415) 964-4777

Family Violence Project
1001 Petrero Avenue
Bldg. 1, Suite 200
San Francisco, CA 94110
B (415) 821-4553
B (415) 552-7550

San Joaquin County

Stockton's Women's Shelter
P.O. Box 424
French Camp, CA 95231
C (209) 982-0396

34.9.5,90   C = 24 hour crisis number; B = Business number.

WOMEN'S SHELTERS BY COUNTY

San Joaquin County cont.

Direction for Abused Women
in Need (D.A.W.N.) House
c/o Women's Center
930 N. Commerce
Stockton, CA 95202
B (209) 941-2611
C (209) 465-4878

San Luis Obispo County

Women's Shelter Program
P.O. Box 125
San Luis Obispo, CA 93406
C (805) 544-6163
B (805) 554-2321

San Mateo County

San Mateo Women's Shelter
P.O. Box 652
San Mateo, CA 94401
(415) 342-0850

Santa Barbara County

Family Violence Counseling
815 S. Park View Ave.
Santa Maria, CA 93454
B (805) 736-5621
B (805) 928-2611

Shelter Services for Women, Inc.
P.O. Box 1336
Lompoc, CA 93436
C (805) 736-0965
B (805) 735-1834

Shelter Services for Women, Inc.
P.O. Box 1536
Santa Barbara, CA 93102
C (805) 964-5245
B (805) 963-4458

Shelter Services for Women, Inc.'
500 S. Broadway
Santa Maria, CA 93454
B (805) 925-2160

Santa Clara County

La Isla Pacifica
South County Alternatives
P.O. Box 1326
Gilroy, CA 95020
C (408) 683-4118
B (408) 842-3118

Mid-Peninsula Support Network
222-D View Street
Mountain View, CA 94041
C (415) 964-2266
B (415) 946-6503

WOMA: The Women's Alliance
160 E. Virginia, Rm 230
San Jose, CA 95112
C (408) 279-2962
B (408) 298-3505

Santa Cruz County

Santa Cruz Women
Against Rape
P.O. Box 711
Santa Cruz, CA 95061
C (408) 426-7273

Women's Crisis Support
and Shelter Services
1025 Center St.
Santa Cruz, CA 95060
C (408) 429-1478/728-2295
B (408) 425-5525

Shasta County

Shasta County Women's Refuge
P.O Box 4211
Redding, CA 96099
C (916) 244-0117
B (916) 335-5388 (East Shasta Co.)
  (916) 243-9057 (Men's Program)

34.9.6,90 C = 24 hour crisis number; B = Business number.

WOMEN'S SHELTERS BY COUNTY

Siskiyou County	Tehama County
Domestic Violence Program P.O. Box 1679 Yreka, CA 96097 C (916) 842-4068 B (916) 842-6629	Women's Refuge B (916) 529-1102

Siskiyou County	Trinity County
	Domestic Violence Program P.O. Box 447 Douglas City, CA 96047 C (916) 623-4357 B (916) 623-2024

Solano County
Solano Center for Battered Women
P.O. Box 2589
Fairfield, CA 94533
C (707) 429-4357
B (707) 429-4950

Sonoma County
Women's Emergency Shelter
Program (YWCA)
P.O. Box 3506
Santa Rosa, CA 95402
C (707) 546-1234
B (707) 546-7115

Tulare County
Emergency Women's Shelter Project
P.O. Box 510
Visalia, CA 93279
C (209) 732-5941

Mary Baker Mission Shelter
P.O. Box 2033
Porterville, CA 93258
C (209) 784-0192

Stanislaus County
Central Cal. Coalition on
Domestic Violence
P.O. Box 3931
Modesto, CA 95352
B (209) 575-7037

Stanislaus Women's Refuge
1700 McHenry Village Way #6
Modesto, CA 95350
C (209) 577-5980
B (209) 522-0331 (Shelter)

Open Gates Ministries
511 K Street
Dinuba, CA 93618
C (209) 591-1241

Tuolumne County
Motherlode Women's Center
P.O. Box 663
Sonora, CA 95370
C (209) 532-4707
B (209) 532-4746

Sutter County
Casa de Esperanza
P.O. Box 56
Yuba City, CA 95992
C (916) 674-2020
C (916) 674-5400

Ventura County
Coalition Against
Household Violence
455 S. Hill Rd #15
Ventura, CA 93003
C (805) 656-1111
B (805) 656-3443

34.9.7,90 C = 24 hour crisis number; B = Business number.

WOMEN'S SHELTERS BY COUNTY

Ventura County cont.

Interface Community
3475 Old Conejo Road
Newbury Park, CA 91320
In Thousand Oaks/Newbury Park
(805) 498-6643
In Simi Valley/Moorpark
(805) 529-0975
In Oxnard/Ventura
(805) 647-7855

Yolo County

Battered Women's Center
of Yolo County
c/o Yolo Sexual Assault Center
203 F Street
Davis, CA 95616
C (916) 758-8400
B (916) 758-0540

Yolo County cont

Harper House
P.O. Box 725
Broderick, CA 95605
C (916) 758-8400
B (916) 758-0540

Crisis Lines of Yolo County
Battered Women's Center &
Harper House:
Davis   (916) 758-8400
East Yolo (916) 371-1907
Wooland   (916) 662-1133

C = 24 hour crisis number; B = Business number.
34.9.8,90 Source: Southern California Coalition on Battered Women,
December 1989 *Directory*.

LARGEST U.S. CITIES WITH FEMALE MAYORS

Rank	Mayor	City
1	Kathy Whitmire	Houston
2	**Maureen O'Conner**	**San Diego**
3	Annette Strauss	Dallas
4	Donna Owens	Toledo
5	**Anne Rudin**	**Sacramento**

34.10,90 Source: Pacific Data Resources.

WOMEN'S ORGANIZATIONS

American Association of University Women 16291 Content Circle Huntington Beach, CA 92649	**California State Coalition of Rape Crisis Centers** Humboldt County Rape Crisis P.O. Box 543 Eureka, CA 95502
Asian Pacific Women's Network P.O. Box 84-012 Los Angeles, CA 90073	**California Women's Lawyers Asso.** P.O. Box 161523 Sacramento, CA 95016
Black Women's Forum P.O. Box 10702 Los Angeles, CA 90001	**Children's Lobby** P.O. Box 448 Sacramento, CA 95802
Black Women United / Bay Area 10966 Cliffland Oakland, CA 94605	**Church Women United** **No. California / Nevada Region** 2791 Laurel Drive Sacramento, CA 95825
California Abortion Rights Action League 4110 Geary Blvd., #204 San Francisco, CA 94118 and 1337 Santa Monica Mall #316 Santa Monica, CA 90401	**Church Women United** Southern California / Nevada Region 1145 East Rubio Street Altadena, CA 91001
California Advocates for Re-Entry Education Merritt College 12500 Campus Drive Oakland, CA 94619	**Coalition for the Medical Rights of Women** 2845 24th Street San Francisco, CA 94110
California Elected Women's Association 1400 K. Street #304 Sacramento, CA 95814	**Comparable Worth Project** 488 41st Street, Suite 5 Oakland, CA 94609
California Family Law Coalition P.O. Box 7596 Van Nuys, CA 91409	**Eagle Forum** P.O. Box 8212 Newport Beach, CA 92658-8212
California Federation of Business & Professional Women's Clubs, Inc. 833 Market Street, Suite 809 San Francisco, CA 94103	**E.X.P.O.S.E.** 5141 Greenberry Drive Sacramento, CA 95841
California Legislative Roundtable 2611 11th St., #1 Santa Monica, CA 90405	**Family Day Care Asso. of Cal.** 5730 Market St. Oakland, CA 94608
California Nurses Association 110 11th Street #200 Sacramento, CA 95814	**Federally Employed Women, Western** 3212 Bona Oakland, CA 94601
	Future Homemakers of America Calif. Asso. / FHA-HERO 712 Capitol Mall, 4th Floor Sacramento, CA 95814

34.11.1,90 Source: California Commission on the Status of Women, 1989.

WOMEN'S ORGANIZATIONS	
Gray Panthers of California 926 J Street, Ste. 917 Sacramento, CA 95814	**9 to 5 L.A. Working Women** 1010 South Flower Street #500 Los Angeles, CA 90015
League of Women Voters of California 926 J Street, Ste. 1000 Sacramento, CA 95814	**Older Women's League** 3800 Harrison Street Oakland, CA 94611
Minority Women's Legislative Roundtable P.O. Box 160084 Sacramento, CA 95816	**Planned Parenthood of California** 1317-A 15th St. Sacramento, CA 95814
National Action Against Rape 477 15th Street #200 Oakland, CA 94612	**Right to Life of S. Cal.** 1616 W. 9th St., #220 Los Angeles, CA 90015
Naitonal Association of University Women 816 W. 123rd Street Los Angeles, CA 90004	**Right to Life of N. Cal.** P.O. Box 460374 San Francisco, CA 94146-0374
National Council of Catholic Women 11590 Circle Way Dublin, CA 94568	**Soroptimist International of the Americas, Inc.** 845 Monterey Blvd. San Francisco, CA 94127
National Council of Negro Women 4214 Monteith Drive Los Angeles, CA 90043	**S.P.B.** 801 Capitol Mall Sacramento, CA 95814
National Island Women's Association 558 East Double Street Carson, CA 94075	**W.E.A.P.** 518 17th Street, Ste. 200 Oakland, CA 94612
National Organization for Women P.O. Box 1404 Sacramento, CA 95807	**Women For:** 8913 W. Olympic Beverly Hills, CA 90211
N.O.W. Legislative Office 926 J Street #523 Sacramento, CA 95814	**Women's Caucus For Art** 2467 Myrtle Ave. Hermosa Beach, CA 90254
	Zonia International 68 Barbaree Way - The Cove Tiburon,CA 94920

34.11.2,90 Source: California Commission on the Status of Women, 1989.

Minorities

Californians have long been proud of being different from inhabitants of the states east of the Sierras. As the state enters the 1990s, its ethnic composition sets it apart from the rest of the United States. Although the proportion of blacks in the state is smaller than that in the country as a whole, the percentage of Latin and Asian residents in California is three times larger. Only Hawaii has a larger proportion of Asians and only New Mexico a higher proportion of Hispanics.

In contrast with American cities of the East and the Midwest, where during the nineteenth and early twentieth centuries European ethnic populations and blacks lived in ghettos, contemporary California is the nation's most residentially integrated state despite its well-known areas of ethnic concentration. The question in the minds of many Californians is whether this residential integration is symptomatic of a broader economic, political, and cultural integration. Specifically, will California's large recent influx of Hispanics and Asians be integrated into middle-class society?

Much of the upward mobility of all groups depends on their commitment to education, a stable family life, and business skills. Asians seem to do best in each of these areas. By contrast, blacks and Hispanics drop out of high school at a high rate and have a low rate of college attendance--depressing statistics that augur a difficult future for these minorities. Many of them entering the work force in the future will have few skills and will thus face daunting obstacles to economic success.

California is a hotbed of new business opportunities, however, for those who can seize them, with far more fast-growing small companies than any other state in the nation. Entrepreneurs among Asians and Hispanics, more than among blacks, seem to be taking advantage of these business opportunities in California. As of the last census of minority businesses, there were 20,000 Asian, 12,000 Hispanic, and 4,000 black business firms with one employee or more. The success of these business ventures will have a measurable effect on the economic mobility of California's minorities.

Recently Native Americans have been getting involved in nontraditional business in a big way. Bingo and other gambling enterprises are springing up on Indian reservations around the state, pumping dollars into tribal accounts but also worrying law enforcement officials concerned about the potential for the influence of organized crime on the reservations.

Crime is also of great concern to blacks and Hispanics in the state's major metropolitan areas as drugs and gang warfare disrupt community life, discourage business development, and ruin the lives of thousands of people.

| HISPANIC PUBLICATIONS ||
Name	City
20 de Mayo	Los Angeles
Americas 2001	Los Angeles
Business Journal	Los Angeles
Dignidad	Oakland
Eastside Sun	Los Angeles
El Azteca	Santa Ana
El Hispano	Sacramento
El Mensajero	San Francisco
El Mundo	Oakland
El Tecolote	San Francisco
Hispanic Business	Santa Barbara
Hispanic Computing	San Francisco
Hispanic in Philanthropy News	San Francisco
Hispanic Today	Chatsworth
La Opinion	Los Angeles
La Voz	Pomona
Latinograma	Los Angeles
Los Atleticos	Oakland
Mexicalo	Bakersfield
Noticias del Mundo	Los Angeles
Saludos Hispanos	Tarzana
The Forum	San Diego
Union Hispana	Sana Ana

35.1,90 Source: Pacific Data Resources. Also see *Hispanic Media, USA 1987* and *U.C. Berkeley Chicano Periodical Index 1987.*

TOP TEN HISPANIC-OWNED BUSINESSES IN CALIFORNIA, 1988				
Rank Among All Hispanic-Owned Businesses in U.S.	Company	Location	Type of Business	1988 Sales (millions)
8	Galindo Finance Corp.	Bell	Real Estate Sales	$118
21	Rosendin Electric	San Jose	Contractor	$71
24	Lloyd A. Wise	Oakland	Auto Sales	$60
25	Komfort Industries	Riverside	Motor Homes	$60
27	La Reina	Los Angeles	Mfg. Mexican Food	$53
29	Telacu	Los Angeles	Holding Company	$51
37	Angel Echnevarria	Los Angeles	Mfg. Matresses	$47
39	Infotec Development	Santa Ana	Engineering	$45
41	Ramos Oil	W. Sacramento	Oil Products	$43
42	Ruiz Food Products	Tulare	Mfg. Mexican Food	$42

35.2,90 Source: *Hispanic Business Magazine.*

HISPANIC MEDIA*

Station	City	Station	City
Television		**Radio cont.**	
KCSO-TV (ch. 19)	Modesto (SIN)	KMPG (AM)	Hollister
KDTV-TV (ch. 14)	San Francisco (SIN)	KNEZ (AM)	Lompoc
KFTV-TV (ch. 21)	Fresno (SIN)	KNSE (AM)	Rancho Cucamonga
KMEX-TV (ch. 34)	Los Angeles (SIN)	KNTA (AM)	Santa Clara
KO7A-TV (ch. 7)	Santa Monica (SIN)	KOFY (AM)	Burlingame
KSCI-TV (ch. 18)	Los Angeles	KOMY (AM)	Watsonville
KSMS-TV (ch. 67)	Monterey (SIN)	KOXR (AM)	Oxnard
KVEA-TV (ch. 52)	Glendale	KPBS (FM)	San Diego
XEWT-TV (ch. 12)	San Ysidro (SIN)	KPMC (AM)	Bakersfield
XHBC-TV (ch. 12)	Calexico (SIN)	KQIQ (AM)	Lemoore
Radio		KQVO (FM)	Calexico
KAFY (FM)	Bakersfield	KRAY (FM)	Salinas
KALI (AM)	Hollywood	KRCX (AM)	Roseville
KAZA (FM)	San Jose	KROQ (AM)	Los Angeles
KBBF (FM)	Santa Rosa	KSDG (AM)	San Diego
KBRG (FM)	Fremont	KSJV (FM)	Fresno
KCAL (AM)	Redlands	KSKQ (AM)	Los Angeles
KCLQ (AM)	Hanford	KSKQ (FM)	Los Angeles
KCTY (AM)	Salinas	KSTN (FM)	Stockton
KCVR (AM)	Lodi	KTIP (AM)	Porterville
KDIF (AM)	Riverside	KTNQ (AM)	Hollywood
KGST (AM)	Fresno	KTRO (AM)	Port Hueneme
KIQI (AM)	San Francisco	KUTY (AM)	Palmdale
KJMB (AM)	Blythe	KVIM (FM)	Indio
KLBS (AM)	Los Banos	KWAC (AM)	Bakersfield
KLIP (AM)	Fowler	KWKW (AM)	Hollywood
KLOC (AM)	Modesto	KXEM (AM)	McFarland
KLOQ (AM)	Merced	KXEX (AM)	Fresno
KLVE (FM)	Los Angeles	KXLU (AM)	Los Angeles
KMAX (AM) or (FM)	Arcadia	KZON (AM)	Santa Maria
KMJC	San Diego		

* Part or full time Spanish Language Programs
35.3,90 Source: Radio America.

SECTION 35 NOTE

In California the Hispanic population of eleven metropolitan areas exceeds 10,000. In three of the eleven areas it exceeds 200,000.

35.4,90

HISPANIC OFFICIALS IN CALIFORNIA

Major Statewide Appointees
Agonia, Henry-Director, State
  Dept. of Parks & Recreation
Avila, Gilbert-Member, Commission
  on the Californias
Baiz, Thomas-Member, Commission
  on the Californias
Dominguez, H.F.-Member, Commission
  for Economic Development
Gonzales, Alice J.-Director,
  Department of Aging
Gutierrez, Chon-Director, State
  Lottery Commission
Marquez, Francisco J.-Director
  Office of California-Mexico Affairs
Martinez, Robert T.-Director of
  State Planning and Research
Martinez, Vilma-Regent, University
  of California
Molinedo, Manuel A.-Member, State
  Parks & Recreation Commission
Padilla, Oscar R.-Chariman, Small
  Business Development Commission
Pena, Manuel-Board of Governors,
  Cal. Community Colleges
Ruiz, Darlen E.-Member, Water
  Resources Control Board
Romero, David T.-Member, State
  Board of Education
Sandoval, Joe G.-Secretary,
  Youth & Adult Correctional Agency
Sepulveda-Bailey, Jamie-Youthful
  Offender Parole Board
Speake, Theresa A.-Director,
  Dept. of Economic Opportunity
Ugalde, Jesse-Director, Department of
  Veterans Affairs
Villanueva, Daniel-Board of Directors,
  Cal. Economic Development Corp.
Vargas, Gilbert-Member, Commission
  on Aging

Members of Congress
Martinez, Matthew
Roybal, Edward
Torres, Esteban

State Senators
Ayala, Ruben
Montoya, Joseph
Torres, Art

Members of the State Assembly
Calderon, Charles
Campbell, Robert
Chacon, Peter

Polanco, Richard
Roybal-Allard, Lucile

County Officials

Supervisors
Santana, Charles-Alameda
Legaspi, Luis-Imperial
Meirelles, Abel-Kings
Lopez, Jess-Madera
Aramburu, Al-Marin
Vasquez, Gaddi-Orange
Ceniceros, Kay-Riverside
Gonzalez, James-San Francisco

City Officials

Mayors
Mirabel, George-Bell
Noreiga Robert-Brawley
Tirado, Antonio P.-Calexico
Aguiar, Fred-Chino
Coba, Yolanda-Coachella
Gonzalez, Frank-Colton
Aldaco, Ruth-Commerce
Velasco, Leonard T.-Delano
Franco, Robert-Del Rey Oaks
de la Montanya, John-Dinuba
Leyva, Ron-Firbaugh
de Leon, Elias-Greenfield
Pili, Renaldo-Guadalupe
Castro, Leroy-Gustine
Navejas, Kathleen-Hawaiian Gardens
Aquila, John F.-St. Helena
Silva, Tony E.-Huron
Miranda, Pat-Irwindale
Rodriguez, Trinidad-Kerman
Guzman, Louis-La Puente
Pena, John-La Quinta
Garcia, Guadalupe A.-Livingston
Lozano, Victor-Mendota
Rodriguez, Marcial "Rod"-Norwalk
Garcia, Elmo-Oakdale
Lopez, Victor-Orange Cove
Viveros, Arcadio-Parlier
Smith, Donna-Pomona
Trujillio, Velma-Red Bluff
Acuna, Daniel-San Fernando
Gomes, Joseph-San Pablo
Souza, Everett-Santa Clara
Ortiz, Richard-Soledad
Perez, Albert-South El Monte
Hernandez, Ronald R.-Waterford
Martinez, Fidel-West Sacramento
Sanchez, Victor-Westmorland
Lopez, Victor A.-Whittier

35.5.1,90

HISPANIC OFFICIALS IN CALIFORNIA

City Council Members

Blanco, Michael-Alhambra
Rocha, Helen-Antioch
Avila, Jennie-Azusa
Naranjo, Anthony-Azusa
Garule, Manuel-Barstow
Rodriquez, Ed-Belmont
Mendoza, Estella-Brawley
Gonzales, Arthur-Brentwood
Katsigeanis, Amalia-Calexico
Legaspi, Victor-Calexico
Ortega, Ricardo-Calexico
Barros, Roque-Calipatria
Medina, J. Roumualdo-Calipatria
DeWitt, Vera-Carson
Sanchez, Arsenio P. Jr.-Clear Lake
Duran, Frank-Coachella
Ramos, Cally-Coachella
Salas, Larry-Coachella
Cisneros, Connie-Colton
Rios, E. Jerry-Colton
Batres, Ruben C.-Commerce
Cornejo, Robert J.-Commerce
Dimas, James-Commerce
Navarro, Artemio E.-Commerce
Lopez, Al-Corona
Mata, Windy-Delano
Abrica, Ruben-East Palo Alto
Gonzalez, Mac-El Centro
Gutierrez, Ernest-El Monte
Torres, Alex-Exeter
Felix, Charles-Farmersville
Fernandez, Henry-Fowler
Casado, Cedro T.-Galt
Valdez, Pete, Jr.-Gilroy
Chavez, Robert-Gonzales
Yniguez, Ralph-Gonzales
Romo, Paul-Greenfield
Almaguer, Frank T.-Guadalupe
Sanchez, Herb-Guadalupe
Rocha, Pat-Gustine
Souza, Fred-Gustine
Jimenez, Matt- Hayward
Escover, Matthew M.-Hollister
Gonzalez, Joe-Hollister
Alamo, J. Sr.-Huron
Cano, Olivia D.-Huron
Dominguez, Ramon R.-Huron
Vargas, Michael-Huron
Grijalva, Arthur Sr.-Imperial

Lopez, Marcos-Indio
Garcia, Manuel A.-Industry
Perez, Patrick-Industry
Breceda, Joe-Irwindale
Chico, Robert-Irwindale
Diaz, Robert-Irwindale
Hernandez, Sal-Irwindale
Garcia, Ron-Kerman
Lopez, Jeri-La Mesa
Madrid, Art-La Mesa
Palacio, Francis-La Puente
Rodriquez, Robert F.-La Verne
Dominguez, Fred-Lake Elsinore
Tom Vargas-Livermore
Soria, Roy-Lingston
Marques, Marvin-Livingston
Diaz, Ed-Lompoc
Alatorre, Richard-Los Angeles
Molina, Gloria-Los Angeles
Garibay, Robert E.-Madera
Hernandez, Gary-Martinez
Aberasturi, Ramon-Marysville
Santiago, Henry-Maywood
Garza, Ruben-McFarland
Capuchino, Leo-Mendota
Gomez, Joe-Mendota
Robledo, John-Mendota
Silva, Robert-Mendota
Lara, Joseph A.-Merced
Cardenas-Jaffe, Victoria-Mission Viejo
Nobrega, John-Monrovia
Payan, Art-Montebello
Perez, Bernardo-Moorpark
Dalla, Michael-National City
Inzunza, Ralph-National City
Cortez, Louis M-Newark
Rodriguez, Kenneth-Newman
Mendez, Michael-Norwalk
Napolitano, Grace-Norwalk
Chavez, Lucy-Oceanside
Barrera, Fred L.-Orange
Celaya, Hector-Orange Cove
Martinez, Frank-Orange Cove
Rodriquez, Roy-Orange Cove
Villarreal, Gary-Orange Cove
Lopez, Dr. Manuel-Oxnard
Casarez, Marcos-Parlier
Lopez, Armando-Parlier
Patlan, Luis-Parlier

HISPANIC OFFICALS IN CALIFORNIA

City Council Members (cont.)

Rodriquez, Nellie-Parlier
Moctezuma, Joe-Portola
Chavez, John-Pico Rivera
De La Rosa, Gilbert-Pico Rivera
Natividad, Alberto-Pico Rivera
Goularte, John-Pinole
Soto, Nell G.-Pomona
Marquez, John-Richmond
Dominguez, Clarke-Rocklin
Serna, Joe-Sacramento
Portyondo, Ralph-Salinas
Estrada, Ester-San Bernardino
Flores, Jess-San Bernardino
Euelio, Franco-San Fernando
Margarito, Jess-San Fernando
Gonzalez, Jim-San Francisco
Castaneda, Jim-San Gabriel
Hernandez, Avelardo-San Joaquin
Alvarado, Blance-San Jose
Sausedo, Patricia-San Jose
Santos, Anthony-San Leandro
Gomes, Joseph M.-San Pablo
Gonzalez, Rene-Sanger
Martinez, Elliot-Sanger
Acosta, John-Santa Ana
Pulido, Miguel A.-Santa Ana
Fuentes, Al-Santa Fe Springs

Sandoval, Lorenzo-Santa Fe Springs
Urias, Alfonso C.-Santa Paula
Grigas, Victor-Seal Beach
Lujan, Dennis-Selma
Ledesma, Joe-Soldedad
Campos, Manuel-Soledad
Gracia, Ignacio-South El Monte
Olmos, Arthur-South El Monte
Quintana, Stan-South El Monte
Fierro, Evelyn-South Pasadena
Sapien, Sal-Stanton
Oliva, Tom-Stockton
Castillo, Pat- Sunnyvale
Morelos, Raymond Jr.-Tracy
Gomez, Thelma-Tulare
Fernandez, Manuel-Union City
Canestro, Albert A.-Upland
Villeneuve, Donald A.-Ventura
Davis, William-Vernon
Gonzales, H. Larry-Vernon
Ybarra, Thomas A.-Vernon
Campos, Tony-Watsonville
Huseth, Anita-Westminster
Esparza, Pablo-Westmorland
Rodriguez, Ron-Westmorland
Rodriguez, Sal-Woodlake

35.5.3,90

HISPANIC JUDGES IN CALIFORNIA

Judges

Federal
Alarcon, Arthur-9th Circuit
Aguilar, Robert-N. District
Fernandez, Ferdinand F.-9th Circuit
Garcia, Edward-E. District
Ramirez, Raul-E. District
Real, Manuel-Central District

Apellate Courts
Ortega, Reuben A.-2nd District
Ardiaz, James-5th District
Nares, Gilbert-4th District

Superior Courts
Gomes, Gene-Fresno
Nunez, Ralph-Fresno
Olmos, Mario G.-Fresno
Baca, Robert-Kern
Baldonado, Arthur-Los Angeles
Barrera, Victor-Los Angeles
Bazan, Alfonzo-Los Angeles
Cardenas, Raymond-Los Angeles
Corral, Jaime-Los Angeles
Godoy-Perez, Ramona L.-Los Angeles
Gutierrez, Gabriel-Los Angeles
Ibaniz, Richard-Los Angeles
Lopez, Robert-Los Angeles
Martinez, Robert M.-Los Angeles
Mireles, Raymond D.-Los Angeles
Montes, Richard-Los Angeles
Munoz, Aurelio-Los Angeles
Perez, David D.-Los Angeles
Torres, Ricardo-Los Angeles
Velarde, Carlos-Los Angeles
Briseno, Francisco-Orange
Cardenas, Luis-Orange
Ramirez, Manuel A.-Orange
Cazeres, Carlos-San Diego
Rosado, Raul-San Diego
Ferandez, William-Santa Clara
Azevedo, Eugene-Stanislaus
Soares, Robert-Ventura

Municipal Courts
Dorado, Leopoldo E.-Alameda
Ynostroza, Carlos-Alameda
Zuniga, Barbara-Contra Costa
Rodriguez, Armando-Fresno
Contreras, Matias-Imperial
Aranda, Benjamin-Los Angeles
Barela, Henry T.-Los Angeles
Chavez, Victoria M.-Los Angeles
Diaz, Rudolph-Los Angeles
Felix, Fred-Los Angeles
Garcia, Albert J.-Los Angeles
Hermo, Alfonso-Los Angeles
Khan, Abraham A.-Los Angeles
Moreno, Carlos R.-Los Angeles
Moreno, Tracy T.-Los Angeles
Obera, Marion-Los Angeles
Otero, S. James-Los Angeles
Paez, Richard-Los Angeles
Romero, Enrique-Los Angeles
Romero, Roy-Los Angeles
Ruiz, Gilbert-Los Angeles
Sarmiento, Cesar C.-Los Angeles
Uranga, Carlos-Los Angeles
Veron, Juaneita-Los Angeles
Moreno, William-Monterey
Elias, Betty-Orange
Firmat, Francisco F.-Orange
Munoz, Frances-Orange
Velasquez, David C.-orange
Cazares, Roy-San Diego
Ramirez, Victor-San Diego
Alvarado, Paul-San Francisco
Garcia, David-San Francisco
Saldamando, Alex,-San Francisco
Ochoa, Frank-Santa Barbara
Days, Virginia Mae-Santa Clara
Navarro, Rene-Santa Clara
Fernandez, Alfonso-Santa Clara
Vilareal, Luis-Solano
Aguilar, Charles-Stanislaus
Gutierrez, Arturo-Ventura

35.5.4,90 Source: California Secretary of State, *California Roster;* California League of Cities, unpublished data; *National Roster of Hispanic Elected Officials* and Pacific Data Resources.

POPULATION OF NATIVE AMERICANS
THE FIVE LEADING STATES

State	Population
California	201,311
Oklahoma	169,464
Arizona	152,857
New Mexico	104,777
North Carolina	64,635

Note: These five states contain 50% of all Native Americans in the U.S.
35.6,90   Source: U.S. Bureau of the Census, 1980 Census.

NATIVE AMERICAN OFFICIALS IN CALIFORNIA

Major Statewide Appointees
Greig, Niza-Member, State Board of Dental Examiners
Reyes, Bruce A.-Member, State Board of Chiropractic Examiners
Myers, Larry-Exec. Sec. Native American Heritage Commission

Judges
Superior Court
Lester, J. Morgan-San Diego

35.7,90

GOVERNMENT AGENCIES
DEALING WITH NATIVE AMERICANS

California Native American Heritage Commission 915 Capitol Mall, Room 288 Sacramento, Ca 95814 (916) 322-7791	U.S. Bureau of Indian Affairs 2800 Cottage Way Sacramento, CA 95825 (916) 484-4862

Bureau of Indian Affairs Field Offices

Northern California Agency P.O. Box 494879 Redding, CA 96049-4879 (916) 246-5150	Central California Agency 1800 Tribute Rd. Sacramento, CA 95815 (916) 978-4337
Hoopa Sub-A P.O. Box 369 Hoopa, CA 95546 (915) 625-4284	Klamath Field Office P.O. Box 789 Klamath, CA 95548 (707) 482-6421
Palm Springs Field Station P.O. Box 2245 441 S. Calle Encilia, Suite 8 Palm Springs, CA 92262 (619) 322-3086	Southern California Agency 3600 Lime Street, Suite 722 Riverside, CA 92501 (714) 351-6624

35.8,90   Source: U.S. Bureau of Indian Affairs, *Tribal Information & Directory, 1989.*

CALIFORNIA INDIAN TRIBES & BANDS BY COUNTY

Cahuilla

Palm Springs Band,
 Agua Caliente
 Reservation-Riverside
Agustine Band of Mission
 Indians of Agustine
 Reservation-Riverside
Cabazon Band of Mission
 Indians of Cabazon
 Reservation-Riverside
Cahuilla Band of Mission
 Indians of Cahuilla
 Reservation-Riverside
Los Coyotes Band of Mission
 Indians of Los Coyotes
 Reservation-San Diego
Morongo Band of Mission
 Indians of Morongo
 Reservation-Riverside
Ramona Reservation-Riverside
Santa Rosa Band of Mission
 Indians of Santa Rosa
 Reservation-Riverside
Torres-Martinez Band of Mission
 Indians of Torres-Martinez
 Reservation-Riverside

Chumash

Santa Ynez Band of Mission
 Indians, Santa Ynez
 Reservation-Santa Barbara

Cupeno

Pala Band of Mission
 Indians of Pala
 Reservation-San Diego

Diegueno

Barona Group of Capitan Grande
 Band of Mission Indians of
 Barona
 Reservation-San Diego
Campo Band of Mission Indians
 of Campo Reservation-
 San Diego

Diegueno (continued)

Capitan Grand Band of Mission
 Indians of Capitan Grande
 Reservation-San Diego
Cuyapaipe Band of Mission
 Indians of Cuyapaipe
 Reservation-San Diego
Inaja and Cosmit Reservations-
 San Diego
Jamul Indian Village Tribe-
 San Diego
La Posta Band of Mission
 Indians of La Posta
 Reservation-San Diego
Manzanita Band of Mission
 Indians of Manzanita
 Reservation-San Diego
Mesa Grande Band of Mission
 Indians of Mesa Grande
 Reservation-San Diego
San Pasqual Band of Mission
 Indians of San Pasqual
 Reservation-San Diego
Santa Ysabel Band of Mission
 Indians of Santa Ysabel
 Reservation-San Diego
Sycuan Band of Mission Indians
 of Sycuan Reservation-
 San Diego
Viejas (Baron Long) Band of
 Mission Indians of Viejas
 Reservation-San Diego

Hoopa

Hoopa-Yurok Tribe of Hoopa
 Valley Reservation-
 Humboldt and Del Norte

Karok

Karok Tribe of California-
 Humboldt and Siskiyou
Quartz Valley Rancheria-
 Siskiyou

35.9.1,90 Source: Bureau of Indian Affairs, *Tribal Information and Directory, 1988.*

SECTION 35 NOTE

For the names of Tribal Leaders in California, consult the "Tribal Leaders List." U.S. Bureau of Indian Affairs. (202) 343-1710

35.10,90

CALIFORNIA INDIAN TRIBES & BANDS BY COUNTY

Luiseno

La Jolla band of Mission Indians
of La Jolla Reservation-
San Diego

Pauma Band of Mission Indians
of Pauma and Yuima
Reservation-San Diego

Pechanga Band of Mission Indians
of Pechanga Reservation-
Riverside

San Luiseno Band of Mission
Indians of Rincon
Reservation-San Diego

Soboba Band of Mission Indians-
of Soboba Reservation-
Riverside

Twenty-Nine Palms Band of
Mission Indians of
Twenty-Nine Palms
Reservation-San Bernardino

Maidu

Enterprise Rancheria-Butte

Tyme Maidu Tribe of Berry Creek
Rancheria-Butte

Greenville Rancheria-
Plumas

Miwok (Me-Wuk)

Jackson Rancheria-Amador

Sheep Ranch Rancheria-
Calaveras

Shingle Springs Rancheria-
El Dorado

Toulumne Band of Toulumne
Reservation-Toulumne

Chicken Ranch Rancheria-
Toulumne

Mono

Cold Springs Rancheria-
Fresno

North Fork Rancheria-
Madera

Northern Paiute

Paiute Tribe of Cedarville-
Modoc

Paiute-Shoshone

Big Pine Band of Owens Valley
Paiute-Shoshone, Big Pine
Reservation-Inyo

Fort Independence Indian
Community of Paiute Indians-
Inyo

Paiute Shoshone Indians of the
Bishop Community of Bishop
Reservation-Inyo

Paiute-Shoshone Indians of the
Lone Pine Community of Lone
Pine Reservation-Inyo

Paiute Tribe of Bridgeport Indian
Colony-Mono

Timbi-Sha Western Shoshone Band
of Death Valley-Inyo

Susanville Rancheria-Lassen

Utu Utu Gwaitu Paiute Tribe
of the Benton Paiute
Reservation-Mono

Pit River-Wintu

Alutras Indian Rancheria-
Modoc

Big Bend Rancheria-
Shasta

Covelo Indian Community of
Round Valley Reservation-
Mendocino

Lookout Rancheria-Modoc

Madesi Band of Pit River
Indians of Montgomery
Creek Rancheria-
Shasta

Pit River Indian Tribe of the
79 Acres Reservation-
Modoc

Redding Rancheria-
Shasta

Roaring Creek Rancheria-
Shasta

35.9.2,90 Source: Bureau of Indian Affairs, *Tribal Information and Directory,*
1988.

CALIFORNIA INDIAN TRIBES & BANDS BY COUNTY

Pomo-Kato
Big Valley Band of Pomo Indians-
  Lake
Cahto Indian Tribe of
  Laytonville Rancheria-
  Mendocino
Cotyote Valley Band of
  Pomo Indians-Mendocino
Dry Creek Rancheria
  of Pomo Indians-Sonoma
Elem Indian Colony of
  Sulphur Bank Rancheria-
  Lake
Kashia Band of Pomo
  Indians of Stewarts Point
  Rancheria-Sonoma
Manchester Band of Pomo Indians
  of Manchester-Point Arena
  Rancheria-Mendocino
Middletown Rancheria of
  Pomo Indians-Lake
Robinson Rancheria-Lake
Sherwood Valley Rancheria-
  Mendocino
Upper Lake Band of Pomo
  Indians-Lake

Serrano
San Manuel Band of Mission
  Indians of San Manuel
  Reservation-
  San Bernardino

Shokowa-ma-Sokow-Shanel
Hopland Reservation-
  Mendocino

Smith River-Tolowa
Big Lagoon Rancheria-
  Humboldt
Elk Valley Rancheria-
  Del Norte

Tache-Tachi-Yokut
Santa Rosa Community of
  Santa Rosa Rancheria-Kings

Tolowa
Elk Creek Rancheria-
  Del Norte

Western Mono
Big Sandy Rancheria-Fresno

Wintun
Susanville Indian Rancheria
  of Washoe Indians-Lassen
Cachil Dehe Band of Wintun
  Indians of the Colusa Indian
  Community of Colusa
  Rancheria-Colusa
Cortina Rancheria of Wintun
  Indians-Colusa
Nomalski/Wintun-Wailaki-Nuimok
  of the Grindstone Creek
  Rancheria-Glenn
Wintun Tribe of Rumsey
  Rancheria-Yolo

Wiyot/Yurok
Blue Lake Rancheria
  Humboldt
Table Bluff Rancheria
  Humboldt
Rohnerville Rancheria-
  Humboldt
Yokut
Table Mountain Rancheria-
  Fresno
Tule River Tribe of Tule
  River Reservation-
  Tulare

Yurok
Trinidad Rancheria-
  Humboldt
Coast Indian Community of
  the Resighini Rancheria-
  Del Norte

35.9.3,90 Source: U.S. Bureau of Indian Affairs, *Tribal Information and Directory, 1988.*

BLACK-OWNED NEWSPAPERS IN CALIFORNIA		
Publication	**City**	**Publisher**
Newspapers		
Bakersfield News Observer	Bakersfield	Joe Coley
Berkeley Post	Berkeley	Tom Berkley
California Advocate	Fresno	Leslie Kimber
California Voice	Berkeley	Dr. Love
Compton Bulletin	Compton	O. Ray Watkins
Herald Dispatch	Los Angeles	John H. Holoman
Los Angles Sentinal	Los Angeles	Kenneth Thomas
Oakland Post	Oakland	Tom Berkley
The Pasadena Gazette	Pasadena	Beverly Hamn
Richmond Post	Richmond	Tom Berkley
Riverside Black Voice	Riverside	Hardy and Cheryl Brown
The Sacramento Observer	Sacramento	Dr. William H. Lee
San Bernardino American News	San Bernardino	Willie Mae Martin
San Bernardino Precinct Reporter	San Bernardino	Brian Townsend
Sun Reporter	San Francisco	Dr. Carlton Goodlett
Voice and Viewpoint News	San Diego	John Warren
New Bayview News	San Francisco	M. Kareem
San Francisco Post	San Francisco	Tom Berkley

35.11,90 Source: National Newspaper Publishers Association, unpublished data.

TOP TEN BLACK-OWNED BUSINESSES IN CALIFORNIA, 1988				
Rank Among all Black-owned Businesses in U.S.	**Company**	**Location**	**Type of Business**	**Sales (millions)**
5	The Gordy Company	Los Angeles	Entertainment	$105
11	Dick Griffey Productions	Hollywood	Entertainment	48.7
21	Surface Protection	Los Angeles	Paints and Coatings	30.0
22	Westside Distributors	South Gate	Beer Distribution	29.6
25	Advanced Consumer Marketing	Burlingame	Systems Integration, Mail Order Products	26.9
29	Beauchamp Distributing	Compton	Beer Distribution	25.6
42	Bay City Marine	National City	Ship Building and Repair	18.2
49	James Heard Mgmt.	Cerritos	Fast-Food Operations	14.2
52	Supurb Electric	Los Angeles	Hardware Distributor	13.0
54	African Development Public Investment	Hollywood	African Imports	12.5
66	Kass Management	Oakland	Food Service	10.5
68	Tem Associates	Emeryville	Automated Support Service	9.4

35.12,90 Source: *Black Enterprise* magazine's Top 100 Black Businesses.

BLACK OFFICIALS OF CALIFORNIA

Major Statewide Appointees

Brewer, Linda Stockdale
  Director, Office of Administrative Law
Burke, Yvonne Brathwaite
  Regent, University of California
Charles Adams-Governor's Office,
  Community Liason
Harvey, Robert L.-Member, Unemployment
  Insurance Appeals Board
Hesse Deborah M.-Member, Public
  Employment Relations Board
Hutchins, Henry T. Jr.-Member, Board of
  Governors, California Community Colleges
Kelley, Michael A.-Director,
  Dept. of Consumer Affairs
Meeks, Larry G.-Director,
  Statewide Health Planning
  and Development
Nelson, Richard B.-Executive Director,
  Office of Small Business
Poole, Susan E.-Superintendant
  Cal. Institution for Women
Thorton, Shirley Ann-Deputy
  Superintendant of Public Instruction

Members of Congress

Dellums, Ronald
Dixon, Julian
Dymally, Mervyn
Hawkins, Augustus

State Senators

Greene, Bill
Watson, Diane

Members of the State Assembly

Brown, Willie
Harris, Elihu

Members of the State Assembly (cont.)

Hughes, Teresa
Moore, Gwen
Murray, Willard
Waters, Maxine

County Supervisors

King, Mary-Alameda
Widener, Warren-Alameda
Brumfield, Voris-Lake County
Davis, Osby-Solano County
Johnson, Grantland-Sacramento
Kennedy, Willie-San Francisco County
Ward, Doris-San Francisco County
Williams, Leon-San Diego County

County Clerk

Davidson, Rene-Alameda County

County Treasurer

White, Donald-Alameda County

County Sheriff

Charles Byrd-Siskiyou County

City Officials

Mayors

Tucker, Walter-Compton
Vines, William-East Palo Alto
Vincent, Edward-Inglewood
Bradley, Tom-Los Angeles
Wells, Evelyn-Lynwood
Wilson, Lionel-Oakland
Livingston, George-Richmond
Mc Clair, Lance-Seaside
Busby, Jim-Victorville

35.13.1,90

TOP FIVE BLACK SAVINGS AND LOANS IN CALIFORNIA

U.S. Rank	Company	City	Staff	Assets (millions)
3	Family Savings and Loan	Los Angeles	66	$153
4	Founders Savings and Loan	Los Angeles	77	$133
6	Broadway Fed. Savings and Loan	Los Angeles	55	$97
7	Time Savings and Loan	San Francisco	41	$65
21	Enterprise Savings and Loan	Long Beach	14	$17

35.14,90 Source: *Black Enterprise* magazine's Top 100 Black Businesses.

BLACK OFFICIALS IN CALIFORNIA

City Councilmembers

Adams, Robert - Compton
Bartlett, Robert - Monrovia
Bazille, Leo - Oakland
Blakely, James E. Jr. - East Palo Alto
Bonner, Alfred - Stockton
Bostic, James - East Palo Alto
Bostic, John - East Palo Alto
Cannon, Aleta - Oakland
Childs, James - Bakersfield
Clarke, Jack - Riverside
Coates, Warnell - East Palo Alto
Davis, Taylor - Pittsburg
Farrell, Robert - Los Angeles
Filer, Maxey - Compton
Gilmore, Carter - Oakland
Griffin, Richard - Richmond
Hammond, Charles - Fairfield
Henning, Robert - Lynwood
Holden, Nate - Los Angeles
Horner, Lawrence - Thousand Oaks

James, Floyd - Compton
Kimber, Les - Fresno
Lange, Enrique - Stockton
Lindsay, Gilbert - Los Angeles
Lively, Ira - Seaside
McMillan, James - Richmond
McNeill, Julia S. - Baldwin Park
Patterson, Richard - Modesto
Polite, J. Theron - Seaside
Pope-Ludlam, Valerie - San Bernardino
Pratt, Wesley - San Diego
Richards, Paul - Lynwood
Riles, Wilson Jr. - Oakland
Shirek, Maudelle - Berkeley
Smith, Clarence - Long Beach
Tabor, Daniel - Inglewood
Wainwright, Mary - Berkeley
Ward, Bill - Haywood
Washington, Jesse Jr. - Perris
Washington, Lonnie - Richmond
Williams, Iola - San Jose

35.13.2,90 Source: *National Roster of Black Elected Officials, 1989* and Pacific Data Resources.

FIVE LARGEST BLACK-OWNED AUTO DEALERS

Rank	Company	Location	Dealership	Sales (millions)
1	Shack-Woods	Los Angeles	Ford	$127
2	Pope Chevrolet	Modesto	GM	37
3	Chino Hills Ford	Chino	Ford	28
4	Royal Carriage	Oxnard	GM	24
5	Mission Blvd. Lincoln-Mercury	Hayward	Ford	17

35.15,90 Source: *Black Enterprise* magazine's Top 100 Black Businesses.

MINORITIES

See Section 1, "Population," for more detailed population information on Hispanic Americans, Native Americans, Blacks, and Asian Americans.

35.16,90

BLACK JUDGES IN CALIFORNIA

Judges

Federal
Poole, Cecil-9th Circuit
Gilliam, Earl-S. District
Hatter, Terry-C. District
Henderson Felton-N. District
Marshall, Consuela-C. District
Williams, David-C. District

Appellate Courts
Broussard Allen
  Supreme Court
Spencer, Vaino
  Court of Appeals-District 2
Thompson, Leon
  Court of Appeals-District 2
White, Clinton W.
  Court of Appeals-District 2
Woods, Arleigh
  Court of Appeals-District 2

Superior Courts
Alston, Gilbert-Los Angeles
Baranco, Gordon-Alameda
Beverly Jr. William-Los Angeles
Brown-Armstrong, Sandra-Alameda
Clay, William-Los Angeles
Cooper, Candice-Los Angeles
Cordell, La Dorris H.-Santa Clara
Cruikshank, John-San Joaquin
Dearman, John-San Francisco
Dorn, Roosevelt-Los Angeles
Eduards, Jr. Raymond-San Diego
Jones, Charles-Los Angeles
Jones, Napoleon-Los Angeles
Long, James-W. Sacramento
Luke Sherrill-Los Angeles
Lytle, Alice-Sacramento
Malone, Stanley Jr.-Los Angeles
Matthews, Albert-Los Angeles
Miller Loren-Los Angeles
Mills, Billy-Los Angeles
Montgomery, Alpha-San Diego
Moore, H. Randolph-Los Angeles
Morgan, William-Sacramento
Morrow, Dion-Los Angeles
Nelson, Henry-Los Angeles
Pickard, Florence-Los Angeles
Pitts, Donald-Los Angeles
Ramsey, Henry-Alameda
Ransom, Gary-Sacramento
Raye, Vance-W. Sacramento
Roberson Jr., Robert-Los Angeles
Scarlett, Charles R.-Los Angeles

Smith Jr., Sherman-Los Angeles
Stephens, William-Marin
Sweeney, Wilmont-Alameda
Tenner, Jack-Los Angeles
Travis, Benjamin-Alameda
Tucker, Marcus-Los Angeles
Ware, James-Santa Clara

Municipal Courts
Aubrey, Ernest-Los Angeles
Blackwell, Glenette-Los Angeles
Brown, Irma J.-Los Angeles
Carroll, George-Richmond
Curtis, Herbert-Ventura County
Dunn, George-Long Beach
Edwards, Raymond-San Diego
Farrer, Dean-Compton
Ford, Judy-Oakland
Forneret, Rodney-Inglewood
Graham, Holly-Chino
Hill, Hugo-Compton
Hutson, Robert-Fullerton
James, Charles-San Francisco
Johnson, Marion-Los Angeles
Jones, Lawrence-Fresno
Littlejohn, Joe-San Diego
Loncke, Rudolph,-Sacramento
MacKey, Robert-Los Angeles
McBeth, Veronika-Los Angeles
McKay, Patti Jo-Los Angeles
McKinley, Pat-Richmond
Meeks, Perker-San Francisco
Milton, David-Los Angeles
Milton, David-Los Angeles
Mitchell, Elvira-Los Angeles
Morris, Carl W.-Oakland
Moss, Wardell-Inglewood
Niles, Alban I.-Los Angeles
Nunley, L.C.-Los Angeles
Obera, Marion-Los Angeles
Ormsby, William M.-Inglewood
Pichon, Rise-Santa Clara
Riggs, Elziabeth-El Cajon
Robinson, Roosevelt Jr.-Inglewood
Shelton, Phrasel-Redwood City
Shepard, Renard-Sacramento
Shumsky, Rosemary-Los Angeles
Sinclair, Harold-Los Angeles
Stevens, Emily-Los Angeles
Thompson, Sandra Ann-Los Angeles
Weeks, Marvin-Westminster
Wheatly, Horace-Oakland
White, James-Oakland

35.13.3,90 Source: Pacific Data Resources.

FIRSTS FOR BLACK POLITICIANS

Position	Name	Elected
First Black elected to the State Assembly	Frederick Roberts (R)	1918
First Black woman elected to the State Assembly	Yvonne W. Brathwaite Burke (D)	1966
First Black elected to the State Senate	Mervyn Dymally (D)	1966
First Black woman elected to the State Senate	Diane Watson (D)	1978
First Black elected to Congress from California	Gus Hawkins (D)	1962
First Black woman elected to Congress from Cal.	Yvonne W. Brathwaite Burke (D)	1972
First Black Speaker of the Assembly	Willie Brown (D)	
First Black elected to statewide office - Supt. of Public Instruction	Wilson Riles (D)	1970-82
First Black elected as Lt. Governor	Mervyn Dymally (D)	1974-78
First Black judge on the Municipal Court	John Bussey (L.A.)	1958
First Black judge on the Superior Court	John Bussey (L.A.)	1962
First Black judge on the Court of Appeal	Bernard Jefferson	1975
First Black appointed to the State Supreme Court	Wiley Manuel	1977

35.17,90 Source: Pacific Data Resources.

METROPOLITAN & REGIONAL AREAS OF CALIFORNIA BY RACE

Metro-Area	White	Asian	Black	Hispanic	Total
Anaheim-Santa Ana	63%	6%	2%	29%	100%
Los Angeles	47%	8%	10%	35%	100%
San Bernardino-Riverside	69%	2%	8%	22%	100%
Sacramento	75%	8%	8%	10%	100%
San Diego	70%	5%	6%	20%	100%
San Jose	69%	15%	3%	13%	100%
San Francisco-Oakland	61%	18%	10%	11%	100%
Rest of the State	71%	3%	4%	22%	100%
Region					
South Coast	66%	5%	4%	25%	100%
Los Angeles & Inland	51%	7%	10%	32%	100%
Mid Coast	66%	3%	4%	27%	100%
Bay Area	65%	15%	8%	12%	100%
San Joaquin Valley	63%	4%	3%	30%	100%
Sacramento Valley	79%	5%	5%	11%	100%
Rest of the State	88%	3%	2%	7%	100%

35.18,90 Source: California Department of Finance, *Current Population Survey*, 1989.

ASIAN-AMERICAN OFFICIALS

Statewide Officials
Eu, March Fong-Secretary of State

Major Statewide Appointees
Bautista, Alfredo-Community Representative,
  Governor's Office
Chan, Agnes I.-Member, State Board
  of Education
Chan, Joan-Chief Deputy Director,
  Office of Criminal Justice Planning
Liang, Walter-Community Representative,
  Governor's Office
Fontanoza, Cecillio-Director,
  Department of Rehabilitation
Kashiwabara, John-Trustee, California State
  University System
Louie, Lisa-Deputy Director,
  Conservation Corps
Murata-Demetre, Marilyn-Commissioner,
  Worker's Compensation Appeals Board
Tong, Edmund-Member, Board of Prison Terms
Wada, Yori-Regent, University of California
Kawahara, Edward K.-Director,
  Cal. Small Business Devel. Center

Congress
Matsui, Robert T.
Mineta, Norman Y.

County Supervisors
Hsieh, Thomas-San Francisco
Miyoshi, Toru-Santa Barbara

City Officials

Mayors
Kitayama, Tom-Union City
Nishino, Ken-Hemet
Takasugi, Nao-Oxnard
Takahashi, George-Marina
Velasco, Leonard T.-Delano

City Council Members
Chinn, Roger-Foster City
Chu, Judy-Monterey Park
Fukai, Masani "Mas"-Gardena
Fukawa, June-Delano
Hon, Audrey-Bradbury
Ichikawa, Garry-Fairfield
Lee, Tim-Lemoore
Chinn, Thomas-Sacramento
Nakano, George-Torrance
Ogawa, Frank H.-Oakland
Solium, Gorgonio-Hercules
Taguchi, Charles-Reedley
Takahara, Art-Mountain View
Tsukahara, Paul-Gardens
Wong, Daniel K.-Cerritos

City Council Members (cont.)
Woo, Michael-Los Angeles
Yokoyama, Jane-Santa Cruz

Judges

Federal
Lew, Ronald-Cent. Dist.
Takasugi, Robert-Cent. Dist.
Tashima, Atsushi Wallace-Cent. Dist.

Appellate
Fukuto, Morio-2nd Appellate Dist.
Low, Harry-1st Appellate Dist.

Superior
Chin, Ming-Alameda
Fujisaki, Hiroshi-Los Angeles
Hiroshige, Ernest-Los Angeles
Hom, Rose-Los Angeles
Ito,Lance-Los Angeles
Kakita, Edward-Los Angeles
Kawaichi, Ken-Alameda
Kayashima, Ben-San Bernardino
Kim, Frank S.-San Joaquin
Louie, Lenard-San Francisco
Matusinka, Jean-Los Angeles
Mihara, Nathan D.-Santa Clara
Nishimoto, Cary-Los Angeles
Palik, Harkjoon-Monterey
Takei, Taketsugu-Santa Clara
Todd, Katheryn Doi-Los Angeles
Tso, Jack Bing-Los Angeles
Watai, Madge S.-Los Angeles

Municipal
Burns, Cerena Wong-Sonoma
Chang, James-Santa Clara
Cowett, Pat-San Diego
Mayeda, Jon-Los Angeles
Doi, David I-Los Angeles
Kaneshiro, Gale E.-San Diego
Kobayashi, Charles C.-Sacramento
Kwong, Owen L.-Los Angeles
Meyeda, Jon-Los Angeles
Nomoto, Barbara T.-Orange
Quidachay, Ronald-San Francisco
Quon, Lillian L.-San Diego
Recana, Mel-Los Angeles
Sing, Lillian-San Francisco
Suzukawa, Steven-Los Angeles
Takahashi, Irene-Contra Costa
Wasserman, Fumiko H.-Los Angeles
Yip, James Sing-Los Angeles

Justice
Ishii, Anthony-Fresno
Uchiyama, Mikio-Fresno

35.19,90 Source: Pacific Data Resources.

FIRSTS FOR CALIFORNIA ASIAN-AMERICAN POLITICIANS		
Position	**Name**	**Elected**
First Asian elected to the State Assembly	Alfred H. Song (D)	1963
First Asian woman elected to the State Assembly	March K. Fong Eu (D)	1966
First Asian elected to the State Senate	Alfred H. Song (D)	1967
First Asian woman elected to the State Senate	None	
First Asian elected to Congress from California	Norman Mineta (D)	1974
First Asian woman elected to Congress from Cal.	None	
First Asian elected to the U.S. Senate from Cal.	H.I. Hayakawa (R)	1976
First Asian woman elected to the U.S. Senate from Cal.	None	
First Asian elected to statewide office	March Fong Eu (D) Secretary of State	1974
First Asian judge on the Municipal Court	John Aiso (L.A.)	1952
First Asian judge on the Superior Court	John Aiso (L.A.)	1957
First Asian judge on the Court of Appeal	Stephen Tamura	1965
First Asian appointed to the State Supreme Court	Joyce L. Kennard	1981

35.20,90 Source: Pacific Data Resources.

SUGGESTIONS

The editors welcome your comments and suggestions regarding additions or changes to the *California Almanac*.

Please write to:

Pacific Data Resources
c/o ABC-Clio, Inc.
P.O. Box 1911
Santa Barbara, CA 93116-1911.

_____

_____

_____

_____

_____

_____

_____

_____

_____

_____

_____

_____

_____

_____

ORDER FORM

For your convenience in ordering additional copies of the *California Almanac*, 4th Edition, previous editions, and future revised editions, fill out the form below and mail to:

Pacific Data Resources
c/o ABC-Clio, Inc.
P.O. Box 1911
Santa Barbara, CA 93116-1911.

☐ Please send _____ (1-4 copies) of the *California Almanac*, 4th Edition, at $17.95 (price includes tax, postage & handling).

☐ Please send _____ (5-14 copies)* of the *California Almanac*, 4th Edition, at $13.95 (price includes tax, postage & handling).

Copies of the 2nd and 3rd edition of the *California Almanac* are available in limited quantities:

☐ Please send _____ copies of the *California Almanac*, 3rd Edition, at $22.95 (price includes tax, postage & handling).

☐ Please send _____ copies of the *California Almanac*, 2nd Edition, at $24.95 (price includes tax, postage & handling).

☐ Please notify me when the next edition of the *California Almanac* is available.

Name_____

Address_____

City_____

State_____ Zip_____

☐ Payment Enclosed ☐ MC ☐ Visa ☐ Am. Exp.

No._____ Exp. Date_____

Signature_____

Total_____

* For educational/classroom use, educational discounts are available. For more information call (800) 422-2546.

NOW AVAILABLE: CALIFORNIA INFORMATION ON DISK

The entire contents of the *California Almanac,* plus additional information not printed in the book, such as all California place names by county, are now available on computer disk in Apple Macintosh®* format. The package includes the tables in a two part format: an editable format (Microsoft Excel®), and a document format (Microsoft Word®). This product will enable you to utilize the information in the *California Almanac* in your own reports and publications.

Included with each set is a license to use the information at a single site, or within documents or data files which are not sold. Information contained on the disks may not be used in any product designated for resale, without express written permission from Pacific Data Resources.

To order, please fill out the form below and mail to:

> Pacific Data Resources
> c/o ABC-Clio, Inc.
> P.O. Box 1911
> Santa Barbara, CA 93116-1911.

Please send _____ sets** of the California Almanac, disk edition, at $145⁰⁰ (price includes tax, postage & handling) each to:

Name_____

Address_____

City_____

State_____ Zip_____

☐ Payment Enclosed ☐ MC ☐ Visa ☐ Am. Exp.

No._____ Exp. Date_____

Signature_____

Total_____

*   For information on IBM format please call (805) 964-0195.

** One set includes approximately 16 disks. Discounts are available on quantity orders. For more information please call (800) 422-2546.

CALIFORNIA POLITICAL ALMANAC

The *California Political Almanac* is a new book edited by Dan Walters and other staff members of the Sacramento Bee. The *California Political Almanac* is the new definitive source for political information on California. To order your copy, fill out the form below and mail to:

Pacific Data Resources
c/o ABC-Clio, Inc.
P.O. Box 1911
Santa Barbara, CA 93116-1911.

Please send _____ copies of the California Political Almanac, at $34.75* (price includes tax, postage & handling) each to:

Name_____

Address_____

City_____

State_____ Zip_____

☐ Payment Enclosed ☐ MC ☐ Visa ☐ Am. Exp.

No._____ Exp. Date_____

Signature_____

Total_____

* Substantial educational discounts and bulk order discounts are available. For more information please call (800) 422-2546.